INTERNATIONAL HANDBOOK OF JUVENILE JUSTICE

International Handbook
of Juvenile Justice

Edited by

JOSINE JUNGER-TAS

*University of Utrecht
The Netherlands*

and

SCOTT. H. DECKER

*Arizona State University
USA*

A C.I.P. Catalogue record for this book is available from the Library of Congress.

ISBN-10 1-4020-4400-3(HB)
ISBN-13 978-1-4020-4400-7(HB)
ISBN-10 1-4020-4970-6(e-book)
ISBN-13 978-1-4020-4970-5(e-book)

Published by Springer,
P.O. Box 17, 3300 AA Dordrecht, The Netherlands.

www.springer.com

Printed on acid-free paper

The Best Interest of the Child

In all actions concerning children, whether undertaken by public or private social welfare institutions, courts of law, administrative authorities or legislative bodies, the best interests of the child shall be a primary consideration.

Convention on the Rights of the Child (UN Doc. Art. 3, 1ˢᵗ para. (1989))

Although young people should be held responsible for their delinquent acts, all sanctions and interventions should be focused on their rehabilitation and reintegration in society and meet the specific needs which impede their growing up into responsible citizens.

Working group on Juvenile Justice (European Society of Criminology)

Contents

Preface

In 2000 several European academics decided it was time to launch a European Society of Criminology. From the start the new Society encouraged the creation of working groups on specialized topics. One of the first such working groups was focused on "juvenile justice," launched by the first author of this book. The idea for this book emerged from concerns about recent developments in juvenile justice in our own countries, developments that were leading toward an evermore punitive, but not necessarily more effective, system in juvenile justice.

To our surprise numerous Society members specializing in the field of Juvenile Delinquency and Youth Justice shared these sentiments and joined the working group. In addition, some American and Canadian experts became ESC members and were interested in joining the working group, adding an international dimension to our undertaking. The working group was guided by several key questions. How have different states developed their juvenile justice system in the last 25 years, and if one compares countries, to what extent are these developments similar or different? To be more precise: to what degree has the Welfare system that had existed for most of the 20th century changed into a Just Desert and more punitive system in these countries? The present book tries to answer these questions for a great number of European and two North American countries in a comparative perspective, including 19 national reports on juvenile justice and legal reforms in these countries. This book is the first comprehensive review of juvenile justice published since Klein's (1984) review of juvenile justice in eight western countries.

A second objective is to analyze a number of fundamental juvenile justice issues and include answers to the question what might be done about this seemingly inevitable trend and what should be done. We also touch on the issue of whether there are perhaps other, more effective ways to prevent and reduce juvenile crime? This will be the specific focus of a second publication.

We were very fortunate in finding a great number of outstanding experts in the field prepared to write a chapter on trends in juvenile justice in their own country. We are grateful to each of them for their contributions to this work. We are also indebted to the members of the Working group for their dedication, their patience and their goodwill to respond to our specific requirements.

In addition, we wish to express our great appreciation to this year's President of the European Society of Criminology, Professor Hans-Jürgen Kerner who shares our enthusiasm for our undertaking and has written the Foreword to the book.

Special mention should also be addressed to those of our English-speaking experts who had offered to correct the English of all authors whose mother tongue is not English – Julian Roberts, David O'Mahoney, and Mairead Seymour. Lindsey Green and Andrea Burch, both graduate students in Criminology and Criminal Justice at the University of Missouri-St. Louis also provided considerable help in proofreading and editing chapters. Considering the fact that the book includes 14 contributions – out of 20 – of non-English authors, this was by no means a light task and we owe them many thanks!

Finally, we hope that this book, which has collected information on juvenile justice systems in so many nations, will find its way to an international public of academics, policymakers and practitioners, and may open the eyes of many to different solutions for similar problems.

Josine Junger-Tas
Scott H. Decker

Foreword

Modern societies seem to look at young people in a rather ambivalent manner. The last decades of the twentieth century provided us with a couple of telling examples from several countries.

On the one hand, children and juveniles are viewed as needing care and protection. If they become delinquent, educational measures are seen to be the appropriate if not pivotal answer to the problems they are causing or may suffer from. This is the prevailing attitude among the general population in the majority of countries in the developed part of the world, so long as the offences committed by youngsters do not rise steeply in numbers and remain petty or moderate in their quality.

On the other hand, more serious crimes cause public concern, and may even spark outrage when considered to be despicable; even more when attributable to youth with a history of repeat offending. Then the notion of the "young delinquent deserving understanding, education and treatment" suddenly is replaced in the public and often even in the professional discourse by the notion of the "young repeat offender" or the "early chronic criminal" or the "young super predator" or similar connoted terms.

Even in nations where the legitimacy of a legally set strict lower age of criminal responsibility is held strongly, there may be pressure to get rid of those limits. By doing so, present-day judicial systems reintroduce age-old concepts in a superficially modern manner. The most striking example is the late medieval legal exception to the rule that children had to be considered not guilty by reason of immaturity (*doli incapax*). Simply put, this exception meant that a young boy or girl could be tried, formally convicted and eventually sentenced in regular criminal court, if his or her status as a minor at the time of committing the criminal act could be legally "substituted" by the heinous circumstances of the offence and/or the morally depraved character of the offender. In a sense, the characteristics of the act were substituted for the status of the juvenile.

Media images, including prolonged campaigns by the tabloid press and reality TV series, contribute directly to the development of an intricate mixture of feelings in the general public that may produce a very punitive attitude set among large segments of the population. The situation may get even worse when crime policy is governed more by shortsighted political considerations than by emotionally distant and empirically sound legislative projects. Penal populism may emerge as the ultimate outcome of such media and political pressures. In the field of juvenile justice such penal populism is *the* ultimate impediment to sound, rational, humane and therefore effective prevention and intervention policies.

All states in the world do not have yet juvenile offender laws and juvenile justice systems operating separately from the adult criminal justice system. But the global trend certainly has been moving in that direction. States with a well-established juvenile justice system vary considerably on a number of important structural characteristics. The age limit of criminal responsibility that distinguishes between the legal categories of children and juveniles shows a modal age range around 12–14 years. However, even in Europe with its rather high cultural homogeneity the whole range spans from 7 (e.g., Scotland) to 18 (e.g., Belgium) years of age. In most European countries the upper age limit for the jurisdiction of the juvenile court or youth court is 17.

There is considerable variation across the European continent. Germany has a very interesting solution: On the one hand young people called "juveniles" (14 to less than 18 years of age) are always tried before the youth courts and given juvenile educational measures, directives or, in more serious cases, the penalty of youth imprisonment. On the other hand young people called "adolescents" (18 to less than 21 years of age) are also always tried before the youth courts. But those courts are then expected to evaluate the particularities of the offences under consideration, and the state of personality of the indicted young defendants. Depending on the results of such considerations the youth courts eventually handle the adolescent defendants either like adults or like juveniles, and to administer the appropriate substantial law, either with the sanctions provided by the rather flexible Youth Court Act or with the adult penalties as provided by the Penal Code.

As far as the basic juvenile justice philosophy is concerned, some European states follow a deliberate welfare model, whereas others prefer a strict justice or due process model. Many states mingle elements of both philosophies into one act or law, while other states have bifurcated systems where above all very young offenders can be handled either way or both ways in a consecutive manner. Courts may be entrusted with the function of so-called children courts or family courts, and the power to administer educational measures if sufficient, and criminal penalties if necessary.

However diverse the legal solutions and the practical implementations might be in detail, the worldwide ground wave of dealing with young offenders is basically *not* diverse at all. It is, on the opposite, clearly and decisively guided by a set of principles, guidelines and international standards which are intelligible, morally sound, and backed up by a mounting number of empirical evidence. This is aptly dealt with in the concluding chapter of this book. So I need not deal with the issue here.

Josine Junger-Tas, the author of the concluding chapter, deserves special thanks in a couple of respects. She has been always on the forefront of modern juvenile justice in Europe and elsewhere, in terms of scholarly research, service in justice policy positions, academic teaching, and international collaboration and cooperation. Also this book is a genuine fruit of those capabilities and enduring efforts. Josine has been the founder and the energetic facilitator of the European Society of Criminology's Division of Juvenile Justice. This division is, not the least due to her stamina and creative communication skills, the most prominent and productive Division of the ESC, also constantly being present at the ESC website. Scott Decker, her co-editor, joined the Division early on. He is an internationally renowned specialist on youth gang research. He is, in addition, one of those American scholars who are genuinely interested in the world outside the realm of the USA, and therefore contributes remarkably to the mutual understanding of scholars across countries and continents, and to the improvement of our knowledge of how juvenile delinquency and crime should and can be dealt with in an equally enlightened, scientifically based, humane, efficient, and effective manner.

Josine and Scott deserve our congratulations for their successful endeavor to instigate, direct, and edit this thought-provoking collection of papers on international modern juvenile justice. The authors providing country reports deserve our thanks for having delivered their drafts in due course of time, for abiding by the rules as discussed and agreed upon during repeated meetings at ESC conferences or other European or International Congresses. I participated in many of them. The cordiality there was always comforting. The intellectual climate was always stimulating. My reading of the final collection published in this volume led me to the conclusion that much of this personal atmosphere fertilized the writing.

I wish this volume a large readership all over the world. It should serve as a means for reading in classes on comparative and international juvenile justice. It should instigate further research, and serve as a blueprint for good policy and practice in states considering an overhaul of their perhaps outdated laws or their all-too-old legal, viz., law enforcement and juvenile court systems.

Hans-Jürgen Kerner
President of the European Society of Criminology
Director of the Institute of Criminology at the University of Tuebingen,
Germany

Biographical Notes

EDITORS

Josine Junger-Tas studied sociology at the Free University of Brussels (Belgium). In 1972 she obtained her PhD in the Netherlands at the University of Groningen with a study on "Characteristics and Social Integration of Juvenile Delinquents," which was the start of her involvement in criminology.

She worked in a research centre in Brussels in the field of Juvenile Crime, but returned to her home country in 1975 where she was employed by the Dutch Ministry of Justice in its Research Institute. In 1979 she was appointed as special Adviser and Director of the Research Unit on Juvenile crime. In 1989 she was appointed as Director of the Institute.

Josine Junger-Tas was active in the Council of Europe. From 1984 to 1988 she chaired an Expert Committee on Juvenile Delinquency which produced two reports with recommendations for member states, the first report treating social reactions to juvenile crime and the second reactions to delinquent behaviour of young people belonging to an ethnic minority. She wrote several basic documents for the Council of Europe and in 1992 was appointed member of its Scientific Council. She was active in the United Nations, where she also did preparatory work for the UN Criminology congresses, and now serves as an expert on Juvenile Delinquency for Central European and Middle Eastern states.

In 1989 she received the Sellin-Glueck Award from the American Society of Criminology for her "International Contributions to Criminology." She wrote a great number of articles and books, as well as reports for the Minister of Justice.

In 1994 she became visiting professor of Youth Criminology at the University of Lausanne in Switzerland and she is also visiting professor at the University of Utrecht. She is member of the Council for the Administration of Criminal Law and the Protection of Juveniles, an independent consultant body for the Minister of Justice, which has a surveillance function with respect to all penitentiary (youth) institutions, and serves as an Appeal court regarding decisions taken by the Supervising committees of the institutions.

In 2000 the University of Lausanne awarded her an honorary doctorate.

Scott H. Decker received his BA in Social Justice from DePauw University in 1972. He earned an MA in Criminology in 1974 and a PhD in Criminology in 1976, both from Florida State University. He is Professor and Chair of Criminal Justice and Criminology at Arizona State University. He received the UM-St. Louis Chancellor's Award for Excellence in Research in 1989. He is the author of eleven books, over onehundred articles, and more than one hundred presentations. His research has been funded by the Harry Frank Guggenheim Foundation, US Department of Justice, US Department of

Health and Human Services, National Institute on Drug Abuse and the State of Missouri.

Professor Decker's primary research focus has been on criminal justice policy, gangs, violence, and juvenile justice. Decker is the author of an ethnographic study of gang members and their families, *Life in the Gang: Family, Friends and Violence*, published by Cambridge University Press in 1996. This book was a finalist for the 1997 C. Wright Mills Award, and received the prize for Outstanding Book from the Academy of Criminal Justice Sciences in 1998. His most recent book, *European Street Gangs and Troublesome Youth Groups* (with Frank Weerman), was published in 2005 by Alta Mira Press.

Contributors

AUSTRIA

Karin Bruckmüller received the Mag. Jur. Law degree from the University of Vienna and she is working there as a research assistant at the Criminal Law Department. Currently, she is writing her thesis for her PhD on the issue of recidivism in Austrian criminal law and in the field of criminology. Special fields of research are juvenile law, crime prevention, the penal system, alternative sanctions, and the evaluation of sanctions. For a period of two years she worked as a volunteer for the Austrian probation service.

BELGIUM

Catherine Van Dijk graduated in Educational Sciences at the Katholieke Universiteit Leuven (KULeuven, Catholic University of Leuven) in 1999 and in Criminological Sciences at the Vrije Universiteit Brussel (VUB, Free University of Brussels) in 2000. As from 2001 she is an assistant at the Vrije Universiteit Brussel, Faculty of Law, Department of Criminology. She has done research on restorative justice practices in Flanders (2000–2001) and is currently preparing a PhD in the field of juvenile justice (subject: "Balancing on the border between juvenile and criminal justice. Serious juvenile offenders: unfit for juvenile justice?"; Promoter: Prof. dr. C. Eliaerts; Co-promoter: Prof. dr. J. Christiaens).

Els Dumortier was engaged in a research project regarding legal rights for minors at the Vrije Universiteit Brussel (project funded by the Belgian National Fund for Scientific Research (FWO)) between 1997 and 2000. On the topic of "Legal Rights for Minors within Restorative Justice", she participated in the annual congresses by the International Network on Restorative Justice for Juveniles and several of her contributions were published. Since 2001 her research activities focus on the figure of the juvenile judge and she is preparing her PhD on this topic (research project funded by the VUB). Especially the birth of the juvenile judge (beginning of the 20th century), his practices during the first half of the 20th century and the criticism surrounding this figure are investigated.

Christian Eliaerts is professor of criminology at the Vrije Universiteit Brussel. He received his Dr. Juris (1969) and his PhD in criminology (1977) from the VUB. He was Head of the Department of Criminology and Dean of the Faculty of Law. His teaching and research concentrate on the fields of juvenile criminology, the rights of children (in the juvenile justice system), community policing and criminal policy.

CANADA

Nicholas Bala has been a professor at the Faculty of Law at Queen's University in Kingston, Canada since 1980, specializing in Family and Children's Law. He has published books and articles on such issues as juvenile justice and youth offending; child welfare law, child abuse and child witnesses in the criminal justice system; family violence; and parental rights and responsibilities after divorce; the legal definition of the family; the *Canadian Charter of Rights* and the family; and child and spousal support obligations. His most recent books are *Youth Criminal Justice Law* (Toronto: Irwin Law, 2003); and Bala et al. (eds.), and *Canadian Child Welfare Law* (Toronto: Thompson Educational Publishers, 2004.)

Julian V. Roberts is professor of criminology and university research chair at the University of Ottawa, and reader in criminology at the University of Oxford. He has published extensively in the area of sentencing for both adult and youth offenders, and public opinion about sentencing issues. His most recent book, *The Virtual Prison*, was published by Cambridge University Press in 2004.

CZECH REPUBLIC

Helena Válková completed a legal curriculum at the Faculty of Law, Charles University in Prague, Czech Republic (1975); habilitation in Criminal Law at the Faculty of Law, Masaryk University in Brno (1997). Lectures on criminal law and criminology at the Faculty of Philosophy, Charles University Prague (1991 to date); lectures on criminal law and criminology at the Faculty of Law, University of West Bohemia in Pilsen (1995 to date); Head of the department of criminal law at the Faculty of Law, University of West Bohemia in Pilsen (1998 to date). Research projects with special reference to juvenile delinquency and non-custodial sentences. Head of the legislative group preparing new Law on Juvenile Justice System in the Czech Republic passed in 2003 (1997–2003). Member of the Criminological Scientific Council of the Council of Europe (2001–2004). Co-author of textbooks on criminology and criminal law and author of various criminological publications and contributions.

ENGLAND

John Graham is currently the Director of the Police Foundation and a professor of criminology at the University of Luton. His previous posts include Associate Director of the Audit Commission, Deputy Director of Strategic Policy in the Home Office and Senior Research and Policy Adviser in the Social Exclusion Unit, Cabinet Office. He has managed to combine a civil service and academic career and has published widely in the fields of juvenile crime, juvenile justice and crime prevention. He has also been a Scientific Adviser to the Council of Europe since 1996 and has worked as a Consultant to the United Nations. He is also a Trustee of Communities That Care and a Non-Executive Director of the Camelot Foundation.

Colleen Moore is currently a senior lecturer in criminology at APU (Anglia Polytechnic University) in Cambridge, as well as deputy head of the Department of Humanities and Social Sciences. She has been involved in research projects which have looked at Community Service, conditions in and the impact of prisons for adults and juveniles and local youth diversion initiatives. More recently, she has been involved in a project assessing and auditing the needs of gypsies and travellers in the Eastern Region of England

FRANCE

Anne Wyvekens is a researcher at the Centre d'études et de recherches de science administrative (CERSA) (French National Centre for Scientific Research, CNRS). Her research field are: local safety policies, urban policies, juvenile justice She is the author of a great number of publications, among which the following books: *Faire la société. La politique de la ville aux Etats-Unis et en France* (avec J. Donzelot et C. Mevel), Paris, Seuil, 2003; *La magistrature sociale. Enquêtes sur les politiques locales de sécurité* (avec J. Donzelot), Paris, La Documentation française, 2004; *Face à la délinquance des mineurs, des acteurs et des actions,* Paris, Profession Banlieue, 2004; *La justice de proximité en Europe: pratiques et enjeux* (ed., avec J. Faget), Toulouse, Erès, 2001.

She is also a member of the Advisory Board of the *European Journal of Criminology* as well as the editor of *Les Cahiers de la sécurité.*

GREECE

Calliope D. Spinellis is Professor Emeritus (Criminology-Penology), Law School, University of Athens. Presently she is teaching postgraduate courses at the same institution. She is also former member the Criminological Scientific Council of the Council of Europe.

Aglaia Tsitsoura is Former Head of Division of Crime Problems, Council of Europe. She is also former Professor of Crime Policy at the Free University of Brussels. Presently she is a Visiting Professor at Panteion University, Athens.

IRELAND

Mairéad Seymour (BSoc.Sc., MSSc., PhD.) lectures at the Department of Social Science at the Dublin Institute of Technology. Previously, she worked as a researcher at the Centre for Social Research (DIT) and at the Institute of Criminology and Criminal Justice at Queen's University Belfast. Her main research interests are in the area of comparative youth justice, alternatives to custody and reintegration.

NETHERLANDS

Peter van der Laan has an MA in Special Education (Orthopedagogiek) from Leiden University. He received his PhD from the Law Faculty of the Free University in Amsterdam for a thesis on alternative sanctions for juveniles.

For many years he has been involved in research concerning criminal justice in general and the impact of (semi-)criminal justice interventions in particular. He has a special interest in issues regarding juveniles. Between 1981 and 1998 he worked in various positions at the Research and Documentation Centre (WODC) of the Dutch Ministry of Justice, followed by two years at the Dartington Social Research Unit in Devon (UK). Since 1999, he is a senior researcher at the Netherlands Institute for the Study of Crime and Law Enforcement (NSCR). He is also professor of social and educational care at the Faculty of Social and Behavioral Sciences of the University of Amsterdam.

He has served as an expert for the Council of Europe and the United Nations on juvenile justice issues. He was involved in drafting two Council of Europe recommendations (Implementation of the European Rules on Community Sanctions and Measures (2000) and New Ways of Dealing with Juvenile Delinquency (2003)). He also participated in numerous juvenile justice missions to member states in Central and Eastern Europe.

POLAND

Barbara Stando-Kawecka is assistant professor at the Law Faculty at the Jagiellonian University in Cracow in Poland. The main field of her research is criminal policy and execution of criminal sanctions, prison systems and human rights of prisoners. Her recent publications include the book *Prawne podstawy resocjalizacji* (Legal Basis of Resocialization) and reports from Poland in: *Imprisonment Today and Tommorrow*, Second Edition; *Community Sanctions and Measures in Europe and North America*; *Youth Violence: New Patterns and Local Responses – Experiences in East and West*.

SCOTLAND

Michele Burman is professor of criminology at the University of Glasgow and a Co-Director of the Scottish Centre for Crime and Justice Research (a partnership between the universities of Glasgow, Stirling and Edinburgh). Her main research interests are in violence, young female offenders, and gender and justice.

Paul Bradshaw is a senior researcher with the Scottish Centre for Social Research, an independent social research organisation. Having also worked as a researcher for the Scottish Children's Reporter Administration and the Edinburgh Study of Youth Transitions and Crime, Paul has been involved in a range of research studies on children and young people in Scotland particularly in the areas of youth crime and youth justice.

Neil Hutton is a professor of criminal justice in the Law School at the University of Strathclyde. His main research interest is in sentencing. He was a leading member of the team which designed and implemented a Sentencing Information System in the High Court in Scotland, and his current research, supported by the ESRC, examines social enquiry reports and sentencing in the sheriff courts. He is a member of the Sentencing Commission for Scotland.

Fergus McNeill is a senior lecturer in the Glasgow School of Social Work (a joint venture of the universities of Glasgow and Strathclyde). Prior to becoming an academic in 1998, he worked for a number of years in residential drug rehabilitation and as a criminal justice social worker. His research interests and publications have addressed a range of criminal justice issues including sentencing, community penalties, and youth justice.

Mary Munro is a freelance researcher and criminology lecturer based in Glasgow. She runs www.cjscotland.org.uk – a news database and information source about Scottish criminal justice issues. Earlier in her career she qualified and practised as a lawyer in England and then as a probation officer.

SLOVENIA

Katja Filipčič is currently assistant professor of criminal law and criminology at the Faculty of Law, University of Ljubljana and research associate at the Institute of Criminology at the Faculty of Law, University of Ljubljana. Her research interests and recent publications include juvenile crime, juvenile victimization, violence in the family, and fear of crime.

SPAIN

Cristina Rechea Alberola, Ph.Dr., is a full professor of psychology and law in the Law Faculty at the Univesity of Castilla-La Mancha in Albacete, where she has directed the master's degree in criminology since 1990 and the doctoral program in criminology since 1992. She has been the director of the Research Centre in Criminology at the University of Castilla-La Mancha since its creation in 2000, where she has developed research interests in juvenile justice, juvenile delinquency (self-reported delinquency, violence, girls' delinquency), battered women, trafficking of women, and drugs in the workplace, and has collaborated with other European research institutes and universities (through European Union research programs such as Youth in Europe, COST, STOP, and AGIS).

Esther Fernández Molina, Dr. iur.3, has been a research member of the Research Centre in Criminology at Albacete since 1999. She received her degree in law in

1996, a master's degree in criminology in 1998, and a doctoral degree in criminology in 2004 at the University of Castilla-La Mancha. The topic of her doctoral thesis was: "Juvenile justice system in Spanish democracy: between education and punishment." Her research interests have always centred on the juvenile justice system. She has undergone specialist training in aspects of the juvenile justice system at the Professional Lawyers Association in Madrid (1997) and at the Pontifical University of Comillas in Madrid (1999). She obtained two student's awards for her papers, in 1997 and 1998, in the student criminology meetings held at the University of Valencia. She has published, in collaboration with Professor Rechea Alberola, a number of papers and book chapters on juvenile justice in Spain.

SWEDEN

Felipe Estrada is associate professor at the Department of Criminology, Stockholm University, Sweden. His dissertation "Juvenile Crime as a Social Problem – Trends, Media Attention and Societal Response" was published in 1999. During 2000–2001 he worked as secretary in the welfare commission that was set up in Sweden to draw up a balance sheet for welfare in the 1990s. This task included an examination of the connection between living conditions, social exclusion and victimization. Part of this work has been published in the *Journal of European Social Policy, The British Journal of Criminology*, and *The European Journal of Criminology*. He is also editor of *Journal of Scandinavian Studies in Criminology and Crime Prevention*. From 2005 he has been working with a project on "Pathways to inclusion and exclusion – risk exposure and turning points in a life course perspective" at the Institute for Future Studies in Stockholm.

Jerzy Sarnecki is professor at, and formerly head of, the Department of Criminology, Stockholm University. He has also been Head of Division on Swedish Council for Crime Prevention. Professor Sarnecki is currently the President of the Scandinavian Research Council for Criminology. He has published several books on *Juvenile Delinquency*. In 2001 his work *Delinquent Networks. Youth Co-offending in Stockholm* was published in Cambridge Studies in Criminology, Cambridge University Press. Currently he is working on publication, *Knowledge-based Crime Prevention: Theoretical Base for Crime Prevention in Stockholm*.

UNITED STATES

Donna M. Bishop is a professor in the College of Criminal Justice at Northeastern University. She received her PhD in criminal justice from the State University of New York at Albany and also holds an advanced degree in mental health counseling from the University of Florida. For more than two decades, Professor Bishop's research has focused on juvenile justice and youth policy. She has written one book and over fifty articles and monographs, many dealing with race and gender inequities in juvenile justice processing; juvenile detention policy and practice; and the origins and consequences of juvenile waiver law reform.

SWITZERLAND

Jean Zermatten was President and Dean of the juvenile court of the canton of Valais (Switzerland) from 1980 to 2005; he is also the Founder and Director of the International Institute for the Rights of the Child (IDE) in Sion/Switzerland and has been Lecturer at the University of Fribourg (Arts Faculty, Social Work and Law Faculty). He has initiated and launched the Executive Master on Children's Rights, in collaboration with the University of Fribourg and the Institut Universitaire Kurt Bösch.

Zermatten was charged by the Swiss Confederation to draft a project for the first unified Law for criminal Procedures for Minors (OFJ). He was also asked by the cantons from the Latin part of Switzerland to draft an inter-cantonal concordat on the implementation of measures for young offenders. This concordat has been accepted in October 2003. In addition, he collaborated to the creation of the first Swiss children's rights network gathering more than 50 Swiss NGOs.

He was the president of the Swiss society for the criminal law for juveniles as well as the president of the International Association of Magistrates for Youth and Family (IAMYF). He is also a member of the UN Committee for the Rights of the Child.

Most recent publications in the field:

2005   *Child Trafficking: A Fatality ?* 270 pp. (editor)
2004   12 petits contes pour ne pas s'endormir
        Editions Saint-Augustin, Saint-Maurice, to be published in September 2004
2004   Droits de l'enfant et SIDA : du tabou aux stratégies d'intervention/The rights of the child and HIV/AIDS: from taboos to intervention strategies IDE 214 pp. (editor)
2003   Les Droits de l'Enfant. Et les filles? IDE 211 pp. (editor)
2002   L'Enfant et la Guerre IDE 162 pp. (editor)
2002   Tribunal des Mineurs Le petit tailleur et autres histoires de galère Editions Saint-Augustin, Saint-Maurice

BOSNIA-HERZEGOVINA

Almir Maljević (1977), LLM, Senior lecturer of Criminal Law at the Faculty of Criminal Justice Sciences, University of Sarajevo. So far, he has published in both the Bosnian and the English language on topics concerning juvenile criminal justice and organized crime related criminal offences. In the course of his studies he received scholarships and fellowships from the Max-Planck-Institute for Foreign and International Criminal Law, the DAAD, UNDP Bosnia and Herzegovina and the Open Society Fund Bosnia and Herzegovina. He participated in numerous national and five comparative international research projects in the fields of criminal law and criminology. He is currently a doctoral student at the Faculty of Law, University of Freiburg, Germany

Frieder Dünkel, born 1950 in Karlsruhe, studied law at the universities of Heidelberg and Freiburg/Germany (second state examination in 1976). His PhD in 1979 dealt with empirical research on the effectiveness of therapeutic treatment in prisons. From 1979 until 1992 he worked as a researcher at the Max-Planck-Institute of Foreign and International Penal Law, Criminological Unit, in Freiburg (together with Prof. Günther Kaiser). The subject of his "Habilitation" in 1989 was "Juvenile imprisonment and other forms of deprivation of liberty in an international comparison." Since 1992, he has taught criminology, penology, juvenile justice, criminal procedure and criminal law at the University of Greifswald in the north-east of Germany. The research at the chair (department) of criminology covers a wide range of empirical studies in juvenile criminology, penology, prisons and alternative sanctions, alcohol and drunk driving, drug policy, etc. (see www.uni-greifswald.de/~ls3). He has widely published in these areas (24 books and 330 articles). He is co-editor of the journal, *Neue Kriminalpolitik*, since 1989 and of the *European Journal of Criminology* since 2003. He has organised many international conferences (duenkel@uni-greifswald.de).

PART I

The Anglo-Saxon Orientation

Punishment and Control:
Juvenile Justice Reform in the USA

Donna M. Bishop and Scott H. Decker

INTRODUCTION

A separate justice system for juveniles has existed in the USA for over 100 years. It was originally intended to function as a social welfare system with dual aims: to shield young delinquents from the corrupting influence of seasoned adult offenders, and to provide delinquents and status offenders[1] with the guidance and treatment necessary to make the often difficult transition through adolescence to become law abiding adults. Over the last century, and most especially since the 1960s, juvenile justice policy has shifted dramatically, undergoing a series of reforms that have reshaped the system and challenged the principles on which it was founded.

In this chapter we examine trends in juvenile justice policy and practice in the USA, with a special focus on changes that have taken place in the last 20 years. Our analysis is presented in several parts. In the first, we set the stage for what follows by providing some background on the context within which juvenile justice operates in the USA. We explain that juvenile justice in the USA varies greatly across state and local jurisdictions. Since the 1970s, there has been a considerable degree of "federalization" of juvenile justice policy, resulting in somewhat lesser heterogeneity across systems than was true in the past. Nevertheless, the US tradition of federalism – which recognizes the autonomy of its 50 states – continues to guarantee wide variation in policy and practice. In this first section, we also present a picture of juvenile crime and juvenile court processing to further contextualize the challenges presented to those who work in the juvenile justice field.

In subsequent sections, we describe juvenile justice policy trends and their intended and unintended consequences. We focus initially on punitive reforms, what motivated them and what research has demonstrated regarding their effects.

---

[1] In the USA, the juvenile justice population is classified into delinquents – those who commit crimes – and status offenders – those who commit special juvenile offenses like truancy, running away from home, and "being beyond parental control" that would not be crimes if committed by adults. The jurisdiction over status offenders has historically been justified on the grounds that these are youth at-risk for delinquency.

J. Junger-Tas and S. H. Decker (eds.), International Handbook of Juvenile Justice, 3–36.
© 2006 Springer.

Here we also discuss the death penalty, and the longstanding but recently reversed stance on the execution of youths under 18. We then turn to a discussion of delinquency prevention. There has been a recent burst of activity in this area whose effects are not yet clear. We describe the nature of several key programmatic efforts and discuss preliminary assessments. In the final section of this chapter, we attempt to step back and assess the whole. We look at the uneasy mix of social welfare and social control that characterizes juvenile justice policy and practice in the USA today, and the very uncertain direction of juvenile justice policy in the future.

1. CONTEXT FOR UNDERSTANDING POLICY

No policy or policies can be understood outside of the context in which they are made and must operate. Thus we provide a brief set of background or contextual issues that provide an important framework for understanding the policies and practices of the juvenile justice system in the USA.[2]

1.1. Historical Context

Twenty years ago, Carter (1984: 36) noted that in order to comprehend juvenile justice in the USA, it is essential to understand three points. First, the size of the system(s) is enormous. All 50 states, the District of Columbia – and to some extent the federal government – have separate systems of juvenile justice. Within minimum constitutional standards set by the US Supreme Court, each jurisdiction is free to establish its own juvenile justice policies and practices. States are not *required* to have a separate justice system for juveniles, although all established separate systems by the mid-1920s and have maintained them ever since. Second, the systems are extremely complex internally and externally. This is especially true of the interaction of juvenile courts and juvenile correctional agencies with other public and private forms of social welfare and social control, including schools, mental health systems, public health agencies, police, and other agencies of government. Third, Carter underscores the dynamic character of the system(s), noting the significance of paying close attention to trends in those systems.

1.2. Social and Demographic Context

A key to appreciating the main policies of prevention, treatment, punishment, and procedural/individual rights is to understand something of the context of

---

[2]It is important to observe at the outset of this essay, that the use of the word "system" is a misnomer. There is no juvenile justice system in the USA. Indeed, some argue that it was not possible to speak of an adult criminal justice system in the USA until the 1960s (Klein, 1984).

the juvenile population, the seriousness and extent of juvenile crime, and the nature of the juvenile justice system.[3] There are approximately 70 million people under the age of 18 in the USA, a figure projected to increase to over 80 million by the year 2030. This projection represents an increase of 21% from 1995 to 2030. The population of 15–17 year olds, the primary population "served" by the juvenile court, is increasing at a similarly dramatic pace. By 2007, it is estimated that there will be roughly 13 million juveniles in this age range, a number similar to that recorded at its peak in the midst of the post World War II baby boom of the 1970s. This increase is projected to be dramatically higher among minorities.

The USA is characterized by much cultural diversity: racial and ethnic minorities make up approximately one-third of the youth population. In 2003, the composition of the 15–17 year old age group was 64% White non-Hispanic, 14% White Hispanic, 16% Black, 4% Asian, and 1% American Indian. While modest growth is expected among non-Hispanic Whites, the projected increase among Asians and Hispanics is several times greater. Complicating this picture is the fact that a large fraction of juveniles live in poverty (roughly 20%), and that the child poverty rate is much higher than that for adults or the elderly. There is good news in that the poverty rates of Black and Hispanic youth have lowered in the past decade. Nevertheless, nearly 40% of Black and Hispanic youth continue to live in poverty, compared to 16% of non-HispanicWhites and 20% of Asians. Family structure has also changed for juveniles in the USA: many fewer youths live in homes with two parents than was the case in the past. In 1997, three-quarters of White children lived with two parents, 64% of Hispanic children lived with both parents, but only 35% of African–American children lived with both parents. While the birth rate among teenaged girls in the USA declined steadily through the 1990s, it remains higher than in the 1980s. In addition, the teenage birth rate of 57 per 1,000 teenaged girls is significantly higher than in other industrialized democracies such as Canada (32), England (26), Australia (22), the Netherlands (6), Norway (15), and Japan (4). High school completion rates have increased for all race/ethnic groups, although Hispanics, Blacks, and American Indians lag behind Whites. Overall, approximately 84% of 18–24 year olds have completed high school.

1.3. Crime

Data on juvenile crime in the USA are available from a number of sources. Major sources of official data include the annual Uniform Crime Reports (UCR) – which include a compilation of arrests for the nation prepared by the Federal Bureau of

---

[3]An excellent website that maintains much of these data, and that allows for individual queries of the data, can be found at http://ojjdp.ncjrs.org/ojstatbb/index.html. Data for much of this section of the paper are drawn from Snyder and Sickmund (1999) and Puzzanchera, Stahl, Finnegan, Tierney, and Snyder (2003).

Investigation based on reports from local police jurisdictions – and *Juvenile Court Statistics*, a document prepared annually by the federal Office of Juvenile Justice and Delinquency Prevention (based on state reports) that describes the juvenile court population and the processing of cases through the juvenile justice system from initial referral to final court disposition. While the UCR and *Juvenile Court Statistics* are case-based data on the nature and frequency of offending by individuals, as well as information on the prevalence of juvenile offending, can be gleaned through self-reports, the most important of which is the National Longitudinal Survey of Youth. Another major source of data on juvenile crime is the National Crime Victimization Survey (NCVS), a program run by the federal Bureau of Justice Statistics. The NCVS gathers data from a representative sample of households regarding criminal victimization, and includes information on incidents of serious violence (rape, robbery, and aggravated assault) and simple assault. The NCVS is somewhat limited in that it does not include homicides or victimizations experienced by persons under the age of 12, but it provides important insight into crimes that do not come to the attention of the police.[4]

1.3.1. Juveniles as Victims

Much of the concern about crime in the USA revolves around violence, especially violence committed by and against young people.

The NCVS indicates that, compared to adults, juveniles are at high risk especially for violent victimization. Indeed, compared to adults, 12–17 year olds are twice as likely to be victims of serious assault and three times as likely to be victims of simple assault. Young males, racial and ethnic minorities, and residents of cities are most likely to be victims of these crimes. Juvenile victimizations occur in a patterned manner with regard to time of day, with the highest risk period being the hours just after the end of the school day. Consistent with a growing body of research about juvenile victimization (Lauritsen et al., 1991), it appears that juveniles who engage in delinquent offending put themselves at increased risk for victimization. This is particularly true for juvenile drug users, who are at highly elevated risk for violent victimization.

Because juvenile violence has had a tremendous influence on recent juvenile justice policy, it is important to understand something about murder (the type of violence that receives disproportionate media attention) in the USA. Data on juvenile homicides are available through the FBI's *Supplemental Homicide Reports*. From 1987 to 1994, the number of juveniles murdered in the USA grew at an unprecedented rate – by 65%. Juvenile homicide victimizations peaked in 1994 – when 2,900 youths were killed – and have declined significantly since then.[5] The vast majority of homicide victims aged 12 to 17 are male (about 80%), Black

---

[4]At least half of all crimes are not reported to law enforcement agencies.
[5]Reflecting this trend, the juvenile arrest rate for murder dropped to 74% between 1993 and 2000 (Snyder, 2002).

(over 50%), and killed with a firearm (over 80%) by an acquaintance of the same race (about 90%). Juvenile homicides are also spatially concentrated. Indeed, eight of the nation's more than 3,000 counties account for 25% of all juvenile homicides. Almost all of the growth in juvenile homicide between 1987 and 1994 was due to killings with firearms, and the use of firearms in juvenile homicides is much higher than in killings of adults. It is important to note in comparative context that homicide victimization rates in the USA (for both juveniles and adults) are consistently higher than those for other industrialized nations.

1.3.2. Juvenile Offenders

According to self-report data from the National Longitudinal Survey of Youth, a large proportion of juveniles have engaged in delinquent behaviors. Some of the more prevalent offenses include: using alcohol (39%), using marijuana (21%), engaging in property destruction (28%), carrying a gun (19%), belonging to a gang (5%), and stealing something valued at more than $500 (8%). In addition, 8% of juveniles report having been arrested in their lifetimes. Males report considerably more involvement in delinquency than females, and race/ethnic minorities report greater involvement in offenses such as assault and gang membership.

The majority of juveniles who enter the juvenile justice system make one appearance never to return again. For boys, this is the pattern for 54% of all referrals; for girls it is the case for 73% of all referrals. This has important implications for focused strategies of prevention and intervention, which we discuss later. Estimates of the cost of a lifetime of offending are of course based on several assumptions, the validity of which cannot be fully assessed. However, best estimates indicate that a juvenile who drops out of high school and engages in a lifetime of offending and drug use generates a cost to society between $1.7 and $2.3 million.

The major source of official data on juvenile offending is the UCR. For calendar year 2000, an estimated 2.4 million juveniles were arrested. The UCR divides arrests into three major categories: Violent Index Crimes (murder/nonnegligent manslaughter, forcible rape, robbery, and aggravated assault), Property Index Crimes (burglary, larceny-theft, motor vehicle theft, and arson), and Nonindex Offenses (21 generally less serious offenses, including drug abuse violations, simple assaults, vandalism, disorderly conduct, and curfew and loitering violations). In 2000, nearly three quarters of juvenile arrests were for Nonindex Offenses. Thus, although a substantial number of juveniles are arrested each year, the vast majority are arrested for minor offenses. Only 4% of juvenile arrests (99,000) were for Violent Index Crimes, of which 1,200 were for murder. Twenty-two percent of juvenile arrests were for Property Index Crimes, over 70% of which involved larceny-theft.

Measured in terms of arrests, juvenile crime in the USA has undergone major shifts in the past 20 years (Table 1.1). Overall juvenile arrest rates and arrest rates for violence rose sharply from the early-1980s to the mid-1990s, while arrest rates for property crimes remained relatively flat during this period. From the mid-1990s

TABLE 1.1. Juvenile Arrest Rates, 1980–2000 (per 100,000 persons aged 10–17)

Offense	1980	1985	1990	1995	2000
All offenses	7414	7425	8031	9286	7299
Violent Index Crime	334	303	428	516	308
Property Index Crime	2562	2371	2563	2439	1609

Source: Adapted from National Center for Juvenile Justice (2003).

to the present, substantial declines were observed in total arrests, and in both Violent Index and Property Index Crimes.

During the period 1991–2000, there were major variations in arrest rates for different offenses, some of which are inconsistent with the overall downward trend (data not shown). During the decade, the sharpest declines occurred in arrests for murder (down 65%), motor vehicle theft (down 51%), and burglary (down 38%). Yet there have been dramatic increases in arrests for drug abuse violations (up 145%) and curfew and loitering (up 81%). It is especially noteworthy that major increases occurred in offense categories where police are generally proactive and where they have a great deal of discretion with respect to the decision to arrest. The increase in arrests for drug abuse violations is undoubtedly connected in part to the continuing "war on drugs," a program of stepped up narcotics enforcement that began in the 1980s. While self-reports of illicit drug use among 8th, 10th, and 12th graders show increases for the same time period, they are of a magnitude less than half that reflected in official arrest data (Johnston et al., 2005). The increase in arrests for curfew violations is also related to shifts in policy. Many jurisdictions have recently established and/or increased enforcement of juvenile curfew laws in an effort to reduce juvenile crime.

Juvenile crime is to a very considerable extent a male phenomenon. In 2000, females contributed 28% of all juvenile arrests, and only 18% of those in the Violent Index category. Recently, much has been made of the fact that while arrest rates for males declined (down 11%) over the past two decades, arrest rates for females increased (by 35%) (Table 1.2.). The increases were concentrated in a few offense categories, especially aggravated and simple assault. This may be linked to the national shift toward mandatory arrest policy in cases involving domestic violence. Intended originally to apply to spousal assaults, the pro-arrest policy has spilled over to intra-family disputes involving parents and children, as well as fights between siblings. Like arrest rates for males, those for females declined over the period 1995–2000, but the rate of decline was somewhat lower than that for males.

Juvenile arrests are also disproportionately concentrated among racial minorities. Table 1.3 presents arrest rates for Whites and Blacks (the two largest racial groups).[6] It can be seen that, although rates of arrest for offenses overall

[6]In the interests of space, arrest rates for Asians and American Indians are not presented. However, it can be noted that arrest rates for Asians are lower than those for Whites. Arrest rates for American Indians fall between those for Whites and Blacks.

TABLE 1.2. Juvenile Arrest Rates by Gender, 1980–2000 (per 100,000 persons aged 10–17)

Offense	1980 M	1980 F	1985 M	1985 F	1990 M	1990 F	1995 M	1995 F	2000 M	2000 F
All offenses	11543	3104	10987	3318	12090	3753	13524	4813	10263	4171
Violent Index Crime	587	70	528	67	736	105	856	158	490	116
Property Index Crime	4082	976	3665	1013	3903	1152	3515	1302	2185	1001

Source: Adapted from National Center for Juvenile Justice (2003).

and for Property Index offenses follow the same general trend for Blacks and Whites, arrest rates for Blacks are approximately double those for Whites. The gap between Whites and Blacks is much more pronounced for violent crimes. In some years, the violent crime arrest rate for Blacks has been nearly six times that for whites. In 2000, there was a dramatic shift, as the arrest rate for violent crime among Blacks dropped to its lowest level in decades and the gap in arrest rates of Blacks and Whites narrowed. Still, Blacks were nearly four times as likely as Whites to be arrested for a Violent Index Crime. In order to understand US juvenile justice policy and practice in recent decades, it is important that the reader be aware that the 15-year rise in violent crime depicted in Table 1.3, especially among Blacks, has received a great deal of media attention. Violent crime has been "racialized," the young Black male has been demonized, and politicians have sought to assuage media-generated fears by advocating simplistic, punitive approaches to juvenile violence.

TABLE 1.3. Juvenile Arrest Rates for Whites and Blacks, 1980–2000 (per 100,000 persons aged 10–17)

Offense	1980 W	1980 B	1985 W	1985 B	1990 W	1990 B	1995 W	1995 B	2000 W	2000 B
All offenses	6906	11600	6781	12155	7226	14063	7985	17496	6764	11541
Violent Index Crime	189	1190	172	1096	254	1434	308	1668	220	820
Property Index Crime	2252	4886	2149	4465	2339	4408	2122	4441	1442	2783

Source: Adapted from National Center for Juvenile Justice (2003).

1.3.3. Youths in Juvenile Court

Juvenile courts process a large number of cases annually, but still only a fraction of all juvenile arrests.[7] Over the last 20 years, the police have chosen to refer an increasing proportion of cases to the juvenile court rather than handling cases informally. The proportion referred to juvenile court rose from 58% in 1980 to 71% in 2000. In 2000, over 1.6 million cases were handled by the juvenile courts of the USA. This figure represents more than four times as many cases as juvenile courts handled in 1960 (Fig. 1.1).

Once a case has been referred to juvenile court, it proceeds through a number of decision steps as shown in Fig. 1.2. The first step in the process is *intake*, where a decision is made to close the case without action, divert it for informal handling by a social service agency, or file a formal petition (the charging document) to be handled formally by the juvenile court. In 2000, 58% of delinquency cases referred to intake resulted in a formal petition. Seventeen percent were closed without action, and the remaining 25% were handled informally. An additional (and unknown) number of cases were referred for prosecution in criminal rather than juvenile court.[8] Youths transferred in this way are treated as adults, and receive the same sentences as adults, including incarceration in prisons. (More will be said about this in the discussion of policy trends below.)

Estimated delinquency cases, 1960-2000

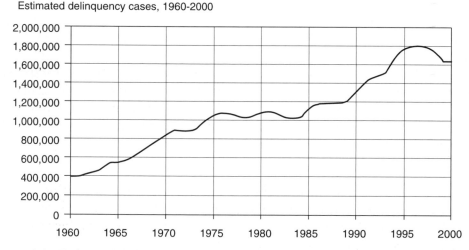

FIGURE 1.1. Estimated delinquency cases, 1960–2000. *Source*: Adapted from *OJJDP Statistical Briefing Book*. Online available at http://ojjdp.ncjrs.org/ojstatcc/court/qa06204.

---

[7]For an excellent description of the juvenile justice system in the USA and the numbers of case processed at each step of the system, see Lundman (2001: 24).

[8]The number of cases transferred at this point is unknown because they are not counted in *Juvenile Court Statistics*, nor are they classified separately from cases involving adults in criminal court statistics.

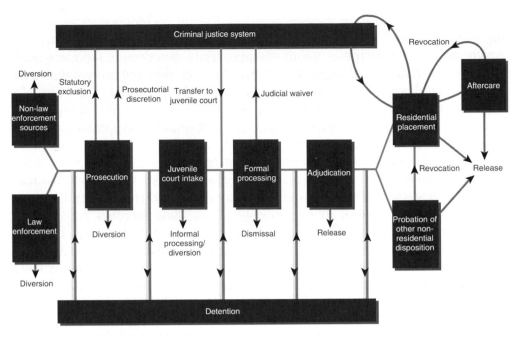

FIGURE 1.2. Case flow diagram of the stages in delinquency case processing. *Source*: Adapted from Snyder and Sickmund (1999: 98).

The second step in the juvenile justice process is the detention decision. About 18% of youth referred to the juvenile court are held in detention pending the outcome of their cases. Juveniles charged with drug or personal crimes are most likely to be detained, with public order and property crimes less likely to receive detention. In 2000, more than 640,000 youth were held in detention. Males were much more likely to be detained than females, and Blacks were more likely to be detained than Whites or members of any other race. Just as the use of detention has increased over time, informal adjustment of cases has declined over time, and formal hearings now account for the process in more than half of all delinquency cases. These two trends reflect the increasing formality of juvenile justice system responses.

In cases where a petition has been filed, youths proceed to the adjudicatory stage (equivalent to a criminal trial). If a youth is found or pleads guilty, he or she is adjudicated delinquent, or adjudication may be withheld contingent upon the youth's completion of some program or sanction. In 2000, 22% of petitioned cases were dismissed (not guilty) at the adjudicatory stage, while the vast majority were adjudicated delinquent or had adjudication withheld (77%). An additional 1% of the cases were transferred to the criminal court by the juvenile court judge through a process called judicial waiver.

Following adjudication, cases proceed to disposition (equivalent to sentencing in the criminal justice system). Disposition generally involves a hearing at which the judge determines the most appropriate sanction or service, usually with the assistance of a predisposition report prepared by the probation department, which describes the youth's background and circumstances and includes a sentencing recommendation. In 2000, 60% of those who were adjudicated or had adjudication withheld were placed on probation, 21% received a residential placement, 17% received some other sanction (e.g., fine, restitution, community work service), and 2% were released unconditionally.

In a one-day count[9] in 1999 (the most recent year for which such data are available), just over 134,000 juvenile offenders were held in residential placement facilities (Sickmund, 2004). The majority of these juveniles were held for a delinquency offense (78%), though 4% were held on status offenses, and 19% were nonoffenders.[10] Roughly 70% of these juveniles were held in public facilities, while private facilities accounted for the balance. Public facilities, generally much larger than private facilities, held the vast majority of youths adjudicated and committed for delinquency. Private facilities held over 70% of delinquents whose adjudication was withheld, and 65% of status offenders.

Over the decade 1991–1999, the number of delinquents held in residential placement increased by 50%. Increases occurred even during the period 1994–1999, when juvenile arrests declined sharply. The custody rate per 100,000 juveniles varied widely across the states, illustrating the difficulty in characterizing a US juvenile justice system, rather than a collection of 51 separate systems. While the average rate for the nation was 371, Hawaii and Vermont (representing the lowest rates) held 96 youths per 100,000, while the District of Columbia (704/100,000) and Connecticut (513/100,000) represented the highest figures. States also differ widely in their use of private versus public facilities.

Similar to the arrest and petitioning stages of the juvenile justice system, minority youth are over-represented in custody. Sixty-five percent of offenders committed to public placement and 55% of offenders committed to private facilities were minority youths. Nationally, the custody rate varied dramatically across racial groups. The custody rate for Blacks (1,004) was five times greater than that for Whites (212). American Indians were held at a rate of 632/100,000 and Hispanics at a rate of 485/100,000. Only the rate for Asians (182) was lower than that of Whites. The ratio of minority to nonminority custody rates also varies widely across states, from highs of over 8:1 in 4 states (Connecticut, New Jersey, Pennsylvania, and Washington), to lows of less than 2:1 in 5 states (Florida, Idaho, Maine, Oregon, and Vermont).

---

[9]One-day counts differ from and substantially underestimate the number of annual admissions.
[10]These include juveniles in placement for abuse or neglect, mental retardation, and emotional disturbance, and those "voluntarily" admitted by their parents.

Females account for a small proportion (13%) of juveniles in custody, but present their own special challenges for management in residential facilities. They tend to be younger (31% under the age of 15) than males in custody (21% under the age of 15), and are more likely to have backgrounds of abuse, neglect, and family conflict. In some states, there are so few females in custody (and so few females relative to males) that residential programs for girls receive fewer resources per capita and have far fewer treatment options.

2. KEY POLICY AREAS

Here we borrow from the framework identified by Klein (1984) in his introduction to an edited volume describing western systems of juvenile justice just two decades ago. At that time, Carter identified seven key policy areas that must be understood to fully appreciate juvenile justice systems in the USA: age, status offenses, discretion, other systems of control, diversion, demographic bias, and trends. We deal with the first six here, policy trends are dealt with separately. It is important to observe that a recent report published by the US Justice Department (Snyder and Sickmund, 1999: 89) concluded that from 1992 through 1997, ". . . legislatures in 47 states and the District of Columbia enacted law that made their juvenile justice systems more punitive."

2.1. Age

There is considerable variation across states in the age of juvenile court jurisdiction. In the USA, each state sets its own age limits. Variation across states occurs with respect to (1) the minimum age of juvenile court jurisdiction, (2) the age at which transfer to the adult court is possible, (3) the upper age of the juvenile court's original jurisdiction (the maximum age at which new cases can be heard), and (4) the upper age of the juvenile court's continuing jurisdiction over youth who have been made wards of the court. The trend across the states has been to lower both the minimum and the maximum jurisdictional limits. Currently, the juvenile codes in 33 states do not indicate a *minimum* age of jurisdiction for delinquency cases, although all have jurisdiction over truancy beginning at ages 5, 6, or 7. In those 17 states where a minimum age of delinquency jurisdiction is specified by statute, one sets a minimum at age 6, 3 at age 7, 11 at age 10, and 1 at age 12 (Sanborn and Salerno, 2005).

At the upper end of jurisdiction, the majority of states use age 17 (37 states and the District of Columbia), while 10 states specify age 16, and 3 states use age 15 as the maximum age of the juvenile court's delinquency jurisdiction. Stated differently, in 10 states, youths aged 17 are automatically treated as adults for all violations of the criminal law, and in 3 states, all youths aged 16 and 17 are automatically treated as adults for all violations of the criminal law. Age limits lower than 18 have been severely criticized on the grounds that they are inconsistent with evidence that persons aged 16 and 17 do not have the maturity of adults and therefore should not be held to adult standards of culpability (see, e.g., Zimring, 1998). They have also been criticized as inconsistent with other laws that fail to grant adult status to 16 and 17 year olds for other purposes (e.g., the voting age is 18, the minimum drinking age is 21) (Scott, 2001).

All states also give the juvenile court statutory authority to retain continuing jurisdiction over juveniles who are already under its supervision or control (e.g., youths on probation or in residential placement). The traditional retention age (age 21) is followed in 30 states, but 16 states have set the retention age between 17 and 20, and 5 states have raised it to age 23, 25, and beyond. To complicate matters further, in many states, juvenile courts have also been granted the authority to impose sanctions on juvenile offenders that extend well into the adult years. At the extreme, for example, Texas juvenile courts can impose sentences of up to 40 years on youths charged with certain serious crimes. Clearly, the age jurisdiction policies of American states have attempted to have it both ways, arguing that responsibility begins early (e.g., at age 6 in North Carolina), but ends late (Sanborn and Salerno, 2005).

2.2. Status Offenses

Status offenses continue to be an important avenue for referral to the juvenile court. As noted above, status offenses are acts that if committed by an adult would not be considered violations of law. In the USA, due to their age, juveniles can be brought under the jurisdiction of the juvenile court for violating curfews, being beyond the control of the parents (incorrigibility), running away from home, and being truant from school. Unlike youths charged with delinquent acts, status offenders have fewer legal rights. For example, they are not entitled to representation by counsel. Legislation in the 1970s attempted to curb court jurisdiction over Children in Need of Supervision and to remove status offenders from secure confinement. However, it is difficult to assess progress on these issues. Although official data indicate that there are fewer juveniles in placement for status offenses than a decade ago, the figures may be somewhat unreliable. In response to the federal mandate that status offenders be removed from locked facilities, there is evidence that many were relabeled as delinquents. "Family problems, even some that in past years may have been classified as status offenses (e.g., incorrigibility), can now result in an assault arrest. This logic explains why violent crime arrests over the past decade have increased proportionately more for juvenile females than males" (Snyder and Sickmund, 1999: 132). In addition, repeat status offenses – especially among females – sometimes result in charges of contempt of court or violation of probation, making youths eligible for secure confinement (Bishop and Frazier, 1992). Finally, there is evidence that many status offenders have been moved into "hidden" systems of social control by their parents (e.g., placed in private mental health facilities). Unfortunately, such private placements do not appear anywhere in official data, making it impossible to determine current practices in this area. Clearly, status offenders continue to be among the most difficult challenges for most juvenile court jurisdictions.

2.3. Discretion

Klein observed in 1984 that the USA was one of two nations that exercised the greatest amount of discretion in its juvenile justice system. Little has changed to alter that perspective, except at the punitive end of discretion. The significant changes in discretion that have occurred over the past two decades, particularly since the early 1990s, have all served to reduce discretion in ways that increase punitiveness. Rather than move toward a system where judges and decision-makers consider the individual circumstances behind the actions of a juvenile, decision-makers find their hands increasingly tied by punishment grids, mandatory minimum sentences, mandatory transfer, and other forms of increased punishment. It is important to note that at the critical stage of intake (i.e., decisions made by police and prosecutors) discretion remains high and is largely unreviewed by higher authorities.

2.4. Other Systems

The juvenile justice system in the USA has long relied on other, related systems of treatment, intervention and punishment. In many European countries, this has meant the use of other governmental functions outside the juvenile justice system (Carlsson and Decker, 2005). In the USA the use of such "other" systems has largely meant the use of systems from the private sector. States such as Florida and Massachusetts rely almost exclusively on private systems of control for secure commitment functions, particularly at the more secure levels of confinement for juveniles.

2.5. Diversion

A trend in the 1970s and 1980s to divert large numbers of youth from formal processing has largely been sidetracked in the past decade by the recent focus on formal, punitive responses. It is not an overstatement to observe that diversion was one of the key policy initiatives in juvenile justice in the USA 20 years ago. However, diversion remains an important function in American juvenile justice, particularly for prevention efforts and first-time or minor offenders.

2.6. Demographic Bias

As we have seen, juvenile justice in the USA continues to include disproportionate proportions of minority youth at every decision-making stage. Whether one examines police referral patterns, court intake, detention, residential placement or length of confinement issues, minority youth, and particularly African – American males, are over-represented. There have been a number of policy initiatives that have attempted to address this reality; to date none have been very successful. In some jurisdictions, the over-representation is so severe that the majority of Black teenaged males will appear in juvenile court.[11] The federal government, several states, local juvenile court jurisdictions and private foundations have engaged in efforts to reduce disproportionate minority confinement, and found these to be tough policy and program choices. Such efforts were complicated by the increases in youth violence in the early 1990s.

3. POLICY TRENDS AND OUTCOMES

In the last 15 years, a vast array of new juvenile justice policies and programs have been introduced in the USA. Reforms have taken place at the local, state, and federal levels and have concentrated primarily on three fronts. The first, which has attracted a great deal of media attention both at home and abroad, involves a movement to "crack down" or "get tough" on serious and chronic offenders. The spirit of this movement is captured in the slogan "adult crime, adult time," and has affected the nature of American juvenile justice in a number of important ways. At the extreme, the US Supreme Court in 1989 upheld the constitution-ality of the death penalty for crimes committed by persons as young as age 16 (*Stanford v. Kentucky*). Between 1989 and 2005, 18 states continued to permit the execution of persons who committed murder at age 16 or 17.

Also representative of the "get tough" movement, nearly every state and the federal jurisdiction amended its juvenile codes in the 1990s to transfer greater numbers of juveniles to criminal court for prosecution and punishment as adults. Many have, in addition, instituted "blended sentencing," a curious and unprec-edented mix of both juvenile and adult sanctions applied to the same individual. These reforms, which have occurred in rapid-fire fashion, have blurred the tradi-tional boundary that separates juvenile from criminal court jurisdiction (in most states, the 18th birthday) and generated a crisis in the juvenile court.

If the first front is aimed at serious, chronic and violent offenders, the second is directed toward the other end of the spectrum, i.e., toward children and youth who are at-risk for delinquency. In the past 10–15 years, governmental support for policies and programs of delinquency prevention and early intervention has grown. Although some prevention programs are delivered to the youth population at large, most are more selective, targeting those who exhibit empirically identified risk

[11]Decker and Curry (2001) report that in St. Louis, Missouri more than half of all 15 and 16 year olds black males will be referred to the juvenile court and have an intake hearing.

factors for delinquency. The contexts in which at-risk children live – their families, schools, and communities – have also become foci of intervention. Prevention programs cover a broad spectrum: they range from efforts to prevent risk factors from developing among children who are yet *in utero* to efforts to divert from the juvenile court first-offenders arrested for nonserious crimes.

A third front, which is still taking shape, is aimed at the very large group of midrange offenders who are formally processed in the juvenile courts. The US approach to these offenders is very much in transition, and philosophies and practices aimed at this group show tremendous variation across jurisdictions. The general trend over the past two decades has been to engraft punitive (deterrent, retributive, and incapacitative) objectives onto the traditional treatment mission that has so uniquely characterized American juvenile courts. While some commentators contend that the rehabilitative mission of the juvenile court has been thoroughly supplanted by these other objectives (see, e.g., Feld, 1999), others maintain that it remains, for the most part, alive and well (see, e.g., Butts and Mears, 2001; Howell, 2003; Sanborn and Salerno, 2005). New, innovative, and empirically grounded approaches to treatment have been implemented (e.g., multisystemic therapy, teaching family homes) alongside approaches that are unequivocally punitive (e.g., determinate and mandatory minimum sentencing, graduated sanctions, most boot camps). These conflicting policy and programmatic developments reflect the juvenile justice system's adaptation to the highly politicized environment of the 1980s and 1990s (see Sanborn and Salerno, 2005; Butts and Mears, 2001).

In the following section, we discuss each of these policy trends in greater detail. However, it is important to place each of these trends in a broader context, as none is unique to the recent generation of juvenile justice reform in the USA. The orientations of rehabilitation and punishment have been central themes in the practice and evolution of American juvenile justice since the origins of the system. Platt's (1977) work on the origins of the juvenile court in the USA illustrates the conflicting orientations of the juvenile justice system. The Illinois Juvenile Court Act (IJCA) of 1899 is credited with beginning the first organized juvenile court system in the USA. However, there are numerous institutions that preceded the IJCA that laid the foundation for the Act in Illinois, as well as for juvenile justice practice. Notable among these institutions were the New York House of Refuge, an early attempt to separate children from adults in confinement. In addition, the reformatory movement attempted to bring a more humane form of incarceration for offenders in the 19th century, albeit with questionable results (Pisciotta, 1994).

The history of juvenile justice and adult criminal justice in the USA is replete with examples of interventions, policies and practices in which rhetoric and reality differed considerably (Rothman, 1971; Platt, 1977; Ainsworth, 1991; Pisciotta, 1991, 1984, 1993). The two competing ideologies that seem to provide a foundation for much of the history of juvenile justice are "the welfare of the child" and "the safety of the community." These two extremes have led to "doing nothing" on the one hand, and intervening with harsh penalties on the other. Bernard (1992) captures the balancing act between these two orientations in his book, *The Cycle of Juvenile Justice*. Bernard argues that there is a cyclical aspect to juvenile justice policy when it is examined over time. The cycle is driven by a perception that juvenile crime rates are excessively high,[12] which leads to harsh punishments throughout the juvenile justice system. In a dialectical sense, this produces an eventual call for increased leniency, in part because the court is faced with a "forced choice" between doing (little or) nothing and reacting harshly. This "leniency" is followed by the perception that juvenile crime rates are "out of control," leading again to harsher, more repressive interventions. Bernard argues that images of juvenile delinquency are central to changes in juvenile justice policy and reform. Legal philosophers such as Allen (1981) argue effectively that the lack of a coherent framework for intervention, policy and legislation leads to "irrationalities" that undermine the effectiveness of a system and create competing goals and in the end a somewhat chaotic system. Because of the lack of coherence in juvenile justice in the USA, the system can alternate between harsh punishments and benevolent social interventions, neither of which has much chance of achieving its goals.

3.1. "Get Tough" Reforms for Serious Offenders

Though it is a fact not widely known, since its inception at the end of the 19th century the juvenile court in the USA has maintained a "trap door" through which young offenders could be removed to the criminal courts for prosecution and punishment as adults (Tanenhaus, 2004). Chronic offenders – those who continued to violate the law despite repeated intervention – posed a direct challenge to the effectiveness (and legitimacy) of the new court. A second group – those who committed truly heinous crimes that provoked public demands for harsh punishments – similarly posed a problem for the new court. Harsh retributive sanctions were not only contrary to the juvenile court's social welfare mission but were also beyond the court's capacity to provide. With little fanfare, the small number of youth who fell into these two categories were sent to criminal court. This action shielded the juvenile court from criticism and allowed it to function as intended for the vast majority of young offenders – that is, as a refuge from harsh criminal punishments and as a welfare agency bent on helping youth make their way through the *sturm and drang* of adolescence.

For a very long time, the trap door remained narrow and functioned largely unnoticed. During the 1980s and 1990s, however, a major shift occurred.

---

[12]In the 1990s this led to the identification of "the young and the ruthless," "a new breed of young killers," and "super-predators" (Bennett et al., 1996).

Prompted by dramatic increases in youth violence that received sensationalized media coverage, popular images of delinquent youth changed. The archetypal delinquent of a generation ago – the pot-smoking kid (of any color) who paints graffiti on walls and steals cars – was replaced by the menacing image of the Black gun–wielding drug dealer who commits random acts of lethal violence. Images of delinquents as dangerous and savvy prompted a stream of punitive legislation. Nearly every state and the federal jurisdiction enacted laws that both expanded the pool of transfer-eligibles and expedited their removal from the juvenile system. During the past 15 years, these and other innovations that blur traditional lines of distinction between juvenile and criminal justice (e.g., "blended jurisdiction" statutes, modifications in the age of criminal responsibility) have generated heated debate in both academic and policy circles regarding core juvenile justice issues: for example, Do we need a juvenile court? What is the rationale for a juvenile court? Who belongs in juvenile court and who should be excluded? No consensus has been reached on answers to these critical questions. Change has proceeded in a theoretical void, and its end is very much uncertain.

To expedite transfer to criminal court, statutes were passed that circumvented the traditional mode of transfer – a waiver hearing in juvenile court. In *Kent v. United States* (1966) waiver hearings were regularized. Recognizing that transfer was a matter of momentous consequence that signaled the end of childhood and threatened the juvenile with adult sanctions that might be permanently disfiguring, the Supreme Court mandated a formal hearing and a thorough investigation into the youth's background and circumstances prior to waiver. Statutes in most jurisdictions specified that waiver required a finding that the youth was either too dangerous to remain in the juvenile system or no longer "amenable to treatment" in the juvenile system. Applying these criteria, juvenile court judges seldom invoked transfer. It was most often applied to repeat offenders who were nearing the age of majority and who had exhausted the court's treatment resources.

New "statutory exclusion" and "prosecutorial waiver" statutes have shifted the responsibility for transfer from the judiciary to the legislative and executive branches. Under "statutory exclusion," state and federal legislatures specify offense or offense/age criteria for "automatic transfer" to criminal court.[13] In many states, they permit or require the transfer of children as young as age 10 who are charged with very serious felonies. "Prosecutorial waiver" allows prosecutors to choose the forum in which cases will be tried, subject to statutory guidelines (age, offense, and prior record criteria) that are frequently very broad. For example, in many states the pool of eligibles includes young people charged with property crimes and misdemeanors.[14] These new transfer methods

---

[13]Actually, the process is anything but "automatic" because it is dependent on what charges prosecutors choose to file.

[14]For example, in Florida, prosecutors may choose to treat 16-year-olds charged with *any* felony as either juveniles or adults. They can also transfer youths as young as 10, although the criteria are more restrictive.

accomplished three things: they expedited the transfer process (unlike waiver, they require no investigations or hearings prior to transfer). They restricted the powers of a judiciary that was perceived as "too soft on crime." And, perhaps most important, they removed the offender-focus that had been the hallmark of the transfer decision. Unlike judicial waiver, the new transfer methods are purely offense-driven.

In addition to changes in transfer policy, many states have instituted blended sentencing, which represents a kind of middle ground between the juvenile and adult systems. Blended sentencing schemes come in a variety of forms, but many "criminalize" the juvenile court, permitting (and sometimes requiring) judges to impose lengthy sentences – served initially in the juvenile system, then in the adult system – for specified offenses. Dawson (1988) has aptly described this as the "third justice system." Blended sentencing is subject to criticism on a number of grounds. Most importantly, it lacks a cogent, underlying rationale and potentially sets up a "slippery slope" leading to a poorly planned merger of the juvenile and adult systems.

In some states, these reforms have greatly increased the numbers of youths entering the criminal courts. However, their impact nationwide has been somewhat less consequential than predicted. Although it was believed by some that prescriptive transfer statutes would literally flood adult jails and prisons with adolescent offenders, the increase in the numbers of youth transferred nationwide has been fairly modest. One reason is that prosecutors have not invoked the laws nearly as frequently as they might have: one recent study found that only 23% of youths eligible for "automatic" prosecutorial transfer for specified violent felonies were actually transferred (Sridharan et al., 2004). Another reason is that criminal courts frequently sentence transferred offenders more leniently than their adult counterparts. These outcomes are consistent with Professor Zimring's observation that criminal law reform frequently serves primarily symbolic functions, allowing politicians to appear tough on crime while producing only modest systemic changes. New laws tend to "bark much louder than they bite . . . [They] . . . satisfy the need for symbols of denunciation without making much difference in the penalties meted out to most offenders" (Zimring, 2001: 5).

If transfer reforms have been underutilized, they have nonetheless had a tremendous impact on the kinds of juveniles who are entering adult corrections systems. Because statutory exclusion statutes most often target serious and violent offenders regardless of their age or offense histories, the proportions of young adolescents, racial minorities, and first-time offenders entering the adult system have increased. The influx of young teens has burdened departments of correction unaccustomed to the special issues and problems associated with this population (e.g., increased risk of victimization, increased suicide risk, special educational needs). In addition, racial disparities in the application of reforms have exacerbated already serious concerns about disproportionate minority confinement and "unequal treatment under the law." Finally, it is unfortunate that, as a result of the reforms, youth who enter the criminal justice system frequently have not had the opportunity to benefit from any sort of rehabilitative intervention (see, Lanza-Kaduce et al., 2002; Sridharan et al., 2004). Often they are first offenders with substance abuse and mental health problems who, under the traditional judicial waiver system, most likely would have been retained in the juvenile system for treatment (Sridharan et al., 2004). In the adult system, where the incarcerated population has trebled since 1980 to a recent peak of over 2 million inmates, overcrowding and simple warehousing are the norm. In that system, the treatment needs of juvenile offenders almost surely remain unmet (Bishop and Frazier, 2000).

Although we could point to numerous other examples of the "get tough" assault on serious juvenile offenders (e.g., subjecting them to sex offender registration laws; counting their prior juvenile convictions as "strikes" for purposes of invoking adult habitual offender statutes that carry capital and life sentences), those we have discussed represent the major punitive reforms. The major exception to this punitive reform movement has to do with the death penalty, a subject to which we now turn.

3.1.1. The Death Penalty for Juveniles

In 1989, the United Nations passed the Convention on the Rights of the Child, which contains 41 articles establishing minimum standards for the protection of children. As of this date, only two countries have not ratified this Convention: the USA and Somalia. "Among the reasons given for the United States' failure to ratify are that its enforcement would interfere with individual state's rights, that rights acknowledged under the UN are not acknowledged as rights in the USA, and that US laws conflict with the principles of the Convention" (Sarri and Shook, 2005). The conflict between US law and principles of the Convention have primarily to do with the Convention's Article 37, which states that "neither capital punishment nor life imprisonment without possibility of release shall be imposed for offenses committed by persons below 18 years of age."

In the very same year that the UN Convention was passed, the US Supreme Court decided the case of *Stanford v. Kentucky*, which found no constitutional infirmity in allowing the death penalty to be applied to 16 and 17 year olds. In its opinion, the Court used an "evolving standards of decency" criterion to determine whether capital punishment of 16 and 17 year olds violated the Constitution's prohibition against "cruel and unusual punishments." Relying largely on evidence that many of the 38 states that permitted capital punishment also permitted the execution of persons under the age of 18, the court held that current standards of decency were not violated by the execution of 16 and 17 year olds.

As this chapter goes to press, the US Supreme Court has overturned its decision in *Stanford v. Kentucky*. In March 2005, it ruled in *Roper v. Simmons* that the death penalty constitutes "cruel and unusual punishment" when applied to persons under the age of 18. Although the same number of states accepted the death penalty and permitted the execution of 16 and 17 year olds in 2005 as was the case in 1989, the Court found that standards of decency had been violated. It was persuaded in part by social science research showing the comparative immaturity, impulsivity, and vulnerability to external pressures of juveniles. Importantly, the Court also looked beyond the borders of the USA in its assessment of evolving standards of decency. It specifically noted that the execution of juvenile offenders violated the UN Convention on the Rights of the Child (as well as several other international treaties) and concluded that the overwhelming weight of international opinion against the death penalty for juveniles supported a conclusion that the death penalty is cruel and unusual punishment for offenders under the age of 18.[15]

It remains to be seen whether the USA will now ratify the UN Convention on the Rights of the Child. It is likely that it will not, in part because the imposition of sentences of life without possibility of parole continues to be approved in many states for juveniles who have been transferred to criminal court (in violation of Article 47). Ratification of the Convention is also unlikely for a more fundamental reason: when the US Senate ratifies an international treaty, it supercedes state laws. The federalization of areas that have previously been governed by state law encroaches on a longstanding and cherished tradition of state's rights with respect to all matters not in conflict with the US Constitution.

We turn now to a discussion of recent trends at the "front end" of the system.

3.2. Delinquency Prevention

At the same time that legislatures were passing punitive reforms for the worst offenders, Congress was authorizing funds for delinquency prevention programs. Some are early intervention initiatives, while others are aimed at youths who have already begun to engage in delinquent behavior.

3.2.1. Early Intervention
In the last decade, early intervention has taken on important new emphases and become increasingly research-based. Early intervention programs are not entirely novel. In the 1960s, for example, we saw the development of Head Start, a well-funded preschool program for young children in disadvantaged neighborhoods

[15]The dissent in the case objected to taking guidance from foreign law and supported state's rights to make decisions on the use of capital punishment. The decision also provoked a backlash against using international law as a benchmark in the interpretation of the US Constitution. Indeed, a nonbinding resolution was introduced into Congress instructing the judiciary to *ignore* the laws of other countries. The representative who introduced the resolution commented that "[I]t is improper for them [the Supreme Court] to substitute foreign law for American law or the American Constitution. To the extent they deliberately ignore Congress' admonishment, they are no longer engaging in 'good behavior' in the meaning of the Constitution and they may subject themselves to the ultimate remedy, which would be impeachment."

in the nation's inner cities. But, at that time, such programs for children were generally not implemented under the umbrella of "delinquency prevention." (Head Start was part of President Lyndon Johnson's "War on Poverty.") Today, that has changed. Influenced by important theoretical and research advances in developmental criminology (e.g., Loeber and Farrington, 2000; Patterson and Yoerger, 1993), policy makers have become more cognizant of the connections between the family, school, and neighborhood contexts in which young children live and their risk of later delinquency and crime. To an unprecedented degree, research in developmental criminology has played a role in shaping at least one part of the nation's prevention policy agenda.

We see this most clearly in the 1992 reauthorization of the federal Juvenile Justice and Delinquency Prevention Act of 1974.[16] The 1992 law[17] created the Title V Community Prevention Grants Program, which is based on the premise that effective delinquency prevention "begins with an understanding of risk and protective factors" (Caliber Associates, 2002: 4). One of the most exciting aspects of this effort is its reliance on (1) what we have learned from criminal careers research and epidemiological criminology about the individual, family, school, and community factors that put children at risk for serious delinquent involvement, (2) what we have learned from this same research regarding protective factors that buffer the exposure to risk, and (3) what we have learned from recent advances in evaluation research about intervention strategies that are most and least promising (e.g., Sherman et al., 1998; Center for the Study and Prevention of Violence, n.d.). Much of the research on which prevention efforts are based – including both long-term longitudinal studies of the etiology of delinquency and sophisticated evaluation research – has been supported by OJJDP and other federal agencies. It is very significant that, in order to be eligible for Title V funding, community-grant recipients must conduct a research-based risk assessment and must choose prevention strategies that have been proven to be effective (e.g., prenatal/postnatal nurse visitation, parent training, antibullying programs).

The Communities That Care (CTC) program, which has been widely adopted, illustrates this new emphasis on risk-focused prevention (Hawkino and Catalano, 1992). Under CTC, entire communities, rather than individual agencies, receive funding and technical assistance to implement coordinated systems of delinquency prevention. CTC involves a systematic, multistep process: (1) rally community leaders to support delinquency prevention; (2) have them appoint a community board comprised of at-risk youth, parents, representatives of business and industry, and representatives of police, courts, corrections, and public and private youth-serving organizations; (3) have the board carry out an assessment of risk and protective factors in the community, make an inventory of existing community resources, and identify gaps in existing resources; (4) with that empirical base as a foundation,

[16]Public Law 93–415: 42 U.S.C. Section 5601 et seq.
[17]Public Law 107–273.

prioritize risks and develop a comprehensive delinquency prevention plan; and (5) to address the community's most pressing problems, coordinate existing resources and implement new programs, selecting from a portfolio of strategies that evaluation research has shown to be effective (Caliber Associates, 2002). The overall goal is to identify children at greatest risk, then to mobilize the community to reduce risk through well-coordinated interventions aimed at families, schools, peer groups, and neighborhoods. Although these are laudable goals, their attainment is hampered by a number of obstacles, of which we will mention just two. First, the program is not well funded: 75% of CTC communities receive annual grants totaling $52,000 or less (Caliber Associates, 2002: 19). Second, in the USA, services at the community-level are fragmented. It is extremely difficult to foster communication and coordination among businesses, police departments, juvenile courts, child welfare agencies, child protection agencies, school boards, health departments, mental health agencies, churches, and private not-for-profit youth-serving agencies. Agencies have domains, many are rule-bound and rigid, and many have neither the time nor the inclination to work together to develop and implement well-coordinated community prevention plans.

It remains to be seen whether programs funded under Title V, as well as other primary prevention programs, will endure and also whether they will be subject to rigorous evaluation to assess their long-term effectiveness. In the past, prevention efforts have been notably difficult either to sustain or to evaluate over the long term. Prevention programs that focus on the long term, and whose effects are difficult to measure, have, at least until recently, been a "hard sell." Politicians responsible for funding anticrime efforts have instead tended to focus on short-term programs that can demonstrate fairly immediate and quantifiable results (Lab, 2004). Prevention programs also have had a faddish quality about them, as each new election cycle brings promises of new and better programs to replace "failed efforts" that came before. There is a current focus on faith-based initiatives that is a prime example. In 2001, not long after the inauguration of President George W. Bush, the Justice Department outlined a plan for future funding that included special funding opportunities for programs that involve the faith community (e.g., through mentoring of elementary school children), despite any evidence that faith-based programs are more effective than secular ones. According to Lab (2004: 687), this prevention strategy is merely a politically motivated effort to win votes by courting the faith community.

3.2.2. Secondary Prevention

Much more well-funded than primary prevention programs are those that target youth who have already begun to exhibit problem behaviors, e.g., by being expelled from school or arrested for the first time, usually for a nonviolent offense. First offenders are frequently diverted from formal juvenile justice processing, continuing a trend that began in the 1960s. The early diversion movement was influenced to no small degree by labeling and societal reactions theories that called attention to the potentially damaging consequences of formal juvenile justice intervention. Although that diversion movement was only a partial success,[18] a number of new diversion programs have emerged in the last decade.

Teen courts (also called youth courts) represent one such innovation. These are "informal courts" to which youth are referred in lieu of formal processing. In order to be tried in teen court, youths must admit responsibility for the offense with which they are charged and agree to abide by the teen court's decision. In return, the charges are dismissed.[19] Referrals to teen court are most often restricted to young, first-time offenders charged with misdemeanor offenses (e.g., vandalism, shoplifting, alcohol possession, simple assault). In teen court, adolescents serve as jurors, attorneys, and sometimes also as judges. Many court personnel are themselves former teen court defendants who come back to serve as jurors and attorneys (Butts et al., 1999). The primary underlying premise of the program is that the judgment of a youth's peers may be more persuasive and beneficial than the judgment of adult officials. Sanctions imposed by teen courts tend to be more severe than those that would have been imposed had these same youths opted for formal processing. Typically, the teen court orders community work service or restitution, and the writing of essays or letters of apology.

Like most other juvenile justice innovations, teen court "caught on" in advance of any empirical research or solid evidence of its long-term effectiveness. Teen courts have proliferated rapidly – from about 50 in 1991 to about 700 at present – and they currently represent the fastest growing alternative to formal intervention. It is estimated that teen courts today handle 100,000 youth per year – or about one of every eight court referrals that are not formally processed. Thus far, there has been only one major evaluation of teen courts (Butts et al., 2002), which was carried out in four sites. Relative to comparison groups, teen court participants had significantly lower levels of recidivism over a 6-month follow-up period in two of the four sites.

Other secondary prevention efforts include the many variations on *Scared Straight*, a program grounded in deterrence theory that was initiated at Rahway State Prison in New Jersey in the late 1970s. In this program, teens are taken to prison for a day and confronted by inmates who intimidate them and relate the horrors of prison life. Although numerous evaluations of Scared Straight and other programs like it have consistently shown that they tend to *increase* rather than reduce recidivism, the popular myth that threats of punishment are effective deterrents helps to insure their continuation (Finckenauer and Gavin, 1999).

A discussion of recent trends in prevention would be incomplete without some mention of "zero tolerance policies." Following upon some tragic shooting

---

[18]Its legacy includes net widening, "bootstrapping" (relabeling status offenders as delinquents to render them eligible for formal intervention), and "transinstitutionalization" (displacement of status offenders from juvenile correctional institutions to mental health facilities).
[19]The only penalty for failure to comply is the reinstatement of charges.

incidents in suburban high schools in which teens killed and injured their class-mates, schools all over the country began introducing policies of automatic suspension or expulsion and arrest for bringing weapons of any type into schools. It was not long before these policies were expanded in many school districts to include the imposition of the same harsh penalties for possession of drugs and other forms of contraband (e.g., cigarettes), for fighting, and even for simple vio-lations of school rules. This approach has been criticized for overbreadth (e.g., students have been expelled from school for giving an aspirin to a classmate, for having a butter knife in a lunch pail, for cursing at a school official) and, thus far, has shown little if any benefit. It has been linked instead to increased rates of dropout and delinquency. Because zero tolerance policies have been implemented disproportionately in inner city schools, they have also had a differentially harsh impact on impoverished minority youths.

Other diversionary reforms flow out of the restorative justice movement, which was "virtually unknown to all but a small group of academics at the beginning of the 1990s" (Bazemore and Walgrave, 1999: 1). Restorative justice programs take a variety of forms, including victim-offender mediation, com-munity reparation boards, family group conferencing, and circle sentencing (Bazemore and Umbreit, 2001). Instead of focusing on the offender, these pro-grams focus on the offense; on its effects on the victim and (with the exception of victim-offender mediation) the larger community of family and friends that sup-port both victim and offender; and on apology, forgiveness, and reparation of harm. Broadly stated, the goals are to educate participants about the harms – especially the emotional harms and fracturing of relationships – caused by the offense; to repair the harms; and to rebuild relationships and strengthen systems of infor-mal social control. The establishment of restorative justice programs in the USA has not kept pace with similar developments in Western Europe, Austra-lia, New Zealand, and Canada, though in some jurisdictions substantial prog-ress has been made.[20] Bazemore and Walgrave (1999: 60) offer the following observations regarding the fact that these programs have not been more widely adopted:

> [J]uvenile justice administrators today are often overwhelmed with responding to policy-maker demands that they get tough (while con-tinuing to provide treatment). . . . In an already overcrowded field where a new "program of the month" and a new "crisis of the week" vie for the attention of juvenile justice administrators, it is questionable whether restorative justice practices and policies will break through as priorities.

---

[20]Minnesota and Pennsylvania have emerged as leaders in the use of family group conferencing. The state of Vermont has made community reparation boards a centerpiece of its juvenile justice system for youth who admit guilt. However, Vermont's program has recently been criticized for low levels of victim participation, the composition of the boards (i.e., civic and business leaders) and, most important, for the tendency to be more punitive than reparative.

3.2.3. Juvenile Court: Processing, Sentencing, and Correctional Reforms for Middle-Range Offenders

The third front in American juvenile justice focuses on the very large group of offenders who are formally processed in the juvenile court. The number of youth formally processed in the juvenile courts rose significantly from 1990 to 1999 (from about 650,000 in 1990 to nearly 1 million in 1999; Puzzanchera et al., 2003), an increase that far outstripped the 3% increase in juvenile arrests over the same time period (Snyder, 2002). The reason for the discrepancy is twofold. First, there were changes in the way that police disposed of juvenile arrests. Over the last 25 years, law enforcement has been "cracking down" by referring a greater proportion of arrestees to the juvenile court. The proportion of arrests that were referred to juvenile court rose from 58% to 64% between 1980 and 1990, and from 64% to 72% in the following decade (Snyder, 2003). Second, changes have taken place in the way that juvenile courts dispose of referrals. Although the numbers of youth transferred to the adult system have increased, the proportions of youth diverted from formal processing have decreased much more significantly (from 50% of referrals in 1990 to 43% in 1999). Consequently, the proportion of delinquency cases in which a petition was filed rose from 50% of all referrals in 1990 to 57% in 1999. Although the greatest numerical increases in prosecuted offenses involved drug crimes,[21] what is perhaps most telling is that the proportion of offenses handled formally increased most for the *least* serious offenses (disorderly conduct and other public order offenses), reflecting the tendency of the court to take even minor offenses more seriously.[22] The proportion of petitioned delinquency cases that resulted in formal adjudications of delinquency (i.e., convictions) also rose over the decade, from 60% of cases in 1990 to 66% in 1999. These increases occurred across all offense categories (Puzzanchera et al., 2003). Of those adjudicated, a smaller percentage were committed to out-of-home placements (32% in 1990 and 24% in 1999), but that may reflect the fact that institutions were already overcrowded. A much greater *number* of delinquents were incarcerated in 1999 than in 1990 (an additional 30,000 youngsters), and more large institutions (detention centers and training schools) were built to house them. In sum, during the 1990s much greater proportions of cases were referred to, prosecuted in, and convicted by the juvenile court, and youth were incarcerated in greater numbers. In terms of processing in the juvenile court, we see clear indications of much greater formal social control than was the case in decades past.

The juvenile court's orientation toward its youth clientele is far less clear. There are many indications that juvenile courts are beginning to converge with the criminal courts in their emphasis on punishment. In the past two decades,

---

[21]Drug prosecutions increased 15.2% over the decade, consistent with the "war on drugs."

[22]This trend is entirely consistent with adoption of the "graduated sanctions" approach, about which we will have more to say shortly.

legislatures in 27 states revised their juvenile codes to endorse either "punish-ment" or "accountability" as objectives of the juvenile court. Twenty-six also endorse protection of the public safety as an explicit juvenile justice goal. How-ever, contrary to the "convergence thesis," legislatures have not abandoned the historical rehabilitative mission that has distinguished the juvenile court from its criminal counterpart. A recent review of juvenile code purpose clauses (Sanborn and Salerno, 2005) revealed that all 50 jurisdictions maintain provisions that are compatible with the juvenile court's traditional mission. Thirty states continue to endorse the view that the court is to act "in the best interests of the child." Thirty-five states encourage the juvenile court to rehabilitate children at home. Twenty-four states indicate that the aim of the juvenile court is to "preserve or strengthen the child's family or the child's ties to the family." Thus, the law on the books suggests that most states are trying to strike a balance between punitive and social welfare objectives. Of course, the law on the books may not match the law in action.

Juvenile code purpose clauses are only one indication of current trends. There are other indications that juvenile courts are beginning to resemble criminal courts. Dating back to the "due process revolution" of the 1960s and 1970s, juve-niles were given important procedural rights to which they had not previously been entitled (e.g., right to notice, right to counsel, right to remain silent, the requirement that guilt be proven "beyond a reasonable doubt")[23] which made court proceedings much more formal and adversarial than they had been previ-ously. Recent changes have not expanded rights, but have instead chipped away at special protections that youth have traditionally enjoyed. Juvenile court pro-ceedings have historically been closed to the public, juvenile records have been confidential and subject to later expungement, and at least nonserious juvenile offenders were exempt from photographing and fingerprinting. In the 1990s, 47 states made juvenile records and proceedings more open (Snyder and Sickmund, 1999: 89), 46 allowed juveniles to be photographed and fingerprinted, and 42 allowed the names – and sometimes the photographs and court records – of juve-niles to be released to the media (Snyder and Sickmund, 1999: 101).

Juvenile courts' sentencing policies have also undergone change. Although in nearly every jurisdiction sentencing for the vast majority of offenders remains indeterminate, legislatures have also passed determinate sentencing, guidelines-based sentencing, and mandatory minimum sentencing for some offenses, all of which are contrary to the offender-focused dispositions that have long been a hallmark of the juvenile court. These are offense-driven, "one size fits all" sanc-tions that are imposed without any consideration of individual needs and cir-cumstances. For example, legislatures in 31 jurisdictions have passed mandatory sentencing statutes for some offenses (Sanborn and Salerno, 2005: 377). While most of these mandatory sentences do *not* involve incarceration, 26 states have

---

[23]"Beyond a reasonable doubt" is the traditional criminal law standard.

adopted minimum mandatory periods of incarceration for certain violent crimes, weapons offenses, and repeat felony offenders (Sanborn and Salerno, 2005: 377–380). Many of these statutes suffer from overbreadth and are subject to misapplication.[24]

Nationally, the trend is toward sentencing youth based on notions of punishment and accountability, rather than rehabilitation. Significantly, the federal government has endorsed a policy of "graduated sanctions" under which youth who have been adjudicated delinquent receive sanctions "proportionate to the offense" to hold them accountable for their actions and to prevent further law violations. This approach has become the centerpiece of OJJDP's Juvenile Accountability Incentive Block Grants program (JAIBG) – now renamed JABG – the largest single source of federal funding for juvenile programs in the country.[25] The program was revised in 2003, in part to make its deterrent objectives more explicit. The new provisions indicate that although participation in the graduated sanctions approach by individual courts is voluntary, states:

> must encourage courts to participate. At a minimum, such systems should impose sanctions for each offense; sanctions should escalate in intensity with each subsequent, more serious charge; and the system should be sufficiently flexible to allow for individualized sanctions and services appropriate for each offender (Andrews and Marble, 2003: 3).

This language surely smacks of the criminalization of the juvenile court. JABG clearly moves federal policy closer to a "pure punishment" approach. None of its 16 provisions mentions "rehabilitation," "help," "development," or "skills building" – language that had been used in OJJDP publications describing its JAIBG predecessor (see, e.g., Beyer, 2003). The only hint of another agenda is found in a provision for "Risk and Needs Assessment" that supports "programs to conduct risk and needs assessments of juvenile offenders that facilitate early intervention and the provision of comprehensive services, including mental health screening and treatment and substance abuse testing and treatment" (Andrews and Marble, 2003: 2).

Other recent developments in the juvenile corrections area similarly suggest that a punishment agenda has taken hold. The 1980s saw the establishment of

---

[24]In research conducted by one of the authors, a youth arrested for throwing a piece of fruit at another was charged with "throwing a deadly missile," one who stole a clown statue from a restaurant play area was charged with" "burglary of an occupied structure," and a youth who took a pickup truck for a brief "joyride" was charged with "armed burglary" because a toolbox containing a hammer and screwdrivers was found in the back of the truck. All of these charged offenses are serious felonies that carry lengthy maximum sentences.

[25]Initiated in 1998 (Public Law 105–119), its annual funding level authorization is $500 million. Compare this to the Title V prevention program discussed earlier, which has an annual funding allocation of $27 million. While prevention is a priority, punishment of past actions clearly takes precedence.

boot camps, first in the adult system (1983), then in the juvenile system (1985). Boot camps are short-term (90–120 day) residential programs where inmates are subjected to military-style basic training, including physical labor, regimented activity, and intense verbal degradation. Some, but not all, include educational and counseling components. OJJDP supported the boot camp initiative and funded an evaluation of three programs in three different states that showed that boot camp participants had higher recidivism rates than controls (Peters et al., 1997). Findings of ineffectiveness are consistent with evaluations of boot camps in the adult system (see MacKenzie, 2000). Despite the negative results, and despite allegations of staff abuse, boot camps have "caught on" in the same way that other deterrence-based programs have. At least two states (Texas and Virginia) have incorporated them into the continuum of graduated sanctions (Howell, 2003: 134).

Other trends in juvenile sentencing include electronic monitoring, random drug testing, a shift in probation that makes it more surveillance- than service-oriented, and simple incarceration. (Detention centers, which have little in the way of programming, are increasingly being used as places to which youth are sentenced.) These are all examples of get-tough reforms, and there is little evidence that any of them is effective.

Although it is clear that the USA has embraced retributive and deterrent objectives for convicted juvenile offenders to a degree not seen since the 19th century, there are some indications that we have not embraced this position single-mindedly. As we have seen, the restorative justice movement, which is inconsistent with a narrow focus on punishment, is gaining ground. In some areas of the country, restorative justice principles and programs are being used at sentencing and as an adjunct to probation.[26] There is also another movement afoot that may be even more important. More specifically, in the midst of all the indicia of a criminalized juvenile justice that we have discussed, there are signs of a revitalization of rehabilitation.

In the last 15 years, there have been major advances in evaluation research, and both private foundations and the federal government have invested significant funding in assessing the effectiveness of various forms of treatment.[27] This research has produced fairly consistent evidence that treatment-oriented

---

[26]We see little potential for the transformation of juvenile justice around principles of restorative justice. Existing bureaucracies (court, probation, prosecutorial, and defense systems) are entrenched, and do not easily accommodate a central role for victims and community members, nor relinquish their focus on adversariness and due process.

[27]Interest in rehabilitation waned in the 1970s, following the release of the highly publicized "Martinson Report" (Martinson, 1974; Lipton et al., 1975), which concluded that "nothing works." Critics of the report responded that the negative results could be explained by methodological problems and weak evaluations, rather than by the absence of effective treatments, but these responses – and even the subsequent retraction of the Martinson Report's conclusion by its authors – fell on deaf ears. Instead, the idea of rehabilitation was increasingly viewed with skepticism. Subsequent increases in juvenile crime, especially juvenile violence, contributed to the view that treatment was ineffective.

programs, especially those that focus on interpersonal skill development and parent/family interventions, are considerably more effective than punishment-oriented ones (e.g., Lipsey and Wilson, 1998; Lipsey et al., 2000). Research has identified effective nonresidential treatment programs for minor and first-time offenders as well as effective residential interventions for serious and chronic offenders. Some show very substantial reductions in recidivism, especially if programs are well-designed and faithfully implemented (Lipsey 1999a, b). In addition to Lipsey's research, which utilizes meta-analysis, the Center for the Study and Prevention of Violence has played a major role in renewing interest in treatment. Center staff have reviewed individual evaluations of rehabilitation programs throughout the country that meet rigorous scientific criteria (i.e., the evaluation must use an experimental design and include at least 1 year of follow-up). They have identified a number of "Blueprint Programs" that have produced statistically significant reductions in recidivism and that have been replicated in at least one other site. (These include multisystemic therapy, life skills training, and multidimensional treatment foster care.)

It is possible that, at the local level, thousands (or even tens of thousands) of rehabilitation programs exist despite policymakers' determination to implement punitive policies. Unfortunately, because most states and the federal government do not maintain program inventories or conduct surveys to determine what kinds of local programs are operating and where, it is impossible to determine the extent of rehabilitative programming in the USA today.

It is still too early to tell, but the punitive tide may be turning. Opinion polls show that the public continues to support treatment for juvenile offenders. In addition, public officials have begun to express real worry about how they are going to manage the financial costs of America's "imprisonment binge" (Irwin and Austin, 1994). In combination with the research evidence showing the substantial advantages of rehabilitative programs over punitive ones, these considerations may support a revival of interest in returning to traditional core principles of juvenile justice.

4. CONCLUDING THOUGHTS

In his seminal book on American street gangs Klein (1995) laments the fact that 30 years of gang intervention and programming have little to show for what works. The situation is not quite that bad with regard to the impact of programs and policies in juvenile justice in the USA, but almost. Lundman (2001: 11) notes the tendency in the USA to choose what he calls "cut-through" programs, programs that ignore root causes of delinquency and are seen as "quick fixes." This predilection for such cut-through programs has led the USA to spend large amounts of money on programs such as DARE, zero tolerance programs, Scared Straight Programs, boot camps, large custodial programs, and curfew and truancy interventions. Evaluation results for these programs have been reviewed extensively (see Howell, 2003) and found wanting for positive results.

Tremendous advances in program evaluation research have taken place in the last 20 years. As a consequence, we have a great deal more evidence of the efficacy of some prevention and intervention strategies. We now know a great deal about ineffective policies and programs, as well as those that produce meaningful beneficial effects. This is not to say, however, that policy makers will look to social science research for guidance. Many ineffective programs continue because the general public continues to believe that they are effective or because they serve retributive aims in an era that is highly punishment oriented. Effective programs may not be popular, or they may be implemented only sparsely among a few communities. Although the USA does not have national juvenile justice policy, there is much that could be done at the federal level to support the proliferation of effective strategies (e.g., by making funds available for communities that want to implement them). However, the current administration has been far more supportive of simplistic and inexpensive punitive programs (that tend to be less effective) than of holistic and generally more costly strategies aimed at providing family intervention, education and training, social skills training, and social support. As important as it is to have good evaluation and research to use as a foundation for programs, it is equally important to have the political will and courage to use these results for effective programming. To date, the USA seldom demonstrates that will. The last decade of policy, legislative and program changes have been overwhelmingly punitive, to the exclusion of considerations of the welfare of juveniles. If Tom Bernard is right that juvenile justice moves from cycles of punitiveness to concern for the welfare of children, the USA should be on the verge of a major change in the orientation of its juvenile justice system. We are not that optimistic.

REFERENCES

Ainsworth, J.E. (1991). "Re-Imagining Childhood and Reconstructing the Legal Order: The Case for Abolishing the Juvenile Court," North Carolina Law Review, 69:1083–1133.

Allen, F. (1981). *The Decline of the Rehabilitative Ideal*. New Haven, CT: Yale.

Andrews, C. and Marble, L. (2003). "Changes to OJJDP's Juvenile Accountability Program." OJJDP Juvenile Justice Bulletin, June 2003 Washington, DC: US Department of Justice, Office of Justice Programs.

Bazemore, G. and Umbreit, M.S. (2001). "A comparison of four restorative justice conferencing models." *Juvenile Justice Bulletin* (February). Washington, DC: US Department of Justice, Office of Justice Programs, Office of Juvenile Justice and Delinquency Prevention.

Bazemore, G. and Walgrave, L. (1999). "Introduction: Restorative Justice and the International Juvenile Justice Crisis," in G. Bazemore and L. Walgrave (eds.), *Restorative Juvenile Justice: Repairing the Harm of Youth Crime*. Monsey, NY: Criminal Justice Press, pp. 1–13.

Bennett, W.J., DiIulio, J.J., Jr., and Walters, J.P. (1996). *Body Count: Moral Poverty and How to Win America's War Against Crime and Drugs*, New York: Simon and Schuster.

Bernard, T.J. (1992). *The Cycle of Juvenile Justice*. New York: Oxford.

Beyer, M. (2003). Best Practices in Juvenile Accountability. JAIBG BULLETIN, April 2003. Washington DC: US Department of Justice, Office of Justice Programs. Online available at http://www.ncjrs.gov/html/ojjdp/184745/contents.html.

Bishop, D.M. and Frazier, C. (1992). "Gender Bias in Juvenile Justice Processing: Implications of the JJDP Act," *Journal of Criminal Law and Criminology*, 82:1162–1186.

Bishop, D.M. and Frazier, C. (2000). "Consequences of Transfer," in J. Fagan and F. Zimring (eds.), The Changing Borders of Juvenile Justice, Chicago: University of Chicago Press, pp. 227–276.

Butts, J.A. and Mears, D.P. (2001). "Reviving Juvenile Justice in a Get-Tough Era," *Youth and Society*, 33:169–198.

Butts, J., Hoffman, D., and Buck, J. (1999). "Teen Courts in the United States: A Profile of Current Programs" *OOJDP Fact Sheet No. 118*. Washington, DC: US Department of Justice, Office of Justice Programs, Office of Juvenile Justice and Delinquency Prevention.

Butts, J.A., Buck, J., and Coggeshall, M. (2002). *The Impact of Teen Court on Young Offenders*. Washington, DC: The Urban Institute.

Caliber Associates. (2002). *2002 Report to Congress: Title V Community Prevention Grants Program*, NCJ 202019. Washington, DC: US Department of Justice, Office of Justice Programs, Office of Juvenile Justice and Delinquency Prevention.

Carlsson, Y. and Decker, S.H. (2005). "Gang and Youth Violence Prevention and Intervention: Contrasting the Experience of the Scandinavian Welfare State with the United States," in S. Decker and F. Weerman (eds.), *Gangs and Troublesome Youth Groups in Europe: Results from the Eurogang Research Program*, San Francisco, CA: Alta Mira.

Carter, R.M. (1984). "The United States," in M. Klein (ed.), *Western Systems of Juvenile Justice*, Beverly Hills, CA: Sage, pp. 17–38.

Center for the Study and Prevention of Violence. *Blueprints for Violence Prevention*. Online available at http://www.colorado.edu/cspv/blueprints/.

Dawson, R.O. (1988). "The Third Justice System: The New Juvenile-Criminal System of Determinate Sentencing for the Youthful Violent Offender in Texas," *St. Mary's Law Journal* 19: 943–1015.

Decker, S.H. and Curry, G.D. (2001). *JAIBG, St. Louis. Third Year Evaluation Report*. University of Missouri-St. Louis: Department of Criminology and Criminal Justice.

Feld, B.C. (1999). *Bad Kids: Race and the Transformation of the Juvenile Court*. New York: Oxford University Press.

Finckenauer, J.O., and Gavin, P.W. (1999). *Scared Straight: The Panacea Phenomenon Revisited*. Prospect Heights, IL: Waveland.

Hawkins, D. and Catalano, R. (1992). *Communities that Care*. San Francisco: Jossey-Bass.

Howell, J.C. (2003). *Preventing and Reducing Juvenile Delinquency: A Comprehensive Framework*. Thousand Oaks, CA: Sage.

Irwin, J. and Austin, J. (1994). *It's About Time: America's Imprisonment Binge*. New York: Oxford University Press.

Johnston, L.D., O'Malley, P.M., Bachman, J.G., and Schulenberg, J.E. (2005). *Monitoring the Future. National Results on Adolescent Drug Use: Overview of Key Findings, 2004*, NIH Publication No. 05–5726. Bethesda, MD: National Institute on Drug Abuse.

Klein, M.W. (1984). "Introduction," in M. Klein (ed.), *Western Systems of Juvenile Justice*, Beverly Hills, CA: Sage, pp. 1–16.

Klein, M.W. (1995). *The American Street Gang*. New York: Oxford.

Lab, S.P. (2004). "Crime Prevention, Politics, and the Art of Going Nowhere Fast" [Academy of Criminal Justice Sciences Presidential Address], *Justice Quarterly*, 21: 681–692.

Lanza-Kaduce, L., Frazier, C.E., Lane, J., and Bishop, D.M. (2002). *Juvenile Transfers to Criminal Court Study: Final Report*. Online available at http://nicic.org/Library/017540.

Lauritsen, J., Sampson, R.J. and Laub, J. (1991). "The Link Between Offending and Victimization Among Adolescents," *Criminology*, 29: 265–292.

Lipsey, M.W. (1999a). "Can Intervention Rehabilitate Serious Delinquents," *Annals of the American Academy of Political and Social Science*, 564:142–166.

Lipsey, M.W. (1999b). "Can Rehabilitative Programs Reduce the Recidivism of Juvenile Offenders? An Inquiry into the Effectiveness of Practical Programs," *Virginia Journal of Social Policy and Law*, 6:611–641.

Lipsey, M.W. and Wilson, D.B. (1998). Effective Intervention for Serious Juvenile Offenders: A Synthesis of Research, in R. Loeber and D.P. Farrington (eds.), *Serious and Violent Juvenile Offenders: Risk Factors and Successful Interventions*, Thousand Oaks, CA: Sage, pp. 313–345.

Lipsey, M.W., Wilson, D.B., and Cothern, L. (2000). *Effective Interventions for Serious Juvenile Offenders*. Washington, DC: US Department of Justice, Office of Juvenile Justice and Delinquency Prevention.

Lipton, D., Martinson, R., and Wilks, J. (1975). *The Effectiveness of Correctional Treatment: A Survey of Treatment Evaluation Studies*. New York: Praeger.

Loeber, R. and Farrington, D.P. (2000). "Young Children Who Commit Crime: Epidemiology, Developmental Origins, Risk Factors, Early Interventions, and Policy Implications," *Development and Psychopathology*, 12:737–762.

Lundman, R.J. (2001). *Prevention and Control of Juvenile Delinquency*. New York: Oxford.

MacKenzie, D.L. (2000). "Evidence-Based Corrections: Identifying What Works," *Crime and Delinquency*, 46:457–471.

Martinson, R. (1974). What Works? Questions and Answers About Prison Reform, *Public Interest*, 35:22–54.

Patterson, G.R. and Yoerger, K. (1993). "Developmental Models for Delinquent Behavior," in S. Hodgins (ed.), *Mental Disorder and Crime*, Newbury Park, CA: Sage, pp. 140–172.

Peters, M., Thomas, D., and Zamberlan, C. (1997). *Boot Camps for Juvenile Offenders*. Washington, DC: US Department of Justice, Office of Juvenile Justice and Delinquency Prevention.

Pisciotta, A.W. (1984). "*Parens Patriae*, Treatment and Reform: The Case of the Western House of Refuge, 1849–1907," *New England Journal on Criminal and Civil Confinement*, 10: 65–86.

Pisciotta, A.W. (1991). "A House Divided: Penal Reform at the Illinois State Reformatory, 1891–1915," *Crime and Delinquency*, 37: 165–185.

Pisciotta, A.W. (1993). "Child Saving or Child Brokerage? The Theory and Practice of Indenture and Parole at the New York House of Refuge. 1825–1935," in A. Hess and P. Clement (eds.), *The History of Juvenile Delinquency: A Collection of Essays*, Germany: Scientia Publishers, pp. 533–555.

Pisciotta, A.W. (1994). *Benevolent Repression: Social Control and the American Reformatory-Prison Movement*. New York: New York University Press.

Platt, A.M. (1977). *The Child Savers: The Invention of Delinquency*. Chicago: University of Chicago Press.

Puzzanchera, C., Stahl, A.L., Finnegan, T.A., Tierney, N., and Snyder, H.N. (2003). *Juvenile Court Statistics 1999*. Pittsburgh, PA: National Center for Juvenile Justice.

Rothman, D.J. (1971). *The Discovery of the Asylum: Social Order and Disorder in the New Republic*. Boston: Little, Brown and Company.

Sanborn, J.B., Jr. and Salerno, A.W. (2005). *The Juvenile Justice System: Law and Process*. Los Angeles: Roxbury.

Sarri, R. and Shook, J. (2005). "Human Rights and Juvenile Justice in the United States," in M. Ensalaco and L. Majka (eds.), Children's Human Rights. Lanham, MD: Rowman and Littlefield, pp. 218–240.

Scott, E.C. (2001). "The Legal Construction of Childhood," in M. Rosenheim, F.E. Zimring, D.S. Tanenhaus, and B. Dohrn (eds.), *A Century of Juvenile Justice*, Chicago: University of Chicago Press, pp. 113–141.

Sherman, L.W., Gottfredson, D., MacKenzie, D., Eck, J., Reuter, P., and Bushway, S. (1998). *Preventing Crime: What Works, What Doesn't, What's Promising*. Washington, DC: US Department of Justice, Office of Justice Programs, National Institute of Justice.

Sickmund, M. (2004). *Juveniles in Corrections: Juvenile Offenders and Victims National Report Series Bulletin*. Washington, DC: US Department of Justice, Office of Justice Programs, Office of Juvenile Justice and Delinquency Prevention.

Snyder, H.N. (2002). *Juvenile Arrests 2000*. Washington, DC: US Department of Justice, Office of Juvenile Justice and Delinquency Prevention.

Snyder, H.N. (2003). *Juvenile Arrests 2001*. Washington, DC: US Department of Justice, Office of Juvenile Justice and Delinquency Prevention.

Snyder, H.N. and Sickmund, M. (1999). *Juvenile Offenders and Victims: 1999 National Report*. Washington, DC: US Department of Justice, Office of Juvenile Justice and Delinquency Prevention.

Sridharan, S., Greenfield, L., and Blakley, B. (2004). "A Study of Prosecutorial Certification Practice in Virginia," *Criminology and Public Policy*, 3:605–632.

Tanenhaus, D.S. (2004). *Juvenile Justice in the Making*. New York: Oxford University Press.

U.N. General Assembly. (1989). United Nations Convention on the Rights of the Child, U.N. General Assembly, Document A/RES/44/25 (12 December 1989) with Annex. Online available at http://www.cirp.org/library/ethics/UN-convention/.

Zimring, F.E. (1998). American Youth Violence. New York: Oxford University Press.

Zimring, F.E. (2001). "The New Politics of Criminal Justice: Of 'Three Strikes,' Truth-in-Sentencing, and Megan's Laws," *Perspectives on Crime and Justice: 1999–2000 Lecture Series*. Washington, DC: US Department of Justice, National Institute of Justice. Online available at http://www.ncjrs.org/pdffiles1/nij/184245.pdf.

CASES

Kent v. United States, 383 US 541 (1966)

Stanford v. Kentucky, 492 US 361 (1989)

Roper v. Simmons, 543 US 551 (2005)

2

Canada's Juvenile Justice System: Promoting Community-Based Responses to Youth Crime

Nicholas Bala and Julian V. Roberts

INTRODUCTION: THE YOUTH JUSTICE CONTEXT IN CANADA

There have been profound changes in Canada's juvenile justice system during the century that it has been in existence, most recently when the Youth Criminal Justice Act (YCJA)[1] came into force in April 2003. A major rationale for enacting the statute was to reduce Canada's high rate of custody for adolescent offenders, based on the belief that community-based responses are more effective for dealing with most young offenders. The YCJA continues to protect the legal rights of youth, such as access to counsel. This chapter discusses the evolution of Canada's juvenile justice system over the past two decades. It considers the policy concerns that led to the enactment of the YCJA and the impact that the new law is having. The new statute addresses some problems in youth justice that have been uncovered by empirical research, and is thus to a significant degree, evidence-driven. Where appropriate, we provide Canadian research findings relevant to the specific policy developments.

By way of introduction it should be noted that Canada is a federal country with 10 provinces and 3 territories. It has a population of about 31.6 million, of whom about 8% are between 12 and 18 years, the age range for jurisdiction under the YCJA; in 2003–2004 about 17% of charges by police were laid against youth.[2] Under Canada's Constitution the jurisdiction for the enactment of criminal laws, including those that govern juvenile offenders, rests with the federal Parliament. However, responsibility for the enforcement of criminal laws and the provision of services for youthful offenders rests with the provinces and territories, which also have full responsibility for the enactment of laws and provision of services in such related fields as child welfare, education and health. As a consequence of this overlap of responsibility, in practice the enactment of new juvenile legislation has involved the federal government consulting extensively with the provinces and territories before enacting the new law, and providing some funding support for its implementation.

---

[1]YCJA., S.C. 2002, c. 1. In force from 1 April 2003.
[2]Statistics Canada (2005), *Youth Court Statistics 2003–04*, Juristat, Vol. 25, No. 4, p. 3.

J. Junger-Tas and S. H. Decker (eds.), International Handbook of Juvenile Justice, 37–64.
© 2006 Springer.

1. A CENTURY OF CHANGE IN CANADA'S JUVENILE JUSTICE SYSTEM

Canada's first national juvenile justice law, the Juvenile Delinquents Act (JDA)[3] of 1908 recognized that children and youths are different from adults and should not be held accountable for violations of the criminal law in the same fashion as adults.

In 1984, the JDA was replaced by the Young Offenders Act (YOA).[4] The introduction of the YOA represented a dramatic change in Canada's response to youth offending, moving from a discretionary welfare-oriented regime that, in theory at least, promoted the "best interests" of juvenile offenders, to a regime that was clearly criminal law. The YOA was in turn replaced by the YCJA in 2003. While there are significant differences between these two most recent statutes, both statutes share some important characteristics, emphasizing respect for legal rights and the accountability of young offenders, albeit not holding youths accountable to the same extent as adult offenders.

2. THE JUVENILE DELINQUENTS ACT (1908–1984)

The JDA had an explicitly welfare-oriented philosophy and stated that juveniles who violated the law were not to be treated as "criminal offenders," but rather as "misdirected and misguided" children, "needing aid, encouragement, help and assistance."[5] Since the focus of the law was on the promotion of the welfare of the child, there was little concern for legal rights, and during much of the time that the JDA was in force many Juvenile Court judges did not have legal training. The express legislative concerns about the special needs and rehabilitation of youth did not, however, necessarily translate into more lenient treatment. Sentencing under the JDA could result in light sanctions for some adolescents, particularly those from "good homes" with middle-class parents, but it also resulted in an intrusive response to some youthful offenders, especially juveniles from marginalized backgrounds who were often placed in custody facilities for much longer periods than adults who committed the same offences. Adolescent girls were sometimes placed in custody for the vaguely worded delinquency of "sexual immorality." Aboriginal juveniles were placed in juvenile correctional facilities in disproportionate numbers.

---

[3]Juvenile Delinquents Act, first enacted as S.C. 1908, c. 40; subject to minor amendments over the years, finally as Juvenile Delinquents Act, R.S.C. 1970, c. J-3. Starting in the mid-19th century provincial governments began to enact legislation that provided for the confinement of children separate from adults in prisons and the establishment of juvenile reformatories.

[4]YOA, R.S.C. 1985, c. Y-1, enacted as S.C. 1980–81–82–83, c. 110.

[5]JDA, s. 38.

The JDA provided for indefinite committals to youth custody facilities, based on the rationale that some juveniles needed the benefit of a significant period of time in a structured environment, away from a corrupting situation at home, and that the length of time needed to effect rehabilitation could not be determined by a court, but only by correctional officials after the youth spent time in custody. Despite the rehabilitative aspirations of the JDA, juveniles inevitably felt that they were being punished, and by the 1970s there were growing doubts about the capacity of the juvenile corrections system to rehabilitate juvenile offenders (Shamsie, 1981). Further, all too often these juveniles, who had few legal protections, were being subjected to physical abuse or sexual exploitation by staff, or intimidation by other inmates in juvenile facilities (Bessner, 1998).

3. THE YOUNG OFFENDERS ACT (1984–2003)

By the mid-1960s the JDA was the subject of increasing criticism,[6] but it was not until 1984 that the YOA replaced the JDA. A strong impetus to action was the constitutional entrenchment of the *Canadian Charter of Rights and Freedoms* in 1982. The informality and lack of legal rights for youths in the JDA were inconsistent with the legal protections recognized in the *Charter*, while the interprovincial variation allowed by the JDA for such issues as age jurisdiction was inconsistent with the equal protection of the law guaranteed by s. 15 of the *Charter*.[7]

Under the JDA, there was variation between provinces in both the minimum age of Juvenile Court jurisdiction (from 7 to 14 years) and in the maximum age (with adult jurisdiction starting from 16 to 18 years). The YOA provided greater recognition of legal rights than the JDA, as well as establishing a uniform national age jurisdiction of 12 through to the 18th birthday (as of the date of the offence), developments consistent with the emphasis in the *Charter* on due process of law and equal treatment under the law. Children under 12 years of age who commit criminal acts can only be dealt with informally or are referred to the child welfare authorities if there are concerns about inadequate parental care.

The YOA abolished the indeterminate sentences of the JDA, which were premised on providing involuntary treatment as long as this was consistent with the needs of a delinquent youth. The YOA used determinate (fixed) custodial dispositions, subject to judicially controlled early release, premised on the notion that holding a youth accountable was the dominant objective of the Act rather

---

[6]See, for example, Canada, Department of Justice, Report of the Committee on Juvenile Delinquency, *Juvenile Delinquency in Canada* (Ottawa: Queen's Printer, 1965).

[7]*Canadian Charter of Rights and Freedoms*, enacted as Part I of the *Constitution Act, 1982*, being Schedule B to the *Canada Act, 1982* (UK), 1982, c. 11 (subsequently referred to as the *Charter*).

than rehabilitation. The YOA was also a much more detailed piece of legislation than the JDA, regulating every stage of the youth justice process, including arrest and police questioning, diversion to alternatives to youth court, access to legal counsel, restrictions on disclosure of information, and the sentencing process. The YOA moved away from the child-welfare philosophy of the previous Act, abolishing the vague status offence of "sexual immorality" and focusing on federal criminal offences.

4. DISSATISFACTION WITH THE YOA: CANADIAN POLITICS AND YOUTH CRIME POLICIES

By the early 1990s the YOA was subject to growing public and political criticism. Concerns were being raised about the perceived inadequacy of the maximum three-year sentence under that Act for violent young offenders, especially those convicted of murder, and about the difficulties encountered in transferring youths to adult court where they might face much longer sentences in adult prisons. While the youth homicide rate in Canada has been quite stable over the past few decades, and the rate has been much lower than in the USA (Hormick et al. 1995),[8] the issue of youth violence, and especially youth homicide, received increased media attention in Canada in the 1990s, with conservative politicians demanding that the government "get tough" with youth crime.

Police reports of youth crime in Canada increased in the late 1980s, and the reported rate of youth crime peaked in the early 1990s. The rise in police reports about youth crime in the late 1980s and early 1990s reflected, at least in part, changes in police charging patterns. During this period "zero tolerance" policies were introduced in many schools across the country, requiring school officials to report to the police about minor assaults that previously would have been resolved informally. While *police and court based statistics* reported significant increases in youth crime in the years after the YOA came into force in 1984, certain key indicators of serious youthful criminality, such as the youth homicide rate, have remained relatively stable in Canada for years, as have measures of youth offending based on self-reports by adolescents (Doob & Cesaroni, 2004). Thus in 1993 the rate of homicide per 100,000 youth population was 2.50; a decade later it was 2.29. The rate of youths charged with a criminal offence declined slightly over the period 1993–2003.

While the actual rate of youth crime reported by police in Canada was slowly falling for much of the 1990s, media reporting about youth crime increased amidst growing political concerns about the YOA. In spite of the fact that the latter half of the 1990s saw a drop in reported youth crime rates, media reports of

[8]The youth homicide rate in Canada is one-sixth to one-tenth the rate in the USA; the lower rate in Canada is attributable to a number of factors; much stricter gun control in Canada is undoubtedly an important factor.

youth violence and public anxiety about the problem of youth crime continued to escalate in Canada.

In Canada, another important element of political concern about youth justice issues relates to the division of responsibilities between the federal and provincial governments.[9] Under the *Constitution Act, 1867*, the federal government has jurisdiction over the enactment of criminal laws, including juvenile justice laws, while the provinces are responsible for the implementation of these laws, as well as having full responsibility for such important related matters as education, health and child welfare.

The federal government has a broad power to enact legislation dealing with young offenders, including regulation of youth corrections facilities and the establishment of noncourt alternative programs.[10] Provincial governments, however, are obliged to implement these laws, including paying for the legal, judicial, correctional, and social services required for youths. The federal government transfers some money to the provinces for some services related to the administration of juvenile justice, but it is not obliged to do so, and after the YOA came into force in 1984, as a result of efforts to reduce the federal deficit, the level of federal financial support for such services declined. For both financial and philosophical reasons, some provincial governments disagreed with various provisions of the YOA.

By the end of the 1990s the decline in the level of federal financial support for provincial spending on youth justice ended. The YCJA is part of a federal "youth justice strategy" that includes some additional federal support for provincial spending on youth justice, although the federal government imposed conditions on how this increased funding is to be spent, with an emphasis on community-based programs and alternatives to custody. The decrease in federal financial support in the early 1990s caused considerable tension between the federal and provincial governments over youth justice. While increased federal funding may help to reduce such tensions, the provinces remain concerned about increased federal controls on their spending.

5. ENACTING THE YOUTH CRIMINAL JUSTICE ACT (1996–2003)

In response to the political pressures to "get tough" on youth crime, amendments were made to YOA in 1992 and 1995 to make it easier to transfer youths charged with murder and other very serious offences to adult court for trial and sentencing, though these amendments did not silence conservative critics

---

[9]Canada has 10 provinces and 3 sparsely populated northern territories. Territorial governments have essentially the same responsibilities as provincial governments with regard to youth justice. For the sake of simplicity, references in this text are only to provincial governments.

[10]See, for example, *Québec (Ministere de la Justice) v Canada (Ministre de la Justice)* (2003), 10 C.R. (5th) 281 (Que. C.A.); *R. v. S.(S.)* [1990] 2 S.C.R.254.,d *B.C. (A.G.) v. S.*, (1967) S.C.R. 702.

(Bala, 1994; Campbell et al. 2001). At the same time as these "get tough" demands were being made, there was an increasing awareness among governments of the high costs associated with the use of expensive custody facilities. In spite of the large increase in the numbers of youth in custody following the enactment of the YOA, more than three-quarters of youth receiving custodial sentences under that Act had not committed violent offences. Under the YOA Canada had a significantly higher rate of use of youth custody than the USA,[11] Britain and European countries. For example, the overall rate (per 100,000 young people aged 12 to 17) was 1,050 in Canada compared to 795 in the USA (Bala et al. 2002). Other countries were making greater use of diversion and informal responses for less serious youth offenders, and greater use of community-based dispositions for youth sent to court.

In response to the public dissatisfaction with the YOA, in the late 1990s the federal government embarked on a process of reform of youth justice laws and policies, including consultation with the provincial governments and Parliamentary Committee hearings.[12] In 1998, the federal government announced a "strategy" for new approaches to youth crime that included but was not limited to legislative reform.[13] The federal Liberal government introduced to Parliament the YCJA in March 1999.[14] The new law was the subject of lengthy Parliamentary Committee hearings, during which it was criticized by conservative politicians for being "too soft," for example for not lowering the age of criminal responsibility from 12 to 10 years of age. The YCJA was also criticized by opposition politicians from Quebec, the province that has a more welfare-oriented approach to youth justice issues and in general more supportive policies for families, who expressed concern that the new law placed too much emphasis on accountability and would result in more youths being treated as adult offenders. Some relatively minor amendments were made in the course of the Parliamentary hearings, and the YCJA came into force on 1 April 2003.

The federal youth justice reform strategy was intended to respond to the belief that there had been a "disturbing decline in public confidence in the youth justice system" in Canada; the most prominently publicized aspect of the strategy was the stated intention "to respond more firmly and effectively to the small number of the most serious, violent young offenders."[15] But there was

[11] See Canada, Department of Justice, The Youth Criminal Justice Act: Summary and Background. Ottawa: Department of Justice Canada, 2002; Canada, Department of Justice Canada, *A Strategy for Youth Justice Renewal* (Ottawa: Ministry of Supply and Services, 1998). Online March 2004 at http://canada.justice.gc.ca.

[12] Canada, House of Commons, *Thirteenth Report of the Standing Committee on Justice and Legal Affairs: Renewing Youth Justice* (Ottawa: Ministry of Supply and Services, 1997).

[13] Canada, Department of Justice Canada, *A Strategy for Youth Justice Renewal* (Ottawa: Ministry of Supply and Services, 1998). Online March 2004 at http://canada.justice.gc.ca.

[14] Bill C-68, First Session, 36th Parliament, First Reading 11 March 1999.

[15] Canada, Department of Justice, Press Release, 12 May 1999, remarks by (then) federal Justice Minister, Anne McLellan.

also a very important recognition by the federal government that Canada had made too much use of expensive and often ineffective court-based responses and custody for the majority of young offenders who are not committing serious violent offences. The federal strategy also called for more use of community-based alternatives to court and custody, and for more resources for crime prevention. The strategy aimed to achieve these objectives by changing the law, and working with the provincial governments and various professional groups to change the way in which the youth justice and corrections systems operate. The federal government also committed a further $200 million to provincial governments to be spent over 5 years, principally to increase community-based alternatives and over $30 million for initiatives to prevent youth crime, mainly directed to local groups.

6. CANADA'S YOUTH CRIMINAL JUSTICE ACT : A SUMMARY

6.1. Preamble and Principles

Under the YCJA, judges are provided with a policy framework for the sentencing of juvenile offenders. The purpose of this framework is made clear from the Preamble to the YCJA, which states that Canada should "have a youth criminal justice system that reserves its most serious interventions for the most serious cases and reduces the overreliance on incarceration for non-violent young persons." Section 3 of the Act contains a "Declaration of Principle" which makes clear that the criminal justice system for young offenders "must be separate from that of adults," with the Act establishing principles and detailed provisions for the youth justice system.

The Declaration of Principle of the YCJA outlines the overall purpose of Canada's youth justice system, with s. 3(1)(a) stating that:
the youth criminal justice system is intended to

(i) prevent crime by addressing the circumstances underlying a young person's offending behavior,
(ii) rehabilitate young persons who commit offences and reintegrate them into society, and
(iii) ensure that a young person is subject to meaningful consequences for his or her offence in order to promote the long-term protection of the public.

Thus rehabilitation is as important as preventing crime and imposing meaningful consequences. Further, the long-term protection of the public is seen as the *consequence* of rehabilitation and accountability, rather than as an independent objective of the youth justice system. Although there is no ranking of priorities, this statement of principle clearly encourages judges and other professionals to focus on responding to youth crime in a fashion that facilitates the rehabilitation of young offenders, rather than on imposing custodial sentences that would merely incapacitate them.

6.2. Youth Justice Courts

Except for those very serious cases that may result in an adult length sentence, trials in youth justice court are almost always resolved by a judge sitting without a jury. In most provinces the youth justice court judges also deal with adult criminal cases, though in some places youth cases are dealt with by judges who are responsible for family law cases. Only Quebec utilizes a court with specialist judges who focus on children and adolescents, dealing only with youth justice and child welfare cases.

The public has the right of access to youth courts, though a judge may exclude members of the public from the court if satisfied that their presence would be "seriously injurious" to the youth.[16] Several provisions of the YCJA are intended to protect the privacy of young offenders. These provisions reflect the principle of the limited accountability of youth and are intended to promote their rehabilitation. There is a prohibition on the publication of information that might identify a young person involved in the youth justice process, with a narrow judicial discretion to allow publication when a youth who is at large poses a serious risk to the public.[17]

While the media can report about proceedings in youth court, there is generally a prohibition on the publication or broadcast of any information that might identify the youth. There are extensive provisions in the Act to restrict access to records and information about youths dealt with by the justice system, and to prevent subsequent use of a prior youth court record if the youth has had a crime-free period, with longer periods of records retention for more serious offences.

6.3. Protection of Legal Rights – Police Questioning and Access to Lawyers

All the protections of the *Charter of Rights* that are afforded to adults also apply to youths who are suspects of criminal offences. Further, s. 146 of the YCJA requires that the police must take special measures to protect the rights of young persons who are being questioned about offences which they are suspected of having committed, including advising the youth of the right to silence and of the right to consult with a parent and a lawyer before making a statement. Most youths, however, are quite unsophisticated and despite being cautioned by the police waive their rights to consultation with a lawyer or parent. The legal rights afforded under the YCJA are very similar to those under the old YOA, except that the courts are given new but limited authority under the YCJA to admit

[16]YCJA, s. 132.
[17]YCJA, ss. 110 and 112.

statements made to police even if there has been a "technical irregularity" in the way in the police advise about rights.[18]

As soon as a youth is arrested, the police must inform the youth of the right to consult a lawyer.[19] If the youth's parents have the means to pay for a lawyer, they may decide to privately retain counsel for their child. If, however, the parents are unable or unwilling to pay for a lawyer, the YCJA provides that a youth has the right to have a government-paid or legal aid lawyer. This is a significantly broader right than what is afforded an adult in the criminal justice system. While an adult always has the right to privately retain counsel, under the terms of legal aid plan regulations adults facing criminal charges can only have a government paid lawyer if they have very limited income *and* are facing serious criminal charges. The YCJA provides for greater access to counsel for youths than for adults, reflecting a desire to ensure that their rights are protected and the belief that adolescents may lack the capacity to meaningfully participate in the criminal justice process without legal representation. Although in practice, some youths waive the right to be represented by counsel in court, and some lawyers for youth may not be very effective, the Act does offer significant legal protections to adolescents.

6.4. Role of Parents

The Declaration of Principles and specific provisions of the Act require that parents are to be notified of the detention of their children, and have the right to attend proceedings and make submissions to the court prior to sentencing.[20] Parents are most likely to attend court with their child if the youth is younger and does not have a significant prior record. While a court may order that parents are to attend court if their presence is considered "necessary or in the best interests" of the youth,[21] such orders are rarely made. Courts may make detention orders or impose sentences that require youths to reside with their parents; these provisions reflect research in Canada that has shown that when charges are serious or youths have significant records, parents seldom attend youth court proceedings. Research in Quebec has demonstrated that the absence of collaboration with parents of young offenders has a negative impact on the success rate of probation orders (Trepanier, 2002). As well, when family members are involved in the treatment of young offenders, recidivism rates were significantly lower (Latimer, 2001). There are, however, no provisions to require parents to allow their child to reside with them, or to require them to take part in counselling, and in cases involving serious or repeat offenders parents often lack the willingness or ability to provide meaningful support for their children (Peterson-Badali & Broekins, 2004).

[18]YCJA, s. 146.
[19]See YCJA, s. 25.
[20]YCJA, ss. 3(1)(d)(iv), 26 and 42(1).
[21]YCJA, s. 27.

6.5. Pre-Court Diversion: Extrajudicial Measures

The provisions of the YCJA that are intended to decrease the use of youth courts are an important element of Canada's youth justice strategy to increase use of community-based responses to youth crime. Under the YOA there was great variation in the use of diversionary measures. In particular in Quebec, which has more of a welfare-oriented focus, there has long been more diversion. Under the YOA the rate of bringing cases to court in Quebec was 16 per 1,000 youths in the population, while the national average was 33 per 1,000, and in some provinces the rate was as high as 82 per 1,000.[22]

The YCJA was intended to encourage greater use of diversion, especially in those jurisdictions, which had high rates of use of court. On a national level there was a 17% decline in police charges against youths in the first year that the YCJA was in force. The smallest decline was in Quebec (6% down to a rate of 15 per 1,000 youth), which already had the lowest charging rate. In some provinces the decline was as high as 28%, while Saskatchewan, the province with the highest youth charging rate experienced a decline of 16% to 71 per 1,000 youths.[23]

A number of statements in the Declaration of Principle and specific provisions in the YCJA are intended to encourage police and prosecutors to resolve youth cases without sending the youth to court but rather to use of "extrajudicial measures" and "extrajudicial sanctions." "Extrajudicial sanctions" are more formal community-based responses and programs, that may, for example, result in restitution to a victim or some form of restorative justice response to youth crime, while the concept of "extrajudicial measures" is broader, including extrajudicial sanctions as well as police cautioning and police referrals to community agencies.

Extrajudicial measures are aimed at reducing the number of youths being processed in youth court, particularly first offenders and juveniles accused of minor offences. The Act affirms the importance of extrajudicial measures, stating that "extrajudicial measures are often the most appropriate and effective way to address youth crime," and further providing that: "Extrajudicial measures are *presumed* to be adequate to hold a young person accountable for his or her offending behaviour if the young person has committed a nonviolent offence and has not previously been found guilty of an offence."[24] There is also a statutory requirement that a police officer "shall" consider whether to invoke an extrajudicial measure prior to commencing judicial proceedings against a young person.[25]

---

[22]Statistics Canada (2004), *Youth Court Statistics 2002–03*, Juristat, Vol. 24, No. 2.
[23]Statistics Canada (2005), *Youth Court Statistics 2003–04*, Juristat, Vol. 25, No. 4.
[24]YCJA, s. 4. Emphasis added.
[25]YCJA, s. 6.

While there is a presumption that extrajudicial measures shall be used for nonviolent first offenders, the Act also reminds police and prosecutors that "nothing . . . precludes their use in respect of a young person who (i) has previously been dealt with by the use of extrajudicial measures, or (ii) has previously been found guilty of an offence."[26] This provision is intended to encourage police and prosecutors to avoid automatically escalating the degree of criminal justice intervention in response to any subsequent offending.

In some communities in Canada, minor violent offences, such as assaults in schools, are dealt with by extrajudicial sanctions programs that, for example, may involve victim-offender reconciliation or family group conferencing, and may result in an apology to the victim, personal service orders, restitution, community service or counseling for the offender. Section 10 of the YCJA provides that extrajudicial sanctions may be used only if a youth "accepts responsibility" for the offence that is alleged to have been committed and consents to the imposition of the sanction. A youth who denies responsibility for the offence or objects to a specific sanction should be referred to youth court. In an attempt to prevent "net widening" the application of these interventions to cases in which the young person is not at risk of a judicial proceeding, s. 10(2)(f) states that an extrajudicial sanction may be used only if there is sufficient evidence to proceed with a prosecution.

If the young person complies with the conditions of the extrajudicial sanction, the case against the young person cannot proceed to youth court. The record of having received an extrajudicial sanction is not technically a finding of guilt, but if in the 2 years following the imposition of the sanction the youth is found guilty in youth court of an offence, the existence of the prior extrajudicial sanction may be used by the youth court and might result in a more severe sentence.[27]

While the YCJA encourages police and prosecutors to make greater use of diversionary programs, it also makes clear that the decision of police and prosecutors to lay charges and send a matter to youth court rather than divert a case is not subject to judicial review.[28] Although a judge may informally signal that a case should be diverted, or may impose the very mild sentence of a reprimand for a case that should have diverted, the success of the diversionary provisions of the YCJA is dependent on the attitudes and policies of police and prosecutors, and or the availability of community-based alternatives. There is substantial variation across Canada in provincial policies and in local attitudes and community programs, but the introduction of the YCJA was accompanied by a significant professional educational initiative funded by the federal government, and as noted above there was 17% decline in police charges against youths in the first year that the new Act was in force (Blackwell, 2003; Daly, 2004).

[26]YCJA, s. 4(d).
[27]YCJA, s. 119(2)(a).
[28]YCJA, ss. 3(1)(d)(i) and 6(2).

6.6. Conferences

The Declaration of Principle encourages the involvement of victims, parents, and members of the community in the youth court process. While the YCJA does not require conferencing, it has provisions that encourage police, prosecutors, and judges to consider having a restorative justice conference where the victim and offender can hear from one another directly. Conferences will generally involve parents and, particularly in Aboriginal communities, elders and other members of the community. For less serious cases, there may be a conference instead of court to develop a voluntary plan, while in more serious cases, the judge may refer a case after a finding of guilt to a conference for a recommendation about sentencing, or the judge may personally preside over a conference, sometimes referred to as "circle sentencing."

The strong emphasis in the YCJA on conferencing and extrajudicial measures reflects research that has found that such measures often result in a successful outcome. In the last major study in Canada (in 1997–1998), of the youth cases referred community-based precourt programs, 89% of the youths successfully completed all the requirements of the program (Kowalski, 1999). There is a growing body of research from around the world about the value of various diversionary and restorative justice-based programs for youth offenders. Some Canadian research on youth diversion did not find a reduction in recidivism from use of youth diversion as opposed to youth court (Morton & West, 1989). However, a meta-analysis of research studies on restorative justice programs in a number of countries found that on average these programs reduce recidivism by 7% compared to nonrestorative programs, but there is wide variation in their effects (Latimer et al. 2001). It would seem that those youths who are most clearly engaged in conferencing and genuinely remorseful are most likely not to reoffend (Hayes & Daly, 2004). While young offenders, parents and victims generally find conferencing preferable to court, many victims find neither experience satisfactory.

It seems safe to conclude that for a range of less serious youthful offenders, use of various forms of extrajudicial measures, including conferencing, has no worse effect than sending a youth to court in terms of recidivism. Further, properly designed and resourced programs may better engage youths and may have the potential to contribute to lower rates of recidivism. Victims who are supported and willing to participate also tend to be better served by conferencing and a restorative justice approach. Some victims, however, will understandably be unwilling to participate, and among those who do, some victims will still leave the process feeling dissatisfied with the outcome, perhaps questioning the sincerity of expressions of remorse or feeling intimated.

6.7. Pre-trial Detention

In more serious cases that are proceeding through the court system, the Crown prosecutor, in consultation with the police, may decide to seek detention of the youth in a custody facility pending trial. The decision about whether to detain a youth is made by a judge at a pre-trial detention (bail) hearing. There were concerns that under the YOA many youths were being detained before trial in situations in which an adult would be released, for example, in cases where a judge was concerned that a youth might be at risk of harm by engaging in street prostitution. In some cases judges may have been detaining youths to "send them a message" about their offending, even though technically such punitive concerns should only be taken into account after a finding of guilt.

Concerns about pre-trial detention are not only based on a concern that this may be a violation of rights, but also reflect the reality that compared to post-sentence centers, pre-trial detention facilities have fewer rehabilitation programs. There may also be greater potential for peer-on-peer abuse in these facilities, due to the absence of programming.[29] Further, the sudden removal from the community that results from detention is very disruptive to a youth's social relationships and education.

Section 28 of the YCJA makes clear that a youth should only be detained *before* sentencing in circumstances in which an adult could be detained. Further, s. 29(1) specifies that pre-trial detention shall *not* be used as a "substitute for appropriate child protection, mental health or other social measures," though s. 35 allows a judge with social concerns to refer a case to a child welfare agency for possible services. Subsection 29(2) creates a presumption that a youth will not be detained if a custodial sentence would not be imposed if there is a conviction, unless there is a legitimate concern that the youth will not attend court. Even if detention is justified, before ordering this, the judge is required to inquire as to whether there is a responsible adult, such as a parent, who is willing and able to supervise the youth pending adjudication. In some large Canadian cities there are now bail supervision programs that provide community supervision and support for youths released pending trial; the establishment of these programs encourages judges to consider pre-trial release.

6.8. The Sentencing Process

If there is a finding of guilt, the youth court judge imposes a sentence on the youth. In some cases, a sentence will be imposed immediately after the finding of guilt. In more serious situations, the case is likely to be adjourned so that a pre-sentence report may be prepared; sometimes a medical or psychological assessment may also be conducted before the sentencing hearing.

The YCJA gives judges a range of sentencing alternatives, from a verbal reprimand to 3 years in youth custody, except for a conviction of murder in youth justice court, the maximum sentence is 10 years. Table 2.1 provides a list of the sentencing options available to youth court judges.

There is no direct equivalent to parole for young offenders. However, if a youth justice court imposes a custodial sentence under the YCJA, normally the

[29]See *Re E.T.F.* [2002] O.J. 4497 (Ont. Ct.J.); and *R v T.M* [1991] O.J. 1382 (Ont. Prov. Ct.).

TABLE 2.1. Sanctions Available at Youth Court Level in Canada, s. 42(2)

(a) Reprimand
(b) Absolute discharge
(c) Conditional discharge
(d) Fine of not more than $1,000
(e) Compensation to victim
(f) Restitution to victim
(g) Restitution to innocent third party in possession of stolen property
(h) Personal services contract for loss, damages, or injury to victim
(i) Community service order of up to 240 hours
(j) Prohibition order for driving or possession of firearms
(k) Probation term not to exceed 2 years
(l) Order for intensive community support and supervision program
(m) Attendance order for nonresidential treatment program
(n) Custody and supervision order not to exceed 2 years for most offences
(o) Custody and supervision order not to exceed 3 years for more serious offences
(p) Deferred custody and supervision order (strict supervision in community with immediate placement in custody for apprehended breach)
(q) Intensive rehabilitative custody and supervision order (e.g., placement in mental health facility)
(r) Custody and supervision order for up to 10 years for murder

Notes: Three sanctions – (l) intensive community supervision; (m) attendance order; and (q) intensive rehabilitative custody – are available only at the discretion of the provincial authorities, and are not available in all jurisdictions in Canada. Table does not include adult sentences that may be imposed on youths found guilty of the most serious offences, provided that certain statutory criteria are met (ss. 61–81).

last third of the total sentence is to be served under community supervision. The period of community supervision is intended to allow for the reintegration of the young offender into the community, while receiving support and supervision from probation services.

The youth justice court retains jurisdiction to review the sentence of a youth, that is, to lessen its severity. For example, a young offender may be released from custody by a youth justice court judge at a review hearing even before two-thirds of the sentence has been served, if there has been sufficient progress toward rehabilitation. Unless a youth is in breach of a term of an original order, a more severe sentence cannot be imposed as part of the review process, but a youth on supervision after release from custody may be returned to custody if any term of the release is breached.

6.9. Sentencing Purposes – s. 38(1)

The YCJA sets out the *purpose* of sentencing in youth court in s. 38 before articulating specific *principles* to govern sentencing in s. 39. At the adult level, the purpose of sentencing as articulated in the *Criminal Code* is a rather confused statement that incorporates a number of considerations, conflating deontological and utilitarian purposes. Section 718 of the *Code* lists all of the conventional sentencing purposes including denunciation, deterrence, incapacitation, rehabilitation, restoration to victims, and acknowledgment of harm. This statement for adult sentencing has been criticized for failing to provide judges with concrete guidance, and leaving them free to pursue their own individual sentencing theories, with a predictable absence of effect on adult sentencing practices (Roberts & von Hirsch, 1995). Section 50 of YCJA, however, provides that the provisions of *Criminal Code* that govern adult sentencing are *not* to apply to the sentencing of young offenders.

The structuring of discretion in youth sentencing in the YCJA is a response to empirical research. It was very well-documented that under the YOA there were wide variations in Canada in youth sentencing patterns across the country, particularly with respect to the use of custody. For example, under the YOA the incarceration rate per 10,000 young persons in 2001 ranged from 9 in one Canadian jurisdiction to 36 in another (Marinelli, 2002). This wide variability should decline as a result of the sentencing provisions of the YCJA.

In contrast to the vagueness of s. 718 of the *Criminal Code*, setting out the objectives of adult sentencing, s. 38 of the YCJA sets out the purpose of sentencing in youth court in a concise fashion:

> The purpose of sentencing under section 42 (youth sentences) is to hold a young person accountable for an offence through the imposition of just sanctions that have meaningful consequences for the young person and that promote his or her rehabilitation and reintegration.

In Canada, it is clear that rehabilitation is more important in the sentencing of youths than adults. While accountability and proportionality of sentences to offences are central themes of sentencing under the YCJA, s. 38(1)(c) creates a hierarchy, with rehabilitation "subject to" proportionality considerations. Thus rehabilitative concerns can modify a sentence to reduce its severity, but a youth court should not impose a disproportionately intrusive sentence to attempt to achieve rehabilitative objectives.

It is also clear that this emphasis on rehabilitation requires a judge to carefully consider whether noncustodial alternatives would be adequate to hold the youth accountable, as a noncustodial sentence will often be more likely to rehabilitate the youth. The emphasis on rehabilitation is consistent with the results of research, much of it conducted in Quebec, that rehabilitation programs and in particular psychoeducational programs, represent the most effective way of reducing youth recidivism (Green & Healy, 2003).

In contrast to the adult sentencing principles in s. 718 of the *Criminal Code*, the YCJA statement of sentencing purpose makes no explicit reference to either deterrence or incapacitation of offenders. A number of judgments have emphasized the absence of explicit mention of deterrence in the Act as a reason for imposing a noncustodial sentence.[30] Other judges, however, held that although not mentioned in the YCJA, it "would be unrealistic and unwise to conclude that the principle of...deterrence has no application in dealing with young offenders."[31] The issue of whether s. 50 of the YCJA precludes youth courts from taking direct account of specific and general deterrence will have to be resolved by the Supreme Court of Canada.

Even if specific and general deterrence are not to be directly taken into account by a judge as the *purpose of sentencing* a youth, the youth justice *system* will have a deterrent effect on the behavior of youths by holding them "account-able" and imposing a sentence that is "proportionate" to the circumstances of the offender and harm done to a victim – principles of sentencing that are explicitly recognized in ss. 3 and 38 of the YCJA. The significance of deterrence being an *indirect effect* of youth court sentencing rather than a *purpose* of sentencing is quite subtle; it would, for example, suggest that the prevalence of an offence in a particular community should *not* be an aggravating factor in youth justice court sentencing, though the court can consider the harm suffered by the victim in the case before the court.[32]

6.10. Sentencing Principles – s. 38(2)

Section 38(2) articulates a number of principles to govern youth sentencing, of which the most important is that in s. 38(2)(c) that any sentence must be "proportionate to the seriousness of the offence and the degree of responsibility of the young person for the offence." This reinforces the statement in s. 38(1) that the purpose of youth sentencing is to hold young persons "accountable" for their criminal acts.

Section 3(1)(b)(ii) of the YCJA makes clear, however, that the accountability of youths must reflect their "limited maturity," and hence youth sentences will nor-mally be less severe than sentences imposed on adults in similar circumstances. Section 38(2)(a) reinforces this limitation on the severity of youth sentencing: the sentence imposed on a youth "must not result in a punishment that is greater that would be appropriate for an adult . . . convicted of the same offence committed in similar circumstances."

The statement of sentencing principles also makes clear that the YCJA is intended to reduce the use of custody, with s. 38(2)(d) stating that "all available sanctions other than custody that are reasonable in the circumstances must be considered" before a sentence is imposed on a youth. Further, s. 38(2)(e) provides that "the sentence must be the least restrictive sentence that is capable of achiev-ing the purpose [of sentencing]."

---

[30] *R. v. B. W. P.* [2004] M.J. 267 (C.A.); under appeal to the Supreme Court of Canada.
[31] *R. v. B. V. N.* [2004] B.C.J. 974 (B.C.C.A.); under appeal to the Supreme Court of Canada.
[32] *R. v. B. R. S.* [2003] S.J. 357, para. 24).

Sections 38 and 39 reflect the policy position taken by the government that the use of custody in youth courts under the YOA was excessive. Under the YOA, over one-third of youth sentences resulted in a term of custody, a similar percentage as at the adult level (Sanders, 2000). In many other countries, the rate of custody is lower for adolescents than for adults. In addition, comparative research suggested that the incarceration rate for youth in Canada was one of the highest in the world, even higher than the rate in the USA (Hornick et al. 1995). One reason for the relatively high incarceration rate is that youth courts have used custody for crimes of relatively low seriousness. For example, statistics revealed that under the YOA approximately half the youth court convictions for theft over $5,000 resulted in a term of custody (DeSouza, 2002).

While the YCJA principles restrict the use of custody, in appropriate cases, especially those involving violence, a proportionate response may require a custodial sentence, especially where a youth has a prior record that indicates that community-based response will not have a rehabilitative effect.[33] If the offence causes sufficient harm, a custodial sentence will normally be appropriate to hold a youth accountable.

The Declaration of Principle makes references to the special social and legal status of Aboriginal youth. Thus s. 38(2)(b) requires a judge to pay "particular attention to the circumstances of aboriginal young persons" when considering a custodial sentence. The reason for this provision is that Aboriginal youth in Canada are significantly overrepresented in the prison population. In 2000/2001, at the juvenile level, Aboriginal persons accounted for 5% of the general population, but one quarter of admissions to youth custody (Marinelli, 2002). It has, however, been stressed by appeal courts that Aboriginal youth must also be held accountable and that judges need to be realistic about their prospects for rehabilitation.[34]

6.11. Restrictions on the Imposition of a Custodial Sanction – s. 39

Under the previous YOA, a judge could not commit a youth to custody unless "the court consider[ed] a committal to custody to be necessary for the protection of society having regard to the seriousness of the offence and the circumstances in which it was committed, and having regards to the needs and circumstances of the young person."[35] This vague provision left a great deal to judicial discretion, and offered little real guidance as to which youths should be imprisoned, even though it was accompanied by an injunction to exercise restraint, and there was very significant variation in the extent to which custodial sentences were imposed by different judges.

[33]*R. v. M.A.M.*, [2003] M.J. 464 (Man. C.A.); and [2004] B.C.J. 320 (B.C.C.A); *R. v. B.L.M.*, [2003] Sask.J. 870 (Sask.C.A.).
[34]*R. v. B.L.M.*, [2003] Sask.J. 870 (Sask.C.A.).
[35]YOA, s. 24(1).

Section 39 of the YCJA gives effect to the more general statements of principle, placing significant restraints on the use of custody for young offenders:
    A youth justice court shall not commit a person to custody unless

1. the young person has committed a violent offence;
2. the young person has failed to comply with noncustodial sentences;
3. the young person has committed an indictable offence for which an adult would be liable to imprisonment for a term of more than 2 years and has a history that indicates a pattern of findings of guilt; or
4. in exceptional cases where the young person has committed an indictable offence, the aggravating circumstances of the offence are such that the imposition of a noncustodial sentence would be inconsistent with the purpose and principles set out in s. 38.

A considerable amount of research in Canada (and elsewhere) has now accumulated to suggest that harsher criminal sanctions for youth, such as imprisonment are no more effective in preventing recidivism than community-based sanctions.[36] The restrictions in the YCJA on the use of custody in youth justice courts in Canada are reducing the use of this expensive sanction, and resulting in more use of less expensive, less intrusive and equally or more effective community alternatives. In the first year that the YCJA was in effect, there was a 37.2% decline on the number of custodial sentences imposed.

While it is difficult to determine precisely how much s. 39 has reduced the use of custody, under the YOA there were significant numbers of youth who were imprisoned but who could not receive a custodial sentence under the YCJA. In particular, it is noteworthy that a youth can only receive a custodial sentence for breach of probation if there has been a breach of previous community-based sentence. Under the YOA one charge in eight was for breach of probation, and almost 40% of these charges resulted in a custodial sentence.[37]

Further, apart from "exceptional circumstances" and cases where a youth has a history of noncompliance with noncustodial sentences, a nonviolent offence can only result in a custodial sentence if the offence is reasonably serious (an offence for which the maximum adult sentence is greater than 2 years) *and* there is a "history that indicates a pattern of findings of guilt," words that suggest there must have been at least three previous findings of guilt.

6.12. Additional Restrictions Regarding the use of Custody: s. 39

If the case before a youth court satisfies one of the four conditions in s. 39(1), a number of other principles must still be considered before a court can imprison the young offender. There is a clear reminder to judges in s. 39(2) of the principle

---

[36]Solicitor General Canada (2002), *The Effects of Punishment on Recidivism.* Corrections Research and Development, Vol. 7, No. 3.
[37]Statistics Canada (2004), *Youth Court Statistics 2002–03*, Juristat, Vol. 24, No. 2.

of restraint in the use of custody, even if one of the conditions of s. 39(1) is satisfied: "if [one of the criteria for custody] apply, a youth justice court shall not
impose a custodial sentence . . . unless the court has considered all alternatives
to custody raised at the sentencing hearing that are reasonable in the circumstances, and determined that there is not a reasonable alternative, or combination
of alternatives, that is in accordance with the purpose and principles of sentencing at the youth court level."

Another provision in s. 39 is intended to discourage judges from escalating the severity of the sentence in response to subsequent offending. Having
imposed an alternative to custody for one offence, some judges shift to custody
if a youth reappears before the court, reasoning that the first sentence was
insufficient to discourage the offender. Section 39(4) addresses this judicial reasoning, providing:

> The previous imposition of a particular noncustodial sentence on a
> young person does not preclude a youth justice court from imposing
> the same or any other non-custodial sentence for another offence.

While s. 39(4) does not prohibit judges from following the "step principle" logic at
sentencing, the provision makes it clear that the same alternative may be imposed
on separate occasions.

A common justification for the imposition of a term of custody in some
cases under the YOA was that the judge could see no other way of providing
necessary social intervention for an adolescent at risk. Under the new youth
justice statute, this justification for the imposition of custody is eliminated, as
s. 39(5) of the YCJA explicitly states that a youth court "shall *not*" use custody
as a substitute for a child protection, mental health, or other social measures.
Hopefully, needed services will be provided under provincial child welfare or
mental health laws, there may be situations in which homeless or mentally ill
may simply not receive needed help due to the absence of appropriate resources
under provincial law.

There are also procedural provisions that are intended to limit the use of
custody. Section 39(6) provides that a youth court is generally obliged, prior to
imposing a custodial sentence, to consider a pre-sentence report as well as any
sentencing proposal made by the young offender or his or her counsel. Further,
s. 39(9) imposes on youth court judges who impose a term of custody an obligation to provide reasons why "it has determined that a non-custodial sentence is
not adequate" to achieve the purpose of sentencing ascribed to the youth court
system.

6.13. New Community-based Sentences

All of the community dispositions, which were available under the YOA can be
imposed under the YCJA; these traditional juvenile sentences include: the absolute discharge, fines (relatively rarely used for youth), restitution to victims and

community service, and probation (the most commonly used disposition under both the YOA and the YCJA). At the very low end, the YCJA adds the "reprimand," which might be used where a judge considers that case should have been diverted by the prosecution.

The YCJA also adds two rehabilitative community-based sentences: the attendance centre order, and the intensive support and supervision order. These two sentencing options, however, require resources for staffing, and are only available where the provincial governments chose to provide them. In some provinces, such as Ontario, in the first year under the new Act, there are many places where these new community-based sentencing alternatives were not available, though gradually they should be become available in all urban centres.

The YCJA provides that in cases in which a custody order should be imposed, the judge may impose a deferred custody and supervision order (DCSO). Under this sanction the youth remains in the community, but is subject to stricter supervision than offenders on probation. The offender serving a DCSO is also subject to placement in custody in the event of an apprehended breach of the condition, subject only to a later judicial review.

6.14. New Blended form of Custody and Community Supervision

Under the YOA juveniles sentenced to custody generally remained in a custodial institution until the end of the sentence; unlike with adults, there was no parole under the YOA. While the YOA did allow for the possibility of judicial review of custody sentences as well for temporary absences arranged by custody staff, in practice, judicial review under the YOA was cumbersome to arrange, and even when a review hearing occurred, many judges were reluctant to modify a previously imposed sanction.

Under the YCJA all custodial sentences are composed of custodial and community phases; for most offences the first two-thirds of the sentence is served in custody and the last third under supervision in the community. For the most serious offences, there is judicial discretion about how to divide the sentence between custody and community supervision, and for all custodial sentences there is the possibility of judicial review to allow early release or detention after the presumptive release date. This reform is intended to ensure that youth have support and supervision during the period following release from custody when they are most vulnerable and most likely to reoffend. The introduction of this new form of sentence will not in itself reduce the number of young offenders committed to custody, but should lower the average number of young persons in custody on any given day.

At the time of sentencing, youth justice court judges are to specify the level of custody – open or secure – but the provincial director has the authority to determine which facility within that level the youth will be placed. There is a great deal of variation in the nature and quality of youth custody facilities in Canada. Some youth facilities are literally just separate wings of an adult jail, with limited rehabilitative resources and significant problems of peer-on-peer abuse. Others, especially open custody facilities, have more programming and rehabilitative services.

For the most serious offences, the YCJA adds the new sentence of the intensive rehabilitative custody and supervision order (IRCS). The IRCS sentence allows a judge to order that a juvenile will serve a portion of the sentence in a mental health facility or some other place where treatment will be provided rather than in custody. This sentence can only be imposed if a youth is suffering from a mental illness or psychological disorder, and further requires that the correctional officials have agreed that a suitable treatment oriented plan is available for the youth. In practice, such treatment oriented sentences are only likely to be imposed if there is evidence that a youth is willing to engage in treatment, as a young offender is still entitled to refuse treatment.[38]

Under the YCJA for most offences, the maximum period of combined custody and supervision is 2 years, but for the most serious offences it is 3 years, and for murder it is a maximum of 10 years. The maximum IRCS order depends on the offence, and is same as the maximum sentence of custody and supervision for that offence.

6.15. Adult Sentencing

While many provisions and principles in the YCJA are intended to reduce the use of youth custody, especially for those who commit nonviolent offences, when the new Act was being introduced there was a concern that for those youth who commit the most serious offences, there would be an increase in the number of adult sentences imposed. As the YCJA was being considered by Parliament, government press releases highlighted the provisions in the Act intended to facilitate the imposition of an adult sentence for those youth who commit "serious violent offences."

Under the old YOA an adult sentence could only be imposed after an often protracted pre-trial "transfer hearing," with a subsequent trial in adult court, and if there was a conviction, adult sentence. Only the most serious cases, such as homicides and attempted murder, were even considered for this process and under the YOA less than one-tenth of one per cent of all cases were transferred to adult court.[39] The YCJA facilitates the process for imposing adult sentences, by permitting a youth court to impose an adult sentence on youths 14 or older at the time of the offence, without the need for a time-consuming pre-adjudication transfer applications. An adult sentence, however, may only be imposed under the YCJA if the youth has notice before trial, and is offered the opportunity for a jury trial,

[38]YCJA, s. 42(8).
[39]Canadian Centre for Justice Statistics, *Youth Court Statistics 2001–02* (Ottawa: Statistics Canada, 2003), Juristat, Vol. 23, No. 3.

albeit still under the provisions of the YCJA, such as the provisions prohibiting the publication of identifying information. In those cases where a pre-trial notice is given and the youth has an opportunity for a jury trial, if there is a finding of guilt, there is a hearing to determine whether an adult sentence is to be imposed. The sentencing judge is to determine whether the maximum youth sentence of 3 years (and 10 years for murder) is sufficient to hold the youth "accountable;" if the youth sentence is not considered adequate to hold the youth accountable, an adult length sentence is to be imposed, though the youth will usually be placed by the court in a youth custody facility until reaching the age of eighteen. Further, for youths who receive a sentence of life imprisonment for murder, there is earlier parole eligibility than for an adult serving the same sentence.

The YCJA, as drafted, significantly increased the range of situations in which an onus would be on the youth to satisfy the court that a youth sentence should be imposed. Under the former YOA, in most cases the onus was on the prosecutor to justify transfer to adult court; a reverse onus was created with respect to transfer for 16- and 17-year old youths charged with one of the most serious offences (murder; attempted murder; manslaughter and aggravated sexual assault); these older youths had to establish why they should *not* be transferred to adult criminal court. Under the YCJA, as it was drafted, for youths 14 to 17 years and found guilty of one of these enumerated very serious offences, there was a presumption that an adult sentence was to be imposed, and an onus was placed upon the youth to satisfy the court that a youth sentence was more appropriate than an adult sentence. Moreover, an additional "three strikes" element was added to the list; young offenders 14 and over and convicted of a third "serious violent offence" also faced a presumption that an adult sentence would be imposed. In other cases, an adult sentence can also be imposed, but only if pre-trial notice is given and the youth upon afforded the opportunity for a jury trial, and the prosecutor satisfies the onus of establishing the need for an adult sentence.

Taken together, these measures of the YCJA would likely have resulted in an increase in the number of adolescent offenders who would receive an adult sentence. However, just before the YCJA came into force, the Quebec Court of Appeal, relying in part on the *United Nations Convention on the Rights of the Child*, held that it is a violation of the Canadian *Charter of Rights* to place an onus on a youth to justify receiving a youth sentence, no matter how serious the offence (Anand & Bala, 2003).[40] The federal government announced that it would not appeal that decision to the Supreme Court of Canada. As a consequence, in all situations under the YCJA, there is an onus on the prosecution to justify an adult sentence, even in situations where under the previous law there would have been an onus on the youth to seek transfer out of the adult court. If the prosecution wishes to seek an adult sentence, the youth must receive pre-trial notice and

---

[40]*Québec* (*Ministere de la Justice*) *v Canada* (*Ministere de la Justice*) (2003), 10 C.R. (5th) 281, [2003] Q.J. 2850 (C.A.). For a detailed discussion, see S. Anand and N. Bala (2003).

have the right to a jury trial, and then if there is a finding of guilt the prosecution must justify the imposition of an adult sentence.

Thus, while the government originally intended that under the YCJA more youth who commit very serious offences would receive adult sentences, it seems likely that as a result of the Quebec Court of Appeal decision, there will be little change in low rate of adolescents receiving adult sentences.

7. CHARGING AND SENTENCING UNDER THE YCJA

The YCJA came into force from 1 April 2003 and it is already clear that it has substantially changed Canada's youth justice system. As intended by its drafters, the Act has resulted in a substantial increase in community-based responses to youth crime. While there continues to be significant variation across the country in youth sentencing and in youth custody rates, populations in youth custody facilities declined by about 50% in the first months that the Act was in force, and a number of youth custody facilities have been closed.[41]

This decline in the number of youths in custody is a result of several factors:

- more use by police and prosecutors of diversion of youth from the courts by increasing the use of warnings, conferencing and extrajudicial measures; nationally the youth charging rate fell 17% in the first year that the YCJA was in effect;[42]
- a decrease in the use of pre-trial detention due to Crown prosecutors and police seeking detention less frequently as well as judges and justices of the peace releasing more youth on supervision;
- judges making less use of custodial sentences and greater use of community-based sentences; in the first year that the YCJA was in force, there was a 37% decline in the number of youth custody sentences imposed;
- the fact that the last third of almost all custodial sentences are to be served in the community under supervision.

Although there have been differences in how the courts have interpreted some of the provisions of YCJA, in general police, prosecutors and judges have responded to the admonition in the Preamble that the Act is intended to "reduce the overreliance on the incarceration of . . . young persons."[43] Youth court judges

---

[41]See, for example, "Fewer Youths Jailed Under New Law," *National Post*, 18 July 2003, p. A1, reporting on the first 3 months of implementation, with a 24% decline in use of custody in Alberta and a 20% to 25% decline in Ontario. In Ontario, custody populations for Phase II youth (16–17 years) in the period 1 April 2003 to 31 January 2004 compared to the prior year: open custody admissions decreased 53%; secure custody admissions decreased 43%; secure detention admissions decreased 14% (Data provided by Ministry of Children's Services).

[42]Statistics Canada (2005), *Youth Court Statistics 2003–04*, Juristat, Vol. 25, No. 4.

[43]YCJA, s. 3(1)(c) and 3(1)(b)(ii).

have generally accepted the principle that a youth sentence must be a "fair and proportionate" response to youth crime, and are not using pre-trial detention or custodial sentencing to achieve child welfare objectives. Further, in fashioning a proportionate response, youth courts have generally recognized the limited accountability of youth in comparison to adults and focused on the need to impose community-based sentences that "promote . . . rehabilitation and reintegration into society."[44] In cases involving more serious offences or youths with lengthy records who clearly are not responding to community-based options, youth courts have generally continued to impose custodial sentences.

8. THE LIMITED ROLE OF THE YOUTH JUSTICE SYSTEM IN RESPONDING TO YOUTH CRIME

In Canada, the appropriate role for the youth justice system and the principles that are to guide that system have been subjects of long-running debate. The *Juvenile Delinquents Act of* 1908 established a highly discretionary regime with little regard for the rights of children and, at least in theory, with a focus on the welfare of the juvenile offender. The YOA, which came into force in 1984, had a clearer criminal law orientation and greater emphasis on respect for the legal rights of adolescents. However, the YOA continued to give judges a significant degree of discretion, and, resulted in substantial variation across the country in how the Act was applied, especially in terms of the use of court and custody.

It is understandable that youth court judges want to ensure that appropriate rehabilitative services are provided to the offenders with whom they deal. Appeal court decisions, however, make clear that it is not for youth court judges to assume this role.[45] While a youth court judge may make recommendations for the provision of specific services to a young offender, and the failure of the government to provide these services might be the ground for the review of the original sentence, this will not result in the provision of services needed by the youth.

The statements in the Declaration of Principle of the YCJA about the importance of crime prevention and rehabilitation require a youth court judge to consider the rehabilitative value of different sentences that might be imposed in accordance with principles of "fair and proportionate accountability." Rehabilitative concerns might, for example, result in a youth court judge deciding that a term of probation should be imposed rather than a custodial sentence that would be warranted on purely accountability-based principles. This could be justifiable in light of the rehabilitative potential of an *available* community-based treatment program that could help reduce the likelihood of a young offender committing further offences. However, the proportionality principle of sentencing and provisions like s. 39(5) of

---

[44]YCJA, s. 38(1).
[45]*R.* v. *L.E.K.*, [2000] S.J. 844 (Sask C.A.), para. 20. To the same effect see, *R.* v. *R.J.H.*, [2000] A.J. 396 (Alta C.A.).

the YCJA make clear that a youth court cannot impose a longer custody sentence than would be justified by the nature and circumstances of the offence if the objective is to provide rehabilitative or social services to the youth.

The YCJA has a number of statements of principle and specific provisions that are intended to establish a new set of principles to direct the youth justice system. Although these provisions could have been drafted in a more concise fashion, when read together, they offer a more coherent set of principles than those in the YOA. While the Preamble of the YCJA clearly recognizes the value of a range of social, educational, and health programs to address the underlying causes of youth crime and prevent youth crime, the YCJA is premised on a narrower, more focused role for the youth justice system. The youth justice system is intended to respond to adolescent offending that has already occurred. A central principle of the YCJA is that there is to be fair and proportionate accountability, which, for many adolescents, may mean an informal response such as a police warning or some form of extrajudicial measures.

The Preamble of the YCJA makes clear that a primary objective of the Act is to reduce overreliance on custody, especially for nonviolent offenders. The YCJA continues to recognize the importance of attempting to rehabilitate young offenders, and thereby prevent future offending, but the attainment of this objective cannot be used to justify a longer custodial sentence than the offence merits. Those responsible for the implementation and interpretation of the Act will continue to face challenges in making decisions on both a systemic and individual case basis. The application of the Act to individual young persons will continue to require professional judgment and a balancing of principles and concerns, made in the context of the resources available.

The more coherent and community focused message of the YCJA has resulted in a very substantial reduction in the use of custody for Canadian youths. However, the Act continues to allow for substantial variation among provinces and territories in terms of policies and resources available to deal with young offenders. The principles in the YCJA are important, but their significance will depend on the actions of justice system officials. In individual cases, these principles will be applied by police officers, prosecutors, judges, and youth court workers, exercising their individual professional judgment. As under the YOA, judges dealing with individual young offenders are constrained by what resources and programs are available. Moreover, the policy and resource decisions of provincial governments will continue to have a profound effect on Canada's youth justice system and on how principles are applied in individual cases. Ultimately, it will be the cumulative effect of these decisions by provincial and territorial governments and by individual professionals that determines whether the hopes of Parliament for the new Act are achieved, namely the aspiration that "the YCJA will correct fundamental weaknesses of the YOA and result in a fairer and more effective youth justice system."[46]

[46]Department of Justice Press Release, "Why New Youth Justice Legislation?" (February 2001).

The YCJA represents an attempt to find a better balance on youth justice issues in Canada. In order to appease the vocal law-and-order critics of Canada's youth justice system, a number of provisions of the YCJA place an emphasis on accountability, especially for serious violent offenders, and address some concerns of victims for greater participation in the justice process. Some provisions of the YCJA were intended to result in a relatively small number of the most serious offenders serving longer sentences, sometimes in adult prisons, and in the publication of identifying information about young offenders who committed very serious offences. While the new statute continues to recognize that young persons have the right to due process of law, there is some weakening compared to the YOA in the protection of legal rights – a further reflection of a law-and-order agenda.

To address the concerns of child-advocacy groups and politicians who wanted a more supportive and preventive approach to youth offending, the YCJA was intended to move youths charged with less serious offences out of custody facilities and the youth courts, and to have more use of more effective community-based responses to youth offending. While it is the responsibility of each province to determine whether more community-based services are being made available, it is clear that the new Act has resulted in more diversion and less use of custody for adolescent offenders in Canada. Whether this ultimately leads to less youth offending and a safer society remains to be seen.

REFERENCES

Anand, S. and Bala, N. (2003). 'The Quebec Court of Appeals Youth Justice Reference: Striking Down the Toughest Part of the New Act. *Criminal Reports* (6th), 10:397.

Bala, N. (1994). 1995 YOA Amendments: Compromise or Confusion? *Ottawa Law Review*, 26:643.

Bala, N., Hornick, J., Snyder, H., and Paetsch, J. (2002). *Juvenile Justice Systems: An International Comparison of Problems and Solutions*. Toronto: Thompson Educational Publisher.

Bessner, R. (1998). *Institutional Child Abuse in Canada*. Ottawa, Canada: Law Commission of Canada. Online available at www.lcc.gc.ca/research_project/98_abuse.

Blackwell, T. (2003). *Fewer Youths Jailed Under New Law*. National Post, July 18.

Campbell, K., Dufresne, M., and Maclure, R. (2001). Amending Youth Justice Policy in Canada: Discourse, Mediation, and Ambiguity. *Howard Journal*, 40:272.

Daly, R. (2004). *Kids Who Hurt can Also Heal.* Toronto Star, March 28.

Dauvergne, M. (2004). Homicide in Canada, 2003. *Juristat*, Catalogue no. 85-002-XPE. Vol. 22, No. 3. Ottawa: Statistics Canada, Canadian Centre for Justice Statistics.

DeSouza, P. (2002). Youth Court Statistics, 2000–01. *Juristat*, Catalogue no. 85-002-XPE. Vol. 24, No. 8. Ottawa: Statistics Canada, Canadian Centre for Justice Statistics.

Doobs, A., and Cesaroni, C. (2004). *Responding to Youth Crime in Canada*. Toronto: University of Toronto Press.

Green, R., and Healy, K. (2003). *Tough on Kids.* Saskatoon: Purich Publishing.

Hayes, H., and Daly, K. (2005). Conferencing and Re-offending. *Australian and New Zealand Journal of Criminology*, 37:167–191.

Hornick, J., Hudson, J., and Bala, N. (1995). *The Response to Juvenile Crime in the United States: A Canadian Perspective*. Calgary: Canadian Research Institute of Law and Family.

Kowalski, M. (1999). Alternative Measures for Youth in Canada. *Juristat*, Catalogue no. 85-002-XIE, Vol. 19, No. 8. Ottawa: Statistics Canada, Centre for Justice Statistics.

Latimer, J. (2001). A Meta-Analytic Examination of Youth Delinquency, Family Treatment, and Recidivism. *Canadian Journal of Criminology*, 43:237–253.

Latimer, J., Dowden, C., and Muise, D. (2001). *The Effectiveness of Restorative Justice Processes: A Meta-Analysis*. Ottawa: Research and Statistics Division, Department of Justice, Canada.

Marinelli, J. (2002). Youth Custody and Community Services in Canada, 2000–01. *Juristat*, Catalogue no. 85-002-XIE, Vol. 22, No. 8. Ottawa: Statistics Canada, Canadian Centre for Justice Statistics.

McLennan, A. (1998). Press Release, May 12, 1999. Ottawa: Department of Justice, Canada.

Morton, M. and West, G. (1983). An Experiment in Diversion by a Citizen Committee, In R. Corrado, M., LeBlanc, and J. Trepanier (eds.), *Current Issues in Juvenile Justice*. Toronto: Butterworths.

Peterson-Badali, M. and Broeking, J. (2006). *Parental Involvement in Youth Justice Proceedings: Perspectives of Youths and Parents*. Ottawa: Department of Justice, Canada.

Roberts, J. and von Hirsch, A. (1995). Statutory Sentencing Reform: The Purpose and Principles of Sentencing. *Criminal Law Quarterly*, 37:220.

Robinson, P. (2004). Youth Court Statistics. *Juristat*, Catalogue no. 85-002-XPE, Vol. 24, No. 2. Ottawa: Statistics Canada, Canadian Centre for Justice Statistics.

Sanders, T. (1999). Sentencing of Young Offenders in Canada, 1998–99. *Juristat*, Catalogue no. 85-002-XIE, Vol. 20, No. 7. Ottawa: Statistics Canada, Canadian Centre for Justice Statistics.

Shamsie, S.J. (1981). Antisocial Adolescents: Our Treatments Do Not Work – Where do We go From Here? *Canadian Journal of Psychiatry*, 26:357–364.

Sprott, J.B. (1996). Understanding Public Views of Youth Crime and Youth Justice System. *Canadian Journal of Criminology*, 38:271.

Sprott, J.B. (2000). *The Youth Criminal Justice Act: Summary and Background. A Strategy for Youth Justice. Youth Court Statistics 1997–98*. Ottawa: Statistics Canada, Canadian Centre for Justice Statistics.

Synder, H., Finnegan, T., Stalh, A., and Poole, R. (1999). *Easy Access to Juvenile Court Statistics, 1988–97*. Pittsburgh, PA: National Center of Juvenile Justice.

Thomas, J. (2003). Youth Court Statistics 2001–02. *Juristat*, Vol. 23, No. 3. Ottawa: Statistics Canada, Canadian Centre for Justice Statistics.

Thomas, J. (2005). Youth Court Statistics 2003–04. *Juristat*, Catalogue no. 85-002-XPE, Vol. 25, No. 4. Ottawa: Statistics Canada, Canadian Centre for Justice Statistics.

Trepanier, J. (2005). *L'avenir des pratiques dans un nouveau cadre legal visant les jeunes contrevenants*. Montreal: Université de Montréal.

Wallace, M. (2004). Crime Statistics in Canada, 2003. *Juristat*, Catalogue no. 85-002-XIE. Vol. 24, No. 6. Ottawa: Statistics Canada, Canadian Centre for Justice Statistics.

Canada, Department of Justice. (1998). A Strategy for Youth Justice Renewal. Ottawa: Ministry of Supply and Services. available at http://canada.justice.gc.ca 2004. Why New Youth Justice Legislation? Press Release, February.

Solicitor General, Canada. (2006). The Effects of Punishment on Recidivism. *Corrections Research and Development* 7(3).

3

Beyond Welfare Versus Justice: Juvenile Justice in England and Wales

John Graham and Colleen Moore

INTRODUCTION

A quarter of a century ago, the prevailing view about how best to respond to juvenile[1] crime was dominated by the orthodoxy that criminal justice interventions had little or no impact on future offending behaviour (and could even be counterproductive) and that juvenile justice policy should, as far as possible, focus on diverting young offenders from the criminal justice system (see, e.g., Morris and Giller, 1987). By the beginning of the 1990s, frustration with the scientific community's reticence to endorse criminal justice interventions and public concern over the frequent offending of a relatively small group of young offenders led to an almost complete reversal of the diversion orthodoxy that characterised the 1980s. This was exemplified by the passing of the 1991 Criminal Justice Act, which moved towards a "just deserts" approach that shifted the focus of sentencing towards the nature and seriousness of the offence, rather than the offender and his/her criminal record.

However, the tragic events of February 1993 and their highly publicised aftermath drove public concern into public panic. The abduction and murder of a young child, James Bulger, by two 10-year-old boys, shocked the nation and confirmed to the public and politicians alike that action was indeed needed "to curb the delinquent tendencies of the new generation of ever-younger and increasingly persistent offenders". Within a year, new legislation – the Criminal Justice and Public Order Act 1994 – introduced stiffer penalties for juvenile offenders, including the extension downwards of long term detention to include 10- to 13-year-olds (see s. 53 of the Children and Young Person's Act 1993)[2] and the introduction of the new Secure Training Order for persistent offenders aged 12–14. This set the tone for the rest of the decade which, in contrast to the preceding decade, witnessed a substantial rise in the juvenile custodial population and an altogether more punitive response to offending by children and young people.

---

[1]The terms 'juvenile' and 'youth' are used interchangeably here, although strictly speaking juveniles are defined in law as those aged 10–17, whereas youth is a more generic term covering a wider age range.
[2]Section 53 of the Children and Young Persons Act 1933 defines the sanctions appropriate for grave crimes committed by juveniles aged 14–17. Grave crimes are serious crimes such as robbery or rape, for which an adult would receive a minimum custodial sentence of at least 14 years. Juveniles charged with committing such an offence are dealt with in the Crown Court.

J. Junger-Tas and S. H. Decker (eds.), International Handbook of Juvenile Justice, 65–92.
© 2006 Springer.

The emergence of the persistent young offender during the early 1990s was confirmed by the first national survey of self-reported offending by 14- to 25-year-olds in England and Wales, which showed that a small minority of juveniles – 3% – were indeed responsible for over a quarter of juvenile crime (Graham and Bowling, 1995). But more significantly, the same report found that, contrary to popular belief, many young men do not appear to simply grow out of crime as they approach adulthood but just switch to offences with lower detection rates, such as fraud and theft from the workplace. Policymakers then questioned the notion that juvenile offenders should be diverted from formal proceedings and proposed quite the opposite – namely intervening as early and as quickly as possible in order to "nip offending in the bud".

Further reforms were then introduced following the publication of Misspent Youth, a report by the Audit Commission that roundly criticised the effectiveness and efficiency of the youth justice system and the services that support it (Audit Commission, 1996). From its analysis, it concluded that the time taken from arrest to sentence was far too long (4 months on average); that most of the £1 billion per annum spent on young offenders was taken up by processing and administration costs with virtually no money being specifically used to address their offending behaviour; and that the management of the juvenile justice system was largely uncoordinated, inconsistent, unsystematic and inefficient. The report concluded that resources should be shifted from the juvenile justice system to more proactive, preventative work with children at risk of offending, which became one of the main philosophical planks underpinning the new approach to juvenile justice as enshrined in the Crime and Disorder Act, 1998. Indeed this legislation introduced a new single statutory aim for the juvenile justice system – to prevent offending and reoffending by children and young people – which helped to circumvent the tensions between the "welfare" and "justice" models and unify practitioners towards a common and shared purpose.

As well as the establishment of a new Youth Justice Board to provide leadership, set standards and monitor performance, the 1998 Act also introduced a wide range of measures that reflected in law much of the new discourse on the nature of juvenile crime and ways to combat it. The latest ways of thinking included extending criminal responsibility beyond the offender himself/herself and towards embracing their parents; the introduction of restorative justice; and confronting young offenders with the consequences of their offending and helping them to develop a sense of responsibility. Reducing costs and improving performance are the driving forces behind a new managerialism, with an emphasis on devising plans, setting targets, measuring performance and reviewing progress.

Many of the new measures have been piloted (they were rolled out nationally in June 2000), which reflects a desire to develop pragmatic rather than ideological solutions. Most importantly of all, the new legislation introduced a network of 155 multi-agency youth offending teams (Yots) across the country to coordinate the provision of juvenile justice services. Each Yot is made up of representatives from social services, probation, police, education and health and is responsible for assessing the risks, needs and circumstances of young offenders, providing reports to the courts and delivering community sentences, accessing the resources of partner agencies as necessary.

The remainder of this report begins with some relevant demographic information, which then leads into a more detailed account of recent developments in juvenile justice in England and Wales. It describes recent patterns and trends in juvenile crime, drawing on self-report as well as recorded crime data, and describes developments in prevention and the operation of the current juvenile justice system in England and Wales (focusing in particular on the new measures). Where relevant, examples of effective, evidence-based practice are presented and key issues are highlighted and discussed.

1. DEMOGRAPHIC INFORMATION IN ENGLAND AND WALES

The United Kingdom has a growing population. In 2003, it comprised over 59 million people and the population of England and Wales constituted just under 53 million.[3] These figures include roughly 13 million under the age of 18 which amounts to almost a quarter of the population (see Fig. 3.1). There

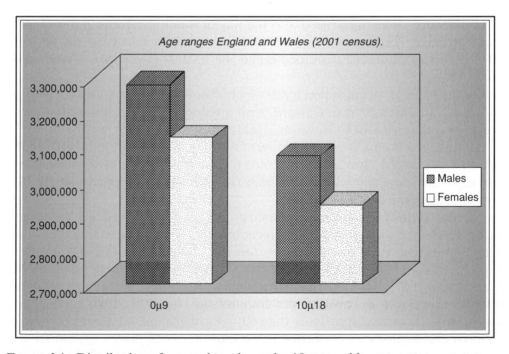

FIGURE 3.1. Distribution of age and gender under 18 years olds.

---

[3]The actual population was 52,793,700 according to national statistics.

are over 300,000 more males than females in this age band, although the population of under the age of 16 as a whole is declining. There are currently about 5 million juveniles (those aged 10–17 inclusive) in England and Wales, which amounts to about 10% of the population. The 2001 census showed that 87% of the population of England and 96% of the population of Wales gave their ethnic origin as White British and White Christians are by far the largest single group. It also showed that there are a higher proportion of younger people within ethnic minority groups (predominantly Black Caribbeans, Pakistanis, Indians, Bangladeshis and Black Africans) than in the general population as a whole.

The total land cover of Great Britain is approximately 15 million hectares and in a medium-sized city the density of population averages about 2,000 people per square kilometre (Office for National Statistics, 2004).

2. TRENDS IN OFFENDING BEHAVIOUR

Overall, the level of crime in England and Wales has fallen quite substantially in the last 10 years. In 1992, the recorded crime rate stood at 10,900 per 100,000 of the population; 6 years later, in 1998, it stood at 8,600 per 100,000 of the population, a fall of 23%, but since then it has increased by about 6%. Because certain changes were introduced into the way in which the crime statistics were recorded and collected, it is not possible to show a full 10-year-trend, but between 1998/1999 and 2001/2002, recorded crime per 100,000 population increased by about 6%.

On the basis of victimisation data, which uncovers a larger proportion of all crimes, again the trend is downward, with a reduction in victimisation of one-third since the mid-1990s. However, against this backdrop of a general fall in crime, there has been a steady rise in recorded violent crime of about 30% in the last 10 years, whilst serious violent crime (including robbery, serious wounding and rape) and drug trafficking have been rising at a rate of approximately 10% per year (Graham, 2002).

Alongside this fall in overall offending, there is limited evidence to suggest that juvenile crime might also have fallen, but not to the same extent. The number of known juvenile offenders (i.e., those cautioned or convicted) fell from approximately 197,000 young offenders aged 10–17 in 1992 to 181,000 in 2002 (a reduction of 8%). However, compared with a decade ago, the number of young offenders cautioned or convicted for drug offences has more than doubled and for robbery has increased by more than 60%. Furthermore, increasingly younger children and adolescents are being drawn into the youth justice system for less serious offences than 10 years ago. However, obtaining a picture of the true scale of juvenile delinquency requires more than arrest and conviction data, as such data only capture a small proportion of all juvenile offending (i.e., many crimes are not reported to the police and of those which are, a considerable proportion are not recorded[4] or do not end up as a conviction).

Self-report surveys are a better method of establishing trends in offending behaviour by young people (although they have limitations too – see, e.g., Coleman and Moynihan, 1996). In England and Wales, annual self-report such data only exists for the last 5 years. It shows that the overall self-reported offending rate for 11- to 16-year-olds[5] has remained stable over this period, with about one in four admitting to committing at least one offence in the previous 12 months (see Audit Commission, 2004).

Prior to 1999, there were two national self-report surveys of offending behaviour, one in 1993 and the other in 1999. Over this 6-year period, the proportion of 14- to 17-year-old boys who admitted offending doubled from 18% to 36%. For girls of the same age, the rise was much smaller – from 17% to 23% (Flood-Page et al., 2000). The increase in offending by boys was mainly due to the proportion admitting fighting and criminal damage, which increased by 12% and 7%, respectively, between 1993 and 1999.

3. DEVELOPMENTS IN PREVENTION

Research evidence suggests that early intervention is hugely beneficial in promoting positive outcomes for children. The current government has introduced a range of measures and programmes to support early intervention schemes to prevent children and young people from offending in the first place, including initiatives within the youth justice system designed to address the predisposing factors associated with youth crime. These, and similar programmes that target a wider population of children at risk, aim to get at the root of why young people get involved in crime and to steer them into more positive prospects. Examples include:

- *Sure Start*, which aims to improve the health and well-being of families with children up to the age of 4, ensuring they are ready to flourish when they go to school;
- *On Track*, which is a small initiative aimed at older children, who have been identified as at risk of getting involved in crime;
- *Connexions*, a new universal support service for 13- to 19-year-olds in England, which aims to provide integrated advice, guidance and access to personal development opportunities to help young people make a smooth transition to adulthood and working life;
- *Youth Inclusion and Support Panels* (*YISPs*), which are multiagency panels set up by the Youth Justice Board to target children at risk;

---

[4]Mirrlees-Black et al. (1996) estimate that approximately 50% of 'crimes' reported to the police in England and Wales are not subsequently recorded.
[5]The survey only covers secondary school children and therefore omits 10- and 17-year-olds.

- *Safer Schools Partnerships* (*SSPs*), which place police officers in schools to reduce truancy, crime and victimisation among young people, challenge unacceptable behaviour and provide a safe and secure learning environment; and
- *Youth Inclusion Programme* (*YIP*),[6] which targets 50 of the most "at risk or most disaffected" 13- to 16-year-olds in the most deprived neighbourhoods. Preliminary research findings (Morgan Harris Burrows, 2003) suggest a substantial reduction in arrest rates for the "top 50" who have been actively engaged in the programme since its inception.

Although inclusion as a principle is one that rightly lies at the core of initiatives such as these, it has been suggested that they are potentially divisive, stigmatising participants as an apparent threat or as someone who deviates from normative expectations (Smith, 2003). Also, with the exception of Connexions (and by the beginning of next year YISPs), these programmes are all targeted initiatives with limited resources. To be really effective, prevention needs to be embedded into mainstream public services for children and young people. This is now emerging as Government policy, with every Local Authority in England now required in law to develop a Local Preventative Strategy for 0- to 19-year-olds which emphases supporting children within the home, the school and in the wider community. There is also a strong focus on supporting parents both in their parenting, and with other issues including domestic violence, counselling, family support and health awareness. These preventative services seek to address the risk factors facing children, maximise access to protective experiences and opportunities, and thus establish a stable foundation from which the young people can develop. Furthermore, local authorities are now required to identify, refer and track children at risk[7] and share information on them with relevant agencies. It will be important to ensure that this more universal approach to prevention does not become just a sophisticated, high-tech information sharing system, but actually leads to the delivery of real improvements on the ground, to those who need them most. And it remains to be seen whether such schemes will be challenged under article 3 of the UN Convention on the Rights of the Child as contributing to the labelling and stigmatisation of children and young people.

4. THE JUVENILE JUSTICE SYSTEM

4.1. The Youth Court

Most judicial proceedings in respect of people under the age of 18 are brought in specially constituted magistrates' courts known as Youth Courts. The procedure in Youth Courts, which is adversarial in nature, is simpler and less formal than

---

[6]More recently 'Junior YIP's have been established, which aim to reduce social exclusion, offending and other adverse outcomes among a target group of 8–12 year olds identified as being at high risk.
[7]Of, for example, offending, drug-taking and teenage pregnancy.

in adult magistrates' courts. Members of the public are generally not admitted to sittings of Youth Courts, but the press may attend and report on the proceedings. Such reports must not identify any young people involved unless the court itself sanctions the lifting of reporting restrictions (e.g., to avoid injustice to the child or young person or facilitate the apprehension of a child or young person who has committed a serious offence and is unlawfully at large).

4.1.1. Lifting Reporting Restrictions

Following conviction, protection from publicity can be lifted if this is considered to be in the interests of justice. The idea behind this is to encourage young offenders to face up to the consequences of their offending behaviour and thus deter further offending. Commonly referred to as "naming and shaming," this relatively new power is controversial in that it is in breach of article 40(2b) of the UN Convention on the Rights of the Child – the right to privacy for offenders under the age of 18 throughout criminal proceedings – as well as the Beijing Rules.[8] Official guidelines provide advice to the courts on cases where the lifting of restrictions may or may not be in the interest of justice.

4.2. Magistrates and District Judges

The magistrates who sit in Youth Courts are chosen from a special panel. The Youth Court must be made up of not more than three magistrates, among whom there must normally be at least one man and at least one woman. Magistrates are unpaid, or "lay" members of the public who rely on justices' clerks (legal advisers) for advice on matters of law. In some of the larger cities, District Judges are appointed; they are full time, salaried professionals with legal qualifications who adjudicate alone.

4.2.1. Specialisation

Unlike other European countries, the Youth Justice system in England and Wales rarely uses professionals to adjudicate. A comprehensive review of the new Youth Justice reforms has recently been undertaken by the Audit Commission (2004), which, as mentioned earlier, played a leading role in formulating the reforms (see Audit Commission, 1996). It concluded that magistrates were insufficiently trained to deal with juveniles, particularly the more serious and persistent offenders whose lives are often complex and chaotic. Young offenders who keep returning to court, whether for breaching their bail conditions or sentences or for reoffending, rarely see the same magistrate and the Commission's recommendation for more specialisation – magistrates who sit in the Youth Court may do so for no more than 7 days a year – could provide greater continuity.

---

[8]Rule 8 recommends that information leading to the identification of an offender under the age of 18 should not be published.

4.3. The Crown Court

Under certain circumstances, a child or young person will be tried in the Crown Court rather than the Youth Court (although they can still be remitted to the Youth Court for sentence). These circumstances include: those charged with homicide; those charged with a serious offence for which a person aged 21 or over could be sentenced to at least 14 years imprisonment; those charged with the offence of indecent assault; and those charged jointly with a person aged 18 or older (who may also be committed to an adult magistrates court).

4.3.1. A Suitable Venue for Juveniles?

Following the trial for the murder of James Bulger in 1993 by two 10-year-old boys (see above), concerns were raised about whether the Crown Court is an appropriate venue for trying juveniles. In 1999, in *V and T v United Kingdom*, the European Court of Human Rights found the United Kingdom to be in breach of articles 3 and 6 of the European Convention.[9] The Court ruled that the Crown Court in the United Kingdom, an adult criminal court, was not a suitable venue for public trials involving juveniles and should be adapted to take account of their age and maturity. In so doing, it should adequately respect their right to privacy, promote their welfare and enable them to understand and fully participate in the proceedings. Despite modifications to judicial proceedings, the European Court held that the proceedings were in breach of article 6 and issued a Practice Direction governing the trial of juveniles.

Since then, special training for judges and lawyers who deal with juveniles in the Crown Court has been proposed and in a major review of the Criminal Justice System, Lord Justice Auld suggested that all cases involving juveniles should be dealt with in the Youth Court, with Crown Court judges sitting alongside magistrates for serious cases (Auld, 2001). This has yet to be taken up by the Government, although they have introduced changes to the layout of some Youth Courts in order to promote better communication and engagement between magistrates and defendants and their parents (see Allen et al., 2000). The recent review of the Youth Justice reforms undertaken by the Audit Commission (2004) recommends that more should be done to improve communication and understanding in procedures involving juveniles and the specialisation of judges and magistrates who deal with juvenile cases.

4.4. The Age of Criminal Responsibility

Currently, the earliest age at which a child can be brought to court in criminal proceedings is 10 years. This is known as "the age of criminal responsibility" and

---

[9]Article 3 is the prohibition of torture (including inhuman and degrading treatment) and article 6 expresses the right to a fair trial.

is one of the lowest age thresholds in Europe. A child below the age of 10 cannot be found guilty of a criminal offence. Despite general appreciation that maturity is a gradual and variable development, it is now the law in England and Wales, that a child of 10 years old is considered to be as criminally liable as an adult. The UN has expressed concern on more than one occasion about the low age of criminal responsibility in the United Kingdom, which is considered to be out of line with prevailing practice in Europe and difficult to understand or defend. But the trend in England and Wales is, if anything, to apply the criminal law to even younger children. Although a child under the age of 10 cannot be found guilty of a criminal offence, concern over the behaviour of a small number of children under the age of 10 led to the introduction of the Child Safety Order in 1998.

4.4.1. Child Safety Order
The Child Safety Order can be used where the local authority can show that:

- a child under the age of 10 has done something that would constitute an offence if he or she were over 10;
- a child's behaviour suggested he or she was at risk of offending;
- a child's behaviour was disruptive or harassing to local residents; or
- a child had breached a Local Child Curfew (see below).

In theory, the order is meant to specify that certain requirements be undertaken to support the child, protect him or her from the risk of being drawn into crime and ensure proper care and control. To secure this, the Family Proceedings Court (such cases are not heard in the Youth Court) may require a child, for example, to attend school, be at home at certain times or stay away from certain people or places. The order is normally for a period of up to 3 months, but in exceptional circumstances may last up to 1 year.

In essence, by intervening with children under the age of criminal responsibility, the Child Safety Order represents a move towards the Scottish Children's Hearings system, where such decisions are embedded within the criminal justice system and the age of criminal responsibility is 8. Concern has been expressed that this new order may in effect reduce the age of criminal responsibility, but since a civil court rather than a criminal court deals with such cases, this concern is likely to be unfounded (although such children may still see themselves as "offenders").

Along with the Parenting Order (see below), the Child Safety Order reflects the state's increasing involvement in the private sphere of the family, which in turn reflects widespread concern about changing family structures and family breakdown. This is the first time in the history of the English criminal law that children who have not committed an offence but are considered to be at risk of so doing may be brought before a court. It reflects the growing concern about increasingly younger out-of-control children, but it looks unlikely to also provide a solution. So far, only a few Child Safety Orders have been passed and they have now effectively been superseded by Anti-Social Behaviour Orders and Acceptable Behaviour Contracts. These are dealt with below.

4.5. Judicial Arrangements for Dealing with Juveniles

The judicial arrangements for dealing with young offenders (those aged 10–17) can be divided into four main sections: pre-court disposals; prosecution; pretrial arrangements and sentencing.

4.5.1. Pre-Court Disposals
The purpose of pre-court disposals is to prevent young people from being sucked into the youth justice system too early, whilst still offering them the help and support they need to stop offending. In England and Wales, there are currently no specialist police for juveniles.[10] When dealing with a young offender, the police have considerable discretion in deciding how to respond, using a variety of pre-court measures and orders, including measures that apply to children under the age of criminal responsibility, such the Child Safety Order described above or the local child curfew. A local authority can apply to the Home Secretary for a local child curfew where children are causing alarm or distress to others living in a particular area. A local child curfew, which can last for up to 90 days, requires all children within the designated area to be in their homes by a designated time. Individual children found outside their homes after the curfew can be made the subject of a Child Safety Order. In practice, very few curfews have been issued.

For those over the age of criminal responsibility, the police may decide in the most trivial cases that an informal warning is sufficient, either given on the spot or at the police station. In either case no further action will be taken. Informal warnings are not recorded and cannot be cited in court. If an informal warning is not considered appropriate, the police may decide to issue a reprimand or a Final Warning. A reprimand is a formal verbal warning given by a police officer to a young person who admits responsibility for a minor first offence. A Final Warning is a formal verbal warning given by a police officer to a young person who admits their guilt for a first or second offence. Unlike a reprimand, however, the young person is also assessed to determine the causes of their offending behaviour and a community intervention programme, involving the offender and his or her family to address the causes of the offending, will usually follow. No offender will be able to receive more than one reprimand and a second Final Warning is only possible if at least two crime-free years have lapsed since the first was issued. It has been suggested that some people may accept a final warning (and the record that accompanies it) in cases where the available evidence may not merit it.

---

[10]However, the local Yots comprise a range of specialists, such as police (police liaison officers), probation officers, social workers and education welfare officers.

4.5.2. Prosecution

If a defendant has already received a reprimand and a Final Warning, the only options left are to prosecute the alleged offender or drop the charges. The initial decision to prosecute is normally taken by the police, but sometimes (and increasingly) they seek advice from the Crown Prosecution Service, especially where there is some doubt about the sufficiency of evidence, before deciding on whether to charge an offender and if so with what offence(s). Once a case has been handed to the prosecution, they must satisfy themselves that there is sufficient evidence to secure a conviction and that it is in the public interest to prosecute the defendant. There are various factors to consider in reaching a decision about whether it is in the public interest to prosecute, such as the seriousness of the offence or whether the defendant has put right the loss or harm caused. If they decide not to proceed, they may refer the case back to the police for a reprimand or a final warning where these have not already been used.

4.5.3. Pretrial Arrangements

The legislation on pretrial arrangements for juveniles in England and Wales is far from straight forward, with 17-year-olds, for example, treated as adults for bail and remand purposes.[11] In principle, magistrates can remand a young person in custody or on bail, with or without conditions, and there is a presumption that any defendant (i.e., not just juveniles) will be granted bail (unless there are very strong reasons for not doing so).[12] Custodial remands are considered only as a last resort, so essentially bail will only be refused if the defendant has a past history of breaching bail conditions, is deemed likely to commit further offences whilst on bail or interfere with witnesses, is deemed unlikely to appear or should be held in custody for their own welfare or protection. Before a decision is reached, most courts will receive detailed information (known as bail information schemes) on whether, if granted bail, the defendant will receive adequate support and supervision to ensure that he/she will turn up in court at the specified date and refrain from committing any further offences. The information is drawn together following a detailed risk assessment undertaken by the youth offending team.

Where bail is granted, the court may nevertheless impose specific conditions, such as residing at a particular address (usually the parental home), not associating with other known offenders, not contacting witnesses, regularly reporting to the police station or being subject to a curfew, which may be enforced by electronic monitoring. Curfew may expressly require the defendant not to enter a specific area or certain types of premises or not to associate with named individuals. Bail support and supervision schemes are used to help young offenders comply

---

[11]The Government has recently announced that this will be changed through new legislation.
[12]The only exception to this is where the alleged offence is very serious (e.g., murder, manslaughter and rape), in which case the court has to justify the decision to grant bail in all cases involving those aged 17 and over.

with such conditions, offering constructive activities to reduce their risk of further offending. Schemes may include regular reporting, measures to ensure school attendance or access to special educational provision, training or assistance with finding employment. They may also include work with families to reduce conflict and increase parental responsibility and supervision. Most recently, Intensive Supervision and Surveillance Programmes (ISSPs) have been extended to persistent and serious young offenders on bail as a mechanism for reducing the number of secure remands. They are referred to in more detail in the section on sentencing below.

Knowledge of support and supervision schemes plays an important part in keeping the use of custodial remands to a minimum, although there is little evidence to suggest that they are being used effectively in this respect. They seem to be more promising, however, in reducing offending on bail. According to the Audit commission's recent assessment of the impact of the new youth justice reforms, bail support and supervision schemes have helped to reduce offending on bail from 1 in 3 young offenders in 1994 to 1 in 5 young offenders by 2002/2003 (Audit Commission, 2004).[13]

If bail is refused, a juvenile offender may be either remanded to local authority accommodation or to prison. Defendants under the age of 17 who are refused bail are normally remanded to local authority accommodation, usually in the area in which the young person resides or where the offence was committed. In exceptional cases, local authorities may apply to the court for a Secure Accommodation Order for juveniles aged 12–16. For a local authority to obtain a secure placement, it must satisfy the courts that the offender has committed a serious violent or sexual offence, or is likely to abscond from nonsecure accommodation, or is likely to injure him/herself or other people if not in secure accommodation.

A wide range of alternative forms of provision is available for juveniles remanded to local authority accommodation, depending on the circumstances of the young person concerned. The different alternatives include supported lodgings, placement with relatives (or in his/her own home), placement in a community home (sometimes in secure conditions) and remand fostering.

Where a local authority decides that a young person is not in great need of supervision or support, it may place him/her in private lodgings. The host family is not usually expected to fulfil a parental role, but to offer a degree of support. Alternatively, the court may decide to place a defendant with relatives. This placement may be used when factors associated with the juvenile's own home suggest that a removal from this environment would be desirable and where relatives are willing and able to offer support and supervision. Community homes provide an alternative to the family home for those who have difficulties with their families. Remand fostering is used where it is felt that the young person needs more individual attention, supervision and support than they might otherwise get in a

---

[13]Part of this improvement will be due to the big reduction in the time taken from arrest to sentence in juvenile cases.

community home. Despite receiving specialist training and payment, it is difficult to find suitable foster parents who are willing to take on what are often difficult young people with serious problems in addition to their offending behaviour. But in principle such schemes are preferred to custodial remands.

The court may attach special conditions when remanding a young person to local authority accommodation. As with conditional bail, he/she may be required to remain indoors between certain hours, to refrain from attending a particular place or meeting particular individuals, or to report to a police station. The court can also impose requirements on the local authority, such as stipulating that the defendant shall not be placed (i.e., accommodated) with a named person. For example, the court may take the view that the home circumstances of the defendant provide insufficient support or supervision and may decide, therefore, to require the local authority not to allow him/her to return to live at home.

Remands in prison are subject to similar criteria as for placement in secure accommodation, with the added criterion of protecting the public from *serious harm* from the young person. Before remanding a young person to prison the court is required to consult a local authority social worker or a probation officer. No young person may be remanded to prison without having been given the opportunity of applying for legal aid. Normally, an initial remand to custody will be for a maximum period of 8 days, but in exceptional circumstances this can be extended to 28 days. Remands to police custody are for a maximum of 24 hours, unless the defendant is 17, in which case it may be for up to 3 days. The maximum period for which a juvenile can be held on remand (whether to local authority accommodation or to custody) is 70 days, although in theory (but rarely in practice) the prosecution can apply to the court for an extension.

From the mid-1970s onwards, it was the aim of successive Governments to phase out the remanding of juveniles to penal establishments and between 1977 and 1981 the powers of the court to remand juveniles in custody were progressively restricted. Fourteen-year-old girls were excluded from the procedure in 1977, 15- and 16-year-old girls in 1979, and 14-year-old boys in 1981. Up to 1994, custodial remands for juveniles were only available for 15- and 16-year-old boys and the numbers remanded in prison fell substantially during the 1980s. However, during the 1990s the number of juveniles remanded to custody increased as Government policy changed. In 1994 custodial remands were extended to 12- to 14-year-olds and more recently to 10- and 11-year-olds.

The average time spent on remand in custody since the reforms were introduced has remained at between 36 and 38 days and the numbers held on remand, after an initial drop, have also remained stable, despite a Government target to reduce the use of secure remands. The suicide rate of young offenders remanded to prison is, at three times the rate of those in the general prison population, of great concern and there is also concern about the disproportionate use of custodial remands for black and mixed race young people. The Audit Commission

(2004) has identified how the already disproportionate use of custodial remands for these two groups has risen considerably over the last few years.

4.5.4. Sentencing

The powers of the courts to sentence offenders under the age of 18 are governed by a number of key principles. First and foremost, sentences must relate primarily to the seriousness of the current offence, and in the case of sexual and violent offences, the need to protect the public from serious harm from the offender. The Criminal Justice Act of 1991 places the seriousness of the offence at the core of the sentencing process and states what the minimum level of seriousness must be before a custodial or community sentence can be imposed. The court has to first establish what range of sentences might be appropriate on the basis of the seriousness of the offence that has been committed before adjusting their decision to take account of any mitigating (e.g., guilty plea, previous good character) or aggravating (e.g., offended on bail, lack of remorse) circumstances. The most important mitigating factors are the offender's age and his/her previous convictions. The Audit Commission (2004) found that in addition to offence seriousness and aggravating/mitigating circumstances, these two factors were the most prevalent influences on magistrate's sentencing decisions, with close to 100% of magistrates listing them.

There are no national sentencing guidelines applicable to juveniles, so in practice there are considerable variations in sentencing decisions between local areas. So, for example, research commissioned by the Youth Justice Board shows that the proportion of custodial sentences given to juvenile offenders varies from under 2% to over 18% (NACRO, 2002) and whilst there is some correlation with the seriousness of offending in the local area, this by no means explains the wide discrepancies in the use of custody. Similar patterns reflecting different levels of punitiveness have also been found in other European countries (e.g., Germany).

A second principle underpinning sentencing is that magistrates should have regard to the welfare of the child or young person, as set out in the Children and Young Persons Act of 1993, although this is always secondary to the principle of seriousness. In practice, the welfare (or care) system is completely separate from the criminal system in England and Wales, so that where serious welfare concerns have been identified, these would necessarily be dealt with by civil proceedings in the separate family proceedings court. There is therefore no mechanism within the Youth Justice System as currently configured for magistrates to take full account of the welfare needs of the young offender and no mechanism for referring the case to the family proceedings court. This is seen by some commentators as a seriousness weakness.

A third principle, which applies to defendants under the age of 15, concerns the role of parents. They are expected to attend court and to pay any fines or compensation and courts are required to bind parents over to take proper care of and exercise proper control of their child where this is desirable in the interests of preventing him/her from committing further offences. The 1994 Criminal Justice and Public Order Act extended these powers by allowing courts to include in any bind-over a requirement that the parent or guardian must ensure that a child complies with the requirements of a community sentence.

A fourth principle relates to the special status of 16- and 17-year-olds who are regarded as being in a transitional stage between childhood and adulthood and for whom it is believed that a flexible approach to sentencing is desirable. The full range of community sentences, both those previously available for juveniles and those currently available for adults, can be imposed and courts have *powers* to involve parents (as opposed to the duty to do so, which applies in respect of younger offenders). In determining how to use these powers, courts are required to take account of a range of factors relating to the offender's stage of development and maturity.

A fifth principle, which relates in particular to demanding community sentences (e.g., Community Punishment and Rehabilitation Orders) and most custodial sentences, is that the court should consider a presentence report (PSR). The report, usually submitted by a probation officer or a social worker, attempts to reach an opinion on the most suitable sentence for the offender based on information relating to the offender and the circumstances of the offence, including mitigating factors. The 1994 Criminal Justice and Public Order Act provided the courts with the discretion to dispense with the requirement to obtain a PSR before sentence where it is satisfied that it can properly sentence without one *and* if it has considered an existing PSR on the offender concerned. (If more than one such report exists, the most recent one must be considered).

With the introduction of the new reforms through the Criminal Justice Act 1998, the main principles underpinning sentencing were influenced, at least in theory, by the introduction of a single statutory aim for the youth justice system, namely the prevention of offending and reoffending by children and young people. Insofar as this is a statutory requirement, sentencing should take account of the extent to which any sentence passed is likely to prevent further offending behaviour. To ensure this is practicable, magistrates would need to know something about the relative effectiveness of different sentences in preventing or reducing reoffending, but the Audit Commission (2004) showed that 3 years after the Act was implemented, only just over half of magistrates take account of reoffending rates in reaching their decisions.

Finally, sentencing is influenced by the need for timeliness. In 1997, a new Government pledged to halve the time from arrest to sentence for all persistent young offenders from the then average time of 142 days. By 2001, this pledge was achieved and similar efficiency gains were achieved with other young offenders (i.e., nonpersistent ones). The average time taken for all young offenders was 55 days in 2003, compared with 81 days in 1999 (DCA, 2003). The main underlying principle here is not just to achieve efficiency gains, but also to help establish a better link in the young offender's mind between the crime and the punishment.

4.6. Sanctions

There is an extensive range of sanctions available for sentencing juvenile offenders. In addition to discharges[14] and fines, the following provides an overview of the range of community and custodial penalties:

4.6.1. Supervision Order
A Supervision Order lasts up to 3 years and a range of conditions, called "specified activities" can be attached, particularly for more serious offences. Examples of "specified activities" include participation in an ISSP, drug treatment (for juveniles aged 16 or 17), curfews or residence requirements, which might require a young person to live in local authority accommodation for the period of the sentence. Yots can also require an offender to take part in specific activities, such as reparation to the victim or the community and addressing their offending behaviour.

4.6.2. Action Plan Order
An Action Plan Order is an intensive, 3-month community-based programme supervised by the Yot and specifically tailored to the risks and needs of the young person. It can include reparation, education and training, attending an Attendance Centre or a variety of other programmes to address a young person's offending behaviour.

4.6.3. Attendance Centre Order
An Attendance Centre Order requires a young person to attend an Attendance Centre. Normally run by the police, they require an offender to participate in physical activities and social skills training for a period of up to 36 hours.

4.6.4. Reparation Order
A Reparation Order is designed to help young offenders understand the consequences of their offending and take responsibility for their behaviour. It requires a young offender to make reparation to the victim or the community, usually through a written apology and/or undertaking a specified number of hours of work to repair or compensate for the damage the offender has caused and, in a few cases, to participate in victim/offender mediation.

4.6.5. Community Punishment Order
The Community Punishment Order is available to courts for young people aged 16–17. It requires a young person to undertake unpaid reparative, community work for a period of 40–240 hours.

---

[14]A young person is given an absolute discharge when they admit guilt or are found guilty, but no further action is taken against them. A conditional discharge, which can only be used in exceptional circumstances, is used for minor offences and require the young person to stay out of further trouble for a specified period (between 6 months and 3 years).

4.6.6. Community Rehabilitation Order
The Community Rehabilitation Order is also only available for young people aged 16–17. It is very similar to a Supervision Order, but geared specifically for this age range.

4.6.7. Community Rehabilitation and Punishment Order
The Community Rehabilitation and Punishment Order involves elements of both the Community Punishment Order and the Community Rehabilitation Order. It extends from 1 to 3 years and includes unpaid community work of 40–100 hours.

4.6.8. Curfew Order
The Curfew Order requires a young person to remain for set periods of time at a specified place. The time period can be between 2 and 12 hours a day and the sentence can last no more than 6 months for those aged 16 years and above or 3 months for those under 16.

4.6.9. Drug Treatment and Testing Order
The Drug Treatment and Testing order is used for young offenders who have drug misuse issues that require treatment. It can only be used with young people who are 16 years of age or older and the young person must agree to comply with the order before it can be made. The order lasts between 6 months and 3 years. Under the order, the young person receives regular drug testing and treatment in the community.

The Criminal Justice Act of 2003 has rationalised this large range of community sentences and whilst not yet implemented, the new sentencing framework will comprise one generic community sentence – the Juvenile Rehabilitation Order – to which a number of interventions can be attached. The list of possible interventions is long, but essentially includes the kinds of interventions already available, such as unpaid work, curfews, supervision, electronic monitoring, drug, alcohol and mental health interventions, etc.

Many of these community penalties are common to the jurisdictions of other European countries, but three in particular – the Referral Order, the Parenting Order and the Anti-Social Behaviour Order – were all introduced as part of the new reform package and are worthy of more detailed comment as they have all shifted the focus of the Youth Justice System in radical but different ways.

4.6.10. Referral Order
The introduction of the Referral Order in 2001 constituted a major shift towards the incorporation of restorative justice into the English Youth Justice System. A young person who is prosecuted for the first time and pleads guilty is now automatically eligible for a Referral Order of between 3 and 12 months. He/she is referred to a Youth Offender Panel, along with his/her parent or guardian. The Panel consists of two trained volunteers from the local community, a representative

of the youth offending team and the victim if he/she wishes to attend. It draws up a contract with the young person in which he/she agrees to make reparation to the victim or the community and is discouraged from further offending. If the contract is successfully completed, the offender will have no criminal record, but if not, the offender is returned to the Youth Court to be resentenced.

Although the legislation does not explicitly exclude legal representation, panels are strongly advised to waive legal representation and since defendants are not eligible for legal aid, legal representation is effectively precluded in practice. Since the drawing up of the contract is still part of the sentencing process, it has been suggested that this is in breach of article 6 of the European Convention on Human Rights (Ashford and Chard, 2000). Most contracts are successfully completed and the majority of magistrates approve of the Referral Order (Audit Commission, 2004), although some complain that their introduction has overly restricted their sentencing options for first time offenders as effectively the only other sentence they can impose (apart from an absolute discharge) is custody. Both young offenders and their parents also seem to like the Referral Order, but victim participation rates are low and in some cases long delays occur before Panels are set up, which can undermine the credibility of the order (Audit Commission, 2004). About a third of all young offenders who appear before the Youth Court (approximately 30,000) receive a Referral Order.

4.6.11. Parenting Order

The Parenting Order is the latest development in the continuing shift towards placing more emphasis on the responsibility of parents for the offending or irresponsible behaviour of their children. It is seen as one of a range of new measures for supporting parents in bringing up children to avoid a wide range of social problems, of which criminality is just one. In the first instance, a court may require an offender's parents to attend regular counselling or guidance sessions for a period not exceeding 3 months or comply with other requirements to help them control their children. In some cases, courts may impose additional requirements, such as requiring parents to ensure their children attend court or school or that they are at home during certain hours of the day or night. Such additional requirements may apply for up to 1 year and where a parent fails to comply with such requirements, they may be liable to a fine of up to £1,000, although the order does not result in the parent/caretaker receiving a criminal record.

Given the overwhelming evidence that now exists on the primary importance of the family in the aetiology of crime, it would seem sensible to reinforce parental responsibility. Research has consistently shown that family relationships and parental supervision are important influences on offending (see, e.g., Graham and Bowling, 1995). But although the court has to assess the effects of such an order on an offender's family circumstances before imposing an order, concern was expressed when it was first introduced. For example, some felt it would be counterproductive if it merely added to the already considerable pressures experienced by the parents of some young offenders, especially lone parents, leading in the worst cases to child abuse, family breakdown and children ending up in care (Family Policy Studies Centre, 1998). For poor parents, the imposition of a fine in cases of breach was also considered to be potentially counterproductive.

In practice, these concerns seem to have been largely unfounded. Findings from an evaluation of the Parenting Order show that the great majority of parents who took part in parenting programmes, whilst somewhat sceptical and even antagonistic at the outset, were very grateful for the help they received. Despite very high levels of need, attendance rates were high and parents reported improvements in their relationships with their children, in their supervision of their children's activities, in their capacity to influence and control their children's behaviour and in their own feelings as parents (Ghate and Ramella, 2002). But despite these promising findings, voluntary parenting programmes are preferred to the compulsory, court-ordered Parenting Order and in most areas Parenting Orders are little used and/or poorly resourced.

Originally, the order was only available where a child or young person had been convicted of an offence, made the subject of a Child Safety Order, an Anti-Social Behaviour Order or a Sex Offender Order and where parents have been convicted of failing to send their child to school. New legislation introduced last year has extended the Parenting Order to include those subject to Anti-Social Behaviour Orders (ASBOs) issued in the Youth Court (see below) and young people excluded from school or who persistently truant and last year a mother was indeed imprisoned for not ensuring her child attended school.

4.6.12. Anti-Social Behaviour Order

In response to concern by all political parties about increasing levels of antisocial behaviour in high crime communities, legislation was introduced to tackle forms of behaviour considered to be inadequately covered by existing criminal law, such as littering, verbal (including racial) abuse, obstruction, minor damage, harassment and persistent levels of nuisance by neighbours and local groups of young people. The lives of some of the most excluded people living in some of the most deprived areas were reputedly a constant misery, living in fear of their neighbours and groups of young people hanging around with nothing to do and nowhere to go. Essentially, they were in need of greater protection and the Crime and Disorder Act of 1998 introduced a new civil measure, the ASBO to tackle forms of antisocial behaviour and local disorder, such as rude, abusive and insulting language and gestures, rowdy disputes with neighbours and persistent nuisance, harassment (including racial harassment) and intimidation, that (apparently) fell short of being defined as criminal and therefore subject to the criminal law.

Under the 1998 legislation, applications for ASBOs can be made either by the local authority or a police authority where they are of the opinion that a person aged 10 or over has acted in an antisocial manner that caused, or was likely to cause harassment, alarm or distress to others. Until very recently, applications could only be made to an adult court, although where an order is being considered for a juvenile, the court must have regard to the welfare of the child or young person. If granted, the order attempts to prevent the named individual from behaving in an antisocial manner for at least 2 years and often longer. Curfews, bans and dispersal powers are the main measures used to achieve this. If the individual is a juvenile, the court may simultaneously pass a Parenting Order. Breach of an ASBO constitutes a criminal offence.

There has been much criticism of this order, such as the discretionary and discriminatory way in which they can be allocated and the way they contradict or undermine evidence-based policy implementation and efforts to promote social inclusion. It has been suggested that the introduction of the ASBO amounts to a circumvention of some of the key principles of due process that apply in criminal proceedings, such as that a person is innocent until proven guilty and that to prove guilt, there must be an element of criminal intent (NACRO, 2003). The introduction of the ASBO as a civil measure means that the civil rather than the criminal burden of proof applies. Therefore an ASBO can be imposed if, on balance, the court decides that the person has probably acted in an antisocial manner, rather than needing proof that he/she has so acted and showing that he/she intended to do harm. Courts can therefore rely on hearsay evidence and grant orders on the basis of Closed Circuit Television (CCTV) footage alone.

The Government's official guidance to the court to consider the imposition of an ASBO as a serious matter (and hence a breach of such an order, which is a criminal offence, as equally serious) has led the Chairman of the Youth Justice Board to raise the concern that ASBOs might be fast-tracking some young people into custody who may not even have committed a criminal act (other than breaching a civil order). In 2000, over half of those sentenced in court for breach of an ASBO received a custodial sentence (Campbell, 2002).

For a number of reasons, not least of which was the amount of time and effort required to secure an ASBO, the number issued in the first couple of years was less than 500. In some areas, voluntary alternatives – Acceptable Behaviour Contracts – were being used instead. Although they do not have the statutory authority of an ASBO, they are seen as a cheaper, less coercive and potentially more constructive alternative, especially for young people.

Nevertheless, the Government passed new legislation to reduce the bureaucratic hurdles and increase the powers of the court through the Anti-Social Behaviour Act of 2003 and whilst the guidance that accompanied the original 1998 legislation suggested that ASBOs would normally apply to adults, this new legislation expressly targets young people. The ASBO has been accompanied by an increase in negative media coverage of young people. Some cities in England and Wales are distributing leaflets and fliers, publicising details[15] of the children and young people made subject of ASBOs (Bateman, 2004). The fact that they

---

[15]Photographs and conditions of the order.

are civil orders and not criminal has led to a media free-for-all with many local newspapers citing a "duty" to name and shame young people who are subject to ASBOs (Ghose, 2004).

The majority of ASBOs are now issued on juveniles (NACRO, 2003), who can also be "named and shamed." There are still real concerns about the new antisocial behaviour legislation, although there are also signs that they are beginning to have some impact on levels of antisocial behaviour. Unfortunately, there is no commonly agreed definition of antisocial behaviour, so it is difficult to measure and assess the impact of interventions. The new measures are considered to be too punitive by some commentators – the maximum prison sentence for breaching an ASBO is 5 years – and there is little sign that they address the causes of such behaviour. There are also real concerns about the extent to which they may breach various articles of the European Convention on Human Rights. The Antisocial Behaviour Bill is currently before the UK Parliament for amendments.

4.7. Custody

The use of custody for young offenders fell into disrepute during the 1980s and during this decade the youth custody population fell dramatically (see, e.g., Allen, 1991). The 1990s, however, witnessed an almost complete reversal of this trend as a consensus across the political spectrum for a more punitive approach emerged, with each party attempting to be "tougher" than its rivals. The main catalysts for change were the tragic murder of the toddler James Bulger (see above) and the emergence of the persistent young offender. Until 1994, with the exception of those who committed very serious offences, custody was only available for juveniles aged 15–17, but in 1994 the Criminal Justice and Public Order Act introduced Secure Training Orders for 12- to 14-year-olds.

4.7.1. Secure Training Order

Five new Secure Training Centres (STC) were proposed to cater for 12- to 14-year-old offenders convicted of at least three imprisonable offences who had failed to comply with the requirements of supervision in the community while on remand or under sentence. Those sentenced to Secure Training Orders would serve sentences of between 6 months and 2 years, of which half would be in custody and half under supervision in the community. The legislation allowed for the new STCs to be managed by public, voluntary or private organisations, but such was the antipathy at the time to the new provisions by the first two that in practice the private sector became the new operators by default.

Despite the provision in the 1994 Criminal Justice and Public Order Act to build five STCs for persistent young offenders aged 12–14, the first STC did not open until 4 years later. Initial doubts about the effectiveness of the new STCs were upheld when news of numerous incidents and internal disturbances reached the outside world (Moore, 2000). They were not cheap either, with one estimate suggesting a place in an STC costs between £4,000 and £5,000 per week (€6,000–€7,500) (Crowley, 1998).

An evaluation, carried out from 1998 to 2000, highlighted the lack of staff training, high staff turnover, inadequate offending behaviour programmes and a lack of communication with outside agencies. One in three children were rearrested within 1 month of their release and 2 out of 3 had offended before the STO had expired (Hagell et al., 2000). The evaluation concluded that STCs and the staff who run them needed to adopt a much more child-centred approach.

4.7.2. Detention and Training Order

In 1998, the Crime and Disorder Act effectively abolished the distinction between STCs and other forms of secure facility when it introduced the Detention and Training Order (DTO). Now, any young offender aged 12–17[16] who is sentenced to a DTO is allocated to any of the three forms of secure facility – an STC, a Young Offender Institute (YOI) or Local Authority Secure Children's Home (LASCH).[17] Placements should be determined by age, gender, vulnerability and home location, although in practice they are usually determined by availability of places. Juveniles (those aged under 18) are now also separated from older young offenders (18- to 21-year-olds).

Offenders are sentenced for a period of no less than 4 months and no more than 24 months,[18] half of which must be served in the community. A DTO should only be used as a last resort for offences that are considered so serious as to warrant a custodial penalty or, where a violent or sexual offence has been committed, to protect the public. The sentence must be for the shortest possible period and any time spent on remand must be taken into account. On release, the offender is supervised by a member of the Yot (usually a probation officer or a social worker), and if the order is breached, the offender can be returned to custody to serve the remainder of his/her sentence.

An evaluation of nearly 6,000 young offenders subject to a DTO identified a number of elements of good practice, including the use of reward and incentive-based systems (rather than punitive ones) for controlling the behaviour of inmates; effective coworking and information sharing with community agencies; and continuity in addressing offending behaviour and providing for their education and health needs. But the evaluation also identified a number of problems and

---

[16]Provision exists within the legislation to extend DTOs to 10- and 11-year-olds at the direction of the Home Secretary.

[17]These comprise what is known as the secure estate. YOIs are essentially prisons for young offenders aged 15–20. LASCHs are run by Social Services and provide secure accommodation for young offenders on remand and (generally) vulnerable young offenders under sentence. STCs, of which there are currently just 3, hold 12- to 17-year-olds who have been identified as vulnerable and/or persistent offenders.

[18]In practice, DTOs are for fixed periods of 4, 6, 8, 10, 12, 18 and 24 months, with some rather limited provisions for early and delayed release for good and bad progress, respectively.

weaknesses, including too many transfers to other institutions mid-placement; too many placements too far away from home; lack of preparation for release and poor postrelease provision and supervision; and high rates of reoffending, particularly in the first few weeks following release (Hazel et al., 2002).[19]

The most common length of a DTO when first introduced was also the shortest one – 4 months in total, 2 months of which was spent in custody. This reflected (despite evidence to the contrary) magistrates' enduring belief in the deterrent effect of the "short, sharp, shock" and their attraction to a sentence that mixed custodial and community provision. As a result, the numbers of young people in custody rose 8% in the first year following the introduction of the DTO. In practice, the short DTO was replacing community penalties and pushing up the juvenile prison population in the process. In direct response, the Youth Justice Board recommended the replacement of the short DTO with a new, high-tariff community programme, the Intensive Supervision and Surveillance Order (ISSP), to take the heat out of an overpopulated prison system.

4.7.3. The Intensive Supervision and Surveillance Programme

In 2001, the Government launched the Intensive Supervision and Surveillance Programme (ISSP) for persistent young offenders as an alternative to custodial remand and (primarily short) custodial sentences. Designed to target the 3% of offenders who are responsible for 25% of all juvenile offending, they run for a maximum of 6 months and must provide at least 25 hours of purposeful activity a week during the first 3 months. They should also include elements of reparation, education and training, intensive offending behaviour courses, training in interpersonal skills and family support and, where applicable, provision for mental health problems or drug rehabilitation. Offenders serving an ISSP are subject to intensive surveillance in the community for up to 24 hours a day, seven days a week. Electronic tagging, voice verification, intelligence-led policing and advocate schemes are used to monitor, track and supervise offenders.

Youth Courts have accepted 3 out of 4 proposals to use an ISSP instead of a custodial sentence, but there are problems of enforcement, with large numbers breaching the strict requirements of the programme and ending up in custody and no evidence to suggest that they are providing an effective alternative to custody (Audit Commission, 2004). They do seem, however, to be targeting the right population: the average number of prior offences is 13, two out of 3 have been permanently excluded from school and the average reading age of clients is 5 years below their chronological age, which is a similar profile to those in custody (University of Oxford, 2002).

---

[19]The average time from release to first arrest was found to be 7.5 weeks. Nearly half were arrested before the end of the community supervision part of the sentence, one in five were convicted of a new offence and one in four were returned to custody for either offending or breaching the order. These outcomes are, however, better than those found for STCs before they were expanded to take 15- to 17-year-olds.

Research comparing the ISSP with short DTOs found that the former offered much more help to young offenders. It found that a young offender in custody received, on average, 12.7 hours of purposeful activity, compared with 25.8 hours for those on an ISSP. It also established that during the community part of a DTO, contact with a YOT worker is, on average, 1.5 hours per week, whereas during the less intensive second 3-month period of a 6-month ISSP, offenders receive on average 20 hours of contact time (PA Consulting Group, 2003a, b).

A recent evaluation of a small-scale ISSP-type programme,[20] targeting persistent young offenders in a county in Southern England, found that reconviction rates were unaffected by the intervention, but that there was a 30% to 50% reduction in the volume of crime committed by programme participants compared with two control groups (Little et al., 2004). The programme only covered 79 persistent young offenders, but its use of random allocation means the findings are very robust. ISSPs are certainly cheaper than custody – a 6-month ISSP costs about £6,000 (€9,000) compared with £21,000 (€30,000) for a 6-month stay in a YOI – but whilst they may not yet provide an effective mechanism for diverting young offenders from custody, the evidence above suggests that they could do so, particularly if they establish the confidence of the courts.[21]

4.7.4. Long-Term Detention

In addition to DTOs, a young offender who commits murder will receive a mandatory indeterminate sentence of "long-term detention" and in the case of other serious offences, such as robbery or rape, the maximum penalty that the court may impose is the same period of determinate custody that an adult offender might receive (see s. 90 and 91 of the Powers of Criminal Courts (Sentencing) act, 2000). Since 1994, the number of young offenders sentenced for serious crimes under s. 90 and 91 (previously referred to as grave crimes and covered by s. 53 of the Children and Young Person's Act of 1933) has risen considerably. In 1970, only 6 sentences were imposed under s. 53. By the early 1990s, this had risen to about 100 juveniles, but by 1997 more than 700 were sentenced for grave crimes. This is partly due to the widening of the range of crimes covered by s. 53 and the lowering of the eligibility threshold to 10, but even taking this into account there has clearly been a real increase in the use of these sentencing powers. It is perhaps not surprising that the United Kingdom (including Scotland and Northern Ireland) have one of the highest rates of custody in Europe and this fuels the concern that

---

[20]The programme was a Dutch initiative called Intensive Supervision and Support Programme, which does not contain the surveillance element of the English programme and includes restorative and supportive measures.

[21]The Government has recently agreed to introduce a new Intensive Supervision and Surveillance Order as a robust alternative to custody through new legislation.

the detention of juveniles in England and Wales is neither used as a measure of last resort nor for the shortest possible period of time.

4.7.5. The Rise in the Prison Population

One of the most striking effects of the shift from diversion to a more interventionist approach has been the rise in the number of juveniles held in custody. Between 1993 and 1998, the number of imprisoned 15- to 17-year-olds almost doubled; the number of imprisoned 15- to 17-year-old boys as a proportion of the total prison population more than doubled; and for girls of the same age, it trebled (Social Exclusion Unit, 2002). By 2002/2003, a total of nearly 7,000 juveniles were issued with a custodial disposal in England and Wales, of which 237 were under the age of 14, as Table 3.1[22] illustrates.

These figures represent approximately 3.1% of the prison population overall and compared to other countries in Europe is rivalled only by Ireland, where the young people's secure estate makes up 5.7% of the overall prison population. When contrasted with the rates of custody in relation to the general population, England and Wales (as well as Scotland and Northern Ireland) incarcerates on average about 1 in 4,000 of its population – this figure is much higher than many other European countries, where the proportion of incarcerated young people is considerably lower (see Table 3.2).[23]

TABLE 3.1. Distribution of Custodial Sentences in England and Wales (2004) – under 18-year-olds

Custody	10	11	12	13	14	15	16	17	Total
Detention and Training Order (4 months)	0	0	10	71	168	487	668	956	2,360
Detention and Training Order (4 months + 2 years)	0	1	31	103	301	751	1,253	1,674	4,114
Section 90–91	5	1	0	15	42	74	137	213	487

[22]Source: Youth Justice Board Annual Statistics, 2002/2003.
[23]It should be noted that the figures are not all from the same year spanning from 2000–2004. This is due to recording inconsistencies across countries and means care should be taken in interpreting these data. Nevertheless, the general pattern is reliable as annual fluctuations in any one country tend not to be that great.

TABLE 3.2. Levels and Proportions of Young People in Custody in
Selected Countries (2004)

Country	Number in Custody (Actual Figures)	Percentage of Prison Population (%)	Custody per 1,000 Population	Under-18 Population 1,000s	Proportion of Youths in Custody
Northern Ireland	71	5.7	0.25	452	1 in 4,000
England and Wales	2,335	3.1	0.24	13,044	1 in 4,166
Scotland	196	2.8	0.23	1,263	1 in 4347
Iceland	54	7.5	0.17	70	1 in 5,882
Hungary	150	0.9	0.09	2,536	1 in 11,111
France	797	1.4	0.08	14,908	1 in 12,500
Ireland	54	1.5	0.08	991	1 in 12,500
Belgium	101	1.1	0.06	2,589	1 in 16,666
The Netherlands	130	0.8	0.05	4,048	1 in 20,000
Italy	471	0.0	0.05	14,330	1 in 20,000
Spain	175	0.3	0.02	10,388	1 in 50,000
Finland	7	0.2	0.01	1,302	1 in 100,000
Norway	11	0.5	0.01	1,131	1 in 100,000

5. CONCLUSION

Establishing the reasons for a rise in the prison population is rarely straight-forward (see, e.g., Graham, 1990). There is little doubt however that during the 1990s the panic generated by a *perceived* rise in juvenile crime in general and persistent juvenile offending in particular was used by politicians and others to justify a more punitive response to juvenile crime and an extension of the use of custody to lower age groups. This led to more young offenders, particularly persistent offenders, being sentenced to custody and for longer periods (Moore, 2000). The introduction of the DTO did nothing to reverse this trend.

Despite the recognition that the juvenile prison population is too high and that some young offenders held in secure facilities might be better placed in community provision, upward pressure on the prison population continues to threaten the quality of programmes delivered to existing inmates. The situation is compounded by a Government that is not quite sure whether reducing the prison population is a priority or not. As a consequence, different policies and practices are working in different directions.

The introduction of ISSPs to discourage short term DTOs and the use of tagging for offenders released early on DTOs and those who might otherwise be remanded to custody should all work to reduce the population. But the recent extension of custodial remands down to 12-year-olds enacted through the Criminal Justice and Police Act of 2001, the introduction of special provisions for remanding young street robbers in custody rather than on bail[24] and the pronouncement by the Lord Chief Justice in January 2002 that mobile phone thieves should go to prison all work in the opposite direction. The most recent developments in penal policy contained in the Criminal Justice Act of 2003, such as increasing the powers of magistrates to impose custodial sentences of up to 24 months as opposed to 12 months, suggest that this ambivalence towards the size of the prison population will continue, despite serious concerns that prison establishments have reached their capacity. So it remains to be seen whether the Youth Justice Board's recently announced target to keep the proportion of young offenders who receive a custodial sentence to no more than 6% will be effective in halting the continuing pressure to incarcerate more and more young offenders.

REFERENCES

Allen, R. (1991). "Out of Jail: The Reduction in the Use of Penal Custody for Male Juveniles 1981–88," *Howard Journal*, 30(1):30–52.

Allen, R. (2000) "New Approaches to Youth Justice" *Criminal Justice Matters*, 40:6–7.

Ashford, M. and Chard, A. (2000). *Defending Young People in the Criminal Justice System*. London: Legal Action Group 2000.

Audit Commission. (1996). *Misspent Youth*. Abingdon: Audit Commission Publications.

Audit Commission. (2004). *Youth Justice 2004: A Review of the Reformed Youth Justice System*. Wetherby: Audit Commission Publications.

Auld, L.J. (2001). *Review of the Criminal Courts in England and Wales*. London: HMSO.

Bateman, T. (2004). "Youth Justice News," *Youth Justice*, 3(3):192–201.

Campbell, S. (2002). *A Review of Anti-Social Behaviour Orders*. Home Office Research Study No. 236. London: Home Office.

Coleman, C. and Moynihan, J. (1996). *Understanding Crime Data: Haunted by the Dark Figure*. Buckingham: Open University Press.

Crowley, A. (1998). *A Criminal Waste*. London: Children's Society.

Departmant for Constitutional Affairs (DCA) 'Departmental Report 2002–2003' www.dca.gov.ule.

Family Policy Studies Centre. (1998). *The Crime and Disorder Bill and the Family*. London: Family Policy Study Centre.

Flood-Page, C., Campbell, S., Harrington, V., Mayhew, P., and Miller, J. (2000). *Youth Crime: Findings from the 1998/99 Youth Lifestyles Survey*. Home Office Research Study. London: HMSO.

Ghate, D. and Ramella, M. (2002). *Positive Parenting*. London: Youth Justice Board.

Ghose, D. (2004). *Newspapers Give Young People a Bad Reputation*. Young People Now. Haymarket, London, England.

Graham, J. (1990). "Decarceration in the Federal Republic of Germany: How Practitioners are Succeeding Where Policy-Makers have Failed," *British Journal of Criminology*, 30(2):150–170.

Graham, J. (2002). "Juvenile Crime and Justice in England and Wales," in N. Bala, J.P. Hornick, H.N. Snyder, and J.J. Paetsch (eds.), *Juvenile Justice Systems: An International Comparison of Problems and Solutions*. Toronto: Thompson Educational Publishing.

[24]This is now in the Criminal Justice Bill and if enacted will apply to all areas of the country, not just the 10 areas which are covered by the street crime initiative.

Graham, J. and Bowling, B. (1995). *Young People and Crime*. Home Office Research Study, No. 145. London: HMSO.

Hagell, A., Hazel, N., and Shaw, C. (2000). *Evaluation of Medway Secure Training Centre*. London: Home Office.

Hazel, N., Hagell, A., Liddle, M., Archer, D., Grimshaw, R., and King, J. (2002). *Detention and Training: Assessment of the Detention and Training Order and its Impact on the Secure Estate across England and Wales*. London: Youth Justice Board.

Little, M., Kogan, J., Bullock, R. and Van der Laan, P. (2004). ISSP: An Experiment in Multi-Systemic Responses to Persistent Young Offenders Known to Children's Services. *British Journal of Criminology*. 44(2): 225–240.

Moore, S. (2000). "Child Incarceration and the New Youth Justice," in B. Goldson (ed.), *The New Youth Justice*. Lyme Regis: Russell House Publishing, pp. 115–128.

Morgan Harris Burrows, (2003) *Evaluation of the Youth Inclusion Programme*. London:Youth Justice Board

Morris, A. and Giller, H. (1987). *Understanding Juvenile Justice*. Beckenham: Croom Helm.

NACRO. (2002). *Differential Patterns of Custodial Sentencing*. London: Youth Justice Board.

NACRO. (2003). *Youth Crime Briefing: Anti-Social Behaviour Orders and Associated Measures* (Part 1). London: NACRO.

Office for National Statistics (2004), *People and Migration-Population, Where People Live*. www.statistics.gov.uk; http://www.statistics.gov.uk/cci/nugget.asp?id=760; http://www.statistics.gov.uk/cci/nugget.asp?id=1306.

PA Consulting Group. (2003a). *The Content of Short DTOs Compared with ISSP*. London: Youth Justice Board.

PA Consulting Group. (2003b). *Repeat Young Offenders Arrested on Bail or Community Penalty*. London: Youth Justice Board.

Smith, R. (2003). *Youth Justice: Ideas, Policy, Practice*. Willan Publishing.

Social Exclusion Unit. (2002). *Reducing Reoffending by Ex-Prisoners*. London: Social Exclusion Unit.

University of Oxford. (2002). *Intensive Supervision and Surveillance Programmes: Evaluation Findings*. Bulletin No 1, March 2002.

4

Mainstreaming Restorative Justice for Young Offenders through Youth Conferencing: The Experience of Northern Ireland

David O'Mahony and Catriona Campbell

1. INTRODUCTION

Though Northern Ireland is a relatively small jurisdiction within Ireland and the United Kingdom with a population of just over 1.7 million (of which about 183,000 are 10–16 years of age – the current age of criminal responsibility for children), it has its own unique system of youth justice which very recently has undergone significant transformation. A restorative justice approach to deal with young offenders and victims has been mainstreamed through a process called "youth conferencing." This new approach offers valuable insights in terms of youth justice policy and practice to the international forum and in this chapter we explore some of its potentials and limitations.

The chapter firstly looks at crime and how the criminal justice system in Northern Ireland deals with young people who have offended. It examines what is known about youth offending in general and looks specifically at a number of innovative approaches to criminal justice practice. The police response to youth offending is examined and their specialist teams of officers who deal with young offenders. The courts and sentencing are then looked at, with attention being placed on the new arrangements for holding children in custody. The range of measures introduced following the Criminal Justice Review are then examined, and specifically the youth conferencing arrangements, which adopt a restorative justice model to deal with young offenders. This chapter draws to a close with a critical overview of the major changes in our system of youth justice and the possible lessons that can be learnt from an international perspective. However, before exploring how this whole new system of youth justice operates it is important to understand the broader criminal justice system in context and a little about crime levels and how young people have been dealt with through the criminal justice system.

1.1. Young People, Crime Levels and Victimisation

Generally speaking, Northern Ireland has relatively low levels of crime, despite the high profile and serious terrorist related offences that have dominated the media, especially in the recent past. Police recorded crime statistics show that

J. Junger-Tas and S. H. Decker (eds.), International Handbook of Juvenile Justice, 93–116.
© 2006 Springer.

recorded crime levels have generally been about half of that recorded in England and Wales. Recently recorded crime levels have increased from 62,222 to 109,053 offences between 1997 and 1999 and have continued to increase to 142,496 in 2003. This has meant that the crime rate has increased from around 37 crimes per 1,000 of the population in 1997 to 87 per 1,000 population in 2003. These changes appear to have largely been caused by new counting rules that came into effect in 1998 which record crimes that were not previously part of the official figures and together with the introduction of a new data collection system have had a significant impact on recorded crime levels. Despite these changes, however, Northern Ireland still has relatively low levels of police recorded crime, especially if comparisons are made with England and Wales or the United States of America.

Much of crime recorded by the police is property related, in fact 74% of offences in 2002/2003 involved property such as theft, burglary or criminal damage, and of these vehicle crime (including theft from and theft of vehicles) accounted for about half of all property crime. Though property related crime makes up the majority of crime recorded, Northern Ireland generally has a higher proportion of violent and sexual related offences, with 23% of offences in 2002/2003 recorded as violent, by comparison to 17% in England and Wales.

Victimisation surveys also confirm the lower levels of police recorded crime in Northern Ireland. For example, the International Crime Victimisation Survey 2000 which surveyed victims of crime in a number of different countries in Europe and North America showed that Northern Ireland actually had the lowest victimisation rate of any of the participating countries. Only 15% of those questioned in Northern Ireland had been a victim compared with an international average of 21% (Hague, 2001).

Self-reported crime data suggest that while many young people admit to committing crimes the majority of incidents are not serious. For instance, McQuoid (1994) conducted a self-reported delinquency study in Belfast in 1993 and found that about 75% of 14- to 21-year-olds surveyed admitted committing at least one delinquent act in their lives and 47% said they had done so in the past year. The vast majority of delinquent acts disclosed were such things as bus fare evasion, graffiti or minor acts of property vandalism. Relatively few admitted committing more serious acts such as violence and few were repeat offenders. These findings are common to other studies (e.g., Wolfgang et al., 1987; Graham and Bowling, 1995) and suggest that while many young people commit delinquent acts at some time in their lives, few commit serious offences or go on to be serious or persistent offenders.

Conviction data in Northern Ireland confirms that young people are much more likely to be convicted of an offence but as they get older they become significantly less likely to engage in crime. These data support the hypothesis that much of the criminality of youth occurs with their transition into adulthood, in a period when boundaries between right and wrong are often tested, but as they mature find employment and stability in their lives they largely grow out of crime (Rutherford, 1992). These general findings are important especially in terms of how youth crime is best dealt with. It is neither necessary nor productive to involve the criminal justice system with every minor act of delinquency, especially given the vast majority of young people desist from offending as they mature into adulthood.

1.2. Youth Justice

Considering how the youth justice system operates in Northern Ireland the police are generally the first point of contact and the main gatekeepers into the criminal justice system. The police have considerable powers of discretion in terms of how they deal with offenders and use specialist juvenile officers for young offenders. A dedicated Juvenile Justice Liaison Scheme has operated since 1975 and dealt with all young offenders (10–16 years of age) who came to the attention of the police. This was replaced in 2003 by a Youth Diversion Scheme and specialist officers review all such cases and make referrals as to how juveniles should be dealt with (prosecutors make the final decision, usually based on police recommendations). The officers have four broad options available, including taking "no further action," in which case the young person is not processed any further than being referred to the scheme. This is most commonly used when there is insufficient evidence to establish that a crime was committed, or the offence and circumstances were so trivial it is not considered worth pursuing. Secondly, the officer may give "advice and warning" which is an informal action and occurs where there is evidence that a crime has been committed, but an informal warning is considered sufficient to deal with the matter. Such warnings are usually given to the young person in the company of their parent(s) but do not result in any formal criminal record for the young person – though a note of these warnings may be kept should the young person come to the attention of the police again. The police may also decide to formally caution the young person. This can only take place if the young person admits to the offence, there is sufficient evidence to prosecute and the young person and their parent give informed consent to the caution. Police cautions are recorded as part of a criminal record and should the young person reoffend it may be cited in court. The last option is for the police to recommend the young person for prosecution through the courts. This is usually reserved for more serious offences or where the young person has had previous warnings or prosecutions.

The Youth Diversion Scheme only resorts to prosecuting a relatively small proportion of the young people that are referred to it. Typically, only about 10% of cases are referred for prosecution and about 10–15% are formally cautioned. The remainder (about 75–80%) are dealt with informally through "advice and warning" or no further police action is taken. In 2002/2003, for example, only about 5% of cases dealt with by the Youth Diversion Scheme were prosecuted through the courts and 14% were given formal cautions. The remainder, which was the majority of cases, were dealt with informally. There has been a general increase in the use of informal measures when dealing with young people who come to the attention of the police and the proportion of cases given "advice and warning" or no further police action has steadily increased over the last 10 years.

Diverting young people away from the courts is seen as a more positive response than formally prosecuting them, and the police have been operating a progressive policy in terms of diverting young people away from formal criminal processing. The police point to encouraging reconviction data to support their policy, which shows that only about 20% of juveniles cautioned in Northern Ireland went on to reoffend within a 1–3-year follow-up period (Mathewson et al., 1998) whereas about 75% of those convicted in the juvenile courts were reconvicted over a similar period (Wilson et al., 1998).

The work of the police in this area has developed recently, and since February 2001 all juvenile cautions are administered by means of a conferencing process known as restorative cautioning (O'Mahony and Doak, 2004). Where possible the victim is encouraged to participate in the conference and meet the offender concerned. The conference also aims to highlight and get the young person to realise the damage or harm caused by their actions. Recent research examining this restorative cautioning method, while finding some evidence of minor or petty offenders being drawn into the scheme, found the process to have distinct advantages over traditional cautioning practice and helped secure some of the values of the restorative justice approach (O'Mahony et al., 2002).

1.3. The Courts and Sentencing

For those young people prosecuted by the police, the next step in the criminal justice system has traditionally been the courts (though this has recently changed – see section on "Youth Conferencing" later). In 2001, 4% (880) of the sentenced population were juveniles (10–16 years). Juveniles (9%) were proportionately more likely to be given immediate custody than adults (7%), whilst adults were about seven times more likely than juveniles to be given a suspended custodial sentence (Digest 4, 2004). Juveniles were much more likely to be given a community-based disposal or conditional discharge than adults and adults were much more likely to be fined.

The majority of juveniles processed through the courts are at the older end of the age spectrum, with 16-year-olds generally accounting for about half of all juvenile prosecutions. Few juveniles under 13 years of age are prosecuted, and over the last decade no more than a few 10-year-olds have been prosecuted in the courts.

Very significant changes have occurred in the use of custody for juveniles in Northern Ireland in recent years. Prior to the end of 1996, juveniles could be placed in custody – primarily Training Schools – if they were found to be in need of care and control (welfare reasons), for school truancy, or for offending. This changed with the introduction of the Children (Northern Ireland) Order 1995 which removed welfare and educational cases from those who could be sent to custody. The Criminal Justice Act of 1996 (Northern Ireland) also curtailed the powers of the courts to impose custodial sentences, limiting them to more serious, violent and sexual offences and the Criminal Justice (Children) Order of 1998 extended the right to bail for children except in the most serious cases and introduced a determinate "Juvenile Justice Order." The Juvenile Justice Order ranges from 6 months to 2 years – half of which is spent in custody and the other half under supervision in the community.

The combined effects of these changes and close management of the custodial arrangements for juveniles have seen the juvenile custody population fall dramatically. About 10–15 years earlier around 200 juveniles were held in custody in the four training schools across Northern Ireland. They were generally held for less serious offences than adults held in custody. Many juveniles spent more time in custody than adults convicted of similar offences. Juveniles in custody were often placed there after placements in children's homes failed or they were considered too difficult to manage in children's homes (O'Mahony and Deazley, 2000). Reconviction data show that the majority of juveniles released from custody reoffend within 3 years. Curran (1995), for example, showed that 86% of juveniles released from secure custody were reconvicted within 3 years and Northern Ireland Office figures show 97% of boys released from training schools were reconvicted within 3 years (Wilson et al., 1998). The evidence clearly shows that custody for juveniles was ineffective in terms of preventing reoffending.

However, the juvenile population in custody has steadily decreased over the past decade to an average of only about 30–35 persons over the 2000/2002 period (which equates to about 20 per 100,000 of the relevant population) – about half of which were held on remand and the other half were sentenced. This has been a considerable achievement in turning around what had been a failing system, which allowed some young people to be placed and held in custody for reasons other than the seriousness of their offence, to a system which now uses custody for juveniles sparingly.

1.4. Youth Justice and the Criminal Justice Review

The most recent and fundamental changes to youth justice in Northern Ireland have taken place over the past few years and many of the changes are only just coming into effect. These changes follow the recommendations of the Criminal Justice Review which was set up in June 1998 under the Agreement signed in Belfast on Good Friday of that year (known as the "Good Friday Agreement" or "Belfast Agreement"). The Agreement sought a political accommodation to the years of conflict in Northern Ireland and as part of that process the government agreed to a fundamental review of policing and criminal justice. The Review reported in March 2000 making 294 recommendations for change across the criminal justice system and these included changes to the youth justice system. Specifically, the Review recommended that a restorative justice approach should be central to how young offenders are dealt with in the criminal justice system. It proposed a conference model to be termed a "youth conference" based in statute for all young persons (including 17-year-olds), subject to the full range of human rights safeguards.

The recommendations of the Criminal Justice Review relating to youth justice were put into legislation under the Justice (Northern Ireland) Act of 2002, and the most important changes included setting out the aims of youth justice, the inclusion of new community and custodial orders and the establishment of the whole new system of youth conferences based around the principles of restorative justice.

1.5. New Principles, Community and Custodial Orders

The Justice (Northern Ireland) Act of 2002 has for the first time clearly spelled out a set of principles that all of those working within the justice system must follow. These are firstly, that the principal aim of the system is to protect the public by preventing reoffending by children. The legislation states that all persons must have regard to this principle aim and also to the welfare of children affected by the exercise of their functions – recognising that delay in dealing with children is likely to prejudice their welfare. The Act goes on to make provision for two additional measures that have been introduced with a restorative theme: reparation orders and community responsibility orders, which are described as "community-based" sanctions.

Reparation Orders which were introduced in England and Wales following the Crime and Disorder Act of 1998 were expanded to Northern Ireland in s. 36(a) of the Justice (Northern Ireland) Act of 2002. Reparation orders require "the offender to make such reparation for the offence, otherwise than by the payment of compensation" and are now available throughout Northern Ireland as a court disposal. The offender must be found guilty of an offence and consent to being subject to an order. Before making an order, a court must consider a written report complied by a probation officer, social worker or other "appropriate person" containing recommendations of suitable restrictions to be imposed on the offender. Such a report must take into account the attitude and consent of the victim to any reparation. There are a number of restrictions placed on the dispensing of reparation orders. For example, if the offender is under 14 years of age only 2 hours a day of reparation is permitted. A reparation order must be sensitive to the religious beliefs of a young person and "must avoid," as far as possible, any potential conflict with these.

In addition, the order must take into account any potential disruption to the young person's education.

Community responsibility orders are similar in nature to reparation orders, but have a particular focus on community and victim awareness. The order is made by a court as the sole disposal for an offence and must be completed within 6 months of it being made. An order can only be made with the consent of the young person. As part of the order the young person is required to undertake "instruction in citizenship" and practical activities which may involve some form of reparation to the victim or their community.

A number of concerns have been voiced regarding the introduction of community responsibility and reparation orders. They are both available as a form of disposal for young people aged 10–17 and it has been suggested that, given differing levels of maturity, such orders will not always be suitable for very young children. The Northern Ireland Human Rights Commission argues that "[very] young children should be excluded from this form of community sentence, as they are unlikely to be able to participate with the order in any meaningful way," adding that "it is not desirable to mix such young children together with older children when serving a sentence" (Northern Ireland Human Rights Commission, 2002: 7). At the time of writing, very few community responsibility or reparation orders have been served, and it remains to be seen what their role will be in the youth justice system in Northern Ireland.

Regarding the new custodial order – the custody care order – s. 56 of the Justice (Northern Ireland) Act of 2002 restricts the use of custody for 10- to 13-year-old children who have been convicted of an offence for which the court could impose a custodial sentence. Such young children are not to be held with older children in a juvenile justice centre, rather they should be accommodated in the child care system. The order replicates the existing juvenile justice centre requirements and when commenced will mean it will no longer be lawful to detain children under 14 years of age in a juvenile justice centre (other than those directed by the Secretary of State). It is expected the numbers of such children will be very small, but this presents practical problems in terms of how they are to be accommodated, and whether children in such facilities for welfare reasons are mixed with those that have offended. It was clearly recognised over 30 years ago in Northern Ireland that children in need of care requiring placement away from their homes should not be held in the same institution as children who had offended (Black, 1979). Those responsible for the establishment of such facilities will need to be mindful of this and not compromise these principles simply for economic savings.

2. YOUTH CONFERENCING

The introduction and mainstreaming of restorative interventions into the youth justice system in Northern Ireland signals a radical departure from previous responses to young offending. It builds upon the use of increasingly diversionary practices by which the young person is side-tracked from the formal court system. Such diversion is employed as an early intervention designed to prevent further offending by the young person, whilst avoiding the potentially stigmatising label of a criminal record (Becker, 1963).

The new youth conferencing model has much in common with the New Zealand family group conferencing system, which has been in operation since 1989 (see Maxwell and Morris, 1993). In a report commissioned as part of the Criminal Justice Review (Dignan and Lowey, 2000) the New Zealand model was highlighted as a potential restorative model for Northern Ireland. Nevertheless, it is apparent that differing local contexts can make the transposition of models of justice into discrete environments problematic. In Northern Ireland, there exists a background of 30 years of conflict which has created an institutional legitimacy deficit. This is characterised by mistrust and hostility towards the police in some areas and has led to the growth of a crime prevention vacuum and emergence of informal community justice measures (Dignan and Lowey, 2000). Implementing a model of restorative justice without examining contextual factors could perhaps be viewed as misguided, particularly as much of the success of the New Zealand model has been attributed to its contextual and cultural sensitivity to New Zealand's Maori population (O'Mahony and Deazley, 2000). In spite of the burgeoning number of community-based restorative justice schemes that emerged in Northern Ireland in the late 1990s (McEvoy and Mika, 2002), it was determined that for reasons of accountability, certainty and legitimacy the model of restorative justice implemented should be based in statute and fully integrated into the formal justice system.

2.1. The Youth Conference Process

The youth conferencing system has statutory footing in part four of the Justice (Northern Ireland) Act of 2002. Additionally, The Youth Conference Rules of 2003 (Northern Ireland) establish the procedures to be followed when convening and facilitating a conference. The Youth Conference Service was introduced in December 2003 in the form of a pilot scheme and initially was available for all 10- to 16-year-olds living in the Greater Belfast area. In mid-2004, the scheme was expanded to cover young people living in more rural areas, including the Fermanagh and Tyrone regions. Section 63 of the Justice (Northern Ireland) Act of 2002 provides for the extension of the youth justice system to cover 17-year-olds when they are to be included in the jurisdiction of the youth courts. It is expected that this age group will fall under the auspices of the Youth Conference Service by the end of 2005. Before it is launched throughout the rest of Northern Ireland, a thorough and independent evaluation of the youth conference system, which is currently underway, is to be completed (Campbell et al., 2006).

The youth conferencing system marks an important new role for the Public Prosecution Service and Youth Courts, as it is anticipated that youth conferencing will become the primary response to nearly all young offenders brought for prosecution. Youth conferencing will also significantly alter how victims and offenders experience the criminal justice system. In theory, it offers both parties increased involvement in the process and the opportunity to "reclaim" their case from a professionalised, often alienating system (Christie, 1979; Shapland et al., 1985).

Typically, a youth conference involves a meeting in which a young person is provided with the opportunity to reflect upon their actions, and offer some form of reparation to the victim. The victim, who is given the choice whether or not to attend, can explain to the offender how the offence has affected him or her as an individual. In theory, this means that a conference gives the offender the chance to understand their crime in terms of its impact, particularly on the victim, and the victim to separate the offender from the offence. Following group dialogue on the harm caused by the young person's actions, a "conference plan" will be devised. This plan will take the form of a negotiated "contract," with implications if the young person does not follow through what is required of him or her. Agreement is a key factor in devising the "contract," and the young person must consent to its terms. Ideally, the "contract" will ultimately have some form of restorative outcome, addressing the needs of the victim, the offender and wider community.

2.2. When will a Young Person be Referred to a Youth Conference?

Two types of youth conferences are provided for in the legislation: *diversionary* youth conferences and *court-ordered* youth conferences. Both forms of conference take place with a view to a youth conference coordinator providing a recommendation to the Prosecutor or court on how the young person should be dealt with for their offence.

A diversionary conference is convened following a referral by the Public Prosecution Service. The Prosecutor will only make a youth conference referral where he would otherwise have instituted court proceedings. Diversionary youth conferences are not intended for minor first-time offenders, who, depending on the seriousness of the offence, will usually be dealt with by the police and given an informed warning with a "restorative theme" or a restorative caution. Instead, diversionary conferences will often be initiated as a "follow-up" intervention to curb offending, particularly where there has been previous contact with the criminal justice system. Two preconditions must be in place for a diversionary conference to occur: firstly, the young person must consent to the process and secondly they must admit that they have committed the offence. Where these conditions are not met the case will be referred to the Public Prosecution Service for a decision on whether to continue and, if so, the case may be dealt with through the ordinary court process.

Secondly, a young person may be referred to a youth conference by a court, known as a court-ordered youth conference. Again, the admission or establishment of guilt and consent of the young person are prerequisites for a court-ordered conference to take place. A distinctive feature of the Northern Ireland system is that a court *must* refer a young person to a youth conference. This is subject to certain restrictions: when a magistrate refers a case they must take into account the type of the offence committed. Only offences with a penalty of life imprisonment, offences which are triable, in the case of an adult, on indictment only and scheduled offences which fall under the Terrorism Act (2000) are not automatically eligible for youth conferencing. In effect, nearly all or the vast majority of young offenders will be dealt with through the conferencing process. The mandatory nature of court-ordered referrals highlights the intended centrality of youth conferencing to the youth justice system. In jurisdictions where referrals are discretionary, the uptake has often been low which has led to the marginalisation of restorative schemes to the periphery of the justice system (Shapland et al., 2004; Miers et al., 2001; Crawford and Newburn, 2003).

2.3. Who may Attend a Youth Conference?

By law, a youth conference coordinator, the young person, a police officer and an appropriate adult must attend a youth conference. Where any of these parties are absent the youth conference cannot proceed. The young person is permitted to have legal representation at the conference, but they may only participate in an advisory capacity and cannot speak for the young person as they are expected to participate fully in the process. Where the young person is under supervision of a criminal justice agency, such as probation, the supervising officer is also entitled to attend. Finally, where the youth conference coordinator deems it appropriate, any other person whose presence would be "of value" is entitled to attend a youth conference. This may include individuals who can offer advice or support regarding potential outcomes, such as a social worker, teacher or community worker.

A victim, or in his or her place a victim representative, is entitled, but not required, to attend the conference. It is important that the victim is aware of the voluntary nature of the process so as not to result in any additional emotional distress or potential "double victimisation." Where a victim chooses not to attend in person they may still contribute to the conferencing process either directly or indirectly. Section 6(4) of The Youth Conference Rules allows direct participation to be facilitated through a video conferencing or telephone link. Such "remote" participation may also be used where the young person is in secure accommodation at the time of the conference so that the victim does not have to visit the secure facilities. Indirect participation may be in form of a written statement, letter, tape or video recording or through a victim representative explaining the impact of the crime on the victim. If the victim is not an individual a representative may attend in their place. For example, where the offence is theft from a shop an employee of the business may attend, or a community representative may participate and explain the impact on the wider community where the offence is disorderly behaviour or criminal damage to public property.

Once it has been established who should attend the conference, the youth conference coordinator must take reasonable steps to inform all parties, orally and in writing, of the time and place of the conference. If notice is not provided and the youth conference goes ahead, it may be declared invalid. The Youth Conference Rules stipulate that a declaration of invalidity will only occur where failure to give notice is "likely to have materially affected the outcome of the youth conference." Where notice is not given to a party *legally obliged* to attend the conference cannot take place.

2.4. Preparation for the Conference

Each case referred to the Youth Conference Service by the Prosecutor or court is designated to a youth conference coordinator. The legislation requires that they are an employee of the civil service and, in practice, many coordinators have backgrounds in other criminal justice agencies such as the probation service. The role of the coordinator is to facilitate the conference process by enabling the preparation and participation of those involved. One of the key indicators of a successful restorative conference has been identified as the extent to which the participants have been informed and are prepared for the conference (Umbreit and Zehr, 1996; Strang, 2002). Effective communication with all participants prior to the conference on the part of the coordinator is therefore paramount. In addition to the legislative guidelines, the Youth Conference Service has produced a practice manual which sets out procedures and best practice to be followed by coordinators when meeting the young person and the victim (Youth Justice Agency, 2003).

Once a referral has been made, the youth conference process operates within a defined timescale. A report on the outcome of the conference must be sent to the Public Prosecution service within 30 working days, Initial contact is made with the young person, the Youth Conference Rules stipulating that a youth conference coordinator is required to make "all reasonable efforts" to visit the young person within 5 working days of the referral. On first meeting the young person, the coordinator will listen to their perspective, establish their readiness to engage in the process and, if they agree to participate, begin preparing them for the conference. The young person should be consulted with regards to a suitable time and a place for the conference to be held, and asked who they feel should attend the conference. Informational material, in the form of leaflets, a DVD and preparation worksheets should be provided and explained to the young person to ensure they fully understand the process. The coordinator will normally have at least two meetings with the young person to prepare them for the conference. If, following a referral by a court, the coordinator determines that the young person is failing to engage or not suitable for conferencing they are required make a written report to the court detailing this. This may occur where the young person has failed to attend preconference meetings or is deemed incapable of understanding the process. If the conference is diversionary the coordinator must only inform the Prosecutor of withdrawal of admission of guilt or consent.

The youth conference looks not only at an offence, but any background factors that may have contributed to the young person's offending. In preparing for the conference, s. 4 and 5 of the Youth Conference Rules enable the coordinator to access to the young persons criminal record and gather "information, advice and reports in relation to the child as he may deem necessary for the purpose of the youth conference" thus providing a contextual background to the offence. Previous offences may be discussed at the conference, however the coordinator must impress upon the young person that any *new* offences should not be raised in the conference; the police officer present is legally obliged to take action if such matters arise.

Only once the young person has consented to taking part in a Youth Conference will the victim be informed about the option of a conference. The Youth Conference Service practice manual states that "if this is not done and the young person does not consent to participate in a Youth Conference the victim may feel disappointed and even more aggrieved" (Youth Justice Agency, 2003: 58). When the coordinator visits the victim for the first time the voluntary nature of the process should be emphasised and the coordinator should explain the various means by which they can participate. Again, informational material should be supplied and explained so the victim is fully aware of the nature of process and any potential outcomes.

2.5. The Youth Conference

The format of the youth conference itself bears much similarity to New Zealand family group conferencing model (Maxwell and Morris, 1993); though with more emphasis on the victim playing an active role. The Youth Conference Rules provide the youth conference coordinator with a considerable degree of flexibility when facilitating a conference, stating that it should be conducted "in such a manner as appears to him to be appropriate." This allows for more "creative" conferences which may be more apposite and sensitive to the particularities of the case than a "scripted" conference may allow. In practice, however, conferences typically follow a more structured format with two distinct parts: discussion of the offence and its impact, and discussion on what can be done to repair the harm. Each conference should take place in a neutral venue – said to be "conducive to victim safety and the generation of positive outcomes" (Miers et al., 2001: 24) – which is convenient to both victim and offender. Most conferences take place at the purpose-built facilities at the Youth Conference Service Headquarters in Belfast; however venues such as community centres and libraries have also been used.

Prior to the conference starting, the coordinator is required by legislation to explain the procedures that will be adopted. Normally, ground rules and practicalities should be established and the coordinator will emphasise the importance of respect amongst the participants and the confidential and voluntary nature of the process. It should be explained that breaks can be called if necessary: for example, if the conference becomes emotional. A conference typically commences with a factual account of the offence read out by a police officer who is specialist in the field of youth diversion and trained in restorative practice. The young person will then be asked to put forward their side of the story and, if there is a victim in attendance, they will be provided with the opportunity to ask the young person questions or to elaborate on their account. Attention will then turn to the victim who will be asked to give their perspective and explain how the offence has affected him or her. If they have a supporter present, they too will be given the opportunity to provide more detail on the impact of the crime.

Once the victim has described the impact of the offence the young person will be provided with the opportunity to apologise. Although an apology is often spontaneous, the practice manual acknowledges that it will have been discussed with the young person prior to the conference and that they "should know from their preparation that this is the cue for an apology" (Youth Justice Agency, 2003: 69). It is, however, stressed that any apology must not be forced and should only be made if the young person wishes to do so. The young person's supporter(s) will be given the opportunity to speak up on the behalf of the offender and highlight the positive qualities or aspects of the young person's life. At this point, focus will turn towards the youth conference plan, and ways in which the young person can make amends to the victim and prevent further offending.

2.6. The Youth Conference Plan

The intended outcome of a youth conference is the devising and agreement of a "youth conference plan" or "action plan." The content of a plan will vary and should take into account the offence, the needs of the victim and the needs of the young person. Typically, a conference plan will include some form of apology, either written or verbal, and some form of material or symbolic reparation to the victim or community. A youth conference plan will cover a period of not more than one year. It is essential that the young person consents to the plan and that the consequences of failing to comply with the plan are made clear to them.

Section 3C(1) of the Justice (NI) Act (2002) provides guidelines detailing what a plan should contain. The legislation states that a young person is "required to do one or more of the following": apologise to the victim, perform unpaid community work or service, make financial reparation to the victim, submit him or herself to the supervision of an adult, participate in activities addressing offending (e.g., drugs and alcohol education), be subject to physically restrictive sanctions such as curfews, and undertake "treatment for a mental condition or for a dependency on alcohol or drugs." Consequently the legislation suggests that for an action plan to be valid at least one of these outcomes is required.

The intention of a diversionary conference is to divert a young person from formal prosecution, however this does not mean that this course cannot be taken, as a diversionary conference plan may still go on to recommend formal prosecution. Furthermore, participation in a youth conference does preclude the option of referring the young person to remand or secure accommodation. If the young person consents, a court-ordered youth conference may recommend custody, however if accepted it is for the court to decide the length of the term.

Once a plan has been agreed, depending on the type of referral, two courses will be followed:

(i) Diversionary conference plans

When a plan is agreed in a diversionary conference it will then be sent back to the Public Prosecution Service. The Prosecutor will consider the plan and make a decision to either accept or reject it. If a plan is accepted by the Prosecutor it will appear on the young person's criminal record, but not as a conviction. Where there is no agreed outcome, the youth conference coordinator must produce a written report to the Prosecutor detailing this. If this occurs, or the plan is rejected by the Prosecutor, the Prosecutor will then make a decision on how to proceed. A young person can then be referred for prosecution and their case streamed back into the formal court system.

(ii) Court-ordered conference plans

Once a referral to the Youth Conference Service has been made the court cannot deal with the offence until it has obtained a written report from a youth conference coordinator. The coordinator can recommend one of three options to the court

1. that the court exercise its powers to deal with the child for the offence,
2. that the child be subject to a youth conference plan in respect of the offence, or
3. that the court exercise its powers to deal with the child for the offence by imposing a custodial sentence and that the child be subject to a youth conference plan in respect of the offence.

If a plan is accepted by the court it then becomes known as a *youth conference order*. In making an order, the court may choose to amend certain aspects of the plan; for example, to increase or decrease the number of hours of reparation work. A youth conference order will appear on a young person's criminal record as a conviction. If there is a recommendation for a custodial sentence in addition to the plan the coordinator cannot specify the form and duration of the sentence. However, if there has been a recommendation that the court exercises its powers by imposing a *non*-custodial sentence the court may then hear recommendations. When a proposal is received by the court it must only make a youth conference order where the offence is "serious enough to warrant it." In theory, this may be viewed as a legislative safeguard to ensure the proportionality of a plan. Interestingly, a similar check is not present in the rules governing diversionary youth conferences.

2.7. Termination of a Youth Conference

The youth conference process may be terminated for a number of reasons. For a youth conference to take place the young person must consent to participate. If at any stage they withdraw this consent the legislation requires that the conference process is terminated. The rationale behind the restorative aspect of youth conferencing is the achievement of an *agreed* outcome, something which is clearly undermined if a conference takes place without the consent of the young person. In addition to consent, a young person must also admit guilt or be found guilty of an offence for a conference to take place. Consequently, if the young person withdraws an admission of guilt the conference process must be stopped.

A court-ordered youth conference may also be terminated where a youth conference coordinator is satisfied that it "would serve no useful purpose." This may occur where young persons refuse to engage in the process or if they have previously taken part in unsuccessful youth conferences. Before making such an application to a court, the coordinator is required to consult the key parties to a conference: the young person, their appropriate adult and police officer.

2.8. Non-Compliance

A designated youth conference coordinator will monitor a young person's adherence to a youth conference plan or order. When non-compliance is first identified, a meeting is immediately convened with the young person in order to discuss this. The youth conference coordinator should seek to identify the reasons behind non-compliance and reinforce the importance of adhering to the plan. Extenuating circumstances which are beyond the young person's control – such as family conflict or homelessness – may be located as the cause of the problem. In such a situation, the youth conference coordinator can recommend to the coordinator that a plan is suspended temporarily until a way forward is agreed. Where it is not possible to come to a resolution, the youth conference coordinator must then make a report to the Public Prosecution Service or court explaining this.

When a young person willingly and repeatedly fails to comply with the terms of the conference plan or youth conference order, a number of steps can be taken. Firstly, a further conference may be arranged addressing the reasons behind the young person's non-compliance. If there is continued non-compliance following a second conference two routes may be taken depending on the type of referral.

(i) Diversionary plans

Proceedings can *only* be actioned or continued against a young person where the plan has been rejected by the Prosecutor or they have failed to comply with the terms of the plan to a "significant extent." The youth conference coordinator is required to produce a written report to the Prosecutor detailing any non-compliance. At this stage, a plan may be varied or proceedings instigated against the young person. A plan can only be amended where it is deemed appropriate and if the Prosecutor, the young person and any other individual of whom action is required consents. If a young person is appearing before a court for breach of a diversionary youth conference order, the court may, *where it is appropriate to do so*, refer the case to the Youth Conference Service for a court-ordered youth conference. As such, a court-ordered conference may be convened for the same offence.

(ii) Court-Ordered plans

If a young person is in breach of a youth conference order the court will follow one of the alternatives available to them under Schedule 10 of the Justice (Northern Ireland) Act of 2002. Breach proceedings can only be instigated where there is non-compliance. As a punishment for breach the court may impose an attendance centre order or a community service order. In addition to this they also have the option of (i) revoking the youth conference order, (ii) amending the youth conference order or (iii) extending the timescale of the youth conference order. If the youth conference order is revoked completely the young person will be resentenced as if they have just been found guilty of the offence. Where a court decides to amend a youth conference order they must obtain the consent of the young person and inform all relevant parties.

3. ISSUES ARISING FROM THE YOUTH CONFERENCE SCHEME

Despite being in its infancy, a number of potential gaps as to how the youth conference process works in theory, and how it might work in practice, can be identified. These include (i) gaining the informed consent of the young person; (ii) guaranteeing the proportionality of outcomes; (iii) net-widening and (iv) securing victim participation.

3.1. Informed Consent

The UN guidelines on the administration of restorative justice programmes require that they "should be used only with the free and voluntary consent of the parties" (United Nations, 2000). In theory, a young person's decision to participate in the youth conference process will be an informed choice, with a full awareness of all the options available to him or her. In practice, given that the alternative is often sentencing by a court, whose sanctions may be perceived as more punitive, a young person may feel there is "no choice." When a young person appears in an often intimidating court environment and is offered a youth conference by the magistrate they are typically required to make their decision "on the spot." If they have not previously discussed this option with their solicitor they may have little understanding of what the process entails. After accepting a conference there may be reluctance to withdraw for fear of being looked upon negatively by the court.

Similar problems may be encountered in a conference scenario where the "negotiation" of a plan has the potential to be undemocratic. The young person may feel that they have no leverage and must agree to suggestions put forward, regardless of their willingness or suitability. Research looking at the detention and questioning of young people by the police in custody has also shown that there are problems in getting young people to fully understand what is happening to them in stressful environments such as police stations (Quinn and Jackson, 2004). The European Court of Human Rights has held that to conform with an individual's right to a fair trial it is essential that the person is dealt with in a manner which takes full account of their age, level of maturity and intellectual and emotional capacities and that steps are taken to promote their ability to understand and participate in proceedings (T and V v United Kingdom (1999) 30 EHRR 121). Article 12 of the UN Convention on the Rights of the Child also states that a child should have the opportunity to be heard in any proceedings affecting them, and be able to express their views freely. Careful attention must be paid by practitioners to ensure that this occurs in practice.

3.2. Proportionality of Outcomes

A key theme throughout the literature on restorative justice is the principle of proportionality, which requires that the outcome reflects the seriousness of the offence. In New Zealand, Maxwell and Morris (1993: 96) have highlighted a number of family group conferences in which the outcome seemed to "outweigh the gravity of the offence." In Northern Ireland, the legislation states that a court should only impose a conference order if it considers it "serious enough to warrant it." In practice, however, a court may be unlikely to reject a plan for being "too harsh," particularly where there has been "agreement" in devising it. Notably, diversionary conference plans have no similar safeguards, bar the recommendation in the *Practice Manual* that a plan should be "proportional to the harm done and the seriousness of the offence" (Youth Justice Agency, 2003: 70). Restorative justice can potentially "trample rights because of impoverished articulation of procedural safeguards" (Braithwaite, 1999: 101). This may mean inequitable outcomes: for example, if a conference fails to reach an agreed outcome a "double jeopardy" situation may occur where a young person is "punished by the court for the failure of the conference as well as the offence" (Warner, 1994: 180). The number of possible youth conference outcomes is potentially wide and, except for the fact that a plan can only be enforced for a year, there are few restrictions as to what can be included. The lack of such safeguards, particularly for diversionary conferences, is an oversight which may require reexamination by legislators and careful attention by the courts and youth conference practitioners.

Proportionality is a particularly important issue where there the victim, whose level of forgiveness will inevitably differ from case to case, has a say in the content of the conference plan. Outcomes may be inconsistent if determined by individual victims, which could result in uncertain and disproportionate disposals. Ashworth (2001: 359). posits that to counter this, upper limits should be established and "decided by reference to publicly debatable and democratically determined policies that show respect for the human rights of victims and defendants." Strang (2002: 4–15), however, notes that research has rejected the notion of a "vengeful victim" and instead suggests that victims prioritise involvement in the *process* rather than in deciding the outcome (see also Hough and Mayhew, 1985: 35). This is particularly important in a restorative context where the victim may be *less* likely to demand a punitive outcome after meeting the offender face to face and learning more about them.

3.3. Net-Widening

Despite the fact that the youth conferencing system operates with the express intention of diverting young people from the formal justice system, the possibility of net-widening remains a key issue. Net-widening occurs when less serious cases are brought into the criminal justice system that would have previously fallen outside it. Evaluations have proved inconclusive in determining if net-widening is occurring as a consequence of restorative practices. In New Zealand, Maxwell and Morris (1993) found no evidence that family group conferencing was resulting in new cases being drawn in. Similarly, in a police-led scheme in Bethlehem, Pennsylvania, it was concluded that "cases were successfully diverted without net-widening effects" (McCold and Watchel, 1998: 108). In a study of the restorative cautioning scheme in Northern Ireland, however, concerns were raised that it was "drawing very young juveniles into the criminal justice system for very petty offences" (O'Mahony et al., 2002: 7). Youth conferencing will usually only be available to young people who have offended previously and have already received some form of restorative caution or warning, or to those who have committed more serious offences where a caution or warning is not appropriate. As such, very minor first-time offenders should normally fall outside its auspices. Nevertheless, to prevent any potential net-widening effects, best practice requires that internal checks are carried out and that there is awareness of who is being referred to youth conferencing and for what.

3.4. Victim Participation

One of the primary claims of restorative justice is that it enables the victim to play an active role in their own case where the traditional court system would otherwise marginalise them. Such involvement is said to address the emotional needs of the victim by performing a cathartic function. Research has shown it is often difficult to secure the participation of victims in practice. The police-led restorative cautioning scheme in Northern Ireland experienced low levels of victim participation (O'Mahony and Doak, 2004), as did youth offender panel meetings in England and Wales, where an average of only 13% of victims took part (Crawford and Newburn, 2003: 186). When a victim does not participate, either directly or indirectly, questions clearly arise as to just how "restorative" the process is (McCold, 2000). Resolving the issue of how to augment the number of victims attending restorative sessions whilst being mindful of their right not to participate is therefore an important one for practitioners.

Finally, if the victim is really to move in from the margins of the criminal justice system equal consideration must be given to the treatment of non-participating victims. This is particularly important with regards to the level of information and feedback they receive from the Youth Conference Service as to the outcome of the conference. Hoyle (2002: 131) has argued that if this does not happen it may lead to a bifurcation in the system between participating and non-participating victims, "the '[non-participating victims]' becoming the forgotten actors in restorative justice."

4. CONCLUSIONS

Northern Ireland offers a number of insights in youth justice practice and policy which are relevant to the international forum. The introduction of the youth conferencing system appears to be a positive development for both victim and young offender. Research on the early operation of the scheme has shown high levels of participant satisfaction; the vast majority of victims interviewed post-conference unequivocally stated that they would recommend the initiative to another person in their position, as did the vast majority of young people (Campbell et al., 2006). If youth conferencing is to continue to prove effective in achieving long-term positive outcomes, high standards of best practice, due process and procedural equity must be aspired to and attained. This will require a great deal of time and resources and, in theory, the quality of the conferences may be affected by the sheer quantity of referrals. In terms of facilitation, formulaic conferences in which the content of the conference plans are decided in pre-conference meetings should be avoided. Less "scripted" conferences which do not simply "go through the motions" are perhaps more desirable in achieving a long-term positive outcome – in New Zealand, research shows that a successful conference contributed to reducing the chance of reoffending (Maxwell and Morris, 2002). Inevitably, not all cases will be appropriate for youth conferencing – when 17-year-olds come under the jurisdiction of the youth court offences such as car tax evasion will be referred to the youth conferencing service. Consequently, the efficacy of mandatory referrals may be something to be reviewed over time.

One of the more successful aspects of youth justice practice in Northern Ireland outside youth conferencing has been adopted by the police and their use of the Youth Diversion Scheme. The scheme manages to divert the majority of young offenders away from formal proceedings and deals with most juvenile offending informally. This has been shown to be effective as recidivism rates of those dealt with informally are considerably lower than those prosecuted through the courts. The police have also been developing their practices with young offenders and now deliver cautions using a restorative framework which should help young people realise the harm caused by their offending and may help victims come to terms with the offence. This new practice has been shown to be a significant improvement to previous methods of cautioning and hopefully will lead to continued low levels of recidivism for such young offenders(O'Mahony and Doak, 2004).

The use of custody is another area where there have been considerable advances. Northern Ireland has moved from a jurisdiction which locked up too many of its young people, sometimes for petty offences. This has changed, and now the numbers in custody is only around 30–35 children (10–16 years). Progressive legislation which has restricted the courts ability to impose custodial sentences on children other than for serious offences and restrictions on custodial remands has helped greatly to keep the number of young people in custody to a minimum. The importance of restricting the use of custody is underlined by the very high reconviction rates of those who have been released from custody, showing it to be really only effective as a means of temporary incapacitation. Best practice shows that custody should only be used as a last resort for juveniles and for the shortest period necessary.

However not all of the recent reforms have been positive – in August 2004 Anti-Social Behaviour Orders (ASBOs) were introduced in Northern Ireland, sitting uncomfortably in a juvenile justice system said to be underpinned by a restorative justice philosophy. ASBOs are civil orders which were first introduced in England and Wales under the Crime and Disorder Act (1998) whose primary purpose is to "protect the public from behaviour that causes or is likely to cause harassment, alarm or distress" by dealing with "persistent unruly behaviour" (Northern Ireland Office, 2004). ASBOs are available in two ways. Firstly, where there is no conviction the police, district council or housing executive may make an application for an ASBO to the magistrates' court as a civil injunction. Notably, hearsay evidence is admissible in civil proceedings so the affected person does not have to give first-hand evidence on any antisocial behaviour and the burden of proof is below that required in criminal proceedings. Furthermore, the type of behaviour the injunction seeks to prohibit includes actions which are not in and of themselves criminal, including acts "likely to cause harassment, alarm or distress," which can include making excessive noise, or acting in an "antisocial manner." Secondly, it is proposed that ASBOs will be available to a court on conviction in criminal proceedings. In both instances an ASBO can only be served where it is deemed necessary to protect a person from further antisocial acts. An ASBO will not appear on an individual's criminal record, as it is a civil order. There are however significant implications for breach, which is classified as a criminal offence and punishable with up to 5 years imprisonment. Effectively the ASBO is a hybrid conviction which takes advantage of the lower standard of proof required in civil proceedings and includes actions or behaviours that are not criminal, but punishes non-compliance with the imposition of onerous criminal sanctions.

ASBOs are perhaps the most controversial of the new criminal justice measures to be established in Northern Ireland. In England and Wales they have proved difficult to implement in practice, with support from local authorities described as "not consistent" and "patchy" (Campbell, 2002; Burney, 2002). More fundamentally, their introduction sends mixed messages about the government's youth justice strategy, as they mark a divergence from the increasingly restorative path youth justice in Northern Ireland has been following. Groups campaigning for the rights of young people have been strongly vociferous in their opposition to ASBOs. In June 2004, the Children's Commissioner unsuccessfully called for a judicial review of the proposed legislation (Belfast Telegraph, 2004) and the Chief Commissioner of the Northern Ireland Human Rights Commission expressed concern that ASBOs would "severely and unjustifiably restrict the human rights of many individuals and possibly leave them open to attack by paramilitary organisations" (Northern Ireland Human Rights Commission, 2004). Whether they ultimately serve to protect the public from persistent unruly behaviour or result in young people being criminalised on shaky evidence remains to be seen.

REFERENCES

Ashworth, A. (2001). "Is Restorative Justice the Way Forward for Criminal Justice?" *Current Legal Problems*, 54:347–376.

Becker, H. (1963). *Outsiders: Studies in the Sociology of Deviance*. London: Free Press of Glencoe.

Beckett, H., Campbell, C., O'Mahony, D., Jackson, J., and Doak, J. (2005). *Interim Evaluation of the Northern Ireland Youth Conferencing Scheme*. Belfast: Northern Ireland Office.

Belfast Telegraph. (2004). *Hooligan Law Faces Court Challenge*, 11 June 2004.

Black, H. (1979). *Legislation and Services for Children and Young Persons in Northern Ireland* (Children and Young Persons Review Group). Belfast: HMSO.

Braithwaite, J. (1999). "Restorative Justice: Assessing Optimistic and Pessimistic Accounts," in M. Tonry (ed.), *Crime and Justice: A Review of Research*. Chicago: University of Chicago Press.

Burney, E. (2002). "Talking Tough, Acting Coy: What Happened to the Anti-Social Behaviour Order?" *The Howard Journal of Criminal Justice*, 41(5): 469–484.

Campbell, C., Doulin, R., O'Mahony, D., Doak, J., Jackson, J., Corrigan, T., and McEvoy, K., Evaluation of the Northern Ireland Youth Conference Service. Research and Statistics Report No. 12. (Northern Ireland Office).

Campbell, S. (2002). *A Review of Anti-Social Behaviour Orders*. London: HMSO.

Christie, N. (1979). "Conflicts as Property," *British Journal of Criminology*, 17(1):1–15.

Crawford, A. and Newburn, T. (2003). *Youth Offending and Restorative Justice: Implementing Reform in Youth Justice*. Cullompton: Willan.

Curran, D., Kilpatrick, R., Young, V., and Wilson, D., (1995). "Longitudinal Aspects of Reconviction: Secure and Open Interventions with Juvenile Offenders in Northern Ireland," *The Howard Journal of Criminal Justice*, 34(2):97–123.

Digest 4. (2004). *Digest of Information on the Northern Ireland Criminal Justice System 4*. Belfast: Northern Ireland Office.

Dignan, J. and Lowey, K. (2000). *Restorative Justice Options for Northern Ireland: A Comparative Review*. Belfast: HMSO.

Graham, J. and Bowling, B. (1995). *Young People and Crime – Home Office Research Study 145*. London: HMSO.

Hague, L. (2001). *NIO Research and Statistical Bulletins 1/2001: International Crime Victimisation Survey 2000; Key Findings for Northern Ireland*. Belfast: HMSO.

Hough, M. and Mayhew, P. (1985). *Taking Account of Crime: Key Findings from the Second British Crime Survey*, Home Office Research Study No. 85. London: HMSO.

Hoyle, C. (2002). "Securing Restorative Justice for the 'Non-Participating' Victim," in C. Hoyle and R. Young (eds.), in *New Visions of Crime Victims*. Oxford: Hart.

Mathewson, T., Willis, M., and Boyle, M. (1998). *Cautioning in Northern Ireland. A Profile of Adult and Juvenile Cautioning and Re-offending Rates* (Northern Ireland Office, Research and Statistics Branch. Research Findings 4/98). Belfast: Northern Ireland Office.

McCold, P. (2000). "Towards a Mid-Range Theory of Restorative Juvenile Justice: A Reply to the Maximalist Model," *Contemporary Justice Review*, 3(4): 357–414.

McCold, P. and Watchel, B. (1998). *Restorative Policing Experiment: The Bethlehem Pennsylvania Police Family Group Conferencing Project*. Pipersville: Community Service Foundation.

McEvoy, K. and Mika, H. (2002). "Restorative Justice and the Critique of Informalism in Northern Ireland," *British Journal of Criminology*, 42(3):534–562.

McQuoid, J. (1994). "The Self-Reported Delinquency Study in Belfast, Northern Ireland," in J. Junger-Taset al. (eds.), *Delinquent Behaviour Among Young People in the Western World*. Amsterdam: Kulger:

Maxwell, G. and Morris, A. (1993). *Family, Victims and Culture: Youth Justice in New Zealand*. Wellington: Social Policy Agency and Institute of Criminology, Victoria University of Wellington.

Maxwell, G. and Morris, A. (2002). "Restorative Justice and Reconviction," *Contemporary Justice Review*, 5(2):133–146.

Miers, D., Maguire, M., Goldie, S., Sharpe, K., Hale, C., Netten, A., Doolin, K., Uglow, S., Enterkin, J., and Newburn, T. (2001). *An Exploratory Evaluation of Restorative Justice Schemes*. London: HMSO.

Northern Ireland Human Rights Commission. (2002). *Initial Comments on the Justice (Northern Ireland) Bill*. Online available: at http://www.nihrc.org/documents/landp/71.doc (2 June 2005).

Northern Ireland Human Rights Commission. (2004). Press Release: Human Rights Commission Gravely Concerned at Haste in Introducing Anti-social Behaviour Orders. Online available at http://www.nihrc.org/ (July 12th, 2004).

Northern Ireland Office. (2004). *Proposal for a Draft Anti-Social Behaviour (NI) Order*. Online available at http://www.nio.gov.uk/pdf/antisocial2004.pdf (2 June 2005).

O'Mahony, D. and Deazley, R. (2000). *Juvenile Crime and Justice*. Belfast: Northern Ireland Office.

O'Mahony, D. and Doak, J. (2004). Restorative Justice – Is More Better? The Experience of Police-led Restorative Cautioning Pilots in Northern Ireland. *The Howard Journal*, 43(5):484–505.

O'Mahony, D., Chapman, T., and Doak, J. (2002). *Restorative Cautioning: A Study of Police Based Restorative Cautioning Pilots in Northern Ireland*. Belfast: Northern Ireland Office.

Quinn, K. and Jackson, J. (2004). *The Detention and Questioning of Young Persons by the Police in Northern Ireland*. Belfast: Northern Ireland Office.

Rutherford, A. (1992). *Growing Out of Crime: The New Era*. London: Waterside Press.

Shapland, J., Wilmore, J., and Duff, P. (1985). *Victims and the Criminal Justice System*. Aldershot: Gower.

Shapland, J., Atkinson, A., Colledge, E., Dignan, J., Howes, M., Johnstone, J., Pennant, R., Robinson, G., and Sorsby, A. (2004). *Implementing Restorative Justice Schemes* (*Crime Reduction Programme*): *A Report on the First Year*. Online available at http://www.homeoffice.gov.uk/rds/pdfs04/rdsolr3204.pdf (2 June 2005).

Strang, H. (2002). *Repair or Revenge: Victims and Restorative Justice*. Oxford: Clarendon Press.

Umbreit, M., and Zehr, H. (1996). "Restorative Family Group Conferences: Differing Models and Guidelines for Practice," *Federal Probation*, 60(3):24–29.

United Nations. (2000). *Basic Principles on the Use of Restorative Justice Programmes in Criminal Matters*. Online available at http://www.restorativejustice.org/rj3/UNdocuments/UNDecBasicPrinciplesofRJ.html (2 June 2005).

Warner, K. (1994). "Family Group Conferences and the Rights of Offenders," in C. Alder and J. Wundersitz, (eds.), *Family Conferencing and Juvenile Justice: The Way Forward or Misplaced Optimism?* Canberra: Australian Institute of Criminology.

Wilson, D., Kerr, H., and Boyle, M. (1998). *Juvenile Offenders and Reconviction in Northern Ireland* (Northern Ireland Office, Research and Statistics Branch Research Findings 3/98). Belfast: Northern Ireland Office.

Wolfgang, M., Thornberry, T., and Figlio, R. (1987). *From Boy to Man, From Delinquency to Crime*. Chicago: University of Chicago Press.

Youth Justice Agency. (2003). *Youth Conference Service Practice Manual*. Belfast: Youth Justice Agency.

5

Transition and Reform: Juvenile Justice in the Republic of Ireland

Mairéad Seymour

The Republic of Ireland has a population of 3.9 million of this figure 29% are under the age of 20 years and 37% are under 25 years. Despite increasing immigration, Ireland still remains a relatively homogenous country with over 90% of individuals categorised as Irish and 88% of the population classified as Roman Catholic (Central Statistics Office, 2002). In April 2005, Ireland had the lowest rate of seasonally adjusted unemployment (4.2%) in the Eurozone compared to an average of 8.9% (Eurostat, 2005). Ireland also had the second lowest rate of youth unemployment (7.9% compared to an average of 19%) in the same period.

This chapter focuses on the juvenile justice system in the Republic of Ireland. It documents the background and history to the Children Act of 2001 which is the first major change in juvenile justice legislation in almost 100 years. Trends in youth crime and crime prevention initiatives are discussed before moving on to discuss the main principles and provisions of the Children Act of 2001 including the use of custody as a measure of last resort, the increased use of community-based sanctions and the introduction of restorative justice initiatives into the system. A common theme throughout the chapter is the slow pace at which the new legislation is being implemented and the implications of these delays for young people in the criminal justice system. The chapter concludes with a reflection on the future direction of juvenile justice in the Republic of Ireland.

INTRODUCTION

The Irish juvenile justice system is in a period of transition following the replacement of the Children Act of 1908 with the Children Act of 2001 as the main legislation governing juvenile justice in the Republic of Ireland. The Children Act of 2001 represents the first major legislative reform of the system in almost 100 years. Despite this, significant delays have occurred in bringing many parts of the new Act into force and this has led to a continued reliance on the outdated legislation in many areas. While the Children Act of 1908 was seen as progressive for its day, not surprisingly, given that its foundations are rooted at the beginning of the last century, it has been severely criticised for being archaic and out of keeping with

J. Junger-Tas and S. H. Decker (eds.), International Handbook of Juvenile Justice, 117–144.

current thinking on juvenile justice (Coghlan, 2000; O'Mahony, 2000; O'Sullivan, 1996; Quinn, 2002). Some of the most common criticisms of it relate to an overemphasis on the institutionalisation of children through detention and imprisonment with less attention being placed on community-based options. The Children Act of 1908 also restricts the way in which children in trouble before the law can be disposed of. However, even with the outdated provisions, it has been suggested that more ingenious and creative measures could be used to deal with young offenders (Burke et al., 1981). Another criticism of the Children Act of 1908 relates to the low age of criminal responsibility for children. The Republic of Ireland currently has the lowest age of criminal responsibility (7 years) in Europe. The Children Act of 2001 has made provision for it to be increased to 12 years however; the relevant part of the legislation was never enacted.[1]

A plethora of committees have been convened and reports produced with significant recommendations for change to the childcare and juvenile justice system in the Republic of Ireland since the late 1960s (Kennedy Report, 1970; Task Force on Child Care Services, 1980; Whitaker Report, 1985); however, the recommendations from these combined committees, with a small number of exceptions, were collectively ignored by successive governments. The impetus for legislative change in the form of the Children Act of 2001 only began in the early 1990s with a report by the Government Select Committee (1992) entitled *Juvenile Crime – Its Causes and its Remedies*. Many of the recommendations emerging from this report formed the basis of the Children Bill (1999), which subsequently became the Children Act of 2001. Pressure from the international community about the government's approach to young people in conflict with the law was another factor driving forward change to the juvenile justice system. The Irish government ratified the UN Convention on the Rights of the Child in 1992 but was later criticised by the UN Committee who expressed concern about the treatment of children deprived of their liberty in the light of the principles of the UN Convention and other international standards[2] (Children's Right Alliance, 1998). Independent and non-statutory organisations, lobbying groups and members of the academic community played a role in the move for change by highlighting the inadequacies in the system. They were often lone voices because in a country the size of the Republic of Ireland, extensive media reporting of an isolated but

[1]Recently proposed amendments to the Criminal Justice Bill of 2004 include a prohibition against the charging of children under 12 years with most offences (with the exception of the most serious offences, e.g., murder, manslaughter, rape or aggravated sexual assault by a child age 10 or 11 years); the abolition of any rule of law which a child aged between 7 and 14 years is doli incapax and; provisions to ensure that prosecutions of children under 14 years must be sanctioned by the Director of Public Prosecution.

[2]For example, the United Nations Standard of Minimum Rules for the Administration of Juvenile Justice (Beijing Rules), the United Nations Guidelines on the Prevention of Juvenile Delinquency (Riyadh Guidelines) and the United Nations Rules for the Protection of Juveniles Deprived of their Liberty.

serious incident of youthful offending can serve to swing the political pendulum towards reactionary punitiveness rather than strategic crime prevention in efforts to still public concern about crime.[3] Over the last number of years, there has been a gradual shift in Ireland towards a focus on children's rights. A number of developments such as the Ombudsman for Children Act of 2002 and the publication of National Children's Strategy (Government of Ireland, 2000) have raised the status and profile of preventative work with children. Such developments coupled with the necessity of updating outdated legislation and international pressure on the government created the context in which change has begun.

1. EXPLAINING THE LACK OF CHANGE IN THE JUVENILE JUSTICE SYSTEM 1908–2001

Before addressing the key changes in the Irish juvenile justice system, an important question in terms of the development of the system relates to why change took so long? O'Dwyer (2002) explains that up to the 1960s, Ireland was a relatively insular and underdeveloped country where the influence of the Roman Catholic Church was strong and crime was not seen as a problem to any great extent. Until recently, the Republic of Ireland experienced minimal immigration resulting in a largely homogenous population; this homogeneity is likely to have created fewer opportunities to question the approach used in dealing with juvenile offenders in the jurisdiction or to explore the diversity of approaches used in others. Numerous voices have highlighted the lack of political interest in juvenile justice as a resounding reason for the lack of change (Kenny, 2000; O'Sullivan, 1996). McCullagh (1991 in O'Sullivan, 1998: 339) argues that because a range of social partners including the trade union movement did not align or associate with the issue of juvenile justice, there was a lack of political pressure placed on the government to reform. Indeed, it has been argued that the very lack of legislative change since 1908 is testimony to a long-standing lack of political interest (Quinn, 2002).

In addition, a major problem underlying the Irish juvenile justice system has been the dearth of research in the area. A variety of commentators (Burke et al., 1981; O'Sullivan, 1996; O'Mahony, 2000) have pointed to the lack of empirical research undertaken on juvenile justice in the Republic of Ireland as hindering the effective development of the system. There is a lack of statistical data on crime (National Crime Council, 2003) and what is available has been criticised as being of sub-standard quality "usually outdated, partial, limited, non-integrated, and

---

[3]In April 2002, following the death of two Gardaí (Irish Police) as a result of a car theft and joyriding incident by juveniles, the Minister for Justice proposed plans for a temporary children's prison wing for 14 and 15 year olds at St. Patrick's Institution. Such a plan would have only been possible under the Children Act (1908) as the Children Act (2001) when fully enacted prohibits the detention of children under 16 years in a place of detention such as St. Patrick's Institution.

poorly explained" (O'Dwyer, 2002: 182). It has also been argued that this has resulted in policy being developed in a "research vacuum" (O'Sullivan, 1996: 5). The lack of published material on juvenile justice in the Republic of Ireland has led to limited debate about the issues, influences and direction of the system, which in turn has placed few demands on the political system to reform. Regardless of the reasons for a lack of change, there is now almost uniform acknowledgement that change is essential and as O'Sullivan (1998: 341) argues "considerable efforts will have to be taken to overturn the virtual neglect of the issue of juvenile justice since the foundation of the Irish State." Before discussing the transition in the juvenile justice system from the Children Act of 1908 to the Children Act of 2001, the context is set by outlining recent trends in youth crime and crime prevention initiatives in the Republic of Ireland.

2. TRENDS IN YOUTH CRIME

Ireland has a low level of recorded crime when examined in an international context (Young et al., 2001). The official source of crime data in the Republic of Ireland is the Annual Report of the Garda Síochána (Irish police). These statistics are inevitably incomplete due to all crimes not being reported to and recorded by the police. Data on juvenile crime are available from the main records of crime held by the Garda Síochána and also from data on referrals to the National Juvenile Office (NJO), both of which are published in the Annual Report of the Garda Síochána. The main records of crime are limited with regard to the information which can be gathered about juvenile crime. Firstly, information is only available on persons convicted or against whom the charge was held proved or an order was made without a conviction. Secondly, data is categorised in age cohorts that do not correspond with the legislative definition of a child or young person. The categories include those less than 14 years, from 14 to 16 years, from 17 to 20 years and 21 years and over; it is therefore impossible to establish the rate of recorded crime against those less than 18 years. Overall, trends suggest that recorded crime involving juveniles has remained steadily low over the last decade, although it has been suggested that this may be due to the increasing numbers receiving a caution under the Garda Juvenile Diversion Programme.[4] The vast majority of headline (indictable) offences involving juveniles relate to crimes of larceny and burglary with only a minute proportion involving offences against the person. The most common non-headline (non-indictable) offences recorded against juveniles are criminal damage, public order, unauthorised taking/interference with vehicles and traffic related offences.[5]

[4]The number of juveniles cautioned decreased from 10,539 in 1996 to 7,784 in 2000, however the numbers have risen steadily in recent years to 10,240 cases in 2002 (An Garda Síochána, 2000, 2002).

[5]A breakdown of the age cohorts for non-headline offences is available for the first time in the Annual Report of the Garda Síochána in 2002.

All juvenile cases are referred centrally to the NJO under the auspices of the Garda Síochána in Dublin where a decision is taken on what action should be taken against them, e.g., a caution, recommended for prosecution etc. Data from the NJO statistics are therefore not comparable to the main crime records but they present a more complete picture of crime amongst those less than 18 years. The total number of offences in respect of which referrals were made to the NJO has increased significantly from 14,488 to 19,080 in the period from 2000 to 2001 and again to 20,647 in 2002. Statistics from the NJO suggest that theft, criminal damage, drink-related offences, public order, traffic offences, burglary, vehicle offences and minor assault are the most common offences for which young people are referred (An Garda Síochána, 1999–2002). A comparison of the principal offences as a percentage of the total referrals received for each year between 1995 and 2002 by the NJO allows broad trends to be derived from the data. Theft, as a percentage of the total offence referrals for each year has fallen dramatically from almost 30% in 1995 to 19% in 2002. There has also been a steady decrease in burglaries from the mid-1990s and especially from 1998 onwards. This trend has continued with burglary representing 8.7% of referrals in 1998 but only 5.5% in 2002. In 2002, drink-related offences, for the first time, became the most common offence for which young people were referred to the NJO. Referrals for drink-related offences have risen steadily since 1995. There was a 6.4% increase in referrals for drink-related offences in the period from 1998 to 1999 and this trend has continued upwards. While drink-related offences accounted for 9.8% of offences for which juveniles were referred in 1999, they rose to 12.4% in 2000, 17% in 2001 and 19.3% in 2002. Public order offences have remained static as a percentage of total referrals received each year (with the exception of 1996 when they rose to approximately 10% of referrals). From 1998 they have risen only slightly from 6.5% to 7.2% in 2002. There has been a downward trend in vehicle offences since 2000 when they accounted for 8.5% of referrals. The percentage of referrals has remained static over the last 2 years accounting for 5.7% and 5.5%, respectively in 2001 and 2002. Serious crime by young people accounts for only a small amount of referrals. For example, serious assaults accounted for approximately 2% of referrals between 1999 and 2002 and referrals for such assaults decreased by 13% during 2002 (An Garda Síochána, 1999–2002: 112).

Unfortunately, the main source of crime data in the Republic of Ireland comes from official sources only. The Republic of Ireland has not previously participated in the International Crime Victimisation Survey, completed a regular National Crime Victimisation Survey or undertaken any major self-report crime survey. While a number of victim surveys (Breen and Rottman, 1984; Central Statistics Office, 1998; Watson, 2000) have taken place, they are often limited by their crime or area specific focus. Similarly self-report studies have been confined to one-off, localised areas or specific to a particular group of the population.

3. CRIME PREVENTION

There has been increased investment in projects to tackle disadvantage and social exclusion amongst children and young people in recent years (Kenny, 2000; O'Mahony, 2000). That said, many crime prevention initiatives in the Republic of Ireland are characterised by their non-integrated approach, lack of long-term investment and limited evaluation (Quinn, 2002). Difficulties with regard to resources and planning continue. However, a number of crime prevention initiatives have developed on a national basis and plans are afoot to move towards a more integrated model of crime prevention. The recently published document *A Crime Prevention Strategy for Ireland – Tackling the Concerns of Local Communities* includes proposals for a National Crime Prevention Model (National Crime Council, 2003). The proposed model would be developed at local, county and national level and would emphasise the importance of early intervention, long-term planning and investment as well as regular, independent evaluation. Various government departments support initiatives which come under the remit of crime prevention, e.g., early school leaver programmes and community programmes for children at risk. The following outlines some of the more widely available crime prevention initiatives in the country[6]:

Springboard Programme – This is a community-based intervention programme funded by the Department of Health and Children to support families with children who are at risk of dropping out of school, entering care or getting into trouble with the law. Considerable improvements in the well-being experienced by parents and children were noted in an evaluation of the programme; however it was also noted that "the problems in vulnerable families tend to be entrenched" and are therefore "not amenable to quick change" (McKeown et al., 2001: 123).

The Early Start Programme – This programme provides pre-school intervention for 3-year-olds who are most at risk in areas of social disadvantage. The aim is to prevent school failure and minimise the effects of social disadvantage.

School Completion Programme – This initiative focuses on children and young people between 4 and 18 years who are at risk of leaving school early. It targets individual children and young people and seeks to support them in removing barriers to access and improving outcomes from education. A range of other programmes to support children at risk are available including the Home School Community Liaison Scheme which promotes partnership between parents and teachers in the interest of the child's learning and the Substance Misuse Prevention Initiative.

Youthreach – Youthreach aims to provide education, training and work experience to young people aged 15–20 years with no formal education or training qualifications. All Youthreach centres provide a substance misuse prevention

---

[6]A more comprehensive account of crime prevention initiatives, particularly locally based programmes is available in the Crime Prevention Directory (CSER, 2003).

programme and a crime prevention programme in association with other statutory bodies.

Garda Schools Programme – The Schools Programme is one strand of the crime prevention work undertaken by the Garda Síochána with young people. The other strands relate to the Garda Special Projects (see below) and the Juvenile Diversion Programme (see Section 6 "Processing, Cautioning and Pre-Court Conferencing"). The Schools Programme involves members of the Garda Síochána visiting schools and talking to children about responsible behaviour and safety. The purpose of the programme is to reduce children's propensity to commit crime and to improve their safety.

Garda Special Projects (*Youth Diversion Projects*) – The projects are targeted at young people up to the age of 18 years who are either involved in crime, at risk of becoming involved, are early school leavers or are unable to participate in other youth activities due to behavioural difficulties. Youth organisations are responsible for the administration of Garda Special Projects at community level. The role of the Garda Síochána in the projects ranges from representation on their management boards, to referral and participation in project activities and programmes (Centre for Social and Educational Research, 2001). An evaluation of the projects suggests that overall they are having a positive impact on antisocial and offending behaviour amongst the target population (Bowden and Higgins, 2000).

Copping On – The Copping On national crime prevention initiative provides training and support to local groups working with young people at risk.

The traditional reactionary, as opposed to preventative response to crime in the Republic of Ireland has resulted in a heavily resourced prison system to the detriment of community-based strategic crime prevention initiatives. The extent to which resources will be invested in crime prevention initiatives in the future will be central to supporting the changes that are underway with the Children Act of 2001.

4. JUVENILE JUSTICE IN TRANSITION: IMPLEMENTING THE CHILDREN ACT OF 2001

The Children Act of 2001 represents a new framework for change in the juvenile justice system in the Republic of Ireland. The key areas of change include an increase in the age of criminal responsibility, provision to separate the care and justice systems, an increased focus on parental responsibility, expansion of the Garda Síochána juvenile cautioning programme, the introduction of restorative cautioning and family conferencing, the enshrinement of the principle of detention as a measure of last resort, the abolition of imprisonment for children and an expansion in the range of community-based sanctions. Many of the provisions of the Children Act of 2001 have yet to come into force, indeed some predict that it will be a number of years before all provisions are in place. The delay means that children and young people continue, in many aspects of proceedings, to be subject to the Children Act of 1908. This has a number of serious implications for the way in which they are disposed of in the system. For example, as outlined in the introduction, provision was made to increase the age of criminal responsibility from 7 to 12 years under the Children Act of 2001, however this aspect was never enacted. Under the 1908 legislation, there is a presumption of *doli incapax* for children from the age of 7 to 14 years but this can be rebutted by proof beyond reasonable doubt that the child knew what he or she was doing was seriously wrong. Furthermore, there appears to be few exact rules as to how the presumption may be rebutted (O'Malley, 1994). When the age of criminal responsibility is increased, the health boards will have responsibility for the majority of children less than 12 years who come to the attention of the Garda Síochána; such children will be dealt with by purely therapeutic and educational rather than criminal justice measures.

The Children Act of 2001 has created separate provisions to meet the needs of non-offending children in a distinct way from offending children. However, until the full implementation of the Act, non-offending children who arc often "deprived rather than depraved" (Coghlan, 2000: 12) will continue to be at risk of being criminalised by the very system which should exist to care for them.[7] Currently, non-offending children may come to be detained with offending children and in some cases even with adults due to a combination of provisions in the outdated Children Act of 1908 including the imprisonment of young people and/or a lack of appropriate placements for children with severe behavioural problems (Kelleher et al., 2000). A review by the Department of Education and Science suggests that 34% of girls admitted to Oberstown Girls Centre (Detention School) were there for non-offending reasons (Department of Education and Science, 2002). The Children Act of 2001 abolishes the imprisonment of all children under 18 years however, in line with many other aspects of the Act, it has yet to come into force namely due to the lack of available, alternative secure placements in the country. According to the Irish Prison Service (2002) a total of 155 individuals under the age of 17 years were committed to prison in 2002.[8] Kilkelly (2003) notes that the Prison Service has expressed concern in the past about the number of children committed to prison, some of whom were non-offenders. As recently as May 2002, the European Court of Human Rights ruled against the Irish Government in the case of *D.G. v Ireland* (2002).[9] The court ruled that Ireland was in violation of the right to liberty guaranteed under Article 5 of the European Convention on Human Rights by detaining a 16-year-old with

[7]The legislation allowing for the imprisonment of young people in the Children Act (1908) states than an individual aged 15 or 16 can be certified and committed to prison if they are seen to be 'unruly or depraved.'

[8]A total of 1702 young people between the age of 17 and 20 years inclusive were also committed in the same year.

[9]35 European Human Rights Report (EHRR) 33.

serious behavioural problems in St. Patrick's Institution[10] (Irish Council for Civil Liberties, 2002).

The delay in implementing the Children Act of 2001 has serious repercussions for the treatment of children coming into contact with the juvenile justice system in Ireland. A common theme throughout the remainder of the chapter is the need for adequate resources and services to properly implement the new Act. The Children Act of 2001 has been described as a "framework for reform" because legislative change without the political commitment to financially support the changes will of itself be wholly insufficient. The following discussion centres on how the system currently operates focusing specifically on the provisions in the new Act as they represent the future direction of the Irish juvenile justice system. The Children Act of 2001 defines a child as a person less than 18 years of age and therefore such terminology will also be adopted throughout this chapter.

5. QUESTIONING CHILD SUSPECTS: PROCEDURAL RIGHTS AND WELFARE PROTECTION

Under the Children Act of 2001 the Garda Síochána are obliged when questioning children suspected of having committed an offence to take special measures to protect their rights. These include informing them of their entitlement to legal representation and how to avail of it in a manner and language that is appropriate to the child's age and level of understanding. Detained children should be kept separately from adult detainees and should only be held in a cell if no other secure accommodation is available at the station. A member of the Garda Síochána is required to contact a solicitor and seek their attendance if a child so requests. Parents or guardians must be informed that their child has been arrested and the child should not be questioned without their presence. There are exceptions however, such as where the parent/guardian is the victim or there is suspicion of complicity in the offence by the parent/guardian.

The Children Act of 2001 places additional responsibilities on the Garda Síochána with regard to the welfare of children in their custody. This part of the Act represents a noteworthy change in practice as it requires a member of the Garda Síochána to inform and seek the intervention of the relevant authorities (i.e., the local health board) if there is reasonable cause to believe that the child in custody in the station may be in need of care or protection. The rationale for such provision is to create greater cooperation between the various agencies coming into contact with children at risk. The Children Act of 2001 also amended the Child Care Act of 1991 with further specific provisions for children with behavioural difficulties in need of special care and protection. Under s. 23D of the Child Care Act of 1991, if a member of the Garda Síochána has reasonable grounds to

---

[10]St. Patrick's Institution is a designated Place of Detention operated by the Irish Prison Service.

believe the child's behaviour poses a risk to their health, safety or welfare or that the child is not receiving adequate care and protection, a member of the force is required to deliver the child to the care of the health board.[11]

6. PROCESSING, CAUTIONING AND PRE-COURT CONFERENCING

The policy of the Garda Síochána is that young offenders are not prosecuted unless their previous offence(s) or gravity of the present offence warrants such an action. This policy is reflected in statistics from An Garda Síochána Annual Report (2002) suggesting that 27% of children were prosecuted, 12% received a formal caution, 52% received an informal caution and no further action was taken in 9% of cases (adapted figures).[12] As outlined above, all juvenile cases should be referred centrally to the NJO under the auspices of the Garda Síochána in Dublin. A decision is then made by the Director of the NJO with regard to the action to be taken against a child. The Director has the option of recommending prosecution (in which case a file is sent to the Director of Public Prosecutions), a formal caution, an informal caution or no further action.

A non-statutory cautioning programme called the Juvenile Liaison Scheme has existed in the Republic of Ireland since 1963. Since the enactment of the Children Act of 2001, the scheme, now known as the Juvenile Diversion Programme has been placed on a statutory footing. All provisions relating to the Juvenile Diversion Programme including restorative cautioning and conferencing by the Garda Síochána have been implemented (Part 4). Under this Programme, young people under the age of 18 years may be cautioned by the Garda Síochána without proceedings being entered before the courts. Such cautions are not recorded as a criminal conviction. The purpose of the Juvenile Diversion Programme is to prevent re-offending and to divert young people away from the criminal justice system. The Programme is operated throughout the country by a network of specially trained Juvenile Liaison Officers under the guidance of the NJO.

Conditions of entry into the Juvenile Diversion Programme include that the child accepts responsibility for his or her offending behaviour and consents to being cautioned. All cautions should be administered in the presence of a parent(s) or guardian(s). A child receives an informal caution when the criminal behaviour is not deemed to warrant a formal caution and is given by the Juvenile Liaison Officer. The formal caution is carried out by a senior member of the Garda Síochána or a Juvenile Liaison Officer trained in mediation skills. Provision is made in the Children Act of 2001 for the Director of the Programme to invite the victim to attend and receive an apology and/or reparation at the formal caution. A formal caution is followed by supervision by a Juvenile Liaison Officer

[11]Section 23D is not yet implemented.
[12]These figures exclude cases pending for the year (5,439).

for a one-year period. The level of supervision is at the discretion of the Juvenile Liaison Officer subject to a number of guidelines including the seriousness of criminal behaviour, the level of care and control provided by the parents or guardians, the officer's perception of the risk of re-offending and any directions from the Director of the Juvenile Diversion Programme.

Following the administration of a formal caution, the supervising Juvenile Liaison Officer can recommend that a conference be held, however, it is the Programme Director's decision as to whether it proceeds; furthermore it can only be held if a parent or guardian is willing to attend. Participants at the conference include the facilitator (a member of the Garda Síochána), the child, the parent/guardian, the victim, representatives from agencies that have contact with the child, or any others perceived to be of benefit to the conference and requested by the child or the child's family. The purpose of the conference is to formulate an action plan for the child that may include a range of provisions including an apology to the victim, financial reparation, participation by the child in pro-social activities, attendance of the child at school or work, restrictions on the child's movements and associations and other initiatives which may help to prevent re-offending. While there is provision for reconvening the conference on a number of occasions, the Act gives little guidance on the consequences of non-compliance. However, O'Dwyer (2004) argues that it is the caution under the Juvenile Diversion Programme which has been deemed the appropriate sanction, therefore, any subsequent action is voluntary and as a result non-compliance cannot be punished.

There have been a number of criticisms levelled at the Juvenile Diversion Programme including net widening (O'Malley, 1994) and preferential selection for the programme[13] (O'Mahony, 2001). The main criticisms relate to concerns about the absence of due process associated with court convictions (O'Malley, 1994) and therefore concerns about the lack of protection for a child's procedural rights. The child is required to decide whether to plead guilty as a condition of entry to the Juvenile Diversion Programme or risk the possibility of a sentence of detention if found guilty by the court. As a result, it may be argued that in consenting to the cautioning programme "the offender relinquishes the rights implicit in the formal criminal justice system" (Griffin, 2004: 5) including the presumption of innocence and the right to a fair trial. Despite the criticisms of the programme, it is seen as one of the main diversionary initiatives in the Irish juvenile justice system, one which acknowledges the limited role of formal intervention in the lives of young people[14] (Duncan, 1982) and which diverts them from custody (Griffin, 2004). The Garda Síochána compile their own statistics on the

[13]O'Mahony (2001) argues that there is some evidence to suggest that the most vulnerable and at risk children are excluded from genuine consideration for the Juvenile Diversion Programme from an early age.
[14]See Doob and Cesaroni (2004) for more in-depth discussion on the impact of formal proceedings on young people.

programme and the most recent statistics suggest that since the inception of the cautioning programme "87.6% of the total involved reached their 18th year of age without being prosecuted for a criminal offence" (An Garda Síochána, 2002: 106). With the exception of one study (O'Dwyer, 1998), little research has been undertaken to follow-up programme participants beyond the age of 18 years; therefore it is difficult to ascertain the overall success of the programme in the long term.

7. CHILDREN COURT

The juvenile court has been replaced by a new Children Court under the Children Act of 2001 and Part 7 of the Children Act of 2001 relating to the Children Court has been fully implemented.

The Children Court has the power to deal with both offending and non-offending children up to 18 years of age – this represents a change from the previous legislation where the court had jurisdiction over those under 17 years only. The Act instructs that the court should sit in a different building or part of the building or at different times to other court proceedings, that children be kept separate from adult defendants (other than codefendants) and that the time children have to wait for proceedings be kept to a minimum as far as practicable. The only personnel permitted to attend court proceedings involving children are officers of the court, parents/guardians and adult relatives of the child, bona fide representatives of the Press and those admitted at the discretion of the court. There are also restrictions on the reporting, publishing or broadcasting of any information about the child, which is likely to lead to their identification (with exceptions such as if a child is unlawfully at large). Although these provisions are in force Kilkelly (2004) queries the extent to which anonymity can be maintained when public waiting areas in the courts are often shared by adults and juveniles, court listings show names, there is a practice of calling names publicly and dedicated courts are well-known. The Children Court has the power to deal summarily with a child charged with most, but not all, indictable offences. The decision to be tried summarily for an indictable offence depends on the age and maturity of the child as well as other relevant factors.[15] Excluded indictable offences include those which are required to be tried by the Circuit Criminal Court or manslaughter. In these cases, young people are treated like their adult counterparts in the adversarial system.

Parents or guardians are obliged to be present at all court appearances relating to the child under the Children Act of 2001. They are required to attend and participate if required in all stages of court proceedings against the child for an offence,[16]

[15]C.A. s. 75(2)(a)(b).
[16]Under the s. 91(4) of the Children's Act (2001) the parent or guardian may be examined with regard to any relevant matters in respect of the offence for which a child is charged.

relating to a family conference in respect of the child or relating to the failure of a child to comply with a community sanction. The court has the power to adjourn proceedings and issue a warrant for the arrest of the parent(s) or the guardian(s) who fails to attend the court without reasonable excuse. Furthermore, their failure to attend is treated as if it were contempt in the face of the court.

8. PRE-TRIAL DIVERSION – CONFERENCING

Conferencing is an integral part of the Children Act of 2001 and represents a new practice in the Irish juvenile justice system. The success of conferencing interventions with young people in other jurisdictions particularly in Canada and New Zealand was central to its adoption into juvenile justice legislation in the Republic of Ireland. In addition to the conferencing executed through the Garda Síochána as outlined above, two further conferencing approaches are provided for, to deal with children charged with an offence. These are the family welfare conference and the family conference.

If it appears that the child before the court is in need of care and protection, proceedings may be adjourned and the child's local health board are directed to convene a family welfare conference. The conference brings together the immediate and extended family and relevant professionals to devise a plan for the child to resolve issues related to childcare, child welfare or child protection. The purpose of the family welfare conference is to decide whether to recommend a Special Care Order or other care option to the court. The court can choose to make an Emergency Care Order or Supervision Order (under the Child Care Act 1991) and if appropriate dismiss the charges against the child. Emergency Care Orders have been criticised on the basis that there are fewer stipulations on their use (including the length of time a child may be subject to such an order) which means that the rights of these children may be less protected than for those detained within the criminal justice system (O'Sullivan, 2000).

The final conferencing format, the family conference, provides a pre-trial diversionary option for children. The court may adjourn proceedings and direct the Probation and Welfare Service to convene a family conference in order to formulate an action plan to prevent further re-offending.[17] The criteria are that the child accepts responsibility for his or her offending behaviour and that the child's parent/guardian agrees to participate in and support the activities of the conference. While the legislation stipulates that the action plan arising from the conference must be written in language understood by the child, there is no mention in the legislation of efforts to ensure their understanding of the proceedings. If the court is satisfied of

---

[17]Under s. 82(2)(a)(b) of the Children Act (2001) if there is not agreement on an action plan as a result of a family conference, the court itself may formulate such a plan or alternatively the court can resume proceedings in respect of the offence for which the child is charged.

the child's compliance, it may dismiss the charge following a review. However, failure to comply may result in a resumption of proceedings in respect of the offence.

All conferencing options under the Children Act of 2001 are facilitated by criminal justice professionals, with the exception of the family welfare conference which is the responsibility of health board professionals.

9. SENTENCING

9.1. Sentencing Principles

The Children Act of 2001 has incorporated a number of principles relating to criminal jurisdiction over children. These principles under Part 9, s. 96 of the Children Act of 2001 have not yet been implemented. Under the first principle, children charged with offences are entitled to the same rights and freedom before the law as adults, specifically a right to be heard and a right to participate in any court proceedings that affect them (Article 12 UNCRC). Furthermore, criminal proceedings should not be used solely to provide any assistance or service needed to care for or protect a child. This represents an important departure from the Children Act of 1908 where children could be placed in custody for primarily welfare reasons. The second principle states that any penalty imposed on a child for an offence should be the least restrictive and a period of detention should be imposed only as a measure of last resort. Under the third principle, the court may take mitigating factors such as the child's age and level of maturity into consideration when determining the nature of any penalty imposed, unless the penalty is fixed by law. The fourth principle posits that the penalty imposed on a child for an offence should be no greater (and may be less) than that which an adult would receive for the same offence. Finally, the fifth principle stipulates that measures for dealing with children's offending should have due regard to the interests of victims. While these principles represent an important departure from the Children Act of 1908, they will be rendered effectively meaningless without the full enforcement of the provisions of the Act relating to community-based sanctions (see below).

9.2. Sentencing Procedures

If after a finding of guilt, the court decides it is appropriate to impose a community sanction or a period of detention, proceedings are adjourned and the child is remanded to allow for the preparation of a Probation and Welfare Officer's report. Such reports are required in the majority of cases with a few exceptions, such as if the penalty for which the child is guilty is fixed by law or a previous report is available and sufficient to serve the purposes of the court. The Children

Act of 2001 lays down a number of conditions with regard to the preparation of the report although Part 9, s. 99–107 of the Children Act of 2001 relating to this are not yet enforced. The conditions are concerned with the child's rights, namely that the place where the report is undertaken should be accessible to the child and that the times he or she is required to attend do not interfere with their educational or work schedule. Provision is also made in the new Act for children to be fully informed in a language appropriate to their level of understanding about the expectations on them at the time the court imposes a community sanction. While this aspect is welcomed, Kilkelly (2004) warns that inadequately equipped courtrooms and poor acoustics often mean that children are physically isolated from proceedings. This is likely to adversely impact on their understanding of proceedings.

9.3. Sentencing: Orders and Sanctions

The Children Act of 2001 makes provision for a range of non-custodial sanctions, however until the Act is fully enforced the main provisions for supervision in the community are limited to a Probation Order under the Probation of Offenders Act of 1907 or for those over 16 years a Community Service Order under the Community Service Act of 1983. The Children Act of 1908 also makes provision for dismissing the charge, recognisance, parental recognisance, a Fit Person Order, a fine and whipping (no longer used).

When the Children Act of 2001 is fully enforced the range of sentencing options will include a conditional discharge or a fine, costs or compensation; orders imposing a community sanction on the child; a Deferment Order; orders imposing sanctions on the parents; and orders imposing a Detention and/or Detention and Supervision Order on the child. Currently the only sanctions enforced under Part 9 of the Children Act of 2001 are fines, costs and compensation (Part 9, s. 108–110); compensation by parent or guardian (Part 9, s. 113–114); and provisions relating to the Restriction on Movement Order (Part 9, s. 133–136). None of the new provisions relating to deferred detention, a Detention Order or a Detention and Supervision Order have been implemented to date.

9.3.1. Fines and Costs
A number of provisions are in place in the new Act to ensure a child is not unduly burdened with the payment of a fine. The fine should not be more than half the amount imposed on an adult in the District Court and the child's financial circumstances and means must be taken into consideration when determining whether to award costs against the child. Furthermore, in keeping with the diversionary ethos of the Act, a child cannot be detained for non-payment of a fine, rather the court may choose to reduce the fine, extend the length of time for payment or impose an age appropriate community sanction on the child.

9.3.2. Order Imposing a Community Sanction on the Child

The focus of the Irish juvenile justice system has not traditionally been on community-based options to divert young people from custody. The lack of viable community-based options is addressed in the Children Act of 2001 and a range of new provisions has been created in addition to existing orders. The provision of additional community sanctions is an essential aspect of the Act in order to affect the principle of detention as a sanction of last resort. In keeping with the spirit of this principle, children who fail to comply with the conditions of a community sanction should not receive a Detention Order unless the court is satisfied that detention is the only suitable way of dealing with the child. The following sections outline the range of options that will be available (when the Children Act 2001 is fully enforced) in addition to the pre-existing Probation Order and the Community Service Order.

Day Centre Order – A Day Centre Order requires the child to attend a specified centre to participate in activities which are likely to be beneficial for him or her for a period of not more than 90 days.

Probation (training or activities programme) Order – This is a Probation Order with the additional requirement to complete a programme of training or activities.

Probation (intensive supervision) Order – Under an Intensive Probation Order a child is required to remain under the intensive supervision of a Probation and Welfare Officer, reside at a specified residence and complete an education, training or treatment programme. The period of intensive supervision should not exceed 180 days.

Probation (residential supervision) Order – The Residential Supervision Order is a Probation Order with the additional requirement to reside in a hostel residence recommended by the Probation and Welfare Service for a specified period of not more than 1 year.

Suitable Person (Care and Supervision Order) – A Suitable Person Order is not unlike the Fit Person Order under the Children Act of 1908. A court may assign a child to the care of a person, including a relative of the child for a period of time, not exceeding 2 years if parental consent is given. A child will be supervised by a Probation and Welfare Officer while under the care of a suitable person.

Mentor Order – Mentoring is increasingly recognised as a positive way of engaging with young people and "bringing marginalized youths back into mainstream society" (Green and Healy, 2003: 193). Provisions in the Children Act of 2001 enable the court to assign a child to a person, including a relative of the child to support the child and their family in efforts to prevent re-offending for a period of not more than 2 years and under the supervision of a Probation and Welfare Officer. Research suggests that mentoring programmes have the potential to impact positively on future criminal activity; indeed findings from the RAND Corporation on the Quantum Opportunities Project (QOP)[18] found that fewer

---

[18]QOP involved random selection of 14-year-old youths from families on welfare living in an impoverished neighbourhood (Green and Healy, 2003: 193).

arrests were recorded for QOP youth than their peers (Green and Healy, 2003). The impact of such programmes on youth offending in the Republic of Ireland remains to be seen.

Restriction on Movement Order – Under the Restriction on Movement Order, the court may either order a child to remain in a specified residence at specified times between 7.00 p.m. and 6.00 a.m. and/or order that a child stays away from specified premises or localities between specified times and during specified days.

Dual Order – A Dual Order combines the requirements that a child be supervised by a Probation and Welfare Officer or attend at a day centre and which also restricts the child's movements for a specified period not exceeding 90 days. The Act stipulates that such an order may be made when either supervision or restriction on movement is not seen of itself to adequately reduce the likelihood of the child re-offending.

9.3.3. Deferred Detention Order

New provisions under the Children Act of 2001 allow for a Detention Order to be deferred for a number of reasons including if it is seen to be in the interests of justice to do so or a place is not available in a Children Detention School (for children under 16 years). O'Dwyer (2002) suggests that the provision to defer detention if a placement is not available in a detention school entered the legislation as a type of compromise and balancing mechanism between the courts and the detention system. Under the 1908 legislation, Directors of Children Detention Schools have the right to refuse a placement to a child under a Detention Order from the courts. This has created immense frustration amongst the judiciary and on occasion grave embarrassment to the government. When the relevant provisions of the Children Act of 2001 are enforced, Directors will be required to accept any child ordered to be detained by the court unless there is no space available in which case a Deferred Detention Order may be used. Under the Act, the Director of the Children Detention School will be required to apply to the court to make a Detention Order when a place becomes available.

The provisions under this aspect of the Children Act of 2001 are of concern in the light of the argument that delays and postponements in the criminal justice system impact on its effectiveness and especially on the effectiveness of the punishment (Feeley, 1979). It also raises concern regarding legitimacy vis-à-vis the administration of justice if in one set of circumstances a child is detained immediately, while in another identical case a child is required to wait until a place becomes available. Furthermore, there is provision for a court to impose a community sanction, rather than deferred detention, if a place is not available in a detention school. Such anomalies in the legislation raise concerns about equality and the equal treatment of children who get into trouble with the law. In many respects it may leave the legislation open to a wider interpretation than was originally envisaged in the drafting of the Act.

9.3.4. Parental Orders

A noteworthy feature of the Children Act of 2001 is the emphasis placed on parental responsibility from the requirement to attend court through to a range of sanctions that can be imposed on parents. Such orders may be appealed by parents however their very existence in the legislation has led to questioning and criticisms from many quarters (Kenny, 2000; O'Sullivan, 1996). A common view is that the state has taken little responsibility for juvenile justice over the last century and now the onus of responsibility is being placed on parents without a corresponding level of accountability being placed on the state for children in their care (O'Sullivan, 2000). Furthermore, as Shannon (2004: 25) argues, parental control mechanisms "demonstrate a reluctance to acknowledge the social context that contributes to a child's delinquent behaviour, such as poverty, drug addiction and disadvantage." A number of parental orders have been incorporated into the Children Act of 2001 including:

Compensation by Parent or Guardian – Parents can be ordered to pay compensation for offences committed by their children. A Compensation Order cannot be made against the parent or guardian unless the court is satisfied that wilful failure of the parent or guardian to take care of or to control the child contributed to the child's criminal behaviour.

Binding over of Parent or Guardian – The court may order the parent or guardian to enter into a recognisance, to exercise proper and adequate control over their child. Consent is not entirely voluntary because if the court considers the parent's refusal as unreasonable, it may treat it as if it were contempt of court. The recognisance by the parent or guardian may be forfeited if the child commits another offence during the period and the court deems that a contributing factor was the parent's failure to exercise proper and adequate control.

Parental Supervision Order – This order may be made where a child is found guilty of an offence and the court is satisfied that a wilful failure of the parents to take control of the child contributed to the criminal behaviour. Under the supervision of the Probation and Welfare Service, parents may be required to undertake any or all of a range of activities including treatment for alcohol or other substance abuse, a parenting skills course, instruction to properly control the child and/or to comply with any other instructions of the court that would assist in preventing the child from committing further offences. The order should not exceed 6 months, parents have a right to be heard in court prior to the making of such an order and also have the right to appeal against it. The implications for the parents of not complying, range from having the order revoked, making an alternative order or it being treated as if it were contempt of the court. If the court so requests, the Probation and Welfare Officer's report should include an indication of whether any lack of care or control by the parent resulted in the child engaging in offending behaviour. One can only speculate on whether the dual responsibility of the Probation and Welfare Service both to deem parents to have wilfully failed to parent on the one hand, and supervise them on a Parental

Supervision Order on the other, will raise problems of legitimacy in the execution of its role.

To date the provisions relevant to the Parental Supervision Order have not been commenced. Supporters of parental control measures, particularly the Parental Supervision Order point to studies of parental education programmes that suggest they positively impact on family relationships. This is significant given the research evidence linking poor family relationships to a higher risk of offending (Flood-Page et al., 2000). Research evidence also suggests that the most effective parental interventions are those which take a holistic approach (Goldblatt and Lewis, 1998). This is reflected somewhat in the legislation by the stipulation that parents and their children are supervised by the same Probation and Welfare Officer, thus enabling a more coherent approach to addressing the underlying issues related to offending. However, it would appear that the parent – child relationship and its relationship to offending is complex and bidirectional[19] and therefore further research is required to inform the development of parental educational programmes for the parents of offenders (Flood-Page et al., 2000: 34).

O'Mahony (2001) highlights the futility of parental control measures by suggesting that the disadvantaged and inequitable position many of the targeted parents hold in society contributes to the manner in which they approach parenting. He argues that in addition to dealing with poverty and sometimes addiction amongst other problems, such parents may have had little experience of effective parenting themselves as children. Quinn (2002: 679) criticises the measures on the basis that they appear to seek retribution without a corresponding acknowledgement of parents' needs or "any suggestion that substantial interventions will be established to encourage and enable positive parenting." The potential for effectiveness will ultimately rely on the extent to which these approaches are adequately resourced, with the challenge being "one of investing in the necessary support services so that parents can get the help they need" (Kenny, 2000: 26). Furthermore, the absence of an element of voluntarism to participate in such orders is of concern given the research on parental interventions which suggests that the most positive outcomes occur with clients who are best able to draw upon their own resources and strengths to solve their problems (McKeown, 2000).

9.3.5. Detention Orders

Detention Order (Children Detention School) – Children aged 15 years and younger are detained in Children Detention Schools which are the responsibility of the Department of Education and Science. The purpose of a Children Detention School is to provide education and training facilities for children as well as providing for their physical, psychological and emotional well-being. When the

[19]Parents both influence their children and are themselves influenced by their child's behaviour (Flood-Page et al., 2000: 34).

Children Act of 2001 is fully implemented the minimum period a child will be allowed to be placed in a detention school will be 3 months and the maximum will be 3 years. Although a period of detention may run consecutively on any period imposed on the child for a previous offence, the total period should not exceed 3 years. However, if a child under the age of 16 years is convicted on indictment of an offence, the court may impose a period of detention exceeding 3 years. No such sentence of detention should exceed that which could be given to an adult for the same offence.

As outlined in the introduction, instances occur where children are inappropriately placed in facilities because there is no where else for them to go. The Act made provision for the establishment, on a statutory basis, of the Special Residential Services Board. These provisions of the Act (Part II, section 225–244) have been implemented in full. While the Board has a number of functions[20] one of its main roles is to coordinate the delivery of residential accommodation and support services to children detained in detention schools and special care units and to ensure such schools are used appropriately. It is hoped that the Board will make significant progress in addressing the historical difficulties regarding the appropriate placement of young people in the Irish juvenile justice system. The Act also seeks to overcome the issue of inappropriate placement by stipulating that Children Detention Centres (see below) must specify the profile of children who may be detained by age and sex and thereby prohibit the detention of children who do not meet the criteria (i.e., those under 16 years of age).

Detention Order (*Children Detention Centre*) – Males aged 16 years and over are currently held in St. Patrick's Institution in Dublin which is run by the Irish Prison Service as a place of detention for young people up to the age of 21 years. At present, females aged 17 years and over can be detained in the Dochas Centre which is a facility for adult female prisoners at Mountjoy Prison. When the relevant provisions of the Children Act of 2001 are enforced all 16- and 17-year-olds will be detained in Children Detention Centres and will be held separately from those 18 years and older in contrast to current practice. The delay in bringing the new provisions into place relates largely to a lack of suitable accommodation to detain 16- and 17-year-olds separately from those over 18 years. For children detained in Children Detention Centres (16- to 18-year-olds) a sentence of detention should not exceed the terms of imprisonment for an adult convicted of the same offence.

10. RIGHTS OF DETAINED CHILDREN

The new legislation requires the establishment of visiting panels in Children Detention Schools.[21] The power of panels as laid out in the new legislation

---

[20]C.A. (2001) s. 227(1)a–i and s. 227(2).
[21]Part 10 (s. 157–224) of the Children Act (2001) relating to Children Detention Schools including their inspection or operation has not been enforced to date.

extends to a reporting role only. This is in contrast to Kilkelly's (2003) argument that international standards require visiting panels be given responsibility for following up any complaints made by children. The Act stipulates that one of the objectives of Children Detention Schools is to recognise the personal, cultural and linguistic identity of each child. However, the Act is less strong on the specific detail of how individual identity will be recognised and fostered. For example, with regard to the opportunity to receive religious instruction and to practice, the Act stipulates that the Director of the school should ensure this occurs "as far as practicable." The rights of detained children aged 16–18 years do not appear to be as strongly emphasised in the legislation. For example, the Act stipulates that the Minister of Justice, Equality and Law Reform *may* (emphasis added) make rules governing the general operation of Children Detention Centres on a range of matters from the treatment of detained children, to the facilities provided for them, recognition of their personal, cultural and linguistic identity, the duties and conduct of staff to the constitution and powers of visiting panels to such centres. It is noteworthy that the creation of such rules is discretionary and the legislation places no mandatory responsibility on the government to do so.

11. REINTEGRATION

The principle and practice of reintegration is not embedded entirely into the new juvenile justice legislation despite the need for such practice being acknowledged in a number of publications (Irish National Teachers Organisation, 1995; National Economic and Social Forum, 2002). The Act provides for supervision in the community following a period in a Children Detention School but such supervision is voluntary. The rationale is that a child has served his or her sentence on completion of the detention period and additional supervision cannot therefore be mandatory. However, the Act stipulates that the Director of a Children Detention School may authorise the placement of the child in the community, to reside with a parent, guardian or responsible person under the supervision of a Probation and Welfare Officer after the child has spent a period of time in detention. While this represents a positive step in terms of reintegrating children into the community, the equity of this measure for children without supportive parents or guardians must be queried. In essence, without the provision of adequate support to families and other responsible persons it raises questions about how this aspect of the Act will operate in practice.

   Research suggests that having follow-up support in the community on release is one of the most effective approaches for reintegrating offenders. Altschuler and Armstrong (1999) refer to this idea as the notion of reintegrative confinement and describe it as a phased out transitional process which clearly begins in custody and moves outwards to the community. It would appear that the most appropriate order to support this model is one which requires a proportion of the sentence to be spent in custody and a proportion in the community. Under the new legislation children between the ages of 16 and 18 years may be sentenced to a Detention and Supervision Order if the court is satisfied that detention is the only way of dealing with the child. The Detention and Supervision Order provides for half the sentence to be spent in detention and half under the supervision of a Probation and Welfare Officer in the community. In common with many of the other provisions of the Act this aspect has not yet been enforced. Furthermore, while the legislation may provide the framework, without sufficient resources to support the transition from custody to the community the potential for reintegration with the Detention and Supervision Order may well be lost.

12. REFLECTION ON THE FUTURE

The issue of juvenile justice in the Republic of Ireland has been drawn in from the political wilderness to a more visible position in Irish society with the introduction of the Children Act of 2001. However, the slow pace at which the Act is being implemented is a major issue and gives further credence to the view that juvenile justice is not a high priority on the political landscape (Dooley and Corbett, 2002). The Irish juvenile justice system has cherry picked from the juvenile justice systems of other jurisdictions namely in choosing to incorporate conferencing and restorative cautioning as well as a range of community-based measures to be used as alternatives to custody. It is of great concern, however, that various approaches to deal with young offenders are being introduced in the context of a dearth of empirical research on juvenile crime and justice in the country. The virtual absence of such research means baseline information is rarely available about the suitability and appropriateness of these planned criminal justice interventions.

Recent developments in the Irish juvenile justice system include the proposal to introduce Anti-Social Behaviour Orders (ASBOs) for children in the Criminal Justice Bill (2004). An ASBO is a civil order used to deal with antisocial behaviour which is defined as behaviour which causes harassment, alarm and distress. The major concern regarding the introduction of ASBOs, especially for young people is that a breach of such an order is a criminal offence punishable by imprisonment. The introduction of the ASBO goes against the philosophy and vision of the Children Act of 2001 which seeks to divert young people from the criminal justice system through the use of restorative justice initiatives and other community-based sanctions. Furthermore, the Irish Youth Justice Alliance (2005: 7) argues that introducing ASBOs "threatens the potential that the Act presents to reform the area of children at risk in the Republic of Ireland."

The significant delay in fully enacting the Children Act of 2001 means that commentary on the potential impact of the new legislation is likely to be tentative only. The extent to which children will be diverted from the criminal justice system in the long-term will be largely dependent on the manner in which services are developed, coordinated and sufficiently resourced to meet their needs. New requirements under the Act stipulate that all juvenile cases are referred and pro-cessed centrally at the NJO of the Garda Síochána. This should ensure greater consistency in the approach used by Juvenile Liaison Officers and reduce the criticisms identified earlier in this chapter with regard to net-widening and selec-tion for the programme. The role of the Garda Síochána and particularly the Juvenile Liaison Officer has significantly developed with the introduction of restorative cautioning and conferencing under the Act. Results from an evalu-ation of the Garda pilot programme of restorative justice cautions and confer-encing reflect international experience which identifies such initiatives as time and resource intensive (O'Dwyer, 2004). Victim attendance during the pilot programme was high with no attendance in only 14 cases of the 68 cases. While victim satisfaction was rated highly, it is important to note that participants' views were gathered using observation sheets and there was no direct victim participant involvement in the research.

Little can be said about the impact of family conferences and family wel-fare conferences under the Children Act of 2001 given that provisions relating to both options have only been implemented in relatively recent times. However, lessons about the effective operation of conferencing from other jurisdictions pointing to the need for sufficient resources, appropriate training and victim participation are all relevant to the Irish context. To date, the most restrictive of the community-based measures (e.g., the Restriction on Movement Order) have been implemented. It would appear that resource issues with regard to the more labour intensive community-based options are stalling the implementation of these aspects. The delay in enforcing all provisions relating to community-based options means that the principle of using detention as a measure of last resort cannot be implemented in practice. The role of the Probation and Welfare Service and related services will expand dramatically once all provisions of the Children Act of 2001 are enforced. Probation and Welfare staff will be involved at all stages of the juvenile justice process from pre-trial conferencing, to commu-nity supervision of children and in some cases their parents, as well as working with children during and after their detention. It is unlikely that the vision in the legislation of custody as a measure of last resort will come anywhere near a real-ity if a corresponding level of resources are not put in place to support the vast expansion in the role of the Probation and Welfare Service. Notwithstanding the difficulties outlined above, it is anticipated that the new legislation will impact on the number and profile of children sent to Children Detention Schools (Depart-ment of Education and Science, 2002). The expectation is that fewer children will be sent to custody. There will be a higher turnover of children in custody and if custody is truly to be reserved as a measure of last resort, the detained popula-tion is likely to be more challenging and criminally mature.

Finally, the aspiration of an effective juvenile justice system will remain as such unless the current inadequacies in social services support for children and their families are appropriately targeted, expanded and sufficiently resourced.

O'Mahony (2001: 5) argues that what is required for the Act to reach its potential is a "much wider social context of positive social policy" ranging from childcare to education, drug and antipoverty initiatives. Such interventions at the level of the family, school and community are required from an early age to be effective in the prevention of crime. These measures are also essential to avoid some young people ending up in a life cycle of social disadvantage, crime and imprisonment. The relevance of this point is highlighted by a recent study of homeless prisoners in Dublin which found that almost two-thirds of those with a history of homelessness had first experienced it as a child or teenager. Furthermore, three-quarters of those homeless on committal to prison had previously spent time in a youth detention facility (St. Patrick's Institution) (Seymour and Costello, 2005). The Children Act 2001 offers a framework to address some of the problems in the current juvenile justice system but it is not a panacea for all. The extent to which it succeeds will largely depend on the level to which diversionary measures in the childcare and juvenile justice system are coordinated, supported and resourced.

ADDENDUM

In December 2005, the Government announced that a Youth Justice Service would be established to implement the key remaining provisions of the Children Act 2001 and to provide a more coordinated approach to youth justice in Ireland. The establishment of the Service arose from key recommendations from a review of the youth justice system in 2004–2005. The review report entitled *Report on the Youth Justice Review* (Government of Ireland, 2006) outlines the remit of the Youth Justice Service as encompassing a range of tasks including the development of youth justice policy; the development and implementation of a national youth justice strategy with links to other child-related strategies; responsibility for detention of offending children under 18 years of age; implementation of the provisions of the Children Act 2001 relating to community sanctions, restorative justice conferencing and diversion projects and the coordination of service delivery at both national and local level. The Report on the Youth Justice Review (Government of Ireland, 2006) also recommends a range of other measures including the establishment of a national Youth Justice Oversight Group, the development of local youth justice teams, in consultation with key agencies, to enhance local service delivery, the development of a parallel structure for special care by the Department of Health and Children and the preparation of a strategy for educational services in the new youth justice structure by the Department of Education and Science. Other recent developments designed to create a more integrated juvenile justice system include a number of amendments to the Criminal Justice Bill 2004 which have recently been approved by the Government. These include provisions to transfer responsibility for the detention of young offenders to the new Youth Justice Service from the Department of Education and Science and provisions to ensure that the Children Detention School is the model for the detention of all children less than 18 years.

REFERENCES

Altschuler, D.M. and Armstrong, T.L. (1999). "Reintegrative Confinement and Intensive Aftercare," *Juvenile Justice Bulletin* (July). Washington, DC: US Department of Justice, Office of Juvenile Justice and Delinquency Prevention, pp. 2–15.

An Garda Síochána (1999–2002). *Annual Report of An Garda Síochána 1999, 2000, 2001, 2002*. Dublin: Stationery Office.

Bowden, M. and Higgins, L. (2000). *The Impact and Effectiveness of the Garda Special Projects*. Dublin: Department of Justice, Equality and Law Reform.

Breen, R. and Rottman, D. (1984). *Crime Victimisation in the Republic of Ireland*. Dublin: Economic and Social Research Institute.

Burke, H., Carney, C., and Cook, G. (1981). *Youth and Justice: Young Offenders in Ireland*. Dublin: Turoe Press.

Centre for Social and Educational Research, Dublin Institute of Technology (CSER) (2001). *Study of Participants in Garda Special Projects*. Dublin: Department of Justice, Equality and Law Reform.

Centre for Social and Educational Research, Dublin Institute of Technology (CSER) (2003). *Crime Prevention Directory*. Dublin: Department of Justice, Equality and Law Reform.

Central Statistics Office (1998). *Quarterly National Household Survey Crime and Victims September – November 1998*. Dublin: C.S.O.

Central Statistics Office (2002). *Population Statistics*. Retrieved 1 June 2005, from http://www.cso.ie/statistics/Population.htm.

Children's Rights Alliance (1998). *Children's Rights Our Responsibilities*. Concluding Observations of the UN Committee on the Rights of the Child Following Examination of the First National Report of Ireland on the Implementation of the Convention on the Rights of the Child. Dublin: Children's Rights Alliance.

Coghlan, N. (2000). "Locating Young Offenders in their Communities," *Perspectives on Youth Crime*. Dublin: Barnardos and the Irish Penal Reform Trust.

Department of Education and Science (2002). *Residential Provision for Children under the Auspices of the Department of Education and Science: A Preliminary Review*. Retrieved 26 July 2004, from http://www.education.ie/servlet/blobservlet/sped_education_review.doc.

Doob, A.N. and Cesaroni, C. (2004). *Responding to Youth Crime in Canada*. Toronto: University of Toronto Press.

Dooley, R. and Corbett, M. (2002). "Child Care, Juvenile Justice and the Children Act 2001," *Irish Youth Work Scene: A Journal for Youth Workers*. Dublin: National Youth Federation.

Duncan, W. (1982). "The Juvenile Justice System at the Crossroads," in G. Cook and V. Richardson (eds.), *Juvenile Justice at the Crossroads*. Dublin: Department of Social Administration, University College Dublin, pp. 14–25.

Eurostat. (2005). *Euro-Indicators News Release*. 71/2005. 1 June 2005. Retrieved 2 June 2005, from epp.eurostat.cec.eu.int/pls/portal/docs.

Feeley, M. (1979). *The Process is the Punishment Handling Cases in the Lower Criminal Courts*. New York: Russell Sage.

Flood-Page, C., Campbell, S., Harrington, V., and Miller, J. (2000). "Youth Crime: Findings from the 1998/99 Youth Lifestyles Survey," *Home Office Research Study 209*. London: Home Office Research, Development and Statistics Directorate.

Goldblatt, P. and Lewis, C. (1998). "Reducing Offending: An Assessment of Research Evidence on Ways of Dealing with Offending Behaviour," *Home Office Research Study 197*. London: Her Majesty's Stationery Office (HMSO).

Government of Ireland (2000) *National Children's Strategy: Our Children Their Lives*. Dublin: Stationery Office.

Government of Ireland (2006) *Report on the Youth Justice Review*. Dublin: Stationery Office.

Government Select Committee (1992). "First Report on the Select Committee on Crime," *Juvenile Justice: Its Causes and Its Remedies*. Dublin: Stationery Office.

Green, R.G. and Healy, K.F. (2003). *Tough on Kids Rethinking Approaches to Youth Justice*. Saskatoon: Purich Publishing Ltd.

Griffin, D. (2004). "The Juvenile Conundrum – Ireland's Responses to Youth Offending," *Cork Online Law Review*, 3 edn. Retrieved 21 June 2004, from http://colr.ucc.ie/2004xii.html.

Irish Council for Civil Liberties (2002). *European Court Condemns Imprisonment of Irish Teenager*. Press Release 17 May 2002.

Irish National Teachers Organisation (INTO) (1995). *Youthful Offending: A Report*. Dublin: INTO.

Irish Prison Service (2002). *Annual Report of the Irish Prison Service*. Dublin: Irish Prison Service.

Irish Youth Justice Alliance (2005) *Anti Social Behaviour Orders (ASBOs): A Briefing Paper Prepared by the Irish Youth Justice Alliance*. Retrieved 2 June 2005, from http://www.iprt.ie/iprt/1230.

Kelleher, P., Kelleher, C., and Corbett, M. (2000). *Left Out on Their Own Young People Leaving Care in Ireland*. Dublin: Oak Tree Press (in association with Focus Ireland).

Kennedy Report (1970). *Report on the Industrial and Reformatory School System*. Dublin: Stationery Office.

Kenny, B. (2000). "Preventing Youth Crime: The Child Care Context," *Perspectives on Youth Crime*. Dublin: Barnardos and the Irish Penal Reform Trust.

Kilkelly, U. (2003). "Children Detention Schools: Learning from International Best Practice," *Irish Criminal Law Journal*, 13(2):15–19.

Kilkelly, U. (2004). *The Operation of the Children Court*. Presentation at the Children Act 2001 Seminar, Faculty of Law, University College Cork, June 2004.

McKeown, K. (2000). *A Guide to What Works in Family Support Services for Vulnerable Families*. Dublin: Department of Health and Children.

McKeown, K., Haase, T., and Pratschke, J. (2001). *Springboard Promoting Family Well Being: Through Family Support Services*. Dublin: Department of Health and Children.

National Crime Council (2003). *A Crime Prevention Strategy for Ireland – Tackling the Concerns of Local Communities*. Dublin: Stationery Office.

National Economic and Social Forum (NESF) (2002). *Re-integration of Prisoners Forum Report No. 22*. Dublin: National Economic and Social Forum.

O'Dwyer, K. (1998). "Juvenile Diversion Programme: Re-offending Rates," *Garda Research Unit Report 2/98*. Templemore, Tipperary: Garda Research Unit.

O'Dwyer, K. (2002). "Juvenile Crime and Justice in Ireland," in N. Bala, J. Hornick, H. Snyder, and J. Paetsch (eds.), *Juvenile Justice Systems: An International Comparison of Problems and Solutions*. Toronto: Thompson Educational Publishing, pp. 153–188.

O'Dwyer, K. (2004). *Restorative Justice Initiatives in the Garda Síochána Evaluation of the Pilot Programme*. Presentation at the Children Act 2001 Seminar, Faculty of Law, University College Cork, June 2004.

O'Mahony, P. (2000). "A Brief Overview of Juvenile Justice in Ireland," in M. Barry, O. Burke, J. Connolly, and J. Curran (eds.), *Children, Young People and Crime in Britain and Ireland: From Exclusion to Inclusion*, Edinburgh: Scottish Executive Central Research Unit, pp. 130–145.

O'Mahony, P. (2001). *Contextualising the Children Bill as a Response to Youth Crime*. Paper delivered at the National Conference of Youthreach Coordinators. Retrieved 24 February 2003, from http://www.youthreach.ie/aatopmenu/Library/Children/Children.html.

O'Malley, T. (1994). "Juvenile Justice," in L. Heffernan (ed.), *Human Rights: A European Perspective*. Dublin: Round Hall Press.

O'Sullivan, E. (1996). "Juvenile Justice in the Republic of Ireland: Future Priorities," *Irish Social Worker*, 14(3/4):4–7.

O'Sullivan, E. (1998). "Ireland," in J. Mehlbye and L. Walgrave (eds.), *Confronting Youth in Europe – Juvenile Crime and Juvenile Justice*. Denmark: AFK, pp. 307–352.

O'Sullivan, E. (2000). "A Review of the Children Bill (1999)," *Irish Social Worker*, 18(2–4):10–13.

Quinn, M. (2002). "Youth Crime Prevention," in P. O'Mahony (ed.), *Criminal Justice in Ireland*. Dublin: Institute of Public Administration, pp. 674–704.

Seymour, M., and Costello, L. (2005). *A Study of the Number, Profile and Progression Routes of Homeless Individuals before the Courts and in Custody*. Dublin: Probation and Welfare Service.

Shannon, G. (2004). *A Critical Overview of the Act*. Paper from Children Act 2001 Seminar, Faculty of Law, University College Cork.

Task Force on Child Care Services (1980). *Final Report*. Dublin: Stationery Office.

Young, P., O'Donnell, I., and Clare, E. (2001). *Crime in Ireland Trends and Patterns 1950 to 1998*. A Report by the Institute of Criminology, Faculty of Law, University College Dublin for the National Crime Council, Dublin: National Crime Council.

Watson, D. (2000). *Victims of Recorded Crime in Ireland: Results from the 1996 Survey*. Dublin, Oaktree Press in association with the Economic and Social Research Institute.

Whitaker Report (1985). *Report of the Committee of Inquiry into the Penal System*. Dublin: Stationery Office.

6

Just Desert and Welfare: Juvenile Justice in the Netherlands

Peter H. van der Laan

INTRODUCTION

The Netherlands is a small but densely populated Western European country. The total number of inhabitants amounts to 16.2 million. Roughly 3.6 million of them are under the age of 18. Juvenile penal law applies to 12- to 17-year-olds (1.2 million). Children under the age of 12 cannot be held criminally responsible. In exceptional cases 16- and 17-year-olds can be tried according to adult law. Similarly juvenile law can be applied to young people aged 18–20 years who function mentally at a much younger age.

In this contribution an overview will be presented of recent trends in juvenile delinquency in the Netherlands and of the ways the police and the justice system deal with young delinquents. The second part is about recent policy developments and practice initiatives in the field of juvenile crime prevention and reactions.

The development of juvenile delinquency in the Netherlands is fairly well documented. The principal development trends can be identified in two ways: by consulting data compiled by the Dutch Central Bureau of Statistics (CBS; Centraal Bureau voor de Statistiek) on minors suspected of a crime and questioned by the police, or by reference to the so-called self-report research studies. Where information is lacking on various relevant background factors, such as age, gender, ethnic origins and recidivism, the missing pieces can be sourced from the continuous stream of studies exploring specific aspects of juvenile delinquency.

The situation is different in respect of societal reactions to juvenile crime. A large number of judicial and pre-judicial interventions have been evaluated in the past years. But until a few years ago, there was no long-term overview of how the police, the public prosecution service and the courts were resolving (criminal) cases involving juvenile delinquents. The CBS and the Research and Documentation Centre of the Dutch Ministry of Justice (WODC; Wetenschappelijk Onderzoek- en Documentatiecentrum) have only recently started again publishing statistics on judicial disposals. The information available still has many gaps and omissions, which make it difficult to establish what is happening, never mind to assess whether our societal responses to juvenile crime are adequate, and achieve their intended aims. This does not, however, discourage those involved in practice, policymaking, and politics from constantly launching new initiatives and more intensive forms of policy. These efforts are often

J. Junger-Tas and S. H. Decker (eds.), International Handbook of Juvenile Justice, 145–170.
© 2006 Springer.

motivated by referring to the – supposed – growth and severity of the problem. But no fundamental consideration is being given to the nature, function, and position of the new approach within the system of resolutions.

This contribution describes the development of juvenile delinquency in the past years, and how juvenile delinquency is dealt with in the Netherlands. A number of recent initiatives are then described, focusing on what is known about their outcomes. After an intermezzo, which locates the Dutch situation in an international perspective, a number of suggestions and follow-up points are made by way of conclusion.

1. DEVELOPMENT OF RECORDED JUVENILE DELINQUENCY[1]

The number of youths aged from 12 to 17 years old (inclusive) who were detained by the police more than doubled between 1960 and 2003: from almost 23,000 to 59,000 (see Fig. 6.1). A period of growth and later some major fluctuations occurred during the 1960s, 1970s and 1980s. This was followed by a period of

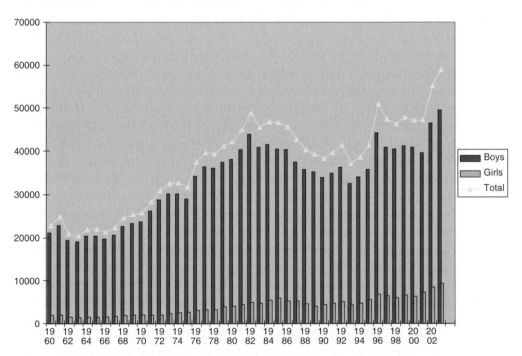

FIGURE 6.1. Trends in the number of minors questioned 1960–2003.
Source: CBS/van der Heide and Eggen (2004).

[1]Figures sourced from Van der Heide & Eggen, 2004.

stability in the second half of the 1990s – around 47,000 juveniles were detained annually at that time. The past few years, however, have seen a remarkable increase. The number of minors detained in 2002 rose by no less than 17% in relation to 2001. The respective increase in 2003 was nearly 7%.

The recent compared to number of suspects questioned by the police is also evident compared to adults. The proportion of minors in the total number of suspects questioned in 2003 is therefore unaltered, remaining as in previous years at around 17%. The development looks different, however, when set against the size of the youth population in the Netherlands. In 1960, 1.8% of minors came in contact with the police. In 1980, the proportion was 2.8%, and towards the end of the 1990s, it was around 4.2%. The marked increase in the number of minors questioned in 2002 and 2003 is reflected in a still higher figure of 5%.

These police statistics say little or nothing about the actual volume of juvenile delinquency in the Netherlands. After all, (by far) not all crime is detected or brought to the attention of the police. Moreover, only a proportion of all recorded crime is solved, so in most cases it remains unknown whether the offenders are minors or adults. Recorded juvenile delinquency therefore comprises only part of all juvenile delinquency actually committed. We do not know which part this is, and it may vary from year to year. Neither the reporting behaviour of citizens nor the detection efforts of the police are stable phenomena. More closely defined insurance policy conditions, reporting via the Internet, camera surveillance, computerisation and other technological developments, political profiling, national and local policy priorities, police and judicial capacity issues, a serious crime that gives rise to much social concern, other far-reaching social events; all of such matters could lead to more or less reporting of crime, a higher or lower ratio of crimes solved, and thereby to more or less recorded (juvenile) delinquency. This means not only that police statistics fail to communicate the absolute extent of juvenile delinquency, but also that developments should be considered with caution. The absolute and relative numbers of underage suspects questioned in the period 1997–2001 may suggest stability. But this "stability" could well have resulted from the police having reached the maximum number of juvenile cases that they could handle. Should the police capacity for dealing with juvenile cases increase or decrease, or should more output be required of the police, as occurred recently, the volume of recorded juvenile delinquency may rise or fall correspondingly.

2. RECORDED VIOLENT CRIME

The discussion above does not mean that statistics on recorded (juvenile) delinquency should be considered meaningless and left out of consideration. By observing not from one year to the next, but across a series of years, certain trends do emerge. The most important of these trends concerns the nature of the crimes committed by juveniles. In 1980, 68% of juveniles were questioned in connection with a property crime, 21% in connection with an act of vandalism or disorderly conduct, and 5% for a violent crime against the person.[2] In 2003, only 44% of cases involved a property crime. The number of violent crimes quadrupled to 20%. The category of vandalism and disorderly conduct remained at the same level, 23%, for years, but increased in 2003 to 29%.[3] The proportion of violent crimes has increased steadily in the last 20 years, while the proportion of property crimes has decreased to the same extent.

In terms of the increase in violent crime, it may be noted for the purposes of differentiation that society may be becoming more sensitised to violence. Certain types of behaviour are sooner perceived as threatening or violent and therefore reported. Some acts are now designated as violent crimes, although in the past they may have been considered to be "straightforward" property crimes or acts of disorderly conduct (Freeling, 1993; Egelkamp, 2002). This cannot, however, "explain away" the overall increase in recorded violent crime. In other words, the increase in recorded violent crime does represent, at least in part, a real increase (see also Bol et al., 1998; de Haan et al., 1999; Meeus et al., 2001).

Half of all cases of violent crime involve assault, and a quarter involve robbery with violence and extortion. Seventeen percent involve crimes against the person – mostly threatening – and 8% are sex offences. All categories of crimes show an (absolute) increase, but in comparison with, 1995, the number of assaults has increased (from 43% to 52%) and the number of violent robberies has decreased (from 32% to 23%).

3. DEVELOPMENT OF JUVENILE DELINQUENCY ON THE BASIS OF SELF-REPORTING

Where police statistics are lacking, the method of self-reporting may fill the gap to a certain extent. By asking a representative sample of juveniles whether they have been guilty of criminal acts during a certain period, insight may be gained into, for instance, delinquent behaviour that has not become known to the police. The outcomes of this research method are considered reasonably reliable, particularly in respect of less serious and fairly uncontroversial criminal behaviours, and they can complement police data in important ways (Junger-Tas and Haen-Marshall, 1999). But self-report research does not ask about all potential delinquent behaviours. It tends to present a restrictive series of criminal acts, and is therefore just as incapable as police statistics of offering insight into the true extent of juvenile delinquency. Repeat research, which always deals with the same items, does reveal the trends though.

---

[2]This category includes property crimes whereby violence was used or threatened.
[3]The increase in the number of minors questioned in 2002 and 2003 is almost entirely due to the increase in this category.

The method of self-reporting has been well established in the Netherlands for some years. Institutions such as the Dutch National Institute for Budget Information (Nationaal Instituut voor Budgetvoorlichting; NIBUD), the Social and Cultural Planning Office of the Netherlands (Sociaal en Cultureel Planbureau; SCP), the CBS and the Trimbos Institute periodically conduct wide-ranging surveys covering various subjects, including antisocial or criminal behaviour. The most specific and extensive research in the field of delinquent behaviour has been carried out by the WODC. The WODC conducted studies every two years from the mid-1980s to 1998, and again in 2001. Some of the findings from these studies are discussed below (Kruissink and Essers, 2001; 2004).

Consecutive measurements show minor fluctuations between individual years, but the overall impression is one of relative stability (see Table 6.1).

All measurements, with the exception of 2001, focused on 10 acts, with questions phrased identically.[4] This produced a total score (index), which is also fairly stable. Through the years, around 38% of the youths reported that they had been guilty of one or more of the acts in the previous year. This is considerably more than the 4–5% who come into contact with the police every year. This difference is inherent in self-reporting, since behaviours are reported that do not come to the police's attention. The behaviours are also such that the police tend not to get involved, or only incidentally involved. Fare dodging, for instance, was consistently the act most frequently mentioned by young people, but according to them only 1% of these cases came to the attention of the police in 2001.

TABLE 6.1. Offences reported by juveniles during "last year" (in %) (period 1988–2001)[1]

Offence	1988	1990	1992	1994	1996	1998	2001
Fare dodging	14.5	17.0	19.0	15.7	16.7	16.2	21.3
Graffiti	10.3	8.8	8.6	10.1	11.1	11.0	9.6
Harassment	9.9	12.0	11.8	14.1	14.6	9.9	–
Vandalism	8.9	9.9	10.5	9.1	14.6	10.6	11.0
Shoflifting[2]	5.4	7.4	6.6	7.0	10.0	7.4	8.1
Arson	3.8	5.0	3.8	4.3	5.3	5.1	–
Receiving stolen goods	3.5	4.1	4.0	4.2	8.6	6.1	6.6
Bicycle theft	2.1	3.0	2.7	1.3	3.1	3.5	3.0
Assault	1.9	2.7	2.7	2.7	3.3	2.6	–
Burglary/illegal entry	1.5	1.6	1.3	1.6	1.2	1.4	2.9

(Cont'd)

[4]Fare dodging, graffiti, harassment, vandalism, shoplifting, arson, receiving stolen goods, bicycle theft, assault, and burglary/illegal entry.

TABLE 6.1. Offences reported by juveniles during "last year" (in %)
(period 1988–2001)[1]—(Cont'd)

	1988	1990	1992	1994	1996	1998	2001
Theft from a phone box or automated machine[3]	–	1.2	1.0	1.1	2.3	2.3	–
Theft at school[3]	–	6.5	8.4	7.2	10.1	7.2	12.6
Involvement in a fight/public disturbance	–	6.7	8.8	11.6	14.7	12.4	11.1
Wounding with a weapon	–	0.6	0.4	0.4	1.1	1.4	0.3
Carrying a weapon[4]	–	–	12.8	20.5	21.5	–	–
Threatening to extort money[4]	–	–	0.4	0.3	0.5	0.3	–
1 or more "original" offences	34.5	38.2	38.2	37.8	40.2	37.3	–

[1]n : in 1988: 994; in 1990: 1,006; in 1992: 1,038; in 1994: 1,085; in 1996: 1,083; in 1998: 1,099; in 2001: 1,056.
[2]In order to enable comparison, the categories of shoflifting to a value of below 10 guilders and to a value of above 10 guilders were combined.
[3]This offence was left out of the 1988 survey and was not introduced again in 1998.
[4]This offence was left out of the 1988, 1990 and 2001 surveys.
Source: Kruissink and Essers (2004).

After the 1996 measurement, it was noted that a number of criminal acts, including some violent or violence-related acts,[5] had shown a small but still constant increase during the present period (van der Laan et al., 1998). This trend did not continue. The 2001 measurement included or reformulated some new items on violence, but no trends could be inferred from these.

The trend identified earlier in the police statistics is partially supported by self-reporting. There is indeed little evidence of a significant increase or decrease in juvenile delinquency; the situation is stable.[6] At the same time, the self-reports do not confirm the decrease in property crimes recorded by the police, or (any longer) the increase in violent crimes.

4. JUVENILE DELINQUENTS: SOME CHARACTERISTICS

Three characteristics of juvenile delinquents are discussed very regularly: gender, age, and ethnic background. The received wisdom is, in brief: more and more

[5]Among others, harassment, assault, involvement in a fight or disturbance, wounding with a weapon, carrying a weapon, and threatening someone to extort money.
[6]Since no self-report research was conducted in 2002 or 2003, the marked increase in the police statistics for those years cannot be verified.

girls are guilty of juvenile delinquency, delinquency is occurring at an earlier age, and excessive numbers of immigrant youths are involved in crime. The validity of such statements can only partly be judged on the basis of the CBS statistics. Police data do differentiate by gender, but not by age or ethnic background. The WODC self-report studies provide information on gender, age and, in the 2001 measurement, ethnic background.

4.1. Gender

Most of the underage suspects questioned by the police in the Netherlands are boys: 84%. The proportion of girls has grown since the beginning of the 1980s, when it was 10%, to 13% at the end of the 1990s, and 16% in the early years of this century.

Initially in the 1980s, girls were responsible for a relatively small share of (recorded) violent crime, 7%, but this share has increased since the second half of the 1990s to nearly 15%. The absolute increase was significant: 140 girls were questioned about a violent crime in 1980, and 1,700 in 2003. Girls are comparatively often involved in assaults (80%) and less often in robberies with violence and extortion (10%); the figures for boys are respectively 54% and 30%.[7]

Self-report research shows a different picture. There is little difference between boys and girls in terms of fare dodging, shoplifting and graffiti. But the differences are once again significant in terms of the more "classic" serious offences, such as housebreaking and violent crimes. In this sense, juvenile delinquency is a boys' affair. We may see a major increase in the recorded number of violent crimes by girls, just as for boys, but neither the police statistics nor the self-reports support the suggestion that girls are "catching up in a spectacular fashion"[8] (see also Mertens et al., 1998).

4.2. Age

Police statistics differentiate between minors in a criminal justice sense and adults, but make no further distinctions on the basis of age. We have no way of knowing how many 12- or 13-year-olds have been questioned, or how many 22- or 55-year-olds. It is therefore not possible to investigate whether the police are detaining ever younger children. But where the statistics fail to consider the age factor, self-report research can provide some insight. Such research consistently reveals a considerably higher percentage of youths aged 15, 16 and 17 years (around 46%) than youths aged 12 or 13 years (23%), who claim to have been guilty of one or more criminal acts. These percentages fluctuate from year to year, without revealing a clear trend.

[7]Figures from 2000; not reported thereafter.
[8]Cf with an article titled 'Meppende meiden' ('Girls who fight') that appeared in HP/De Tijd on 28 June 2002.

Respondents are also always asked at what age they committed a particular act for the first time; the responses do not yet indicate that delinquency is starting at a younger age (Kruissink and Essers, 2004).

Children below 12 years old form a category of their own. They are believed to be committing more and more criminal acts. Because they are younger than 12 years, they cannot be prosecuted. For this reason, any criminal acts that these children commit are not recorded in the Dutch police identification service system. Self-report research was carried out among 8- to 11-year-olds (inclusive) in 1994 (van der Laan et al., 1997). Not surprisingly, this research showed that the youngest children reported far less delinquent behaviour than the 12- to 17-year-olds, while the oldest children generally reported about the same extent, although different acts tended to be committed. This research has not been replicated, however, so the development of trends can only be estimated.

4.3. Immigrant Youths

Police statistics are equally uninformative on the numbers of immigrant youths who come into contact with the police. Research studies using data from the police identification system have indicated that some groups of immigrant juveniles are disproportionately involved in particular types of crime (Leuw, 1997; Junger et al., 2001). For instance, juveniles from Morocco and the Antilles are relatively often arrested in connection with violent crimes. The situation is not clearcut, however, because the studies did not employ uniform age limits or categorisations by offence and ethnic background. Young asylum seekers and refugees are currently a new focus of attention. The police and the judiciary are concerned that these young people may be involved in serious and organised crime (Kromhout and van San, 2003).

Until recently, self-report research conduced by the WODC could not offer much insight, because of the small sample sizes and the resulting (too) small numbers of immigrant youths. In its latest measurement, the WODC approached a larger number of immigrant youths. In comparison with Dutch youths, immigrant youths reported more fare dodging and involvement in fights, and the same amount of shoplifting, theft at school, vandalism and graffiti (Kruissink and Essers, 2004).[9]

The overrepresentation of immigrant youths in both police statistics and self-reporting can partly be explained by demographic and socio-economic background factors, such as a different age composition, and disadvantages in areas such as residence, education, and employment. When those factors are controlled for, however, there is still evidence of some overrepresentation of certain ethnic groups (Leuw, 1997).

---

[9]The reliability of self-report research among certain ethnic groups was questioned at the end of the 1980s (Junger, 1990). There appeared to be (a higher level of) underreporting. This situation may have improved since, because immigrant youths are now more likely to have been born and raised in the Netherlands, leading to perhaps less of a 'cultural distance' to certain research methods.

5. JUDICIAL RESPONSES

In line with the welfare or protectionist approach that characterises so many Western societies, juvenile delinquency in the Netherlands has always been tackled with a primary focus on the person and interests of the juvenile offender. The criminal act committed is important, but the following factors are directive for the way the case is dealt with: the offender's personal characteristics and background, the degree to which the youth can be considered guilty on the grounds of their physical and moral development and their age, and any psychosocial problems that may be signalled by the offence committed. These factors could result in the underlying problems being tackled by means of a civil law intervention (child protection measure), rather than a criminal justice response. If the criminal justice route is chosen, in contrast with communal criminal law, special prevention is the guiding principle under juvenile criminal law. The primary objective of any punishment is behaviour modification: restoration, the award of damages and general prevention play less prominent roles. This goes together with a measure of reserve and moderation: only respond and take action if that is really necessary, do not make the response more severe than needed with a view to behavioural change, and certainly do not punish for punishment's sake. This approach is also known as a policy of minimal intervention: not every criminal act is prosecuted through the criminal justice system, not every case is brought before a judge, and a guilty verdict does not always receive the heaviest penalty possible (Hermanns and van der Laan, 2002).

The sections below give a broad view of how the police and the judiciary deal with criminal acts by juveniles. The view is broad, because the necessary information is not recorded and published at fixed points by a single institution, and it is anything but complete. Moreover, different figures are given for one and the same case resolution in one and the same year, meaning that some caution in respect of the reliability of the data is justified. Table 6.2 contains some key figures for 2003.

The data are sourced from the CBS, the WODC, the Dutch prison and judicial institution service (Dienst Justitiele Inrichtingen; DJI) and "Halt Nederland," as

TABLE 6.2. Key statistics related to police and judicial responses in 2003

Police or judicial response	N
Referral to Halt (police)	23,255
Summons (police)	31,188
Dismissal (public prosecutor)	3,849
Out-of-court settlement (public prosecutor)	12,698
Indictment (public prosecutor)	10,805
Punishments and measures (court)	15,652
Alternative sanction (public prosecutor + court)	15,521

Source: CBS/WODC (van der Heide and Eggen, 2004).

compiled in *Criminaliteit en rechtshandhaving in cijfers* ("Crime and law enforcement in statistics"; van der Heide and Eggen, 2004).

6. CASES HANDLED BY THE POLICE

The police in the Netherlands can respond in roughly four ways. They may refrain from any further criminal justice action and instead refer a case to support services. They may issue a warning or reprimand, but take no further action. Cases of vandalism or small property crimes, such as shoplifting, may be referred to "Halt." Halt is an institution where juveniles carry out up to 20 hours of restorative or other types of activities, or possibly damage compensation. In other cases, the police may issue a summons and send this to the public prosecution service for further handling.

Whether and how often the police *refer cases on to support service institutions* or to the Council for Child Protection,[10] thereby refraining from issuing a summons or otherwise recording the case, cannot be determined from the recording systems, annual reports or suchlike. These cases cannot be traced through the administration of the Council for Child Protection either, because they are recorded as complaint cases rather than criminal cases.

The same applies when *warnings* are given without a summons being issued (the police dismissal or the police reprimand). This only happens from time to time. Guidelines[11] from the Board of the Procurators General have reduced the police's freedom to act in this way. The guidelines advise that nearly all cases should be referred to Halt. Alternatively, a summons should be issued and sent to the public prosecution service for further processing. The number of Halt referrals and summonses recorded at public prosecution offices is approximately the same as, or sometimes even higher than, the number of minors questioned by the police. In line with the minimal intervention policy, an informal approach is undoubtedly still taken in trifling cases, but the police dismissal, whereby the act is recorded but no summons issued, seems a thing of the past.

In less than 20 years, referral to *Halt* has developed into an important way for the police to handle cases. In 1987, almost 1,200 youths were sent to Halt. Since 1996, the annual figure has been around 21,000, and in 2003, it was as high as 23,255.[12]

---

[10]The Council for Child Protection is a government body, responsible for research and for advising the courts on civil and criminal cases.

[11]The following guidelines are relevant: guidelines on the policy of issuing a summons and a description of legal proceedings against minors (*Aanwijzing verbaliseringsbeleid en procesbeschrijving minderjarigen*, 1999), guidelines on the 'Halt' resolution (*Aanwijzing Halt-afdoening*, 1999) and guidelines on the 'Stop' response (*Aanwijzing Stop-reactie*, 1999).

[12]From 1999 on, this figure also covered the 'Stop' response. This response is comparable with the 'Halt' resolution, but designed for children younger than 12 years old.

Juveniles are referred to Halt primarily for shoplifting and other small property crimes, lawless behaviour, vandalism and firework offences. Some 20% of Halt clients are girls, so clearly more than the 12% of the number of minors questioned. This is almost certainly due to the fact that juveniles are referred to Halt in cases of shoplifting, one of the few offences that girls commit to the same extent as boys, and other less serious acts, and that Halt clients are more often *first-time offenders*. For the same reason, mostly 14- and 15-year-olds are to be found at Halt, rather than 16- and 17-year-olds. A consistent 95% of juveniles have always complied with their Halt obligations. Between 5% and 8% of all Halt juveniles have attended Halt before.[13]

At the start of the 1980s, the police sent over 25,000 *summonses* to the public prosecutor, but in subsequent years that number dropped by 25%. The number started to increase again from the mid-1990s. Over 31,000 cases were recorded with public prosecution offices in 2003, 9% more than in 2002.

7. CASES HANDLED BY THE PUBLIC PROSECUTION SERVICE

At the level of the public prosecution service, the policy of minimal intervention is expressed in restraint in proceeding to a prosecution. Traditionally, many cases in the Netherlands are (conditionally) dismissed or, for example in the framework of an out-of-court settlement, dealt with by imposing an alternative sanction. The prosecutor only issues an indictment in a minority of cases.

Over 70% of all cases were not prosecuted in the 1980s. There was initially no real evidence of a decrease, but conditions such as damage compensation or alternative sanctions were increasingly associated with dismissals, while the number of unconditional dismissals reduced significantly. In the second half of the 1990s, out-of-court settlements started to become more evident. Such settlements comprised 62% of all public prosecutor resolutions (excluding indictments) in 2003, as compared to 19% dismissals; in 1995 this ratio was reversed. In many cases, the out-of-court settlement is the framework within which an alternative sanction is imposed (the "prosecutor's model"). Public prosecutors imposed more than 8,600 alternative sanctions in 2003.

The number of *indictments* issued remained constant at 6,000 for a long time, but started to increase from the mid-1990s. While 7,000 cases were presented to the judge in 1995, in 2003 the number was 10,800. The number of indictments has grown from less than 30% to 35% of all public prosecutor decisions in 2003.

---

[13]This percentage should not be taken as an indication of recidivism. Young people may be referred to Halt twice at most, but it is unknown to what extent that happens in practice.

8. CASES HANDLED BY THE COURTS

In 2003, the Dutch courts imposed over 15,650 punishments and measures in 10,800 cases (Table 6.3).

The *alternative sanction* has been the punishment most frequently applied to minors for years. Over 15,500 alternative sanctions were applied in 2003, 6,880 of which were imposed by the court; this equates to 44% of all sanctions imposed. Of all alternative sanctions, including those applied by the public prosecution service, around 70% requires some form of unpaid community service and 30% involves an educational programme, sometimes in combination with community service. The percentage of "failed" alternative sanctions is 12–15%, and has remained constant for years. In comparison with the Halt resolution, the proportion of girls is smaller, at 13%, and the youths are older (more 16- and 17-year-olds). Alternative sanctions are generally imposed together with a conditional punishment.

Before the alternative sanction emerged in the 1980s, *fines* were the juvenile punishment most frequently applied, but this is no longer the case. Only 5% of all sanctions now involve a fine (650 in 2003), mostly ranging from 45 to 225 euros.[14]

In 2003, nearly 5,500 conditional and (partly) unconditional imprisonments were ordered. These included 5,200 *youth detentions* and, in the framework of adult criminal law, 210 *prison sentences*. The number of imprisonments had increased greatly in relation to previous years; by 67% in comparison with 1997. The proportion of conditional and unconditional imprisonments within the total number of sanctions imposed had not changed, however, and has remained at 35% for years.

TABLE 6.3. Punishments and measures imposed on minors in 1997 and 2003

Sanction	1997	2003
Prison sentence	284 (3.0%)	217 (1.4%)
Youth detention	2,988 (31.9%)	5,242 (33.5%)
Alternative sanction	4,026 (43.0%)	6,880 (44.0%)
Fine	952 (10.2%)	651 (4.2%)
Additional punishment	155 (1.7%)	206 (1.3%)
Placement in a juvenile institution	192 (2.0%)	202 (1.3%)
Other[1] and unknown	756 (8.1%)	2,254 (14.4%)
Total	9,353 (100%)	15,652 (100%)

[1]Including damage compensation measure
Source: CBS/WODC (van der Heide and Eggen, 2004).

[14]Excluding police transactions and similar.

Almost 1,800 (partly) unconditional youth detentions were imposed in 2003. This is a fraction less than in 2002, but nearly twice as many as in 1996. The average duration of these unconditional youth detentions comprised just under three months (83 days). This is almost seven weeks shorter than the average duration in 1998, which was four and a half months. The average duration has decreased since then.

The number of criminal justice measures imposed in 2003 increased to nearly 2,400. The majority (2,010) consists of the *damage compensation measure. Placement in a youth institution*, comparable with adults being admitted to a secure psychiatric unit, was applied to 202 juveniles in 2003. The number of these placements ordered on an annual basis varies widely; a clear upwards or downwards trend is not evident. How long youths subject to this measure remain in a judicial youth institution, secure or not, is unknown.

Not only are more sanctions being imposed, young people are increasingly being supervised by the *juvenile rehabilitation service*. This service supports and guides youths from when they are taken into custody up until their case being heard, within the framework of a conditional sentence, while supervising an alternative sanction, and during and after detention. In 2002, almost 8,700 youths were in contact with the juvenile rehabilitation service, three times as many as in 1995.

9. DETENTION ON REMAND

The application of detention on remand deserves separate attention. The actual imprisonment of minors in the Netherlands predominantly happens within this framework. Data from the Dutch prison and judicial institution service reveal that around 930 unconditional custodial sentences were imposed and enforced in 2003. This is approximately half of all unconditional custodial sentences ordered. The other half presumably spent the unconditional part in detention on remand. The final verdict will have involved an unconditional custodial sentence, with the remand period to be deducted and no further punitive aspect remaining. The number of youths who are remanded in custody and deprived of their freedom for some time is considerably larger than the number of youths sentenced to a (partly) unconditional custodial sentence. A reliable recording system is lacking, however. Occupation and intake figures recorded by the receiving institutions show that nearly 4,800 youths were taken in during 2003. Over 40% of them were received in the framework of detention on remand, which equates to over 2,000 youths. The average stay in an institution is 75 days. No youths were turned away because of lack of space in 2003, and only one or two were turned away in earlier years.

Detention on remand is an important stipulation in respect of juvenile delinquents for another reason besides imprisonment. Many districts are increasingly employing the suspension of detention on remand as an alternative to imprisonment, relatively quick yet still involving a "big stick" (the suspension could be removed). Actual imprisonment does not occur in these cases.

10. RECENT INITIATIVES AND POLICY DEVELOPMENTS

In addition to the trends and developments in the area of juvenile delinquency described above, and the judicial responses to these, all kinds of concrete initiatives and events have taken place. Undoubtedly the most important of these was the review of juvenile criminal law in 1995. The package of sanctions was formally extended to include alternative sanctions, and the number of custodial punishments and measures was reduced to a single punishment (youth detention) and one measure (placement in a juvenile institution). In relation to the old situation, the maximum duration of the detention was doubled to one year for 12- to 15-year-olds (inclusive), and quadrupled to 2 years for 16- and 17-year-olds. The maximum value of the fine was increased from 500 to 5,000 gilders. The Halt resolution was entered into statute. Criminal procedure also underwent some changes, including an extension of the potential for applying adult criminal law to 16- and 17-year-olds. Apart from further increases in the application of alternative sanctions and referrals to Halt, the review did not lead to major changes. Contrary to expectations (van der Laan, 1995), custodial sentences have not become longer and the increased potential to apply adult criminal law has not been exploited on a large(r) scale (Kruissink and Verwers, 2001).[15]

Another important alteration to the law was the (revised) legal regulation of alternative sanctions for minors and adults, on 1 February 2001. This regulation formally ended the option of applying alternative sanctions, including intensive educational requirements such as the "quarterly course" or the "day training centre," within the framework of suspending detention on remand. In practice, possibilities were found to use the suspension of detention on remand in order to be able to take preventive action comparatively quickly. However, the number of referrals to the most intensive forms of supervision reduced nonetheless.[16]

In addition to changes in the law, various important guidelines and memorandums have appeared: "Faced with the facts" (*Met de neus op de feiten*, 1994) by the Van Montfrans Committee, the memorandum "Crime and integration in relation to ethnic minorities" (*Criminaliteit en integratie in de relatie tot etnische*

---

[15]Further research is needed to establish whether minors who are sentenced under communal criminal law receive harsher penalties than young adults who have committed the same kinds of offences, as occurs in the United States (Kurlychek and Johnson, 2004).

[16]The Restriction of Freedom Committee (Otte Committee) is attempting to provide for this through proposals for regulation of the conditional sentence, conditional release and the conditional suspension of detention on remand (*Vrijheidsbeperking door voorwaarden* ('Restriction of freedom through conditions'), 2003).

minderheden, 1997) by the minister of the Interior and the minister of Justice, the memorandum produced by the Dutch police "Vision of police care for juveniles" (*Visie op politiele jeugdzorg*, 1997), memorandum "Tenacious and effective" (*Vasthoudend en effectief*, 2002) by the second "purple" cabinet,[17] the report "Preventing and combating juvenile delinquency" (*Preventie en bestrijding van jeugdcriminaliteit*, 2002) by the Netherlands Court of Audit and the memorandum "Juveniles and the law" (*Jeugd terecht*, 2003) by the first and second Balkenende cabinets.[18] These publications placed the issue of juvenile delinquency prominently on the social, political and administrative agendas. The outcome was a series of new interventions and policy initiatives, and more intensive phases of initiatives, which for the time being seem to be continuing. This is not the place to discuss all of these initiatives and developments, but the most important will be mentioned.

11. PREVENTION

Prevention is always the order of the day. The 1980s saw a powerful drive towards situational, administrative and technological prevention. The focus shifted in the 1990s, towards early, individually oriented prevention. Longitudinal (criminological) research, which follows large groups of children over the long term until late into adulthood, has shown that children who are confronted with a sum of risk factors, in domains such as person and personality, family and friends, school and work, and neighbourhood and environment, are more likely to end up in problematic situations and, perhaps, develop a criminal career. The following factors are particularly likely to contribute to an unfavourable prognosis: problem behaviour at a very young age, a range of unfavourable family circumstances such as a harsh rearing style, parental delinquent behaviour, but also poverty, and unsafe and unhealthy living conditions (Junger-Tas, 1996). These factors represent starting-points for preventive action (Junger-Tas, 1997). This has resulted in discussion about the need for preventive action, for example through mandatory or voluntary parenting support, the introduction of the "Stop" response for children younger than 12 years old who have committed criminal acts (Slump et al., 2000; van den Hoogen-Saleh, 2000), and broad prevention programmes such as *Communities that care*, which aims to make neighbourhoods and residential areas safer, cleaner and more healthy, and to promote social cohesion (Ince et al., 2004). Education, too, is increasingly seen as an obvious area where prevention activities can take place (Junger-Tas, 2000). Measures are taken to prevent truancy and school

---

[17]A coalition of social democrats (PvdA), conservative liberals (VVD) and progressive liberals (D66).
[18]Coalitions of Christian democrats (CDA) and conservative liberals (VVD) and conservatives (LPF).

drop-out. Space is created in the curriculum to offer advice and to cover concrete activities, such as learning effective ways of resolving conflict (van Lier, 2002). Parents are easier to reach through school, so they can be offered help and advice with difficulties in bringing up their children.

12. SUPERVISION AND TREATMENT

The large-scale application of alternative sanctions and rehabilitative supervision has made it difficult to provide juveniles with intensive, individual attention and supervision. This despite the fact that such attention and supervision is appropriate for youths who have committed more serious offences more often, and produces comparatively the best results (Spaans and Doornhein, 1991). Building on experience with the "hard core" projects (Kleiman and Terlouw, 1997), an individual form of supervision has been developed (the "ITB" or "individuele trajectbegeleiding"; Krechtig and Menger, 2001). Within the ITB framework, youths are intensively supervised, with clear agreements, by a member of the juvenile rehabilitation service. Compared with regular rehabilitative supervision, this form of supervision lasts longer and involves a higher level of contact with the supervisor (whose case load is lower). Important objectives include: returning to school, finding employment, restoring and/or developing relationships with family and friends, finding a permanent home, developing worthwhile, perhaps organised leisure activities, and avoiding excessive alcohol and drug use. A more recent variant is ITB-CRIEM, an intensive type of supervision specially designed for immigrant youths who may be on the brink of a criminal career.

13. RESIDENTIAL SUPERVISION AND TREATMENT

As mentioned several times above, more and more youths in the Netherlands are being placed in open and secure judicial youth institutions. The number of places in open and secure judicial youth institutions has more than doubled in the last 10 years, from under 1,000 to over 2,000. A further increase of another 1,000 places is anticipated in coming years. Although the judicial youth institutions are investing heavily in the development of treatment methods and in encouraging parental involvement, and are also trying to initiate aftercare (Bernasco, 2001; Boendermaker and van Yperen, 2003; Helmantel et al., 2003), they have not been able to prevent the perception of youth institutions becoming ever more strongly that of custodial facilities. Partly because of the increase in capacity, a great deal of new construction and redevelopment work has been carried out. To comply with the safety requirements of the Dutch prison and judicial institution service, this has involved high fences and walls being built, powerful lighting and the roofing-over of exercise areas. The outside of most youth institutions now looks identical to adult prisons or detention centres. This has initiated discussion about the long-standing phenomenon of youths being handled under civil law (in the framework of a supervisory order) and those being handled under criminal law (in the framework of detention on remand, youth detention or placement in a youth institution) being placed together in a single institution in a single group. In the view of many people, civil law juveniles, some of whom will not have committed any offence, do not belong in an institution that so clearly serves a punitive purpose. Moreover, these youths should not associate with youths who have committed offences, because that could lead to "criminal infection" (Goderie et al., 2004; Boendermaker et al., 2004).

A number of institutions, which through word and gesture seem to attach great importance to re-education, order, rules and discipline, are contributing to the increasingly "heavy" image of the judicial youth institutions.

14. DETENTION ON REMAND

The Netherlands makes extensive use of detention on remand, often, incidentally, in order to suspend it and speed up the start of focused treatment or support. The disadvantages of detention are widely described: extracting youths from their home environment, potential interruption to school or work, being subjected to negative group influences. Partly as a result, in the past years experiments have been run with two alternatives to detention on remand: night detention and electronic monitoring. In night detention cases, juveniles only stay in the institution overnight and attend school or work during the day. Electronic monitoring also enables youths to continue school or work, spending the rest of their time at home. Both alternatives combine, as considered desirable, surveillance and control with continuity in education, work or other daily occupation, while avoiding a range of undesirable side effects of detention. Both experiments have been evaluated, which revealed that both night detention and electronic monitoring were considered appropriate alternatives to detention on remand (Bos and Mehciz, 2001; Terlouw and Kamphorst, 2002). The number of night detention places has since been extended. The electronic monitoring experiment, on the other hand, was stopped because of a lack of suitable candidates.

15. ORGANISATION AND STRUCTURE

After a major reorganisation of the Dutch police towards the end of the 1980s, there was no longer scope for separate juvenile and vice departments, where all juvenile cases would be handled. Police officers were expected to deal with all cases by themselves. In special cases, they could turn to a small number of specialists, or officers responsible for particular areas. Partly through the involvement of the Van

Montfrans Committee,[19] which highlighted the police's loss of specific knowledge and expertise in the area of juvenile justice, appreciation for the juvenile role has revived in recent years. This does not mean the reinstatement of the old bureaus for juvenile affairs, where all juvenile cases were sent. It means that central departments have been created to support the police service and its staff in developing policy and dealing with juvenile cases. It also means that the district offices once more have youth judges who take responsibility for dealing with the more serious juvenile cases ("Vision of police care for juveniles"; *Visie op politiele jeugdzorg*, 1997; van de Riet et al., in preparation).

Juvenile delinquency is not only receiving more attention from the police, but also from other organisations. At a local level, policy is being developed by forums involving collaboration between the following bodies, under direction of the public prosecution service: the police, family guardianship, youth rehabilitation, the Council for Child Protection, Halt, youth care and youth support services, local administration and sometimes also education (compulsory education officials), health care, and services for addicts.

Another project within the area of organisation and structure focuses on reducing the time required for processing cases. The period between a juvenile being detained by the police and their case being fully resolved is very long. It is considered undesirable for youths to have to wait between six months and a year, and sometimes a year and a half, before the court reaches a decision. Specific targets have been set to address this problem. Eighty percent of cases handled by Halt must start within 60 days, 80% of cases dealt with by the public prosecutor must be completed within three months, and verdicts should have been issued by court within six months in 80% of cases. An initial evaluation has shown that processing times have been reduced, but that the primary objective has not (yet) been achieved (van Dijk et al., 2003). It is proving particularly difficult for courts to issue verdicts within six months. In 2002, 40% of cases were handled within six months. In the first months of 2003, the figure was 44%.

16. EFFECTIVENESS

The final important theme focuses on the effectiveness of criminal justice interventions. Dutch juvenile criminal law has always emphasised its pedagogical aspect: criminal justice actions should lead to behavioural change and prevent re-offending. At the same time, we must point out that few efforts have been made to check the extent to which this aim is being achieved. The issue of recidivism only started to receive more attention when alternative sanctions were introduced on a large scale, midway through the 1980s. At this point in time, more was expected

---

[19]The Van Montfrans Committee was established in the early 1990s, to advise the State Secretary for Justice on the approach to juvenile crime.

of alternative sanctions than of the traditional financial and freedom restricting punishments. Since then, publications on the subject of recidivism and the
effectiveness of youth sanctions have appeared regularly (Kruissink and Verwers,
1989; van der Laan and Essers, 1990; van der Laan, 1991; Spaans and Doorh-
nein, 1991; Vreeman, 1992; Kleiman and Terlouw, 1997; Boendermaker, 1999).
The differences between the "new" and the "old" sanctions are mostly minor, but
they do tend to favour the "new" interventions. So the ratio of juveniles who reoffend is smaller among youths who received, for instance, an alternative sanction,
than among youths who received youth detention or a fine. If youths subjected to
alternative sanctions do re-offend, they, moreover, do this less often, less quickly
and by committing less serious offences.

The consideration of effectiveness was stimulated further, in the adult sector too, by the publication of a number of large-scale foreign overview studies
or meta-evaluations (Andrews et al., 1990; Lipsey, 1995; Sherman et al., 1997).
These revealed that particular interventions, using particular methods, can
achieve important results with particular categories of offenders, under particular circumstances. The insights taken from such meta-evaluations enable the
development of intervention programmes that might be expected to truly help
reduce recidivism. They also offer departure points for evaluating the potential
effectiveness of current interventions. Following the lead of England and Wales,
where an Accreditation Panel has been active since 1996, the Netherlands is
preparing to formalise a similar evaluation structure and to develop a recognition or accreditation ruling of criminal justice interventions. The starting point
is eventually only to allow and finance those interventions that an independent
accreditation committee has judged to be either promising or actually effective.
The Council for Child Protection has already started the process with regard to
educational sanctions (Ceelen, 2003).

17. INTERMEZZO II: THE NETHERLANDS FROM A EUROPEAN PERSPECTIVE

The recent expansion of the European Union and the increasing influence of
"Brussels" on national policy – in the third pillar[20] too – raise the question of
where the Netherlands stands in relation to other European countries. The international comparison of law is a difficult task, since many countries do not have
reliable recording systems or because recording systems differ greatly from each
other. In addition, while judicial systems may share common features, they also
display significant differences. Nevertheless, some tentative observations can be
made on the basis of information that was collected and discussed in a committee
of the Council of Europe, which issued a new recommendation on the approach

[20]EU policies that co-ordinate police and judicial co-operation in criminal matters.

to juvenile crime in the period 2000–2003 (see also van der Laan and Graham, 2004). This recommendation, *New ways of dealing with juvenile delinquency and the role of juvenile justice* [Recommendation Rec(2003)20], was accepted by the Council of Ministers on 23 September 2003. Two different streams can be identified in the development of juvenile delinquency in Europe. The border lies roughly between Western Europe on the one hand, and Central and Eastern Europe on the other hand. Reports on Western European countries indicate that juvenile delinquency is relatively stable, with perhaps an increase in violent crime (Pfeiffer, 1998) but perhaps not (Estrada, 2001). The situation in Central and Eastern Europe is more difficult to map out, because of inadequate statistical services. The impression is, however, that the volume of juvenile delinquency in these countries is currently smaller but showing a clearly increasing tendency, particularly in respect of property offences. Almost all member states, in both Eastern and Western Europe, are concerned about the relatively strong and increasing involvement in crime among youths from minority groups.

In terms of the development of juvenile delinquency, the Netherlands is no better or worse off than other (Western) European countries. The same seems to apply in terms of the approach to juvenile delinquency. No other country within Europe has seen the enormous growth in the application of alternative sanctions that the Netherlands has. Others regard both the Halt disposal, and community service and educational punishments with interest and respect. Some see the Netherlands as a shining example in this field. There is great restraint in taking action, which is manifest in the discretionary powers of the police (diversion) and the public prosecution service (non-prosecution). It is also evident in the much shorter (average) duration of youth detention. At the same time, the Dutch situation causes surprise. With the exception of England and Wales, in no other country has the capacity of the judicial youth institutions increased by so much so rapidly, and have so many young people been deprived of their freedom. Nowhere else has detention on remand been applied on such a scale as in the Netherlands. The Netherlands is no different in terms of the age limits of juvenile criminal law (12 and 17 years old), but it is different in terms of the exceptions allowed to these limits. The Stop response for children younger than 12 years old may not be a criminal justice intervention, but the measure does have a criminal justice flavour, by virtue of falling under the responsibilities of the public prosecutor. Only England and Wales have a comparable "judicial" focus on young children. The application of adult criminal law to minors is possible in several countries, but appears to happen more frequently in the Netherlands than elsewhere. Such matters, and also the flirtation with electronic monitoring, though short-lived, and some lagging behind in the field of restitution law, point towards a tougher approach than previously taken. From a European perspective, then, the Dutch approach to juvenile delinquency must be characterised as increasingly repressive, but at the same time still very moderate and restrained.

18. THE PROS AND CONS WEIGHED

18.1. Juvenile Delinquency

The information available on juvenile delinquency in the Netherlands still has many gaps and is, as far as police statistics are concerned, strongly dependent on priorities and the efforts reserved by the police for this purpose. The actual extent of juvenile delinquency is unknown, and it is not possible to say with certainty how it has developed. Taking everything into account, however, it seems that the last two decades have seen stabilisation rather than growth or decrease. The extent to which the increase signalled by the police in 2002 and 2003 might buck the trend remains to be seen. The conclusion that juvenile delinquency has become harder does seem justified. Young people are committing violent crimes more often, even if this increase is probably smaller than the police statistics suggest. Girls are getting more involved in delinquent behaviour in only a limited way. It is unknown how the involvement of immigrant youths in delinquency has manifested itself through the years, but some groups are certainly over-represented in the statistics. Despite all reports to the contrary, it is unlikely that younger children are increasingly involved in delinquency. This is not to say that young children are not a focus for attention. All kinds of behaviours displayed by children under 12 years old are, rightly or wrongly, taken more seriously than was the case for a long time. As an extension of this, such behaviours are increasingly officially recorded, bringing a risk that behaviour formerly noted as children's mischief will enter the books as criminality (cf, van der Laan, 2000).

The fairly one-sided political, policy and research focus on children and adolescents means that young adults, aged from 18 to 24 or 25 years old, are generally left out of consideration. We may assume, however, that some of these will be equally active in a criminal sense, or perhaps more active. The number of suspects per 10,000 members of the population is highest among 18-, 19-, and 20-year-olds, not among 16- and 17-year-olds (Eggen et al., 2003). Focused preventive and repressive attention should therefore be paid to this age category. We may well be chasing minors too hard, and young adults too little.

18.2. Judicial Responses

Since the end of the 1980s, the police have tended to issue more summonses, send more juveniles to Halt and probably deal with fewer cases with a reprimand. In the same period, we have seen that the public prosecution service dismissed fewer cases, offered more transactions and, moreover, prosecuted more cases. The courts were given more juvenile cases to handle, imposed a considerably higher number of alternative sanctions, increased the number of (partly) unconditional custodial sentences, and remanded more juveniles. In addition, the number of juveniles supervised by the juvenile rehabilitation service has also increased greatly.

These developments suggest that the policy of minimal intervention has come under pressure and that the police and judicial approach to juveniles has become more punitive. By contrast, the average duration of juveniles' loss of freedom was somewhat reduced. This brings us to the conclusion that the judicial climate in the Netherlands in respect of minors has become more punitive in the last 20 years: more juveniles have faced a formal sanction. But restraint is still the order of the day in applying sanctions. The principal response is in the area of alternative sanctions and supervision. If juveniles lose their freedom, this is, certainly from an international perspective, for a short time, and there are clear indications that the duration is becoming shorter rather than longer.

The judicial response cannot, of course, be separated from the development of juvenile delinquency. The hardening of juvenile crime has repercussions for how cases are dealt with. Comparatively more summonses and indictments will be issued, and the chance of imprisonment being imposed will also be greater. This development is evident in the types of cases that the public prosecution service and the courts are dealing with. In 2003, the proportion of violent crimes in the police statistics was 20%. In the cases handled by public prosecution offices, the proportion was 22%, and in cases handled by the courts, it was 29%. Twenty-two percent of all alternative sanctions and 45% of all youth detentions were imposed because of a violent crime. The change in the nature of the crimes committed thus offers a partial explanation for the departure from the policy of minimal intervention.

The relationship between juvenile delinquency and law enforcement remains complex. As described above, developments in law enforcement can be related to an extent to the (perceived) development of juvenile delinquency, but the reverse is less straightforward. As long as the number of crimes committed by minors and detected and solved by the police remains basically dependent on police capacity and priorities, the effects of particular measures will not be very visible in official, recorded crime trends. Even if measures do produce effects, these will take time, meaning a delay before they are apparent in the statistics. For the time being, therefore, making statements about the success of policy measures, on the basis of developments in juvenile delinquency as recorded by the police, remains a precarious business. Thorough research, for example into recidivism among juveniles who have experienced a certain intervention, will support statements about the special preventive effect of particular interventions. But whether such an intervention will have a generally preventive effect is uncertain, and can certainly not be established on the basis of general trends in delinquency.

18.3. The Public Debate

The conclusion that the judicial approach to juvenile delinquency in the Netherlands has become more punitive in certain ways, but still remains characterised by restraint, does not apply to the political and public debate on how juvenile delinquency should be tackled. The tone of that debate has unmistakably hardened. This is evident in the current cabinet's memorandum on juveniles and the law (*Jeugd Terecht*). The proposals made in this memorandum may not represent a break with the past but a, sometimes subtle, difference can be detected. With a measure of exaggeration, one could say that the Dutch government is sick and tired of delinquent youths – particularly multiple offenders – and is no longer prepared to tolerate them. To quote from the memorandum (page 7): "Lenience, understanding and restraint have had insufficient effect in tackling juvenile delinquency." Actions speak louder than words, is the message. The "big stick" is becoming ever more evident: increased opportunities for detention on remand, stricter execution of alternative detention, compulsory aftercare, and so on. Nor are parents let off lightly. They must meet their responsibilities, or risk compulsory parenting support or a reduction in child benefit.

It is notable that concepts such as youth custody centres, actually abolished in the last review of juvenile criminal law, and corrective education are back in common use. The hard approach taken by some judicial youth institutions is likely to meet a great deal of approval, primarily because of their robust image based on order, rules and discipline. The same applies for calls from police chiefs and other administrators for setting curfews, applying adult criminal law, publishing photographs, and even reintroducing the pillory. But no fundamental discussion is taking place about the value or senselessness of such extreme and other less invasive proposals, their acceptability or unacceptability. The question of whether there is a place and need for such provisions is rarely addressed or thoroughly researched. The same applies in respect of potential outcomes. It is considered self-evident that particular measures or interventions will have an effect. Discussions on such matters did take place at the end of the 1970s and during the 1980s. Extensive consultations were held and careful experimentation took place around the introduction of alternative sanctions. No chances were taken in reaching the decision to make these a statutory regulation. Many principle-based discussions took place about the desirability of alternative sanctions being carried out by the public prosecutor or within the framework of a suspension of detention on remand. The introduction of provisions such as night detention and electronic monitoring at the end of the 1990s was a far more pragmatic affair. No fundamental theoretical discussion happened then. The perceived need for such provisions sufficed, without the underpinning of a thorough analysis of the issue and its outcomes. The simple fact that night detention was used, and that most parties involved were satisfied, was enough to continue and extend the practice. Electronic monitoring, on the other hand, was used very little and the experiment was consequently closed.

The arguments that lead to the introduction of a provision, or the decision to either continue or stop one, are generally pragmatic rather than based on principle. This seems to apply to the new behaviour modification measure. It is typical of current thinking about the problem of juvenile delinquency and how it should be tackled. The pragmatic approach has its roots in a report by the Van Mont-frans Committee. Apart from an appendix on issues related to immigrant youths, the considerations in this report do not involve theoretical analysis and interpre-tation of identified developments. They steer mainly towards concrete measures, with the mantra "timely, quick and consistent." One after the other proposal or initiative has followed since, with no time being taken for analysis and (thorough) evaluation. In fact, it is high time for a moment of reconsideration. Reconsidera-tion, removed from the latest "hot" issues and the heat of the (political) battle, that allows the problem of juvenile delinquency to be investigated and, above all, that allows the system of police, judicial and other societal responses to be judged on its fundamental merits.

REFERENCES

Aanwijzing verbaliseringsbeleid en procesbeschrijving minderjarigen (1999). Den Haag: College van Procureurs-Generaal.

Aanwijzing Halt-afdoening (1999). Den Haag: College van Procureurs-Generaal.

Aanwijzing Stop-reactie (1999). Den Haag: College van Procureurs-Generaal.

Andrews, D.A., Zinger, I., Hoge, R.D., Bonta, J., Gendreau, P., and Cullen, F.T. (1990). "Does Cor-rectional Treatment Work? A Clinically Relevant and Psychologically Informed Meta-analysis," *Criminology*, 28: 269–404.

Bernasco, W. (2001). Trajectvorming in de justitiële jeugdinrichtingen. Den Haag: WODC (Onder-zoeksnotities 2001/5).

Boendermaker, L. (1999). Justitiële behandelinrichtingen voor jongeren,populatie en werkwijze. Leuven/Apeldoorn: Garant.

Boendermaker, L. and Yperen, T. van (2003). Kansen in de keten. Den Haag: DJI/NIZW.

Boendermaker, L., Eijgenraam, K., and Geurts, E. (2004). Crisisplaatsingen in de opvanginricht-ingen. Utrecht: NIZW.

Bol, M.W., Terlouw, G.J., Blees, L.W., and Verwers, C. (1998). Jong en gewelddadig. Den Haag: WODC (Onderzoek en beleid 174).

Bos, J. and Mehciz, M. (2001). Evaluatie nachtdetentie. Amsterdam: Regioplan Onderzoek Advies en Informatie.

Ceelen, T. (2003). Je wilt garanties dat een leerstraf bijdraagt aan gedragsverandering. Perspectief, 11, 8, 17–18.

Criminaliteit en integratie in de relatie tot etnische minderheden (1997). Den Haag: Ministerie van Binnenlandse Zaken/Ministerie van Justitie.

Dijk, B. van, Heerwaarden, Y. Van, and Amersfoort, P. van (2003). Evaluatie project verkorting doorlooptijden jeugdstrafrechtketen. Amsterdam: DSP-groep.

Egelkamp. M. (2002). Inflation der Gewalt? Strafrechtliche und kriminologische Analysen von Qualifikationsentscheidungen in den Niederlanden und Deutschland. Groningen: Universit-eitsdrukkerij RuG.

Eggen, A.Th.J., Kruissink, M., Panhuis, P. Van, and Blom, M. (2003). Criminaliteit en opsporing. In W. van der Heide en A.Th.J. Eggen (red.) Criminaliteit en rechtshandhaving 2001. Den Haag/ Meppel: CBS/WODC/Boom (Onderzoek en beleid 211).

Estrada, F. (2001). "Juvenile Violence as a Social Problem," *British Journal of Criminology*, 41: 639–655.

Freeling, W. (1993). De straf op tasjesroof; hoe het strafklimaat strenger werd. Proces, 72, 76–82.

Goderie, M., Steketee, M., Mak, J., and Wentink, M. (2004). Samenplaatsing van jongeren in justitiële jeugdinrichtingen. Utrecht: Verwey-Jonker Instituut.

Haan, W.J.M. de, Bie, E.F.A.E. de, Baerveldt, C., Bouw, C., Doreleijers, Th.A.P.H., Ferwerda, H.B., Hermanns, J.M.A., and Laan, P.H. van der (1999). Jeugd & geweld. Een interdisciplinair perspectief. Den Haag: Van Gorcum.

Heide, W. van der and Eggen, A.Th.J. (2004). Criminaliteit en rechtshandhaving in cijfers. Den Haag: WODC/CBS.

Helmantel, A.M., Lodewijks, H.P.B., and Smit, R.C.T. (2003). Traject op maat. Groningen/Zutphen: J.J.I. Het Poortje/ J.J.I. Rentray.

Hermanns, J. and Laan, P.H. van der (2002). Perspectief in jeugdreclassering. Utrecht: Stichting Vedivo.

Hoogen-Saleh, T. van den (2000). Hoe eerder hoe beter. Den Haag: Politie Haaglanden/Stichting jeugdzorg den Haag/StichtingHalt Haaglanden/Raad voor de Kinderbescherming.

Ince, D., Beumer, M., Jonkman, H., and Vergeer, M. (2004). Veelbelovend en efectief. Utrecht: NIZW.

Jeugd terecht (2003). Den Haag: Ministerie van Justitie.

Junger, M. (1990). *Delinquency and Ethnicity*. Deventer/Boston: Kluwer Law and Taxation.

Junger, M., Wittebrood, K., and Timman, R. (2001). Etniciteit en ernstig en gewelddadig crimineel gedrag, in R. Loeber, N.W. Slot, and J.A. Sergeant (eds.), *Ernstige en gewelddadige jeugddelinquentie. Omvang, oorzaken en interventies*. Houten: Bohn Stafleu Van Loghum, pp. 97–127.

Junger-Tas, J. (1996). Jeugd en gezin. Preventie vanuit justitieel perspectief. Den Haag: Ministerie van Justitie.

Junger-Tas, J. (1997). Jeugd en gezin II. Naar een effectief preventiebeleid. Den Haag: Ministerie van Justitie.

Junger-Tas, J. and Haen-Marshall, I. (1999). "The Self-report Methodology in Crime Research," in M. Tonry (ed.), *Crime and Justice: A Review of Research*. Chicago:University of Chicago Press, pp. 291–367.

Junger-Tas, J. (2000). Diploma's en goed gedrag. Den Haag: Ministerie van Justitie.

Kleiman, W.M. and Terlouw, G.J. (1997). Kiezen voor een kans. Den Haag: WODC (Onderzoek en beleid 166).

Krechtig, L. and Menger, A. (2001). Intensieve begeleiding van de harde kern. Den Haag: Ministerie van Justitie.

Kromhout, M. and San, M. van (2003). Schimmige werelden. Nieuwe etnische groepen en jeugdcriminaliteit. Den Haag/Meppel: WODC/Boom (Onderzoek en beleid 206).

Kruissink, M. and Verwers, C. (1989). Halt: een alternatieve aanpak van vandalisme. Arnhem: Gouda Quint bv (onderzoek en beleid 97).

Kruissink, M. and Verwers, C. (2001). Het nieuwe jeugdstrafrecht. Den Haag: WODC (Onderzoek en beleid 193).

Kruissink, M. and Essers, A.A.M. (2001). Ontwikkeling van de jeugdcriminaliteit: periode 1980–1999. Den Haag: WODC (Onderzoeksnotities 2001/3).

Kruissink, M. and Essers, A.A.M. (2004). Zelfgerapporteerde jeugdcriminaliteit in de periode 1990–2001. Den Haag: WODC (WODC-cahier 2004–1).

Kurlychek, M.C. and Johnson, B.D. (2004). The juvenile penalty: a comparison of juvenile and young adult sentencing outcomes in criminal court. Criminology, 42, 2, 485–517.

Laan, P.H. van der and Essers, A.A.M. (1990). De Kwartaalkursus en recidive. Arnhem: Gouda Quint bv (Onderzoek en beleid 99).

Laan, P.H. van der (1991). Experimenteren met alternatieve sancties voor jeugdigen. Arnhem: Gouda Quint bv.

Laan, P.H. van der (1995). Het nieuwe jeugdstrafrecht. Op weg naar onnodige repressie? Tijdschrift voor Familie- en Jeugdrecht, 17, 11, 242–247.

Laan, P.H. van der, Spaans, E.C., Essers, A.A.M., and Essers, J.J.A. (1997). Jeugdcriminaliteit en jeugdbescherming. Ontwikkelingen in de periode 1980–1994. Den Haag: WODC.

Laan, P.H. van der, Essers, A.A.M., Huijbregts, G.L.A.M., and Spaans, E.C. (1998). Ontwikkeling van de jeugdcriminaliteit: periode 1980–1996. Den Haag: WODC (Onderzoeksnotities 1998/5).

Laan, P.H. van der (2000). Van opgeschoten jeugd tot aangeschoten wild. Over jeugdcriminaliteit en beeldvorming omtrent jongeren. J*-tijdschrift over jongeren, 1, 1, 45–51.

Laan, P. van der and Graham, J. (2004). Nieuwe manieren om jeugddelinquentie aan te pakken. Tijdschrift voor familie- en jeugdrecht, 26, 6, 144–151.

Leuw, E. (1997). Criminaliteit en etnische minderheden. Een criminologische analyse. Den Haag: WODC.

Lier, P.A.V. van (2002). Preventing disruptive behavior in early elementary schoolchildren. Rotterdam: academisch proefschrift Erasmus Universiteit.

Lipsey, M.W. (1995). What do we learn from 400 research studies on the effectiveness of treatment with juvenile delinquents? In J. McGuire (ed.) What works: reducing reoffending, guidelines from research and practice. Chichester: Wiley (pp. 63–78).

Meeus, W., Rie, S.M. de la, Luijpers, E., and Wilde, E.J. de (2001). De harde kern; ernstige, gewelddadige en persistente jeugdcriminaliteit in Nederland. In Loeber, R., Slot, N.W., and Sergeant, J.A. (red.) Ernstige en gewelddadige jeugddelinquentie. Omvang, oorzaken en interventies. Houten: Bohn Stafleu en Van Loghum (pp.51–71).

Met de neus op de feiten (1994). Rapport van de Commissie Jeugdcriminaliteit (Commissie Van Montfrans). Den Haag: Ministerie van Justitie.

Mertens, N.M., Grapendaal, M., and Docter-Schamhardt, B.J.W. (1998). Meisjescriminaliteit in Nederland. Den Haag: WODC (Onderzoek en beleid 169).

Pfeiffer, C. (1998). "Juvenile Crime and Violence in Europe," Crime and Justice: A Review of Research, 23: 255–328.

Preventie en bestrijding van jeugdcriminaliteit (2002). Rapport van de Algemene Rekenkamer. Den Haag: Sdu.

Recommendation Rec (2003)20 (2003). New ways of dealing with juvenile delinquency and the role of juvenile justice. Strasbourg: Council of Europe.

Riet, M. van de, Bernasco, W., and Laan, P.H. van der (in voorbereiding). Politie en jeugdigen.

Sherman, L., Gottfredson, D., Mackenzie, D., Eck, J., Reuter, P., and Bushway, S. (1997). Preventing crime: what works, what doesn't, what's promising. Washington DC: Report to the US Congress.

Slump, G.J., Dijk, E. van, Klooster, E., and Rietveld, M. (2000). Stop-reactie. DenHaag: Ministerie van Justitie.

Spaans, E.C. and Doornhein, L. (1991). Evaluatie-onderzoek jeugdreclassering.: de effectmeting. Arnhem: Gouda Quint (Onderzoek en beleid112).

Terlouw, G.J. and Kamphorst, P.A. (2002). Van vast naar mobiel. Den Haag: WODC (Onderzoek en beleid 195).

Vasthoudend en effectief (2002). Rapport van de Commissie Vrijheidsbeperking. Den Haag: Ministerie van Justitie.

Visie op politiële jeugdzorg (1997). Z.pl., z.u..

Vreeman, M.J. (1992). Leerprojecten orthopedagogisch gewikt en gewogen. Groningen: Stichting Kinderstudies.

Vrijheidsbeperking door voorwaarden (2003). Rapport van de Comissie Vrijheidsbeperking (Commissie Otte). Den Haag: Ministerie van Justitie.

PART II

Western Continental Europe

7

The French Juvenile Justice System[1]

Anne Wyvekens

INTRODUCTION

Current French law on juvenile justice has a long story. It originated in the imme-diate aftermath of World War II and is still governed by an ordinance of 2 Febru-ary 1945. In this paper we would like to consider especially the most recent part of this story and to examine whether and to what extent the French juvenile jus-tice system possibly shows a trend towards becoming more repressive. Its found-ing principles – specialised jurisdiction, mitigated criminal responsibility due to age[2] and priority placed on educational rather than law enforcement measures – were indeed at the beginning of the 2000s at the heart of a virulent debate, with the ministries of Justice and the Interior on opposing sides of the issue. Although several laws, including one adopted on 9 September 2002, introduced changes that could be interpreted as a movement towards a more punitive approach to juveniles, the original principles were nevertheless officially reaffirmed.

1. GLOBAL OVERVIEW OF DELINQUENCY TRENDS IN FRANCE

The common discourse in France over the past years holds that juvenile delin-quency is on the rise and that young delinquents are becoming younger and more violent. A debate has been launched on these assertions, not so much to discount the statistics themselves as to question whether or not they are sufficiently well-grounded to substantiate the policies they are presumed to legitimise. Although the limits and biases of statistical approaches are well known, there is also a limit

---

[1] I extend my thanks to Ms Flavie Le Sueur, deputy prosecutor for minors at the Pontoise Tribunal de Grande Instance, for her assistance in preparing this report.

[2] Following art. 1 of the ordinance of 2 February 1945, minors (i.e., youth under 18) are to be judged by juvenile courts, not by ordinary ones. By way of comparison, on a total population of 62 millions inhabitants, 23.8% are under the age of 20 (*INSEE Première,* n° 1001, janvier 2005).
If educational measures are supposed to be administered in priority to these minors, different ages have to be taken into account in order to determine what kind of measures will be choosen. An "educative sanction" can be taken for a minor aged 10 (see below), a sanction can be pronounced against a minor aged 13 and, on the contrary, youth between 18 and 21 can request to receive edu-cational measures like minors.

J. Junger-Tas and S. H. Decker (eds.), International Handbook of Juvenile Justice, 173–186.
© 2006 Springer.

as to how far they can be questioned. On the whole, any reservations tend to concern the extent of the evolution rather than whether it exists or not.

Several sources are now available in France. The first is a long-standing institutional source: figures from the police and judicial system (*Aspects de la délinquance . . . 2003;* Ministère de la Justice, 2003). Another more recent and as yet relatively undeveloped source is surveys on self-reported delinquency. Various forms of monitoring agencies have also come into being over recent years.

1.1. Figures from the Police and Judicial System

As summarised in a 2002 report prepared for the Senate (Commission d'enquête sur la délinquance des mineurs, 2001–2002: 163 & sq.),[3] the number of offences where minors were placed under suspicion rose 20.4%[4] from 1977 to 1992, and 79% from 1992 to 2001.[5] A sharp rise observed from 1994 (17.7% increase over 1993 figures[6]) continued at the same rhythm over the ensuing years: 15.4% higher in 1995,[7] 13.9 % in 1996,[8] 7.3 % in 1997,[9] and 11.2 % in 1998.[10] After a slight drop observed in 1999 (down 0.81%[11]), the figures rose again, but more moderately, with an increase of 2.86% in 2000 and 1% in 2001. These last figures (published in 2004) reflect a stabilisation, or even a slight decrease in the number of offences involving minors.

1.2. Self-reported Delinquency

Self-report delinquency surveys, a common methodological tool in the Anglo-American countries for a number of years now, have been used in France in a systematic and detailed manner only since the late 1990s (Bègue, 2000; Roché 2000, 2001), and as yet not at the national level. These surveys provide information on the risk factors of delinquency, profiles of the perpetrators and criminal processing of the infractions. The study conducted by Sebastian Roché in two cities points to "overactive groups" of delinquents: 5% of the 13- to 19-year-olds in one city committed between 55% to 88% of the crimes (according to the type of crime). Roché's findings also support the hypothesis of an overrepresentation of delinquency among youths of foreign origin. The study shows that school

---

[3]The most recent figures are also annexed to this report.
[4]Rising from 85,151 to 98,864.
[5]177,010 minors placed under suspicion in 2001.
[6]109,338 minors placed under suspicion.
[7]126,233 minors.
[8]143,824 minors.
[9]154,437 minors.
[10]171,787 minors.
[11]170,387 minors.

drop-out is a reliable indicator of delinquent behaviour. Lastly, the study shows that criminal proceedings are rare: the delinquent is seldom arrested.

1.3. Monitoring Boards for Delinquency and School Violence

Another source of quantitative information on juvenile delinquency comes from various "monitoring boards." The National French Delinquency Monitoring Board (*Observatoire national de la délinquance*), established by the Interior Ministry in 2003, aims to pull data together from various sources in order to complete police statistics, the traditional source of information. Juvenile delinquency, however, does not appear to be one of the Board's current priorities. On the other hand, a whole new series of local agencies monitoring school violence and truancy, as well as partnerships formed to pool data on juvenile delinquency, are starting to yield interesting indicators.

2. THE PREVENTION OF DELINQUENT BEHAVIOUR

Crime prevention in France is an area closely associated with the general issue of minors. French-style prevention is known for its primarily social and educational dimension, unlike the notion that prevention may have in Anglo-American cultures where the situational component prevails. Crime prevention experienced a renaissance in the early 1980s on the basis of the work done by a commission of mayors of medium and large cities, the now-famous "Bonnemaison report" (Commission des maires sur la sécurité, 1982). This report promoted what would later be termed local public safety policies or partnerships around the authority of the mayor, under the banner of *prevention*. While the institutions and partnerships that were set up following this report focus on crime prevention in the broad sense of the term, their preferred field of action is juvenile delinquency, since that still relates to social forms of prevention.

2.1. Early Prevention

France as yet has hardly developed practices for early prevention of juvenile delinquency. It is easy to understand how delicate the process can be: can we reasonably expect to early identify risk factors enabling us to undertake action with young children? And the corollary refers to the risk this type of policy involves: that of diluting the notion of crime prevention (for example "anti-social behaviour"), and the more onerous stigma caused when the services and agencies become involved long before any delinquent act has been committed. An experiment along these lines is presently under way in the Paris region. The early prevention actions presently conducted in France are oriented towards assisting the parents and helping them exercise their authority. One example is the "parent centres" that have sprung up in the framework of Local Security Contracts (*contrats locaux de sécurité,* CLS); their overall objective is to help parents by advising them or referring them to other agents (especially psychologists) who can provide support in coping with their children.

2.2. Special Prevention

Until the early 1980s, prevention of juvenile delinquency was the almost exclusive domain of specialised educators who worked in "prevention clubs" in the street in contact with youth, in the attempt to build an individualised relationship. These prevention clubs, which can still be found, have been criticised against the background of the increase in juvenile delinquency and the fact that it starts at ever younger ages. Their workers are seen as ineffective, or even guilty of a certain laxness towards their young protégés. It is also hard for them to find a place in new partnership arrangements, particularly when they must deal with "repressive" agencies, the police and justice system.

2.3. New forms of "Social" Prevention

Several types of actions focussing on youth were designed following the "Bonnemaison report" – at first in the framework of City Councils for Crime Prevention (*conseils communaux de prévention de la délinquance,* CCPD), and then under the Local Security Contracts. These actions consist of community initiatives, extra-curricular and general recreational activities, proposed mainly to youth in the most troubled neighbourhoods and organised in the context of "urban" policy. These campaigns are increasingly organised in partnerships, associating a broad range of agents consisting of educators, social workers, the police, municipal services and occasionally businesses. They include, for example, school monitoring, national education relay services and police recreational centres.[12]

Although "school monitoring" (*veille éducative*) is not explicitly linked to preventing delinquency, it is nevertheless closely tied to endeavours to distance youths from occasions of delinquency and to preserve public order. The aim is "in urban policy priority sites" to "mobilise and co-ordinate educational and social agents, professionals involved in public health and social integration to identify youths who have dropped out of school or are in danger of dropping out, and to propose educational and integration solutions."[13] The programme takes the form of local partnerships having as a *basic principle* to develop responses that are educational rather than law enforcement-oriented, and to

[12]For more recent examples, see the "summary of local actions" published by the Délégation interministérielle à la Ville (2004).
[13]Cf. the letter from the Prime Minister on 21 January 2002 referring to a joint circular by the Ministries of National Education and Urban Policy of 11 December 2001.

build a network in which all the agents, including the national education system, are on an equal footing. The mayor is designated as the system's "guarantor." Its *action modes* are to implement tutoring and mentoring by volunteers outside the school environment: local residents, members of the city council, elected parent representatives.

Along the same lines, the national education system has initiated a series of "relay services" for young dropouts. Although the form can vary depending on the school level and age of the youths, the duration (from a few weeks to a whole school year) and other aspects, they share the common aim to offer "a temporary solution adapted to [students] who are in danger of school marginalisation or have already dropped out of school" (Ministère de l'Education nationale, 2003). The various services are based on volunteering: by the youths themselves, families and the instructors. The intention is to provide a stable context and behavioural limits, and to exert authority but without imposing sanctions. The activities are varied such as calling on outside participants such as artists. The youth is not seen as a student, but as someone who needs help "to situate himself as a student." The objectives are "a type of learning different from that which occurs in school" and "reconciling youths with the constant presence of an adult." Since the relays are partnerships, the Judicial Youth Protection Service (*Protection judiciaire de la jeunesse*, PJJ) (see below) was closely associated with the programme's design and is represented on the board of admissions. However, it is not involved in the daily operation of the classes and workshops, which is handled by the national education system together with other partners (child psychiatrists, youth centres, etc.). As regards the "results," statistics after nine years show that approximately 70% of the youths returned to school. As for "real" results, that is whether the youths who return to school actually graduate, something has to change in the school system itself to achieve full success.

Another novelty related to the prevention policy is various schemes to get the police involved. Police officers have begun to invest their time in recreational, sports or cultural activities for youths. They organise these projects either in the framework of "summer prevention campaigns" (*opérations prévention été,* OPE), now referred to as "City-Life-Holiday" ("*Ville-Vie-Vacances,*" VVV), coordinated by the Ministry of Youth and Sports, or else in the framework of Youth Recreational Centres (*centres de loisirs des jeunes, CLJ*) which are run by the national police service itself.

2.4. The Question of Assessment

Assessment is not France's strong point. Experiments are rarely evaluated, and it is even rarer to draw lessons when an evaluation is made. As for *evidence-based* programmes, the French are even less acquainted with this method.

3. POLICE INTERVENTION

3.1. Specialised Police

A 1998 parliamentary report on "Responses to Juvenile Delinquency" (Lazerges & Balduyck, 1998) highlighted two points: that the police forces did not have a clear vision of the State's policy on minors, and that they lacked specialisation in dealing with juvenile delinquents. Although "juvenile brigades" do indeed exist, they mainly deal with minors who are victims. The report cited various explanations for this situation. Some were "negative" choices: not enough staff available, and little taste for a specialisation that police functionaries do not consider as prestigious. Other arguments were more "positive:" both minors and adults are involved in the same crimes, and juvenile delinquency is becoming diversified making it hard to determine the criteria for such a specialisation.

A second report, prepared in 2002, observed that "the juvenile brigades had begun to re-invest efforts to deal with delinquency following the [1998] report of Ms Christine Lazerges and Mr. Jean-Pierre Balduyck" (Commission d'enquête sur la délinquance des mineurs, 2002). The central director for Public Security, when interviewed for the 2002 report, indicated that 109 juvenile brigades with an extended competence could now be found in 462 public safety districts. The French *départements* also have juvenile brigades, but the small number of police investigators restrict their work to the most serious cases. And lastly, the *gendarmerie* has no specialised service for minors.

The question of police specialisation in minors is under study: the movement is taking shape although it has yet to be thoroughly consolidated.

3.2. Discretionary Powers of the Police

The police do not have discretionary powers. When a minor is arrested he cannot be held in police custody without the agreement of the prosecutor's office (*'parquet'*). To avoid police custody, the prosecutor occasionally asks the police to call the minor back for voluntary questioning. The prosecutor also has the right to decide whether the minor will be brought before him or not. He can ask the police to proceed with a *"rappel à la loi,"* whereby the police officer informs the minor, with his parents present, of the sentence he can incur for the offence of which he is accused. If the minor does not have a police record and the charges are not serious, the prosecutor can also impose a settlement; this is accomplished by means of the judicial police officer. And lastly, in areas that have a community justice centre (*maison de justice et du droit,* MJD), the prosecutor can order the minor to be brought before the prosecutor's representative (see below).

3.3. Minors and Police Custody

In principle, minors under the age of 13 cannot be held in police custody. One exception to this rule was expanded by the law of 9 September 2002: "On an exceptional basis, a minor of 10–13 years of age against whom there is serious *or* concordant evidence that he has committed or attempted to commit a serious felony or an offence punishable by at least *five* years imprisonment can, for the needs of the inquiry, be held in custody of a judicial police officer with the prior agreement and under the control of a prosecutor or an examining magistrate specialised in juvenile protection or a juvenile court judge, for a period determined by the prosecutor, but which cannot exceed *twelve* hours." This period can be extended for an additional *twelve* hours maximum.[14]

In all cases, the minor's parents must be informed at the very onset of the custodial sentence, unless there has been an exceptional decision by the public prosecutor or examining magistrate. If the minor is under 16 years of age, he must also be examined by a doctor. As soon as custody begins, the minor can request to speak to a lawyer and must be informed of this right. Police custody of a minor of 13–16 years of age cannot be extended if the offence is punishable by a sentence of less than five years imprisonment.

Police custody of minors is under the control of the prosecutor. The exercise of this control can vary from one court to another. For example, a court in the Paris suburbs makes it mandatory for police investigators to contact the prosecutor on duty whenever they decide to place a minor in custody, even during the night. The prosecutor of this court has also established a custody inspection duty for the deputy prosecutors: they have to inspect the police register (indicating names, hours for the custody, times for the breaks, meals, hearings), the state of the custody cells, blankets, etc. These inspections have the added effect of enabling the deputy prosecutors to get to know the police investigators better as well as their working conditions.

4. INTERVENTIONS OF THE PROSECUTOR

The prosecutor's role in French juvenile justice has evolved noticeably. In order to fully appreciate this evolution, which cannot be reduced to replacing education

---

[14]"On an exceptional basis, a minor of 10 to 13 years of age against whom there is serious or concordant evidence leading to presume that he has committed or attempted to commit a serious felony or an offence punishable by at least five years imprisonment can, for the needs of the inquiry, be held in custody of a judicial police officer with the prior agreement and under the control of a prosecutor or an examining magistrate specialised in juvenile protection or a juvenile court judge, for a period determined by the prosecutor, and which cannot exceed twelve hours."
The previous text state "serious *and* concordant evidence." *seven* years imprisonment, *ten* hour in custody.

by law enforcement measures, we need to summarise the structure of juvenile justice and the way it was practised over many years. French juvenile court judges have a dual competence: criminal in the case of a *delinquent* minor, based on the ordinance of 2 February 1945, and civil when protecting a child *in danger*, based on article 375 and following of the Civil Code.[15] In both cases, the measures that the judge may impose are essentially educational: the 1945 ordinance gives priority to the educational measures over criminal sanctions, and affirms the right to education for delinquent minors. When the juvenile court was first set up, at the same time a directorate for Correctional Education (*Direction de l'Education surveillée*) was created to implement these educational measures. It is now called Directorate for Judicial Youth Protection (*Direction de la Protection judiciaire de la jeunesse*, PJJ). For many years juvenile court judges tended to open a file for educational assistance rather than a criminal file whenever possible, based on the idea that a young delinquent was above all a child in danger. Therefore, although the prosecutor has the legal power to launch criminal proceedings and oblige a minor to appear before a judge, until recently he actually seldom exercised this right. As for criminal files, due to the quasi-monopoly exercised by juvenile court judges coupled with the prosecutors' lack of interest in cases involving minors, their presence at hearings was often more of a formality. The same held for lawyers, who were considered useless in this protection and guardianship perspective that only saw the interest of the child.

The prosecutor's low profile began to change about ten years ago, when the rise in petty and minor offences and the growing fear of crime led to a search for new forms of response: participation by agents other than those solely involved in public order. For their part, this latter group, especially the prosecutors, have also instituted new responses (see below). Nevertheless, the juvenile court judges are still involved throughout the whole process, they do not merely hand down a decision along the lines of traditional criminal justice.

4.1. Prosecutor Specialisation

Some courts have a special prosecutor for minors, others do not. This primarily depends on the size of the prosecutor's office (for practical reasons a "small" prosecutor's office with four deputy prosecutors cannot have a specialist in minors). However, it does not necessarily follow that all large prosecutor's offices have a specialised service for minors; this depends on the policy they adopt[16]. The

---

[15]"If the health, safety or morality of a non-emancipated minor are in danger, or if the conditions for his education are seriously compromised" ("*Si la santé, la sécurité ou la moralité d'un mineur non émancipé sont en danger, ou si les conditions de son éducation sont gravement compromises . . .*").
[16]For example, Nanterre, a large office, does not have a "minors" specialisation, while Melun, "very medium sized," recently added one, and Poitiers, a small office with 8 prosecutors, is trying to set up a specialisation thanks to a motivated deputy.

current tendency is for a specialisation to develop: juvenile court judges appreciate the presence of prosecutors specialised in dealing with minors. They see them as privileged and habitual interlocutors who gain experience in working with minors and also know these youths personally, their background and evolution, just like the judges.

4.2. Procedure to Launch Criminal Proceedings

The prosecutor's office has a fair amount of leeway when deciding whether to send a minor before the court. The deputy prosecutor is the one who decides, in application of criminal justice policy. Guided by the police investigator, he considers how serious the charge is, the minor's record and personal situation, and other elements. In the case of criminal proceedings the judge can never bring charges against the minor on his own, unlike the educational assistance procedure where he himself can summon the minor before him.

New practices introduced by the prosecutors are components of what was originally called "proximity justice" (Wyvekens, 1998). In correctional law (for adults) and juvenile delinquency, the notion of employing mediation for petty crime, deemed to be better adapted to minor offences than criminal proceedings, progressively led to the prosecutors' practice for some offences of dropping a case if certain conditions were met. This "Praetorian practice" was set down in law in 1993 under the following terms: "The Public Prosecutor, the jurisdiction responsible for investigating a case, or the sentencing jurisdiction have the right to propose to a minor a measure or activity that assists or compensates the victim or is in the interest of the community."[17]

This type of action can also take place earlier on, with the aim of prevention. The "Community Justice Centre" in Paris's 11th *arrondissement*, for example, summons parents whose children the police have found several times loitering in the street late at night. This prosecutor's initiative enters into a broader partnership context where, if necessary, in addition to a warning, social services are also called in. Six months into the project, a drop in the number of children out "after hours" was observed. This experience gave rise to a debate: is this type of action still in the realm of the justice system or rather is it not social work? And do we have here an example of "penalising the poor," or rather the emergence of a "new response at the frontiers of social work"?

The prosecutor's office's involvement in the form of conditionally dropping cases developed at the same time as another scheme called "real-time processing" of criminal cases. Whereas previously the police transmitted the files in writing to the prosecutor, where they were processed more or less rapidly, real-time processing consists in verbal reporting, by phone, as soon as police custody has ended. The (judicial) police officer calls the prosecutor, describes the case and

---

[17]New Art. 12–1 of the ordinance of 2 February 1945.

the prosecutor immediately advises on the follow-up to be given (proceedings by the prosecutor's office, transfer to the judge, etc.). In other words, this evolution combines in practice a diversity of responses with a quicker response.

In this train of events, in some prosecutor's offices at least, where practices can vary noticeably from one office to another - the prosecutor's role before the juvenile court has come to be more like the one foreseen by the law. Furthermore, the lawyer has also assumed his place, amidst a more general movement of increased attention to "children's rights."

4.3. Probation

Minors of 13–18 years of age can be put on probation under certain conditions. Depending on the case this is handled by the juvenile court judge, the examining magistrate or the "*juge des libertés et de la détention*" - the judge responsible for civil liberties and detention. The law of 9 September 2002 stipulated the obligations of a minor on probation: either to submit to measures of protection, assistance, supervision and education implemented by the Judicial Youth Protection Office or a licensed private facility; or – and this is one of the main novelties of this law – to respect the conditions for placement in an educational centre, in particular a closed educational centre (*centre éducatif fermé,* CEF), and this for a maximum period of six months, renewable once for another six months.

4.4. Pre-trial Detention of Minors

In the spirit of legal texts, pre-trial detention of minors, just like (or even more so) for their incarceration, is an exceptional measure. Even the latest amendment to the law in this area (the law of 9 September 2002) states this explicitly. This law foresees two distinct ways of extending the possibilities to detain minors before trial. The first is to broaden existing possibilities (pre-trial detention serving both to further the investigation and, in some cases, to "make a point"): minors at least 16 years old can henceforth be placed in pre-trial detention if under suspicion for an offence punishable by a prison term of three years or more (and not only for a serious criminal offence sentence). The second is a new possibility linked to a recent measure: placement in a closed educational centre (see below), a new form of placement in which the term "closed" refers precisely to the fact that the sanction for failure to respect this obligation (legally tantamount to judicial control) will be placing the minor in pre-trial detention in jail.

Pre-trial detention of minors is subject to various forms of control:

- By the rules of procedure themselves which limit this detention according to the minor's age and the seriousness of the charge
- By the jail's incarceration commission for minors
- By educators of the Judicial Youth Protection Office who follow the detained minors and report to the magistrates

- By the lawyers who handle applications for release
- By the judge

As for the involvement of social or educational services, pre-trial detention is not principally the time for this work. A social-educational supervision is foreseen throughout the procedure, through the court's educational service (*Service éducatif auprès du tribunal,* SEAT) and "centres for educational action" (*centres d'action éducative,* CAE).[18] The SEAT is responsible for providing guidance to juvenile delinquents under their jurisdiction and proposes educational solutions. The role of this service is to consult with the minors and their families, ensure the follow-up of incarcerated minors and perform the measures of *liberté surveillée* (a special form of probation for minors), community service, and reparation. The CAE's are responsible for investigations to assist the magistrate in his or her decision process.[19] They are also responsible for the education of delinquent minors or minors in danger who continue to stay in their families. These centres are multidisciplinary; they work with the minor as well as with his social environment and his family. They are also responsible for implementing restitution measures applied to delinquent minors.

5. SENTENCING AND SANCTIONS

During the sentencing phase of a case, jurisdiction for minors has three different "faces." Once the court has made the necessary investigations (after referral by the prosecutor) the *youth court magistrate* can either judge the case in chambers, alone, only handing down educational measures, or he can send the case to the juvenile court. This is mandatory if the infraction would incur a sentence of seven years or more imprisonment. The *juvenile court* is composed of the youth court magistrate (who presides) and two assessors (non professional magistrates). This court primarily judges offences (*délits*) committed by minors or serious offences (*crimes*) committed by minors under 16. It can order educational measures or else a penalty. Lastly, serious offences committed by minors of 16–18 years of age are tried by the *juvenile assizes court*, composed of three professional magistrates (a chief magistrate and two assessors who are youth court magistrates of the court district) and a jury of citizens. This court can either order educational measures, or impose fines and prison sentences.

The issue of sanctions is subject to much current debate. After establishing (art. 1) that delinquent minors would be referred to a specialised jurisdiction, the ordinance of 2 February 1945 states (art. 2) that "the juvenile court and the juvenile assize court shall hand down, according to the case, the measures of *protection,*

---

[18]The SEAT and CAE are governed by the Judicial Youth Protection.
[19]Social inquiries and measures for investigation and education (*enquêtes sociales et mesures d'investigation et d'orientation éducative,* IOE).

assistance, supervision and *education* deemed appropriate." Until 2002, the article was retained with one explicit exception to the principle: "They can, nevertheless, when the circumstances and the personality of the delinquent seem to so require, impose a *penal sentence* to a minor of over 13 years of age . . ."[20].

The word *sanction* did not appear until 2002, in the expression *educational sanction*. The second part of art. 2 was amended to read: "They can, nevertheless . . . either impose an educational sanction for minors aged 10 to 18 . . . or impose a penalty on minors from age 13 to age 18 taking into account their diminished criminal responsibility . . ."

The expression "educational sanction" is essentially intended to enable the courts to apply a *sanction* to minors who have not reached the age of criminal responsibility (13 years) and who until the 2002 amendment escaped all punishment. The educational sanctions (art. 15–1) now applicable from the age of 10 include confiscating an item belonging to the minor and linked to the infraction, interdiction to frequent certain places or people (victims or co-authors of the infraction), the obligation to follow a civic training course,[21] an assistance measure, and restitution.

Without going into too many details (applicability according to age, accumulation of offences), the measures that the juvenile jurisdiction can order, in addition to the so-called educational sanctions (applicable until the age of 18), are judicial protection (*protection judiciaire*), supervision (*liberté surveillée*), placement (in various types of living units), fines,[22] community service work (minors of 16–18 years), control by electronic monitoring, a suspended incarceration sentence, and incarceration.

In the case of incarceration (art. 20–2), juvenile judges cannot impose a custodial sentence longer than half that of the sentence that would be incurred by an adult. And this can only be imposed in exceptional cases and only on minors over 16 years of age. Minors can only be incarcerated in a special prison section or in a specialised penal establishment for minors.

In addition to non-residential centres for educational action (*centres d'action éducative en milieu ouvert*), the Judicial Youth Protection Office manages various types of residential facilities. The secure educational centres (*centres éducatifs renforcés,* CER)[23] are adapted to the treatment of minors who are delinquent

---

[20]"The Juvenile court ad the juvenile assize court shall hand down, according to the case, the measures of *protection, assistance, supervision* and *education* deemed appropriate." Until 2002: 'They can, nevertheless, when the circumstances and the personality of the delinquent seem to so require, impose a *penal sentence* for a minor of over 13 years of age [. . .]" 2002 amendment: "They can, nevertheless [. . .] either impose an educational sanction for minors from 10 to18 years of age [. . .] or impose a penalty for minors from 13 to 18 years of age taking into account the mitigation of their criminal responsibility [. . .]"

[21]A decree of 5 January 2004 organises this training.

[22]Not over half of the fine incurred by an adult, or not exceeding 7,500 euros.

[23]"Invented" in 1996, initially called "*unités à encadrement éducatif renforcé* (UEER)." Presently 47 CER are operational.

or seriously marginalised, and are in danger of recidivism and imprisonment." They work on "the danger of disintegration in an educational perspective."[24] The objective is to "create, through the discovery of a new way of life outside their normal environment, the conditions capable of producing a transformation of their image of the adult world and life in society." The sessions last from 3 to 6 months, with a group of 5 to 7 youths. Emergency placement centres (*centres de placement immédiat*, CPI),[25] must be able to cope with emergency placements (3–4 months) of minors, in particular delinquents. The objective is both to put them in a situation that "breaks from the environment and lifestyle that led them before the court" and to enable the services involved to "evaluate the situation of the minor and elaborate proposals leading to long-term educational solutions."[26] The guidance objective is thus more important than that of the final emergency placement. Closed educational centres (*centres éducatifs fermés,* CEF) are one of the main innovations of the law of 9 September 2002. They are addressed to minors of 13–18 years of age placed by judicial decision, either by a supervision order or under a conditional detention sentence, for a period of 6 months. The term "closed" should not be taken in the physical sense, as barred windows (such as politicians tend to convey), but refers to the fact that the placement is in the framework of judicial control and thus entails the threat of incarceration in prison if the youth attempts to escape from the centre. Eleven centres were operational in January 2005.

Lastly, we should note that since the Perben law of 2002 the juvenile judge[27] can impose sanctions on parents: when summoned by the court, they are fined if they fail to appear.

6. CONCLUSIONS

The French juvenile justice system has undoubtedly been the subject of attempts to make it tougher, as a way of answering to an increase in youth delinquency and to the consequences of it. Measures like the creation of closed educational centres seems to go in that direction and has been interpreted in that way. Similarly, in France as in other countries, an increase in the prosecutor's power can be noticed which has given rise to concern about the double risk of more repressive answers and less protection of civil liberties. Those two examples can be read

[24]Source : web site of the Ministry of Justice – http://www.justice.gouv.fr
[25]Decided in 1999. Presently 37 have been set up.
[26]Ibid.
[27]The Criminal Code (Art. 227–17) punishes with two years prison and a 30,000 euros fine the parents who heavily compromise the health, security, morality or education of their minor children ("*Le fait, par le père ou la mère légitime, naturel ou adoptif, de se soustraire, sans motif légitime, à ses obligations légales au point de compromettre gravement la santé,la sécurité, la moralité ou l'éducation de son enfant mineur est puni de deux ans d'emprisonnement et de 30000 euros d'amende*").

in another way, less pessimistic. We would like to suggest, as a hypothesis to be confirmed (or not) by the evolution of practice, that an important part of the intention of the "Perben law" was to show that the issue of juvenile delinquency really was addressed, not only through "soft" measures, but also around ideas like getting some places to get rid of the most harmful young delinquent. Thus the French law indeed has created "closed educational centers," but they are *not* closed with fences, and they are a place where to develop educational measures specific for youth instead of locking them up in prison with adults. As for the evolution in the prosecutors' practice, it precisely shows that only the observation of what really happens in the field allows to qualify a trend. French prosecutors indeed have got more power within the juvenile justice system. But it was out of a concern for giving quicker answers and had as a result the implementation of more various diversion measures by those prosecutors, and the comeback of the lawyer in the juvenile court.

REFERENCES

Aspects de la criminalité et de la délinquance constatées en France par les services de police et de gendarmerie (2003). Paris, La documentation Française.

Bègue, L. (2000). *Attachements sociaux, croyances conventionnelles et délinquance*, research report. Paris, IHESI.

Commission d'enquête sur la délinquance des mineurs (Commission of Inquiry into juvenile delinquency) (2001–2002). *La République en quête de respect*. Les Rapports du Sénat, n° 340.

Commission des maires sur la sécurité (1982). *Face à la délinquance : prévention, répression, solidarité*. Paris, La Documentation française.

Délégation interministérielle à la Ville, département "Citoyenneté, prévention, sécurité" (Citizens, prevention, security) (2004). http://i.ville.gouv.fr/divbib/doc/prevention-delinquance.pdf

Lazerges, Ch. and Balduyck, J.-P. (1998). *Réponses à la délinquance des mineurs*, rapport au Premier Ministre, Paris, La Documentation Française.

Ministère de l'Education nationale, direction de la programmation et du développement (2003). note d'information n° 03–07, février.

Ministère de la Justice, direction de l'Administration générale et de l'Equipement, sous-direction de la Statistique, des études et de la documentation (2003). *Les chiffres-clés de la justice*.

Roché, S. (ed.) (2000). *Enquête sur la délinquance autodéclarée des jeunes*, research for the MAIF foundation, the Ministry of the Interior (IHESI), the Ministry of Justice (GIP "Droit et justice" et Protection judiciaire de la jeunesse), le Centre de prospective de la Gendarmerie nationale, la Semitag, Grenoble, CERAT.

Roché, S. (2001). *La délinquance des jeunes. Les 13–19 ans racontent leurs délits*. Paris, Seuil.

Wyvekens, A. (1998). Délinquance des mineurs: justice de proximité vs justice tutélaire, *Esprit*, March–April, pp. 158–173.

8

Survival of the Protection Model?
Competing Goals in Belgian Juvenile Justice

Catherine Van Dijk, Els Dumortier, and Christian Eliaerts

INTRODUCTION

Belgium is a small (with a surface of 32.545 km²) but well-situated country in the northwest of Europe. It consists of over 10 million citizens (10,396,421 on 1 January 2004) of whom 6 million live in the Northern, Dutch-speaking part (Flanders), almost 3.4 million in the Southern, mostly French-speaking part and close to 1 million in the region of Brussels (bilingual). As in other European countries, families in Belgium are becoming smaller and smaller. The fertility rate is 1.56 children per woman. So Belgium is faced with an aging population, 15% of whom are older than 65. The portion of juveniles (0–19 years) has diminished from 24.6% in 1990 to 22.4% in 2003 and the prognosis is a further decrease to 20.2% in 2021 (VRIND, 2003). On 1 January 2004 Belgium consisted of approximately 875,000 juveniles aged 12–17,[1] almost half a million of them live in the Flemish region, more than 300,000 in the Walloon part and over 75,000 in the region of Brussels.[2]

Due to a federalization process (1970–1988) Belgium has been transformed into a Federal State consisting of three communities (French, Dutch, and German) (De Vroede and Gorus, 1997). This metamorphosis resulted in the reorganization of the competencies concerning juvenile delinquency. The judicial reaction to youth delinquency remained a federal matter, while the execution of the educational measures ordered by the youth court has become a community matter.

This means that each community has its own regulation concerning the execution of measures ordered by the youth court. The judicial response on criminal offences committed by minors however is still based upon the federal Youth Protection Act of 1965 and therefore remains equal for all communities (Eliaerts, 1999). Despite fierce criticism on the rehabilitative orientation of this Act and

---

[1] We give the statistics for the 12- to 17-year-old youths since this is the most relevant age group with respect to the topic of juvenile delinquency. Juvenile jurisdiction is operative under the age of 12 as well, however the judicial interventions will be more regarding educational and familial problems than about youth crime. Exceptionally, juvenile jurisdiction can be prolonged after the juvenile's 18th birthday (up until 20).

[2] See http://statbel.fgov.be; http://www.Belgium.be (dd. 26/04/2005).

J. Junger-Tas and S. H. Decker (eds.), International Handbook of Juvenile Justice, 187–224.
© 2006 Springer.

ongoing theoretical debate between adherents of different paradigms, the legal situation remains – aside from a few minor changes – unchanged until today.

In Belgium, juveniles under the age of 18 years have no *criminal responsibility* (with some exceptions as from the age of 16, see Section 5). There exists no lower age limit to the jurisdiction of juvenile law.

In this contribution we will first briefly go over some Belgian figures on juvenile delinquency. Statistics on this topic are however scarce and unreliable. The Section 2 elaborates on the Belgian prevention policy with regard to youth crime. The interventions on the level of the police and Public Prosecutor are discussed in paragraphs 3 and 4, with specific attention for diversion experiments and the fundamental legal safeguards of juveniles. Section 5 initiates the basic principles of sentencing in Belgian juvenile law. Juveniles are still tried according to the Act of 1965, but a new Bill has been submitted by the Minister of Justice Onkelinx and is being discussed in the Chamber of Representatives.[3] Finally, a great deal of attention is being paid to the variety of sanctions that juvenile judges can impose during the preliminary and the trial phase (paragraph 6). In the past years academics and practitioners have been searching for alternatives for the traditional, residential treatment of juveniles and its protective, rehabilitative philosophy. We elaborate on the experiments with community service, educational training, victim-offender-mediation and Family Group Conferences and discuss their implications for the minor's legal rights. Notwithstanding these alternatives, a significant amount of juveniles still end up in juvenile institutions: we go in to some figures and to the juveniles' rights during detention. To close we also focus on the evaluation of judicial interventions, with regard to recidivism as well as regarding the experiences of the juveniles themselves.

1. GLOBAL OVERVIEW OF DELINQUENCY TRENDS

An accurate quantitative picture of the actual practice with regard to youth crime in Belgium appears difficult to obtain. The lack of reliable figures concerning the different aspects of juvenile justice is a major bottleneck.

1.1. Availability and Reliability of Belgian Figures on Juvenile Crime

The systematic gathering of data on crime and crime control has been a problem in Belgium for decades. This situation – despite increasing computerisation – is dramatic, especially regarding juvenile delinquency. Figures, if available, are scattered over several federal, regional and local agencies and hence neither reliable nor

---

[3]"Bill considering the modification of the youth protection act and the supervision of minors that have committed acts of delinguency." November 29th 2004, Parliamentarian Document 51K1467, http://www.dekamer.be (dd. 28/04/2005).

comparable. Official criminal statistics are in brief *little accessible, pretty unreliable and very incomplete* (Goedseels, 2002: 30).

We will, however, attempt to draw a picture of juvenile delinquency in Belgium on the basis of results of self-report studies and official statistics,[4] e.g., figures of the public prosecution and the youth court (see Section 1.4) and data on sentence implementation (juvenile facilities (see Section 6.5) and alternative measures (see Section 6.3)).

1.2. Self-report Data

During the physically and emotionally turbulent period of adolescence, committing (petty) offences can be considered as part of typical juvenile experimenting behaviour. In this respect juvenile delinquency can be looked upon as *statistically normal*, standard behaviour that comes with the process of growing up. International self-report studies confirm this thesis (Junger-Tas, Terlouw, and Klein, 1994). An extensive research project of the KULeuven (the Catholic University of Leuven) on Flemish youth included an inquiry into the offending behaviour of 12- to 18-year-old students (Goedseels, Vettenburg, and Walgrave, 2000). Despite the known distortions of self-report data,[5] they reveal interesting information on undetected, unreported, and unresolved crime (the "dark number").

Students were asked about eight types of offences or problem behaviour, committed during the past year. Fare dodging was reported the most (25.5%), followed by theft (23.4%), vandalism (20.7%), use of drugs (17.4%), carrying weapons (12.7%), assault and battery (12.6%), running away from home (6.5%), and drug dealing (5.7%). With regard to the use and dealing of drugs, in 90% of the cases it involved only soft drugs.

Half of the respondents (52%) committed at least one of the offences. One-fifth committed only one of the offences, a same proportion two to three acts, 10% claimed for four or more crimes. The latter group can be considered as *career delinquents*: they not only committed more types of offences, but also more frequently and their acts were detected more often by the police. These career delinquents suffered more from depression, suicidal thoughts, experienced less parental support and control and their school careers tended to be problematic.

These figures correspond well with another Belgian study of French-speaking juveniles (14–to 21 years old): the total prevalence of delinquent behaviour during the last year aggregates 56.1%, the total prevalence in the total course of their young lives amounts to 82.5%. Only the drug-related offences are remarkably less

---

[4]We would like to emphasise that official data do not necessarily reflect the criminal reality (the offences actually committed by minors). These figures also express the efforts of victims (willingness to report crime), police (willingness to register), magistrates (willingness to prosecute and sentence) and priorities set in policies.

[5]Bias provoked by social desirable answering, by memory distortion, and by the drop-out of truants.

prominent among the Walloon youths (8.8% drug use and 1.6% drug selling during the past year) (Born and Gavray, 1994).

Most offences are committed only once (especially "assault and battery" and "running away") or occasionally. Carrying weapons, drug use and dealing are committed more recurrently (Goedseels et al., 2000). Criminal acts classified as serious have a rather low frequency (Born and Gavray, 1994). Consistent with other research, girls are less delinquent, although the differences are less striking for running away, drug use and fare dodging. Regarding age, the same curve as in international studies occurred: a peak at the age of 15–16 and a decline from age 17 (apart from the use of drugs). Vandalism and especially drug use typically take place in groups, while running away, assault and battery and drug dealing are committed alone (Goedseels et al., 2000).

The variance between Belgian and non-Belgian juveniles is small, only for fare dodging, assault and battery and carrying weapons the latter group presents slightly higher percentages. Students with a higher educational level commit significantly less offences. Most crimes (70–90%) are never discovered; vandalism, assault, and battery are the most detected by the police. Noteworthy is that the group of offenders was also more victimised (Goedseels et al., 2000).

Generally – as far as a comparison with other research studies[6] is allowed – Belgian youths nowadays do not seem to be more criminal than their peers in the past or their peers abroad. Quite the contrary, international research postulates 70% or more of all 13- to 18-year-old juveniles committing yearly at least one offence. Remarkably, the figures vary little over time. So the idea that juvenile delinquency is increasing could be inaccurate. Yet, these statistics do not reveal anything on the seriousness of the offences.

1.3. Police Statistics

Because age is not a variable in Belgian police statistics, there are no specific youth statistics available at this level. Only regional and diffuse figures exist, for example, regarding local phenomena such as street gangs.

1.4. Statistics of the Public Prosecutor and Youth Court

For some insights in to Belgian judicial statistics we refer to a research study that analysed all decisions of the prosecutor and the juvenile judges regarding juvenile delinquents in eight Belgian judicial districts[7] during three months (Vanneste, 2001).

---

[6]See: J. Junger-Tas, G-J. Terlouw, and M.W. Klein (eds.) (1994). *Delinquent Behavior Among Young People in the Western World: First Results of the International Self-report Delinquency Study.* Amsterdam: Kugler Publications..
[7]Belgium consists of 27 judicial districts.

On the *level of the prosecution*, almost three quarters (71%) of the determinative decisions encompassed a dismissal of the case. One-fifth implied a referral to the youth court. Alternative sanctions occur relatively rarely (4.2%), although the use of alternatives can vary significantly over districts (in some districts this percentage can double). Finally, 4.5% of the decisions leads to a referral to Special Youth Services.

The mentioned research study also managed to gather some more specific long-term (1980–1997) data concerning the largest (and hence most important) judicial district, Brussels. These data do not support the hypothesis that juvenile delinquency is rising the contrary, the figures show that the amount of juvenile delinquency communicated to the Public Prosecutor by the police diminished between 1994 and 1997. The supposition that delinquent minors are becoming younger, cannot be supported either. We can however conclude that the nature of committed offences is changing; while the amount of property offences is diminishing, personal offences are on the rise. Besides, these findings need to be put against the background of a diminished portion of juveniles in the total population (see introduction).

Regarding the 20% referred cases to the youth court; the juvenile judge can pass provisional decisions (in the preliminary phase) as well as judgments in the final trial-stage. For all decisions the proportion preliminary decisions versus judgments is 60–40%, and the proportion residential (with outplacement of the juvenile) versus ambulatory (with preservation of the minor in his own environment) measures is more or less equally dispersed. Residential confinement (49.7%) usually involves custody in a (half-)open or closed institution of the Flemish or French-speaking community (26%), but also in private institutions (18%), and before 2002 confinement in a detention centre for adults for maximal 15 days took place in 4% of the cases (Art. 53 of the 1965 Act was abrogated January 1, 2002). Other residential options such as placement in charge of a reliable person (0.7%) or a psychiatric institution (1%) are less frequently used, although the need for more facilities in juvenile psychiatry is pressing. Ambulatory measures (48%) involve putting the minor under supervision of Special Youth Services (18%), imposing a community service or an educational training (16%), or giving the minor a reprimand (14%). Transferring juveniles to adult court (Art. 38) remains an exceptional decision (3% of all judgments).

By means of analysis of files on the level of the prosecution and the youth court a profile of the juveniles could be made, which of course cannot be equated with the profile of the delinquent in general. The profile covers offence characteristics as well as socio-demographic features.

With respect to the offence characteristics, it is striking, but not surprising, that the profiles on the level of the youth court are far more serious than those on the level of the prosecution. The juveniles brought before the judge committed more offences, often in group, using more violence and weapons and had a longer criminal record than those whose case was being handled by the Public Prosecutor.

Juveniles who enter the juvenile justice system can be profiled as being socially and economically vulnerable. They often experience familial problems (e.g., judicial interventions in the family, harmful familial atmosphere) and their school career evolves adversely and involves problem behaviour, bad grades and truancy. Profiles also show an overrepresentation of boys, especially of minority groups. These socio-demographic features are even more significant in case of the juveniles brought before the youth court.

Whether these profiles give rise to more delinquent behaviour, facilitate a referral to judicial instances, or else a combination of both, cannot be determined.

2. PREVENTION OF DELINQUENT BEHAVIOUR

The Belgian prevention landscape can be labelled as highly chaotic: there is no consensus of used concepts, no united theoretical perspective, and there remain gaps and overlaps (Burssens, Goris, and Vettenburg, 2004). The complex allocation of competences between the Federal State and the Communities is partially responsible for this chaos. National prevention programs directly aimed at preventing juvenile delinquency are rare. Most often they are part of a larger and more general societal oriented project. The Federal State usually plays the role of financier (except in case of projects organised by the police, see Section 3). With federal or regional subsidies, local communities and agencies can, for example, organise programs for youth at risk in cities (e.g., in Antwerp).

Since the emergence of crime and feelings of insecurity have become political priorities; local, regional and national authorities have launched several preventive measures. We will briefly point at some of these initiatives. For example, the Belgian Ministry of Social Integration has created "integration contracts" for youngsters up to 25 without an income. In cooperation with the welfare sector the Ministry of Education has set up projects for schools with problems of discipline, motivation of students and violence. With regard to the prevention of drugs and alcohol, several initiatives are taken by the health sector. Especially worth mentioning are the prevention initiatives of the Ministry of Internal Affairs (1989). These integrated projects – a collaboration between as many local instances as possible such as the police and the administrative, political, social and educational agencies – were directed at so-called petty street crimes and the feelings of insecurity. From the beginning of 1993 municipalities can close Prevention and Security Contracts with the Ministry of Internal Affairs to obtain more resources for the necessary extra security measures. The content of these measures can be very diverse: specialised policemen training, drug treatment centres, social prevention programs for football-hooligans, job training for societal vulnerable youngsters, etc.

Globally, prevention has shifted from early detection and treatment of individual cases, to global action at social, economic and cultural level (Walgrave, Berx, Poels, et al., 1998)[8].

3. POLICE INTERVENTION

According to the Youth Protection Act of 1965, children are not criminally responsible below the age of eighteen.[9] The youth court imposes no punishments like in adult courts, but "educational measures" (see Section 5). Besides criminal cases, the youth court is also competent to try cases of children in need of care, and deviant behaviour (i.e., truancy). The law demands that the decisions of the Public Prosecutor and the youth court should be taken in the best interest of the child, considering his personality and family situation. This legal framework influences, or should at least do so, the tasks and the functioning of the police forces in youth cases.

According to the law, the police act under the authority of the Public Prosecutor, to whom they have to report all crimes. In theory, they cannot decide to drop the charges. In practice, the police often give unofficial warnings (cautions) or provisionally register the facts. Depending on additional information or new offences, they still can decide to make an official report and to send it to the Public Prosecutor. In principle, diversion programs cannot be set up without intervention of the Public Prosecutor (see Section 4). In practice, it occurs that the police demand juveniles to participate in educational training such as traffic courses or to restore small damages. If the deviant behaviour of a young person reveals a "problematic educational situation," they can refer him (and his parents) to social support agencies (yet without conditions).

There exist no specific legal rules for arrest and police custody of minors. Recently the *Cour de Cassation* decided that, like in adult cases, deprivation of liberty of a minor should be confirmed within 24 hours by a (juvenile) judge.[10] The minor should then be transferred to a youth institution.[11] The individual rights of juveniles during police custody aren't clearly regulated. Assistance of a lawyer is only provided by law if the minor is brought before the youth

---

[8]See also C. Strebelle (2002). *Les contrats de sécurité. Evaluation des politiques de prevention en Belgique*. Bruxelles: Bruylant; Ph. Mary (ed.) (2003). *Dix ans de contrats de sécurité: évaluation et actualité*. Bruxelles: Bruyant.

[9]See below, 5.1., for a few exceptions.

[10]According to the law on pre-trial detention (20/6/1990). *Cour de Cassation*, 15/5/2002.

[11]Since 1/1/2002, a minor can no longer be locked-up in a prison (abrogation of art. 53 of the 1965 Act), unless he has been sentenced by an adult court. Due to regular overcrowding in the institutions of the Communities, a federal detention centre was set up in March 2002 (the Federal Centre Everberg), where juvenile delinquents can be sent to (under certain conditions) as a provisional measure (for a max. period of 2 months and 5 days).

court. It appears that the parents are not always (immediately) warned. Research revealed that juveniles (especially ethnic minority groups) sometimes complain about their treatment during police custody (Vanderhaegen and Eliaerts, 2002). They maintain that arrest and police custody (especially spending a night at the police office) is abused to obtain confessions or testimonies or even to "punish" some offenders.[12] The circumstances of detention are sometimes reported to be bad (i.e., no food). To control the actions of the police in juvenile cases no specific independent complaint bodies exist.[13] In the Flemish and the French Community there is an "ombudsman" for children who (only) can ask questions and report to political authorities.[14]

The law does not demand a special youth section within a police force. However, since the reform of the Belgian police law in 1998, the function of "specialized head-inspector" was created in the local police (formerly called "police assistant") (De Naeyere and Gossé, 2004). This function requires an additional diploma in the humanities, i.e., criminology. The specialized head-inspector works mostly for the youth (and family) section of the office of the Public Prosecutor and performs inquiries related to the Youth Protection Act. The juvenile judge can also give him instructions, such as controlling the execution of his decisions.

In the larger police forces, however, there often is a special youth section. They also have detectives and sometimes even social workers. Special equipment facilities are often available, like separate rooms for interrogation of juveniles (also victims of crime) and anonymous cars. The assignment of a youth section is rather large. They undertake preventive actions, make inquiries in "problematic educational situations," and they deal with cases where children are victims of crime, like child abuse. Besides that, they offer special support in tackling specific youth crimes (e.g., street crimes, car-jacking, drugs): profiling, crime-analysis, coordination of special actions (on hot spots). Concerning their preventive tasks, school visits can be mentioned (e.g., information about drugs, traffic regulations). They can also participate in networks of social support and victim aid agencies. Much depends on the initiatives taken by local authorities or the police management.

---

[12]Some police officers are of the opinion that prosecutors or juvenile judges are too "soft" with juvenile delinquents, especially recidivists, and that they are sent back home too easily (sometimes because of overcrowding in youth institutions).

[13]Control of the police is exercised by the "General Inspection" of the police (Police Law of 1998) and by an independent committee (Comité permanent de contrôle des services de police, law of 18/7/1991) that reports directly to the "Chambre des représentants du peuple" of the Belgian Parliament.

[14]The "Kinderrechtencommissaris" in the Flemish Community and the "Délégué general aux droits de l'enfant et à l'aide à la jeunesse" in the French Community.

4. INTERVENTIONS OF THE PUBLIC PROSECUTOR

4.1. Legal Framework

Every judicial district has a specialised Youth Division, competent for all cases involving minors. When confronted with an offence committed by a minor, the Public Prosecutor has only three legal options at his disposal:

1. He can dismiss the case.
2. He can consider the offence as a symptom of underlying personal, social or familial problems and consequently send the minor and/or his family to Special Youth Services.
3. Finally, if the Public Prosecutor assesses a judicial measure necessary, he can refer the case to the juvenile judge.

In practice however, Public Prosecutors also employ alternative options. Because these new practises take place in absence of any legal basis, they create several problems for the legal rights of minors (see Section 4.3).

4.2. Diversion Experiments

4.2.1. Developments over the last 20 years

Since the beginning of the eighties, Public Prosecutors of several judicial districts experimented with measures to divert young offenders from the formal juvenile justice system. The reasoning behind these experiments was the observation that a great number of the offences were not prosecuted at all, because of its minor importance. Nevertheless, the dismissal of these cases had several negative side effects such as a sense of impunity with the offender, risk of recidivism, and frustrations with the victim and society in general. By giving the Public Prosecutor additional modalities to react to juvenile crime, a more immediate response that can prevent the further development of a criminal career became possible (Defraene, 2001; Devroede, 1997). The introduction of community-based agencies that organise and supervise the execution of alternatives increased the use of community service on the level of the Public Prosecutor (Spiesschaert et al., 2001).

From a more general and theoretical perspective, these new practices can be considered as a result of the dissatisfaction with the Youth Protection Act of 1965, its rehabilitative philosophy and its implementation. The past twenty years and especially during the nineties we see a revival of a punitive discourse on youth delinquency. The criminal responsibility of juveniles, the presumed increase in youth delinquency and a renewed belief in a just desert instead of a rehabilitative approach, are central issues in the recent public debate on the reform of the Belgian juvenile justice system. While in some countries this movement has lead to a new legislation, in Belgium, this retributive or repressive tendency remains rather a matter of the political discourse[15] (Eliaerts, 2001). Instead, community service increasingly became a means to sanction young offenders within the legal framework of the rehabilitation paradigm (Eliaerts, 2001). However, from a theoretical point of view, these new practises are associated with the sanction or justice model.

During the 1990s, a third way of thinking about justice emerged in Belgium. A lot of researchers felt dissatisfied with both the protection/treatment and the sanction/penal model. Following an international movement, they advocated a new model: the restorative justice paradigm. Within the restorative justice literature, community service and victim-offender mediation are presented as two prototypes of this new philosophy. One of the key principles of restorative justice that distinguishes it from the traditional rehabilitative and retributive paradigms is the focus on the harm caused by the offender. Therefore, the main goal of the judicial response is to restore this harm. Retributive and re-educational goals are subsidiary and not intentionally strived for. As a consequence, the content, aims and philosophy of community service are evolving in a restorative direction (Walgrave, 2000), or at least in theory.

Influenced by the restorative justice movement and a supportive policy towards restorative justice practises, several Belgian judicial districts introduced victim-offender mediations in the mid and late nineties. As voluntariness is considered an essential characteristic of victim-offender-mediation, many claim that it should be proposed on the level of the Public Prosecutor, before initiating any judicial procedure.

Because a clear legal framework is lacking, the practice is very fragmented and diverse. According to district, the Public Prosecutor, the juvenile judge or both have the competence to impose a community service and/or a victim-offender mediation. Moreover, judicial districts diverge highly in the application of alternatives and in the way they employ selection criteria.[16]

4.2.2. Implementation of Diversion: Rehabilitative, Retributive and Restorative Features

(a) Community service

Some studies suggest that judicial actors often use alternatives as a means to sanction juvenile offenders in a constructive way, or even to reinforce the punitive features of the intervention (Vanderhaegen, 1999). With this punitive intention, Public Prosecutors in some judicial districts impose community service in addition to victim-offender-mediation, in case the minor has a prior record or has committed a rather serious offence.

---

[15]With the Acts of 1994 and 2002, however, some adjustments have been made (see below section 6.4.2 and 6.6.1).
[16]For related issues to the legal rights of minors, see below 4.3.

Research also reveals that alternative measures have a net-widening effect. First, community services are not only used as an alternative for prosecution or traditional welfare measures, but often as an alternative for dismissal (Eliaerts, Dumortier, and Vanderhaegen, 1998; Geudens, 1996; Geudens and Walgrave 1996). However, not all judicial actors experience this net-widening effect as negative. From the victim's point of view, more victims can have their damages repaired. From a pedagogical point of view, moreover, it may be better to react (in a restorative way) to a minor's first offence, than not to react at all. Community service can make young offenders and their parents more responsible and it gives the minor the opportunity to symbolically restore the damages caused to society. On the level of the prosecution, community service can avoid stigmatising and coercive judicial interventions. This might prevent further, more persistent delinquency and, accordingly more severe judicial interventions (Devroede, 1997; Vanderhaegen, 1999).

Secondly, this net-widening effect may result in a bifurcation policy: minor offences will be handled alternatively, while serious crimes will still be pursued within the traditional system. Besides the restorative goals of community services, a great number of magistrates value punitive objectives. Influenced by some mediatised incidents concerning young delinquents, public safety as well, is becoming a more legitimised goal of judicial interventions (Eliaerts, 2001). Community services, imposed for minor offences, when unsuccessful, can result in even more severe interventions than an initial traditional juvenile justice measure. After all, when juveniles do not complete their community service, judges can feel the need to react strongly in order not to lose their credibility (Dumortier, 2000).

However, not only restorative or punitive philosophies are at stake: community services are also still influenced by the rehabilitative paradigm. Different studies show disproportion between the seriousness of the offence and the length of community service. Besides offence characteristics, more subjective factors and personal circumstances of the young offender (e.g., age, family and school situation and attitude of the minor), influence the decision making process of Public Prosecutors and judges (Eliaerts et al., 1998; Geudens 1996; Geudens and Walgrave 1996). Therefore, in order to re-educate and rehabilitate them, some juvenile offenders are dealt with more harshly than their fellow offenders with less personal problems. Because of the lack of legal rules and the discretionary power of judicial actors, unequal practices are very common in the Belgian juvenile justice system. According to the individual prosecutor or judge, the restorative, the retributive or else the pedagogical objectives gain the upper hand (Eliaerts et al., 1998; Puccio, 2001; Van Paesschen, 2000).

(b) Victim-offender mediation
Although with a different impact, the same general comments can be made regarding victim-offender mediation. There is empirical evidence that victim-offender mediation is used in addition to other measure in order to broaden

social control processes (Eliaerts et al., 1998). The problem of net-widening also reflects situations where victim-offender mediation is applied even in case of mischief (Puccio, 2001). In some judicial districts it is the explicit policy to select only cases of minor importance with clear, minor and easy identifiable damage, with the principle objective to restore the financial damage of the victim. Some empirical data show that mediation can be employed in a punitive way, or at least result in punitive practices. For example, after mediation young offenders can be confronted with high damage claims and therefore experience an even more severe reaction than they would have experienced within the traditional procedure. Moreover, fear of being sentenced and pressure of victims, parents or others can push offenders to restore more then they think is just. Furthermore, the introduction of the victim in the judicial process, can lead to double punishment: on the one hand the youngster is obliged to restore the harm caused to the society, on the other hand he has the duty to repair the damages of the victim. Moreover, in some judicial districts community services are imposed together with victim-offender mediation to obtain a more punitive judicial reaction (Dumortier, 2000, Dumortier and Eliaerts, 2002).

Despite these punitive side effects or retributive practices, victim-offender mediation is also characterised by rehabilitative and restorative elements. In line with the rehabilitation model, the personal characteristics and needs of the offender and his or her environment play a major role in the decision to propose a victim-offender mediation. For example, the diversion from a stigmatising judicial procedure, the opportunity for the offender to gain insight in the victim's moral and financial needs and to empathise with the victim can be important considerations. From a pedagogical point of view, a quick and adequate reaction, even to minor offences, is preferable (Puccio, 2001).

4.2.3. Profile of Diverted Offenders

A large survey in several Belgian judicial districts in 1999 that questioned the decision making process of the Public Prosecutor, gives us an indication of the characteristics of minors engaged in community service and/or victim-offender mediation (Vanneste, 2001; see Section 1.4). Neither offence history, nor prior conviction, ethnic origin nor additional problem behaviour stand in the way of diversionary strategies (e.g., community service victim-offender mediation). On the other hand, school and family problems decrease the use of alternative measures. In fact, alternatives are especially employed in cases that formerly would have been dismissed by the Public Prosecutor (Vanneste, 2001).

The profile of young offenders selected for community service by the Public Prosecutor can be described as follows (Geudens, 1996; Geudens and Walgrave, 1996). In comparison with offenders sentenced by a juvenile judge to community service (see Section 6.3.1), minors are younger (age 14 or 15, with an average of 15.1 years), study on a higher educational level (one-third attend general secondary education), but strikingly they are more often part of broken homes.

Both however, are mostly male and belong to lower social classes. As in the study of Vanneste (2001), ethnic origin is well represented (nearly half of the cases). As opposed to the level of the juvenile judge, most minors committed only one offence and have no prior record. Nearly half of these offences concerned acts of vandalism, another 40% consists of property offences. Almost invariably, community service on the level of the prosecution amounts to 20 hours (which is substantially less than the average community service imposed by the juvenile judge, see Section 6.3.1). In over 85% of the cases, the juvenile completed his community service successfully. Of the remaining 15%, the Public Prosecutor dismisses half; the other half is referred to the juvenile judge.

4.2.4. Figures

While community services are preferably imposed by the judge[17], relatively more mediations take place on the level of the prosecution. In this paragraph we will therefore present only the figures regarding victim-offender mediation; for quantitative information on community services we refer to Section 6.3.1. In 2002, the judicial authorities in Flanders referred 935 files to the twelve mediation centres, an increase with 42% compared with 2001 (659 files). 84.7% of these files were referred by the Public Prosecutor, 14.7% by the juvenile judge. Altogether, 1,437 victims and 1,604 juvenile offenders were involved (Geudens, 2003; Ondersteuningsstructuur Bijzondere Jeugdzorg (OSBJ), 2003). The committed offences are mostly property offences (62%), followed by acts of violence (25%). The figures suggest much willingness of offenders and victims to engage in mediation processes (61%), when they are given this opportunity. In 86% of the cases, the victim-offender mediation resulted in a full or partial settlement between the parties. This agreement involved in nearly half the cases apologies of the youngster, in over 60% a financial settlement, and sometimes (15%) the minor makes some promises (e.g., to attend school on a regular basis). The active participation of the parties leads to an overall high degree of satisfaction of victims and juvenile offenders (Geudens, 2003).

4.3. Legal Rights of Minors on the Level of the Public Prosecutor

We would like to stress the fact that legal rules are lacking and consequently, the discretionary power of judicial actors is large. The resulting unequal practices are often object of critiques.

More specifically regarding community service one might question whether this "measure" does not belong solely to the juvenile judge. Although community service might incorporate some restorative characteristics (like repairing in a symbolic way the harm caused to society), the repressive characteristics obviously stay present. After all, community service implies a limitation of freedom.

---

[17]See the discussion on the legal rights of minors in paragraph 4.3 and 6.4.

Especially when no legal framework is present, it seems that only a judge should impose this "restorative" sanction/punishment. The same thing can be said on the educational trainings.[18] Although pedagogical aims obviously are present, it still implies a forced limitation of freedom. Nevertheless, following some discourse (more precisely the previous Minister of Justice, Verwilghen) community service should always take place on the level of the juvenile judge (taken into account the clearly repressive aims), but educational training (seen as less repressive and more educative) should also be possible on the level of the Public Prosecutor. Following the latest project of the new Minister of Justice Onkelinx (2004), however, nor community service, nor educational trainings would be possible on the level of the Public Prosecutor.

As contrasted with community service and educational training, victim-offender mediation is seen as a clear representation of the restorative model. The offender and the victim are considered as primary parties in a decision making process involving the voluntary restoration of the material and immaterial harm caused by the offence. As a consequence it is quite commonly accepted that it can (following some restorative justice advocates should) take place on the level of the Public Prosecution. In this way diversion (one of the aims of the restorative justice movement) becomes possible. In practice we notice that much mediation takes place on the level of the Public Prosecutor. A lack of (legal) rules however leads to serious bottlenecks also with regard to some fundamental legal safeguards for minors.

First of all, it is unclear *for what kind of crimes* mediation can and/or should be used. Also the *influence of a successful or unsuccessful mediation* on the judicial procedure is not clarified. Within certain judicial districts a successful mediation (in practice this terminology seems to cover the execution by the minor of an agreed repair-arrangement) leads to all charges being dropped. In other judicial districts, however, the Public Prosecutor can still prosecute (for example when the Public Prosecutor also wants the damage of the society being repaired). In Belgian practice, these issues tend to be settled in local co-operation agreements between the Mediation Centre and the Public Prosecutor. This lack of legal rules obviously creates *judicial* uncertainty and an inequality between minors, depending on the district they live in.

The right to legal assistance for minors who (want to) enter mediation seems to pose problems as well. In the beginning lawyers did not seem to be very welcome within mediation. Nevertheless, serious criticism seems to have altered this situation. Nowadays the right to legal assistance of a lawyer is quite accepted in Belgium – at least according to discourse – and some mediation centres have already concluded local co-operation agreements with the Bar, Public Prosecutors and the youth courts. However during the mediation process itself the presence of a lawyer appears to remain problematic in some districts. It is feared they

---

[18]For more detailed information on this intervention modality, we refer to Section 6.3.2.

will take over the mediation process. Much seems to be dependent on initiatives of the local Bar.

The "restorative" principle of voluntary acceptance, profiled by different mediation-services, is also criticised. After all, it is hard to pretend that, in practice, a minor has a free choice and is in no way obliged to participate, when his unwillingness to co-operate can be sanctioned by prosecution before the youth court and/or a harsher punishment from the juvenile judge (Trépanier, 1993). Therefore, we wonder if the terminology informed consent (as used in some Belgian Districts) instead of "voluntary" is not more desirable. Indeed, before giving their consent to participate in a restorative justice-process, the young offender as well as the victim *should be fully informed of their rights, the nature of the process and the possible consequences of their decision* (European Recommendation, no. 10; see also a UN Draft Declaration, no. 12b).

The *presumption of innocence*, although almost always claimed, does seem problematic in practice. After all, in Belgian practices a minor has to acknowledge the facts before he can enter a mediation process. But, is it actually possible to acknowledge criminal facts, without admitting guilt? Are juvenile judges not going to interpret earlier participation in mediation as an admission of guilt? Hence the question arises whether it would not be more clear to state that minors who want to participate in a mediation process waive their right to be presumed innocent (of course only for the facts they acknowledge). This waiver could be formalised by signing a document that, at the same time, explicitly refers to all rights, duties and consequences of entering a mediation process.

Also the *principle of confidentiality* is not as easy to realise in practice as discourse might suggest. After all, within some judicial districts Public Prosecutors are interested in the attitude of the involved minors, while in other districts they are only interested in whether the damage has been restored. Hence within different districts, different ways of reporting by the mediation centre to the Public Prosecutor can be noticed.

Finally, *the principle of proportionality* remains a difficult burden within restorative justice practices. After all, the proposed "restorative proportionality" based on the seriousness of the harm caused to the victim and society (Declaration of Leuven, 1999), might imply severe restorative actions from the minor. For example a minor who writes his signature on a wall (graffiti), might cause more material damage than another young offender who intentionally breaks someone else's nose. When the restorative actions are only in function of degree of the material damage, less serious offences with a high material damage degree would become more difficult to restore than serious offences with a low material damage degree. Moreover, coercion, pressure and fear of being pursued or punished severely, might encourage young offenders to restore more than they think is just. Besides, especially in the event of substantial damage, the use of restorative proportionality easily results in more severe measures.

For, as you know, minors are often not in the position to repay the damage without some financial help of their family. Hence, when their family refuses to help or when the victim demands the minor to restore himself, often, the minor has got no other choice than to work to pay back his debts. In Belgium, mediation centres have created Restitution Funds in order to pay a certain amount of money towards the victim for each hour the minor labours in favour of the community. Such a situation, however, obliges some minors to work for many hours in favour of the community in order to repair the damage and finish the mediation successfully. Sometimes, a *restorative measure* that is in proportion to the seriousness of the harm can turn out quite harsh for a young offender, even more severe than an *alternative sanction* (like community service) taken by the traditional juvenile justice system.

Therefore, we wonder whether there should not be guidance available that would leave freedom to negotiate, but that would also avoid unwarranted disparity (Van Ness, 1999: 274–275). A legally based, but not strict retributive proportionality, might also prevent mediation from leading to more severe reactions on young people's offences than is the case in the traditional juvenile justice system.

In summary, we can conclude by stating that, following the latest project of the Minister of Justice in Belgium, it seems that only victim-offender-mediation will be tolerated on the level of the Public Prosecutor. From a legal rights approach, only a judge can impose sanctions. Nevertheless, a clear legal framework organising and guiding the restorative justice practices on the level of the Public Prosecutor is still lacking and does not seem to be foreseen by the new Minister of Justice.

5. SENTENCING: BASIC PRINCIPLES

From the beginning of the 20th century with the *Children's Act of 1912*, the underlying premise of the Belgian juvenile justice system – as in most countries of the European Union – has been the concept that children need not be punished but rather protected and (re)educated. The purpose of the intervention is the protection of society and the protection of the child. The central criterion of the intervention is "the best interest of the child"; emphasis is laid on reintegration and rehabilitation of the child (Eliaerts, 2001).

A first important feature of the protection model is that minors are not criminally responsible. Besides, their actions are not considered as criminal offences as such, but rather as symptoms of an underlying problematic (personal, social, family) situation. Interventions are therefore feasible not only for delinquent behaviour, but also for a wide variety of troublesome behaviour (e.g., truancy, mischief, running away from home) and situations (broken homes, child abuse). In this respect the principle of legality is being deserted (Put and Senaeve, 2003; Verhellen, 1996).

Secondly, the judicial reaction towards the juvenile is no longer based upon the committed acts, but on the personality and environment of the minor (Walgrave, 1998). The classic principle of proportionality is being replaced by far-reaching judicial discretion of the juvenile judge to intervene in the best interest of the child. Moreover, the judge can revise his decision at any time. In order to assess the personality and situation of the minor and possible evolutions, there is only one judge throughout all the stages of the procedure (Christiaens and Dumortier, 2004).

These and other specific characteristics of the rehabilitation model have resulted in fierce criticism regarding the legal rights of minors (see Sections 4.3, 6.4, 6.6).

The rehabilitation tradition was re-affirmed in the *Youth Protection Act of 1965*: until their 18th anniversary juveniles are presumed to lack penal responsibility and are dealt with separately from adults.[19] We point out that the juvenile justice system – along with the federalisation process – has been divided in two sections. One section deals with children in need of care on a voluntary basis, the other – judicial – section (youth court) deals with delinquent juveniles, civil matters and cases where the voluntary assistance has failed and the situation demands a judicial intervention to preserve the integrity of the child (Verhellen, 1996).

While most delinquent minors appear before youth court, the juvenile judge can however, exceptionally decide to refer a juvenile offender aged over 16 to the Public Prosecutor with the intent of prosecuting and sentencing the minor in adult court ("transfer to adult court"). Besides this form of transfer, decided by the juvenile judge (judicial waiver), there also exists the modality of automatic waiver, that is to say referral prescribed by law (legislative waiver). When a minor, 16 years or older, commits a violation of traffic regulations or related violations, he or she is automatically prosecuted before the police court (this is the lowest level of penal jurisdiction). Nevertheless, the police-magistrate still has the possibility to refer the youngster to the juvenile judge when he or she assumes a juvenile measure to be more adequate than the adult (penal) procedure ("reverse waiver") (Tulkens and Moreau, 2000).

Despite some adjustments made by the Acts of 1994 and 2002, the current juvenile justice system in Belgium is still merely based upon the 1965 Act and therefore one of the last European countries with such a far-reaching protection model.

While the debate on the reform of the juvenile justice system has been ongoing for several decades, with the new Bill[20] it is becoming more tangible.

---

[19]We notice that there is no lower age limit.

[20]"Wetsontwerp tot wijziging van de wetgeving betreffende de jeugdbescherming en het ten laste nemen van minderjarigen die een als misdrijf omschreven feit hebben gepleegd." November 29th 2004, Parlementair Document 51K1467, http://www.dekamer.be (dd. 28/04/2005).

Although many had wished for a fundamental rethinking of the whole system and its traditional rehabilitative philosophy, the Bill preserves the Act of 1965 and the protection model as fundaments.

The Bill strives for two main goals. Firstly, it intends to provide a legal basis for the restorative justice practices that have emerged during the past years (see Sections 4.2 and 6.3): reparative measures will be possible at any stage of the proceedings. The restorative paradigm will therefore gain a prominent place, alongside the protection model. The more active role of the youngster and the extension of the victim's rights emanate from this ideological perspective. Secondly, the Bill proposes a diversification of the measures the juvenile judge can impose, as well as the extension of their continuation after majority. The procedure of transferring juvenile offenders to adult court will also be revised and the juvenile court will gain jurisdiction over mentally ill delinquents.

Throughout the Bill, we notice a pursuit for a more objective approach. In order to reduce judicial discretion juvenile judges will need to motivate their decision in line with the listed criteria (e.g., personality, maturity and environment of the youngster, the seriousness and circumstances of the offence, past measures and results, public safety, etc.). Furthermore, the legal requirements for confinement to an open or closed section of the youth institutions of the community will be more stringent. Nevertheless, the juvenile judge keeps a wide range of options; the interest of the child remains the guiding principle and the education of the youngster still is the goal of the intervention. Thus, the risk for disparity continues to be a concern and is further instigated by the (geographical) diversity in the available services that are responsible for the execution of the judge's decisions. The Bill also aims at increasing the participation of the parents and making them take the responsibility along with the minor (i.e., parental training).

It is clear that this Bill contains elements of different philosophies and paradigms. It is the result of numerous reformation attempts in the past, and constitutes a typical compromise between the Flemish and Walloon regions. Considering the current political context, we believe it is likely that this Bill will become a law.

6. SANCTIONS

The Youth Protection Act (1965) does not offer the possibility to inflict punishments or sanctions on juvenile delinquents. The juvenile judge can only impose "educational measures." In practice however, we notice that the answers to juvenile delinquency in our neighbouring countries are named differently ("sanctions," "punishments," and "sentences") but in reality are very similar to the Belgian interventions.

We notice that – while the age of penal majority is 18 – under certain conditions, the measures can be prolonged until the age of 20.

6.1. Provisional measures

The objective of the preliminary phase is to gather information on the committed offence(s), as well as on the personality and the environment of the minor. During this phase of the procedure, the judge can command social investigations (executed by social service of the youth court) and/or a medico-psychological research (performed by a psychiatrist). The youth court can also impose provisional measures during this phase.

The juvenile judge can impose following provisional measures:[21]

1. A supervision order
2. A conditional supervision order
   (a) Specific conditions (e.g., attend school/a guidance centre)
   (b) Community service/educational training
   (c) Mediation[22]
3. Placement
   (a) In a private institution or confinement by a private individual
   (b) In a youth institution of the Community
      (i) (Half-)open
      (ii) Closed
   (c) In the Federal Centre (closed)

The preliminary phase can last *six months*; afterwards the Public Prosecutor has *two months* to summon the minor. Whether or not the provisional measures are applicable until the session of the court remains unclear.

The judge has to specify whether the youngster needs to be confined to an (half-)open or closed institution of the Community. The minor can only be placed in a closed section in case of consistent misbehaviour, dangerous behaviour or when required by the judicial inquiry. Confinement of the juvenile to a closed institution of the Community is possible for *three months*, once extendible for another *three months*. After six months, detention in such an institution can only be extended on a *monthly* basis and at the latest until the juvenile turns twenty (art. 52 quarter, altered by the Act of 1994). These decisions however, have to be motivated by the judge and be indispensable when taking in consideration the public safety and the personality of the minor. Incarceration in the closed Federal Centre is regulated more strictly by the Act of 2002 (see further paragraph 6.6 were the legal rights of minors during detention are discussed).

All provisional measures are open to appeal.

---

[21]We notice that the possibility to send a minor to prison for maximum 15 days (art. 53 of the 1965 Act) has been abolished since 2002, but has been replaced by the Act of March 2002 (see paragraph 6.6.1).

[22]Mediation (victim-offender mediation or family group conferences) is not as such enlisted in the Youth Protection Act of 1965.

6.2. Judgments

The second phase includes the public trial. Here the judge analyses the file of the minor once again. The Public Prosecutor demonstrates proof of the facts and can claim a certain measure, the lawyer of the minor assures his or her defence and the parents can be present as liable party.

By judicial decision the juvenile judge can nullify or re-enforce the provisional measures taken earlier, or he or she can take another appropriate measure. In this decision the judge takes not only the facts and circumstances at the time of the offence into consideration, but also the evolution of the youngster and/or the family have gone through (possibly as a result of the provisional measures). This explains why in many cases the provisional measures are more far-reaching than those in the trial-phase.

The juvenile judge can pronounce the following judgments:

1. A reprimand
2. A supervision order
3. A conditional supervision order
    (a) Specific conditions (e.g., attend school/a guidance centre)
    (b) Community service/educational training
    (c) Mediation
4. Placement
    (a) In a private institution or confinement by a private individual
    (b) In a youth institution of the Community
        (i) (Half-)open
        (ii) Closed
    (c) In a psychiatric institution
5. Transfer to adult court (exceptional)

The law sets no maximal time limit for (conditional) supervisions. However, for alternative measures specific arrangements concerning the duration and nature of the measure are usually made (see 6.3). The judgments mentioned under 4a and 4b can be imposed for maximum one year. After this period, but possibly earlier, the measure needs to be reconsidered by the judge. Confinement to a psychiatric institution is problematic. There are no psychiatric institutions specifically for delinquent minors; the existent institutions are not obligated to hospitalise the juvenile offender if they believe that the minor does not fit into the profile of the institution. In that case the minor will probably be referred to a public institution[23] – even if these do not have the expertise to treat juveniles with psychiatric disorders. As in the preliminary phase, all judgments are open to appeal.

We can conclude by saying that juvenile offenders – theoretically – cannot be "punished" or "sanctioned" within juvenile law. The only way a "real" punishment

[23]Public institutions are obligated to admit all youngsters referred by the juvenile judge.

can be obtained, is by transferring the minor to adult court. The minimal legal requirements to transfer a youngster to adult court are that he or she committed an offence, while at the time being 16 years or older. The central criterion the law prescribes judges to consider in their decision is whether or not the available measures within the juvenile justice system are still adequate for the particular offender. By "adequate" the legislator meant that the principle objective of these interventions – re-education – would still be attainable for the offender. Within this evaluation the personality of the offender and his or her environment play a critical role. Therefore the legislator prescribes that social and medical-psychological inquiries have to be carried out in order to guide the judge in this evaluation (Tulkens and Moreau, 2000).

With the Act of 1994 the transfer procedure has been slightly facilitated, as a new procedure of transfer is not necessary when a minor has already been convicted before adult court and the judgment can no longer be appealed (automatic waiver). When committing any other offence, the youngster is automatically being prosecuted within the penal system (Smets and Cappelaere, 1995).

In case of referral, the juvenile can be sentenced with all penalties of the Penal Code. However, the Bill currently under debate in the federal parliament seeks to abolish the infliction of life sentences on transferred youngsters (Onkelinx, 2004).[24]

6.3. Alternatives

As mentioned earlier (Section 1.4) alternative sanctions occur relatively rarely on the level of the Public Prosecutor (4.2%); decisions of the juvenile judge include 16% alternatives (Vanneste, 2001). We need to stress the fact that there are substantial differences between districts and that it concerns a rapidly evolving field. For theoretical insights we refer to Section 4.2 were the emergence and implementation of alternatives on the level of the prosecution are discussed. Sections 4.3 and 6.4 deal with the legal rights of minors engaged in these alternatives.

We will here present some figures of the implementation of alternative measures (community service, educational training and mediation) in Flanders in 2002, but only from those agencies that are for the greater part subsidised by the Flemish Government. The presented statistics are accordingly an underestimation of the real figures (Geudens, 2003; Ondersteuningsstructuur Bijzondere Jeugdzorg (OSBJ), 2003). Agencies, subsidised by the federal Government organise alternatives as well; however, their target group consists mainly of adult offenders. Additionally we will illustrate these statistics with some qualitative results of studies on community service and educational training.

We will also briefly discuss a new experiment on family group conferences (January 2001 – October 2003).

---

[24]For more information regarding the transfer of juvenile offenders to Adult Court in Belgium we refer to Van Dijk, Nuytiens and Eliaerts (2005) and Nuytiens, Christiaens and Eliaerts (2005).

6.3.1. Community service

In 2002, ten agencies, mostly subsidized by the Flemish Government, guided 658 youthful delinquents in the execution of a community service (OSBJ, 2003). The minors can carry out their community service in a variety of non-profit organisations, like rest homes, the street cleaning or technical services of the municipality, hospitals, animal homes, etc. (Depoortere, 2002). The duration of the services can amount from 20 to over 200 hours. In the judicial district of Brussels the mean duration of a community service was 52 hours in 1998, 69 hours in 1999 and 47 in 2000. Compared to other districts this is a relatively low number, e.g., the average community service in Antwerp takes up to 80 hours. Most juveniles are age 16 to 18, male, Belgian, with a lower educational level and living in a relatively stable home situation. Most frequently qualified for a community service are drug-related offences or thefts; proportionality between the severity of the offence and the length of the sanction can be considered satisfactory (Vanderhaegen and Eliaerts, 2002).

6.3.2. Educational Training

In 2002, twelve services, mostly subsidized by the Flemish Government, rendered assistance to 780 juvenile offenders who were referred by the Public Prosecutor or the juvenile judge for an educational training (OSBJ, 2003).

There is a great variety in programs. Some projects are short-termed (10–50 hours), others can take up to several months or a year. There are programs who focus solely on the minor, others also include his or her environment (friends, family, neighbourhood), or even the victim. Some projects are only organised on individual basis, others take place mainly or exclusively in group. Whether or not the project takes place in a group or rather on an individual basis, depends on pragmatic considerations (preference and experience of the counsellor, long waiting lists) or merely theoretic arguments (characteristics of the minor and of the program). Within the individual approach it is easier to meet the specific needs of the juvenile. On the other hand the group-dynamic that arises from the group-sessions offers the minors an opportunity to confront each other with their different opinions, values and moral standards. They can learn from each other and this can increase the insights in their behaviour (Van Dijk, 2004).

With regard to the content the programs can aim to inform or sensitise (e.g., about drugs, alcohol, vandalism, sexual harassment, gambling), to teach how to cope with aggression (or other problems), or to train social, practical, school or labour skills. Other projects intend to provide the young offender a deeper understanding of the causes and consequences of his or her delinquent behaviour, or offer insights in the position of the victim and aim empathy with the victim's suffering (Van Dijk, 2004).

We will now look in depth at some projects for minors organised by the Flemish community. In view of the diversity we will only discuss the most important and frequently imposed projects (Van Dijk, 2004):

- **Social skills training:** This program focusses on social vulnerable juveniles who lack certain skills to be self-reliant and assertive individuals. They cannot for example resist peer pressure. An individual training aims at increasing their social competence, since a lack of social skills is often causally related to the offences committed. The program teaches the minors to gain insight in their shortcomings and creates the opportunity for them to acquire new skills.
- **The program "coping with drugs":** This project is designed for minors who have committed a drugs related offence. It does not concern occasional drug-takers, neither heavily addicted youth, however, they have to meet some criteria of problematic drug use, sometimes in combination with drug dealing (when it solely concerns dealing, usually another program is imposed, because of the different, more profit-oriented moral intention). The education informs the juveniles about the possible advantages and disadvantages of their drug-(ab)use with regard to their personality and environment, and it gives them the opportunity to reflect upon it in group.
- **The program "coping with aggression":** This training addresses minors who have committed violent crimes and experience problems with physical and psychic aggression. The causes and consequences of frustration-aggression are being examined and alternative behaviours explored.
- **The program "victim in-sight":** Young offenders who poorly empathise with the victim and/or have little insight in the damages and the consequences of their actions can engage in this project. Its intention is not only to increase their knowledge about the material damages and physical and emotional injuries of the victim, but also to alter their attitudes towards the victim and the harm they have caused. Ultimately it wants to encourage the minor to take responsibility and to restore the damage inflicted by his actions.
- **The context-project:** This is a long-term project (six months to a year) meant for young offenders who have lost their link (relation) with their environment and society at large (cf. de-linquere). Its intention is to restore some of these links: the relation with oneself, with the family, with the community and the society (focussing on school, work, social assistance) and with nature and the transcendent. Its starting-point is not just the minor or even only the family but the entire context surrounding the juvenile.

6.3.3. Victim-offender-mediation
To ensure authenticity and voluntariness, most victim-offender mediations (84.7%; Geudens, 2003; OSBJ, 2003) take place on the level of the Public Prosecutor, before initiating any judicial procedure (see Section 4.2.1). More detailed figures are therefore presented in Section 4.2.4.

6.3.4. Family Group Conference (FGC)
Within the framework of restorative justice the *KULeuven* (the Catholic University of Leuven) conducted an experiment with family group conferences in

Flanders (Vanfraechem, 2002). The juvenile judge can hereby propose a FGC
in case of youngsters who have committed a serious offence or a series of minor
offences. The juvenile and his or her parents have to engage freely; the victim(s)
can actively or passively participate. Both parties can also bring their own support system (e.g., a friend, a confidant); other participants are a police officer
who symbolises the societal involvement, the juvenile's lawyer who vouches for
his or her rights. A neutral mediator guides the communication process between
the participants towards a "declaration of intent" settled by all parties. The juvenile judge validates this declaration and evaluates the execution of the settlement
afterwards.

From January 2001 to October 2003, 98 juveniles were referred for a FGC. For
58 of them, 53 conferences were organised (four of them included two offenders). For 33 youths, the FGC could eventually not take place, mostly because
the juvenile offenders denied or minimised the offence(s) or else, social assistance prevailed. Victims participated in half of the cases, in an additional fifth
of the FGC's they were represented by relatives. The "declarations of intent" can
entail restoration towards the victim, reparation towards society and prevention
of future offending. Most commonly the offender makes amends, apologies and
other compensations towards the victim, but also performing a community service or following a treatment can be part of the settlement. Most "declarations of
intent" are executed properly although some youngsters need to be urged to carry
on with their restorative actions (Vanfraechem, 2002).

6.4. Legal Rights of Minors on the Level of the Juvenile Judge

6.4.1. The Act of 1965 (8th of April 1965)
As mentioned earlier, the judicial reaction towards delinquent minors in Belgium is still largely falling within the Youth Protection Act, dating from 1965.
Since the seventies this model has been criticised within Belgium, in particular
in academic circles and in the Flemish part. Especially the lack of legal rights
and informality poses some serious problems. By wanting to meet the *needs* of
each individual child, traditional concepts of criminal justice are overturned
(Christiaens, 1999; Eliaerts, 1999). To make easy participation of the juvenile
possible, the open court is abandoned during the preliminary stages. Instead
an informal procedure is implemented with a specialised juvenile judge. In this
preliminary stage there was[25] no right to legal assistance for this might hamper
a "good," informal contact between the judge and the juvenile. The adversarial
roots of a legal formal procedure, whereby each party has the right to prove
or refute elements *à charge* and *à décharge*, is deserted as well. After all, the
personality and the environment of the minor and especially its prognosis for
the future are the main concern and not so much the committed acts in the

---

[25]Adapted with the 1994 Act, see below.

past. With the same kind of rhetoric reasoning, victims too are pushed to take a back seat "in the best interests of the child." Also the lack of proportionality helped contribute to the criticism of the 1965 Act. For as you know, a protective measure aims at assuring youths' *future welfare;* rather than it intends to punish them for their *past offences*. Finally, even the principle of legality faints away, for juveniles can be in need of help even when they have not committed a crime. Hence, large possibilities to intervene have been created by the 1965 Act (see above, section 5, basic principles).

6.4.2. The Act of 1994 (2nd of February 1994)

The absence of basic penal principles of due process (legality, equality for the law, legal assistance, proportionality or the relation between the offence and the penal punishment), was and is a source of fundamental criticism. At the centre of this criticism stands the observation that stating in books that minors must not be punished anymore but protected, does not mean, in practice, that no more minors will be (or will feel) punished. Indeed, through the evolution of the juvenile justice system, we see the application of different models (paradigms), leading to conflicting goals and interpretations of the protective measures in practice (see also Christiaens, 1999; Eliaerts and Dumortier, 2002). These goals can change during the different stages of the procedure. Moreover, the actors who participate in the procedure can defend different (possibly conflicting) views on the goals and the characteristics of the measures. As a consequence of the lack of legal rights, juvenile judges have great discretionary power to determine the finality of the measure which of course leads to disparity. Thanks to a "justice movement" on international (see UN Convention on Children's Rights), European (Belgium was condemned for its lack of legal rights by the European Court of Human Rights: Bouamar-arrest) and national levels (the installation of a working-group on youth sanction law[26]), in 1994 an act was voted, which offers more due process guarantees to juveniles (most importantly the right to legal assistance during the preliminary stages). At the same time however, the 1994 Act seems to have been the starting point of a re-penalisation of minor's offences (facilitating for example transferring 16- to 18-year-olds towards the adult courts) (see also above, section 5).

6.4.3. Community Service and Educational Training

Following this "justice movement," "alternative sanctions," like community service and educational training became, at least in certain districts, a more common means of sanctioning young offenders. As contrasted with traditional "measures," these new "sanctions" were seen as offering more legal guarantees to youngsters. After all, there is a clear limitation in time (number of hours) for the involved youngster.

---

[26]This workgroup, composed by academics and practitioners, stresses especially the respect for the minor's legal rights. See Decock and Vansteenkiste (1995).

Besides, the juvenile judge should only impose it after a fair trial. Finally, once the "alternative sanction" has come to an end, the youngster can get on with his life. The legal basis for these new "sanctions" was found in the 1965 Act and its possible "conditional supervision order" (a supervision accompanied with certain "educational or philanthropic tasks" for the minor). In 1997 the *Cour de Cassation* confirmed that these sanctions or "educational or philanthropic tasks" could only be imposed after a trial in order not to violate the presumption of innocence (art. 6 ECHR). However within several districts, juvenile judges kept imposing these "tasks" during the preliminary stages in order to react juvenile delinquency in an effective and fast way. It is clear that this way of imposing "alternative sanctions," was contrasted to the views of the highest Court and soon became heavily criticised by those who defend children's *due process rights*. In 2003 the *Cour de Cassation* was again asked to rule. A juvenile judge had liberated a boy during the preliminary stage under the condition of fulfilling a community service. This time, the *Cour de Cassation* overruled its previous arrest. Following the recent arrest of the *Cour de Cassation* the aim of the imposed "task" becomes crucial. When the "educational or philanthropic task" is imposed in order to sanction the minor or to restore the damage caused to society, the "task" should be imposed after a fair trial. On the contrary, when the task is "imposed"[27] in order to unfold the child's personality and/or home situation, it is not a *sanction* but a *measure of protection and research* in the interest of the child. Hence it can be imposed during the preliminary stages.

It is clear that this new arrest does not bring a lot of judicial security towards the minors involved. By claiming that community service or educational training is "imposed" in order to unfold the minor's personality, the juvenile judge is always in the position to "impose" it before any fair trial has been organised (Christiaens and Dumortier, 2004). Within the recent project of the Minister of Justice no clear position is taken either, thus confirming this judicial uncertainty. Besides, other criticism can be noticed concerning the imposition of "alternative measures." Since a clear legal framework is lacking, there is no maximum foreseen in the number of hours an alternative measure might imply. The way of reporting from the private counselling services towards the juvenile judge is not regulated either. What information on the execution should the judge receive? In what way the minor is allowed to take part in the decision making process concerning the content of the measure is also obscure. Besides, many other questions remain unanswered. How many chances should a minor get before his community service or educational training must be seen as a failure? What are the legal consequences of a failure or on the contrary a successful "alternative sanction"?

---

[27]We need to make a distinction for the term "imposed" in this context: in principle the judge can only propose a task and the youngster needs to accept it voluntarily.

6.4.4. Victim-offender mediation

Although victim-offender mediation originally only took place on the level of the Public Prosecutor, since the ending of the nineties we notice this procedure also on the level of the juvenile judge. It seemed that on the level of the Public Prosecutor only less serious cases were sent to mediation centres. In order to be able to work with more serious cases, mediation centres created local co-operation agreements with juvenile judges. Moreover the legal rights of minors are better guaranteed on the level of the juvenile judge, since the right to legal assistance is always foreseen and the interference of a judge can be seen as a judicial safeguard for the minors involved. Nevertheless, the aim of diversion (diverting the case away from the "penal" judge) becomes hard to meet by this way of working.

Because there exists no legal framework for victim-offender mediation, judges try to fit this new way of reacting within the old 1965 Act. Hence it is imposed, as is the case with the already mentioned "alternative sanctions," as a measure of research (during the preliminary stages) or as a sanctioning measure to restore the victim's damage (during trial). Within some districts mediation is imposed during the preliminary stages but the outcome of the mediation (for example working during some hours for the victim) must be confirmed during a trial and hence before its execution actually takes place. This can be seen as a judicial control on the content of the mediation, and more specifically the mediation's outcome.

As is the case on the level of the Public Prosecutor a lack of legal rules governing mediation leads to different bottlenecks and uncertainties as regards the legal rights of minors (see above, 4.3).

6.5. Juveniles in Institutions

In the past decade, the number of Flemish juveniles who are within the province of the Special Youth Services has increased from 6,346 in 1989 to 7,194 in 1999 (Florizoone and Roose, 2000). This number encompasses the private institutions (residential and ambulatory, such as social assistance at home, daycentre, support for adolescents in independent living), foster care and the (half-)open or closed public institutions of the Flemish government. The population of these institutions and facilities includes delinquent youths as well as minors in (familial, educational, social) trouble and their family ("problematic educational situation").

Even confinement to the *(half-)open or closed youth institutions* of the Flemish government[28], considered to be the harshest measure the judge can take, is possible for both groups, although the juvenile delinquents compose the greater part

---

[28]"De Kempen" ("De Markt," (half-)open institution for boys; and "De Hutten," closed institution for boys) and "De Zande" ("Beernem," closed insititution for girls; and "Ruislede," closed and (half-)open insititution for boys).

(ratio 3:1). In 2002 a new federal closed juvenile correctional facility (the Federal Centre Everberg) was established specifically for delinquent boys age 14 to 18. In 2002 all these (half-)open and closed public institutions for Flanders held a *capacity* of 246 (by comparison: in 1999 this capacity entailed 208) (Vlaamse Overheid, 2003). Yearly over one thousand minors are confined to one of these facilities. This stands for a slight, but consistent rise since 1995 (from 930 confinements in 1995 to 1,097 in 2002). The mean detention period amounts to two to three months. This short term enables a quick referral to other facilities with diminished security and more lenient regime, but at the same time it complicates treatment (Florizoone and Roose, 2000).

The juveniles confined to these public institutions are for the greater part of the Belgian nationality (although the proportion of *non-natives* is relatively higher). However, a closer look on the individual institutions reveals a geographic disparity, as in one facility (i.e., "De Markt") over 40% is of non-EU (mostly Moroccan) citizenship (Florizoone and Roose, 2000).

In the French-speaking part of the country, there are five youth institutions of the French government with open and/or closed sections ("Institution publique de protection de la jeunesse").[29] Unlike the Flemish institutions they are only accessible for delinquent youth from the age of 12 (younger ones only in very exceptional situations), and not for the juveniles who find themselves in "problematic educational situations." Altogether there is a capacity of 39 places for girls, of which 34 open and 5 closed. For Walloon boys there are 150 places: 110 open and 40 closed.

The *length* of the placement depends on the institution or section in which the juvenile resides. For example, a stay in the orientation and observation institution can last maximally 40 days in the open section and three months at most in the closed section. Residence at an education-oriented institution is in principle undetermined for the open section. For the closed sections this stay takes 75 days, once extendible with three months, after that extendible every month. Transfers between sections are of course possible and can extend the total stay.[30]

A study revealed that confinement to a public institution did not seem to enable social reintegration: the lack of personnel and the institutional rigidity hinder a personal treatment. Stigmatisation and the risk of social and scholar rejection are additional barriers for successful reintegration. The public security is well enhanced: youths do perceive this security, especially when resided in closed sections. For most juveniles a stay in a public institution is a negative experience, but it provides a means to wipe the slate clean. Some youth do benefit from a placement: especially for those in a "problematic educational situation"

[29]There are four institutions for boys: Braine-le-Château (closed section), Fraipont (open and closed sections), Wauthier-Braine (open section) and Jumet (open section). One is reserved for girls, i.e. Saint-Servais (open and closed sections).
[30]http://www.cfwb.be/aide-jeunesse/IPPJ/index.htm (dd. 22/03/2004)

the period in the institution enables restoration of family bonds; others realise that this might be their last chance and use the opportunity to reflect upon their future. However, the positive aspects of a placement seem to be merely exterior to the institution (family, grow to maturity) and are not inherent to the pedagogical program (Delens-Ravier and Thibaut, 2002).

6.6. Control of Juveniles' Rights During Detention

The same kind of criticism surrounding the "alternatives" (see Sections 4.3 and 6.4.3–4) exists with regard to detention during the preliminary stages. A large majority of youngsters placed in Belgian institutions never had any fair trial. Often they are released before the trial takes place. During the trial they are reprimanded or placed under supervision (with or without the imposition of an "educational or philanthropic task").

6.6.1. The Act of 2002 (1st of March 2002)

When confined to an institution during the preliminary stages the legal rights position of the minor depends on the institution he or she is placed in. Since the first of January 2002, minors can no more be placed in adult prisons during the preliminary stages. As a consequence however, certain juvenile judges claimed they had to liberate several "dangerous young criminals." Hence the Belgian Federal Government rapidly created in less than two months time a new juvenile "Centre" (in fact a youth prison in order to replace the old adult prison) in order to protect society. Nowadays there exist two kinds of institutions in Belgium: the regional institutions of the Community (with the primary aim to protect youngsters) and the new Federal Centre Everberg (with the primary aim to protect society). In practice it is not very clear what the differences between these two kinds of institutions exactly are, unless the obvious procedural differences as a consequence of the differences in pursued goals. Within the regional institutions (goal of protecting minors) juveniles can be held for three months (see Section 6.1). Then the juvenile judge has to revise their case and determine whether the placement should be prolonged for another three months. Following these three months the case has to be revised again and from that moment on the minor can only be placed on a monthly base and under specific conditions (and maximum until the youngster becomes 20). Within the Federal Centre (goal of protecting society) the juvenile judge has to revise the minor's case after five days and then on a monthly base. The minor can only be held for a maximum of two months and five days in the Centre. Afterwards he has to be placed in an institution of the Communities. Hence, the judicial control on minors' placements is better insured within the Federal Centre than within the regional institutions. It has to be mentioned that only boys can be placed within the Federal Centre. As a consequence girls are always placed within regional institutions governed by the "three monthly revision" rule.

When the judge wants to impose a placement during trial, only confinement to a regional institution is possible (see Section 6.2). Following the 1965 Act the juvenile judge can always soften a measure and liberate a minor. Moreover, the minor's case has to be revised on a yearly basis. The juvenile judge has to visit the minor on a regularly base in order to evaluate whether the minor's legal rights are respected during the execution of the detention. The minor can also always write to the juvenile judge. Besides, the French and Flemish Community both have their "Children's Rights Commissioner." These commissioners are allowed to visit the institutions. Within the Flemish Community mention can be made of the "Minorius Project" (which tries to indicate some minimum rights for minors involved within the Flemish Protection System) and the "Jo-Lijn" (where all minors and parents confronted with the Flemish Protection System can call for information and complaints). These projects however do not result in "hard to rights" for placed minors. In fact, in Belgium, when placed in an institution as a minor, no specific regulation exists concerning the *right to complaint*.

If a minor is transferred to the adult courts and penalties, he becomes like an adult and his legal position will differ in no way from that of an adult. Unfortunately, he will also be treated as an adult and no special institutions, regulations or reduced punishments are foreseen for these minors. Within the recent Bill of the Minister of Justice Onkelinx (2004) a certain improvement can be noticed (e.g., no life sentences, special institution for some of the transferred youngsters). However, at the same time it seems that the possibility of transferring youngsters towards the adult system will be facilitated. Again we notice the trend of improving the legal position of minors while, at the same time, re-penalising their delinquent behaviour (see the 1994 and 2002 Act).

6.7. Evaluation of Judicial Interventions

6.7.1. Results and Recidivism

Research on the effectiveness of juvenile sanctions and interventions is scarce in Belgium. Only limited studies on recidivism, on the experience and satisfaction of the sentence by offender and/or victims exist. Usually they constitute small a segment of a larger research project. For example an extensive study on the use and impact of community services involved an investigation of recidivism after a community service in comparison with recidivism after traditional measures (Geudens, 1999). The study revealed that juvenile offenders who carried out a community service re-offended significantly less than the offenders of the matched control group who received a traditional measure,[31] i.e., 50.5% versus 74.5%. Recidivism encompasses a by the Public Prosecutor registered offence within the eighteen months following the intervention. Regarding the traditional

[31]These traditional measures encompass reprimands (11.5%), supervision orders (25%), placements in private (24.5%) or public institutions (39%).

interventions recidivism was especially problematic for the confined youth (84% of the placements in private institutions and 79% of the placements in public institutions). The reprimanded youths did not differ significantly from the community service group (52%), explicable by the higher share of petty offenders in the reprimanded group. Recidivism increases as the juvenile has a longer offence history, however the positive effect of community service on recidivism does apply for the "career delinquents" as well as for the first offenders. A logistic regression analysis pointed out that ethnic minority origin, a broken home situation, a low educational level, traditional sentencing and a serious offence profile are significant predictors for recidivism (Geudens, 1999).

Within the research experiment on family group conferences (see Section 6.3.4; Vanfraechem, 2002), an evaluation with a control group was not made: the researcher only compared the recidivism of the juveniles who successfully completed the FGC with the recidivism of those who didn't. This comparison revealed that more than half of the latter group re-offended as opposed to less than a quarter of those who closed the FGC positively. Juvenile offenders and their parents estimate the risks of re-offending as low, but victims are less optimistic. Considering the high acknowledgement of the involvement and communication of the parties, an inquiry into the experience of the participants of the FGC was an indispensable part of the research. Globally the satisfaction of the participants with the procedure of the FGC was high. They all felt well informed; juveniles appreciated the fact that they could take responsibility and avoid incarceration in a youth institution, parents assessed the procedure and outcome as just and fair, and victims especially valued the opportunity for communication, participation and processing of emotions. However, for many the process is considered to be (too) intensive and time-consuming and not all victims are completely satisfied with the settlement (Vanfraechem, 2003).

The evaluation of alternative sanctioning in Brussels revealed that these options are often used as "passe-partout" and create a net-widening effect. Judicial actors and practitioners do not experience this necessarily as a negative effect: from a pedagogical point of view it is better to respond actively to the misbehaviour of juveniles than to do nothing or to just reprimand them, they need to take responsibility (see Section 4.2.2). The greater part of the community services is completed successfully. However the only criterion used, is that the juvenile performed the total amount of hours; the quality of the work or problems during the execution are not included in this evaluation. Although the motivation of many young offenders is limited and they often experience difficulties complying with engagements, the decision to abort the execution of the sanction and to send the juvenile back to the judge is not lightly taken. With regard to the drug program, the evaluation is not clear-cut: its goal is merely to inform and sensitise, not necessarily to bring juveniles to stop using drugs. This attitude often conflicts with the objectives of judicial authorities. In respect of these conflicting goals, measuring recidivism is not desirable (Vanderhaegen and Eliaerts, 2002).

6.7.2. Experiences of Juveniles

The Brussels research study (see above, 6.7.1) also entailed interviews with offenders[32] on their experiences. The contacts with police officers are for many offenders an unpleasant and highly emotional experience: they often feel intimidated and manipulated. A lack of information and participation characterises the hearing and trial in front of the juvenile judge: the juveniles feel like they're not involved or taken seriously. The imposed sanction is usually experienced as just, proportional and fair, except if a co-offender is sentenced more leniently or if the offence involves the use of soft drugs. The juveniles consider an educational training as the most useful and beneficial measure: the link with the offence is clear and they feel they have learned something, as opposed to community service where the link with the offence is not as clear-cut. In the latter case they agree to perform the service in order to avoid a detention, and not so much because they are convinced of its benefits. First offenders are more prone to believe that they won't re-offend; career delinquents are less optimistic about their ability to change. The most beneficial factors to keep offenders to "the straight and narrow path" are a steady relationship and a good job (Vanderhaegen and Eliaerts, 2002).

A Walloon research study (Delens-Ravier and Thibaut, 2002) focussed as well on the perspectives of the youngsters themselves. Interviews revealed that most youths have a negative image of the *police* system, mostly caused by the methods police officers employ (e.g., interrogation style, display of power). The role of the *Public Prosecutor* is highly vague and not well understood by the young offenders. In accordance with the Act of 1965, for young offenders the *juvenile judge* occupies the central position in the whole system and is perceived as the organ that follows them closely during their track in the juvenile justice system. Juveniles feel themselves captured in a system where they have absolutely no power or say in. In order to get out of the system as quickly as possible, they try to behave in a conformist way.

7. CONCLUSION

Because of the lack of reliable figures, gathered on a regular basis, it is difficult to uncover trends in juvenile crime. Self-report studies do not suggest that Belgian juveniles commit more offences than their foreign peers. While there is no evidence that juvenile delinquency is rising, nor that offenders are becoming younger, the nature of committed offences does seem to have changed. The amount of property offences is diminishing and personal offences (i.e., violent street crimes) are on a rise. In particular, a small portion of older juveniles (+16),

---

[32]Because the juveniles whose sanctions evolved more problematic did not want to co-operate, we can only offer a highly distorted picture.

often from ethnic minority groups, seems to be responsible for a disproportionate amount of the more serious and violent delinquency in the big cities. Problematic as well is the outdated legal framework and the lack of adequate institutions and (treatment)programs for these so-called difficult offenders or career delinquents.

With regard to the number of youngsters that end up in Special Youth Services, we can perceive a slight rise. More specifically, the capacity of the (half-) open and closed public youth institutions in Flanders expanded from 208 "beds" in 1999 to 246 in 2002. Yearly over one thousand minors are confined to these facilities. Whether the expansion of detention in closed institutions can only be attributed to a rise or hardening of youth delinquency, cannot be determined. The more repressive climate and diminished tolerance towards certain groups of juvenile offenders can also be important factors. Besides, the lack of appropriate intervention modalities (confinement, care, and treatment) for troubled youngsters (who suffer from substance abuse, psychiatric disorders, behavioural problems . . .) "forces" judges to confine these juveniles to other (public) institutions that are not adapted to their specific needs.

Whereas the Belgian juvenile justice system nowadays is still founded upon the Youth Protection Act of 1965, experiments and legislative adaptations have moved the system away from its initial protective and rehabilitative mission. Strikingly, this movement evolves in two opposite directions.

On the one hand, diversion experiments and measures as community service, mediation and educational training, have offered an alternative for formal judicial reactions or residential interventions. While punitive and rehabilitative features are still present, these alternatives also promote restorative goals. These measures are, however, for the greater part (though not solely) applied in cases of petty offences. A clear-cut trend is hard to uncover considering the substantial differences between policies of judicial districts, personal beliefs of magistrates and hence the disparity in practice.

On the other hand, the Acts of 1994 and 2002 have introduced some characteristics of the justice model (better legal safeguards and due process rights for juveniles), but at the same time these Acts contain more punitive features and may give occasion to a re-penalisation of the juvenile justice system (cf. facilitation of the waiver procedure). Furthermore public safety becomes a more legitimate goal of juvenile justice.

Nevertheless, the current Minister of Justice in her recently voted Bill (Onkelinx, 2006) desires to preserve the protection model from 1965 for the greater part of the juvenile offenders. Hence, Belgium will still have a *sui generis* justice system for delinquent youth until age 18. The traditional features of the rehabilitative paradigm will be preserved, i.e., the judicial discretion, decisions and judgments in function of the personality and environment of the minor. All the same time however, the Bill also introduces punitive elements, for a new "extended youth court" will be able to impose adult punishments. Besides, we also notice the introduction of the restorative Justice paradigm mediation and family group conferences will become important ways of handling juvenile delinquency. As a consequence, the new Bill reflects a wide variety of paradigms and stated goals: protection, retribution and restoration. Yet, little is known about the practical outcomes of the present policies concerning the effective reduction of delinquency. Belgian authorities do not have a coherent (research) policy in order to develop "evidence based programs" and to make prevention and intervention more effective and individual rights better respected. This is partially due to the complex division of competencies in the matter of juvenile justice between the Federal State and the Communities.

REFERENCES

Bazemore, G. and Walgrave, L. (eds.) (1999). *Restorative Juvenile Justice: Repairing the Harm of Youth Crime*. Monsey/New York: Criminal Justice Press.

Burssens, D., Goris, P., and Vettenburg, N. (2004). "Preventie en jeugd. Voorstellingen van een onderzoek," in D. Van Daele and I. Van Welzenis (eds.), *Actuele thema's uit het strafrecht en de criminologie*. Leuven: Universitaire Pers, pp. 103–121.

Born M. and Gavray C. (1994). "Selfreported delinquency in Liège, Belgium," in J. Junger-Tas, J. Terlouw, and M. Klein (eds.), *Delinquent Behaviour Among Young People in the Western World: First Results of the International Self Report Delinquency Study*. New York: Kugler Publications, pp. 131–155.

Centrum voor Beroepsvervolmaking in de Rechten (ed.) (2003). *Jongeren en recht*. Antwerpen: Intersentia.

Christiaens, J. (1999). "The juvenile delinquent and his welfare sanction," *European Journal of Crime, Criminal Law and Criminal Justice,* 1: 5–21.

Christiaens, J. and Dumortier, E. (2004). «Gemeenschapsdienst nu (toch) ook voor (nog) onschuldige jongeren?" *Nieuw Juridisch Weekblad*, 57: 74–97.

Declaration of Leuven (1999). "On the advisability of promoting the restorative approach to juvenile crime," in G. Bazemore and L. Walgrave (eds.), *Restorative Juvenile Justice: Repairing the Harm of Youth Crime*. Monsey: Criminal Justice Press, pp. 403–407.

Decock, G. and Vansteenkiste, Ph (1995). *Naar een jeugdsanctierecht (Implementation of a Youth Sanction Model)?* Gent: Mys & Breesch.

De Fraene, D. (2001). "L'évolution de la justice des mineurs et le pratiques restauratrices. Idéologie et réalités sociales," in Ph. Mary and T. Papatheodourou (eds.), *Délinquance et insécurité en Europe: vers une pénalisation du social? Crime and insecurity in Europe: a penal treatment of social issues?* Bruxelles: Bruylant, pp. 195–214.

Delens-Ravier, I. and Thibaut, C. (2002). "Jeunes délinquants et mesures judiciaires: la parole des jeunes, une synthèse," *Journal du Droit des Jeunes*, 215: 5–18.

De Naeyere, B. and Gossé, D. (2004). "Wat is de rol van de gespecialiseerde hoofdinspecteur?" *Politiejournaal-Politieofficier*, 1: 21–23.

Depoortere, H. (2002). "Bas! en de praktijk van de alternatieve sancties," in C. Eliaerts (ed.), *Constructief sanctioneren van jeugddelinquenten. Een commentaar bij vijf jaar werking van Bas!* Brussel: VUB Press, pp. 29–100.

De Vroede P. and Gorus J. (1997). *Inleiding tot het recht*. Antwerpen: Kluwer Rechtswetenschappen.

Devroede, N. (1997). "Les mesures de diversion: l'expérience du parquet de Bruxelles," in Ph. Mary (ed.), *Travail d'intérêt général et médiation pénale. Socialisation du pénal ou pénalisation du social*. Bruxelles: Bruylant, pp. 263–266.

De Witte, H., Hooge, J. and Walgrave, L. (eds.) (2000). *Jongeren in Vlaanderen: gemeten en geteld. 12- tot 18-jarigen over hun leefwereld en toekomst.* Leuven: Universitaire Pers.

Dumortier, E. (2000). "Herstelrechtelijk jeugdsanctierecht: een breuk met het beschermings-verleden" *Orde van de Dag*, 11: 27–34.

Dumortier, E. (2003). "Legal rights and safeguards within Belgian mediation practices for juve-niles," in E. Weitekamp and H.J. Kerner (eds.), *Restorative justice in context. International prac-tice and directions.* Devon: Willan Publishing, pp. 197–207.

Dupont, L. and Hutsebout, F. (eds.) (2001). *Herstelrecht tussen heden en verleden.* Leuven: Univer-sitaire Pers.

Eliaerts, C. (1999). "Jeugddelinquentie en jeugdrecht: een moeilijke relatie," in E. Verhellen et al. (eds.), *Kinderrechtengids.* Gent: Mys & Breesch, deel 1.8, pp. 1–48.

Eliaerts, C. (2001). "Zalven of slaan? Het eeuwige pendelen tussen hulp en straf in de jeugdbes-cherming," in C. Lis. and H. Soly (eds.), *Tussen dader en slachtoffer. Jongeren en criminaliteit in historisch perspectief.* Brussel: VUB Press, pp. 371–393.

Eliaerts, C. and Bitoune, R. (2001). "Herstelrecht voor minderjarigen. Theorie en praktijk," in L. Dupont and F. Hutsebout (eds.), *Herstelrecht tussen heden en verleden.* Leuven: Universitaire Pers, pp. 225–245.

Eliaerts, C. (ed.) (2002). *Constructief sanctioneren van jeugddelinquenten. Een commentaar bij vijf jaar werking van Bas!* Brussel: VUB Press.

Eliaerts, C. (2003). "Gerechtelijke bescherming van de jeugdigen. De wet van april 1965. In Centrum voor Beroepsvervolmaking," in de Rechten (ed.), *Jongeren en recht.* Antwerpen: Intersentia, pp. 135–174.

Eliaerts, C. and Dumortier, E. (2002). "Restorative justice and its need for procedural safeguards and standards," in E. Weitekamp and H.J. Kerner (eds.), *Restorative Justice: Theoretical Foun-dations.* Willan Publishing, pp. 204–223.

Eliaerts, C., Dumortier, E., and Vanderhaegen, R. (1998). "Critical assessment of community ser-vice and mediation for juvenile offenders in Brussels," in L. Walgrave (ed.), *Restorative Justice for Juveniles. Potentialities, Risks and Problems.* Leuven: Universitaire Press, pp. 351–366.

European Recommendation on Mediation in Penal Matters (N° R (99) 19), adopted by the Com-mittee of Ministers of the Council of Europe, 15 September 1999.

Florizoone, B. and Roose, R. (2000). "De bijzondere jeugdbijstand: feiten en cijfers," *Welzijnsgids – Welzijnszorg, Bijzondere jeugdbijstand*, 35: 87–130.

Geudens, H. (1999). "Gemeenschapsdienst en recidive. Een vergelijking met de traditionele jeug-dbeschermingsmaatregelen," *Tijdschrift voor Criminologie*, 1: 57–72.

Geudens, H. (2003). "Verwerking gegevens herstelbemiddeling voor minderjarige daders m.b.t. 2002," *Tijdschrift voor Jeugd en Kinderrechten*, 5: 269–283.

Geudens, H. (1996). *De toepassing van de gemeenschapsdienst in het kader van de Belgische jeugdbe-scherming. Deel 1: de doelgroep en de gerechtelijke context.* Leuven: K.U.Leuven Onderzoeks-groep Jeugdcriminologie.

Geudens, H. and Walgrave, L. (1996). "De toepassing van de gemeenschapsdienst door de Bel-gische jeugdrechtbanken," *Panopticon*, 5: 499–520.

Goedseels, E. (2001). "Onderzoek naar de toepassing en de effecten van een gemeenschapsdienst," *Nieuwsbrief Suggnomé*, 209: 14–25.

Goedseels E. (2002). "Cijfers met betrekking tot jeugddelinquentie," in L. Walgrave and P. Goris (eds.), *Van kattenkwaad en erger. Actuele thema's uit de jeugdcriminologie.* Leuven: Garant, pp. 29–38.

Goedseels E., Vettenburg N., and Walgrave L. (2000). "Delinquentie," in H. De Witte, J. Hooge, and L. Walgrave (eds.), *Jongeren in Vlaanderen: gemeten en geteld. 12- tot 18-jarigen over hun leefwereld en toekomst.* Leuven: Universitaire Pers, pp. 253–282.

Junger-Tas, J., Terlouw, J., and Klein, M. (eds.) (1994). *Delinquent Behaviour Among Young People in the Western World: First Results of the International Self-report Delinquency Study.* New York/ Amsterdam: Kugler Publications.

Lis, C. and Soly, H. (eds.). (2001). *Tussen dader en slachtoffer. Jongeren en criminaliteit in historisch perspectief*. Brussel: VUBPress.

Mary, Ph. (ed.) (1997). *Travail d'intérêt général et médiation pénale. Socialisation du pénal ou pénalisation du social*. Bruxelles: Bruylant.

Mary, Ph. and Papatheodourou, T. (eds.) (2001). *Délinquance et insécurité en Europe: vers une pénalisation du social? Crime and insecurity in Europe: a penal treatment of social issues?* Bruxelles: Bruylant.

Mary, Ph. (ed.) (2003). *Dix ans de contrats de sécurité: évaluation et actualité*. Bruxelles: Bruylant.

Mehlbye, J. and Walgrave, L. (eds.) (1998). *Confronting Youth in Europe. Juvenile Crime and Juvenile Justice*. Kopenhagen: AKF Forlaget.

Nuytiens, A., Spiesschaert, F., Vanthuyne, T., and Van Grunderbeeck, S. (2002). *Herstelgerichte afhandelingen van delicten gepleegd door minderjarigen: leerprojecten-gemeenschapsdienst-herstelbemiddeling. Eindrapport*, Een interuniversitair onderzoeksproject tussen de Vrije Universiteit Brussel, de Katholieke Universiteit Leuven en de Universiteit Gent.

Nuytiens, A., Christiaens, J. and Eliaerts, C. (2005). *Ernstige jeugddelinquenten gestraft? Praktijk van de uithandengeving*. Gent: Academia Press.

Ondersteuningsstructuur Bijzondere Jeugdzorg (OSBJ) (2003). *Cijfers*. Persconferentie 6 November 2003.

Onkelinx, L. (2004). *Kadernota betreffende de hervorming van de wet van 8 april 1965 betreffende de jeugdbescherming*, 13 February 2004.

Onkelinx, L. (2006). Wet tot wyziging van de wet van & April 1965 betreffende de jeugdbescherming, *Belgisch greatsblade,* 2 June 2006.

Puccio, G. (2001). *Invloed van de bemiddeling op de afhandelingspraktijk van het parket Leuven,* Ongepubliceerde licentiaatverhandeling. Brussel: VUB.

Put, J. and Senaeve, P. (2003). Compendium van het jeugdbeschermingsrecht. Leuven: Acco.

Smets J. and Cappelaere G. (1995). De gerechtelijke jeugdbescherming na de wet van 2 februari 1994 (deel II), *Panopticon*, 6: 369–392.

Spiesschaert, F., Vanthuyne, T., Van Dijk, C and Van Grunderbeeck, S. (2001). *Herstelgerichte afhandelingen van delicten gepleegd door minderjarigen: leerprojecten-gemeenschapsdiensten-herstelbemiddeling. Tussentijds rapport, eerste onderzoeksjaar,* Een interuniversitair onderzoeksproject tussen de Vrije Universiteit Brussel, de Katholieke Universiteit Leuven en de Universiteit Gent.

Strebelle, C. (2002). *Les contrats de sécurité. Evaluation des politiques de prevention en Belgique*. Bruxelles: Bruylant.

Terlouw, J. and Bruisma, G. (1994). "Selfreported Delinquency in the Netherlands," in J. Junger-Tas, J. Terlouw, and M. Klein (eds.), *Delinquent Behaviour Among Young People in the Western World: First Results of the International Self-report Delinquency Study*. New York: Kugler Publications, pp. 102–130.

Trepanier, J. (1993). *La justice réparatrice et les philosophies de l'intervention pénale sur les jeunes*. Paper presented at the 9th Journées internationales de criminologie juvénile, Vaucresson, June 1993.

Tulkens, F. and Moreau, T. (2000). *Droit de la jeunesse. Aide, assistance, protection*. Brussel: Larcier.

UN Preliminary Draft Elements of a Declaration of Basic Principles on the Use of Restorative Justice Programmes in Criminal matters, annexed to the ECOSOC Resolution 2000/30-E/CN.15/2000/7.

Van Daele, D. and Van Welzenis, I. (eds.). (2004). *Actuele thema's uit het strafrecht en de criminologie*. Leuven: Universitaire Pers.

Vanderhaegen, R. (1999). *Onderzoek naar de toepassing van alternatieve sancties in het gerechtelijk arrondissement Brussel-Halle-Vilvoorde*. Brussel: VUB, Vakgroep Criminologie.

Vanderhaegen, R. and Eliaerts, C. (2002). "Drie jaar onderzoek in het arrondissement Brussel-Halle-Vilvoorde," in C. Eliaerts (ed.), *Constructief sanctioneren van jeugddelinquenten. Een commentaar bij vijf jaar werking van Bas!* Brussel: VUB Press, pp. 182–221.

Van Dijk, C. (2004). Leerprojecten. Een vorm van herstel? *Tijdschrift voor Herstelrecht*, 4:20–33.

Van Dijk, C., Nuytiens, A., and Eliaerts, C. (2005). "The Referral of Juvenile Offenders in Belgium: Theory and Practice," *The Howard Journal*, 2:151–166.

Vanfraechem, I. (2002). *Een wetenschappelijk onderzoek over de toepassing van family group conferences (herstelgericht groepsoverleg) in Vlaanderen: eindrapport*. Leuven: KULeuven, Faculteit Rechtsgeleerdheid, Afdeling Strafrecht, Strafvordering en Criminologie.

Vanfraechem, I. (2003). *Herstelgericht groepsoverleg in Vlaanderen. Verslag van een wetenschappelijk begeleid pilootproject. Samenvatting*. Leuven: KULeuven, Faculteit Rechtsgeleerdheid, Afdeling Strafrecht, Strafvordering en Criminologie.

Van Ness, D. (1999). "Legal Issues of Restorative Justice," in G. Bazemore and L. Walgrave (eds.), *Restorative Juvenile Justice: Repairing the Harm of Youth Crime*. New York: Criminal Justice Press, pp. 263–284.

Vanneste, C. (2001). Een onderzoek over de beslissing en genomen door de parketmagistraten en de jeugdrechters. *Tijdschrift voor Jeugdrecht en Kinderrechten*, 5:193–202.

Vanneste, C. e.a. (2001). *Les décisions prises par les magistrats du parquet et les juges de la jeunesse à l'égard des mineurs delinquants. Rapport de recherche*. Brussel: NICC-afdeling criminologie.

Van Paesschen, N. (2000). Interview met F. Raes, jeugdrechter te Leuven, *Nieuwsbrief Suggnomé*, 2:7–11.

Verhellen, E. (1996). *Jeugdbeschermingsrecht*. Gent: Mys & Breesch.

Verhellen, E. et al. (eds.). (1999). *Kinderrechtengids*. Gent: Mys & Breesch.

VRIND (2003). Vlaamse regionale indicatoren. Brussel: Ministerie van de Vlaamse Gemeenschap, Administratie Planning en Statistiek.

Walgrave, L., Berx, E., Poels, V., and Vettenburg, N. (1998). "Belgium," in J. Mehlbye and L. Walgrave (eds.), *Confronting Youth in Europe. Juvenile Crime and Juvenile Justice*. Kopenhagen: AKF Forlaget, pp. 55–95.

Walgrave, L. (ed.) (1998). *Restorative Justice for Juveniles. Potentialities, Risks and Problems*. Leuven: Universitaire Press.

Walgrave, L. (2000). *Met het oog op herstel. Bakens voor een constructief jeugdsanctierecht*. Leuven: Universitaire Pres.

Walgrave, L. (ed.) (2002). *Restorative justice and the Law*. Cullompton: Willan.

Walgrave, L. and Goris, P. (eds.) (2002). *Van kattenkwaad en erger. Actuele thema's uit de jeugdcriminologie*. Leuven: Garant.

Weitekamp, E. and Kerner, H.J. (eds.) (2003). *Restorative justice in context. International practice and directions*. Devon: Willan Publishing.

http://www.Belgium.be

http://www.cfwb.be/aide-jeunesse/IPPJ/index.htm

http://www.dekamer.be

http://statbel.fgov.be

9

Juvenile Justice in Germany: Between Welfare and Justice

Frieder Dünkel

INTRODUCTION

Germany is situated in central Europe and shares borders with Denmark, Poland, the Czech Republic, Austria, Switzerland, France, Luxemburg, Belgium, and the Netherlands. The country has a geographical area of 357,026.55 km^2. With about 82 million inhabitants the population density is 231/km^2.

Germany, with its capital city Berlin, is a parliamentary democracy. Article 20 of the Constitution (*Grundgesetz*) defines the political system as "a democratic and social welfare state under the rule of law." Germany is a federal republic consisting of 16 federal states, which dispose of a certain degree of autonomy, particularly concerning questions of education and culture, but not in criminal and prison law as well as juvenile justice. Therefore, the same federal law applies for all federal states.

In 2004 the gross domestic product was €108 per capita and the unemployment rate lay at 12% (about 10% in West Germany; 20% in East Germany, i.e., the five states that formed the former German Democratic Republic before the reunification of Germany in 1990).

The age structure is as follows (1 January 2004): children under 8 years: 7.4%; children 8–14 years: 6.1%; juveniles 14–18 years: 4.7%; young adults 18–21 years: 3.4%; young adults 21–25 years: 4.8%; adults 25–30 years: 5.7%; adults 30–40 years: 15.5%; adults 40–50 years: 15.7%; adults 50–60 years: 12.0%; adults 60 years and older: 24.6%.

Approximately 9% (7.3 million) of the population has a foreign passport, of which 25% is of Turkish nationality. A further 25% comes from other EU member states, particularly from Italy, Greece, and Spain. Population growth in Germany has been on the decline for years despite the increase in the number of immigrants, which played a significant role in the 1980s and early 1990s. Immigrants from the former Soviet empire with German roots have been issued German passports and they are not classed as foreigners.

J. Junger-Tas and S. H. Decker (eds.), International Handbook of Juvenile Justice, 225–262.
© 2006 Springer.

1. HISTORICAL ASPECTS OF JUVENILE JUSTICE IN GERMANY: THE COMPROMISE BETWEEN WELFARE AND JUSTICE

The history of a system of specific social control for minors in Germany goes back to the beginning of the previous century. Since 1908, some courts, like those in Berlin, Frankfurt/Main, or Cologne, started developing special court chambers that specialised issues concerning young delinquents. Only after World War I could the idea of specific legislation successfully be pursued by opting for the "dualistic" approach of welfare *and* justice. Thus, in 1922, the Juvenile Welfare Act (JWA – *Jugendwohlfahrtsgesetz* of 1922) dealing with young persons in need of care was passed and in 1923 the Juvenile Justice Act (JJA – *Jugendgerichtsgesetz*, literally translated as the Juvenile Courts Act)[1] dealing with juvenile offenders who had committed a delinquent act prescribed by the general penal law (*Strafgesetzbuch*, StGB). A totally welfare oriented model of juvenile justice did not fit with the German "mentality," which remained intent upon keeping the penal option to deal with young offenders. The compromise was a "mixed" system of juvenile justice, combining elements of educational measures with legal guaranties and a procedural approach in general, which is characteristic of the justice model. The JJA did not create a new "juvenile penal law." Punishable crimes are the same as for adults, i.e., so-called status offences do not form an element of the JJA. The JJA consists of a specific system of reactions/sanctions applicable to young offenders and of some specific procedural rules for the juvenile court and its proceedings (e.g., the principle of non-public trials).

In comparison with the general penal law for adults the legislator of 1923 for the first time "opened the floor" for *educational measures instead of punishment* (the corresponding slogan was *Erziehung statt Strafe*), particularly of imprisonment. Also opened was the possibility to abandon the otherwise strictly applied principle of obligatory prosecution (principle of legality, *Legalitätsprinzip*). The JJA thus was a forerunner of the notion of giving the prosecutor a discretion whether to, and how to, prosecute or to dismiss a case because of the petty nature of the offence or educational measures taken by other institutions or persons (see §§ 45, 47 JJA and below). The third pillar of innovation of the 1923 legislation was to increase the age of criminal responsibility from 12 to 14 years.

In this context one can mention that only in the period of the Nazi regime between 1933 and 1945 was the 12- to 14-year age group "re-criminalised" for certain offences and behaviour. Today, the lowering of the age of criminal responsibility is only an issue (of a more rhetoric or symbolic nature, particularly in times of elections) for a few conservative politicians of the Christian Democratic

---

[1]The literal translation of *Jugendgerichtsgesetz* reflects the historical roots of the JJA. It goes back to the adjudication of specialised judges of youth chambers at some courts of bigger cities like Berlin, Cologne or Frankfurt. The *Jugendgerichtsbewegung* ("movement for establishing juvenile courts") had a major influence on the first JJA in 1923 (see Schaffstein/Beulke, 2002: 34 ff.)

Parties (CDU/CSU), but without any chance of being accepted by the majority of the political parties.

The law of 1923 and the amendments that followed did not define the principle of "education". History has demonstrated that this lack of precise definition of "education" – under certain ideologies – can lead to a totally different meaning and use of the educational principle. Thus the Nazis defined "education" as *education by* (not instead of) *punishment*, i.e., a certain repressive meaning of education prevailed. The introduction of so-called disciplinary measures, particularly the short-term detention centre (up to four weeks of detention as a short sharp shock), by an administrative decree of 1940 and an amendment to the JJA in 1943 can be seen as a demonstration of the repressive *Zeitgeist* of the Nazi era.

After World War II the legislator decided to keep these measures, as they also existed in other European legislation (see e.g., the British detention centre). The reforms of the Nazi system are ambivalent insofar as they also included educational innovations that had been discussed in the previous era of the Weimar democracy of the 1920s. On the other hand it can be seen that a totalitarian ideology of education was linked to the general totalitarian ideology of the Nazis (see Wolff, 1986; 1989).

The Juvenile Welfare Act of 1922 was a classic law providing intervention in the sense of the "parens patriae" doctrine. The state replaces parents who are not able or willing to fulfil their educational duties. The educational measures were similar to or even the same as the educational measures stipulated in the Juvenile Justice Act, like supervisory directives, care orders, orders to improve the educational abilities of parents, placement in a foster family or in residential care, etc. In the years that followed the interventions of the JWA were neither changed nor criticised very much. However, in the late 1960s, following social and political movements and changes, the reform debate emerged. The main criticism concerned closed institutions ("homes") as stipulated by the JWA; in the field of the JJA the concern was the disciplinary measures, particularly youth detention of up to four weeks (a kind of shock incarceration for repressive purposes). The reform movement in the early 1970s was strongly in favour of a unified welfare model (excluding classic sanctions of the justice model as far as possible). However, this idea was abandoned in 1974 already (see in detail Schaffstein and Beulke, 2002: 41ff.). Thereafter reform proposals were made under the dualistic approach of separate welfare and justice legislation. Finally, in 1990, the JWA was replaced by a modern law of social welfare (under the concept of the *Sozialstaat*). The juvenile welfare boards should function as a help and offer help, not as agents of "intervention." At least in theory, the repressive measures of education, like the detention in secure (closed) residential care ("homes") have been abolished. In the late 1980s and early 1990s a few closed welfare institutions were re-opened (about 150 places in total in some federal states – which is about 0.2% of all measures of placement in the welfare system; see Sonnen, 2002: 330).

The juvenile justice system has experienced major changes since the 1970s. This has happened without any legislative amendmend and has been called "reform through practice" (*Jugendstrafrechtsreform durch die Praxis*), meaning that innovative projects have been developed by social workers, juvenile court prosecutors and judges. As a consequence the number of juvenile prison sentences in the 1980s were reduced considerably after the introduction of "new" community sanctions (see Section 5 and Heinz, 2003).

2. THE SANCTIONS SYSTEM OF THE GERMAN JUVENILE JUSTICE ACT (JJA – *JUGENDGERICHTSGESETZ*, JGG)

In cases of crimes the interventions of the JJA are characterised by the principle of "subsidiarity" or "minimum intervention" (see the diagramme at the end of the article).[2] This means that penal action should only be taken if absolutely necessary. Furthermore, sanctions must be limited by the principle of proportionality. The legislative reform of the JJA in 1990, passcd in the same year as that of the JWA, underlines the principle of juvenile court sanctions as a last resort (*ultima ratio*). Therefore, the primary sanctions of the juvenile court are educational or disciplinary measures.

The most important response to petty offences is the dismissal of the case without any sanction. In this context one should emphasise that police diversion, like the British form of cautioning, is not allowed in Germany. The underlying reasoning is the abuse of police power that occurred under the Nazi regime. Therefore all forms of diversion are provided for only at the level of the juvenile court prosecutor or the juvenile court judge. The police are strictly bound by the principle of legality. All criminal offences have to be referred to the public prosecutor. The situation is different from the one in England where police cautioning plays a considerable role.

The 1990 reform of the Juvenile Justice Act in Germany extended the legal possibilities for diversion considerably. The legislature has thus reacted to the reforms that have been developed in practice since the end of the 1970s (see Bundesministerium der Justiz, 1989; Heinz in Dünkel/van Kalmthout/Schüler-Springorum, 1997). The law now emphasises the discharge of juvenile and young adult offenders because of the petty nature of the crime committed or because

---

[2]The application of the JJA is restricted to crimes defined by the general penal law (StGB). The Juvenile Welfare Act (JWA) is applied when a child or juvenile in his personal development seems to be "in danger" and needs help or measures provided by the JWA. The measures are chosen according to the estimated educational needs. They are not imposed in an "interventionist" style, but offered and taken according to a request of the parents. Partially, the measures are the same as the ones provided by the JJA (e.g., social training courses, special care). The residential care order exists in both laws, too. If the youth welfare department wants to bring a child or juvenile to such a home (against the parents' will), it must ask the family court judge for a specific order. Such homes are usually open facilities.

of other social and/or educational interventions that have taken place (see § 45 (1) and (2) JJA). Efforts to make reparation to the victim or to participate in victim-offender reconciliation (mediation) are explicitly put on par with such educational measures. There is no restriction concerning the nature of offences; also felony offences (*Verbrechen*) can be "diverted" under certain circumstances, e.g., a robbery, if the offender has repaired the damage or made another form of apology (restitution/reparation) to the victim.[3]

Four levels of diversion can be differentiated. Diversion without any sanction (*non-intervention*) is given priority in cases of petty offences. Diversion with measures taken by other agencies (parents, the school) or in combination with mediation is the second level (*diversion with education*). The third level is *diversion with intervention*. In these cases the prosecutor proposes that the juvenile court judge impose a minor sanction, such as a warning, community service (usually between 10 and 40 hours), mediation (*Täter-Opfer-Ausgleich*), participation at a training course for traffic offenders (*"Verkehrsunterricht"*) or certain obligations like reparation/restitution, an apology to the victim, community service or a fine (§ 45 (3) JJA). Once the young offender has fulfilled these obligations, the juvenile court prosecutor will dismiss the case in cooperation with the judge. The fourth level is the introduction of levels one to three at the juvenile court proceedings after the charge has been filed. Fairly often in practice the juvenile court judge will face the situation that the young offender has, in the mean time (after the prosecutor has filed the charge), undergone some educational measure like mediation, and therefore a formal court seems unnecessary. Section 47 of the JJA enables the judge to dismiss the case in these instances.

Also *formal sanctions of the juvenile court* are structured according to the *principle of minimum intervention* (*Subsidiaritätsgrundsatz*; see the diagramme at the end of the text). Juvenile imprisonment has been restricted to a sanction of last resort, if educational or disciplinary measures seem to be inappropriate (see §§ 5 and 17 (2) JJA). The reform of the Juvenile Justice Act of 1990 extended the catalogue of juvenile sanctions by introducing new community sanctions like community service, the special care order (*Betreuungsweisung*), the social training course (see Dünkel, Geng, and Kirstein, 1998) and mediation (see Dünkel, 1996, 1999; Bannenberg, 1993). The educational measures of the juvenile court, furthermore, comprise different forms of directives concerning the everyday life of juvenile offenders in order to educate and to prevent dangerous situations. Thus the judge can forbid contact with certain persons and prohibit going to certain places ("whereabouts," see § 10 JJA). Disciplinary measures comprise of the formal warning, community service, a fine and detention of one or two weekends or up to four weeks in a special juvenile detention centre (*Jugendarrest*).

---

[3]The situation is different in the general penal law for adults (between 18 and 21 years old) where diversion according to §§ 153 ff. of the Criminal Procedure Act is restricted to misdemeanours. Felony offences (i.e., crimes with a minimum prison sentence provided by law of one year) are excluded.

Youth imprisonment is executed in separate juvenile prisons (see § 92 JJA). Youth prison sentences are only a sanction of last resort (*ultima ratio*, see §§ 5 (2), 17 (2) JJA), in line with the view espoused by international rules like the so-called Beijing-Rules of the United Nations of 1985.[4] The minimum length of youth imprisonment is six months, the maximum five years, for 14- to 17-year-old juveniles. In cases of very serious crimes for which adults could be punished with more than ten years of imprisonment, the maximum length of youth imprisonment is ten years. In the case of 18- to 20-year-old young adults sentenced according to the JJA (see Section 4) the maximum penalty is ten years, too (see §§ 18, 109 JJA). The preconditions for youth imprisonment are either the "dangerous tendencies" of the offender that are likely to exclude community sanctions as inappropriate, or the "gravity of guilt" concerning particular, serious crimes (e.g., murder, aggravated robbery; see § 17 (2) JJA).[5]

Youth imprisonment sentences of up to two years can be suspended in case of a favourable prognosis; in all cases the probation service gets involved. The period of probationary supervision is one to two years; the period of probation two to three years.

3. HUMAN RIGHTS ASPECTS OF CRIMINAL PROCEDURE IN THE JUVENILE JUSTICE SYSTEM

Juvenile justice systems, particularly those following the welfare model, are often criticised for failing to guarantee human rights. Compared to the general criminal procedure for adults, the right of access to a legal defence counsel or other basic human rights issues, seem to be underdeveloped and some critical scholars denounce the juvenile justice system as "second class justice."

The German juvenile justice system shares these criticisms only to a very minor extent, as in general the legal procedural rules are very similar for juvenile and adult criminal justice. The JJA states that the procedural rules, e.g., the rules of evidence, are the same as for general criminal procedure. Deviations from this general rule are based on educational aims. So, for example, the court hearings are not open to the public (see § 48 JJA) in order to protect the juvenile's privacy and to avoid stigmatisation. In juvenile trials the participation of the so-called social court assistant (*Jugendgerichtshilfe*), i.e., a social worker of the community

---

[4]See United Nations, 1991; Dünkel, 1994: 43; No. 17.1. of the Beijing Rules restricts youth imprisonment only to cases of serious violent crimes or repeated violent or other crimes if there seems to be no other appropriate solution.

[5]The precondition of "dangerous tendencies" for imposing a prison sentence is very often heavily criticised as it provides stigmatisation and possibly contributes to an "inflation" of prison sentences where the juvenile court judge cannot find appropriate alternatives, see Dünkel, 1990: 466f.; law reform proposals urge for abolishing the term "dangerous tendencies" and for keeping only the precondition of the "gravity of guilt," see Albrecht, 2002; Deutsche Vereinigung für Jugendgerichte und Jugendgerichtshilfen, 2002; Dünkel, 2002 with further references.

youth welfare department, is required (see § 38 (2) JJA). They have to prepare a social report and are required to participate in the court trial in order to give evidence about the personal background of the juvenile and to assist the judge in finding the appropriate sanction. The right to a defence counsel, in principle, is more extended in the juvenile justice system, as every juvenile who is put in pre-trial detention has to have an advocate appointed immediately (see § 68 No. 4 JJA), whereas in criminal cases for adults this right is realised only after having suffered three months of pre-trial detention. Furthermore, there are restrictions for imposing pre-trial detention on juveniles, particularly for 14- and 15-year-old offenders (see § 72 (2) JJA). Residential care in a juvenile home should always be given priority to pre-trial detention. The reality, however, sometimes indicates that the legal preconditions are not always complied with. Therefore the criticism against inappropriate forms of pre-trial detention cannot be refuted.

Another problematic issue is the appeal against juvenile court decisions. A court decision cannot be appealed solely in order to receive another educational measure (see § 55 (1) JJA). This seems to be problematic in cases where the judge imposes a rather "severe" educational measure like several hundreds of hours of community service. Unlike in other countries in Germany the community service order is not limited by a maximum period (in Austria e.g. 80 hours, in other countries 120–240 hours). Thus, in individual cases, a violation of the principle of proportionality has been observed.

Another critical issue concerning the system of judicial review in juvenile justice is that the juvenile can only appeal once, either to the district court (*Landgericht*) in order to get a second hearing, or to the high court of a federal state (*Oberlandesgericht*) for a review of legal questions (see § 55 (2) JJA). This shortening of review procedures has been introduced in order to speed up trials and to enforce the educational approach of juvenile justice. However, from a legal and human rights perspective this puts juveniles at a disadvantage compared to their adult counterparts. On the other hand, juveniles profit from the exclusion of a joint procedure by the victim or their representative counsel (*Nebenklage*) and of the so-called private criminal procedure (*Privatklage*, i.e., the private charge if the public prosecutor refuses prosecution in the public interest), both of which are disallowed in the juvenile justice system (see § 80 (1), (3) JJA).

A few (practically unimportant) rules disadvantage juveniles for the sake of educational concepts. For example, the period of pre-trial detention shall not be taken into account if the remaining period of a juvenile prison sentence is less than six months and therefore estimated as being insufficient for the educational process of reintegration (see § 52a JJA).

In general one can say that the orientation of the German juvenile criminal procedure to preserve fundamental rights is quite well developed and that disadvantages compared to adults are restricted to more exceptional cases. Thus the German juvenile justice system does not share the shortcomings of welfare systems relying more on informal procedures (e.g., round tables, family conferences) than on formal legal rights.

4. TRENDS IN JUVENILE DELINQUENCY, PARTICULARLY OF VIOLENT OFFENCES

In Germany no longitudinal studies of victimisation and delinquency on the basis of representative surveys, like in the USA or some European countries, exist. Police and court-based data are, besides the well-known shortcomings, problematic as the counting methods were changed in the 1970s and 1980s. Thus, more or less comparable data is at our disposal only from 1984 onwards. These indicate that juvenile delinquency has been stable or has even slightly decreased in the 1980s up until 1989, and then increased until the mid-1990s. From then onward a rather stable rate of young offenders and of violent offenders, in particular, can be seen when looking on the rates of convicted offenders (see Figs. 9.1–9.3).[6] Police data indicate, however, a stabilisation only for robbery offenders, whereas serious and bodily injury after 1993 was still increasing for juveniles and young adults. A particular increase can be observed in the five new federal states of former East Germany (Brandenburg, Mecklenburg-Western Pomerania, Thuringia, Saxony, Saxony-Anhalt). The rates for certain offences, particularly violent offences, even surmounted the ratio of the western federal states (see Fig. 9.4). In the last eight

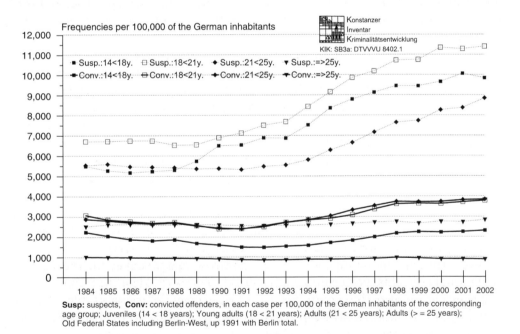

Susp: suspects, **Conv:** convicted offenders, in each case per 100,000 of the German inhabitants of the corresponding age group; Juveniles (14 < 18 years); Young adults (18 < 21 years); Adults (21 < 25 years); Adults (> = 25 years); Old Federal States including Berlin-West, up 1991 with Berlin total.

FIGURE 9.1. Male German suspects and convicted offenders by age groups, 1984–2002. All offences (without traffic offences).

[6]For a comprehensive overview of the development of juvenile crime in Germany see Bundesministerium des Inneren/Bundesministerium der Justiz, 2001; for a similar development in other European countries see Estrada, 1999, 2001.

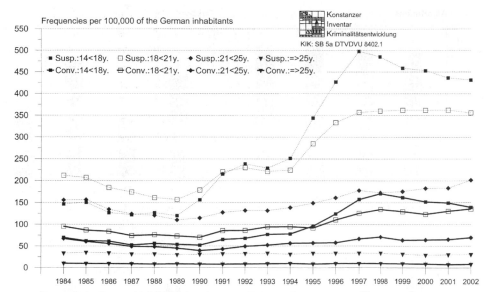

FIGURE 9.2. Male German suspects and convicted offenders by age groups, 1984–2002. Robbery (sect. 249–256, 316a PC).

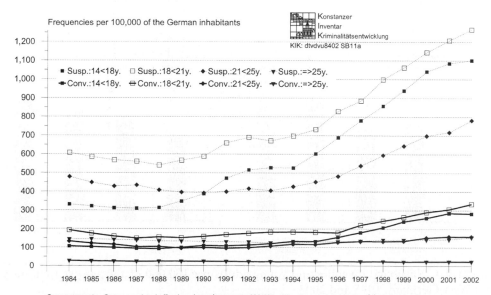

FIGURE 9.3. Male German suspects and convicted offenders by age groups, 1984–2002. Serious and dangerous bodily injury.

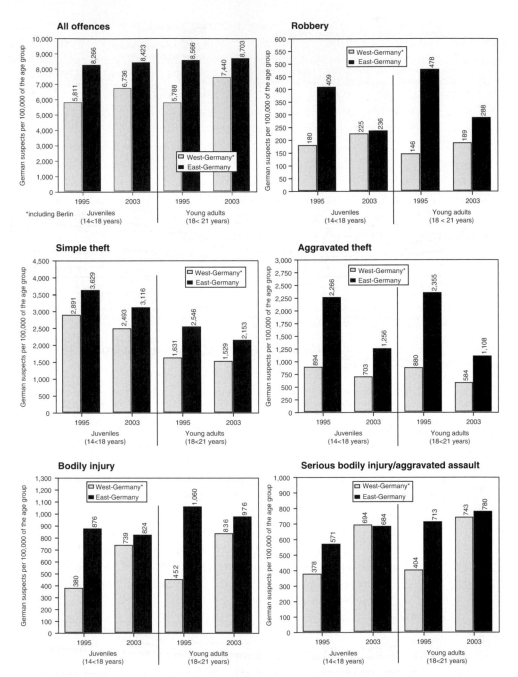

FIGURE 9.4. Suspected juveniles and young adults per 100,000 of the age group in East- and West-Germany, 1995 and 2003.

years however the violent and other young offender crime rates in West and East Germany have grown closer together because of an increase in West and a stabilisation or even reduction in East Germany. This development could be interpreted as a kind of normalisation after a period of particular problems of social transition and anomie or normlessness in East Germany.

Young migrants and members of ethnic minorities have become a major problem for the criminal justice system in Germany. They are over represented particularly concerning violent offences. For the time period of 1984–97 83% of the increase of the police registered juvenile and young adult offender's crime rate (persons aged between 14 and 21) is due to foreign citizens (see Pfeiffer et al., 1998: 48). Most of these foreigners are born in Germany. The Turkish minority plays a specific role in this problem. Self-report studies reveal that the rate of violent offenders is double as high in the Turkish compared to the German juvenile age group (Pfeiffer et al., 1998: 81). Looking at different groups of ethnic minorities or foreigners up to 1993 asylum seekers played a predominant role explaining the increase of the general crime rate, but also the increase of pre-trial detainees and sentenced prisoners. This problem has disappeared after a change of immigration legislation in 1993 reducing the flux of immigration considerably.

A specific problem has emerged with the *Aussiedler*, regularly people from the former empire of the Soviet Union with a German passport, who show severe problems of integration because of language deficiencies and other problems. They often are sentenced for serious violent crimes and build a rather explosive prison subculture (see Dünkel, 2005; Dünkel and Walter, 2005).

All the phenomena described here concerning young migrants and ethnic minorities are only valid for the old federal states of former West Germany. The East German *Länder* in so far face very different crime problems. These are connected with the German native population. As there live very few foreigners they do not really contribute to the crime problem. However, they deserve particular interest as they are over represented as victims of violent crimes, particularly committed by xenophobic or right wing extremists (see Dünkel, Geng, and Kunkat, 2001; Dünkel and Geng, 2003). However, right wing extremist and xenophobic attitudes as well as self-reported violent crime since 1998 in East Germany has declined, too (see Wilmers et al., 2002: 101 ff.; Sturzbecher, 2001; Dünkel and Geng, 2003; all with further references).

There are many possible reasons for the increase of crime, and particularly violent crime, that occurred after the German reunification and the opening of borders in Eastern Europe in general and the concomitant social changes. One of the most popular explanations is Heitmeyer's theory of social disintegration (see Heitmeyer, 1992; Heitmeyer et al., 1996). The East German development can also be connected with the increase of opportunity structures and a lack of social control at the beginning of the 1990s, when police forces where re-established. One general argument for explaining the violent crime increase of the 1990s is a changed sensibility to and reporting rate of violent crimes. One of the very few longitudinal victimisation studies that was conducted by Schwind et al. in the city of Bochum in 1975, 1986, and 1998 showed that a changed reporting rate accounted for the major portion of the increase of violent offences (assault/serious bodily injury; see Schwind et al., 2001). Thus the officially registered assault rate increased by 128%; the non-reported rate only by 9%. The overall increase was only 24% from 1975 to 1998. What really had changed considerably, was the reporting rate: whereas in 1975, 7.2 unreported crimes were added to one reported crime, in 1998 the ratio was only 3.4:1. That means that the dark figure had diminished by half and the "real" increase of violent crime is much less impressive than police data would suggest (see Table 9.1).

Another important statement is that the development of police registered crime rates is not on par with court-based crime rates. The increase of sentenced young offenders is much less important than one would presume when looking at the police data. This can be seen in Figs. 9.1–9.3. The gap between police registered and convicted (sentenced) young offenders has increased considerably. One reason is the practice of diversion by juvenile court prosecutors and judges (see Section 5), which partly is the result of an increase particularly of petty property offences. There are, however, indicators that reported violent offences too often are not very serious crimes and therefore available for mediation and diversion as well (see Pfeiffer et al., 1998). For instance, in Hannover during the 1990s, apparently, robberies with very minor damages (of less than 15 euros) have increased.

Although violent crime rates, particularly robbery and (serious) bodily injury increased in the early 1990s, it is still true that the vast majority of juveniles and young adults are not violent offenders. Non-violent property offences make for about 70% of all crimes reported for young offenders (see Bundesministerium des Inneren/Bundesministerium der Justiz, 2001; Walter, 2001: 201ff.; H.-J. Albrecht, 2002, D 32). The victims of such crimes regularly are the peers of young offenders. Victims of violent adult offenders very often also are children or young persons (see, e.g, the crimes of sexual child abuse or child maltreatment). Considering also domestic violence the First Periodic Security Report (*Erster Periodischer Sicherheitsbericht*) of the German government states: "Young persons deserve

TABLE 9.1. Development of police registered and not registered violent crimes (assault) in Bochum 1975–1998

	1975	1998	*Changes: 1998 compared to 1975 (%)*
Police registered offences	865	1,976	+128
Non reported offences	6,214	6,772	+9
Police registered *and* non reported offences	7,079	8,748	+24
ratio of reported to non reported offences	1:7.2	1:3.4	

Source: Schwind et al. (2001: 140).

attention and the protection of society not so much as perpetrators than as victims of violent crimes" (Bundesministerium des Inneren/Bundesministerium der Justiz, 2001: 2).

Violent and other crime is not equally distributed over the different regions. It is more widespread in cities than in rural areas and the official crime rates indicate an elevated prevalence rate in the northern compared to the southern federal states of Germany (to the differences between East and West Germany, see Fig. 9.4). If these differences are "real" or the product of different reporting and selection strategies, is not so clear. Looking at the different federal states, an interesting observation is that the relatively high police-registered general crime rates for juveniles and young adults in the northern and north-eastern states like Bremen, Berlin, Hamburg, Schleswig-Hostein, Mecklenburg-Western Pomerania, or Brandenburg, in comparison with those of southern states like Bavaria or Baden-Württemberg, diminish if we take the ratio of court-sentenced young persons (always calculated per 100,000 of the age group). The ratio of sentenced young offenders in the southern states is even higher than in the above mentioned northern states (see Figs. 9.5 and 9.6). This is not only a result of different reporting rates, but of very distinct and different styles of diversion as will be amplified upon in Section 5.

5. SENTENCING PRACTICE IN THE GERMAN JUVENILE JUSTICE SYSTEM (DIVERSION AND JUVENILE COURT DISPOSITIONS IN PRACTICE)

Diversion became the principal reaction utilised in the 1980s in juvenile justice in West Germany. In this context it has to be stressed that police registered crime of juveniles during the 1980s had been rather stable; violent crimes had even diminished (see Heinz, 2001a). The extension of diversion even continued in the 1990s when official crime rates and particularly of violent offences increased (see 4. above). A real increase of crime took place after the opening of the borders in Eastern Europe and the occurrence of phenomena of anomie and social disintegration in the youth subcultures in West, but particularly in the East German federal states. The rate of young violent offenders registered by the police in East Germany until 1995 has tripled; since then it has been stable or has slightly decreased.[7] The practice of using diversion as a measure of controlling the input into the juvenile justice system clearly can be shown in the Eastern federal states as well as in the "city-states" Berlin, Bremen, and Hamburg. The elevated crime rates in these states have been reduced by a more extensive diversion practice.

---

[7]From 1995 onward one can observe a (slightly) diminishing juvenile crime rate in East Germany and a increasing crime rate in West Germany (also concerning violent offences), which results in a "convergent" situation in both parts of Germany, see Heinz, 2003.

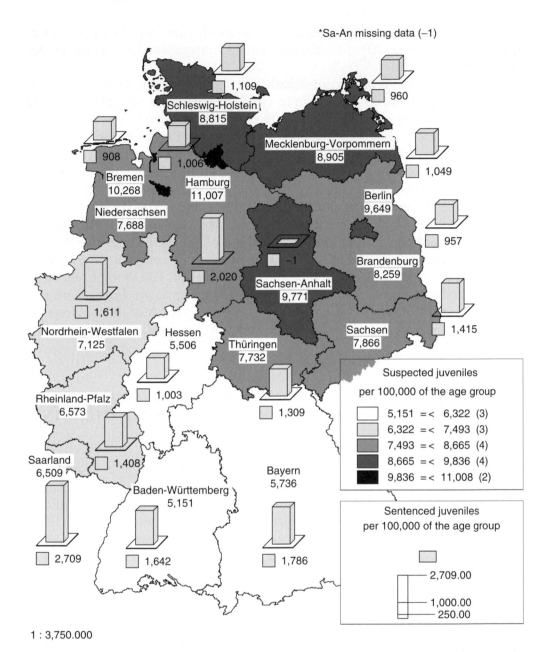

FIGURE 9.5. Suspected and sentenced German juveniles in a comparison of the federal states in 2003.

Before the law reform the discharge rates (diversion) in West Germany had already increased from 43% in 1980 to 56% in 1989. The steady increase continued to 69% in 2003 (see Heinz, 1994, 2003; Heinz in Dünkel, van Kalmthout, and Schüler-Springorum, 1997). It should be stressed that the increase concerns particularly diversion without intervention (according to § 45 (1) JJA), whereas the

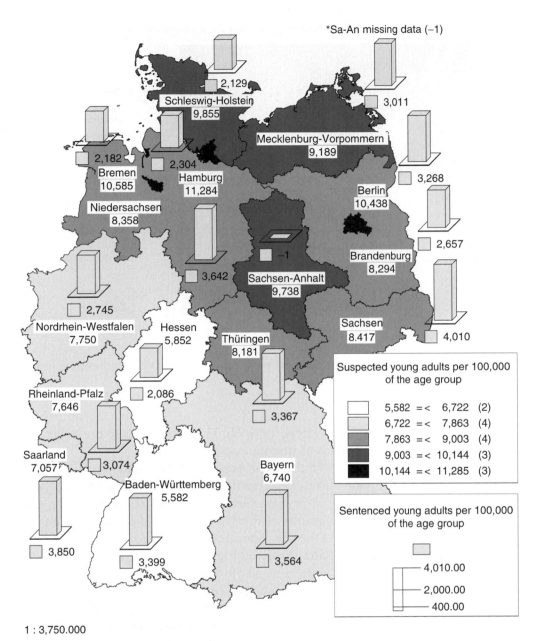

FIGURE 9.6. Suspected and sentenced 18–21 year old German young adults in a comparison of the federal states in 2003.

proportion of diversion combined with educational measures remained stable (see Fig. 9.7).

However, the large regional disparities had not been eliminated. The discharge rates varied in 2003 between 61% in Bavaria and 85% in Bremen or 84% in Hamburg. Apparently in all the federal states of Germany discharge rates in cities are higher

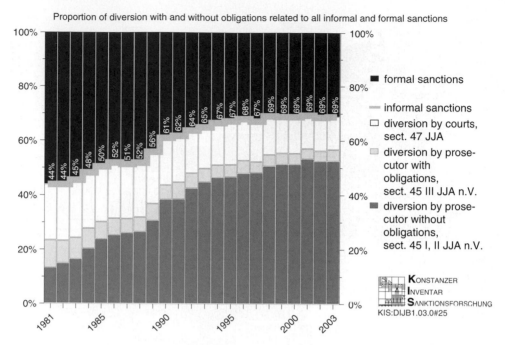

FIGURE 9.7. Diversion rates (dismissals by prosecutors or courts) in the juvenile justice system of Germany, old Federal States, 1981–2003.

than in the rural areas (see Heinz, 1994, 1998/99). This contributes to the rather stable conviction rates and caseloads of juvenile court judges.

It is interesting to compare the diversion practice of East and West Germany. Statistics for a comparison have only recently become available. It had been presumed that the penal culture in East Germany would be more severe and repressive. However, first calculations of diversion rates gave evidence of a even wider extended diversion rate in the new federal states with an overall rate of 77% (Brandenburg even 82%; see Heinz, 2003 and Figs. 9.8 and 9.9). In Mecklenburg-Western Pomerania statistical data is available since 2001. Its diversion rate of 82% is similar to the other new federal states (see Dünkel, Scheel, and Schäpler, 2003). Here too, the "economic" strategy of controlling the input and workload of the juvenile courts is evident. There is, however, also another explanation that seems to be plausible. The expanded diversion rates could also be a reaction to different reporting behaviour. In East Germany possibly more petty offences are reported to the police, which later are excluded from further prosecution by the juvenile court prosecutors.

The strategy of expanding informal sanctions has proved to be an effective means, not only to limit the juvenile court's workload, but also with respect to special prevention. The reconviction rates of those first-time offenders that were "diverted" instead of formally sanctioned were significantly lower. The

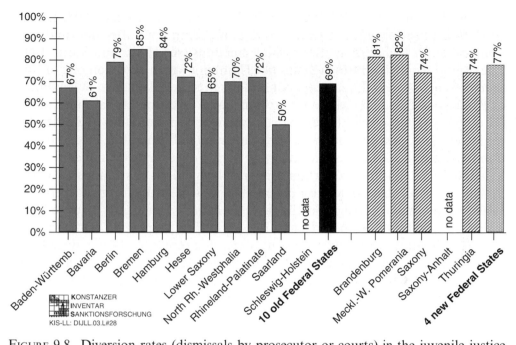

FIGURE 9.8. Diversion rates (dismissals by prosecutor or courts) in the juvenile justice system of Germany in comparison of the Federal States, 2003.

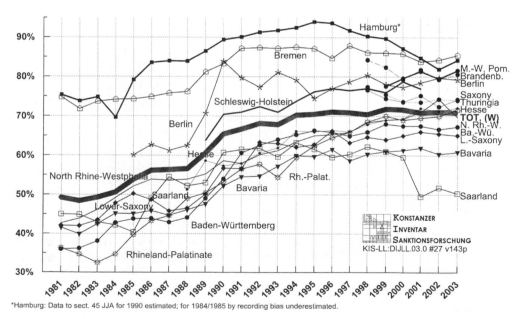

*Hamburg: Data to sect. 45 JJA for 1990 estimated; for 1984/1985 by recording bias underestimated.

FIGURE 9.9. Diversion rates (dismissals by prosecutror or courts) in the juvenile justice system of Germnany in comparison of the Federal States, 1981–2003.

re-offending rates were 27%:36% (see Fig. 9.10 and Heinz, 1994, 2003; Dünke,l 2003: 94). Even for repeat offenders the re-offending rates after informal sanctions were not higher than after formal sanctions (see Heinz and Storz, 1992). The overall recidivism rates in States like Hamburg with a diversion rate of more than 80% or 90% was the same (about 25%) as in States like Baden-Württemberg or Rhineland-Palatinate where the proportion of diversion at that time counted for only about 40%. Thus the extended diversionary practice has had at least no negative consequences concerning the crime rate and general or special prevention. It also reflects the episodic and petty nature of juvenile delinquency.

At the same time the proportion of "formal" sanctions has diminished to only 31% of all cases that could have entered the system at the juvenile court level. Interestingly, major changes in the juvenile court's sentencing practice in the 1980s and 1990s can be observed (see Fig. 9.11). The proportion of the sanction of sentencing to short-term custody in a detention centre has been reduced from 11% to only 6% (which amounts to a reduction of 45%) in the West German federal states. Unconditional youth imprisonment (six months up to five, in exceptional cases, to ten years, see Section 2) accounts only for 1.5%; the suspended

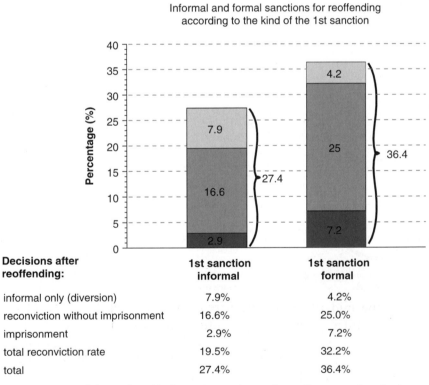

Informal and formal sanctions for reoffending
according to the kind of the 1st sanction

Decisions after reoffending:	1st sanction informal	1st sanction formal
informal only (diversion)	7.9%	4.2%
reconviction without imprisonment	16.6%	25.0%
imprisonment	2.9%	7.2%
total reconviction rate	19.5%	32.2%
total	27.4%	36.4%

FIGURE 9.10. Rates of formal and informal sanctions after a first sanction for larceny and a risk period of 3 years (juveniles, cohort 1961).

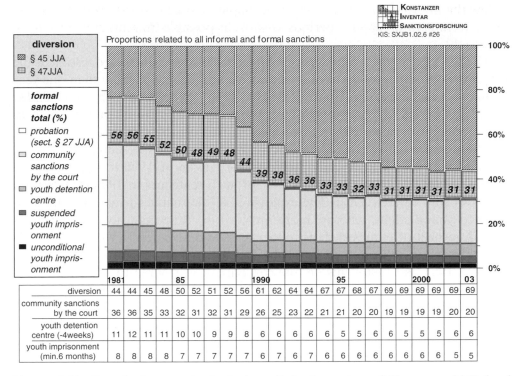

FIGURE 9.11. Sanctioning practice in the juvenile justice system of Germany. old Federal States, 1981–2003.

youth prison sentence for 3.5% of all formal and informal sanctions against 14- to 21- year-old offenders. The reduction of youth prison sentences from 8% to 5% means a 38% reduction over the time period since 1981. This is remarkable insofar as in the 1990s the proportion of youth prison sentences has remained stable, although the number of violent offenders has increased considerably. The reduction of community sanctions by the court from 36% to 20% is attributable to the extended diversion practice.

About 70% of youth prison sentences are suspended (combined with the supervision of a probation officer). Prison sentences of up to one year since the mid-1970s are suspended in about 80% of the cases. Even the longer prison sentences of up to two years now are suspended in about 60% of the cases, whereas in the mid-1970s this occurred only in exceptional cases (less than 20%). The extended practice of probation and suspended sentences (even for repeat offenders) has been a great success, as the revocation rates dropped to only about 30%. The probation service apparently has improved its efficiency, but on the other hand, the courts also have changed their practice by trying to avoid a revocation of the suspended sentence for as long as possible (see Dünkel, 2003: 96ff.). Again it becomes clear that German juvenile court judges follow the internationally recognised principle of youth imprisonment as a last resort (*ultima ratio*) and for periods as short as possible (minimum intervention approach).

The average length of youth prison sentences has slightly increased insofar as the proportion of sentences up to one year decreased, the one of more than one year up to two years increased. However this has been "compensated" by an extended rate of suspended sentences (see below). The proportion of youth prison sentences of more than two or more than three years remained stable (see Fig. 9.12).

The practice of repeatedly suspending even youth prison sentences between one and two years had already preceded the reform of 1990 to a great extent by the suspension of not less than 54% of such sentences in 1990 (the ratio in 2003 went up to even 59%). The expansion of alternatives to youth imprisonment to young adults, who are more involved in crime than juveniles, particularly in respect of crimes such as robbery, have contributed to the considerable decline, by about 40%, in the rate of imprisonment of juveniles and young adults between 1983 and 1990. This decline can only be attributed to a limited extent (5%) to demographic changes. Since 1990 the youth prisoners' rates, however, have increased considerably. But as can be shown by Figs. 9.13 and 9.14, for crimes of robbery and assault this is not a result of more severe punishment by way of longer prison sentences, but simply because of the increase of the absolute figures of sentenced persons.

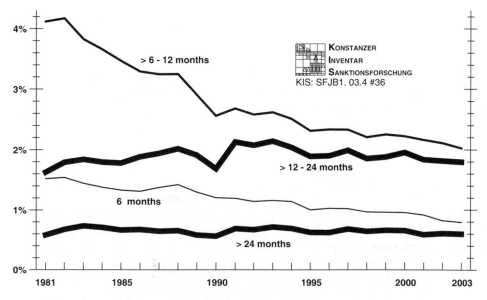

Rate of youth prison sentences 7,8 8,2 7,9 7,5 7,2 7,2 7,2 7,4 6,7 6,0 6,7 6,5 6,6 6,4 5,8 5,9 6,0 5,7 5,8 5,8 5,5 5,4 5,2

= proportion of youth prison sentences related to all formally and informally sentenced juveniles and young adults

FIGURE 9.12. Length of youth prison sentences under juvenile criminal law, 1981–2003.

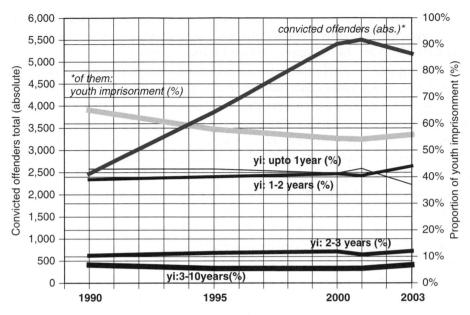

FIGURE 9.13. Length of youth prison sentences under juvenile criminal law, 1990–2003, Robbery.

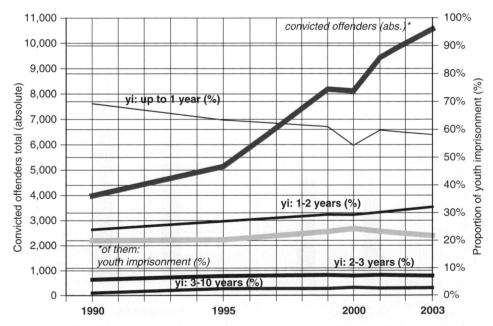

FIGURE 9.14. Length of youth prison sentences under juvenile criminal law, 1990–2003, Serious and dangerous bodily injury.

89% of "youth" prisoners in Germany are young adults between 18 and 25 years of age, whereas only 11% of the total population of 7,455 youth prisoners (31 March 2002) are 14–18 years old (see Dünkel, 2003a).

We do not know much about the court sentencing practice in East-German federal states, as statistical data until recently has not been available. A doctoral dissertation at Greifswald concerning the three states, Brandenburg, Saxony and Thuringia, showed that (contrary to the presumption of some scholars) the sentencing practice is not more repressive in the East. There are some differences in sentencing certain crimes, and particularly violent crimes are punished more severely. The youth detention centre option is widely rejected by the judges, whereas suspended youth prison sentences are more widespread than in West Germany (see Kröplin, 2002). Although the violent crimes rates differed between East and West Germany in the mid-1990s the number of youth prison sentences was about the same, as can be demonstrated by Fig. 9.15 that itemises robbery offences. The main disparity between East and West Germany is the considerably lower risk for a young suspect in East Germany to be sentenced by the juvenile court, which again reflects the extended practice of diversion (see Dünkel, Drenkhahn, and Geng, 2001; Kröplin, 2002).

In a recent analysis of the statistical data of Mecklenburg-Western Pomerania the pattern of extended diversion rates and the few sentences to a detention centre has been confirmed. One peculiarity, however, was the lower rate of suspending youth prison sentences (up to one or two years). Only 55% of youth prison sentences have

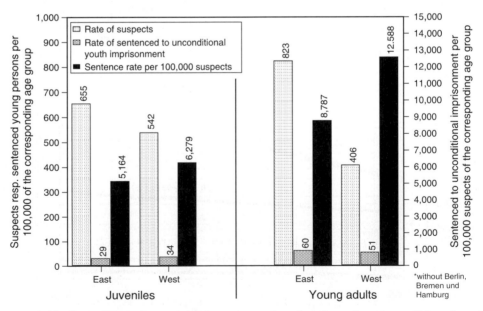

FIGURE 9.15. Juveniles and young adults suspected and sentenced to unconditional youth imprisonment for robbery offences in comparison of East and West Germany* 1997.

been suspended, whereas the average in West Germany is about 80%. Particularly in cases of violent offences, juvenile court judges seem to rely on "sharp shock" incarceration. On the other hand the study showed that "new" community sanctions, like social training courses, made up 15% of all formally sanctioned young offenders (10% of young adults, 20% of juveniles, see Dünkel, Scheel, and Schäpler, 2003). One-third (36%) of all formally and informally sanctioned offenders received a community service order (16% of young adults and almost 80% of juveniles). Mediation, making up about 8% (the same ratio for juveniles as for young adults), ranged far behind. However, like the care order (11%, 8% for young adults, 18% for juveniles) it is apparently not only an alibi for a "repressive" sentencing practice, but an integrated part of a juvenile justice system that greatly relies on the educational ideal.

6. YOUNG ADULTS (18–21 YEARS OLD) UNDER THE JURISDICTION OF THE JUVENILE COURTS (§ 105 JJA)

In Germany, since the reform law of 1953, all young adults are transferred to the jurisdiction of juvenile courts. Comparing practices internationally, this decision is remarkable, because it points the way to extending the scope of juvenile courts for young adults between the ages of 18 and 21. So, for example, Spain in 2000 introduced regulations for young adults that are very similar to those of Germany. Austria and Lithuania, in 2001, also introduced a flexible system to deal with young adult offenders, and the option to choose an appropriate sanction from either the juvenile or the adult criminal law, when dealing with the aspect of the personality and maturity of the offender. Other countries, like the Netherlands and the former Yugoslavia, have long provided for the possibility of avoiding sentences according of the general penal law (see Dünkel, 2002a). But, if in these latter cases the application of educational measures remained the absolute exception, the development in Germany has been in the opposite direction. Undoubtedly a major reason is that the reform of 1953 created the jurisdiction of the juvenile court for all young adult offenders independently of whether sanctions of the JJA or of the general Penal Law (StGB) are to be applied (see § 108 (2) JJA).

Section 105 (1) No. 1 of that law provides for the application of juvenile law if

> a global examination of the offender's personality and of his social environment indicates that at the time of committing the crime the young adult in his moral and psychological development was like a juvenile, he should be punished according to the JJA (*Reifeentwicklung*).

Furthermore, juvenile law has to be applied if it appears that the motives and the circumstances of the offence are those of a typical juvenile crime (*Jugendverfehlung*, see § 105 (1) No.2 JJA). In 1965 only 38% of young adults were sentenced in terms of the Juvenile Justice Act, but by 1990 this proportion had nearly doubled to 64%. In 1995 the ratio decreased slightly to 60%, but then increased again to 64.5% in

2003 (see Dünkel, 2002a; these data refer to the "old" West German federal states). This makes it clear that the full integration of young adults into the juvenile justice system has been accepted in practice. The regulations mentioned above have also been interpreted very widely by the courts to provide for the application of juvenile law in all cases where there are doubts about the maturity of the young offender (see BGHSt 12: 116; BGH Strafverteidiger, 1989: 311; Eisenberg, 2004: notes 7ff. to § 105). The Supreme Federal Court (*Bundesgerichtshof*, BGH) held that a young adult has the maturity of a juvenile if "elements demonstrate that a considerable development of the personality is still to be seen" (BGHSt 12: 116; 36: 38). This is the case in the majority of young adult offenders. Thus the court does not rely on an imaginative (prototype of) juvenile, but at aspects of each individual's personal development. There is no doubt that these arguments also hold for a further extension of the juvenile court's jurisdiction, for example for 21- to 24- year-old adults (see Section 9). The interpretation of a "typical juvenile crime," which is extensively used, follows a similar logic.[8]

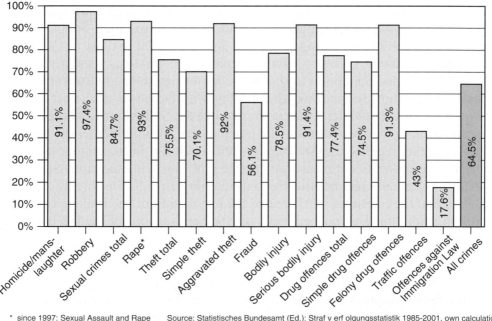

* since 1997: Sexual Assault and Rape   Source: Statistisches Bundesamt (Ed.): Straf v erf olgungsstatistik 1985-2001, own calculations.

FIGURE 9.16. Proportion of young adult offenders sentenced under juvenile criminal law (sect. 105 JJA) according to different crimes, 2001, old Federal States.

[8]The examples mentioned in the cases are crimes committed in groups or under the influence of a group, also hooliganism, sometimes very violent crimes that have derived from a specific situation (possibly in combination with alcohol abuse) etc. (see Eisenberg, 2004, notes 34ff. to § 105).

However, in practice there are considerable regional differences with respect to specific crimes and different regions. For most serious crimes such as murder, rape or robbery nearly all (more than 90%) young adult offenders are sentenced in terms of the (in these cases, milder) juvenile law (see Fig. 9.16). The reason is that the higher minimum and maximum sentences provided by the "ordinary" criminal law do not apply in the juvenile law (see § 18 (1) JGG). Juvenile court judges, therefore, are not bound by the otherwise obligatory life sentence for murder or the minimum of five years of imprisonment in the case of armed robbery. The German practice seems to be contrary to the so-called waiver decisions of the USA, where the most serious offenders are transferred to the "ordinary" criminal justice system (see Stump, 2003).

Only in the case of traffic offences are the majority of young adult offenders (in 2003, 57%) in Germany sentenced in terms of the criminal law for adults, because in these cases there is the procedural possibility of imposing fines without an oral hearing (*Strafbefehl*, which is excluded from the juvenile penal law).

There are constitutional reservations about the regional inequalities that have emerged in practice. In North Rhine-Westphalia, for example, the convictions in terms of the juvenile law according to a research of the 1980s ranged between 27% and 91% of all convicted juveniles (see Pfeiffer, 1988: 96). When the (old) federal states are compared, the range in 2003 was from 48% in Baden-Württemberg, 49% in Rhineland-Palatinate to 86% in Hamburg and 91% in Schleswig-Holstein. Apparently juvenile court judges have different conceptions of the "typical" personality of juvenile offenders and of the "typical" nature of juvenile delinquency. Overall, there is a north-south divide, with the federal states in the north increasingly applying juvenile criminal law, whereas in the south juvenile court judges rely to a greater extent on the criminal law for adults. As to the new federal states again a shortage of available data must be conceded. From individual studies we know that in 1998 the proportion of young adults sentenced according to the JJA was only 30% in Brandenburg, 34% in Saxony, but 60% in Thuringia (East German average: 38%; West German average: 59%; see Heinz, 2001: 79ff.). In Mecklenburg-Western Pomerania the proportion in 2001 was 55%, in 2003 56% (see Dünkel, Scheel, and Schäpler, 2003 and Table 9.2). The low rates in Brandenburg and Saxony are not due to the "distrust" of juvenile court judges towards the JJA, but are the result of a specific bureaucratic routine in the application of the *Strafbefehlsverfahren*, a summary procedure with only a written file in cases of less severe offences.

In this context two discourses can be differentiated. On the one hand the "symbolic" debate in the field of criminal policy and the critique of conservative parties of too-lenient sanctioning by applying the sanctions of the JJA instead of the general criminal law.[9] Conservative politicians argue for young adults to

---

[9]These arguments do not consider that in fact sometimes the application of sanctions of the JJA may be a disadvantage rather than a benefit, as can be shown by the fact that in the juvenile justice system the minimum prison sentence is six months, in the general criminal law only one month (for some empirical evidence of disadvantages in sentencing see Dünkel, 1990; Pfeiffer, 1991).

TABLE 9.2. Proportion of (18–21 years old) young adults sentenced according to the JJA (§ 105 JJA)

Federal states	Proportion of young adults sentenced according to the JJA (all crimes) (%)			Proportion of young adults sentenced according to the JJA (traffic offences) (%)		
	1998[1]	2001	2003	1997[2]	2001	2003
Baden-Württemberg	43	47.9	47.9	20	17.3	19.2
Bavaria	55	60.5	64.8	35	36.7	39.3
Berlin	57	52.8	54.4	30	45.5	36.3
Bremen	62	70.8	78.2	61	71.8	77.8
Hamburg	92	83.2	86.4	95	80.6	82.3
Hessen	71	74.4	77.2	67	64.8	69.7
Lower Saxony	71	69.6	71.9	61	56.9	60.0
Northrhine-Westfalia	63	65.7	69.4	45	47.9	52.5
Rhenania-Palatinate	47	51.4	49.2	19	20.2	19.5
Saarland	84	87.4	84.1	77	81.7	68.9
Schleswig-Holstein	89	90.0	91.2	93	87.8	89.6
Old federal states total	59	62.3	64.5	38.8	40.5	43.0
Brandenburg	30	no inf.	no inf.	23	no inf.	no inf.
Mecklenburg-Western Pomerania (2003)	no inf.	55	56	no inf.	41	37
Saxony	34	no inf.	no inf.	12	no inf.	no inf.
Thuringia	60	no inf.	no inf.	44	no inf.	no inf.
New federal states (1998 resp. 1997 without Saxony-Anhalt and Mecklenburg-Western Pomerania)	38	no inf.	no inf.	21	no inf.	no inf.

Sources: [1]Heinz (2001); [2]Kröplin (2002); Strafverfolgungsstatistik (2001, 2003); Strafverfolgungsstatistik Mecklenburg-Western Pommerania (2001, 2003), own calculations.

be given increased "responsibility," thereby allowing for the imposition of more severe punishment. On the other hand the practitioners have other problems. They want to eschew application of the general criminal law in order to avoid the imposition of more severe punishment, but would like to be able to impose fines in a summary procedure (without an oral hearing), which up to now is not provided by the JJA (*Strafbefehl*). This procedure is very economical and time-saving and – as indicated above – used particularly for traffic offenders (e.g., drunk driving).

7. REFORMS SINCE THE 1970S IN WEST GERMANY: INNOVATION FROM THE GRASSROOTS OF THE JUVENILE JUSTICE SYSTEM – THE NEW COMMUNITY SANCTIONS (MEDIATION, COMMUNITY SERVICE, SOCIAL TRAINING COURSES, CARE ORDER)

As indicated earlier (see Section 1) Germany experienced a reform movement that evolved from the "grassroots" of the juvenile justice system. Practitioners of private or community organisations (youth welfare departments in the cities) and juvenile court prosecutors and judges developed so-called new community sanctions (for one of the first projects of "Brücke"initiatives see Pfeiffer, 1983) from 1974 on when it became evident that legislative reforms would not be achieved in the near future. These projects were established close to the juvenile courts at the community level, very often by the communal welfare boards, but were then transferred to private organisations. This is a peculiarity of the juvenile welfare system that gives priority to privately run projects (principle of subsidiarity of state versus privately run organisations, see § 4 (2) JWA). The idea of the 1970s and 1980s was to establish appropriate and educational alternatives to the traditional more repressive sanctions, such as short-term incarceration in a detention centre (*Jugendarrest*, see Section 2). The first "new" community sanction to be implemented was the community service order. It was followed or accompanied by the special educational care order. This care order means that a social worker is attached to a juvenile offender like a mentor for a period of, usually 6–12 months. It is seen as an alternative to the classic probation sanction where a probation officer sometimes has 70 or more cases. The care order amounts to more intensive oversight, as a social worker in practice will have not more than 10–15 cases. It is evident that the care order can be much more efficient in providing help and social integrative services than a suspended prison sentence with supervision by a probation officer.

Since the beginning of the 1980s another "new" community sanction has been developed: the social training course. This is a group-centred educational measure that targets both leisure-time problems and day-to-day living problems. Its aim is to improve social competence and skills required in private and professional life. Social training courses are organised as regular meetings once or twice per week, often in combination with intensive weekend arrangements (e.g., sports activities, "adventure" experiences like sailing, mountain climbing), for a period usually of up to six months (see Dünkel, Geng, and Kirstein, 1998).

The first mediation projects started in the mid-1980s (see Dünkel, 1999: 108). At the beginning of the 1990s already 60% of the youth welfare departments reported that a mediation project had been established. In 1995 a national poll revealed a total of 368 mediation projects, which is a 68% increase since 1992 (see Wandrey and Weitekmap in Dölling et al., 1998). However, the authors reported that the majority of mediation schemes runs on an "ad-hoc basis" to cater for individual cases and not as a priority measure within the ambit of educational measures provided by the JJA (see Wandrey and Weitekmap in Dölling et al., 1998: 130ff.)

With the reform law of 1990 the legislator recognised the development of "new community sanctions" by creating legal provision for their further and wider application. Mediation, in particular, in the draft bill was mentioned as "the most promising alternative to the more repressive traditional sanctions."[10]

The current JJA in Germany offers many opportunities for arranging mediation or damage restitution. Juvenile court prosecutors may waive prosecution if reformatory measures have already been implemented or introduced (§ 45 (2) JJA). The 1990 reform Act explicitly equates mediation with such a reformatory measure. Significantly, the legislator already recognises sincere efforts by juveniles to resolve conflicts or to provide restitution. This arrangement protects juvenile and young adult offenders if the victim of the crime refuses to cooperate. Successful damage restitution more frequently leads to a dismissal because of "reduced culpability" (pursuant to § 45 (1) JJA; similar to § 153 of the Criminal Procedure Act in adult criminal law). Under the same conditions that apply to juvenile court prosecutors, juvenile court judges may waive prosecution to enable subsequent consideration of mediation efforts by the young offenders. Material losses restitution, as well as mediation as an independent sanction of the juvenile court are peculiarities associated with German juvenile law (see §§ 15, 10 JJA). The juvenile justice system, furthermore, provides for damage restitution in conjunction with a suspended term of detention in a remand home or imprisonment (the same applies for release on probation; for a summary, see Dünkel, 1999).

Providing mediation as a court sanction in juvenile justice (see § 10 (1) No. 7 JJA) was rightly criticised for violating the voluntary principle of mediation efforts. In practice mediation as a juvenile court educational directive is almost never used (see Rössner and Klaus in Dölling et al., 1998: 115), because suitable cases are dealt with in an informal proceeding (diversion in the sense of § 45 (2) JJA, see above) prior to a court trial and therefore do not enter the level of formal court proceedings.

All taken into account, it demonstrates that elements of restorative justice at different levels have been implemented in the German juvenile justice system.[11]

The juvenile law reform of 1990 somehow acted like a "booster detonation" for the further extension of new community sanctions. In a nation-wide poll

---

[10]The legal justification referred to the favourable experiences with assorted pilot projects launched since 1985, which increase consideration for the victim's special circumstances and "settle the conflict between the offender and the victim that results from the criminal act more appropriately and more successfully (. . .) than traditional sanctions have done in the past," see *Bundesratsdrucksache*, No. 464/89: 44.

[11]After the juvenile justice legislation of 1990, the legislator also passed reforms of the general penal law and the Criminal Procedure Act (StPO) which included some innovation with empasising mediation, see § 46a Criminal Law (StGB) of 1994 and §§ 155a, 155b Criminal Procedure Act (stop), see Dünkel, 1999: 110.

TABLE 9.3. Increase of projects of "new community sanctions" (offered by private or public organisations) in the old federal states before and after the amendment of the JJA in 1990

Educative Measures	Increase before the law amendment (1 December 1990) (%)	Increase after the law amendment (1 December 1990) (%)	Relation
Mediation	23	60	1:2.6
Care order	17	37	1:2.2
Social training course	16	30	1:1.9
Community service	2	5	1:2.5

conducted by the Department of Criminology at Greifswald we looked at the period of two years before and two years after the law came into force (1 December 1990). There was a 23% increase in the number of projects before and even a 60% increase after the statutory amendment in the case of mediation, which amounts to a relation of 1:2.6 (see Table 9.3). Considerable further increases can also be observed for the care order and for social training courses, but in absolute terms not for the community service order. This is, however, due to the fact that already before 1990 almost all youth welfare departments ran community service schemes and therefore scope for a further increase was rather limited.

8. THE IMPLEMENTATION OF NEW COMMUNITY SANCTIONS IN EAST GERMANY AFTER THE RE-UNIFICATION IN 1990

The main aim of the nation-wide Greifswald study on new community sanctions was to obtain empirical data about the establishment of these sanctions in the federal states, particularly in East Germany in the general context of implementing the JJA in the former GDR. The process of social transition went very quickly in terms of legal reforms. The JJA came into force simultaneously with re-unification in October 1990, shortly before the amendment of the law in all of Germany. The poll was conducted in 1994 and 1995 and included a questionnaire sent to all community welfare departments, private organisations running mediation and other community sanction schemes and to juvenile court judges (see Dünkel, Geng, and Kirstein, 1998). The question was to what extent the new federal states had been able to implement the structure of juvenile welfare compared to the established infra-structure in West Germany.

   The results were astonishing as a mere four years after reunification East German *Länder* had not only reached equivalent structures and quality of juvenile welfare, but had even overtaken the "old" federal states (see Table 9.4).

   This development continued in the five years that followed, as can be demonstrated by several further studies, particularly in the field of mediation (see

TABLE 9.4. "New" educational community sanctions (offered by private or state organisations) in the old and new federal states of Germany in 1994

	Youth welfare departments	Social training course		Mediation		Care order		Community service	
	N	n	%	n	%	n	%	N	%
Old federal states (FRG)	479	350	73.1	336	70.1	408	85.2	461	96.2
New federal states (former GDR)	127	96	75.6	112	88.2	119	93.7	127	100
Total Germany	606	446	73.6	448	73.9	527	87.0	588	97.0

Steffens, 1999; Schwerin-Witkowski, 2003). The German federal government has sponsored and promoted many projects that focused on specific violent offender groups, such as right-wing extremist skin-heads. At present the police authorities estimate that there are about 10,000 right-wing, violence-prone skin-heads, etc. in the whole of Germany. About half of them live in East Germany, although the East German population accounts only for 20% of the total German population (for an overview of right-wing extremism in Germany and particularly the East German federal states see Dünkel and Geng, 1999, 2003; Dünkel, Geng, and Kunkat, 2001). The overrepresentation of right-wing extremists in East Germany is a very striking phenomenon and can no doubt partly be explained by the specific problems generated by the economic situation (the unemployment rate is double compared to West Germany), the lack of professional and personal perspectives, particularly in young people, and also the authoritarian style of rearing in East German families.

In consequence of the specific East German problems the youth welfare authorities face a tough workload. Nevertheless, the infrastructure and the number of social workers today is comparable to that of West Germany. In the old federal states youth welfare authorities and the juvenile justice system in general face different problems, particularly with young migrants and young drug addicts which are not (yet) a prevailing problem in the eastern part of Germany. The "classic" drug in the Eastern *Länder* is alcohol. The illegal drug market has only recently increased there, too, although the real hard drugs (heroine, cocaine) scenario is not yet prevalent.

Community sanctions have made progress in the East, too. However, it is mainly the community service order that has gained major importance in the practice of juvenile justice. Table 9.3 shows that the other community sanctions, which are more educational and "constructive" than community service or other traditional sanctions, have made little progress. Consequently, half of the community youth departments stated that they had no more than eight young offenders participating in mediation per year. In 50% of the cases of youth departments no more than eight young persons in West and seven young persons in East Germany were under special educational care, and the number of participants at social training courses was 18 and 11, respectively. On the other hand 80 and 78 community service orders were counted in 50% of the youth departments (see Table 9.5). The total number of young offenders sentenced to community service was six to eight times as much as that for the other educational sanctions mentioned in Table 9.5.

9. ACTUAL TENDENCIES IN JUVENILE CRIMINAL POLICY – BETWEEN TOLERANCE AND REPRESSION

The actual tendencies in juvenile criminal policy are ambivalent. Conservative parties demand the lowering of the age of criminal responsibility from 14 to 12, since the registered crime rate of children has increased (an argument that is not convincing as most of the increase is attributable to petty non-violent offences). Furthermore, they urge that the widely extended practice of sentencing young adults according to the JJA should be removed in order to impose harsher punishment for this age group and that the application of the JJA should be the exception and not the rule. The simple but enticing argument is that young adults have many responsibilities in civil law and therefore should be responsible like adults in penal matters, too. These arguments totally neglect the psychological and pedagogic foundation of the JJA. Today the development of personality and integration into the life of adults takes even longer rather than shorter. Therefore, German juvenile criminologists and most of the practitioners in juvenile justice urge for the retention of current age limits for young adults and even for going further in extending the application of the JJA to young adults, without any exception (for arguments of comparative law see Dünkel, 2002a), and to include even 21- to 24-year-old adults in certain cases where the sanctions of the JJA seem to be more appropriate (see Deutsche Vereinigung für Jugendgerichte und Jugendgerichtshilfen, 2002). Indeed, in Europe the age limits are not yet harmonised. On the one hand, in some countries the tendency to lower the age of criminal responsibility has been actualised, to as low as ten years like in England and Wales (similar tendencies can be observed in the Netherlands), on the other hand the Scandinavian countries have retained their moderate approach with 15 as the age of criminal responsibility. It will be difficult to harmonise the different approaches in Europe, and perhaps it is not even desirable if one looks at the influence of the English "getting tough" policy. However, the majority of countries, particularly in the Baltic and Central and Eastern European countries, have more or less developed a consensus about age limits of 14, 18 and 21 years (see Table 9.6). So, in conclusion, it seems to be desirable that

TABLE 9.5. Number of participants at educational measures of youth welfare departments in 1993

	Mediation			Care order			Social training course			Community service		
	25%[1] n =	50%[2] n =	75%[3] n =	25% n =	50% n =	75% n =	25% n =	50% n =	75% n =	25% n =	50% n =	75% n =
Old federal states												
Participants at the measure	4[1]	8[2]	20[3]	4	8	16	9	18	32	41	80	152
Departments of youth welfare, n =	210			263			200			233		
Total participants, n =	3,346			3,758			4,926			28,130		
New federal states												
Participants at the measure	3	8	20	3	7	20	7	11	19	43	78	124
Departments of youth welfare, n =	107			99			47			106		
Total participants, n =	1,836			1,933			815			9,985		

[1]This means 25% of the departments had X clients in the specific measure.
[2]This means 50% of the departments had X clients in the specific measure (= Median).
[3]This means 75% of the departments had X clients in the specific measure.

TABLE 9.6. Comparison of the age of criminal responsibility in Europe

Country	Diminished criminal responsibility (juvenile criminal law)	Criminal responsibility (adult criminal law can/must be applied)	Legal majority
Austria	14	18/21	18
Belgium	16²/18	16/18	18
Belarus	14³/16	14/16	18
Bulgaria	14	18	18
Croatia	14/16¹	18/21	18
Czech Republic	15	18	18
Denmark⁴	15	15/18	18
England/Wales	10/12/15¹	18	18
Estonia	14	18	18
Finland⁴	15	15/18	18
France	10⁶/13	18	18
Germany	14	18/21	18
Greece	8⁶/13	18/21	18
Hungary	14	18	18
Ireland	7/15¹	18	18
Italy	14	18/21	18
Latvia	14	18	18
Lithuania	14³/16	14/16	18
Macedonia	14³/16	14/16	18
Moldova	14³/16	14/16	18
Netherlands	12	18/21	18
Norway⁴	15	18	18
Poland	13⁵	15/17/18	18
Portugal	12⁵/16	16/21	18
Romania	14/16	18	18
Russia	14³/16	14/16	18
Scotland	8/16	16/21	18
Serbia/Montenegro	14/16¹	18/21	18
Slovakia	15	18	18
Slovenia	14³/16	18	18
Spain	14	18/21	18
Sweden⁴	15	15/18	18
Switzerland	7/15¹	15/18	18
Turkey	12	15/18	18
Ukraine	14³/16	14/16	18

[1]Criminal majority concerning juvenile detention (e.g., youth imprisonment).
[2]Only for road offences.
[3]Only for serious offences.
[4]Only mitigation of sentencing without a separate juvenile justice act.
[5]No criminal responsibility "strictu sensu," but application of the Juvenile (Welfare) Law.
[6]Only educational sanctions (including closed residential care) and measures.

Germany maintains its juvenile crime policy and even expands the application of
the JJA to young adults without exception.

A major reform debate took place in September 2002 when the German
Juristentag (a biannual meeting of German lawyers) discussed the issue "Is the
German juvenile justice system still up to date?" The principal expert opinion
was presented by *Hans-Jörg Albrecht*, director of the Max-Planck-Institute for
Foreign and International Penal Law at Freiburg. His main conclusion was to
abolish the idea of education, but nevertheless to keep a separate juvenile justice
system with proportionate (and with respect to adult offenders milder) sanctions
(see Albrecht, 2002). Concerning the abolition of the *"leitmotiv"* of education
his ideas have been rejected by almost everyone in the German lawyers' assembly,
as well as by juvenile criminologists and penal lawyers (see e.g., Dünkel, 2002;
Streng, 2002; Walter. 2002). Some of Albrecht's concrete proposals, however,
corresponded with proposals of the Deutsche Vereinigung für Jugendgerichte
und Jugendgerichtshilfen (DVJJ), an organisation of juvenile court judges, prosecutors, social workers active in juvenile justice and welfare, and criminologists.
This organisation has influenced the reform debate of the last 30 years quite considerably. The DVJJ wants to keep the idea of education in the sense of special
prevention and also to extend the scope of constructive solutions, like mediation
and other community sanctions. In this context a "reconstruction" of the system
of community sanctions is being advocated as well as the restriction (limitation)
of youth prison sentences (abolishing the possibility to impose a prison sentence
because of "dangerous tendencies") and of pre-trial detention. They urge for
young adults generally to be included into the JJA, an extension of the maximum
penalty from 10 to 15 years (in cases where a life sentence would be imposed for
adults) and for a form of a summary written procedure to be introduced for this
age group in order to deal with minor traffic or property offences (see Deutsche
Vereinigung für Jugendgerichte und Jugendgerichtshilfen, 2002 and the recommendations of the Deutsche Juristentag 2002, see www.djt.de).

Although the government of the Social-democratic and the Green party in
Germany have not been ready to follow a "populist" and "hysterical" criminal
policy, it remained uncertain whether reform bills, including a reduction of penal
severity, would pass through parliament successfully, if the conservative and liberal party should win the elections of 2005. Feelings of insecurity are exploited
by most political parties (except the Green party) and right-wing populist parties
in some state parliaments, like in Hamburg, have campaigned successfully during
elections with law and order paroles. The role of mass media is very important in
this context. The German Social Democratic party is sometimes badly influenced
by the more repressive ideas of criminal policy of the British Labour party. On
the other hand, the "culture of education" of those working in the juvenile justice
is strongly engendered in Germany by permanent further education of practitioners organised by the *Deutsche Vereinigung für Jugendgerichte und Jugendgerichtshilfen* and other organisations. The latest news of the new coalition of the

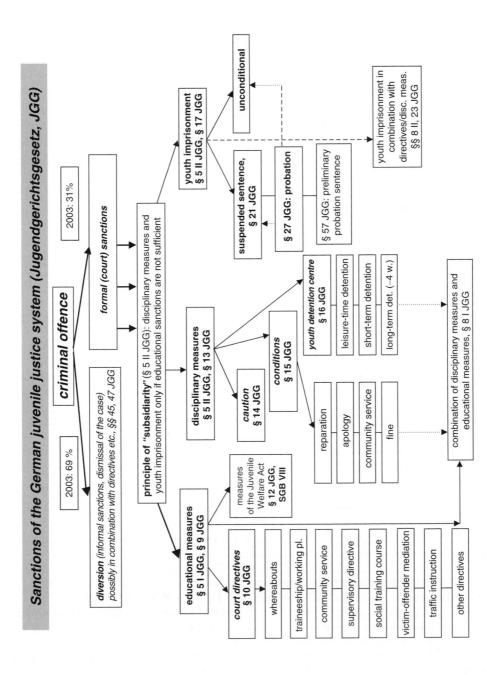

Sanctions of the German juvenile justice system (Jugendgerichtsgesetz, JGG)

criminal offence

2003: 69 %

diversion (informal sanctions, dismissal of the case) possibly in combination with directives etc., §§ 45, 47 JGG

2003: 31%

formal (court) sanctions

principle of "subsidiarity" (§ 5 II JGG): disciplinary measures and youth imprisonment only if educational sanctions are not sufficient

educational measures § 5 I JGG, § 9 JGG

measures of the Juvenile Welfare Act § 12 JGG, SGB VIII

court directives § 10 JGG
- whereabouts
- traineeship/working pl.
- community service
- supervisory directive
- social training course
- victim-offender mediation
- traffic instruction
- other directives

disciplinary measures § 5 II JGG, § 13 JGG

caution § 14 JGG

conditions § 15 JGG
- reparation
- apology
- community service
- fine

youth detention centre § 16 JGG
- leisure-time detention
- short-term detention
- long-term det. (~4 w.)

combination of disciplinary measures and educational measures, § 8 I JGG

youth imprisonment § 5 II JGG, § 17 JGG

unconditional

suspended sentence, § 21 JGG

§ 27 JGG: probation

§ 57 JGG: preliminary probation sentence

youth imprisonment in combination with directives/disc. meas. §§ 8 II, 23 JGG

Conservative and the Social-democratic party (starting in November 2005) is that there will be no substantial change in Juvenile Justice policy, which means that the age of criminal responsibility will be kept with 14 and that young adults of 18–21 years of age regularly will be sentenced according to the measures and sanctions of the Juvenile Justice Act.

It was the honourable *Franz von Liszt*, who, shortly after 1900 stated that a good social policy would be the best criminal policy. The idea of crime prevention has been developed more and more in the past 20 years in Germany. Successful projects have been established, e.g., to prevent violent or xenophobic crimes, in quite a few cities and communities (see e.g., Dünkel and Geng, 2003). This development does not detract from the need for reforms of the juvenile justice system, but it points the way to dealing with the causes of crime. Juvenile justice can play only a marginal role in this regard and cannot solve general societal problems (e.g., poverty, unemployment, discrimination).

REFERENCES

Albrecht, H.-J. (2002). *Ist das deutsche Jugendstrafrecht noch verfassungsgemäß?* Gutachten für den 64. Deutschen Juristentag. Munich: C.H. Beck.

Bannenberg, B. (1993). *Wiedergutmachung in der Strafrechtspraxis.* Bonn: Forum-Verlag.

Bundesministerium des Inneren, Bundesministerium der Justiz (2001). *Erster Periodischer Sicherheitsbericht.* Berlin: BMI/BMJ (published also under www.BMI.de/Berichte)

Bundesministerium der Justiz (ed.) (1989). *Jugendstrafrechtsreform durch die Praxis.* Bonn: Ministry of Justice.

Deutsche Vereinigung für Jugendgerichte und Jugendgerichtshilfen, 2. Jugendstrafrechtsreformkommission (2002). Vorschläge für eine Reform des Jugendstrafrechts. Abschlussbericht. *DVJJ-Journal Extra*, 5 (see also *DVJJ-Journal*, 13:228–276).

Dölling, D., et al. (1998). *Täter-Opfer-Ausgleich in Deutschland. Bestandsaufnahme und Perspektiven.* Bonn: Forum-Verlag.

Dünkel, F. (1990). *Freiheitsentzug für junge Rechtsbrecher. Situation und Reform von Jugendstrafe, Jugendstrafvollzug, Jugendarrest und Untersuchungshaft in der Bundesrepublik Deutschland und im internationalen Vergleich.* Bonn: Forum-Verlag.

Dünkel, F. (1994). Les orientations actuelles de politique criminelle, in F. Dünkel et al. (eds.), *Jeunes délinquants et jeunes en danger en milieu ouvert: utopie ou réalité? Cadres légaux et nouvelles pratiques – approche comparative.* Toulouse: Erès, pp. 41–78.

Dünkel, F. (1996). Täter-Opfer-Ausgleich. German experiences with mediation in a European perspective. *European Journal on Criminal Policy and Research*, 4:44–66.

Dünkel, F. (1999). La justice réparatrice en Allemagne. *Criminologie*, 32:107–132.

Dünkel, F. (2002). Jugendstrafrecht – Streit um die Reform. Anmerkungen zum Gutachten von H.-J. Albrecht zum 64. Deutschen Juristentag 2002. *Neue Kriminalpolitik*, 14:90–93.

Dünkel, F. (2002a). Heranwachsende im Jugendstrafrecht – Erfahrungen in Deutschland und aktuelle Entwicklungen im internationalen Vergleich. in R. Moos et al. (eds.), *Festschrift für Udo Jesionek.* Wien, Graz: Neuer Wissenschaftlicher-Verlag, pp. 51–66.

Dünkel, F. (2003). Entwicklungen der Jugendkriminalität und des Jugendstrafrechts in Europa – ein Vergleich, in F. Riklin (ed.), *Jugendliche, die uns Angst machen. Was bringt das Jugendstrafrecht?* Luzern: Caritas-Verlag, pp. 50–124.

Dünkel, F. (2003a). Situation und Reform des Jugendstrafvollzugs in Deutschland. *Recht der Jugend und des Bildungswesens*, 51:318–334.

Dünkel, F. (2005). Migration and ethnic minorities: impacts on the phenomenon of youth crime. The situation in Germany. In: Queloz, N., et al. (Eds.): *Youth Crime and Juvenile Justice. The challenge of migration and ethnic diversity*. Bern: Staempfli, pp. 45–71.

Dünkel, F., Drenkhahn, K., Geng, B. (2001). Aktuelle Entwicklungen der Sanktionspraxis und des Strafvollzugs in Ost- und Westdeutschland, in V. Bieschke, and R. Egg (eds.), *Strafvollzug im Wandel: Neue Wege in Ost- und Westdeutschland*. Wiesbaden: Kriminologische Zentralstelle, pp. 39–81.

Dünkel, F., Geng, B. (1999). *Rechtsextremismus und Fremdenfeindlichkeit. Bestandsaufnahme und Interventionsstrategien*. Mönchengladbach: Forum Verlag Godesberg.

Dünkel, F., Geng, B. (eds.) (2003). *Jugendgewalt und Kriminalprävention. Empirische Befunde zu Gewalterfahrungen von Jugendlichen in Greifswald und Usedom/Vorpommern und ihre Auswirkungen für die kommunale Kriminalprävention*. Mönchengladbach: Forum-Verlag Godesberg.

Dünkel, F., Geng, B., Kirstein, W. (1998). *Soziale Trainingskurse und andere neue ambulante Maßnahmen nach dem JGG in Deutschland*. Mönchengladbach: Forum-Verlag.

Dünkel, F., Geng, B., Kunkat, A. (2001). Einstellungen und Orientierungen zu Rechtsextremismus, Fremdenfeindlichkeit und Gewalt in Mecklenburg-Vorpommern. Available at: www.uni-greifswald.de/~ls3/Veröffentlichungen, pp. 1–71.

Dünkel, F., Lang, S. (2002). Jugendstrafvollzug in den neuen und alten Bundesländern: Vergleich einiger statistischer Strukturdaten und aktuelle Entwicklungen in den neuen Bundesländern, in M. Bereswill and T. Höynck (eds.), *Jugendstrafvollzug in Deutschland. Grundlagen, Konzepte, Handlungsfelder*. Mönchengladbach: Forum-Verlag, pp. 20–56.

Dünkel, F., Scheel, J., and Schäpler, P. (2003). Jugendkriminalität und die Sanktionspraxis im Jugendstrafrecht in Mecklenburg-Vorpommern. *Zeitschrift für Jugendkriminalrecht und Jugendhilfe*, 14:119–132.

Dünkel, F., van Kalmthout, A., Schüler-Springorum, H. (eds.) (1997). *Entwicklungstendenzen und Reformstrategien im Jugendstrafrecht im europäischen Vergleich*. Mönchengladbach: Forum-Verlag Godesberg.

Dünkel, F., Walter, J. (2005). Young foreigners and members of ethnic minorities in German youth prisons. In: Queloz, N., et al. (Eds.): *Youth Crime and Juvenile Justice. The challenge of migration and ethnic diversity*. Bern: Staempfli, pp. 517–540.

Eisenberg, U. (2004). *Jugendgerichtsgesetz*, 10th edn. Munich: Beck.

Estrada, F. (1999). Juvenile Crime Trends in Post-War Europe. *European Journal on Criminal Policy and Research*, 7:23–42.

Estrada, F. (2001). Juvenile Violence as Social Problem. *British Journal of Criminology*, 41:639–655.

Heinz, W. (1994). Flucht ins Prozeßrecht? Verfahrensrechtliche Entkriminalisierung (Diversion) im Jugendstrafrecht: Zielsetzungen, Implementation und Evaluation. *Neue Kriminalpolitik*, 6(1):29–36.

Heinz, W. (1998/99). Diversion im Jugendstrafrecht und im allgemeinen Strafrecht. Teil 1, *DVJJ-Journal*, 9:245–257; Teil 2, *DVJJ-Journal*, 10:11–19; Teil 3, *DVJJ-Journal*, 10:131–148; Teil 4, *DVJJ-Journal*, 10:261–267.

Heinz, W. (2001). Die jugendstrafrechtliche Sanktionierungspraxis im Ländervergleich, in D. Dölling (ed.), *Das Jugendstrafrecht an der Wende zum 21. Jahrhundert*. Berlin: Walter de Gruyter, pp. 63–97.

Heinz, W. (2001a). Jugendkriminalität in Deutschland. Available at: www.uni-konstanz.de/rtf/kik

Heinz, W. (2003). Das strafrechtliche Sanktionensystem und die Sanktionierungspraxis in Deutschland 1882–1999. Available at: www.uni-konstanz.de/rtf/kis Version 6/2003

Heinz, W., Storz, R. (1992). *Diversion im Jugendstrafverfahren der Bundesrepublik Deutschland*. Bonn: Bundesministerium der Justiz.

Heitmeyer, W. (1992). Soziale Desintegration und Gewalt – Lebenswelten und Perspektiven von Jugendlichen. *DVJJ-Journal*, 3:76–84.

Heitmeyer, W. et al. (1996). *Gewalt: Schattenseiten der Individualisierung bei Jugendlichen aus unterschiedlichen sozialen Milieus*. 2nd edn. Munich: Juventa.

Kröplin, M. (2002). *Die Sanktionspraxis im Jugendstrafrecht in Deutschland im Jahr 1997 – ein Bundesländervergleich*. Mönchengladbach: Forum-Verlag.

Pfeiffer, C. (1983). *Kriminalprävention im Jugendgerichtsverfahren*. Köln et al. (eds.). Heymanns.

Pfeiffer, C. (1988). *Jugendkriminalität und jugendstrafrechtliche Praxis – eine vergleichende Analyse zu Entwicklungstendenzen und regionalen Unterschieden*. Expertise zum 8. Jugendbericht. Hannover: Kriminologisches Forschungsinstitut Niedersachsen.

Pfeiffer, C. (1991). Wird nach Jugendstrafrecht härter gestraft? *Strafverteidiger*, 11:363–370.

Pfeiffer, C. et al. (1998). *Ausgrenzung, Gewalt und Kriminalität im Leben junger Menschen: Kinder und Jugendliche als Täter und Opfer*. Sonderdruck der DVJJ zum 24. deutschen Jugendgerichtstag (Special print of Deutsche Vereinigung für Jugendgerichte und Jugendgerichtshilfen e. V., DVJJ). Hannover: DVJJ.

Schaffstein, F., Beulke, W. (2002). *Jugendstrafrecht*, 14th edn. Stuttgart, Germany: Kohlhammer.

Schwerin-Witkowski, K. (2003). *Entwicklung der ambulanten Maßnahmen nach dem JGG in Mecklenburg-Vorpommern*. Mönchengladbach: Forum-Verlag Godesberg.

Schwind, H.-D. et al. (2001). *Kriminalitätsphänomene im Langzeitvergleich am Beispiel einer deutschen Großstadt. Bochum 1975–1986–1998*. Neuwied, Kriftel: Luchterhand.

Sonnen, B.-R. (2002). Juristische Voraussetzungen des Umgangs mit Kinderdelinquenz. *DVJJ-Journal*, 13:326–331.

Steffens, R. (1999). *Wiedergutmachung und Täter-Opfer-Ausgleich im Jugend- und Erwachsenenstrafrecht in den neuen Bundesländern*. Mönchengladbach: Forum-Verlag.

Streng, F. (2002). Referat zum 64. Deutschen Juristentag, in Ständige Deputation des Deutschen Juristentages (ed.), *Verhandlungen des vierundsechzigsten Deutschen Juristentages*, vol. II/1, Munich: C. H. Beck, N 69-N 108.

Stump, B. (2003). Adult time for adult crime. Jugendliche zwischen Jugend-und Erwachsenenstrafrecht. Eine rechtshistorische und rechtsvergleichende Untersuchung zur Sanktionierung junger Straftäter. Mönchengladbach: Forum Verlag Godesberg.

Sturzbecher, D. (2001). *Jugendtrends in Ostdeutschland: Lebenssituationen und Delinquenz*. Opladen: Leske und Buderich.

United Nations (1991). *The United Nations and Crime Prevention*. New York: United Nations.

Walter, M. (2001). *Jugendkriminalität*, 2nd edn. Stuttgart, Germany: Richard Boorberg-Verlag.

Walter, M. (2002). Das Jugendkriminalrecht in der öffentlichen Diskussion: Fortentwicklung oder Kursänderung zum Erwachsenenstrafrecht? *Golddammer's Archiv für Strafrecht*, 149:431–454.

Wilmers, N. et al. (2002). *Jugendliche in Deutschland zur Jahrtausendwende: Gefährlich oder gefährdet?* Baden-Baden: Nomos-Verlag.

Wolff, J. (1986). Die Geschichte der Gesetzgebung im Jugendstrafrecht. *Zeitschrift für Rechtssoziologie*, 7:123–142.

Wolff, J. (1989). Spurensuche. *Neue Kriminalpolitik*, 1(1):26–30.

10

Austria: A Protection Model

Karin Bruckmüller

INTRODUCTION

This chapter gives a review of the juvenile delinquency and law in Austria. Austria is a relatively small country with a surface of about 83,860 km² in the middle of Europe. It entered the European Union in January 1995. Its frontiers border both "old" EU and "new" EU member states and Switzerland. The country has approximately 8,174,700 inhabitants (2003). Of these about 1,245,300 children are aged under 14 (637,700 males and 607,600 females), 378,700 minors aged 14–18 years (194,400 males and 184,300 females); about 296,900 are "young adults" (18–21 years). The birth rate rose by 2.5% from 2003 to 2004.

The outcomes of a study of Grafl and Beclin (2000) on the development of juvenile delinquency from 1989 to 1998 and the current situation are presented in Section 1. The crime prevention programmes that take place in school and during leisure time are included in Section 2. Sections 3 and 4 illustrate the intervention possibilities of the police and the prosecutor in cases of juvenile delinquent behaviour. The last two sections present our comments on the Austrian sentencing policy (Section 5) and the system of sanctions (Section 6).

The reactions possible under Austrian criminal law to cases of juvenile delinquency behaviour are covered by a special Act, the Juvenile Court Act (*Jugendgerichtsgesetz* 1988 – JGG). This Federal Act contains substantive and procedural regulations, including regulations on the enforcement of imprisonment, for those aged up to 18 years. Though the law defines "juveniles" as persons from 14 to 18 years of age (JGG, 1988), it theoretically also allows for extra-penal measures, according to family law or the law of youth welfare. However, if deemed necessary, such measures can be applied in a criminal court.

In view of the history of the Austrian JGG, the main policy trends can be understood as follows (Jesionek, 2003). In 1928, the first Act of JGG arose from the idea of education. Conventional punishments, both fines and imprisonment, should only be used as last resort when juvenile delinquency is involved

The author wishes to thank Professor Frank Höpfel as well as Professor Christian Grafl and Dr Katharina Beclin (University of Vienna), Judge Norbert Gerstberger (District Court of Criminal Affairs, Vienna) and Manfred Aahs (Bundeskriminalamt, Vienna) for valuable assistance.

J. Junger-Tas and S. H. Decker (eds.), International Handbook of Juvenile Justice, 263–294.
© 2006 Springer.

(Neumair, 1996). This was also the goal of the dramatic and all-encompassing reform of 1988 (Jesionek, 2001; Bogensberger 1992) that was designed with the aim of achieving decriminalisation, while continuing to provide justice for the victims of crime (Jesionek, 1990). On this basis, a new form of immunity from punishment was introduced for misdemeanours committed by juveniles aged 14 and 15 years old at the time of the offence. The age of criminal majority was raised from 18 to 19 years.

In addition to procedural simplifications, special regulations with regard to custody were introduced. Release of information pertaining to criminal records was restricted, and sentences for juveniles shortened in order to avoid the stigmatisation of offenders as much as possible.

For the same reason, the potential for non-intervention and diversion was expanded significantly. Efforts were made to replace traditional convictions and/or sentences imposed by a criminal court, on the basis of a successful practical experiment at some courts and offices of prosecution.

For cases in which conventional criminal penalties prove unavoidable, legislation made sentencing more flexible by the removal of minimum sentences. Equally in the spirit of the principle of last resort, emphasis has been put on special deterrence (*Spezialprävention*), as opposed to general deterrence (*Generalprävention*) that can be taken into consideration only in exceptional cases.

Another important matter was to continue cooperative, coordinated activities in the interest of the juvenile. The juvenile judge, therefore, has no longer been concerned purely with criminal matters, but is also in charge of related aspects of youth welfare. A system of separate juvenile courts exists in the larger cities, whereas for the rest of the country only special departments for juvenile cases have been established within the regular criminal courts.

In recent years, Austrian legislation has moved "backwards," that is, it has moved to a more punitive system. An amendment in 2001 changed the age of civil majority from 19 to 18 years in the General Civil Code (Allgemeines bürgerliches Gesetzbuch). For this amendment it was argued that the 1988 reform had granted access to the more flexible and milder juvenile justice system to an age group commonly associated with a great deal of criminality. As limited compensation for this move, certain new regulations of procedure were introduced for "young adults," i.e., persons from 18 to 20 years. This legislation recognised that crime levels in this age group can rise temporarily, due to the difficulties associated with the adjustment to adulthood. However, it was not consistent with the popular demand for a more comprehensive set of rules for "young adults" (covering only the three years up to the age of 20 or going further, e.g., by including all adults under 25).

On 1 July 2003, the famous old Vienna Juvenile Court (*Jugendgerichtshof Wien*) was closed. It was integrated into several county courts (*Bezirksgerichte*) and the Vienna District Court for Criminal Matters (*Landesgericht für Strafsachen Wien*). Whether the good network (in regard of an effective exchange of information), which existed between criminal and family judges as well as with the Vienna Juvenile Court Assistance (*Jugendgerichtshilfe*) and the Youth Welfare Authority, can continue to be maintained remains to be seen.

1. GENERAL OVERVIEW OF THE DEVELOPMENT OF CRIME

In this chapter the long-term development from 1989 to 1998 will be explored on the basis of the empirical study by Beclin and Grafl (2000) which covers the first ten years of the JGG. Then we review the current situation of juvenile delinquency, based on data of the last three years (2001–2003). The years 1999 and 2000 are not included, due to the redefinition of statistics in relation to the preparation of the new legislation which brought down the upper age-limit of the JGG on 1 July 2001 and, at the same time, in part included young adults (18 to less than 21) into the juvenile criminal justice system.[1] In regard to the age-groups, the methodology is confronted with the problem that from 2001 forward, offenders over 18 years have not generally been considered juveniles. This must be taken into account when reading the following tables.

1.1. The Development from 1989 to 1998: The Beclin and Grafl Study (2000)

At the end of the 1990s, several Austrian newspapers claimed that the rise in juvenile delinquency was alarming and a particular cause for concern (Die Presse, 2000; Salzburger Nachrichten, 2000). Due to this debate, Beclin and Grafl (2000:821–22) analysed the change in juvenile crime in Austria from 1989 to 1998.[2]

During the time period studied (1989–1998), a record rise of over 61% in total juvenile delinquency was observed. The number of registered juvenile suspects (i.e., persons who have been identified by police and referred to the public prosecutor) was about 18,300 (of which 2,400 were due to a crime) in 1989, which rose to 29,500 (4,300 due to a crime) in 1998 (Beclin and Grafl, 2000: 821–23). Further details from the Beclin and Grafl study are presented below.

1.1.1. Gender
It is interesting to note the difference in delinquency rates between girls and boys. Rates of delinquency by girls are still significantly lower than those for boys, but this difference has been slowly diminishing. Hence, there is a clear increase in the percentage of suspects that are girls. Among girls the increase totals 110%, whereas that for boys totals only 50%.

Despite the increase among girls, their percentage of all juvenile suspects for criminal acts rose from 15% to 20%; for crimes it rose from 6% to 11%.

---

[1] For a special treatise on the crime rate and the convictions of this group see: Burgstaller and Grafl (2002).

[2] It should be noted, that during the time period of the study, the young persons of 18, but 19 years still were subject to the regime of the JGG, and therefore they also are counted as minors in this study.

1.1.2. Special Crime Rates

In order to demonstrate change in crime patterns, Beclin and Grafl (2000) examined demographic changes, by referring to the Special Crime Rates ("Besondere Kriminalitätsbelastungszahl" – BKBZ. The BKBZ refers to the number of suspects among 100,000 inhabitants of the same age). Although every crime burden rate has the weakness of disregarding persons who are not officially resident in the country, it is without doubt an important measure of crime statistics. Using the BKBZ (considering the 9% decrease of youth population) an even more pronounced increase in juvenile crime can be seen. From 1989 to 1998, the BKBZ rose by 76% (BKBZ figures: from 3,468 to 6,116), and even as much as by 97% when regarding crimes (BKBZ: from 459 to 902). Both trends are contained in Fig. 10.1.

The study brought to light some surprising and interesting results regarding age: The biggest increase was among minors 14–15 years of age, despite the fact that in general, older minors are perceived as being more criminally active than younger ones. Between 1989 and 1998, the BKBZ of 14- to 15-year-olds rose by 129%, that of 16- to 17-year-olds by 74%, and that of 18-year-olds by 51%. However, in the last two years of the study period, the trend was essentially flat for all age groups as seen in Fig. 10.2.

1.1.2.1. Specific categories of offences Narcotic drug offences have increased more than any other offence category. Here the BKBZ increased by a factor of 10, from 82 at the starting point to 830 in 1998. In the other offences presented in

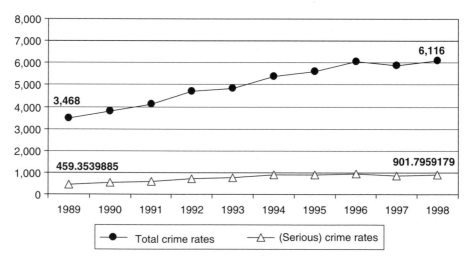

FIGURE 10.1. Crime rates (BKBZ) per 100.000 juveniles of the same age in Austria, 1989–1998.
● Total crime rates; △ (serious) crime rates.
Source: Beclin and Grafl (2000).

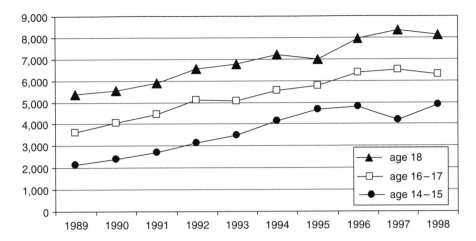

FIGURE 10.2. Crime rates trends in different age-groups per 100.000 of the same age (BKBZ) in Austria, 1989–1998.
▲age 18; □ age 16–17; ● age 14–15.
Source: Beclin and Grafl (2000).

Table 10.1, an increase of up to 2.6% is observed. Only offences against persons caused by negligence decreased slightly. Concerning the distribution of offences in the year 1998, it is evident that property offences come in first, followed by offences against persons and by narcotic drug offences. Based on Table 10.1, the following picture evolves. Theft and criminal damage comprise 70% of all offences against property. The development of *theft* cases during the study period shows a rise in the BKBZ of 55% among boys (987 in 1989 to 1,533 in 1998), and 141% among girls (329 in 1989 to 794 in 1998).

TABLE 10.1. Percent Distribution of offences of juvenile suspects 1998

Offences	*N = 29.486*
	%
Offences against property	53
Offences against the person	15
Drug offences	14
Negligent offences against life and limb	10
Serious threats and coercion	3
Sexual offences	1
Other	5
Total	100

Source: Beclin and Grafl (2000).

The majority of theft cases concern shoplifting (in 1998 being 97% of girls' thefts and 58% boys'). The rise in shoplifting during the total study period is mirrored in the BKBZ (boys + 90% and girls +165%). Beclin and Grafl (2000) conclude that this rise is due to the increased incidence of businesses reporting theft to police, and a greater use of security technology (Brenner, 2000). Hence, at least some of the increase may be due to a rise in the reporting of theft, not an increase of theft itself.

In the category of offences against the persons, the dominant category consists of grievous bodily harm (85%) and public order offences (13%). As for the gender distribution, absolute figures for girls are minimal, but there was a significant increase in terms of the BKBZ: from 86 to 163, a 90% increase, and for boys from 810 to 1,376, a 70% increase. Not surprisingly, public order offences have remained a "male domain."

The same is true for robbery. Female minors represent a small fraction of all offenders. During the study period, the BKBZ for boys rose from 54 to 166, for girls from 3 to 14. The majority of cases consist of mugging, for example, snatching the handbag of an elderly woman. Cases of violent extortion of small sums of money from fellow school pupils also play a role in these figures. Robbing of mobile phones also seems to account for a significant portion of this category of offence.

According to Beclin and Grafl (2000), the increase of violent crime demonstrates a greatly reduced capacity for conflict resolution. Minors are not willing or able to resolve conflicts peacefully. This behaviour may be influenced by the amount of brutality present in films and in computer games which often are used by minors as a sort of "socialisation tool" to balance out the weakening support of the family. As noted above, narcotic drug offences rank third, and have increased dramatically. Here the BKBZ for boys grew from 98 to 1,120 (approximately 11.4 times), and for girls from 52 to 345 (an increase of about 6.6 times).

It is remarkable that by 1998 the proportion of juvenile suspects committing drug offences rose from 2% in 1989 to 13% in 1998 for males. Police strategies, such as increased raids, have had an impact on this increase. As illustrated above (see Section 1.1 and Figs 10.1 and 10.2), the current situation shows a drop both in narcotic drug offences and shoplifting. The extension of security measures in department stores and in self-service shops as well as increased checks for narcotics in bars or pubs, in pop concerts and the more frequent presence of police in places known for drug dealing may have had a deterrent effect.

1.2. The Current Situation

1.2.1. Overall Figures
The number of suspects in the three years (2001–2003) are included in Table 10.2.

As can be seen, total criminal activity in both age groups has increased, yet, the proportions across the age groups remained essentially stable. A similar pattern occurred for felonies and misdemeanours. For a gender-specific picture, the distribution of figures of suspects (age 14 to more than 18) appears in Table 10.3.

TABLE 10.2. Percentage of juveniles and young adults charged on total number of recorded offences, 2001–2003

Year	2001	%	2002	%	2003	%	Change in % from 2002 to 2003
Total number of offences	N = 198,899		N = 206,203		N = 223,915		+ 8.8
14 to <18	21,873	11.0	21,561	10.5	25,804	11.5	+19.7
18 to <21	25,347	12.7	26,011	12.6	28,736	12.8	+10.5

Source: *Sicherheitsbericht 2003*, p. 122.

TABLE 10.3. Gender distribution of juveniles charged for crimes and misdemeanours, 2001–2003

	2001		2002		2003	
	Males	*Females*	*Males*	*Females*	*Males*	*Females*
Total number charged	*N = 17,210*	*N = 4,663*	*N = 16,775*	*N = 4,786*	*N = 20,788*	*N = 5,016*
	%	%	%	%	%	%
All offences	78.7	21.3	77.8	22.2	80.6	19.4
Crimes	88.6	11.4	86.5	13.5	89.5	10.5
Misdemea-nours	77.1	22.9	76.4	23.6	78.8	21.2

Source: Sicherheitsbericht (2003), p. 187.

1.2.2. Specific Offence Categories

Tables 10.4–10.7 examine offences against persons, against property – in particular shoplifting – and drug offences. As these groups play a special role in the Beclin and Grafl study (2000) that examined delinquency from 1989 to 1998, the figures for the years 2001–2003 (suspects) are reported. In this regard, however, it is important to understand the different methodologies used in collecting such data. In the overall statistics (Figs 10.1, 10.2, and Table 10.1) all offenders, even if suspected of multiple offences, have been counted once. In 2001, this was also true for the following statistics. Therefore the increase from 2001 to 2002 is, at least in part, a reflection of these changes. A further question might be provoked by the development from 2002 to 2003. As the trends (see last columns of the tables) show, the overall crime rates have risen significantly, whereas the single groups of offences seem to show considerable decreases from 2002 to 2003. A possible explanation of this phenomenon lies in a peculiar shift in the structure of criminal activity, as multiple offenders apparently have receded into the background.

Offences against persons (including traffic offences) are shown in Table 10.4.

As can be seen, among young adults there was a decrease, in offences against the person, of 3.5%. Statistics regarding offences against property are shown in Table 10.5.

Offences by young adults decreased by about 2.4%, but also for minors a decrease of 1.4% is noted. This development can also be seen in the Table 10.6, specifying shoplifting.

Shoplifting statistics (thefts by customers in self-service shops or department stores) are seen in Table 10.6.

TABLE 10.4. Percentage of juveniles and young adults charged for offences against the person, 2001–2003

	2001	%	2002	%	2003	%	Change in % from 2002 to 2003
Total	75,899	100	89,895	100	87,591	100	−2.6
14 to <18	4,536	6.0	5,953	6.6	6,112	7.0	+2.7
18 to <21	8,884	11.7	10,398	11.6	10,032	11.5	−3.5

Source: Sicherheitsbericht (2003), p. 136.

TABLE 10.5. Percentage of juveniles and young adults charged for property offences, 2001–2003

	2001	%	2002	%	2003	%	Change in % from 2002 to 2003
Total	70,802	100	90,731	100	88,586	100	−2.4
14 to <18	11,057	15.6	15,278	16.8	15,065	17.0	−1.4
18 to <21	8,103	11.4	11,376	12.5	11,100	12.5	−2.4

Source: Sicherheitsbericht (2003), p. 149.

TABLE 10.6. Percentage of juveniles and young adults charged for shoplifting, 2001–2003

	2001	%	2002	%	2003	%	Change in % from 2002 to 2003
Total	20,640	100	23,363	100	20,179	100	−13.6
14 to <18	3,574	17.3	3,701	15.9	3,072	15.2	−17.0
18 to <21	1,885	9.1	2,111	9.0	1,778	8.8	−15.8

Source: Kriminalitätsbericht (2001), p. B 13; and (2003), p. B 13.

TABLE 10.7. Percentage of juveniles and young adults charged for Drug offences, 2001–2003

	2001	%	2002	%	2003	%	Change in % from 2002 to 2003
Total	21,082	100	21,647	100	21,401	100	−1.0
14 to <18	1,772	8.4	1,615	7.5	1,451	6.8	−10.2
18 to <21	5,858	27.8	6,169	28.5	5,747	26.8	−6.8

Source: Kriminalitätsbericht (2001),2, p. B 17; (2002), p. B 19; and (2003), p. B 21.

Narcotic drug offence patterns are displayed in Table 10.7.

A decline in shoplifting and narcotic drug offences is observed in the tables. As was shown above, the situation in the time period from 1989 to 1998 was different, as in that period there was a rapid increase in narcotic drug offences and shoplifting among minors.

2. THE PREVENTION OF DELINQUENT BEHAVIOUR

Preventive measures are implemented starting in pre-school. They are intended to prevent "anti-social behaviour" in a very general sense as well as specific criminal behaviour. A range of programmes for minors has been developed. The programmes are offered in schools as well as in recreational places for the children alone or with their guardians. Peaceful conflict resolution, prevention of violence, integration, addiction problems, as well as the recognition of right and wrong, are the main points of focus in these programmes. The aspects are described in detail in the following sections.

2.1. Prevention in School

As many of the problems of youth are related to conflict resolution, school projects and/or courses run by social workers are focused on avoiding crisis situations and on preventing criminal activity. Anti-drug education is also increasingly being offered in schools.

2.1.1. Through Social Workers

Social workers from the parole board (in Austria, a private organisation called *"Neustart"*) go to schools to inform the pupils about methods of coping with crisis situations. Furthermore, conflict resolution is acted out in special groups with concerned pupils. The intention is for to learn early that conflicts can be resolved through compromise and to have positive experiences to which they later can refer. As aptly stated on the *Neustart*: "If many can receive help when it is needed, they can go without our intervention later on" (http://www.neustart. at/angebote/praevention2.php:2004).

2.1.2. Through Teachers

In some schools teachers carry out prevention efforts on a weekly basis. This takes place in two schools in Vienna, where "KoKoKo"–Lessons (*Kommunikation, Kooperation, Konfliktlösung = KoKoKo*), an exemplary concept, were developed. The school schedule is extended by one such lesson a week, during which communication, cooperation and joint conflict resolution is practised by the students. A class supervisor, in some cases also by the teacher, generally supervises this lesson. An example of the content of the lesson would be asking the following questions: What is communication? Which types of communication and which types of conflicts do exist, and how can the latter be removed? The KoKoKo classes aim to achieve stronger consideration of the social, emotional, and communication structures of the classroom (Sengstbratl, 1999; http://www.sozialeslernen.at/vielfalt/kokoko.htm:2004). This type of education provides the pupils with a tool, which helps them to recognise, analyse, and remove communication problems and conflicts in the future.

2.1.3. Mediation by Pupils

Conflicts are mediated by a pupil who is volunteering in the course, and has been trained as a so-called dispute helper (*Streithelfer*) or dispute guide (*Streitlotsen*) (Horvath, 2003; http://www.ahs-rahlgasse.at/streithelfer/data/evaluationsbericht. pdf:2004 and http://www.evrahlgasse.at/diverse_info/Ev-Endbericht.doc:2004). The volunteers are familiar with conflicts among their classmates and can resolve such conflicts in a manner appropriate to their age. At the same time, pupils learn to take responsibility for their actions and to resolve conflicts in a constructive, non-violent manner. Here the role of the teacher is limited to the training of the pupil as a mediator and to acting as coach. Older pupils would undertake the mediation of the problems of the younger ones. Contact with a mediator can be made by putting a slip of paper into a postbox, or by directly talking to the desired mediator. Sometimes anonymous requests received by mail are also considered. The KoKoKo lessons, as well as peer mediation, have resulted in excellent feedback from pupils, parents, and teachers.

2.1.4. Prevention of Drug-addiction

The social workers of the Mobile Youthwork in Vienna-Favoriten (as part of *Mobile Jugendarbeit Favoriten*) offer drug-abuse prevention to several secondary schools in Vienna. In the first phase of the project, interested headteachers and teachers are familiarised with the subject at hand. The social workers then go into the classroom and work on the problem with the pupils. They introduce such institutions as the help centre and drug advice centres. Furthermore, meetings with teachers and local authority councillors are arranged in order to develop cooperation between schools on this issue.[3]

Some specialist drug abuse advice centres, e.g., the drug advice centre of the General Hospital, Vienna (Allgemeines Krankenhaus Wien), work closely with schools. Therapists, social workers, and sometimes the police, work together with families and schools. They do not stop at explaining the results of drug-addiction, but focus on the discovery of the roots of addiction, in order to be more effective in preventing it.

2.2. Prevention in Leisure Time

For about ten years, many parks in Austria have had "supervision" (*Parkbetreuung*).[4] This is primarily concerned with the integration work for immigrants, but also includes crime prevention. The initial reason for this project was the increasing amount of conflicts in the parks, stemming from the different social, ethnic, and religious backgrounds of the children. This led to unrest and drug problems. To control these problems, the minors (target group: 6–13 years, but also minors up to 18) are offered a broad, free play programme (mainly group games). The participants learn a peaceful way to treat others, such as making common plans. The interaction with each another furthers their communication skills, the development of social skills, and peaceful conflict resolution. The supervisors are not simply coordinators, but also trusted third persons.

Such programmes for minors are provided in numerous youth centres[5] throughout Austria. Support for peaceful conflict resolution or for drug-related problems is offered by a frontline social worker, such as *Mobile Jugendarbeit Favoriten*.[6]

2.3. Police Prevention Work

The police offer prevention work to schools and leisure centres, as well as seminars for parents. This work is presented here, as it is closely related to the issues of police intervention (see Section 3).

---

[3]For details of how the project works: http://backonstage10.jugendzentren.at/projekte/index.htm.
[4]http://www.parkbetreuung.org, http://www.wien.gv.at/stadtentwicklung/spielraeume/parkbetreuung.htm, http://wien.kinderfreunde.at/index.php?page_new=5410, http://www.se-zeitung.at/se12002/integration.htm.
[5]Further information under: http://www.jugendzentren.at.
[6]The names of other programmes are "back bone" and "*Rettet das Kind*," http://www.wien.gv.at/vtx/vtx-rk-xlink?DATUM=20041014&SEITE=020041014003.

2.3.1. Advice service within Criminal Investigation Departments and Juvenile Police.

Criminal Investigation Departments and Juvenile Police offer victim-prevention-programmes in the form of information evenings for parents and teachers. They also advise young people in youth centres and clubs. Materials suitable for minors are being developed in dedicated working groups.

The issue of violent crime – in particular, xenophobia is increasingly being addressed in lectures – is handled differently. Networking with other institutions is of particular importance in this field. The advice services in the Criminal Investigation Departments see themselves as coordination and contact points.

The police authorities have "contact officers" ("Kontaktbeamte") who are to serve as a liaison between the public and the police. Special "youth contact officers" are meant to establish good rapport and personal contact with young persons. In addition, contact officers provide general education on youth-relevant legal matters, e.g., by lectures in schools or workshops in youth centres on the issues of accountability, violent crimes, youth protection, administrative penal law, and fascism. They also undertake traffic education, an important point in crime prevention, as many minors first come in contact with penal law due to traffic accidents with bodily harm by negligence. Similarly, special contact officers are an important part of juvenile crime prevention in the soccer scene. These officers are not simply on duty at home, but also would go along with the fans to games, in order to prevent hooliganism.

2.3.2. Special Police Projects

In Vorarlberg, a prevention programme named "children's police" (*Kindergendarmerie*)[7] for children from 5 to 12 years is in place. In a playful way, they learn how not to become an offender, by learning to recognise wrongs. These programmes focus on shoplifting, bodily harm, criminal damage and arson. At the same time, parents are involved and offer support and advice on how they should behave responsibly. In the City of Salzburg, the programme "Out – die Aussenseiter" deals with the youth violence problem. This concept, initiated by the Salzburg police, educates minors about violence and its results. Visits to courts have been included.[8]

2.4. Legally Determined Preventative Measures

2.4.1. The Youth Welfare Act

Legally, prevention is covered by the Youth Welfare Act (*Jugendwohlfahrtsgesetz – JWG*, 1989). The main role of public welfare is "to further the development of

---

[7]http://www.kindergendarmerie.at/info/index.html.
[8]See: *"Jung und gewaltfrei. Im Rahmen der Kampagne, Out – die Au&Eszett;enseiter' diskutierten Exekutivbeamte innerhalb von vier Monaten mit 60.000 Schülern über Gewalt und Jugendkriminalität."* (2001) *ÖS*, issue 7/8, p. 19 http://www.bmi.gv.at/oeffentlsicherheit/2001/07_08/artikel_8.asp.

children under 18 years by offering support for care and child raising, and by providing education" (*Jugendfürsorge*). The contact persons are parents as well as the children themselves. If measures have to be taken without the parent's consent family courts impose them. In cases of educational emergency of a criminal nature, the jurisdiction of the criminal courts is involved. The social services offered are, direct preventative and therapeutic support, as well as support through organisations for the early recognition of deviant behaviour amongst children and its treatment. The JWG employs organisations of the Child and Youth Legal Centre (*Kinder-und Jugendanwaltschaft*)[9] that provides advice and support. Furthermore, the supervising of the minor can be followed up with front line social work and supervised emergency night shelters (Höpfel, 2004).

2.4.2. School education standards

School education rules should also function as a preventive measure, as they stipulate the duties of the pupil. A general outline of duties can be found in the School Education Act (*Schulunterrichtsgesetz* – SchUG, *1986*) (Höpfel, 2004). According to the latter, pupils are obliged to attend lessons regularly and punctually, while furthering the school's function as a whole by participating in and adapting to the classroom and the school community. In addition, they are obliged to respect the school rules, i.e., the house rules, in which their duties are highlighted.

As for pedagogical reactions, the pupil should receive praise and encouragement for good behaviour. In the case of bad behaviour, the child should be reprimanded, if possible, in an advisory talk; in extreme cases the pupil can be expelled. If the disciplinary situation induced by anti-social behaviour requires it, a guardian should be informed.

Since 2001, it has been possible to agree on a "behaviour agreement" (*Verhaltensvereinbarungen*) through the school's community board. Thus, disciplinary measures adapted to the age of the child and the situation are provided, and early conflict resolution is supported.

3. POLICE INTERVENTION (INCLUDING ADMINISTRATIVE PENAL LAW)

3.1. General Aspects

The police play a role in both criminal law and administrative penal law (in particular in the domain of traffic offences). Yet youth police officers are only found in the field of crime prevention.

[9]http://www.kija.at; http://www.wien.gv.at/kja/kjaaufg.htm

3.2. Criminal Law

In Austria, the police do not have the right to make decisions regarding criminal interventions, including the decision to drop the charges or opting for diversion (see Chapter 4). Police, in criminal matters, have a more supportive function. They are responsible for the actual enforcement of an arrest or detention as well as for the questioning and interrogation of suspects and potential witnesses.

Detention by security officials is dealt with under the general rules. Therefore, in normal cases an arrest warrant issued by a judge is required. Only when the delay caused by obtaining a warrant, or at least a prosecutor's request, would be prejudicial, may police act autonomously. As is explained in Section 4, regarding minors and young adults, special evaluation of whether the arrest is suitable to the age of the suspect is required. In addition, there exists the obligation to inform either a legal guardian or relative who lives with the suspect, if the suspect is not to be released immediately. If necessary, an already involved parole officer and a youth welfare officer must be informed as well.

Minors and young adults have the right to have a trusted adult (including a legal guardian, teacher, or representative of parole) present throughout interrogation by organs of the security services and formal hearings of the security authorities. The suspect must be informed of this right in a timely manner. The interrogation or questioning must be delayed until the requested adult arrives, unless this is out of proportion with the punishable act. The principal reason for the presence of a trusted adult is to provide the minor with psychological support (though they may not ask questions or participate in the proceedings), since an arrest can cause considerable shock, particularly among minors. This may even lead to later misbehaviour and the ensuing grave consequences. Another role of the presence of the trusted adult is that of an independent monitor, whose presence leads to transparency of the conditions under which the interrogation takes place.

Apart from during legal proceedings, minors can be arrested by public security services in order to testify in a case, if they are suspected of having committed an offence that would carry a penalty of one year imprisonment. They must have been caught in the act or they must fall under suspicion within a very limited time after the offence has been committed. The arrested person has the right to inform a relative. After the deposition, the underage child must be handed over to the guardian or youth welfare officer. However, the guardianship court can issue a court order regarding the guardianship of the child.

3.3. Administrative Penal Law

The age of accountability in administrative penal law is 14 years, as stipulated in the JGG. Administrative penal law contains exceptions for minors, though not young adults similar to those of the JGG (Walter and Mayer, 2003). However, these no longer apply after the minor has reached their 18th birthday. A "delayed-maturity" clause has been included in the law. A minor will not be charged with the offence if he or she was, for any reason, not mature enough to understand the unlawfulness of the action committed and to act accordingly.

Whenever possible, the authorities are encouraged to make use of the assistance of public education institutions, youth welfare departments, and people and organisations involved in youth welfare. Such assistance can be particularly useful in determining the personal situation of the minor, in caring for his or her person, and in providing the necessary moral support during the hearing.

Upon request, minors may make use of their right to have a legal representative (legal guardian or other) present during questioning or interrogation, as long as the ensuing delay does not lead to an unnecessary extension of the holding of the suspect. A young suspect can request the presence of two trusted persons at oral negotiations. The minor must be informed of this right. Their legal representative has the right to take legal action in the minor's interest, even if it is against his or her will. The court may appoint a lawyer for the minor if the legal representative is personally involved in the case or if it is necessary due to the diminished mental capacity of the suspect, and thus it is not possible for the legal representative to defend the person. This rule allows the function of monitor and moral supporter to be retained. If the authorities judge that measures must be taken regarding guardianship, a guardianship court must rule on these issues.

In principle, all general penalties apply, although, the minimum sentence of minors cannot exceed half of the sentence for adults. Furthermore, minors under the age of 16 at the time of the commission of the offence may not be sentenced to imprisonment. In special circumstances, minors over this age threshold may be charged with up to two weeks imprisonment. A suspended sentence, which should not exceed two weeks, may be served even in the absence of special grounds. In the case of a sentence being served in a penal institution, the regulations of the JGG are to be applied, although the Act on Administrative Penal (*Verwaltungssrtrafgesetz* – VStG) specifically states that young prisoners and adults should be separated.

3.3.1. The Youth Protection Acts

A special tool of administrative (penal) law that focusses specifically on minors is the Youth Protection Acts of the *Länder* (provinces). These define types of undesirable behaviour that are seen to place the minors in danger. For example, selling alcoholic beverages or tobacco is not legally permitted to minors under a certain age specified by the law, and the hours young people go out at night must be controlled. In principle, such matters are viewed as the responsibility of the parents or adults in general, but the law does reserve the right to sanction minors from 14 years on (Höpfel, 2004).

4. INTERVENTIONS OF THE PROSECUTOR

4.1. General Aspects

The principle of legality has an old tradition in Austria. However, the public prosecutor[10] has considerable discretion regarding steps in the pre-trial proceedings. In case of sufficient evidence, the prosecution authority must decide whether the minor shall be tried in court or whether one of the other measures outlined in the JGG shall be adopted. The JGG does allow for the possibility of diversion (Schwaighofer, 2001),[11] and the court may also decide on diversion options.

As to coercive measures, to a large extent the prosecutor is not entitled to act on his own, but must come forward for a judicial warrant. In particular, it is not up to the prosecution authorities to order search and seizure, including any interception of telecommunication, and they do not rule over pre-trial detentions (as the questionnaire contains this issue in connection with the public prosecutor, as discussed in Section 4.4.).

It is important to note that Section 44 JGG excludes any private party from filing a charge for one of the offences that normally are left up to the victim, e.g., defamation. It is up to the public prosecutor to decide if the prosecution of these cases is in the interest of justice. There is no right to step into the position of the public prosecutor, should he or she dismiss the case (Höpfel, 1988).

4.2. Non-Intervention

According to Section 6 JGG, the prosecutor may drop the case of a juvenile, though not of a young adult. This may occur if the offence is punishable by a fine or not more than five years of imprisonment, unless more serious measures, in particular any form of diversion, are called for. If it seems appropriate, upon request of the public prosecution, the guardianship court officially informs the accused about his or her wrong-doings and the ensuing consequences. The premise of presumed innocence should be noted.

4.3. Diversion with Intervention

As the only practical expression of the idea of a "rapid reaction" to criminal offences, Austrian legislation includes the concept of 'diversion with intervention'. The public prosecutor decides on diversion as an intervention when it is not possible to simply drop the case and yet there are no grounds of general prevention that make it seem

---

[10]In Austria the function of the *"Staatsanwalt"* is not adequately described by the English expression "prosecutor." It rather should be a "procurator" who has the obligation to be objective (see Section 3 StPO). This is particularly relevant in the field of juvenile justice.
[11]For empirical data, see the studies of Pilgram (2000) and Grafl (2001).

indispensable to institute criminal proceedings including the pronouncement of a sentence (Section 7 JGG) that applies to juveniles but not young adults. Furthermore, the prosecutor may only use this instrument in the case of criminal offences that carry the penalty of a fine or not more than five years of imprisonment, and if the remaining general pre-conditions of a diversion measure are met. Excluded are cases of "severe guilt," a resulting death, or when there are grounds of special prevention that require punishment (Schütz, 1999). The implementation of diversion is independent of the agreement or cooperation of the victim, but is based on the principle of consent of the suspect (Höpfel, 2002). The palette of diversion options ranges from suspending prosecution for a probation period to out-of-court settlement, such as victim-offender mediation (known as Außergerichtlicher Tatausgleich).

Whenever possible, compensation or a settlement should bear a direct relation to the diversion measure, although it must be appropriate to the capabilities of the minor, and not unnecessarily render reintegration into society more difficult.

Diversion measures implemented by the public prosecution, or the court, are recorded in the court register for a period of five years. However, no entry in police records is made, hence there is no criminal record.

4.3.1. The field of narcotic drug offences

In the field of narcotic drugs, the public prosecution must drop the charge for a probation period of two years (Schwaighofer, 1997) if a person only possessed or purchased a small amount of narcotic drugs for their own consumption, or committed a criminal act in order to finance the purchasing of drugs. This special form of diversion – which actually is one of the historic roots of the entire system – must be deemed more appropriate on special preventative grounds than to reach a conviction.

Prior to withdrawing the charge, information must be gathered from the Ministry of Employment, Health and Social Welfare and an opinion be obtained from the local health authority in the case of a small amount of cannabis on whether or not the accused must undergo health-related treatment. Such treatments may include, among others, being monitored by a doctor or taking part in a rehabilitation or substitution programme, or even undergoing psychotherapy. The preliminary withdrawal of the charge may also take place if the accused agrees to being supervised by a parole officer. In the case of withdrawal symptoms, the ministry, and in some cases also the local health authorities must be informed.

4.4. Pre-trial Detention

Outside preliminary arrest (*Verwahrungshaft*), only the judge, not the public prosecutor, has the authority to make decisions regarding pre-trial detention. But the judge may impose, and extend the detention only on the basis of a motion made by the prosecutor.

In addition to the general rules of pre-trial detention – which requires its application to be in proportion to the offence, i.e., to the probable punishment and as short as possible – detaining minors in pre-trial custody is limited more strictly. Not only is the maximum duration shorter, but the special criteria are also narrower. Pre-trial detention is not permitted – even if the legal preconditions exist – if the purpose of detention can be achieved by a family law, or youth welfare law, albeit with softer methods. This is the case, for example, if the aim can be achieved by the minor undergoing treatment for drug addiction. Moreover, the minor can only be detained in pre-trial detention if the related disadvantages for the personal development or for the reintegration into society of the minor are not out of proportion with the offence, though in practice this occurs rarely. Thus, a rapid evaluation of interests must be made. The younger the suspect (Jesionek, 2001), the greater the likelihood of rejecting detention as an option. However, the proportionality rule applies not only to detention in relation to the offence, but also to the probable punishment. In a recent ruling, the Supreme Court has taken the view to interpret this literally and thus exclude any pre-trial detention as long as no punishment at all is to be expected (conviction without sentence, conviction with suspended sentence).

To avoid the unnecessary extension of the time in custody and the delays in legal proceedings, the duration of police arrest should generally not exceed 48 hours. Remand in custody is reviewed according to the general regulations of the Code of Criminal Procedure (*Strafprozessrecht* – StPO). Thus, the first control should take place at a hearing after 14 days, the second after a month and all further hearings every other two month. The maximum period for pre-trial detention of minors may not exceed three months, in cases within the jurisdiction of mixed courts or juries trials six months, in extraordinary cases one year.

To protect the rights of minors as comprehensively as possible, the JGG grants the minor a special right of participation of trusted adults from the first pre-trial proceedings forward. Moreover, a parole officer already appointed to the minor can act as a trusted adult. This specific figure also has the right to attend the main trial and to be heard in it.

Furthermore, the legal representative is granted all the same legal rights as the accused minor, though this does not apply to young adults. In addition, the court must appoint a pro-bono attorney, if necessary. This must be accomplished by the first legal proceedings in court (first questioning in the presence of a judge after the arrest).

5. SENTENCING

This chapter is meant to give a broad description of how the Austrian juvenile justice system reflects the basic principles of juvenile justice as expressed by the Council of Europe. According to the general sentencing rules of Austrian Criminal

Law, the sentence must fit the offence and the responsibility of the offender (Section 32 Penal Code – *Strafgesetzbuch* – StGB). It depends on the circumstances and motivation that led to the act, as well as on the personality of the offender.[12] Youth *per se* is a mitigating factor for "young adults." If the offence was committed under the age of 18, reduced punishments apply from the outset.

The JGG pays a lot of attention to special prevention when determining suitable punishment (Section 5 (1) JGG); this requires the actual person, as well as his or her living conditions, to be more thoroughly considered. The crucial issue is not so much the aim of education, but the consideration and furthering of the young offender's chances for reintegration into society. The following observations must be made.

5.1. Special Prevention vs Educational Theory – a Tense Relationship

Regarding sentencing in juvenile justice, the primacy of special prevention is embedded in the language of the above-cited Section 5 (1) JGG. Further, when pondering abstaining from prosecution, diversionary measures, conviction without sentencing, and conviction with suspended sentence, it is only under exceptional circumstances that the court will consider general prevention when determining whether to convict or punish a juvenile offender. Such exceptional reasons to take the demand for general prevention into account often in court practice, are presumed in cases of traffic offences under influence of alcohol or of professional drug dealing.

As the JGG acknowledges the principle of special prevention, it also clarifies the limits of educational theory (Jesionek, 2001; Burgstaller, 1997; Triffterer, 1988; Köck, 1999) within juvenile criminal law. Although historically the JGG developed out of educational thinking, any educational needs can be considered in the determination of sentences only in so far as this is justified and necessary within the legal framework of special prevention. Even in cases of an urgent need for educational measures, the legal judgment is ultimately determined by the boundaries of penal law, based on the principle of responsibility (*Schuldstrafrecht*). This means that the sentence is determined by the gravity of the individual offence and that the future of the life of the individual in society must also be considered. Also in the case of diversion, where compensation or community service is part of the sentence, for the law the relevant basis is the behaviour, and not any educational theory.

The need for education over and above punishment can only be met outside the boundaries of penal law, through the family or youth welfare organisations. Thus, Austrian legislators have given a clear answer to an internationally much disputed issue: "juvenile penal law is limited to the reaction to concrete criminal

---

[12]For empirical data about the reasons for judges' rulings on the taking of sanctions, compare the study of Grafl (1995).

behaviour; whereas the protection of minors through educational measures is the responsibility of youth welfare bodies," i.e., the guardianship court. When the *Jugendgerichtshof Wien* existed, these two institutions worked together and networked in an exemplary manner. Only time will tell how this will develop since the abolition of this special court.

5.2. Preparation of Decisions Through Youth Inquiries

Youth Inquiries are designed to assist the court in decisions regarding pre-trial detention and especially appropriate sentence for each case when considering punishment of guilty minors and young adults. It is therefore necessary to research the living conditions and family circumstances of the accused, along with his development and all other circumstances that could help to establish the bodily, mental, and spiritual state of the minor. The protection of privacy and family life as stipulated in Article 8 European Convention on Human Rights – ECHR should be noted as under Austrian law, the European Convention on Human Rights has the range of constitutional law. The gathering of information from schools is no longer provided by the law, as this proved to be unfeasible (Jesionek, 2001). In case of doubt, a medical expert or a psychologist should be consulted. It is left to the judge's discretion which inquiries are necessary on a case by case basis. However, these are to be carried out every time there is any doubt about the necessity of taking accompanying guardianship or youth welfare measures. Such inquiries may be avoided if the offence committed renders in-depth investigation of the person *per se* to be unnecessary. This mainly applies to cases of petty offences, where the invasion of the private sphere of the minor or others involved would not be proportionate to the offence (Jesionek, 2001).

In juvenile cases, inquiries and the development of proposals to the judge are the responsibility of the juvenile court aid. The court can also seek the counsel of other social welfare bodies, such as that of the parole or youth welfare officer, or request medical, psychological, psychiatric, or paediatric reports. In the case of foreign minors who do not have sufficient command of the German language, psychologists and psychotherapists who speak the language of the accused should be obtained. When a minor or young adult is arrested or taken to pre-trial detention, a brief psychological test establishing possible reactions to the detention is compiled (Jesionek, 2001).

5.3. Principle of Social Reintegration in the Different Stages of Juvenile Justice

The principle of social integration permeates juvenile penal law. Its influence can already be seen at the pre-trial stage during detention negotiations that, as already mentioned, can only be imposed in exceptional circumstances so as not to unnecessarily rip the minor out of his or her life. Similarly, the influence of the social reintegration principle can be seen in the suitability of the sentence, as well as the way the sentence is served.

5.3.1. Legal Action, Legal Reaction, and Sentence Determination

So as not to negatively impact the future career of the minor and not to endanger or destroy any future chances in the workplace, the releasing of information on juvenile penal cases is strictly restricted.

During legal proceedings, all television and radio recording and transmission, filming and photographing, as a general rule, are prohibited. Moreover, the identity of minors (only to a reduced extent for adults) accused or convicted of an offence is specifically protected under media law from being revealed in the mass media. Hence, even in the case of the accused being guilty, he or she may sue for compensation if any report in mass media would make the person concerned identifiable. Moreover, Section 42 JGG restricts the principle of a public trial "if this is in the interest of the juvenile" a section that also applies to young adults.

When determining the legal reaction, the judge must choose the option that least impacts the lifestyle of the minor. Fines and imprisonment are, therefore, only options of last resort. As mentioned above, the determination of the sentence is governed by the general sentencing regulations of the StGB. This means that guilt including the circumstances that led to the commission of the offence, but also the impact the sentence will have on the "future reintegration into society" of the offender, must be considered (Kienapfel and Höpfel, 2005).

5.3.2. Serving of the Sentence

If a prison sentence has been passed, serving of the sentence may, in juvenile cases, be deferred up to one year if necessary, because of resocialisation of the juvenile or other reasons including health, family, and financial reasons. This includes allowing the accused to finish a job-training programme, such as an extended job-training programme or preparation for a professional qualification or university studies. This only holds true if the sentence to be served does not exceed one year. If a prison sentence is to be served, the minor should be "educated in law-abiding behaviour fitted to the circumstances." To what extent this is actually possible and will be useful to the minor upon his or her release remains to be seen.

The educational and job possibilities offered during imprisonment have educational value. Section 58 JGG allows the development of "motivation workshops," in which minors can learn about the working conditions of certain jobs and professions (Jesionek, 2001). They can only work outside the institution if it can be guaranteed that the minor will not be stigmatised, i.e., the (uninformed) general public should not recognise that he or she is an offender. In the case of minors serving a longer sentence, they should, "if the length of the sentence so permits, receive professional training suited to their knowledge, capabilities, talents and their previous occupation" (Löschnig-Gspandl, 2002). The prisoners receive payment for their work, part of which is paid out as pocket money and part of which is paid upon their release.

In some special institutions, even those remanded in custody for further questioning are offered regular mandatory and professional school education. The lessons should avoid gaps in the education of the detainees and further their general knowledge. The success of the lessons should be determined in an appropriate manner. The time spent in lessons counts as work time.

5.3.3. Social Integration after Trial/Serving a Sentence: Restricted Access to Information on the Criminal Record

Reintegration into society should be encouraged and stigmatisation should be avoided by restricting access to police records and by shortening the length of the period before the records of minors are deleted. After the termination of a specific time period the police record is deleted automatically, the convicted person being considered to have a clean criminal record. Except for multiple convictions, juvenile offences are deleted after five years.

6. SANCTIONS

6.1. Introduction

Juvenile law covers a wide range of sanctions in JGG, under the title "Juvenile Penal Law" (*Jugendstrafrecht*). It includes sanctions that we are familiar with from adult penal law, but which have been adapted to the needs of juveniles and include special options that only apply to minors but not young adults. Thus Sections 4–13 JGG offer grounds for immunity, methods of diversion, conviction without punishment, and conviction with a suspended sentence. Also included are the traditional fine and prison sentences, for which Section 5 contains modifications. These last two sanctions may only be implemented as a last resort (*ultima-ratio* principle). The court and the public prosecution, respectively, on a case by case basis, must always choose the sanction that causes the least impact on the lifestyle of the minor, yet which at the same time has the best special preventative effect (Jesionek, 2001; Löschnig-Gspandl, 2002).

All possible sanctions for juvenile offences are presented below, in the order of increasing impact from zero to the maximum intrusion into the rights of the accused.

6.2. Grounds for Immunity

Beyond the defences that also apply in adult cases, there are two rules to be noted in Austrian juvenile criminal law, in cases of (1) delayed maturity and (2) moderate misdemeanours committed by juveniles under the age of 16.

Next to the minimum age of 14 years, Section 4 excludes punishment when the juvenile offender, due to certain circumstances, was not capable of distinguishing right and wrong, or of acting accordingly. This so-called delayed maturity, which must be demonstrated by an "unusual level of development retardation," must be examined in relation to the single criminal act. It may be caused, e.g., by social or psychological defects, child neglect, or by illness. As a rule, such cases are cleared up with the help of expert witnesses. There is another reason for non-punishment for juveniles under 16. There is immunity for members of this privileged group for any moderate misdemeanour. If the juvenile, having committed a misdemeanour without serious guilt does not show special reasons which speak for the enforcement of juvenile penal law to prevent the offender from committing further acts, immunity is given the threshold of serious guilt (*schweres Verschulden*) is reached when, in a specific case, the guilt and unlawfulness of the act concerned surmounts the typical; an example would be serious bodily harm (*schwere Körperverletzung*) by an act of hooliganism.

In all such cases the public prosecutor must drop the charges and notify the guardianship court, which in turn can take appropriate family or welfare measures. Should the case be prosecuted, the court must cease all legal proceedings, i.e., acquit the accused. Logically, these issues of substantive criminal law must be examined before considering possible diversion measures (Section 6.3.).

6.3. Diversion

Possible diversion measures when taken by the court, never mean a conviction. The rules described above for diversion by the prosecutor also entitle the judge to dismiss the case either in the form of non-intervention or with an intervention component. There is only one significant difference: diversion by the court is allowed in more severe cases. As opposed to the prosecutor, the court can go beyond the limit of offences with a maximum sentence of five years of imprisonment. However, there is a doctrinal controversy as to how far the extension of the rule goes.

6.4. Conviction Without Sentence

After the trial, instead of pronouncing a low sentence – up to three months of imprisonment – the court may convict the juvenile offender and abstain from passing sentence, if it is considered that the official conviction is sufficing to prevent the offender from committing further criminal acts and no exceptional general preventative grounds are found that speak against such an approach (Schroll et al., 1986). Hence, a formal conviction is made, yet no sentence is passed. Thus the offender has received a slap on the wrist, but no further damage has been caused. No sentence may be passed in retrospect. Whether or not a conviction without sentence can be passed is left to the discretion of the court.

6.5. Conviction with Suspended Sentence

The first alternative to a conviction without sentence is retaining the right to pass a sentence in retrospect within a certain probation period between one and three years. A prerequisite is that the court considers that a conviction and the mere threat of a sentence, alone or in combination with other measures, serve as enough of a deterrent. There must be no general preventative concern of extraordinary weight against such action being taken. Once again, the implementation of this measure is left to the discretion of the court.

A conviction with a suspended sentence can be joined with a personal directive and/or the appointment of a parole officer, if this is deemed necessary or advisable on grounds of special prevention. The passing of a sentence in retrospect is only possible with the public prosecutor's consent. A prerequisite is that the convicted person commits another criminal offence within the probation period and reasons of special prevention speak in favour of such action or, at least on paper, if the offender disregards a court directive with bad intent or stops seeing his or her parole officer.

6.6. Fines and Imprisonment

6.6.1. General Aspects
In passing a judgment with a fine or prison sentence, the court must consider the minimum and maximum punishments provided in the penal code. For fines, as well as for prison rates, the maximum possible sentence for juveniles is halved, while for imprisonment minimum sentences, as will be described below, usually do not apply at all.

To avoid short prison terms (up to six months), they can be replaced by a fine if the maximum sentence for the criminal offence in question does not exceed five years (i.e., for juveniles, ten years) of imprisonment. Both fines and imprisonment can be suspended, in whole or in part. The probation period is from one to three years. However, the probation period may be terminated after one year, provided that new facts are supporting the good prognosis.

6.6.2. Fines
In Austria, the prevailing system of fines is the day fine. In passing the sentence, the first step includes the setting of a number of daily rates that fit the offence and the degree of responsibility of the young offender. These are set according to the general rules on sentencing. The second step is to determine the amount of the daily rate. Here the personal circumstances and the financial capability of the convicted to pay are the main determinants when passing the sentence (Leukauf and Steiniger, 1992; Fabrizy, 2002). The minimum amount of a daily rate is 2 euros.

The relevant values for calculating the daily rate are the net daily income of the offender setting the upper limit, and the minimum required to live setting the lowest limit. Yet in the case of minors, such as those still at school, they frequently do not have any income. In such cases the limits are determined by the pocket money, which would fit to the offender's lifestyle. Also to consider is the amount of the family income that is being spent on the offender, as well as the monetary value of sport, hobbies and holidays, and potential sources of income of the minor, such as holiday jobs, if a real possibility of this exists and if the job is suited to the offender. This would not be case if the offender is a mediocre student who needs time to study (Platzgummer, 1980; Lässig, 2002).

6.6.3. Imprisonment

The shortest prison sentence possible is one day. Any police arrest or pre-trial detention must be deducted. As mentioned above, the maximum sentence is halved, and there are no minimum sentences. However, there are two exceptions. Life, or 10–20 years punishment is replaced by 1–15 years, if the juvenile committed the offence when he or she was 16 or older, and 1–10 years if the offence was committed before the age of 16. A possible sentence of 6 months up to 10 years replaces a possible prison sentence of 10–20 years.

The possibilities of a suspension of a prison term are twofold: the suspension in whole or in part. These special regulations do not apply to "young adults." However, for an adult who has committed the crime under age 21 there is no life sentence (maximum sentence: 20 years of imprisonment). Minimum sentences are reduced; for offences with a maximum sentence of not more than five years there is no minimum sentence at all.

Early release from serving an unconditional prison term is possible after half of the term if there is a fair prognosis. After two-thirds of the term, however, release must be granted, unless there is a high risk of reoffending. There is a minimum of one month of prison to be served before any early release. For minors, a further rule in excludes any consideration of general prevention.

Early release of persons who have committed an offence under age 21 must be combined with allocation of a parole officer unless there are reasons to believe there will be no relapse.

6.7. Preventive Measures

Along with, or in lieu of punishments, Austrian penal law also allows for a different track, so-called preventive or prophylactic measure. This "track 2" is not determined by the culpability of the offender, but exclusively by the dangerousness he or she represents to others. Hence, the public's need for security is met in terms of special prevention. Whereas punishment focuses on the past, these measures look to the future.

Considering deprivation of liberty, only the placement of insane offenders or of criminal offenders with a diminished mental capacity in an institution, and the placement of criminal offenders in need of rehabilitation in an institution are of theoretical relevance for juveniles. This sanction is used rarely, as it was invoked in only three cases for mentally abnormal minors in 2003.

6.8. Adverse Consequences of Legal Rules

According to the Austrian legal code, many regulations lead to adverse consequences that the defendant will suffer in addition to the direct consequences of the conviction. These so-called legal consequences may be an automatic loss of one's job, of one's driver's licence or of a residence permit.

However, the juvenile penal law prohibits such adverse consequences in the case of young people. The reason is that the legal consequences should not render the future path in life for the juvenile offender impossible or more difficult (Jesionek, 2001). Despite this provision, in reality it often happens that administrative authorities illegally deny a driver's license or residence permit as a result of a previous conviction for a juvenile offence.

6.9. Orders by Family and Youth Welfare Services Courts

Along with penal sanctions, the JGG also deals with family and youth welfare services court orders; these apply to minors, i.e., those who have not yet reached their 18th birthday. Thus, for example, a court order may be issued to support the guardian in caring for the child, or the right of custody for a child may be taken away, including the admission of the child to a home or a flat-sharing community. It must be verified that such a court order is indeed necessary, when the underage person is being charged with a punishable offence (either criminal or administrative) and there is a concern that his or her personal development is endangered.

These are not reactions within penal law, the court orders are regarded as extra-penal law. In principle, the procedure follows the rules of family law, and it belongs to the jurisdiction of the guardianship and social welfare courts. Only in exceptional circumstances can the criminal judge, if it is deemed necessary, pass a family and youth welfare court order for the duration of the accompanying penal case. Upon the completion of the penal case, the file must be immediately handed over to the competent family judge.

Jesionek (2001) believes the reason for this concentration of responsibility to be "the need of a reaction as quickly as possible to a concrete endangerment of the minor." In legal practice, this regulation is extremely rarely implemented, as the same effect can be achieved within the jurisdiction of the social welfare court.

6.10. Enforcement of Imprisonment Sentences

The rules on the enforcement of prison sentences and their length do not differ significantly from that of adults. Generally, minors are subject to the provisions of the Act on the Enforcement of Penal Sanctions (*Strafvollzugsgesetz* – StVG), special regulations of the JGG having to be considered. These special rules concern specific issues that need to be taken into consideration for the treatment of minors, such as the need for schooling, the appropriate nutrition required for their physical development, as well as physical exercise in the fresh air. Furthermore, it is important to note that prisoners are not publicly exposed, in particular during transfer or when working outside the penal institution. In addition, visiting times and the right to receive parcels are expanded, and the regulations regarding house arrest and solitary confinement are milder, both of which are intended to maintain social ties between the juvenile and other relations.

Moreover, the special regulations of the JGG are also supposed to prevent "criminal infection" by avoiding contact with adult inmates. For this reason, minors should serve their sentences in special institutions, or at least in a special prison section separated from the adults.

As a rule, minors serve their sentences in more relaxed conditions. This means that the doors to the common rooms, sometimes even the gates during the day, are not locked. The prisoners are only guarded – if at all – in a limited manner when working outside the premises, and there is the possibility of leaving for work or for educational purposes. While petitioning for early release, leave of up to five days may be granted (Jesionek, 2001).

Similarly to the judges and public prosecutors who are involved with juvenile cases, all those dealing with minors should have some pedagogical knowledge and an understanding of the basics of psychology and psychiatry. Because no specific training for guards in juvenile institutions exists at present, this requirement is only rarely met. There is, however, a "mentor system" in which a guard is appointed to each prisoner to watch over him or her and in whom he or she can confide. In this way, conflicts and problems should be more easily spotted and countered.

"Enforcement commissions," composed of seven adults, who are interested in penal institutions and have comprehension for the enforcement (but one of them must be an official of the justice ministerial department), monitor the treatment of prisoners and lawfulness of the enforcement. They report to the Ministry of Justice and, if necessary, make comments. But they are not allowed to give any instructions.

Court decisions on parole (early release) influence the possibility of attaining conditional release from prison. If this is granted to a minor or young adult, a parole officer is allocated to them.

The enforcement of any imprisonment should always be supervised by a social worker and, where necessary, psychotherapeutic support should be provided. The law also allows the offender to undergo therapy as an outpatient (Jesionek, 2001).

6.11. Empirical Data on Punishments and on Incarceration Rates

6.11.1. Empirical Data on Punishments Imposed
In 2003, roughly 3,180 juvenile offenders were convicted, on which the court imposed the sentences[13] seen in Table 10.8.

---

[13]See also Grafl (1988).

TABLE 10.8. Punishments imposed on juveniles in 2003

Conviction without sentence	68 cases	2.1%
Convictions with suspended sentence	402 cases	12.6%
Suspended penalties	1,503 cases	47.3%
	(287 fines, 1216 prison sentences)	
Penalties suspended in part	374 cases	11%
	82 fines and 266	
Non-suspended penalties	799 cases	25.1%
	499 fines and 300 prison sentences	
Total (2003)	3,187 cases	100%

Source: Sicherheitsbericht (2003), p. 415.

6.11.2. Empirical Data on Incarceration Figures

In 2003, the actual average daily number of prisoners was 7,880, including approximately 5,080 prisoners who served their sentence and 2,060 persons in detention on remand. The incarceration rate per 100,000 inhabitants, as of 1 September 2003 (Council of Europe,) was 96.9. About 2% of the inmates were minors (between 14 and less than 18), and around 6% "young adults" (between 18 and less than 21) (http://www.justiz.gv.at/justiz/justizanstalten/statistik.html:2004).

Over the year 2003, approximately 1,440 minors and 1,380 adolescents were taken into (pre-trial) custody, which is an enormous figure considering this should only be applied in exceptional circumstances. For the years 2000–2002, Pilgram (2003) describes a continuous increase in the number of youth entering into Austrian justice institutions.

6.11.3. How Effective are the Sanctions?

In 1994, Pilgram published a study on recidivism of young offenders, which shows the following picture of recidivism after a sanction by the court in the year 1983 in Table 10.9.

Not surprisingly, the heavier the intrusion, the more likely is recidivism. In 1983, the system of diversion as it is today did not yet exist. There was only Section 12 (2) JGG which allowed for dismissal of the case if the prosecutor anticipated a mere conviction with admonition, but without any sentence, by the criminal court.

With respect to diversion and other techniques of social work (particularly in parole and probation), there is no special study concerning juveniles. In a recent study, Pilgram et al. (2001) try to find an answer to the question what kind of influence the measures of diversion and the means of social work during parole or probation have on the number of formal adjudication and of prison sentences. Their answer is a very sceptical one.

TABLE 10.9. Juveniles convicted by Austrian Courts in 1983 who were reconvicted in the next 5 years

Sanction by court	Absolut figures of cases	Percentage of the use of the specific sanction	% of recidivism
Section 12 (1) JGG	980	12	38
Section 13 JGG	3315	45	44
Suspended fine	244	3	59
Fine (unconditional in whole or in part)	1021	14	62
Suspended Imprisonment	1533	21	61
Imprisonment (unconditional in whole or in part)	271	4	82
Total	7292	100	51

Source: Pilgram (1994).

7. CONCLUSION

In Austria juvenile delinquency currently amounts to 12% of total delinquency. Offences against property (particularly shoplifting) and against the person as well as narcotic drug offences are predominantly committed by (male) juveniles and young adults. The past years have seen a steady increase of criminal activity among young people. This increase (especially violent offences) is to some extent based on a reduced capability to resolve conflicts peacefully. Intensified security measures, such as reinforced policing of areas notorious for drug dealing by means of raids and CCTV or the employment of detectives in department stores seem to be responsible for this increase in offence rates although they also should have a crime preventive effect.

In order to reduce the delinquent behaviour of juveniles a number of crime prevention programmes are offered by social workers, police officers and teachers. These programmes concentrate on peaceful conflict resolution and drug counselling. Also communication skills and social skills are taught and furthered. Feedback from juveniles as well as parents and teachers to these programmes has been very positive. As there is most regrettably no official evaluation, we have no information on which programmes work effectively against delinquency.

If a young person between 14 and 18 years of age commits an offence, the Austrian Juvenile Criminal Law (JGG) offers a considerably broad range of measures, from non-intervention, diversion, conviction without sentence and conviction with suspended sentence to ordinary sanctions like fines and imprisonment. Thus, after having made a comprehensive evaluation, judges are offered the possibility to find the most effective answer to the young offender's situation. Indeed, judges of the Juvenile Court apply all these possibilities. But regrettably the above mentioned options are only applicable for minors and not for young adults. For the age group of 19 and 20 the law only provides some procedural regulations. It would be desirable to apply the wide range of sanctions of the JGG to young adults until the age of 25, or to even design a special law for young adults.

Prosecutors and judges should predominantly use non-intervention or diversion measures like suspending prosecution for a probation period, training, community service or victim-offender mediation. Rehabilitation has proven more successful if the young offender is not sentenced. Moreover, by using mediation with the victim the juvenile delinquent is encouraged to reflect about his offence.

Fines and imprisonment should only be applied as a last resort. Generally this is also put into practice but since the closure of Vienna Juvenile Court the number of fines and also the length of terms of imprisonment have risen constantly as juvenile offences are not only dealt with by prosecutors in the juvenile justice system but also by prosecutors who deal with adults. It is hoped that the latter will change their views. Unfortunately, pre trial detention is also imposed much too fast, without considering carefully whether custody is actually necessary.

Although imprisonment is applied as a last resort, about 2% of all prisoners are minors and around 6% are young adults, which is a high percentage indeed. But if such sanction seems indispensable, penal institutions offer at least several occupations even outside the prison itself. This however is only done if it can be guaranteed that the minors are not stigmatised. In future more attention should be paid to juvenile inmates so that they will be able to stay in contact with their families.

REFERENCES

Beclin, K. and Grafl, C. (2000). Die aktuelle Entwicklung der Jugendkriminalität – Anlass zur Sorge? Österreichische Juristen-Zeitung (ÖJZ), p. 821 et seq.

Bogensberger, W. (1992). Jugendstrafrecht und Rechtspolitik: eine rechts- und sozialwissenschaftliche Studie zur Genese des österreichischen Jugendgerichtsgesetzes. Wien: Manz-Verlag.

Burgstaller, M. (1977). Ist der Einsatz des Strafrechts eine sinnvolle Reaktion auf delinquentes Verhalten Jugendlicher? Österreichische Juristen-Zeitung (ÖJZ), p. 114 et seq.

Burgstaller, M. and Grafl, C. (2002). Daten zur Kriminalität und Verurteilung junger Erwachsener in Österreich, in R. Moos et al. (eds.), Festschrift für Udo Jesionek zum 65. Geburtstag. Wien-Graz: Neuer Wissenschaftlicher-Verlag, p. 35 et seq.

Brenner, G. (2000). Diebstahl, Drogen und Gewalt, Öffentliche Sicherheit (ÖS), issue 3, p. 9 (http:// www.bmi.gv.at/oeffentlsicherheit/2000/03/artikel_5.asp:2004).

Fabrizy, E. (2002). Strafgesetzbuch. Kurzkommentar, 8th edn. Wien: Manz-Verlag.

Grafl, C. (1988). Jugendliche Tatverdächtige und ihre Sanktionierung nach der Strafrechtsreform, Österreichische Juristen-Zeitung (ÖJZ), p. 519 et seq.

Grafl, C. (1995). Entscheidungsgrundlagen für strafrechtliche Reaktionen bei Jugendlichen. Eine empirische Untersuchung am Jugendgerichtshof Wien, Monatschrift für Kriminologie und Strafrechtsreform, vol. 78, p. 69 et seq.

Grafl, C. (2001). Ein Jahr Diversion in Österreich – Anspruch und Wirklichkeit, Österreichische Juristen-Zeitung (ÖJZ), p. 411 et seq.

Höpfel, F. (1988). Staatsanwalt und Unschuldsvermutung. Wien: Orac-Verlag.

Höpfel, F. (2002). Das Freiwilligkeitselement bei der Diversion, in R. Moos (ed.), Festschrift für Udo Jesionek zum 65. Geburtstag. Wien-Graz: Neuer Wissenschaftlicher-Verlag, p. 329 et seq.

Höpfel, F. (2004). National Report for the XVII International Congress of Penal Law. Austria. Criminal Responsibility of Minors, Revue internationale de droit penal, vol. 75, p. 121 et seq.

Jesionek, U. (2003). 80 Jahre Jugendgerichtsbarkeit in Österreich – Rückblick and Ausblick (Parts I–IV), Österreichische Richterzeitung (RZ), p. 66 et seq. (Part I); p. 94 et seq. (Part II); p. 118 et seq. (Part III); p. 142 et seq. (Part IV).

Jesionek, U. (2001). Das österreichische Jugendgerichtsgesetz, 3rd edn. Wien: Juridica-Verlag.

Jesionek, U. (1990). Zum Jugendgerichtsgesetz 1988, Österreichische Juristen-Zeitung (ÖJZ), p. 51 et seq.

Kienapfel, D. and Höpfel, F. (2005). Grundriss der Strafrechts. Allgemeiner Teil, 11th edn. Wien: Manz-Verlag.

Köck, E. (1999). Der Erziehungsgedanke im Jugendgerichtsgesetz, Journal für Rechtspolitik (JRP), p. 269 et seq.

Kriminalitätsbericht (Crime Report) 2001, 2002, 2003. Attached to the Sicherheitsbericht – Bericht der Bundesregierung über die innere Sicherheit in Österreich (annual reports from the Austrian Federal Government to Parliament).

Lässig, R. (2002). Kommentierung zu § 19. In: Höpfel F./Ratz E. (ed.) Wiener Kommentar 2nd edn. Wien: Manz-Verlag.

Leukauf, O. and Steiniger H. (1992). Kommentar zum Strafgesetzbuch, 3rd edn. Eisenstadt: Prugg-Verlag.

Löschnig-Gspandl, M. (2002). Österreich. In: Albrecht H.-J./Kilchling M., Jugendstrafrecht in Europa, edition juscrim, Freiburg i. Br., p. 269 et seq.

Maleczky, O. (2001). Österreichisches Jugendstrafrecht, 3rd edn. Wien: Manz-Verlag.

Neumair, M. (1996). Erziehung und Strafe. Rechtshistorische Untersuchung über Herkunft und Entstehung des österreichischen Jugendgerichtsgesetzes 1928, Doctoral dissertation, University of Vienna.

Pilgram, A. (1994). Wandel und regionale Varianten der Jugendgerichtspraxis auf dem Prüfstand der österreichischen Rückfallstatistik, Österreichische Juristen-Zeitung (ÖJZ), p. 121 et seq.

Pilgram, A. (2000). Studie über die Strafprozessnovelle 1999 und ihre Auswirkungen auf Diversion und Strafverfolgung, Annex to Sicherheitsbericht 2000 – Bericht der Bundesregierung über die innere Sicherheit in Österreich (annual reports from the Austrian Federal Government to Parliament).

Pilgram, A. (2003) Die Entwicklung der Haftzahlen in Österreich – Darstellung und Analyse der Ursachen, Annex to Sicherheitsbericht 2003 – Bericht der Bundesregierung über die innere Sicherheit in Österreich (annual reports from the Austrian Federal Government to Parliament).

Pilgram, A., Hirtenlehner, H., and Kuschej, H. (2001) Erfüllen (intervenierende) Diversion und Bewährungshilfe die Erwartung, Strafverfahren und Freiheitsstrafen zurückzudrängen? Österreichische Juristen-Zeitung (ÖJZ), p. 210 et seq.

Platzgummer, W. (1980) Probleme der Geldstrafe, Österreichische Juristen-Zeitung (ÖJZ), p. 29 et seq.

Schroll, H.-V. et al. (1986). Das Linzer Konfliktregelungsmodell, Richter Zeitung (RZ), p. 100 et seq.

Schütz, H. (1999). Das schwere Verschulden als Diversionsgrenze, in R. Miklau et al. (eds.), Diversion. Ein anderer Umgang mit Straftaten. Wien: Verlag Österreich, p. 19 et seq.

Schwaighofer, K. (1997). Das neue Suchtmittelrecht. Wien: WUV- Univ.-Verlag.

Sicherheitsbericht – Bericht der Bundesregierung über die innere Sicherheit in Österreich (annual reports from the Austrian Federal Government to Parliament) 2001, 2002, 2003.

Triffterer, O. (1988). Dogmatische und kriminalpolitische Überlegungen zur Reform des Jugendstrafrechts, Juristische Blätter (JBl), p. 343 et seq.

Walter, R. and Mayer, H. (2003). Grundriss des österreichischen Verwaltungsverfahrensrechts, 8th edn. Wien: Manz-Verlag.

11

The Swiss Federal Statute on Juvenile Criminal Law

Jean Zermatten

INTRODUCTION

Switzerland is a country of 7.5 millions inhabitants, of whom about 1 million are children and youths from age 7 to 18. The political system is a Federation of States, each with important decentralized power. The States making up the Helvetica Confederation are called "cantons" and there are 26 of them.

Juvenile Criminal Law is regulated by arts. 82–99 of the Criminal Code (Basic Law). As for procedures and judiciary organization, they come under the cantons' competence. A procedures standardization project is being examined by the central government; it will be submitted to Parliament in the near future.

Accordingly each canton has a specific procedure and organization, making Swiss magistrates and lawyers the champions of comparative law.

Moreover, cantons are also competent as far as the implementation of sentences and measures are concerned, notably to provide facilities to accommodate young offenders. They can associate with other cantons to meet common needs. In that case they will sign an inter-canton agreement (called *concordat*), grouping the cantons' resources for a specific institution. A new federal law requiring new institutions is consequently a source of problems: cantons will need a certain time to respond to these new requirements.

In Switzerland, the minimal age of penal intervention is currently seven years, and it will be raised to ten years under the new law. The age of criminal majority is 18 years. Between these two landmarks, protections limit imposing fines and the deprivation of liberty for minors younger than 15 years.

The aim of this chapter is to present the new Federal Law ruling the Juvenile offender's regime, approved by Parliament on 20 June 2003.

1. RECENT CHANGES IN LEGISLATION

After a long gestation period lasting almost 20 years the new juvenile criminal law was born following a vote held at the Federal Assembly (the Swiss Parliament) on 20 June 2003 in which the first draft law on juvenile justice was adopted. The process had begun back in 1985 when Professor Martin Stettler of the University of Geneva first proposed a new draft law. This was submitted to a committee of

J. Junger-Tas and S. H. Decker (eds.), International Handbook of Juvenile Justice, 295–308.

experts who worked on it from 1986 until 1993. The draft law then went through the consultation procedure, was sent back to the Federal administration for slight revision and was then submitted to the National Council which presented it to Parliament in 1998. It may seem surprising that a text for which the main parties concerned (juvenile courts, youth welfare services) as well as by the major political parties had reached an agreement in principle would have such a laborious delivery. And all the more so in that the parliamentary debate not brought about much change to the text.

The law is expected to come into force on the first of January 2007.[1] Such a long time-frame seems rather surprising but the reason is that the cantons, which retain sovereign authority not only regarding judiciary procedure and organization but also concerning institutional facilities, had requested extra time before the new law was implemented.

It should be recalled that the current legal code had been adopted in 1937 and entered into force in 1942. It had undergone a "face-lift" in 1971 but it needed to be revisited and updated. The law needed to be adapted to the change in the pattern of juvenile delinquency that had taken place since 1990–1995, and the significant statistical changes that had ensued. In general it can be said that the new law did not trigger a revolution, and that it had picked up many of the provisions enshrined in the existing legal regime, whilst modernizing and adapting them to current realities.

In the following presentation I would like to show you above all how the pattern of juvenile crime has changed in Switzerland and then briefly highlight the innovative elements of the text.

2. JUVENILE CRIME TRENDS IN SWITZERLAND

2.1. General Comments

Generally speaking, delinquency in Switzerland is characterized by four distinct findings. First, there has been a sharp rise in the number of minors charged and convicted in juvenile court. Second, there has been a shift from adult delinquency toward juvenile delinquency. And third, there has been a drop in the age at which minors commit offenses.

2.2. A Rise in the Number of Reported Offenses

Federal statistics on juvenile delinquency have been recorded in a generalized fashion since 1986 and systematically recorded since the "Jusus" system was

---

[1] Not yet decided by the Swiss Department of Justice (Ministry).

introduced by the Swiss Federal Statistical Office in 1999.[2] It can be affirmed that the number of convicted minors remained much the same until 1990, that it rose slightly between 1990 and 1995 (6,803–7,983 and since 1995 the number has risen sharply (7,983–13,483).

Figure 11.1[3] clearly illustrates that between 1990 and 2003 there was an increase in the number of minors convicted in Switzerland.

Figure 11.2 shows the number of minors reported to have committed an offense in the French-speaking cantons. This mirrors the change in the actual workload of juvenile courts, since a certain number of cases will not lead to convictions. This may lead to a nonprosecution, no further action, dismissal, acquittal, withdrawal of the complaint, a conciliation arrangement, or withdrawal of the judge.

The breakdown per canton is given in the following Fig. 11.2[4].

Please note that statistics about French-speaking cantons are more or less homogeneous, since their care and custody systems for young offenders are conceived in a very similar way. In German-speaking Switzerland, systems

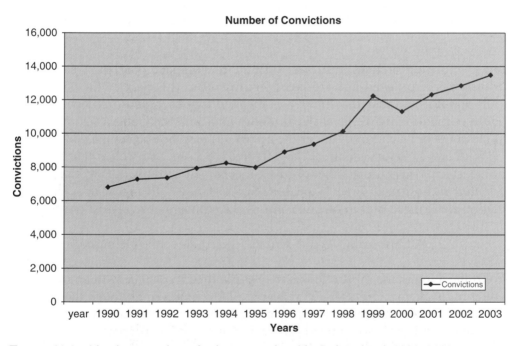

FIGURE 11.1. Absolute number of minors convicted in Switzerland, 1990–2003.

[2]Statistics on criminal convictions of minors in 1999 (Jusus), Swiss Federal Statistical Office, Bern, April 2001.
[3]Statistics on criminal convictions for minors in Switzerland ("Condemnations pénales des mineurs en Suisse"), Swiss Federal Statistical Office, Bern and Neuchatel.
[4]Statistics provided by the "juvenile Courts for French-speaking Switzerland."

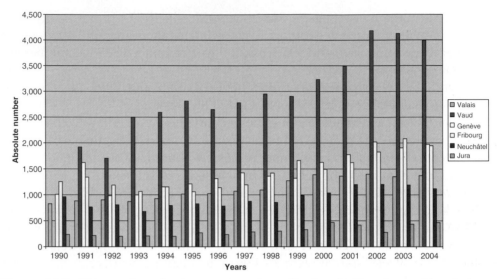

FIGURE 11.2. The number of minors reported as offenders in French-speaking Switzerland 1990–2004.

reveal more differences, and are difficult to compare. For this reason, the author has renounced not produced figures about this part of the country.

It should be noted that these are absolute figures which are dependent on youth population figures in each canton. In addition, the Geneva figures include adolescents only; children (under the age of 15) have not been included.

With just a cursory glance at these figures it becomes very clear that there has been a sharp rise in the number of juveniles charged with offenses by the juvenile criminal authorities in French-speaking Switzerland. With a more detailed examination we realized that in certain cantons the numbers have almost doubled.

2.3. A Shift from "Adult" Crime Towards Juvenile Delinquency

For quite a long time most offenses were committed by adults, with an overrepresentation of young adults (18–25 years old). Now however, although the majority of those brought before the law enforcement authorities are adults, the numbers of juveniles subjected to criminal proceedings is becoming proportionately higher. This is the second key finding in this chapter, the increasing representation of juveniles in criminal proceedings, and the growth of the juvenile population over time in that regard.

Thus, from approximately 15% of all recorded offenses being committed by minors the figures have risen by almost one third,[5] peaking at 44% for example in the canton of Fribourg in 2001.[6]

---

[5]2001 statistics from the Cantonal police of Valais, Sion, February 2002, p. 27.
[6]2001 statistics from the Cantonal police of Fribourg.

2.4. Increasingly Younger Offenders

The fourth characteristic of the new data on juvenile delinquency is that offenders are committing their offenses at an increasingly younger age. This holds true throughout the Western world. In Switzerland juvenile courts have found themselves in the middle of this trend. But since 1999, there is a decrease of the cases of young offenders under 15 years (from 24% to 21%[7]).

The situation of this 20% of very young adolescents in conflict with the law poses additional difficulties since the age of these young offenders often corresponds to a delicate period following the state of latency that precedes adolescence. This is compounded by the educational status of the young delinquents who at times are no longer accepted at normal educational institutions, and have been expelled from them, more or less overriding the legal requirement of compulsory education. The lack of appropriate structures to deal with this type of situation has created enormous difficulties.

A delicate piece of the institutional puzzle needs to be resolved: the offenders' young age precludes strict penalties, although the behavior of these very young people often exceeds what their families, classrooms, and traditional educational institutions can bear. The conundrum is exacerbated further by the need to ensure minimal school attendance.

3. PRESENTATION OF THE NEW LAW

3.1. A Law Outside of the Swiss Criminal Code

There is no specific law in Switzerland at present concerning juvenile offenders; provisions that apply to young offenders are an integral part of the Swiss Criminal Code and are enshrined in arts. 82–99 of the code. Until the new juvenile criminal law enters into force the provisions applying to juvenile offenders will thus remain in the Swiss criminal code,[8] and be the same as apply to adults. Nevertheless the Swiss parliament's intention with the new legislation is to move away from this text and enact a distinct law that applies to juveniles exclusively. This is the new Swiss Federal Statute on Criminal Juvenile Law (CJL) (abbreviation in French: DPMin).

This is above all a symbolic gesture giving young offenders their own law so as to differentiate clearly between the way adult and juvenile offenders are treated. This endeavor to separate the two requires a provision indicating which rules of the Swiss Criminal Code also apply to juveniles, since most of the general rules contained in it continue to be applicable to juveniles (cf. art. 1 para 2 in CJL/DPMin).

---

[7]Statistics OFS, 2003, p. 24, figure 13.
[8]Arts. 82 to 99, Swiss Criminal Code.

3.2. A Law with an Educational Perspective

Historically, juvenile justice has been kept separate from adult criminal law and its system of retribution in order to highlight the concept of individualized care and attention which focuses on the problems underpinning the commission of offenses so as to avoid recidivism/repeat offenses wherever possible. During the past century throughout the Western world lawmakers have enacted increasingly complex laws which have placed such emphasis on the idea of the underlying causes of crime that the judicial systems have swung back and forth between an interventionist approach aiming to correct and cure known as the "welfare model" and a more procedural and punitive approach linked to the "justice model."[9] This trend was quite apparent in the Anglo-Saxon countries where at the end of the 20th century there was a shift to increasingly stringent responses which gave priority to the deprivation of liberty.[10]

In the aftermath of the Convention of the Rights of the Child,[11] the major international texts such as the Beijing Rules,[12] the Riyad Guidelines,[13] and the Havana Rules,[14] or the draft law proposed to states by the United Nations Vienna office in charge of crime prevention on juvenile justice to serve as a model for national legislators[15] do not reveal a choice for one model over another, but repeatedly accentuate the need for clear procedural guarantees for young people in conflict with the law (with the leitmotiv that the juvenile must not be subject to worse treatment than an adult) and on the fact that any deprivation of liberty (pre- and post-trial detention and custody) should be adopted as a last resort. Emphasis is placed on developing alternative measures and out-of-court procedures.[16]

Swiss lawmakers have not allowed themselves to be influenced by the current trend to favor security as the highest value, thus requiring dissuasive penalties for young delinquents but have clearly articulated their endorsement of the protection principles. This is proclaimed unequivocally in art. 2 of the CJL

---

[9]Zermatten J., *Face à l'évolution des droits de l'enfant, quel système judiciaire: système de protection ou système de justice?*, in *Revue internationale de criminologie et de police technique*, n° 2, Geneva, 1994.

[10]Namely in several states in the USA and in England.

[11]Convention of the Rights of the Child, 20 November 1989.

[12]United Nations Standard Minimum Rules for the Administration of Juvenile Justice, 29 November 1985.

[13]United Nations Guidelines for the Prevention of Juvenile Delinquency (The Riyadh Guidelines).

[14]United Nations Rules for the Protection of Juveniles Deprived of their Liberty, 14 December 1990.

[15]Draft law on juvenile justice (United Nations – Vienna), September 1997.

[16]Namely art. 37 and 40, Convention on the Rights of the Child.

(principles). This means that the Swiss legislators have underscored, in this new type of protective law:

- The need to consider the personal and family circumstances of the child (cf. art. 9 CJL);
- The need to provide for protective measures (art. 12–15 CJL)
- The need to give these measures priority over punishment (art. 32 CJL)

3.3. A Law with Elements of Restorative Justice

The way youthful offenders are treated has evolved and it has been affirmed that there is now a third model,[17] that of restorative justice which includes the victim in the process and tries to raise awareness in offenders of the impact of their wrongdoing so they can repair the harm and make amends. This does not in our view constitute a third model but is an approach that can be included within the protection system as well as in the system of justice.

The Swiss lawmaker has picked up on this idea of restitution and confrontation with the victim through the introduction of *mediation*, in arts. 8 and 21, para. 3 (CJL). The confrontation between offender and victim follows a procedure used in mediation. The stakeholders reach agreement on symbolic reparation, be it partial or total, so as to complete the mediation during the preparatory inquiry or at the time sentence is passed.

The concept of *community service order* as seen in art. 23 CJL reflects elements of restorative justice, the idea being to find a way of repairing harm that has an educational grounding (active participation in classes) or reintegrating the society in which the law was broken thanks to a symbolic reparation (community work).

3.4. A Law with Punitive Elements

Although the main concern of the new CJL is to provide protection, it is undeniably more stringent than the current law in that it provides for two forms of deprivation of liberty that are significantly harsher:

- **Qualified deprivation of liberty** for up to four years for juveniles above the age of 16 who have committed grave offenses and who pose a danger to society.
- **Institutionalization in closed establishments** to prevent self-harm or safeguard the public from serious harm (art. 25 para. 2 CJL).

The aforementioned affirmation of the stringency of the new law must be nuanced, however, by the fact that this will depend on the conditions under which the sanctions are implemented. These conditions should be more akin to protective

---

[17]D'Amours, O., *100 ans de justice juvénile*, IDE (Institute of the Child's Rights), 2002, pp. 106–115.

measures than deprivations of liberty in the traditional sense of the term. Institutionalization of a juvenile in a closed establishment must be decided on the basis of objective criteria following medical and psychological examination by an expert.

3.5. Minimal Age of Criminal Responsibility

At present juvenile courts in Switzerland are processing child offenders aged 7–15 and youth offenders between 15 and 18 years old. The new CJL will only apply to children as of the age of 10, thus raising the threshold for the minimal age for criminal responsibility from 7 to 10 years. This decision has given rise to much discussion, with some holding the view that the ages of 12, 14, or 16 would be better suited. It should be noted that the current threshold is amongst the lowest in the world (with that of Scotland and the Republic of Myanmar) and that arguments in favor of such a young age for criminal responsibility (i.e., the myth of early detection) disappeared with the mushrooming of youth social welfare services. In the end it was the emergence of serious crimes committed by very young children and the continual drop in the age of young offenders that prompted the choice for the minimal age for criminal responsibility to be set as of the age of 10 (art. 3 CJL).

The ceiling for criminal responsibility under juvenile justice remains at 18 years of age as is the case in most countries in the world.

The relatively artificial distinction made between children and young people disappears and a sole category remains, that of juveniles. The age limit of 15 years remains for qualified community service orders (art. 23 para. 3 CJL), for fines (art. 24 CJL) and for the deprivation of liberty (art. 25 para.1 CJL), and 16 years for qualified deprivation of liberty (art. 25 para. 2 CJL).

3.6. Protective Measures

Swiss legislation has tried to harmonize protective measures enshrined in the Swiss Civil Code with those adopted by the criminal judge. That is why measures qualified in the new law as "protective" – whereas they are "educational" in positive law – are treated similarly to measures under the Swiss Civil Code.

It should be noted that today there is great variety in the types of correctional facilities for juveniles[18] but this system – which does not stem from an objective analysis of needs but from a rather discriminatory definition of the attitude or character of the institutionalized juveniles – now disappears in favor of the broader heading "institutionalization." Now pride of place will be given to needs analysis, monitoring of the juveniles and potential modification of measures through transfer to another institution.

Naturally the idea of *institutionalization in closed establishments* merits attention, as provided in art. 15 para. 2 CJL as mentioned above. The innovative nature

---

[18]Arts. 91, 93 bis 93 Swiss Criminal Code.

of this type of institutionalization will pose certain problems regarding the availability of appropriate establishments, i.e., in relation to the mental health problems of the young delinquents since such establishments are, at present, sadly lacking.

Concerning remaining issues, in the new provisions we find the same ambulatory and institutional measures that exist at present and that criminal juvenile law uses abundantly and will continue to use.

It should be noted, nonetheless, that Swiss lawmakers have responded to an oft-made request by those dealing with juveniles at risk or juvenile offenders, regarding the exchange of information and collaboration, so as to avoid unnecessary duplication. Art. 20 of the CJL will impose comprehensive collaboration between civil authorities and juvenile criminal authorities and will resolve a certain number of situations where these authorities should not only exchange information but will be called upon to make the corresponding decisions.

3.7. Penalties

The new law has taken up sanctions from positive law such as reprimands, fines and work duty, and rejuvenated them. The CJL has above all underscored community service order as

- A means of making amends to oneself or to society
- A genuine alternative to short periods of deprivation of liberty

Art. 23, para. 2 CJL offers the possibility of fulfilling this service by following a course and not only by doing work. This is reminiscent of other mandatory measures imposed by juvenile courts in Switzerland, regarding road safety courses, health education or sessions for juvenile sexual abusers (e.g., the experience of Famille Solidaire[19]), etc.

But para. 3 of the same article also provides for the imposition of community work duty for juveniles who were over the age of 15 at the time of the offense and up to *three-month qualified community service order*, allowing the judge to assign fixed residence during the work period. This is new and shows the clear will of the legislator to highlight "reparative" and "alternative" aspects, rather than favoring a return to the traditional form of deprivation of liberty. If we set this provision alongside art. 24 of the CJL and with art. 26 of the CJL we see that the juvenile who has been sentenced to a fine or deprivation of liberty for up to a three-month period can request these sentences to be converted into a community service order.

---

[19]Activity Report 2001 of Association Familles Solidaires, Pl. Be-Air 2, 1003, Lausanne. "Familles solidaires" is a nongovernmental organization (NGO), namely an association founded in the beginning to take care of the victims of sexual abuse. After a few years' experience, this association decided to provide care for the perpetrators of abuse as well, and set up self-help groups for minor delinquents charged of sexual abuse. Minor Courts can dispose of these measures.

That means that in the future community service orders are expected to *hold a pivotal role* in the sentencing of juveniles. It should be recalled that most offenses committed by juveniles are generally relatively minor and that art. 23 CJL should provide a useful settlement framework for them.

The same does not hold true for *qualified deprivation of liberty, which should remain the exception*. The conditions set by art. 25 para. 2 CJL are quite strict:

- The offender must have reached the age of 16 at the time of the offense, and
- The offender must have committed an offense punishable under adult law by at least three years of deprivation of liberty (at the present time: murder, manslaughter, aggravated burglary, the taking of hostages, sexual duress, rape, arson), or
- The offender must have committed an offense provided for in art. 122 of the Swiss Criminal Code (SCC), such as serious bodily harm, art. 140, number 3 SCC aggravated robbery or art. 184 SCC (deprivation of personal liberty, aggravated abduction and forcible confinement) and shown a particular lack of scruples, especially if the offender's motives, action, or intention has revealed a highly blameworthy state of mind.

We thus understand that this punishment can only be applied to exceptional circumstances that are not the common fare of the justice system. The fact of the matter is that such situations, however, do exist, and it is a sign of change in the new law that an adapted form of punishment has been found which lacks the excessive paternalism that at times it had formerly been criticized for. It certainly represents the price to be paid for the public to accept a "tailor-made" law for young offenders. Not providing for stringent punishment for more serious offenses would be tantamount to a rejection of this comprehensive, remedial, and educational form of justice.

The conditions set for implementation of this punishment under art. 27 (CJL) (the requirement to have appropriate facilities and to foster integration and training goals) show clearly that we do not seek to have prisons for young people but rather appropriate facilities where the educational, training and integration goals the CJL has set will be attained.

3.8. The Principle of Dualism (Optional)

Current law applies the principle of legal monism, a theory that holds that he who provides treatment cannot mete out punishment at the same time, hence the second principle that punishment should be in proportion to the crime. Thus, at present, insofar as a juvenile needs special care, punishment is excluded (except for a minor exception[20]). This leads to somewhat indefensible situations, i.e., when juveniles

---

[20]Art. 95, ch. 1 para. 2, Swiss Criminal Code.
VS = Valais, VD = Vaud, GE = Genève, FR = Fribourg, NE = Neuchâtel, JU = Jura

commit offenses in groups and where very different responses are possible for the different offenders, not because of the offenses committed but because of vastly different educational needs.

Whereas the idea that the punishment should fit the crime appears fair (treat first, punish later), this does not rule out punishment for wrongful conduct. The idea is to confront the juvenile with his or her wrongful conduct and possibly with the victim as well, so as to make amends. This is necessary from an educational point of view (gaining awareness, accepting accountability, learning appropriate social behavior) and does not rule out the provision of treatment at the same time. It is thus to meet this dual need to treat root causes and punish wrongful behavior that CJL has introduced the possibility of combining protective measures and punitive penalties. This principle of dualism is seen in art. 11 of the CJL.

Yet this dualism is optional, not compulsory, in the sense that the judge is not obliged to punish a person who has been sentenced by him to a protective measure and that the judge must waive punishment, when the conditions of art. 21 (exemption from punishment) of the CJL have been met. Furthermore, under art. 32 of the CJL (combining protective measures with those providing for a deprivation of liberty) the lawmaker has clearly shown his preference for protective measures in situations where, upon enforcement of protective measures a clash arises with sentences calling for deprivation of liberty.

3.9. Rules of Procedure in Substantive Law

So as to harmonize certain basic rules of procedure, the Swiss legislator has incorporated rules of procedure into substantive law. It is true that criminal rules of procedure concerning juveniles in different Swiss cantons greatly differ from each other or at times do not exist at all. In the view of the European Court of Human Rights and major international instruments on juvenile law, it is no longer possible to ignore rules of procedure. That is why CJL addresses the following procedural points:

1. art. 6 CJL Pre-trial detention
2. art. 39, para. 2 CJL In Camera Proceedings
3. art. 39, para. 3 CJL Personal Appearance of the Parties
4. art. 40 CJL Rights of Defense
5. art. 41 CJL Right to Appeal

These rules are important as they address the specificity of the intervention of juvenile criminal law in regards to young delinquents and extremely delicate situations where, far too often, cantonal codes are conspicuously silent or imprecise. The incorporation of this basic corpus of rules of procedure into substantive law is thus to be welcomed even if in terms of a legal rationale this is rather unorthodox. Nonetheless the existence of these basic rules clearly strengthen the juvenile's position during his trial, protect him against the arbitrary notion of doing something "for the child's best interests," so often used as a pretext, while they safeguard the specific objectives of judicial intervention by averting excessive formalism of certain procedures.

The Swiss cantons therefore will have to enact legislation to bring these rules of procedure into force and implement them. In the event such rules already exist, the cantons will have to either add to or amend their provisions on procedure. Later the unified code on juvenile criminal law, expected in 2007/2008 will apply.

3.10. Implementation Issues

In the new law implementation issues have not been sidestepped nor has the buck been passed to the cantons, far from it. Key principles have been articulated both for protective measures (art. 16–20 CJL) and for penalties (art. 27–31 CJL).

Notwithstanding, the major question that arises at this stage of the innovation process is whether the appropriate facilities as provided under CJL – i.e., closed establishments, establishments for pre- and post-trial detention – and planned mediation bodies or community service orders will be made available to juvenile authorities. It is true that art. 48 of the CJL obliges the cantons to provide for the necessary establishments under arts. 15 and 27 of the CJL within the next ten years. Nonetheless previous examples can lead us to believe that this will remain a dead letter, e.g., the current law provides for therapeutic facilities to be in function, meant for young offenders in need of specific care. However, no such institution has ever become a reality.

Therefore preparatory work must be done for the new law. In our view, above all, an effort must be made by the cantons to reach inter-cantonal agreements. Given the nature and the degree of the demands made by these establishments both in terms of care given as in terms of the number and training of staff, it seems highly unrealistic to assume that each canton will be endowed with each type of institution.

Lastly, it is essential that all services working in the domain of child welfare, be it the civil or criminal authorities, administrative or private services, will be informed of the content of this new law and will be able to carry out its work in a concerted fashion. In this domain as far as possible the different areas of competence of the different stakeholders must be harnessed and unnecessary overlapping avoided. Work with young people and their families should remain based on quality contacts and personal relationships and should strive for minimal adherence to contemplated measures. For that to happen all parties must necessarily collaborate.

4. CONCLUSION

The new juvenile criminal law had a long gestation period but it appears particularly well adapted to new types of delinquency in Switzerland. In my view, the new law meets to a greater extent the challenges resulting from observations on juvenile Offending first, because its basic inspiration remains protection-oriented. Second, because it leads the young offender to face his or her responsibility and his or her deeds (mediation and restorative justice elements). Finally, because, the new law has acquired the instruments necessary to tackle the most difficult of minors, namely the new institutions. Concerning minors committing very serious offences, the law has raised the possible duration of confinement. It is not drifting away from the benevolence characterizing the Swiss system, but it is reinforcing itself, to better respond to young offenders' new expressions.

It is not a revolutionary law, but one that maintains its trust in a protective system, yet still includes elements of restorative justice and tightens its line concerning delinquents who commit grave offenses.

It is also a law that is in keeping with international standards and which hopes to see minimal rules of procedure imposed throughout Switzerland. In this regard, it can be said that it is a law that respects children's rights, and does not adopt a paternalistic stance in regard to the young offender but remains objectively well-intentioned, offering basic procedural guarantees to juveniles and yet desires to treat root causes rather than punish symptoms.

Translated from French by Mrs Lisa Godin-Roger,
ETI, University of Geneva, Switzerland

12

The Emerging Juvenile Justice System in Greece

Calliope D. Spinellis and Aglaia Tsitsoura

INTRODUCTION: THE SOCIO-DEMOGRAPHIC AND LEGAL BACKGROUND

The aim of this chapter is to describe the juvenile justice system of modern Greece and examine the extent to which the legislative initiatives of the 21st century are in conformity with the relevant main conventions and recommendations of the European Union, the Council of Europe and the United Nations. In the first place an attempt is made to sketch the modern Greek state using some social and demographic data, and then to examine the legal background. Emphasis is put on the recent legislative enactments referring to juvenile offences and the state's reaction to them.

Greece is located in the south-eastern part of Europe and more specifically on the southern tip of the Balkan Peninsula and covers an area of 131,957 sq. km. The country has more than 14,880 km of coastline and approximately 1,400 islands – both an advantage because of the picturesque landscape – and a disadvantage because of the difficulty to control various criminal activities (Spinellis/Spinellis, 1999).

The Modern Greek State gained its independence from the Ottoman Empire in 1830 and in 1981 accessed to the European Community. The language – modern Greek – preserves many elements of its classical predecessor dating back 3,500 years. The Greek population is estimated by the National Statistical Service of Greece as of mid-2002: 10,987,559 (Table 12.1). However, earlier estimates (June 1999) of the US Department of State give a higher population size: 11.5 million (US Department of State, Greece, 1999). Most probably the latter estimation includes, non-registered, clandestine economic immigrants. The exact figure of illegal immigrants or the total number of non-natives is unknown. The Ministry of Labour gives an estimate of 500,000–600,000 (Davanelos, 1999). As of 1998 a legalization process of clandestine immigrants and granting of green cards was initiated. The most important nationalities represented among the non-natives, neo-immigrants are people coming from Russia – many of them of Greek origin – 300,000, Albania; 200,000, Egypt; 80,000, Poland; 65,000, Ukraine; 18,000, Palestine; 2,000, Philippines, Nigeria, etc. (*Kathimerini*, 1999).

Until the 1990s Greece was a homogeneous society: 99% of the population had Greek as mother tongue and 98% were of Greek orthodox religion, 1% Muslims

J. Junger-Tas and S. H. Decker (eds.), International Handbook of Juvenile Justice, 309–324.
© 2006 Springer.

TABLE 12.1. Estimated population of Greece in mid of the year 2002

Age brackets	Total	Males	Females
Total	10,987,559	5,439,332	5,548,227
0–4	505,514	260,008	245,506
5–9	536,683	275,314	261,369
10–14	575,629	298,236	277,393
15–19	675,068	351,918	323,150
20–24	814,041	425,415	388,626
25–29	853,007	441,024	411,983
30–34	868,506	443,853	424,653
35–39	819,244	412,050	407,194
40–44	787,024	391,774	395,250
45–49	736,053	365,747	370,306
50–54	684,481	337,951	346,530
55–59	627,657	304,990	322,667
60–64	596,857	278,460	318,397
65–69	630,906	290,715	340,191
70–74	552,082	251,819	300,263
75–79	375,946	164,979	210,967
80–84	204,113	86,689	117,424
85 and above	144,748	58,390	86,358

Source: Statistical Service of Greece.

and 1% other (*Kathimerini*, 1999). This homogeneity made informal controls of family and neighbourhood effective and kept both adult criminality and juvenile delinquency at low levels.

Since 1950, the Penal Code and the Code of Penal Procedure have been the basic texts for the administration of Criminal Justice in Greece (Lambropoulou, 2004). These texts, drawn up after many years of preparatory work, were inspired by the prevailing criminal law and procedure in the country as well as the relevant German, Italian, and Swiss penal and criminological theories and practices. During the half-century of the implementation of these Codes, there have been various amendments, via new legislative Acts, when new situations or ideas rendered modification necessary.

The part of the Greek Penal Code (PC) (articles 121–133 PC) concerning juvenile justice included provisions meant to promote assistance to, and re-education and therapy for young offenders, aged 13–17 years. Children under 12 years were treated by educative or therapeutic measures only. For those of 13–17 years old the Penal Code abolished the (previously accepted) criterion of *discernment* and adopted the idea that the judge must consider, in the light of circumstances of the committed act and of the personality of the juvenile, if educative and therapeutic measures would be sufficient to avoid re-offending. In the negative, young offenders were sentenced to a particular penal sanction.

On the other hand, the Code of Penal Procedure (CPP) (e.g., articles 1, 4, 7, 27, 130, 239, 305, 316, 489, and 549 CPP) and special Acts setting up the institutions, for instance, of Juvenile Courts (Acts 5098/1931, 2135/1939, 3315/1955), of probation services for juveniles (Act 2793/1954), of Societies for the Protection of Minors (Decree of July 1943), of Centres for the re-education of juvenile delinquents and their compulsory primary education (Act 2724/1940 and Decree 71/ 1973) preceded or supplemented the provisions of the Codes.

Although some of the means for implementation of the law were not available (e.g., there have never been centres for the scientific observation of the juveniles' personality) these provisions set the ground for a modern system of juvenile justice in Greece.

As stated above, during the last decades of the 20th century and the beginning of the 21st century, it became evident that changing socio-economic factors made the existing legislation concerning the treatment of juvenile offenders obsolete. Hence, this required revision and – when necessary – even in-depth amendment. Some of these social factors are equally found in the larger European space:

- Urbanization and industrialization modified the living conditions of the population (Council of Europe, 1979); in particular, internal migration resulted in a considerable increase of the population of the main Greek cities (e.g., the greater Athens area has now 3.7 million inhabitants, and Thessaloniki – the second biggest city – about 1 million);
- Political and economic changes in Eastern Europe resulted in a great movement of populations; Greece received an important number of external migrants (migration rate: 2.35 migrants per 1,000 population), some of them accompanied by their families;
- Drug trafficking threatened Greece (Madianou, 1992; Spinellis, 1999), as almost all other European countries, and was often combined with other forms of delinquent behaviour;
- Family and community solidarity and control, although still existing in Greece to a considerable degree, have been weakened (Spinellis, 1999).

It was clear that any revision had to take into account the new ideas and methods developed during the last decades of the 20th century in the field of criminal justice, such as restorative justice, community service, and care for victims.

These ideas and methods were developed in many texts adopted by international organizations and especially by the United Nations[1] and the Council of

[1]United Nations Convention on the Rights of the Child and its optional Protocols, United Nations Standard Minimum Rules for the Administration of Justice (the Beijing Rules), United Nations Guidelines for the Prevention of Juvenile Delinquency (the Riyad Guidelines), United Nations Rules for the Protection of Youths deprived of their Liberty, etc.

Europe.[2] The European Union also granted considerable attention to questions relating to juvenile justice and children victims.[3]

In 2003, the Greek Parliament adopted Act 3189/2003 on the "reform of the legislation concerning minors." The Act has been incorporated in the Greek Penal Code. The same procedure was followed with the amendments of certain provisions or additions to the Code of Penal Procedure. On the other hand, the Act 3064/2002, equally incorporated in the Penal Code, strengthened the protection of juvenile victims. Last but not least, a Bill establishing "Units for the Care of Youngsters" (at risk, delinquents, and victims) is in preparation.

1. JUVENILE CRIME TRENDS IN GREECE

The absence of systematic self-report surveys in Greece (Spinellis et al., 1991) compels us to rely on crime statistics solely, despite the well-known limitations and possible defects of them (Pitsela, 2004).

Tables 12.2–12.4 indicate that juvenile crime is increasing in Greece. However, this increase is not alarming, if one studies carefully the existing formal statistical data collected by (a) the Ministry of Public Order (Hellenic Police: offenders known to the Police), and (b) the Ministry of Justice (offenders convicted by the courts). It should be noted that the latter refer to Juvenile Court data given that Greek Juvenile Courts have exclusive jurisdiction in almost all cases of minors up to 18 years of age (previously 17) and sometimes, even above that age. The statutory "minimum age of criminal responsibility is the 13th year" as of 2003 (see also Section 2.2.2).

The year 1973 is the first year of publication of uniform statistical data covering all Greece, and 1996 the last year for which such data are published due to the reorganisation and computerisation of the system.

Table 12.2 indicates a considerable increase in the offences known to the Police for the age brackets 7–17.[4] In fact the increase is more than 200% between

[2]European Convention of Human Rights, Recommendation N° R (87) 20 on social reactions to juvenile delinquency, Recommendation N° R (88) 6 on social reactions to juvenile delinquency among young people coming from migrant families, Recommendation Rec (2000) 20 on the role of early psychosocial intervention in the prevention of criminality, Recommendation N° R (2003) 20 concerning new ways of dealing with juvenile delinquency and the role of juvenile justice and Recommendations No R (91) 11 on sexual exploitation, pornography, prostitution of and trafficking in children and young persons, and No R (2001) on the protection of children against sexual exploitation.

[3]For example, in May 2001, the Council established the European Union Crime Prevention Network (EUCPN)(2001/427/JHA). The EUCPN focuses its efforts on three areas, according to Council Decision: one of them being juvenile crime. With respect to children victims of sexual exploitation see, e.g., the relevant frame-decision concerning trafficking of human beings (document 8135/02 DROIPEN 26, MIGR 35, 19 April 2002).

[4]The changes of the law which increased the age limits from 7–17 to 8–18 are not reflected in these statistics.

TABLE 12.2. Offences of minors (7–17 years of age) known to the Police and adjudicated by the Juvenile Courts (1973–1996)(Traffic violations included)

Year	Police	%[1]	Juvenile Courts	%[2]
1973	5,948	2.9	5,566	4.9
1974	5,881	2.8	4,577	4.3
1975	5,900	3.1	6,105	5.4
1976	7,041	2.7	6,498	5.8
1977	7,332	2.8	6,056	5.2
1978	7,997	3.0	5,789	5.0
1979	9,480	3.1	5,216	4.3
1980	8,577	2.8	5,476	4.5
1981	8,794	2.8	5,454	4.0
1982	12,272	3.6	6,762	4.8
1983	13,770	3.5	7,819	6.5
1984	12,357	3.5	8,530	7.5
1985	11,456	4.1	7,374	6.8
1986	10,773	3.9	7,767	6.3
1987	10,345	3.6	8,374	6.0
1988	9,060	3.1	6,393	4.8
1989	8,485	3.2	5,107	4.7
1990	15,298	4.9	6.794	6.2
1991	18,535	5.6	6,317	5.6
1992	16,530	5.7	7,964	7.2
1993	17,061	5.7	6,095	6.6
1994	16,530	6.1	5,469	6.5
1995	17,061	6.1	6,388	7.0
1996	17,940	6.0	5,666	6.6

[1]Percentage of the total of alleged offenders known to the police with known age.
[2]Percentage of the total of persons convicted by all Courts.
Source: A. Pitsela, Penal Reaction to the Criminality of Minors, 5th edn., Athens, Thessaloniki, 2004, 471.

the years 1973 and 1996. This situation, however, is not reflected in the Juvenile Court statistics (increase by 1.7% only). This discrepancy could be explained with the help of the realist theory stating that statistics are the reflection of the production of the criminal justice system. Thus, statistics give us nothing more than the number of cases that the Juvenile Courts had the capacity to handle during a particular year (Bottomley, 1979). On the other hand, one could also argue that the above Police statistics are closer to reality and the number of offences committed by juveniles did increase significantly because during this period Greece, as already pointed out, has experienced abrupt social changes and an attempt to computerize criminal justice. (Change between the years 1973 and 1976: from 2.9% to 6.0% or 106.8%).

Certain more recent data are included in Tables 12.3 and 12.4, covering the five-year period 1999–2003 such as detailed information concerning the age, gender, and nationality-ethnicity of offenders, as well as the seriousness of offences known to the Police. Police statistics of the years 1999–2003 present an increasing trend of juvenile crime and delinquency (traffic violations included). The change is significant especially between the years 1973–2003. In fact during this 30-year period there was an increase of 267.1%. Table 12.3 also reveals that around 7% of the reported crime for the age brackets of 7–17 concerns foreigners.

A careful reading of Tables 12.2–12.4 reveals that:

- the increase of the offences known to the Police, in particular after the 1990s is more obvious than that of the Courts – especially, if the percentage of the total of alleged offenders known to the Police is compared with the percentage of the total of all persons convicted by all Courts (Table 12.2);
- the overwhelming majority of offences allegedly committed by juveniles belong to the category of special laws (Nebengesätze) which do not include property crimes or crimes against persons but traffic violations, violations of drug laws, violations concerning illegal entry into the country, violation of laws regulating illegal electronic games, etc. (Table 12.4);
- the most prevalent offences known to the Police for persons 7–17 are: (a) traffic violations (90%), (b) theft (less than 4%), (c) violations relating to drugs (drug use included), and begging (both less than 2%), and finally (d) involvement in illegal games and illegal entry into the country (1%) of the total offences reported (Table 12.4);
- the fluctuations of the particular offences during the examined five-year period (1999–2003) do not suggest remarkable changes, and some of them are related with the intensified, for various reasons, police practices during a specific period (e.g., begging, illegal entry into the country) (Table 12.4);
- the offences that are attributed to persons 7–17 years of age seem to be under control as they represent no more than 6% of the total number of reported crime (Table 12.2);

TABLE 12.3. Offenders 7–17 years of age Greeks and foreigners known to Police (1999–2003)

Year	7–12	13–17	Greeks 7–17	Foreigners 7–17	Males 7–17	Females 7–17	Total
1999	463	21,784	20,811	1,435	20,470	1,777	22,247
2000	489	23,572	22,461	1,600	21,557	2,504	24,061
2001	545	25,629	24,459	1,716	23,945	2,229	26,174
2002	455	25,936	24,373	2,016	24,183	2208	26,391
2003	212	21,627	19,810	1,019	20,281	1,558	21.839

Source: Ministry of Public Order (unpublished data; the table is constructed by C. D. Spinellis).

TABLE 12.4. Most prevalent crimes[1] known to the Police: Offenders 7–17 years of age (1999–2003)

Offences	1999	2000	2001	2002	2003	Change 2000– 1999 (%)	Change 2001– 2000 (%)	Change 2002– 2001 (%)	Change 2003– 2002 (%)
Homicide	6	3	–	–	–	−50.0			
Assault	34	27	28	36	17	−20.0	3.7	28.5	−52.7
Serious theft	83	118	71	56	59	42.1	−39.8	−21.1	5.3
Begging	233		258	152	55	−100		−41.0	−63.8
Theft	771	544	680	748	547	−29.4	25.0	10.0	−26.8
Robbery	50	9	23	27	23	−82.0	155.5	17.3	−14.8
Drugs	283	193	112	119	113	−31.8	−41.9	6.2	−5.0
Illegal entry	136	180	102	104	129	32.3	−43.3	1.9	24.0
Illegal games	108	123	89	75	3	13.8	−27.6	−15.7	−96.0
Accomplice to theft	59	73	57	52	81	23.7	−21.9	−8.7	55.7
Traffic violations	19,786	25,083	25,122	24,860	20,806	26.7	0.1	−1.0	−16.3

[1]In the Table, with the exception of homicide, are included offences whose reported figure, in the year 1999, was 30 and over.
Source: Ministry of Public Order (unpublished data; the table is constructed by C. D. Spinellis).

- males are responsible for approximately 90% of the reported offences (Table 12.3);
- minors belonging to the age bracket 7–12 are responsible for no more than 2% of the total offences reported (Table 12.3);
- foreigners, on the average, are responsible for 6% of the total crime attributed to juveniles 7–17 years of age; however, since the total foreign population in Greece is estimated to be no more than 1,000,000, the population of the relevant age bracket should be less than 300,000 and the 6% shows an overrepresentation of foreigners (Table 12.3).

2. PREVAILING PHILOSOPHY OF THE NEW GREEK LEGISLATION CONCERNING MINORS

2.1. The New Legislation

Acts 3189/2003 and 3064/2002 do not contradict the philosophy of the previous provisions of the Greek Penal Code concerning minors but, in a spirit of continuation, enrich such philosophy in the light of new ideas developed in this field. The main directing principles of these provisions remain and emphasize:

- the respect of the individual rights and interests of the minor;
- the prevention of delinquent behaviour by means of adequate mainly non-custodial measures of assistance, education and treatment.

2.2. Legislative Novelties and Amendments

The recent enactments concerning juvenile offenders and the state's reaction towards them present interesting features which are in accordance to current international and European standards and norms. It is worth mentioning the following amendments to the relevant legislation.

2.2.1. Increase of both the Minimum and Maximum Year that the Juvenile Court has Jurisdiction, and Abolition of the Distinction between "Children" and "Adolescents"

The 7–17 years age bracket has been dysfunctional. The minimum age has been construed by case law as 6 years and one day and the age of 17 was not in accordance with the end of minority status. Thus, in the new provisions, the age limits are stated clearly and they refer to the 8th and 18th birthday. Furthermore, the new Act abolishes the term "criminal" with respect to minors. Finally, in the new provisions the terms "child and adolescent" are not used mainly for two reasons: the term "child" in the UN Convention on the Rights of the Child, which as of 1992 became national law in Greece (Act 2101/1992), covers the ages 0–18 years and misunderstandings might be created since "a child," under the Penal Code, was the person of 7–12 years of age. The second reason is based on the finding that maturity varies among individuals – especially minors – some of them being, from a mental or psychological point of view, less or more developed than what their real age indicates. Thus, the new provisions refer, when necessary, to the age limits of the minors concerned, instead of the term "adolescent."

2.2.2. Age of Penal Responsibility

According to the new rules minors of 8–13 years of age are not penally liable. Those of 13 years (completed) to 18 years are penally liable in some cases (see, 3.3). According to these amendments (a) children of less than 8 years of age who violate the penal law are now under the jurisdiction of welfare services, and (b) youngsters between 8 and 18 years are under the jurisdiction of the Juvenile Court and they are neither referred to the Criminal Courts nor are they sentenced to adult penal sanctions. With the adoption of the age limit of 18 years and the subsequent increase of number of cases that are tried by these Courts, the Juvenile Courts, sometimes due to court delays, have jurisdiction on youngsters older than 18 years. This might happen, since the jurisdiction of the Juvenile Court depends not on the age that the minor has at the moment of the hearing but on the age that the offender had, when he or she committed the act. The Juvenile Court jurisdiction to persons older than 18 is in accordance with modern views concerning penal treatment of young adults (see also Section 4).

2.2.3. Diversion – Restorative Justice

These procedures – new in the Greek legislation concerning children of 8–18 years of age – have been developed in most countries in the past decades. The dubious success of penal measures, the stigmatization of the convicted person, the need for diminishing the workload of the criminal justice system are among the factors which led theoreticians and practitioners of the penal and criminological field to seek solutions to the conflict created by the offence in a dialogue and conciliation between the author of the offence and the victim (A.Tsitsoura, 2001). Intervention of a mediator or of the prosecutor facilitates this dialogue that results in reparation of the damage suffered by the victim and the abandonment of prosecution. Measures of diversion are now provided both in the Penal Code (art. 122 e) and in the Code of Penal Procedure (see below, 5)

2.2.4. Increase of Non-custodial Measures

Although such measures existed already in the Penal Code of 1950, new ones such as placing the minor in a foster family or community service are introduced (A. Tsitsoura, 2002). Non-custodial treatment has become, thus, the rule.

2.2.5. Abolition of Indeterminate Sentences

Such sentences have been recently abolished in most countries in order to safeguard the individual rights of minors. Under the modern Greek juvenile justice system Juvenile Court orders imposing measures or sanctions should not be indeterminate, i.e., the court decision should indicate the time that the measure or sanction will terminate.

2.2.6. Promotion of the Care to Victims

Measures, reflecting the wide movement for the protection of victims, include:

(a) Compensation of the victim as an educative measure imposed on the adjudicated offender;
(b) Measures for the protection of child victims (0–18 years of age) of certain serious offences such as trafficking of human beings and crimes against sexual freedom, child pornography, etc.(Act 3064/2002).

The revised provisions grant the offenders an active role in their treatment and incite them to develop a feeling of responsibility for their own development. However, this perspective should take into account the specific difficulties of certain categories of juveniles such as those coming from migrant families. Special structures for assistance to these juveniles should be a necessary condition for the success of the new legislation. The creation of an "Ombudsman for the Child" is also an important step in this direction (Act. 3094 /2003, The Ombudsman and other provisions).[5]

3. MEASURES AND SANCTIONS

3.1. Educative Measures (Art. 122 PC)

These measures are applicable to all minors 8–18 years of age (unless, those aged 13–18 years are penally liable because of their personality or the circumstances under which the offence has been committed).

Such measures are:

(a) Reprimand or a warning administered by the Juvenile Court Judge during the hearing (art. 122, 1 a. PC);
(b) Placing the minor under the responsible supervision (custody) of parents or guardians (art. 122, 1 b. PC) – this provision may be supplemented by a sanction in case the parents fail to prevent their child from being involved in prostitution or committing an offence (art. 360 PC);
(c) Placing the minor under the responsible supervision of a foster family (art. 122, 1 c. PC);
(d) Placing the minor under the responsible supervision of: (i) a "society for the protection of minors," (ii) an institution for the education of minors, or (iii) a probation officer, the "supervisor of minors" (art. 122, 1, d, PC);
(e) Mediation between the minor and his or her victim(s) through the intervention of probation officers of the Juvenile Court. (In Greece, mediation societies or individual mediators do not exist at present, and hence this task is undertaken by the probation officers for minors employed by the Ministry of Justice and working in every Juvenile Court) (art. 122,1, e, PC);
(f) Payment of compensation to the victims or reparation of the damage by any other means (art. 122, 1, f, PC);
(g) Community service by the minor (art. 122, 1, g, PC). It is expected that inciting the minor to contribute to the welfare of the community may have an educative value. The consent of the minor or of his or her parents is not necessary although efforts will be made by the Court to find a consensus, given that intense opposition of the minor would result in an ineffective measure;

---

[5]Art. 1 of this Act provides: "The independent authority entitled 'The Ombudsman,' has as its mission to mediate between citizens and public services, local authorities, private and public organizations as defined in article 3, para. 1 of this Act, with the view to protecting citizens' rights, combating misadministration and ensuring respect of legality. *The Ombudsman also has the mission of defending and promoting children's rights.*" (Emphasis ours)

(h) Participation of the minor in social or psychological programmes in public, municipal or private services (art. 122, 1, h., PC);

(i) Professional or other training (art. 122, 1, i. PC) – such training would aim at developing the minors' personality, to achieve their vocational training and divert them from delinquent activities;

(j) Traffic education (art. 122, 1, j, PC) – an important measure, given the great number of traffic violations;

(k) Intensive probationary supervision (art. 122, 1, k., PC);

(l) Placing the minor in a public, municipal or private educational institution (art. 122, 1, 1 PC) – this measure may be enforced only to boys, since there is only one such public institution and since no institutions set up by NGOs, the Church or the municipality exist.

Interestingly enough various supplementary conditions may accompany the above measures, e.g., curfew hours, avoiding certain neighbourhoods, working in a certain place, etc. According to the explanatory report of Act 3189/2003 modalities of the above measures should be discussed by the competent authority and the minor. The latter should be personally responsible for the compensation of the victim.

3.2. Therapeutic Measures (Art. 123 PC)

Therapeutic measures concern minors, who are in need for a particular treatment because of a mental or an organic disease, causing dysfunction as well as those who are alcoholic or drug users or present mental retardation or difficulties in developing moral and ethical values.

With regard to these minors, the Juvenile Court may order one of the following educative measures:

- placing the minor under the responsible supervision (custody) of parents or guardians, (see above under 3.1.b.)
- placing the minor under the responsible supervision of a foster family (see above under 3.1.c).

The Juvenile Court in more serious cases may order:

- participation of the minor in an open or day-care therapeutic programme
- placement in a therapeutic or other adequate closed institution.

These measures are ordered after diagnosis and advice by a specialised team of doctors, psychologists and social workers. The psychiatric expertise is necessary for habitual drug users before deciding on the applicable therapeutic measures. The provision of the diagnostic team solves the previous problem of the absence of a diagnostic center for the personality of minors. Such diagnostic teams exist in Public Children's Hospitals and Day Care Centres.

3.3. Detention in a Special Institution for Persons 13–18 Years of Age (Art. 127 PC)

Detention in a special institution can be imposed when the Juvenile Court, taking into account the circumstances of the offence and the personality of the juvenile offender, considers that a penal sanction is necessary to deter persons belonging to the age bracket 13–18 from re-offending, orders reffered to a "Special Detention Institution for Youngsters" (Art. 127 PC). This measure is of a determinate duration.

Two such special institutions operate in Greece: one in Avlona, some kilometers away from Athens, and one in Volos – the former covering the needs of southern Greece and the latter those of the northern part of the country. In the institution of Avlona on 1 October 2004 were detained: 224 juveniles, and in that of Volos: 76 – the capacity of these institutions is 308 for the former and 65 for the latter.[6] The above figures indicate that judges follow the principle that custodial sanctions should be the *ultimum refugium*.

The explanatory report of Act 3189/2003 specifies that, although detention in such a "Special Institution" is a penal sanction and not an educative measure, the institution's aim is essentially educative and it tends to promote the social reintegration of the detainees.

4. THE CASE OF YOUNG ADULTS (ART. 133 PC)

The adult penal court has the discretion to impose to young adults who have committed a crime after their 18th birthday and before their 21st birthday (a) either relatively milder penal sanctions than those provided for adults or (b) the sanctions provided for adults. Young adults who have committed an offence before the age of 18 and who are tried after their 18th birthday, due to delays in the administration of juvenile justice, are tried by the Juvenile Court and measures or sanctions provided for persons 8–18 years of age may be imposed.(See also Section 2.2.2.)

5. THE NEW ROLE OF THE PROSECUTOR FOR MINORS

A diversion procedure is instituted by the new Art. 45A of the Code of Penal Procedure (CPP) which provides that in the case of petty offences or misdemeanours committed by a minor, the Prosecutor may refrain from the exercise of the prosecution, if he or she is convinced, in the light of the circumstances of the act and of the personality of the offender that such prosecution is not necessary to avoid the commission of new offences. One or more educative

---

[6]Unpublished Statistics of the Ministry of Justice.

measures may be imposed on minors or they may be required to pay a sum to a non-profit institution.

The legislation of 2003 has assigned an additional important role to the Prosecutor for minors. Under the revised art. 549, para 5 CPP *eo ipso* this Prosecutor supervises and controls (a) the enforcement of all decisions of the Juvenile Courts (1st instance and Courts of Appeal) and (b) the execution of all educative and therapeutic measures and sanctions.

6. PROTECTION OF VICTIMS 0–18 YEARS OF AGE

Act 3064/2002 (incorporated in various articles of the Penal Code) deals with the protection of victims 0–18 years of age but in general with all victims of human trafficking. These victims attracted particular attention of both policymakers and the public during the recent years. They are victims of so-called crimes against sexual self-determination or of trafficking in human beings, i.e., trafficking with the objective of sexual or work exploitation or selling human organs.

The aforementioned Act also covers in particular pornography using children and cyber child pornography as well as advertisements facilitating child prostitution. It is worth noticing that sexual crimes against children may be prosecuted *ex officio*. Most of these crimes are punished even if committed outside the country by an offender of Greek nationality.

Moreover, most crimes committed by adults against minors are punished as felonies; the clients of child prostitutes are punished as well. Furthermore, agencies, shops, clubs, etc., facilitating child pornography or trafficking are submitted to administrative sanctions (e.g. suspension or withdrawal of premises' licence).

Finally, a Presidential Decree 233/2003 specifies the measures of assistance: (a) medical, (b) psychological, (c) legal via a special 'legal assistant' for victims available throughout the legal proceedings, (d) educational, (e) protection of witnesses in trials concerning the above offences, (f) avoidance of repatriation in case of foreign victims, (g) equal protection of all victims - Greeks and foreigners, etc.

The draft law on "Units for the Care of Youngsters" will expand these provisions and will specify the means for implementing this multifaceted assistance to victims (see below).

7. UNITS FOR THE CARE OF YOUNGSTERS (YOUNG ADULTS UP TO 21 YEARS OF AGE INCLUDED)

A Bill on the "Units for the Care of Youngsters" is pending. The main characteristics of this future enactment, which concerns children at risk, offenders, drug addicts, delinquents with psychological or mental problems and victims, are:

- emphasis on the physical and psychological well-being as well as the fulfillment of the best interest and welfare of children;
- safeguarding the rights of the youngsters served (*inter alia* provisions for interpreters, procedures for complaints), and avoiding their stigmatization and social exclusion while imposing certain reasonable duties to them;
- setting up a variety of Units: open, semi-open or closed institutions, hospitality homes for victims, youngsters at risk and released delinquents, outpatient therapeutic Units for diagnosis or treatment – Units for the social integration of delinquents, a special section for minors in the existing model Therapeutic Centre for the treatment of adult drug users or addicts;
- provision for a global scheme of a sufficient number of interrelated and integrated facilities for persons (males and females) 8–21 years of age to be located in various parts of the country (in this scheme the existing ones are included) – the innovative element of this Bill is that not all of the institutions will be set up at once; every time that a special need arises one or more of the already rationally and globally planned institutions will be established;
- licensing and supervision by the Ministry of Justice of all institutions offering services for the above categories of children and operating under the auspices of the local government, NGOs, etc. – institutions operating under the auspices of the Ministry of Health and Solidarity are excluded;
- yearly evaluation of all Units, old and new ones.

8. CONCLUSIONS AND RECOMMENDATIONS

The new Greek legislation concerning Juvenile Justice appears to be in conformity with the principle of protection of children mentioned in the Greek Constitution (art. 21), the European Convention on Human Rights as well as with the other main conventions and recommendations of international organizations, and in particular those of the United Nations, the Council of Europe, and the European Union.

The measures provided are mostly of a non-custodial nature. Diversion and mediation are introduced. The institution of the Ombudsman for the Child has been introduced. Particular attention is given to the protection of victims.

However, the reorganization of services for the implementation of new provisions (see Section 3) will require a considerable effort.

Social services for Juvenile Justice are at present under-equipped and the personnel is lacking adequate experience - especially in certain sectors, such as diversion, mediation and community service. Professional staff must be increased and the involvement of voluntary workers – rather rare in Greece, with the exception of those assisting in the Olympic Games – must be encouraged.

Particular attention must be given to the training of personnel. It would be desirable to have specialized social work trainers coming to Greece to help Greek staff to familiarize itself with new methods. This solution seems preferable to sending staff abroad, because the number of persons benefiting from fellow-ships would be necessarily limited. Instead, a relatively lengthy seminar in Greece by experienced trainers from European countries with an advanced system of administering restorative justice and community based measures would benefit a considerable number of trainees. In addition, the trainers would have the oppor-tunity to evaluate the needs and the possibilities *in situ*. The cooperation of inter-national organizations for the planning, structuring and possibly financing of such training must be envisaged.

Together with the reorganization of services, a particular effort must be deployed to inform the public, to accept and collaborate in the new measures provided by the legislation.

Many of these measures are not familiar to the Greek public and may be mis-interpreted either as repressive or humiliating (e.g., community service) or as too lenient (e.g., diversion or in particular mediation). Thus intensive information campaigns, through mass media or other means (conferences, publications) is necessary for the success of such measures.

Finally, the new legislation and its implementation should be the object of evaluation from the beginning of its implementation. A research group should be set up to follow the experience and assess periodically the progress of the implementation of the new legislation, the problems presented and the solutions found or desirable. The evaluation of the impact of new legislation in the evolu-tion of offences committed by persons aged 8–18 in Greece would also be neces-sary after some years of implementation (crime proofing). Last but not least, the improvement of crime statistics and the introduction of periodic Crime Surveys are urgently needed.

REFERENCES

A. Keith Bottomley, Criminology in Focus, Oxford, 1979, p. 23.

Conseil de l'Europe, Direction des droits de l'homme, Convention de Sauvegarde des Droits de l'Homme et des Libertés fondamentales, Strasbourg.

Council of Europe, Transformation sociale et delinquance juvenile, Strasbourg, 1979.

Council of Europe, Recommendation N° R (87) 20 on social reactions to juvenile delinquency.

Council of Europe, Recommendation N° R (88) 6 on social reactions to juvenile delinquency among young people coming from migrant families.

Council of Europe, Recommendations No R (91) 11 on Sexual exploitation, pornography, prosti-tution of and trafficking in children and young persons.

Council of Europe, Recommendation Rec (2000) 20 on the role of early psychosocial intervention in the prevention of criminality.

Council of Europe, Recommendation No R (2001) on the protection of children against sexual exploitation.

Council of Europe, Recommendation Rec (2003) 20 concerning new ways of dealing with juvenile delinquency and the role of juvenile justice.

N. Courakis, Juvenile Justice System, Athens/Komotini, 2004 (in Greek).

A. Davanelos, Labor Issues, in: Hermes, No 20, February 1998, in http://www.ana.gr/hrmes/1998/feb/labour.htm

Frame-decision concerning trafficking of human beings (document 8135/02 DROIPEN 26, MIGR 35, 19 April 2002).

J. Junger-Tas, J. J.Terlouw, and Malcolm Klein (eds.), International Self-Report Delinquency Study in Western European Countries, Chapter on Greece, by C.D.Spinellis, et al. The Dutch Ministry of Justice, 1994.

Kathimerini (newspaper), 2 May 1999 (in Greek).

E. Lambropoulou, Crime, Criminal Justice and Criminology in Greece, in: European Journal of Criminology, v.2 (2): 221–247.

D. Madianou et al., Drugs in Greece, vol III: The use of Narcotic Substances by the General Population, Athens,1992, 219 et seq.(in Greek).

A. Pitsela, Penal Reaction to the Criminality of Minors, 5th edn., Athens/Thessaloniki, 2004 (in Greek).

C. D.Spinellis, A. Chaidou, and T. Serasis, Victim Theory and Research in Greece, in: Kaiser, Kury, and Albrecht (eds.), Victims and Criminal Justice. Victimological Research: Stocktaking and Prospects, 1991, 123–158.

C. D. Spinellis, Drugs. : From the Phenomenon to the Models or the Legal Policy for Dealing with the Problem, in: Festschrift für G.-A. Mangagis (G. Bemman and D. Spinellis Herausgeber), Athens, 1999, 715–747, and esp.717–721 (in Greek).

D. Spinellis and C. D.Spinellis, Greece, Criminal Justice Systems in Europe and North America, HEUNI, Helsinki, 1999.

A. Tsitsoura, Mediation en matiere penale, Nouvelles perspectives de politique criminelle. In: volume to honour Prof.Dr.Dionysios Spinellis, Athens/Komotini, 2001, 1145 et seq.

A. Tsitsoura, Community Sanctions and Measures. in H.-J. Albrecht and A. Kalmhout, Community Sanctions and Measures in Europe and North America, 2002, 271 et seq.,

United Nations Standard Minimum Rules for the Administration of Justice (the Beijing Rules).

United Nations Guidelines for the Prevention of Juvenile Delinquency (the Riyad Guidelines).

United Nations Rules for the Protection of Youths deprived of their Liberty, etc.

United Nations Convention on the Rights of the Child and its optional Protocols

US Department of State Background Notes, Greece, June 1999, in: http://www.state.gov/www/background_notes/

13

Continuity and Change in the Spanish Juvenile Justice System

Cristina Rechea Alberola and Esther Fernández Molina

Spain is one of the Mediterranean countries that belong to the EU. It is the third biggest country in Europe, behind Russia and France, with a surface of 504.782 km². According to the National Institute of Statistics, there were 43,026,982 inhabitants by January 2004; i.e., the mean population density is of 86 inhabitants/km². Nevertheless, there is a great inequality in the distribution of the population among regions. Most of the people live in the coastal regions and in big urban agglomerations; i.e., the region of Madrid has 724 inhabitants/km², while Castilla-La Mancha, an inland region, has 23 inhabitants/km² only.

The Kingdom of Spain is composed of 17 autonomic communities and the towns of Ceuta and Melilla in the African border of the Mediterranean Sea. Although these communities have limited self-government, they have a high level of competences. Most of them are competent in health, education, agriculture, welfare, etc.

The Spanish society had suffered a radical transformation in the last 25 years: from 40 years of a dictatorial regime to a democratic country. The rhythm of legal, political, economical and social reforms was accelerated since 1986, when Spain joined the EU. From the point of view of the economy, data from EURO-STAT show that the PIB has increased more than 10 points in the last 10 years.

The recent prosperity and the geographical situation of the country have transformed it, in a very short period, from an emigrant country, into an immigrant recipient country. In 1991 there were 353,367 foreigners living in the country, which represents a 0.9% of the total population, while in 2004 they were 1,977,291, which represents a 4.6% of the population. Most of these immigrants come from Ecuador (15.7%), or Morocco (13.9%).

The juvenile population, younger than 18 years amounted in 2004 to 7,504,473 youngsters, a 17.4% of the total population. According the Spanish Juvenile Report (2000), the number of juveniles at compulsory school was 6,968,168. And following the same report, among the young people aged 15–19 years, 67.4% were studying fulltime, 12.9% had a job, while a 11.4% were studying with a part time job. The percentage of people of this age unemployed is of a 6.2%.

In this chapter we are going to analyse the Spanish Juvenile Justice System. First, we are going to describe how the juvenile delinquency has evolved during the recent years and then explain the organization of the system that regulates the new

J. Junger-Tas and S. H. Decker (eds.), International Handbook of Juvenile Justice, 325–348.
© 2006 Springer.

Juvenile Criminal Act of 2000. To learn about the functioning of this system we will review the results of the main action lines on which the system lies.

INTRODUCTION

The juvenile justice process in Spain has evolved considerably in recent years. Such evolution is manifest in the legislative transition from the OL 4/1992, Juvenile Court Reform Act of 1992 (JCRA) to the OL 5/2000 Juvenile Criminal Act of 2000 (JCA). The 1992 act was the legal text which first allowed the implementation of the "model of responsibility" in Spain, a "dual" framework striving for a balance between education and punishment in juvenile justice, as proposed by the United Nations. This act was largely criticized since it was a provisional act, not changing the overall performance of the juvenile justice system in an organized manner. However, such balance was finally achieved due to the efforts of those involved in the implementation of the act, mainly through the work that was done around two courses of action established by this act: *decriminalization* and "de-institutionalization" (Rechea Alberola and Fernández Molina, 2003).

The JCA attempted a legislative consolidation of this "model of responsibility," which was being implemented in legal practice. This was an issue for actmakers involved in juvenile justice. Yet, such consolidation came late, since it came about at a time when other countries were turning to new views on criminal policy. The international context, within which this new act fell, had more to do with the English *No more excuses* report than with the UN *Beijing Rules* or the UN *Rights of the Child Convention* (ChRC). Following a social outcry that demanded "act and order" policies, the act incorporated tougher action against offenders. Consequently, both during the act-making proceedings and through further amendments, the new act accepted concessions towards social defence, thus abandoning its initial purpose of "individual justice" aimed at defending the juvenile's best interest and at reaching a balance between education and punishment.

JCA is the first act in Spain since 1948 to compile all juvenile justice regulations as a single and complete system. To many interested people, this reform arrived too late, but the delay can be understood as a consequence of the Spanish political agenda of the moment; the reform of the Criminal Act, the "Spanish Criminal Act of Democracy," in 1995. Nevertheless, the delay may also be an indication of the importance that Juvenile Justice has had in Spain, as it has always been a peripheral subject matter.

According to JCA, justice for juveniles is to be administered by a separate system within the general legal system with its own specific and specialized court. Jurisdiction of the juvenile court is determined by the offender's age and his or her conduct. With respect to conduct, the system is exclusively a criminal responsibility system. The legislators' intention was to make juveniles responsible for their criminal acts, and at the same time, to protect young and adolescent delinquents against any arbitrariness throughout the decision-making process. Therefore, juvenile justice is concerned only with those youth who commit acts that are defined as crimes according to the adult Criminal Act. It does not include children who are in poverty, neglected or abused, or those who are unruly or are at risk of becoming offenders. These juveniles are the concern of civil jurisdiction. This division can also be found in other European countries such as Denmark (Mehlbye and Sommer, 1998), Germany (Weitekamp, Kerner and Herberger, 1998), and Italy (Gatti and Verde, 1998), but other countries have maintained a unique system for protection and reform, among others the Netherlands (Junger-Tas, 1998), Belgium (Walgrave et al., 1998), France (Gazeau and Pierre, 1998), and Scotland (Asquith, 1998).

With respect to age, the act applies to young people under the age of 18 and older than age 14.[1] The limits of the previous act were established at 12–16 years of age. To change the lower limit was a very controversial decision that legislators decided to take against the opinion of many juvenile judges and regional social services.[2] However, all agreed to changing the upper age limit because the Spanish Criminal Act established the age of adulthood at 18.[3] Within this age range, the JCA established two differentiated groups of young people with regard to the consequences of their responsibility and the measures to be applied to each group; for juveniles aged 14 and 15 measures would not last more than 2 years, while for those aged 16 and 17 any measure, even custody, could last for 5 years. The JCA intends to give more criminal responsibility to the older young people, as a kind of transition in order to avoid the abruptness of becoming fully responsible before an adult criminal court for crimes committed after their eighteenth birthday.

1. GLOBAL OVERVIEW OF SPANISH DELINQUENCY TRENDS

In Spain, official data about juvenile delinquency can be obtained from three different sources: the Police, the Prosecutor's Office, and the Juvenile Courts. However, it is important to note that the data obtained from each of these institutions

[1]Art. 4 of JCA allowed juveniles between 18 and 21 years, under some circumstances, to be judged by the Juvenile Court, to get the benefits of a more lenient system. However, this article was suspended, initially, for a period of two years by OL 9/2000 of 22 December. This period has been extended recently to last until 2007 by a new OL 9/2002 of 10 December.

[2]We do not want to enter into a controversy, but in a world where the trend is frequently for younger children to be considered as criminals, the new Act has increased the age for criminal responsibility of juveniles. In the Netherlands young people of 16 and 17 can be treated as adults (Junger-Tas, 1998), and in the UK the 1998 reform considered that a child of 10 can be responsible (Muncie, 2004).

[3]The Criminal Act of 1995 established that 18 was the age for criminal majority. However, this same text also said that this would not be put into effect until an act was passed for juvenile criminal responsibility that would imply the definitive reform so needed by the Spanish Juvenile Justice System. That is, the age for criminal majority would not be changed from 16 (the age established by the former criminal act) to 18 (established by the new criminal act) until this new act was passed.

refer to different aspects of the juvenile justice system. While Police statistics[4] come from a survey of the number of arrests carried out, the statistics of the Prosecutor's Office and the Courts consist of the actions carried out annually by each of these institutions; i.e., they do not refer to the number of offences reported but the number of actions that each institution takes for each one of these offences. In Figure 13.1 we can clearly see the implications derived from the differences in criteria.

The data regarding Police arrests must be treated with caution as noted above. In addition, in the Spanish system it is possible to file an accusation directly to the Juvenile Prosecutor's Office, the Duty Magistrate's Court or the Autonomous[5] or Local[6] Police.

Data from 2001 confirm that the differences in the information provided by the different institutions are very large as shown by the spectacular increase in the number of files initiated in the Prosecutor's Office. This big difference is mainly

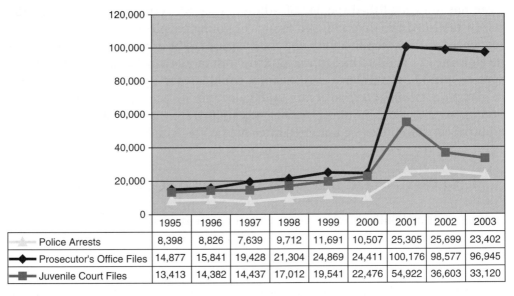

	1995	1996	1997	1998	1999	2000	2001	2002	2003
Police Arrests	8,398	8,826	7,639	9,712	11,691	10,507	25,305	25,699	23,402
Prosecutor's Office Files	14,877	15,841	19,428	21,304	24,869	24,411	100,176	98,577	96,945
Juvenile Court Files	13,413	14,382	14,437	17,012	19,541	22,476	54,922	36,603	33,120

FIGURE 13.1. Number of arrests by the Police, preliminary files initiated by the Prosecutor's Office and files initiated by Juvenile Courts (1995–2003).
Source: Ministry of Home Affairs, Attorney General Office and the General Council of the Judiciary.

[4]These data are supplied by the National Police, that is, the number of arrests by the Autonomic or Local Police is not mentioned (except for the Basque Country which is included).
[5]In Spain, Catalonia and the Basque Country are the regions that have Autonomous Police. As has already been mentioned, the data regarding the Basque Country Police are included.
[6]In research carried out at the Juvenile Courts of the Autonomous Community of Castilla La-Mancha, we could verify that 77.3% of the cases are reported to the National Police (Criminology Research Centre, 2003).

the result of the fact that this is precisely this year when the JCA came into effect. This means, among other things, a more exact regulation of the different competences of each of the institutions that control crime. This act precisely regulated the actions to be taken by the Prosecutor's Office. Thus, this institution has become the main reference point for the Spanish Juvenile Justice System which has adopted a new way of working and, as a result, a new system for gathering information on its actions. This way, the Prosecutor's Office must open a preliminary file for every case referred by the Police, as well as any other actions that must be taken related to these cases (joinders, inhibitions, dismissal, etc.).

The Juvenile Court data refer to those files that the Prosecutor decides to follow for the judge to rule. As the Prosecutor's data, these data refer to the amount of work that the files generate in the Juvenile Court. We want to pay attention to the fact that all the Prosecutor's files as well as the Court ones are files by fact instead of files by person; that means that in the same file more than one minor can be involved. On the contrary, the Police data refer to arrested minors, which means that the same fact could be taken into account more than once.

Despite the numeric differences in magnitude, the trends in data from the different institutions coincide, which is without doubt, very useful information for the verification of the reliability of these data and confirm the value of these sources as instruments of measurement, at least to analyse general tendencies.

Figure 13.1 shows that the data sources diverge in 2001 with a substantial increase in the number of cases: this is the year the new act came into effect. This increase is due to the modification of the age margins established by the new Act to enter the system. Data from 1993 to 2000 refer to the number of juveniles between 12 and 16 years of age who had committed a criminal infraction, whereas data from 2001 refer to the number of juveniles between 14 and 18 years of age who have committed an infraction.

We must also point out that the transition period between one system and the other has been longer than desired. One problem that made the transition period longer was that ordinary Courts refrained from processing the files of juveniles of 16 and 17 years of age in view of the imminent reform. These files were automatically sent from the criminal court to the juvenile jurisdiction on 13 January 2001 and have been processed and settled gradually in subsequent years. This has made the system face a much heavier workload than usual, which is an aspect to be considered.

To avoid the problem of comparisons across two time periods, Figure 13.2 uses the number of Police arrests from 1997[7] to 2003 of all delinquents under the age of 18. We can see that after an increase in the number of arrests in 1999, figures remained constant in subsequent years showing a light decrease in the last year. It is remarkable that the stability that the data show since 1999, mirrors the adult criminality.

[7]In 1997, the police started a new information gathering system, so as to avoid any distortion of the information that could be caused by the different measurement instruments; the number of arrests before this year has been ignored.

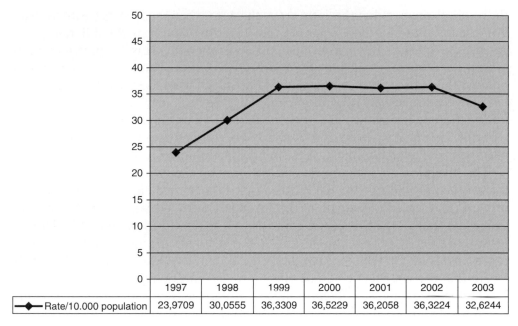

	1997	1998	1999	2000	2001	2002	2003
Rate/10.000 population	23,9709	30,0555	36,3309	36,5229	36,2058	36,3224	32,6244

FIGURE 13.2. Police arrests (0 to 17 years old) Rate/10.000 Population of this age.
Source: Ministry of Home Affairs.

Regarding the type of delinquency, the authors of this report were interested in whether Spain, as in other countries (Barberet, 2001) experienced an increase of violent behaviour. As can be observed in Figure 13.3, the conclusion can be reached that in Spain violent crimes have increased consistently since 1997.

Unfortunately, there are no self-report data for juveniles. Only one survey of this kind was carried out in 1992 (Barberet et al., 1994) but it is so dated as to not be useful.

2. PREVENTION

In the Spanish system there is no specific plan to prevent juvenile delinquency. However, some actions are taken towards preventing criminal behaviour.

Preventive actions in Spain focus on the development of social conditions to achieve more equality and so to make committing crimes "unnecessary." This tendency comes from the southern European countries that promote the protection of children's rights as policies to prevent social maladaptation (Bernuz Beneitez, 2000). The actions are strategies of secondary prevention that imply working with groups at risk and take place through the systems of youth protection. These systems do not have a national structure but are the responsibility of regional governments.

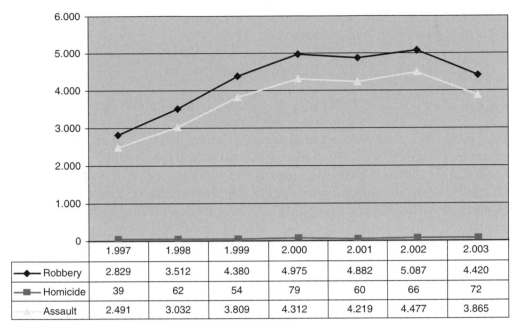

	1.997	1.998	1.999	2.000	2.001	2.002	2.003
Robbery	2.829	3.512	4.380	4.975	4.882	5.087	4.420
Homicide	39	62	54	79	60	66	72
Assault	2.491	3.032	3.809	4.312	4.219	4.477	3.865

FIGURE 13.3. Number of arrests (0 to 17 years old) for violent crimes.
Source: Ministry for Home Affairs.

In addition, there are a series of programmes in the framework of primary intervention at the national level promoted by the Ministry of Education. Among them, we draw attention to a programme to prevent school violence and "bullying,"[8] and the programmes developed within the *Health Promoting School*.[9] However, these are very specific and limited experiences without a strong economic and political commitment and they are very rarely evaluated.

3. AGENTS OF THE SPANISH JUVENILE JUSTICE SYSTEM

The juvenile justice system in Spain is made up of a group of professionals. Since 2001 (in compliance with the rules of the United Nations), these individuals must be specialized in this field, thus guaranteeing that all actions taken will be in the juvenile's best interest.

Although it is the Prosecutor's Office that leads the actions in this system, the new act has conferred upon all professionals a specific role within the juvenile justice system, on an equal level of importance. This has created a horizontal juvenile justice system that traditionally had a pyramidal structure (Bailleau and

[8]For reference, check http://www.cnice.mecd.es/recursos2/convivencia_escolar/
[9]For reference, check http://wwwn.mec.es/cide/jsp/plantillaIn.jsp?id=inn03

Cartuyvels, 2002: 279). In this section we are going to analyse the influence of each professional's role in the system.

3.1. The Role of the Prosecutor

As has been said, the Prosecutor is the main figure in the Spanish juvenile justice system. The leading role of the Prosecutor was first introduced in the reform of 1992 as an innovation in criminal-policy that incorporated the figure of an investigating judge (Fernandez Molina and Rechea Alberola, 2005). In the Spanish justice system the judge is the jurisdiction's authority, and is in charge of adopting the decisions concerning the procedure. There is an investigating judge and a sentencing judge in order to guarantee the impartiality of the latter.

The reform of 1992 attempted to complement practices established in other countries where the Prosecutor is in charge of the instruction of the procedure using juvenile justice as a laboratory to test what could be the future reform of the entire criminal system. This experience was positive since this professional has been consolidated in the system, replacing the Spanish traditional judge (Rechea Alberola and Fernández Molina, 2003). Because of its success, the current government is studying the possibility of introducing this reform in the adult criminal system.

The Prosecutor conducts the preliminary investigation while the Juvenile Court Judge is responsible for safeguarding the rights of the person under investigation. At this stage the Prosecutor is also assisted by the Police to determine the juvenile's participation in criminal acts (art. 6) and by the Social Team to determine the most appropriate measure for the juvenile's psycho-social situation (art. 27.1).

Apart from the investigation of the facts, the Prosecutor also has the important role of procedural efficiency. This implies that he or she is not only going to intervene in the instruction but in the whole procedure: the hearing (art. 8, 31 and 32), possible pre-trial measures (art. 28), in carrying out the measure (article 14, 44b and 50), in substitution or suspension of the measure (articles 40 and 51), and in the appeal system (art. 43). In Spain, each province has a special Juvenile Section within the Prosecutor's Office where there is, at least, a specialized Prosecutor (in some cases there could be many more, and in other cases there might be several but not exclusively devoted to juvenile justice).

The time between committing the crime and the Prosecutor's acknowledgement of the case is usually 10 months. Nevertheless, the new Act has meant a difficult and laborious transitional process that is still affecting the system. For example, crimes committed by 16 and 17 year olds before 2001 are still dealt with today. The adult court was handling them when the Act came into effect and were transferred to be dealt with under the new Act that was considered more benevolent than the adult process. So if we do not take into account the average time needed to complete a case but the value of the median, the time the Prosecutor takes to deal with a case is 3.4 months.

3.2. The Role of the Police

Although the JCA recognizes the need for specialized Police Groups, called GRUME (Juvenile Groups), they have not been assigned many functions. In Spain the Police do not act differently with juveniles than with adults, as opposed to what happens in other countries like the Netherlands (Junger-Tas, 1998), the United Kingdom (Bottoms, Haines, and O'Mahony, 1998), or Ireland (O'Sullivan, 1998) where they can caution the juvenile or adopt diversionary measures.

The GRUME are in charge of arresting the juvenile delinquent and helping the Prosecutor clarify the facts. JCA only mentions the Police twice, first, when it rules on the functions of the Prosecutor and entrusts them to order the Police to verify the facts and the juvenile's participation (art. 6), and second, when it regulates the arrest of juveniles (art. 17).

However, although it is not mentioned in the Act, there is no doubt that the GRUMES' actions are wider. First, because the groups have responsibilities with juvenile delinquents as well as with juvenile victims, their work has undoubtedly preventive potential. On the other hand, in practice the groups become an important element in the juvenile justice system since they are in permanent contact with all its institutions: Juvenile Courts, Prosecutors, Social Services, etc.

The first action to be taken with juvenile delinquents is to determine their age. If the juvenile is under 14 years old (thus excluded from the actions of the juvenile justice system), the Police must restrict their actions to the field of juvenile protection. Once the juvenile's age and identity are determined, the rules of juvenile protection[10] will be applied. The Prosecutor will be informed of the known facts and circumstances by sending the Police report, referring the juvenile either to his actful attorney or to the public entity for juvenile protection.

Another of the main actions carried out by the Police is detaining the juvenile. In this case, the action must be most respectful of the juvenile's rights, in particular when they must guard the juvenile's protection (art.17).

The Police can also keep juveniles in short-term custody, but only for 24 hours before formally accusing them of a crime. During that time, juveniles have the

---

[10]Specifically, it refers to the enforcement of the Juvenile Protection Act, which is the Act that designs the state juvenile protection system and the corresponding acts in the Autonomous Communities where the juvenile might come from. Since Spain is a quasi-federal state, regional governments have transferred competences in some fields, like it is the case of juvenile protection.

same constitutional rights as adults, as well as some specific rights due to their juvenile status such as:

- enforcement officers must use clear and understandable language according to the offender's age;
- before a statement is taken, a written notice of the time, place and purpose of the taking of the statement is given to the parents or guardians, the actyer and the Prosecutor; and
- during these 24 hours, the juvenile must be kept in a special room away from adult offenders.

3.3. The Role of the Social Team

One of the main roles of the Social Team (ST), which includes psychologists, social educators, and social workers, is to prepare a "technical report" at the prosecutor's request. The report must be an objective statement about the juvenile's family, his or her social and educational history, and any previous involvement with private or public agencies of the juvenile. The report also describes the juvenile's physical and mental health, and makes a recommendation as to which treatment alternatives should be advisable in this case.

JCA also establishes the intervention of the ST in other phases of the procedure in an effort to guarantee that all decisions are to be made respecting the juvenile's psycho-social situation.

Apart from this advisory role, the ST accomplishes other functions that turn it more into a consulting team. Among these functions we find the option of a foster-home, the de-judicialization of the proceedings (art. 19 and 27.4), social and psychological assistance while the juvenile is detained (art. 17.3.), and providing all the care, protection and social and psychological assistance required, bearing in mind his age, sex and personal characteristics.

3.4. The Role of the Juvenile Judge

The new act specifies a constrained role for the Spanish juvenile judge. During instruction, he or she will be the *Guarantee* Judge of the juvenile's rights, the *Sentencing* Judge during the procedure at the hearing and when pronouncing a sentence, the *Enforcing* Judge when the measure is carried out (in the same way as the role of the Penitentiary Surveillance Judge in the adult system). He or she must make sure that the Administration executes the sentence, and finally he or she will be a *Civil* Judge when in charge of processing his or her civil responsibilities.

3.5. The Role of the Regional Government

Since the reform of 1992, the services of regional governments are in charge of carrying out the measures adopted by Juvenile Judges. This decision was significant for two reasons: first, because it implied the decentralization of the juvenile criminal enforcement system; and second, because of support for of a global child policy, ranging from the protection of juveniles at risk to a judicial response to criminal behaviour.

This way, in Spain, juvenile educational intervention has a different dimension in every region, based mainly on the uneven supply of resources and the different degrees of social conditions in each region, in terms of differential crime rates, social isolation, and importance of immigration movements. In this respect, Madrid and Catalonia are very different from other regions like Castilla-León or Castilla-La Mancha, or smaller regions like Asturias or Cantabria.

3.6. The Role of the Defence Lawyer

The new Act requires lawyers to follow the same specialized training as judges and Prosecutors. As in the adult system, the attorney in the juvenile justice system is involved in each phase of the process in order to safeguard the juvenile's rights.

4. MAIN ACTIONS DURING INSTRUCTION

In this section we will analyse two actions that occur during instruction which are especially interesting because they are more specific than in the ordinary system. They are focused on the juvenile's best interest (the adoption of pre-trial measures and the possibility of decriminalizing the proceedings).

4.1. Pre-trial Measures

One of the most problematic aspects during instruction is the need to adopt a pre-trial measure. Once the Police have referred the juvenile to the Prosecutor, he or she has 24 hours to make a decision between (art. 28) releasing the juvenile for a later appearance in a formal hearing or asking the judge for pre-trial measures.

If the judge is asked for pre-trial measures, he or she has 24 hours to impose such a measure. For the judge to impose a pre-trial measure, he or she must take into account the juvenile's safety, the protection of the person or property of others, the juvenile's subsequent presence at the hearing, and the seriousness of the offence, the juvenile's record, and the social upheaval caused by the offence. The pre-trial measures that can be applied include custody,[11] probation, or living with another family.

---

[11] Pre-trial detention is the temporary and safe custody of a juvenile who is accused of a serious crime (never for minor offences) while pending legal action. The maximum length of custody is 3 months (the time limit for the prosecutor's investigation of the case). If the case is very complicated the maximum length can be 6 months.

4.2. Decriminalization in the JCA

The fact that the Prosecutor has the monopoly of criminal action in the Spanish juvenile justice system means, among other things, that decriminalization strategies are in his or her hands. The new act allows the proceedings to be dismissed in the best interest of the juvenile, thus avoiding a formal response either by the Prosecutor at his own Office or by the judge immediately after initiating proceedings.

4.2.1. "Decriminalization" carried out by the Public Prosecutor

The new legislation allows the Public Prosecutor to act more freely. Following former acts, the Prosecutor had to ask the judge to dismiss proceedings in the juvenile's best interest. After the enactment of the new act, the Prosecutor may dismiss proceedings without asking the judge, if the offence is minor and committed by a first offender (art. 18). In this way, the Prosecutor carries out an important "filtering" task in the juvenile justice system because first offenders committing minor offences will stay out of the system.

4.2.2. "Decriminalization" carried out by the Judge

The other method of preventing trial and punishment is requested by the Prosecutor but is decided by the judge. In this case it is possible to drop the charges (art. 19) when the juvenile has carried out any kind of activity guided by the principles of "Restorative Justice" (victim-offender mediation, reparation of the damage or an educational task). The Prosecutor has the power to request dropping the charges through this alternative, depending on the seriousness and circumstances of the offence when it is a non-serious offence and when the mere promise of the juvenile to repair the damage or injury caused to the victim seems insufficient. If the mediation process is successfully completed, the prosecutor can request that the judge dismiss the case.

The judge may also dismiss proceedings (art. 27.4) when, although the juvenile is not a first offender, the ST recommends a second chance in the juvenile's best interest. This is possible provided that the offence is not serious, when the measures carried out have been sufficient to make the juvenile responsible for his acts, or because of the time elapsed since the acts were committed makes any intervention unnecessary.

4.3. Implementation of Decriminalization in the Spanish Juvenile Justice System

Next, we analyse the application of this course of action that avoids formalization of the responses in less serious cases. To do so, we use data from the Prosecutor's Office, comparing national data with those of the region of Castilla-La Mancha.

The information in Figure 13.4 shows the number of reform proceedings that have been taken by the prosecutor and the juvenile judge because of an alternative disposal (art. 19) or a dismissal in the juvenile's interest advised by the ST (art. 27.4). Therefore, it is not possible to distinguish between which proceedings are dismissed for which reason.

As can be seen in Figure 13.4, nationwide, the Prosecutor's "decriminalization" has more impact than that of the judge. However, if national data are compared with data from a particular region such as Castilla-La Mancha, the distribution of strategies is different. In this region, although the number of charges dropped by the Prosecutor remains high, the number of cases dismissed by the judge greatly exceeds the national average.

Such differences may be due to the uneven development of "restorative" practices throughout Spain. The Prosecutor may dismiss a lower number of proceedings in order to come to some kind of agreement with the victim in regions where there are enough staff and resources to carry out such practices, despite the fact that this involves higher levels of intervention. Nevertheless, the Prosecutor may avoid excessive criminalization by dismissing cases from the beginning whenever staff and resources are limited.

The problem with resources is due to the fact that the act orders the ST to carry out actions related to mediation with the victim and reparation of the damage. The ST has a great deal of work to do within the framework of justice enacted by the new act, and, as a consequence, ST's have become overworked.

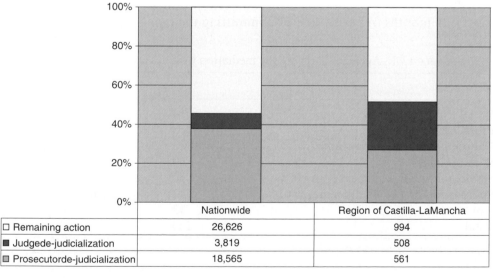

FIGURE 13.4. Decriminalisation in the Spanish Juvenile Justice System.
Source: Prosecutor's Office (2002).

This is the reason why only regional administrations that have their own teams carrying out restorative action, are able to foster this practice. Occasionally, local social services, or even NGOs (through some kind of agreement), cooperate in the implementation of restorative action in some regions. Castilla-La Mancha is one of the regions that carry out their action through agencies such as those that can be seen in Table 13.1.

The final balance of decriminalization in the Spanish juvenile justice system is quite acceptable since it allows half of the cases to be dismissed before the hearing. However, most cases are dismissed in the Prosecutor's Office and not in the Juvenile Court. This means that the charges have been dropped mainly because they were first offenders and because of the non-seriousness of the facts, and not because of the personal evaluation of the case or the juvenile's psycho-social circumstances have advised so.

On the other hand, through this decriminalization strategy, the system is not only trying to avoid criminal procedures for juveniles but also to give a quick response in the case of petty offences. Table 13.2 shows the time the proceedings take when the case is dismissed in the juvenile's interest (art. 27.4), a restorative action process has been carried out (art. 19), or the case has been resolved by means of a formal process where a measure[12] has been adopted.

To sum up cases that are dismissed in the juvenile's interest take the least time, 4.6 months, as opposed to 5.6 months when there has been conciliation, restorative action or socio-educative tasks and 9.3 months when an educational measure has been adopted. However, the proceedings "dismissed in the juvenile's interest" take longest to be resolved from the time of committing the acts, 20.2 months. The data of the median is the most relevant since half the dismissed cases took 17.8 months from the time of committing the crime. This data reveals that

TABLE 13.1. Agencies carrying the mediation task in Castilla-La Mancha

	N	%
Social team	4	3%
Prosecutor's Office	3	2.2%
Community intervention team	23	17.2%
Social services	60	44.8%
Services through agreement with NGOs	30	22.4%
Spontaneous action by different parties	1	0.7%
Not stated	13	9.7%
Total	134	100%

Source: Fernández Molina (2004).

[12]The data in this analysis are from a study carried out in the Juvenile Courts, and that is why we cannot access the information regarding the files dismissed by the Prosecutor since they are never referred to the Court, and so remain the Prosecutor's work in his Office.

TABLE 13.2. Time elapsed between different moments of the process (mean and median)

	Average	Median
Dismissing in the juvenile's interest		
Since the commission of the crime	20.2 months	17.8 months
Since the opening of the procedure	4.6 months	3.4 months
Dismissing by restoration process		
Since committing the crime	8.1 months	6.3 months
Since the opening of the procedure	5.6 months	5 months
Adoption of a measure		
Since committing the crime	13.8 months	11.1 months
Since the opening of the procedure	9.3 months	8.6 months

Source: Fernández Molina (2004).

of the two reasons the ST can use to request a dismissal in the juvenile's interest, as established in art. 27.4, the reason most widely used is *considering inappropriate, in the juvenile's interest, any kind of intervention, taking into account the time elapsed since the acts were committed.*

5. SENTENCING

Once the Prosecutor decides not to dismiss the case, the process continues and the formal adjudication process begins. The next phase is the trial, where the "hearing" takes place informally. The judge must hear everyone including the juvenile, the parents, the prosecutor, the ST, and the defence actyer, and make a decision. In order to make this decision in the juvenile's best interest, the judge must bear in mind the seriousness of the offence, the juvenile's family, and his or her social and educational history.

The juvenile's best interest is the underlying premise of the Juvenile Justice System, addressed by the JCA, which is one of the fundamental rights according to the ChRC: in all legal actions concerning those under the age of 18, the "best interests of the child" shall be a primary consideration (art. 3.1).

One should understand this principle as a juvenile's right, because we know that juvenile delinquency is *something different from adult crime*, and the social reaction to it cannot be punitive but rehabilitative and educative (Giménez-Salinas, 2000). But how can this principle be applied? The legislator does not answer this question directly, but while using the act, states *how* to evaluate it (*with technical and non-formal criteria*) and *who* has to do so (*a team of professionals specialized in sciences other than the legal ones*). That means that the evaluation of the juvenile's best interest, following art. 27 of the JCA, must be done at the prosecutor's request by an interdisciplinary team, the ST, which must write a *report* that will determine the action taken during the process.

The main objective of this report is to provide the judge and the prosecutor with knowledge about the juvenile's situation, indicating his or her deficits and resources. The report must indicate an action plan for each juvenile in order to individualize the decision the judicial agents must take. The report and its use by these agents during the process shows that, at least initially, we are now dealing with a specific criminal process different from the adult one, in which the reaction of the justice system to act-breaking does not follow *general deterrence criteria* but instead tries to provide the juvenile with a more appropriate response to his or her needs.

The measure to be chosen must be guided by the principle of rehabilitation (i.e., it must be educative). However, any intervention in juvenile criminal cases must be proportional to the seriousness of the offence the juvenile has committed.

Once the Prosecutor decides to continue with the case and files a formal charge, the ST's report must be taken into account not only by the Prosecutor and the defence lawyer in their proposals, but also by the judge in his or her sentence. The judge is obliged to motivate the sentence, that is, to explain why he or she decided to apply a certain measure and its duration, as a way to control the evaluation he or she has made of the ST's report, which is the concrete technical expression of the juvenile's best interest. This motivation will prevent arbitrariness, because although the judge's decision will rest on his or her discretionary power, the decision criteria must be formally justified (Fernández Molina, 2002).

The task of the Juvenile Judge is an arduous one. He or she must evaluate the juvenile's best interest in the most sophisticated and exhaustive way, since the evaluation will serve to decide the educative response to be applied to the juvenile. The legislator requires the judge to consider the juvenile's best interest as an essential element of his or her decision (art. 7.3).

5.1. Limits to the Juvenile's Best Interest in the Action of the Judge: the OL 7/2000

Although the JCA declared solemnly that the aim of the measures to be taken in the juvenile process is educative (i.e., *specific deterrence*), and although the Act committed itself to flexibility in the adoption and enforcement of the measures (art. 7.3), in some cases, other aspects of the situation must be taken into consideration. These include age, the kind of crime committed and its seriousness, and recidivism.

On the other hand, and despite the legislation's initial focus on the juvenile's best interest, once the JCA was published and before it came into effect,[13] the government presented another act – the OL 7/2000 of 22 December – modifying the Criminal Act and the JCA with respect to acts of terrorism. But this new act was not only limited to acts of terrorism; rather, terrorism was the pretext for the introduction of other modifications to the JCA that the government did

---

[13]The Government established a *vacatio legis* of a year for the system to prepare itself for change. During this period, a new legislature gave absolute majority to the Government.

not dare to introduce before, given its progressive character. These modifications aggravated the responses to some kinds of crimes or crimes committed by juveniles that were considered especially uncomfortable (in particular in cases of recidivism and of serious crimes), and they did not take into consideration the juvenile's best interest.

5.1.1. Age

Age is one of the factors to be taken into account by the Juvenile Judge. As we have already explained, according to the two age ranges established by act, the consequences regarding his or her responsibility and the length of the measures that can be imposed on the child will differ. So, according to age, the length of the measure might vary from 2 years for juveniles aged 14 and 15 to 5 years for those aged 16 and 17.

5.1.2. Circumstances and Seriousness of the Acts

The motivation of the act regarding the procedure to be used with the juvenile and how to measure the juvenile's best interest at the time of giving a response seems to have been forgotten by the legislator when writing the rest of the act. The judge must take into account the judicial qualification of the acts (i.e., the nature of the committed crime and its seriousness), to decide on a sentence. In some cases, this will prevent him from taking other measures that, from the juvenile's point of view, could be more beneficial for the offender (art. 39). The content of this article is more in line with a general deterrent and social defence point of view than with the rehabilitative principle that seems to govern the proceedings of juveniles according to the OL 7/2000.

5.1.3. Extreme Seriousness

Even stricter limitations are found in art. 9.5. This article establishes the rules to be followed in cases of extreme seriousness, including cases of recidivism. It seems that the legislator is harsher with the group considered to be the hard core of juvenile delinquents. In these cases, the judge is obliged to put the juvenile into custody in a closed centre for 1–5 years without the possibility of modifying the measure during the first year (the sentence may be revised after termination of the first year).

One of the problems with this article is to establish what "extreme seriousness" means. Initially, the text of the JCA of January 12th included recidivism and a limited list of crimes including terrorism, murder or homicide, and sexual assault. But the OL 7/2000 maintains recidivism as an aggravating matter and creates an especially harsh regime for the crimes included in the aforementioned list.

5.1.4. Length of Measures

The duration of the measures established in the JCA is considered too long if the aim of the act is focused on the juvenile's best interest. As Ornosa (2000) points out, if rehabilitation has not succeeded in 2 years, whatever the seriousness of the crime committed or the juvenile's personal or familiar circumstances, the likelihood of success with this juvenile is minimal. That means that measures longer than 2 years do not have a rehabilitative character but rather a retributive one.

5.1.5. Other modifications introduced by the OL 7/2000 of 22 December

As mentioned above, this act is not consistent with the spirit of the JCA that tried to look for a balance between society's right to defend itself and the rehabilitative objective (Gimenez-Salinas, 2000), because it aggravated the measures and created some other punitive concepts. Although the act was created to respond to the escalation of the terrorist acts by the "kale borroca" (terrorist vandalism by juveniles in the Basque Country), it was expanded to include crimes (murder, homicide and sexual assault) committed by any juvenile.

Reviewing the changes instituted by this reform, the two most relevant are first, the creation of a Central Juvenile Court at the National Court (in Madrid) for terrorist acts where all juvenile terrorists will be judged. That means that a judge located far away from the home region of the offender will judge the juvenile, and that eventual custody measures will be applied away from his or her home milieu. This option is a far cry from the "juvenile's best interest," and the fact that he or she will now be labelled as a terrorist renders any rehabilitative intervention very difficult (Ornosa Fernández, 2000). Second, the extension of the length of the measures for offences mentioned in this act, especially the provision that these measures cannot be modified until half of the sentence has been served (see Table 13.3).

TABLE 13.3. Exceptions to the JCA introduced by the OL 7/2000, with respect to terrorist acts and very serious crimes

Age/ kind of crime	Murder, homicide, sexual assault and terrorist crimes	Very serious terrorist crimes (with more than 15 years of prison in the adults Criminal Code)
14-15 year olds	From 1 to 4 years of custody in a closed centre + 3 years of probation (the sentence cannot be modified until half the measure of t custody has been served)	From 1 to 5 years of custody in a closed centre + 3 years of probation (the sentence cannot be modified until half the measure of custody has been served)
16-17 year olds	From 1 to 8 years of custody in a closed centre + 5 years of probation (the sentence cannot be modified until half the measure of custody has been served)	From 1 to 10 years of custody in a closed centre + 5 years of probation (the sentence cannot be modified until half the measure of custody has been served)

6. SANCTIONS

6.1. Educative Intervention in the Spanish Juvenile Justice System

Social Welfare institutions must deal with young offenders. When the judge imposes a measure, the professionals of the Social Welfare system implement the program.

As has been noted above, the regional governments in Spain have competence in the social welfare system. This means that each region of the country has a different social welfare structure as well as different resources. This difference in resources can make a big difference in the kind of measures the judges can apply to juveniles (Rechea and Fernández Molina, 2003).

6.2. Types of Sanctions

6.2.1. Custody measures

Custody is imposed when other measures are deemed insufficient because of the juvenile's criminal tendencies as demonstrated in the offence, or because of the seriousness of the offences. The main aim of this measure is to provide a good and healthy environment in order to redirect the juvenile's antisocial behaviour, even though it might be necessary to restrict the juvenile's freedom. This loss of freedom can vary depending on the kind of restrictions the judge imposes. The judge can only impose custody in a 'closed centre' when the juvenile has committed a serious and violent crime. All measures of custody must be followed by a period of probation. There are several types of custody:

In a closed centre: When a juvenile stays in this kind of centre, the system tries to instil in him or her some degree of social competence to encourage later responsible behaviour in the community.

In a half-open centre: In this case a socio-behavioural plan is implemented in collaboration with community social services. The offenders live in the centre.

In an open centre: Juveniles are required to do all activities in the community. However, their residence is in the centre.

Therapeutic custody: Juveniles with drug or psychiatric problems need a certain context to implement a therapeutic program, either because his or her environment is not adequate for treatment, or because there are risk factors that require custody in a closed centre.

6.2.2. Intermediate measures

Weekend custody: Juveniles must stay in their homes or in a Centre for 36 hours over the weekend. They must perform some educational tasks that are imposed by the judge (i.e., road safety education). This measure is usually applied to those juveniles that have committed assault and vandalism offences during the weekend.

Community therapeutic treatment: Juveniles must periodically attend a centre to follow a specific plan to treat their problem, which could be drug-related or psychiatric. In this case it is necessary to have the juvenile's consent.

Attendance at a 'Day Centre': Young offenders are diverted to community centres to perform activities to improve their social competence. This measure attempts to provide a structured environment for young offenders. The educational activities try to compensate for family deficits. The young offenders continue to live at home.

6.2.3. Community Measures

Probation: Young offenders must be subjected to the supervision and guidance of a 'Probation Officer,' within a time period that has been decided by the judge, usually not exceeding 2 years.

The probation officer's role is of assistance, guidance and care. These officers must promote the juvenile's education and they work with parents or guardians, using community resources as much as possible. The main aim will be to improve the juvenile's skills, abilities, and attitudes. The probation officer is appointed by the court and may be given instructions by the judge for their activities. They must report on the behaviour of the juvenile at intervals specified by the judge, and they must inform the judge of any change in behaviour.

While being on probation, the judge can require the juvenile to comply with the following conditions: attend school, participate in a training course (e.g., a social competence training or a professional course), abstain from going to specific places of public entertainment, obey the rules of the institution where the juvenile lives, as well as other obligations that the judge may impose that do not violate the juvenile's constitutional rights.

Living with another person, another family, or educative group: provide the young offender with a positive socialization environment. The person, the family, or the educative group offer him or her the possibility to live in a family-like environment that tries to develop pro-social and affective responses in the juvenile.

Community service: applicable in those cases where young offenders have infringed the rights or well-being of the community. In order to enhance the educational factor, the nature of the activity should be related to the type of crime committed or to the damage inflicted to the community. If possible, the activities will be done during the offender's leisure time.

Socio-educative measures: The young offenders must do some educational tasks in order to achieve their rehabilitation. This measure attempts to satisfy some needs which are delaying the juvenile's full development. The measure can be the obligation to attend a community activity that already exists or to create a specific activity for each specific case.

6.2.4. Other Measures

Finally, there are other measures that include cautioning, deprivation of a licence to drive a motorcycle or motor vehicle, or to have a gun and game licence, and absolute disqualification for terrorism crimes.

6.3. Implementation of Educative Measures: De-institutionalization

Next we are going to analyse the result of the decisions made by the judge, comparing the data from the current system to those of the former one in order to analyse the trends of the educational intervention system the new JCA sets up (see Table 13.4). First, we would like to state that the average time for the juvenile to be in the judge's hands is 14.4 months from the opening of proceedings to the sentencing.

As has been said before, the new legislation enacted in 2000 considered "decriminalizing" only minor offences. Therefore, and contrary to the juvenile's best interest, the JCA requires that the juvenile who committed a serious offence must be taken to trial and undergo subsequent intervention through an educational measure decided by the judge. Because the rate of serious offences is not very

TABLE 13.4. Educational Intervention 2000/2002

	2000			2002		
	N	%[1]	%[2]	N	%[1]	%[2]
Caution	2,015	25.4%	10%	1,581	11.4%	5%
Community measures:	4,349	54.84%	21.62%	8,502	61.3%	26.84%
Educational task	0	0	0	0	0	0
Community service	1,689	21.35	8.4%	3,463	24.9%	10.9%
Living with another family	4	0.04%	0.02%	14	0.10%	0.04%
Probation	2,563	32.3%	12.7%	4,664	33.7%	14.6%
Therapeutic treatment	93	1.2%	0.5%	361	2.6%	1.3%
Attendance to day centre	0	0	0	0	0	0
Custody:	1,485	18.7%	7.4%	3,512	25.4%	11%
Open/Half-open custody	643	8.1%	3.2%	2,296	16.6%	7.2%
Closed custody	842	10.6%	4.2%	1,216	8.8%	3.8%
Restriction of rights	6	0.06%	0.03%	83	0.6%	0.3%
Not stated	79	1%	0.4%	181	1.3%	0.5%
Total of measures	7,934	100%	39.4%	13,859	100%	43.6%
Total of proceedings	20,143		100%	31,850		100%

Source: NIS (National Institute of Statistics).
[1]Percentage regarding the total of measures.
[2]Percentage regarding the total of proceedings.

high (no more than 11%), the impact of the legal requirement for this kind of offence is very small.

Nevertheless, it prevents the juvenile's best interest from determining the judicial response since it is exclusively the seriousness of the offence that triggers intervention. Former legislation did not restrict the juvenile's best interest and, consequently, the new system slightly increased the number of cases where the judge will impose some kind of measure, although it ranges from 39.4% to 43.6% (see Table 13.4).

Considering Table 13.4 the first data worth emphasizing is the substantial increase of the measure of confinement, from 18.7% in the year 2000 to 25.4% in 2002. This means an increase in the custody rate from 8.1 to 19.3 per 10,000 inhabitants from 14 to 17 years of age.

On the one hand, the strict rules the legislator has established for those cases where custody is an option, might have been the cause for this increase in its use. If this explanation would be confirmed, it would imply that according to the former legislation some serious cases would have had a community intervention since that was considered more beneficial, bearing in mind the juvenile's psycho-social situation. That is, the greater the flexibility available to juvenile judges when adopting measures, the more likely they would have been to choose community intervention, which they seemed to prefer. So, the great restrictions when adopting a measure under the JCA, might have caused the legislator's criteria to take priority over those of the judge, obliging him or her to adopt custody measures where he or she might have preferred to adopt a community measure.

On the other hand, another explanation for this increase could be the changes in juvenile justice due to the modifications in age range, with the new rules simply following this change. That is, the entry in the system of older juveniles might have brought more serious situations that require a more intensive intervention.

Regarding community measures, official data offer quite surprising information. Despite having a catalogue with a widened number of possible community measures, in practice only two of the already existing measures are being applied: *probation* and *community service,* in 33.7% and 24.9% of the cases where a measure is adopted. That is, in the first years of the application of the Act the expected diversification of community measures has not taken place. In fact, the application of the two new measures has not been put into effect.

The non-application of the new measures might be due to several reasons. Firstly, we could point out a problem already mentioned when analysing the content of the Act: there is some confusion regarding these two new measures and their scope does not seem to have been very well understood.

It is also possible that these measures have not been applied because of a lack of resources; that is, if there are no day centres or not enough staff to carry out concrete educational interventions, they could hardly be applied.

Finally, there is another important reason for the small impact of these measures: if the legislator wanted to guarantee wider and more diverse community intervention, he should have provided a more flexible procedure that allows individualizing the intervention based on the juvenile's special situation rather than just enumerate a wide catalogue of measures. The truth is that the success of community intervention will only be possible if there are enough resources and programmes, adequate for each Autonomous Region, allowing an individualized intervention taking into account the juvenile's psycho-social situation.

In this sense we could say that, precisely as a consequence of more resources offered by the Act in most Autonomous Regions, the percentage of cautions has decreased: from 25.4% to 11.4% of cases where a measure is applied. This confirms the explanation that the excessive use of this measure in juvenile justice in Spain for so many years was, to a great extent, due to a lack of resources available for carrying out other types of educational interventions (Rechea Alberola and Fernández Molina, 2003).

Nevertheless, there is still a long way to go in community interventions, although resources have been created, we need a more coordinated action to guarantee more efficiency and real provisional interventions. In the same way, there is no doubt that the strict rules on custody after successive reforms is making it difficult to a large extent to experiment with alternatives to the deprivation of liberty, since the JCA obliges a minimum length of time in custody in some concrete cases.

7. CONCLUSIONS

The changes in legislation that have taken place in the last years in juvenile justice in Spain have, to a large extent, toughened the response to juvenile offenders, the best interests of the juvenile being no longer the only reference criterion in the juvenile judges' and Prosecutors' decisions.

However, in spite of this, the results in practice are not so extreme. Juvenile Prosecutors and judges continue to fight every day for juvenile justice to be as far as possible an individualized justice, offering juveniles an opportunity for change.

REFERENCES

Asquith, S (1998). "Scotland." In Mehlbye, J. and Walgrave, L. (eds.), *Confronting Youth in Europe. Juvenile Crime and Juvenile Justice*, pp. 425–458. Denmark: AKF.

Bailleau, F. and Cartuyvels, Y. (2002). "Introduction," *Déviance et Societé*, 26, 279–282.

Barberet, R. Rechea, C. and Montañés, J. (1994). "Self-Reported Juvenile Delinquency in Spain: Results from the Spanish Survey of the International Self-Report Delinquency Project," In Jünger-Tas, Terlouw and Klein (Coords.), *Delinquent Behaviour Among Young People in the Western World.* Amsterdam: Kugler.

Barberet, R. (2001), "Youth Crime in Western Europe: Will the Old World Imitate the New?,." in Susan O. White (ed.), *Handbook of Act and Social Science: Youth and Justice.* New York: Plenum.

Bernuz Beneítez, Mª.J. (2000). "Protección de los derechos de la infancia y prevención de la delincuencia juvenil," *Revista aragonesa de Administración pública*, 16, 597–617.

Bottoms, A., Haines, K., and O'Mahony, D. (1998). "England and Wales," in Mehlbye, J. and Walgrave, L. (eds.), *Confronting Youth in Europe: Juvenile Crime and Juvenile Justice*, pp. 139–216. Denmark: AKF.

Fernández Molina, E. (2002). "La valoración del interés del menor en la LO 5/2000, de 12 de enero, reguladora de la responsabilidad penal de los menores," in Martín Ostos, J. (Dir.), *Anuario de Justicia de Menores*, 2, 55–77.

Fernández Molina, E (2004). *La justicia de menores en la España democrática: entre la educación y el castigo* (unpublished doctoral thesis). Albacete: University of Castilla-La Mancha.

Fernández Molina, E. and Rechea Alberola, C. (2005). "Policies transfer: the case of juvenile justice in Spain," *European Journal on Criminal Policy and Research*, 11, 51–76.

Gatti, U. and Verde, A. (1998). "Italy," in Mehlbye, J. and Walgrave, L. (eds.), *Confronting Youth in Europe: Juvenile Crime and Juvenile Justice*, pp. 355–388. Denmark: AKF.

Gazeau, J.F. and Peyre, V. (1998). "France," in Mehlbyc, J. and Walgrave, L. (eds.), *Confronting Youth in Europe: Juvenile Crime and Juvenile Justice*, pp. 217–250. Denmark: AKF.

Giménez-Salinas Colomer, E. (2000). "Comentarios a la exposición de motivos y al titulo preliminar," in Giménez-Salinas Colomer, E. (coord.), *Justicia de menores: una justicia mayor*, pp. 27–43. Madrid: CGPJ.

Junger-Tas, J. (1998). "The Netherlands," in Mehlbye, J. and Walgrave, L. (eds.), *Confronting Youth in Europe: Juvenile Crime and Juvenile Justice*. (pp. 389–424). Denmark: AKF.

Mehlbye, J. and Sommer, B. (1998). "Denmark," in Mehlbye, J. and Walgrave, L. (eds.), *Confronting Youth in Europe: Juvenile Crime and Juvenile Justice*, pp. 97–138. Denmark: AKF.

Muncie, J. (2004). "Youth justice: Globalisation and multi-modal governance," in Newburn, T. and Sparks, R. (eds), *Criminal Justice and Political Cultures: National and International Dimensions of Crime Control*, pp. 152–185. Devon: William Publishing.

O'Sullivan, E. (1998). "Ireland," in Mehlbye, J. and Walgrave, L. (eds.), *Confronting Youth in Europe: Juvenile Crime and Juvenile Justice*, pp. 307–354. Denmark: AKF.

Ornosa Fernández, R. (2000). *Derecho penal de menores.* Barcelona: Bosch.

Rechea Alberola, C. and Fernández Molina, E. (2003). "Juvenile justice in Spain: Past and Present," *Journal of Contemporary Criminal Justice*,19, 384–412.

Walgrave, L., Berx, E., Poels, V. and Vettenburg, N. (1998). "Belgium," in Mehlbye, J. and Walgrave, L. (eds.), *Confronting Youth in Europe: Juvenile Crime and Juvenile Justice*, pp. 55–96. Denmark: AKF.

Weitekamp, E., Kerner, H. J., and Herberger, S. M. (1998). "Germany," in Mehlbye, J. and Walgrave, L. (eds.), *Confronting Youth in Europe: Juvenile Crime and Juvenile Justice*, pp. 251–306. Denmark: AKF.

PART III

Eastern Europe

14

Continuity in the Welfare Approach:
Juvenile Justice in Poland

Barbara Stando-Kawecka

INTRODUCTION

Poland is a relatively large country in central Europe. The area of Poland amounts to 312,000 km². According to current statistics, Poland's population as of 30 June 2004 numbered 38,180,249. As for the age structure, over one-fifth of the population (21.5%) had not attained the age of 18. The number of juveniles, who were at least 13 but below 17 years of age, amounted to 2,235,865 (Statistical data of the Central Statistical Office are available online, www.stat.gov.pl).

In 1989 Poland experienced a radical change in the political, social, and economic systems; after the collapse of the communist system in that year, the Republic of Poland re-emerged as an independent and democratic law-abiding State. Since 1991 Poland has been a member state of the Council of Europe and in 2004 it entered the European Union.

As many other post-communist countries, in the 1990s Poland faced an increasing number of offences recorded by the police, including offences committed by juveniles, and also negative changes to the structure of the crimes committed. This chapter focuses on basic recent trends in juvenile crime rates in Poland as well as on legal provisions concerning reactions to juvenile offences.

1. A BRIEF HISTORY OF THE POLISH JUVENILE LAW

1.1. The Juvenile Justice System under the 1932 Penal Code

It was not until 1918 that Poland became independent after a long period when the country had been divided between Austria, Germany, and Russia. After having regained independence it was a matter of great urgency to unify both the penal and civil law. As far as the penal law is concerned, the legislative commission set up to prepare the draft of the Penal Code stressed continuously that children and youths who had broken the law should not be treated as "little adults"; as a result, they should not receive the same penalties as adult offenders. Finally, the Penal Code of 1932 contained a separate chapter on juveniles which introduced a separate system of juvenile justice.

J. Junger-Tas and S. H. Decker (eds.), International Handbook of Juvenile Justice, 351–376.
© 2006 Springer.

According to s. 69(1) of the 1932 Penal Code a juvenile was a person who had committed an offence before having reached 17 years of age. Juveniles who had committed an offence before his or her 13th birthday could not be accountable for their illegal actions. As a result, only educational measures might be imposed that ranged from a reprimand through the supervision of parents, guardians, or a probation officer to placement in an educational institution. The same measures were imposed on juveniles who had committed an offence after the 13th birthday, but before the 17th, provided that they were not competent to understand the nature of the act and direct their behaviour. Under s. 70 of the 1932 Penal Code, juveniles aged 13–16 who had committed an offence, while having been able to understand the nature of the act and direct their behaviour, should be sentenced to placement in a house of correction. It was possible, however, to impose educational measures on such juveniles as well, if the court found placing them in a house of correction useless on the basis of the circumstances of the offence, the juvenile's character or conditions of his or her life and environment.

As in many other countries there was a shift at the beginning of the last century towards a discretionary welfare-oriented model of juvenile justice. In Poland juveniles placed in a house of correction under the Penal Code of 1932 could be institutionalized until the age of 21. However, they might be granted conditional release earlier. Section 73 (1) of the Code gave courts the authority to suspend conditionally the execution of the placement of a juvenile in a house of correction provided that the crime committed was not punished by the death penalty or life imprisonment in the case of adult perpetrators.

The nature of the placement of a juvenile in a house of correction under the Penal Code of 1932 was a matter of great controversy. According to some lawyers placing a juvenile in a house of correction constituted a special educational–preventive measure, different from other educational measures provided by the Code. In the opinion of others, however, placing a juvenile in a house of correction for an indeterminate term was a specific penalty or quasi-penalty that combined some retributive elements and a predominant rehabilitative goal (Stando-Kawecka, 1993: 10–15).

It should be added that in Poland, immediately after having regained independence, separate juvenile courts were set up in some of the biggest cities. The Code of Penal Procedure enacted in 1928 also introduced separate proceedings in juvenile cases. In fact, there were only a few juvenile courts in Poland before World War II. It was only in the 1960s that the number of separate juvenile courts started to grow significantly (Marek, 1988: 42–43).

1.2. The Juvenile Act of 1982

The Penal Code and the Code of Penal Procedure of 1969 did not contain any provisions on juveniles with one exception; the 1969 Penal Code introduced the possibility to transfer a juvenile aged 16 who had committed a very serious offence to an adult court. Generally, however, the provisions of the 1932 Penal Code and the 1928 Code of Penal Procedure concerning juveniles were still valid after the Codes of 1969 had come into force. It was only in May 1983 that they were replaced with the Juvenile Act (JA) enacted in 1982. The JA covers substantive legal questions and procedural matters as well as matters related to the execution of measures imposed on juveniles. It is worth emphasizing that although during the 1980s in many Western countries a shift could be observed from a welfare model that promoted the "best interests" of juvenile offenders towards a more legalistic approach to juvenile crime that stressed personal accountability as well as legal rights of juveniles, which was not the case in Poland. On the contrary, the JA as compared to the 1932 Penal Code strengthened the paternalistic welfare approach (Wojcik, 1995: 73). Strong educational and social rehabilitation elements of the Act are evident not only from the Preamble, but also from its provisions concerning the notion of a juvenile, measures applied to juveniles, and the central role of family judges and family courts in all stages of the proceedings in juvenile cases.

According to the Preamble to the JA, its main objectives are:

1. To counteract the demoralization and delinquency of juveniles;
2. To create conditions for those who have come into conflict with the law or with the rules of acceptable social behaviour, to return to normal life;
3. To strengthen the care and educational functions of the family and its sense of responsibility for the development of children.

Under s. 1(1) of the JA its provisions relate both to

(a) Juveniles aged 13–16 who committed offences and selected misdemeanours (the JA uses the notion "punishable acts"); and
(b) Juveniles who are under 18 years of age and display signs of problem behaviour, referred to as signs of "demoralization."

The JA does not define the notion of demoralization. In s. 4 of the JA only the signs of demoralization are enumerated: prostitution, use of alcohol or drugs, running away from home, association with criminal groups, systemic truancy of compulsory school or vocational training, and so forth. It should be noted that there is no minimum age limit for juveniles displaying signs of demoralization. The commission of an offence by a minor less than 13 years of age is considered to be a sign of demoralization, not a punishable act. Punishable acts may be committed only by juveniles at or above 13 but below 17 years of age.

As a rule, only educational, medical, and corrective measures may be imposed on juveniles. All educational and medical measures may be applied both to juveniles who have committed punishable acts (offences or selected misdemeanours) and to juveniles between 13 and 16 years of age but less than 18 years of age displaying serious problem behaviour. As far as corrective measures are concerned, they may be imposed only on juveniles who have committed offences after the 13th birthday, but before the 17th provided that a high degree of the perpetrator's demoralization and the circumstances and the nature of the act warrant that, and especially when educational measures have proved or are not likely to lead to rehabilitation of the offender. Corrective measures in the meaning of the JA are the suspended and immediate placement of a juvenile in a house of correction. Similar to the 1932 Penal Code, the placement in a house of correction under the JA is imposed on juveniles for an indeterminate term; they could be institutionalized until the age of 21.

Undoubtedly, the next important feature of the welfare approach to juvenile crime in Poland is the central role of family judges and family courts in proceedings in juvenile cases. Family courts were set up in Poland at the end of the 1970s. Since that time they have acted as family and juvenile departments in district courts. The concept of family courts in Poland is based on the assumption that the same judge should deal with cases concerning different members of the family. As a result, the scope of family courts authority ranges from cases heard according to family and guardianship law (with the exception of divorce and separation cases which were transferred to civil regional courts in 2001), cases regarding enforcement of compulsory treatment of alcoholics and drug addicts, and juvenile cases related to the prevention and reaction to problem behaviour of persons under the age of 18, as well as punishable acts committed by those between the age of 13 and 16.

As far as juvenile cases are concerned, family court judges conduct and control all the stages of the proceedings, i.e., the preliminary inquiry, court proceedings and proceedings related to the execution of the measures imposed on juveniles. It is the family judge who institutes proceedings in the case that a juvenile commits a punishable act or displays signs of problem behaviour. On being been notified of the circumstances justifying the institution of proceedings, however, the family judge may refuse to institute proceedings or discontinue them at any time based on the principle of expediency. During the preliminary inquiry the family judge assigns different actions to the police and to probation officers as well as decides – alone or in some cases with two laymen – on provisional measures to apply to a juvenile. The same judge alone or with two laymen decides on the imposition of educational, medical, or corrective measures on a juvenile. What is more, he or she supervises the execution of the imposed measures which to a large extent might be changed during the stage of their execution.

Generally, family court judges in Poland have enormous power in juvenile cases. They have a great deal of discretion in deciding to drop the case or continue the proceedings, to apply provisional measures, to impose educational, medical, or corrective measures as well as to revise or repeal those measures at the stage of their execution. No principle of proportionality between the seriousness of the offence committed and the measure imposed is provided by the JA. According to s. 3(1) of the JA in cases involving juveniles, including perpetrators of offences, the chief consideration should be their welfare, with an emphasis on bringing about favourable changes in their personality and behaviour and, when necessary, on ensuring the proper transfer by parents or guardian of their obligations, as well as the public interest. Under s. 3(2) basic criteria that should be used to choose proper measures are the personality of a juvenile, with particular reference to his age, health, mental and physical development, character and behaviour, as well as the causes and degree of demoralization, his or her environment and the conditions of his or her upbringing. As far as the placement of a juvenile in a house of correction is concerned, however, the circumstances and nature of the offence have to be taken into account.

The JA does not use the notion of "accountability" of juvenile offenders. Since the JA came in force in 1983, the Polish penal law has been based on the assumption that children and youths below 17 years of age are generally not mature enough to be capable of recognizing the dangerousness of their behaviour for society, or controlling their actions (Bogdan et al., 2004: 161). There is, however, an exception to the assumed lack of criminal responsibility of juveniles provided by the Penal Code. According to s. 10(2) of the 1997 Penal Code, a juvenile may be criminally responsible provided that he or she committed one of the most serious crimes enumerated in this section while being 15 or 16 years of age and the circumstances of the offence and the offender, the level of his or her maturity as well as the ineffectiveness of previously imposed educational or corrective measures, justify directing the case to a penal court for adults.

In comparison with the Penal Code of 1969, the 1997 Code lowered the age limit of exceptional criminal responsibility of juveniles in serious cases by 1 year (from 16 to 15 years of age) and slightly broadened the scope of offences for which 15- and 16-year-old perpetrators may be sentenced by an ordinary penal court. At the same time, however, the maximum penalty for juveniles exceptionally tried by an ordinary penal court was limited to two-thirds of the maximum penalty provided for adult offenders; while instead of life imprisonment a maximum penalty of 25 years of imprisonment might be imposed on juveniles.

1.3. Recent Amendments to the Juvenile Act of 1982

In the last decade the juvenile justice issue received a great deal of attention in Poland . On the one hand, efforts were made in the mid-1990s in order to introduce victim-offender mediation as well as some other elements of the restorative approach in juvenile law and praxis. On the other hand, however, the public shared the opinion that there had been a dramatic rise in juvenile crime. There is no doubt that, to a large extent, the media contributed to this opinion. The media frequently raised the problem of young people committing crimes. In their reports on juvenile crimes, the media frequently presented juvenile offenders as psychopathic monsters (Ministry of Justice, 1998: 3). As a result, demands for more stringent punishment were often voiced in the media and the current juvenile law is widely criticized for being "too soft" on young offenders. Such demands were supported by a large number of politicians, who placed great emphasis on the need for radical changes, making juveniles responsible for their acts and demanding more severe punishment. It should be noted that some Polish criminologists were of the same opinion. They stressed that the sharp rise in the number of registered juvenile offences, particularly violent offences, in the 1990s was "a dangerous phenomenon" and stated that current legislation on the treatment of juvenile offenders was out of date, by far too liberal and totally failing to meet the challenge of the new profile of juvenile crime (Siemaszko, 2000: 18). At the same time, the welfare-oriented paternalistic approach to juvenile offenders raised a great deal of doubts concerning the legal status and legal rights of juveniles during the proceedings, particularly with respect to the principles of proportionality and the presumption of innocence as well as the right of a juvenile to be adjudicated by an impartial tribunal (Stando-Kawecka, 1998: 40).

Despite the fact that the JA was strongly attacked for many reasons, it is still in force. What is more, only relatively limited changes to the juvenile justice system were enacted in the last decade. One of the most important changes to the JA was introduced in June 1995 in respect of the situation of persons who had been sentenced to imprisonment by an ordinary penal court for a crime committed after having reached 17- or exceptionally 16- years of age, while having been placed in a house of correction for an indeterminate term, which might have resulted in staying there up to 21 years of age. Before the correctional order, this placement in the house of correction should be executed first and the prison sentence afterwards. The family court, however, had a great deal of discretion as regards the execution of the prison sentence; it was up to the family court whether the prison sentence imposed by a penal court should have been executed after the inmate's release from the house of correction. The family court had the power to modify the penalty imposed by a penal court by suspending it conditionally or even remitting the whole of the sentence. According to s. 92 of the JA after the amendment of 1995, the prison sentence imposed on an inmate staying in a house of correction should be executed immediately. In such a case the execution of the correctional order cannot be continued and it has to be dropped, although the inmate who started to serve the prison sentence is under the age of 21. Under s. 93 of the JA, however, it is still up to the family court, whether the penalty of liberty deprivation of imposed by a penal court on an offender staying in a house of correction, should be executed. Before releasing the inmate from the house of correction, the family court is obliged to make a decision concerning the execution or remission of that penalty.

In September 2000 a further amendment to the JA was issued by Parliament. The main goal of the amendment, which came into force in January 2001, was to adjust the juvenile law to international standards and to harmonize it with other legal instruments, particularly with the 1997 Penal Code and the Constitution, to strengthen victim rights, and to provide a more effective procedure for juvenile cases. As a result, s. 3a was added to the JA which enables family judges and family courts to send juveniles, on request or with the agreement of both victim and offender, to an institution or trustworthy person in order to carry out mediation. At the same time, a number of changes were introduced with regard to the rights of juveniles placed in educational institutions and houses of correction.

Other provisions of the 2000 amendment were aimed at a more restrictive approach to juveniles who have committed serious crimes subsequent to being given a suspended order to a house of correction and after being granted parole from such a house or during their stay in it – provided that there are no grounds for referring the case to an ordinary penal court – in order to impose on the perpetrator a penalty provided for adults. Under the 1997 Penal Code the case is to be referred to a penal court if the offence was committed by a person at or above 17 years of age, because a 17-year-old offender is an adult in the meaning of the penal law. Exceptionally the case may also be referred to a penal court if the perpetrator committed one of the most serious crimes while being 15 or 16 years of age. Provided that the offender is sentenced by a penal court, the further execution of the suspended or unsuspended correctional order depends on the type of the penalty imposed; the correctional order has to be dropped if an unsuspended prison sentence was adjudged. In cases in which a juvenile under 17 years of age at the time of the offence cannot be exceptionally tried by a penal court because conditions set down by s. 10(2) of the Penal Code are not fulfilled, the amended JA provides the following provisions:

1. In terms of the s. 11(3) of the JA the family court has to place a juvenile in a house of correction if he or she has committed a serious crime during the period of a suspended order of placement in such a house.
2. According to s. 91(2) of the JA a juvenile with serious problem behaviour who has committed a serious crime during his stay in a normal house of correction may be sent to a treatment institution with restrictive educational supervision, to a psychiatric hospital or to another appropriate health care institution; earlier conditional release from the house of correction for juveniles who require restrictive educational supervision is possible in such a case after at least a 1-year stay in the house.
3. Under s. 87(3a) of the JA the family court has to revoke the earlier release if the juvenile committed a serious crime while on parole; the juvenile could be granted a renewed conditional release, but not before he has spent no less than 1 year in a house of correction.

Another important amendment to the JA was enacted in 2003. According to it, juveniles both having committed offences and displaying other signs of problem behaviour cannot be placed even provisionally in the same educational institutions as children deprived of parental care. Undoubtedly, the division between institutions designed for juveniles on whom educational measures were imposed under the JA and institutions for neglected or abused children without the history of offences and other antisocial behaviours undermines the welfare philosophy of the JA based on the assumption that both problem behaviour and lack of parental care are symptoms of a child being in the need of care and protection and require the same protective measures.

2. CRIME TRENDS IN POLAND AFTER 1989

2.1. Overall Crime Trends

Like other central and eastern European countries Poland experienced a very rapid increase in the number of recorded offences after the totalitarian state had collapsed. As can be seen from Fig. 14.1 the most dramatic growth of the number of recorded offences was observed between 1989 and 1990; in that period the number of offences had grown by 61%, and the official crime rate in Poland by about 63% (Siemaszko et al., 2003: 16; Krajewski, 2003: 12–13, 2004: 383–384).

According to some Polish criminologists such an explosion of offences limited to 1 year only is hardly imaginable (Krajewski, 2003: s. 13). At the same time they stress that it is difficult to assess to what extent the rapid increase in the number of recorded offences between 1989 and 1990 was compatible with the increase in the number of offences in reality and to what extent it was caused by several other factors, such as the increasing willingness of citizens to report crimes to the police or some radical changes in patterns of recording offences by the police (Błachut et al., 1999: 205–207; Krajewski, 2003: 12, 2004: 384). Unfortunately, it is impossible to verify official data with the help of victimization data, because victim surveys were completely unknown in Poland before 1989 and even after that date they have not been routinely used as a way of collecting data on crime. As a result they provide only very limited data on the development of crime trends during the last decade (Siemaszko et al., 2000: 69–75, 2003: 187–203).

In the early 1990s the number of offences recorded by the police stabilized or even dropped a little. Since 1994 it had started to grow again, with a small interval in 1996, when it dropped. However, the dimensions of this growth were not comparable with the dramatic increase in 1989 and 1990. More recently, the number of offences registered during 2001–2003 were strongly influenced by changes in the penal law. Since December 2000 drunken driving, that previously constituted a misdemeanour and was not included in the statistics of offences, has been penalized as an offence under the Penal Code. As a result, about 120,000–140,000 cases of drunken driving per year have been registered by the police as traffic offences (Siemaszko et al., 2003: 16; *Statistical Yearbook of the Republic of Poland*, 2003: 64). Having these changes in criminalization in mind, it is easy to observe that since 2000 the amount of recorded offences in Poland has increased.

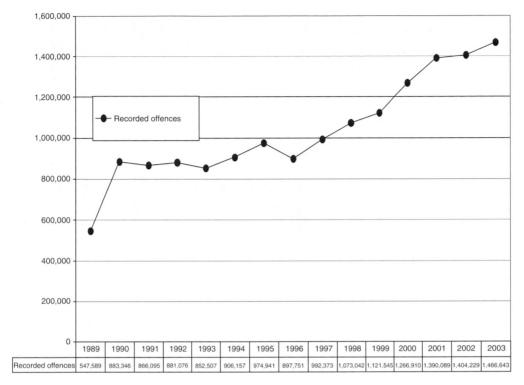

	1989	1990	1991	1992	1993	1994	1995	1996	1997	1998	1999	2000	2001	2002	2003
Recorded offences	547,589	883,346	866,095	881,076	852,507	906,157	974,941	897,751	992,373	1,073,042	1,121,545	1,266,910	1,390,089	1,404,229	1,466,643

FIGURE 14.1. Recorded offences in Poland during 1989–2003. The number of offences registered by the police does not include misdemeanours (*wykroczenia*). According to the Polish penal law, misdemeanours are petty offences, such as petty traffic offences and petty thefts, penalized under the Code of Misdemeanours with a fine, deprivation of liberty up to 1 month, or detention for 5 – 30 days.
Source: Adapted from *Police Statistics*; available at www.kgp.gov.pl.

As far as absolute numbers of the most serious offences are concerned, these are offences against life, health, and robbery, which did not stabilize in the early 1990s but continued to grow steadily. For selected offences against life and health (homicide, bodily injury, assault, and battery) the trend persisted up to 1997 and for robbery up to 2000 (more information in Siemaszko et al., 2003: 20–24; Krajewski, 2003: 14). On the other hand, however, the percentage of offences against life and health during the whole period was relatively small and increased from 1.7% in 1990 up to 3.6% in the late 1990s. Figure 14.2 illustrates that for robbery the situation was much the same; the share of robberies was 1.7% in 1989 and 4.2% at its peak level in 2000. At the same time, however, quite different patterns could be observed for property offences. The percentage of burglaries rose significantly between 1989 and 1990, after which it started to drop constantly with small intervals in 1996 and 1998. As for theft, the percentage has been fluctuating strongly and without any clear pattern.

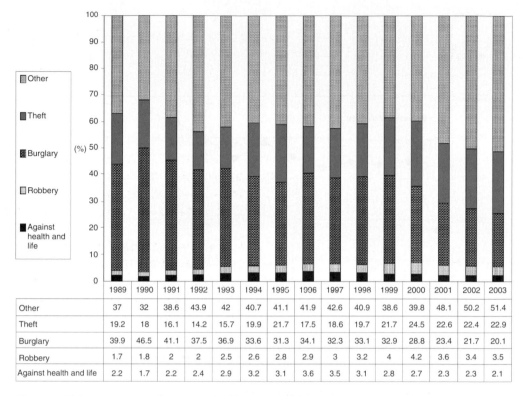

	1989	1990	1991	1992	1993	1994	1995	1996	1997	1998	1999	2000	2001	2002	2003
Other	37	32	38.6	43.9	42	40.7	41.1	41.9	42.6	40.9	38.6	39.8	48.1	50.2	51.4
Theft	19.2	18	16.1	14.2	15.7	19.9	21.7	17.5	18.6	19.7	21.7	24.5	22.6	22.4	22.9
Burglary	39.9	46.5	41.1	37.5	36.9	33.6	31.3	34.1	32.3	33.1	32.9	28.8	23.4	21.7	20.1
Robbery	1.7	1.8	2	2	2.5	2.6	2.8	2.9	3	3.2	4	4.2	3.6	3.4	3.5
Against health and life	2.2	1.7	2.2	2.4	2.9	3.2	3.1	3.6	3.5	3.1	2.8	2.7	2.3	2.3	2.1

FIGURE 14.2. Structure of recorded offences during 1989–2003. Offences against health
and life cover homicide, bodily injury, brawl and battery.
Source: Adapted from *Police Statistics*; available at www.kgp.gov.pl.

2.2. Juvenile Offences According to Police Statistics

Police statistical data on juvenile offences relate to offences committed by persons who at the time of the offence are at least 13 years old but younger than
17 years. Unfortunately, no statistical data are available as far as the number of
recorded juvenile offences in 1989 is concerned; police statistics as well as the
Statistical Yearbook of Poland provide for only the number of juvenile suspects
in that year. For this reason it is impossible to say, whether there was a similar
dramatic increase in the official number of juvenile offences between 1989 and
1990 as was the case of adult crime.

   Figure 14.3 shows that juvenile offences developed between 1990 and 2003 in a
substantially different way from overall recorded offences. Total number of juvenile offences did not stabilize in the early 1990 as was the case of all recorded
offences but grew continuously between 1990 and 1995. In 1996, however, a sharp
decrease in juvenile offences could be observed followed by a rise during the next
2 years. Since 2000 juvenile offences have been dropping steadily while the number

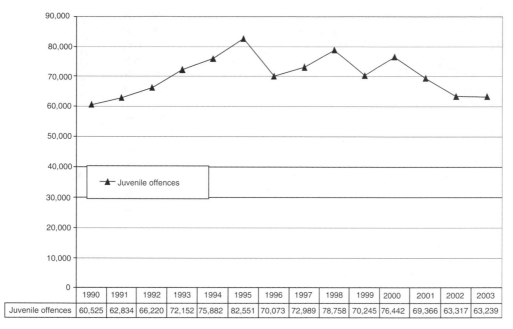

	1990	1991	1992	1993	1994	1995	1996	1997	1998	1999	2000	2001	2002	2003
Juvenile offences	60,525	62,834	66,220	72,152	75,882	82,551	70,073	72,989	78,758	70,245	76,442	69,366	63,317	63,239

FIGURE 14.3. Recorded juvenile offences during 1990–2003 (absolute numbers). *Source*: Adapted from *Police Statistics*; available at www.kgp.gov.pl.

of all recorded offences has continued to grow mainly due to the criminalization of drunken driving.

Generally, trends in juvenile offences compared to trends in overall crime level seem to point out that the former did not contribute significantly to the overall growth of recorded offences in Poland after 1989. Data concerning the proportion of juvenile offences to all offences, as illustrated in Fig. 14.4, lead to much the same conclusion. It should be mentioned, however, that in Poland the overall figures in police statistics refer to the category "confirmed offence," i.e., incidents reported to the police that are confirmed after the investigation following the report as having constituted a criminal offence. "Confirmed offences" are thus recorded independently of whether the perpetrators are known or not. As regards juvenile offences, it is only possible to classify an offence as that committed by a juvenile if the perpetrator is known. In fact, the number of juvenile offences recorded by police statistics may be strongly influenced by a variety of additional factors, such as different clearance rate for different offences and for different age groups of offenders (Krajewski, 2003: 20). Having in mind these reservations, it could be observed that the proportion of juvenile offences to all recorded offences grew between 1990 and 1993. In 1990 juvenile offences constituted 6.9% of all offences recorded by the police, while in 1993 they amounted to 8.5%. In the following years, however, no further increase of this proportion took place. On the contrary, since 1995 the proportion of juvenile offences has

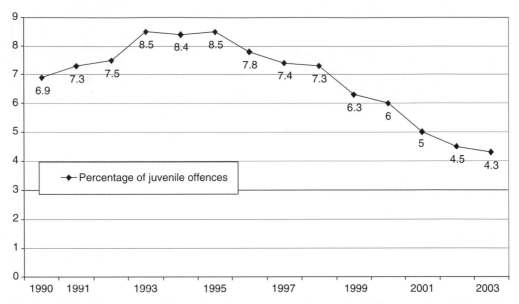

FIGURE 14.4. Proportions of juvenile offences among all recorded offences during 1990–2003. *Source*: Adapted from *Police Statistics*; available at www.kgp.gov.pl.

been falling continuously and in 2003 it amounted to 4.3%, i.e., the percentage is much more lower as at the beginning of the 1990s. As regards the proportion of juvenile suspects to all suspects recorded by the police, Fig. 14.5 shows relative stabilization in the early 1990s followed by an increase during 1993–1995 when it was at its peak and amounted to 16.1%. After 1995, however, the proportion started to drop and in the late 1990s it remained relatively stable, while at the same time the share of juvenile offences among all offences was decreasing significantly. This may suggest some changes in social, and particularly the police, attitudes towards juveniles committing offences in the late 1990s, for example, growing readiness of victims to report such offences or paying more attention by the police to juvenile delinquents. A sharp decrease in the share of juvenile suspects observed in 2001 seems to be connected with the sudden growth in the number of adults suspected of drunken driving that started to be penalized as an offence under the Penal Code.

Juvenile suspects' rates computed for 100,000 of the population aged 13–16 during the 1990s reveal much the same trends as percentages of juvenile suspects among all suspects recorded by the police (see Fig. 14.6). After a relative stabilization in the early 1990s the biggest rise in juvenile suspects' rate took place in 1994 when it grew by about 41% in comparison with that in 1993. This increase continued in 1995 when the juvenile suspects' rate was at its peak. In 1996, however, it dropped sharply and during next years it stabilized again. It should be noticed, however, that in 2001 the juvenile suspects' rate per 100,000 youths did

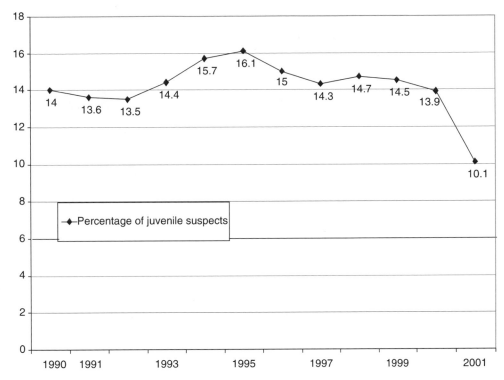

FIGURE 14.5. Proportions of juvenile suspects among all suspects during 1990–2001. *Source*: Adapted from Siemaszko et al. (2003).

not decrease as the proportion of juvenile suspect on all suspects did. Undoubtedly, this justifies the conclusion that the sudden drop in the percentage of juvenile offenders to all suspected offenders in that year was mainly due to changes in the number of adult suspects.

The changing structure of juvenile deliquency was a matter of great concern in Poland during the 1990s. The percentage of juvenile violent offences, such as offences against life and health as well as robbery, was continuously on the rise in the 1990s. It was only in 2000, as is evident from Fig. 14.7, that some stabilization appeared in this respect. Offences against life and health constituted 1.6% of all offences committed by juveniles in 1990, while in the late 1990s the proportion was about four times the 1990 rate. As for robbery, there was a similar substantial growth in the percentage of that offence; in 2000 over six times the 1990 rate. At the same time the proportion of burglaries committed by juveniles has dropped steadily with some intervals in 1994 and 1996.

Data on the proportion of juveniles suspected of selected violent offences, such as homicide, bodily injury, brawl and battery, and robbery, to all persons suspected of such offences confirm to a large extent the conclusion concerning

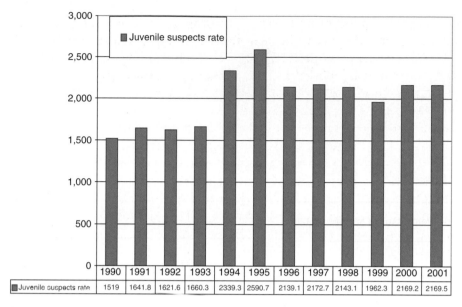

FIGURE 14.6. Juvenile suspects' rates per 100,000 of the population aged 13–16 (1990–2001). *Source*: Adapted from Siemaszko et al. (2003).

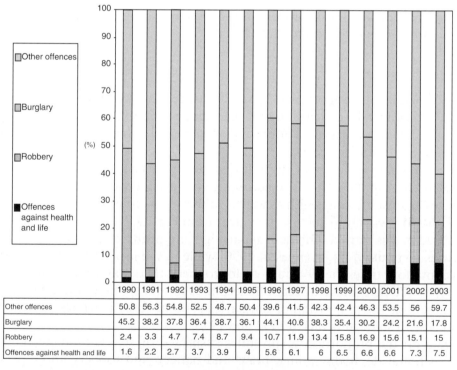

FIGURE 14.7. Structure of juvenile offences during 1990–2003 (percentages). *Source:* Adapted from *Police Statistics*; available at www.kgp.gov.pl.

changes to the structure of juvenile crime. The proportion of juveniles suspected of committing homicide, as can be seen from Fig. 14.8, was relatively stable after 1989. As regards juveniles suspected of bodily injury as well as brawl and battery, a substantial increase in the percentage of juvenile suspects took place during the 1990s. In 1999 the proportion of juveniles suspected of bodily injury amounted to 22.6% in comparison with 8.3% in 1989; the proportions for brawl and battery were, respectively, 5.9% in 1989 and 19.8% 10 years later. The proportion of juveniles suspected of robbery was on a sharp rise between 1989 and 1995, followed by a steady decrease during the next years. In 2001, however, this proportion was much higher as the 1989 rate. On the other hand, the percentage of juveniles suspected of property offences, that is burglary and theft, was significantly lower in 2001 than was the case in 1989 (for more information on trends in juvenile property offences, see Krajewski, 2003: 31).

Generally, the evaluation of changes in juvenile delinquency in the 1990s has been the subject of a great deal of controversy. Some Polish criminologists and educators emphasize that the rise in juvenile crime was very steep. At the same time they put particular emphasis on the fact that the changes in juvenile delinquency

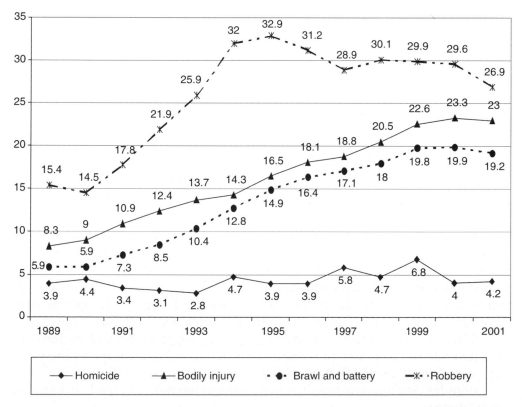

FIGURE 14.8. Proportions of juveniles among persons suspected of selected violent offences during 1989–2001. *Source:* Adapted from Siemaszko et al. (2003).

were not merely quantitative, but also qualitative, since juvenile crime was becoming increasingly violent. Finally, they consider this trend in juvenile crime a dangerous phenomenon (Siemaszko, 2000: 18; Urban, 2000: 194).

In the opinion of others, however, the situation had not been so dramatic, because the increase in juvenile delinquency in the 1990s was no greater than that in adult crime, and more importantly violent crimes still constitute only a small part of juvenile crime. Additionally, they point to the fact that in the 1990s the number of juvenile suspects was growing significantly faster than the number of juvenile crimes. The reason for this was probably the changing criminal policy towards juveniles. As a result, a rise in the number of recorded juvenile crimes could be explained, to a certain extent, by the growing readiness of the police to react to juveniles committing offences (Blachut et al., 1999: 374–375; Czarnecka-Dzialuk, 2000: 137; Krajewski, 2003: 32).

3. THE BASIC PHILOSOPHY UNDERLYING THE JA

Generally, the philosophy underlying the JA is not quite clear. On the one hand, if a juvenile commits a delinquent act, it is considered to be a symptom that the welfare of the child is endangered. As a result, the same educational and (mental) health measures aimed at protection, education, and re-socialization of the child may be applied to both juveniles committing offences or to those being in danger by their own behaviour, such as drinking alcohol, taking drugs, and running away from home. On the other hand, however, the possibility of more restrictive reactions is provided by the law with respect to serious offences committed by juveniles aged 13 or more.

Firstly, only juveniles who committed offences after their 13th birthday may be placed in houses of correction. As regards juveniles with behavioural problems other than committing an offence, their placement in such correctional institutions is excluded by the JA. When choosing between educational, medical, and corrective measures in cases concerning juvenile offenders, the family court should take into account not only the welfare of the perpetrator, with an emphasis on bringing about favourable changes in his or her personality, but also the nature and circumstances of the offence (ss. 3 and 10 of the JA).

Secondly, only juveniles who committed one of the most serious crimes enumerated in s. 10(2) of the 1997 Penal Code after their 15th birthday may be exceptionally tried by the penal court and sentenced to penalties provided for adults. According to s. 3 of the JA, a family judge who transfers the case of a juvenile to the public prosecutor in order to bring a charge to the ordinary penal court should first of all take into account the welfare of the juvenile offender. Such provisions, however, seem to be not only unclear but also contradictory.

4. THE PROCEEDINGS IN JUVENILE CASES

4.1. Limited Activity of the Police and Prosecutors

As a result of the principle that family judges and family courts are competent at all stages of the proceedings in juvenile cases it is the family judge who institutes the preliminary inquiry after having been informed that a juvenile has serious behavioural problems or has committed an offence. The activity of the police and public prosecutors in juvenile cases is very limited.

In terms of ss. 37 and 39 of the JA the police are competent to collect and preserve evidence of punishable acts, including the interrogation of a juvenile suspect, in urgent cases. The interrogation of a juvenile by the police should be carried out in the presence of parents, guardian, or a lawyer. According to s. 40 of the JA, a juvenile suspect at or above 13 years of age may be detained in a special police institution for juveniles for a period not exceeding 72 hours. Detention of a juvenile in such an institution should be immediately notified to parents or guardian as well as to the family court. If within 72 hours of the detention of the juvenile no decision concerning provisional measures has been issued by the family judge, the juvenile should immediately be released and transmitted to the custody of his or her parents or guardian. Provisional measures imposed by a family judge or a family court range from the supervision of a youth by a probation officer, other trustworthy person, a workplace or a youth organization to the placement to a public health institution, a youth educational centre, or a special detention facility for juveniles.

According to the JA, the police have no discretionary powers; on the contrary, they are obliged to report every juvenile case immediately to a family judge after having collected and stored the necessary evidence in urgent penal cases. There are some reasons for assuming that in fact the police do not report all juvenile cases to a family judge, but make an informal selection; however, no research related to this police selection has been carried out. Some research on police activities in juvenile cases revealed that in practice in many cases the police do not report juvenile offences to a family judge immediately after having collected the evidence in urgent cases, but they do it after having made further investigations (Korcyl-Wolska, 2001: 420). Another problem is the time juveniles spend in the police institution for juveniles. Because of lack of place in the youth educational institutions and youth detention facilities where they have been placed by family judges under provisional measures, juveniles suspected of an offence tend to remain in the police institutions for a period exceeding 72 hours (Korcyl-Wolska, 2001: 199–200).

As far as public prosecutors are concerned, they institute and conduct an investigation only exceptionally in juvenile cases, i.e., if:

1. A juvenile has committed an offence acting in association with an adult, the offence of the juvenile being strictly connected to the offence of the adult, and if the welfare of the minor does not preclude the investigation; when the

investigation is completed the prosecutor refers the case to a family court or – provided that a joint trial of the case is essential – submits the indictment to a penal court which should follow the provisions of the JA in adjudicating the juvenile suspect.

2. The proceedings refer to an offence committed between 13 and 16 years of age, but they have been instituted after the offender's 18th birthday.

4.2. Preliminary Inquiries

Under s. 33 of the JA the main object of the preliminary inquiry is to determine whether there is evidence of problem behaviour or of a punishable act, as well as to determine whether there is a need to apply to the juvenile measures provided by the Act. During the preliminary inquiry and apart from the collection of evidence, the family judge should also gather information concerning the juvenile and his or her educational, health, and welfare situation. In terms of s. 37 of the JA, the family judge may order specific measures by a probation officer or the police. If necessary a juvenile may be referred by the family court to a family diagnostic–consultative centre in order to be diagnosed or placed under psychiatric observation in a public health institution for a period not exceeding 6 weeks (ss. 25 and 25a of the JA).

Generally, the preliminary inquiry in juvenile cases is based on the provisions of the Code of Civil Procedure. As regards the collection and storage of evidence by the police as well as the appointment and functions of a lawyer, however, the provisions of the Code of Penal Procedure are to be followed. The family judge conducting the preliminary inquiry may at any time drop the proceedings. Further, during the preliminary inquiry the family judge may refer the case to a mediation project. This is obviously on a voluntary basis and depends on the victim's and offender's motivation and agreement.

During this stage of the proceedings provisional measures may be applied by family judges which are similar to educational and medical measures imposed on juveniles by family courts after adjudicating the cases. In some cases the placement of a juvenile in a youth detention centre (the JA uses the notion *shelter for juveniles*) may be ordered as a provisional measure, i.e., if circumstances have come to light that recommend placement in a house of correction and additionally there are grounds for fearing that he or she may go into hiding or destroy evidence, or if it is impossible to establish his or her identity. In contrast to youth educational centres that are under the authority of the Ministry of Education, youth detention centres are under the authority of the Ministry of Justice. As a rule, juveniles cannot be detained in remand prisons designed for adult offenders. Under s. 18 (1) of the JA, however, in exceptional cases a juvenile at least 15 years old may be temporarily placed in a remand prison provided that there are grounds for sentencing him or her to a penalty provided for adults under s. 10(2) of the Penal Code and placement in a youth detention facility would not be acceptable.

On completion of the preliminary inquiry the family judge may drop the proceedings unconditionally if there is no evidence that the juvenile committed a punishable act or showed problem behaviour. Additionally, the family judge may drop the proceedings on the principle of expediency if the imposition of educational or corrective measures serves no purpose, in particular when such measures had been imposed on the juvenile in a previous case. Apart from discontinuing of the proceedings the family judge may also take one of the following decisions:

1. To refer the case to the school attended by the juvenile or a social organization to which he or she belongs if the judge is of the opinion that the educational measures available to the school or organization are adequate; in practice, however, such referrals are very rarely: e.g., in 2002 only 213 cases of offences and 58 cases of problem behaviour were transferred to schools and social organizations (*Statstical Yearbook of the Republic Poland*, 2003: 81).
2. In order to refer the case to tutelary and educational proceedings, the judge must be convinced, on the basis of the gathered evidence, that educational or medical measures should be applied to the juvenile.
3. If there are grounds for placing the juvenile in a house of correction, the case will be referred to correctional proceedings.
4. If in the course of the preliminary inquiry circumstances come to light which warrant sentencing the juvenile by the penal court to a penalty provided for adults, the case will be referred to the public prosecutor who brings the accusation to the penal court; in fact, this happens in only very exceptional cases: e.g., in 2000–2001 there were respectively 4 and 1 juveniles sentenced to imprisonment by the penal court (*Statistical Yearbook of the Republic Poland*, 2003: 85).

4.3. Proceedings Before the Family Court

According to the decision taken by a family judge on completion of the preliminary inquiry, juvenile cases may be dealt with by family courts in one of the following proceedings:

1. The tutelary–educational proceeding; or
2. Correctional proceeding.

The latter proceeding may be used only in cases of juveniles suspected of having committed an offence after having reached 13 years of age and only if there are grounds for placing them in a house of correction. Furthermore, tutelary–educational proceedings is used in cases of juveniles in danger as well as in penal cases if there are no grounds for applying corrective measures to them.

The main difference between these two proceedings relates to the provisions governing procedural issues. Tutelary–educational proceedings are governed by the provisions of the Code of Civil Procedure; there are, however, some legislative modifications added by the JA. In these proceedings a family judge deals with the case alone and in a rather informal way. In the correctional proceedings the case is dealt with by a family judge who presides and two laymen. A juvenile offender has to have a lawyer in correctional proceedings. In cases concerning serious offences the public prosecutor has to attend the hearing. In both tutelary–educational and correctional proceedings the judge dealing with the case at the trial stage usually conduct the preliminary inquiry.

According to ss. 45 and 53 of the JA, in juvenile cases hearings are not public, unless public hearings are justified on educational grounds. More information on the proceedings in juvenile cases are in Stando-Kawecka (1997: 424–425) and Stando-Kawecka and Dünkel (1999: 412).

5. FAMILY COURTS' DECISIONS IN JUVENILE CASES

5.1. The Number of Juvenile Cases Brought to Family Courts

Figure 14.9 illustrates the number of juvenile cases in family courts during 1989–2002. According to the accompanying statistical data, the proportion of cases of juveniles in danger amounted to 16–22%, while the proportion of cases of juveniles committing offences was 78–84%. The number of both

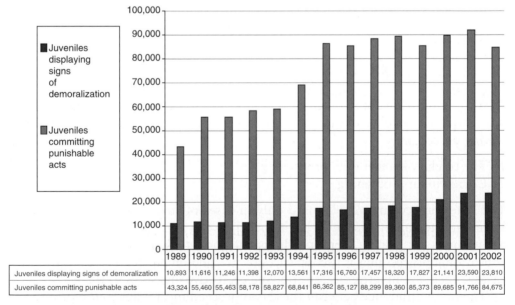

	1989	1990	1991	1992	1993	1994	1995	1996	1997	1998	1999	2000	2001	2002
Juveniles displaying signs of demoralization	10,893	11,616	11,246	11,398	12,070	13,561	17,316	16,760	17,457	18,320	17,827	21,141	23,590	23,810
Juveniles committing punishable acts	43,324	55,460	55,463	58,178	58,827	68,841	86,362	85,127	88,299	89,360	85,373	89,685	91,766	84,675

FIGURE 14.9. Juvenile cases brought to family courts during 1989–2002.
Source: Adapted from Ministry of Justice.

these categories increased significantly in the period between 1993 and 1995 and then remained relatively stable with some increase in the period between 1999 and 2001.

5.2. Measures Applied to Juveniles by Family Courts

As was mentioned earlier, only educational and medical measures may be imposed on juveniles displaying problem behaviour. The JA provides for a wide range of educational measures, most of which are not connected with changes in the living place of a juvenile. In terms of s. 6 of the JA the educational measures include:

1. A reprimand
2. Supervision by parents, guardian, a youth - or other social organization, a work-place, a trustworthy person or a probation officer
3. Applying special conditions, such as redressing the damage, making an apology to the victim, doing unpaid work for the benefit of the victim or local community, taking up school education or a job, taking part in educational or therapeutic trainings, avoiding specific places, refraining from the use of alcohol and other intoxicants
4. A ban on driving
5. Forfeiture of objects gained through the commission of a punishable act
6. Placing a juvenile in a youth probation centre
7. Placing a juvenile in a foster family
8. Placing a juvenile in a youth educational centre or another suitable institution providing vocational training

Traditionally, under the JA juvenile offenders and juveniles in danger have been placed in the same tutelary and educational institutions as children and youth in need of care. As was mentioned above, this situation changed in January 2004. According to the amended provisions of the JA, *youth educational centres* are designed only for juveniles placed in them on the basis of this Act. These centres are under the authority of the Ministry of Education, and separate from tutelary institutions, such as orphanages, designed for children deprived of parental care and who have not committed any offence nor problem behaviour. As far as the latter institutions are concerned, they are under the authority of the Ministry of Labour and Welfare.

As for medical measures, they may be applied to juveniles suffering from mental deficiency, mental disease, some kind of mental disorder, or from alcohol and drug addiction. These measures consist in placing juveniles in a psychiatric hospital or other suitable health care institution. According to s. 12 of the JA, if there is a need to ensure only care and protection, the juvenile may be placed in a social welfare institution or in a suitable educational centre. In practice, however, the possibility to place a juvenile in a health care or social welfare institution is used only in very exceptional cases. Educational and medical measures are applied to juveniles for an indeterminate period of time. As a rule these measures terminate on the 18th birthday of a juvenile and in some rare cases on his or her 21st birthday. The family court that executes the measures may revise or repeal them at any time if that is advisable on educational grounds.

All educational and medical measures may also be applied to juveniles who have committed offences whilst aged 13–16. Additionally, in such cases corrective measures may be used, such as placing them in a house of correction for an indeterminate period. However, in terms of s. 73(1) of the JA, a juvenile placed in a house of correction can stay there not longer than up to 21 years of age, although he may be granted conditional release earlier. Section 11 of the JA states that placement of a juvenile in a house of correction may be conditionally suspended if the personal and environmental circumstances and the nature of the act give grounds for supposing that, despite the waiving of custodial treatment, educative aims will be achieved. Conditional suspension of placing a juvenile in a house of correction may be applied for a period of probation of 1–3 years; while the court imposes educational measures during the period of probation.

Houses of correction are administered by the Ministry of Justice. The Ministry of Justice Ordinance of 2000 provides for separate houses of correction for juveniles with mental disorders and personality disorders, for alcohol and drug addicted juveniles, and for those that are HIV-positive. Juveniles without such problems are referred to common houses of correction, which are divided into open, semi-open and closed establishments. Juveniles who had previously escaped from an open and semi-open house of correction will be placed in the closed establishments. The Ordinance provides for a further type of house of correction designed for juveniles with serious problem behaviour demanding restrictive educational supervision.

5.3. Measures Imposed on Juveniles due to Punishable Acts

In the 1990s the proportion of corrective measures, which are suspended and unsuspended orders placing juveniles in a house of correction, covered 4% to 9% of all measures imposed on juvenile offenders (Stando-Kawecka, 2003a: 200–201; 2003b: 505–507). Thus, in practice, educational measures imposed by the family court form the vast majority of dispositions for juvenile offenders. Figure 14.10 shows that this tendency has not changed during 2000–2001.

As far as the types of educational measures imposed on juvenile offenders are concerned, Fig. 14.11 indicates that the most common measure that was applied to juveniles was placement of the juveniles under supervision of a probation officer. Of all educational measures, the reprimand and supervision of parents

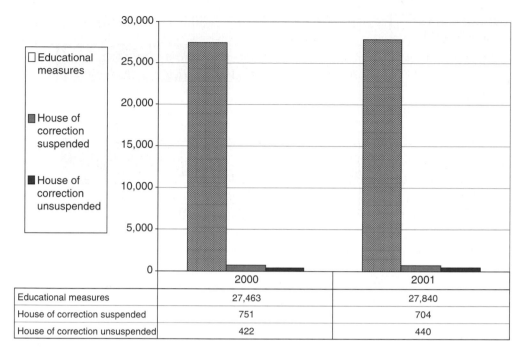

	2000	2001
Educational measures	27,463	27,840
House of correction suspended	751	704
House of correction unsuspended	422	440

FIGURE 14.10. Educational and corrective measures imposed on juveniles due to punishable acts during 2000–2001.
Source: Adapted from *Statistical Yearbook of the Republic of Poland* (2003).

were also frequently imposed on juveniles. Special measures, such as repairing the damages, apologizing to the victim, taking up school education or a job, and placement in an educational institution, do not seem to play a significant role in practice.

6. CONCLUSIONS

The first separate juvenile justice system in Poland established by the 1932 Penal Code combined elements of both the welfare and justice model. The JA of 1982 strengthened the paternalistic welfare approach to juvenile offenders. The welfare juvenile justice system has remained unchanged despite the fact that proportions of the most serious offences committed by juveniles were on the rise in the 1990s. However, juveniles committing repeated offences while being placed in houses of corrections have been seen as a significant problem. In addition, the paternalistic approach has been criticized not only for being too liberal for young offenders, but also for the lack of the principle of proportionality as well as some procedural rights of juveniles. In 2003 a

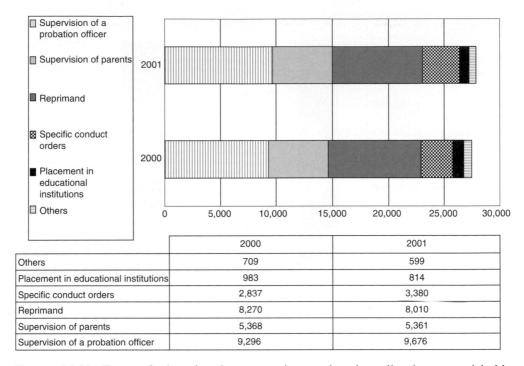

	2000	2001
Others	709	599
Placement in educational institutions	983	814
Specific conduct orders	2,837	3,380
Reprimand	8,270	8,010
Supervision of parents	5,368	5,361
Supervision of a probation officer	9,296	9,676

FIGURE 14.11. Types of educational measures imposed on juveniles due to punishable acts during 2000–2001. Category *others* contain such measures as placement in a foster family or in a day centre for juveniles run by a probation officer, a ban on driving, and forfeiture of goods. *Source*: Adapted from *Statistical Yearbook of the Republic of Poland* (2003).

team was set up by the Ministry of Justice in order to prepare the draft of a new juvenile law. According to basic principles of the draft published in April 2005 the main goals of the team were to unify the proceedings in cases due to offences and other problem behaviour as well as to strengthen the procedural rights of juveniles. Juvenile offenders, however, are still perceived as children lacking the competence to recognize the dangerousness of their acts to society and to direct their behaviour. Offences committed by juveniles are treated as symptoms of problem behaviour similarly to prostitution, use of alcohol or drugs, running away from home, association with criminal groups, or systematic truancy of compulsory school and vocational training. Family judges and courts have a broad scope of discretionary power in their efforts to provide juveniles with care and education, including the possibility to institutionalize children displaying problem behaviour other than committing offences for an indeterminate term (Gaberle, 2005: 12–22). Untill now, the draft of the new "Juvenile Code" has not been officially published nor subject to a public discussion.

REFERENCES

Blachut, J., Gaberle, A., and Krajewski, K. (1999). *Kryminologia* (Criminology). Gdansk: Arche.

Bogdan, G., Cwiakalski, Z., Kardas, P., Majewski, J., Raglewski, J., Szewczyk, M., Wrobel, W., and Zoll, A. (2004). *Kodeks karny. Komentarz. Tom I* (Penal Code. Commentary, Vol. I). Zakamycze: Kantor Wydawniczy Zakamycze.

Czarnecka-Dzialuk, B. (2000). "Juvenile Delinquency," in A. Siemaszko (ed.), *Crime and Law Enforcement in Poland on the Threshold of the 21st Century*. Warsaw: Oficyna Naukowa, pp. 137–143.

Gaberle, A. (2005). "Kontynuacja i zmiana (Continuation and Change)," *Panstwo i Prawo* (State and Law), 4: 11–22.

Korcyl-Wolska, M. (2001). *Postę powanie w sprawach nieletnich w Polsce* (The Proceedings in Juvenile Cases in Poland). Zakamycze: Kantor Wydawniczy Zakamycze.

Krajewski, K. (2003). "Patterns of Juvenile Delinquency and Juvenile Violence in Poland," in F. Dünkel and K. Drenkhahn (ed.), *Youth Violence: New Patterns and Local Responses – Experiences in East and West*. Mönchengladbach: Forum Verlag Godesberg, pp. 10–35.

Krajewski, K. (2004). "Crime and Criminal Justice in Poland," *European Journal of Criminology*, 1(3): 377–407.

Marek, A. (1988). "Są downictwo dla nieletnich w Polsce na tle porównawczym (Juvenile Courts in Poland in Comparative Aspects)," in T. Bojarski (ed.), *Postę powanie z nieletnimi* (Treatment of Juveniles). Lublin: Uniwersytet Marii Curie-Skłodowskiej, pp. 40–54.

Ministry of Justice (1998). *Raport o stanie wdrazania reformy resocjalizacji w zakładach poprawczych* (Report on the Implementation of the Reform of Resocialization in Houses of Correction). Warsaw: Ministry of Justice.

Ministry of Justice. *Statystyka są dowa i penitencjarna. Czesc I* (Court and Penitentiary Statistics. Part 1). A yearly publication. Warsaw: Ministry of Justice.

Ministry of Justice. *Statystyka są dowa* (Court Statistic). Available at www.ms.gov.pl.

Police Central Headquarter. *Police Statistics*. Online available at www.kgp.gov.pl.

Siemaszko, A. (2000). "Crime and Criminal Policy in Poland: A Look Back and into the Future," in A. Siemaszko (ed.), *Crime and Law Enforcement in Poland on the threshold of the 21st Century*. Warsaw: Oficyna Naukowa, pp. 15–25.

Siemaszko, A., Gruszczynska, B., and Marczewski, M. (2000). "Facts and Figures," in A. Siemaszko (ed.), *Crime and Law Enforcement in Poland on the Threshold of the 21st Century*. Warsaw: Oficyna Naukowa, pp. 29–83.

Siemaszko, A., Gruszczynska, B., and Marczewski, M. (2003). *Atlas przestępczości w Polsce 3*. (A Crime Atlas in Poland 3). Warsaw: Oficyna Naukowa.

Stando-Kawecka, B. (1993). *Charakter prawny zakładu poprawczego w Kodeksie karnym z 1932 r.* (Legal Character of the House of Correction Under the 1932 Penal Code). Przeglad Wieziennictwa Polskiego (Review of the Polish Prison System), 4–5, pp. 3–16.

Stando-Kawecka, B. (1997). "Polen," in F. Dünkel, A. van Kalmthout, and H. Schüler-Springorum (ed.), *Entwicklungstendenzen und Reformstrategien im Jugendstrafrecht im europäischen Vergleich*. Mönchengladbach: Forum Verlag Godesberg, pp. 419–435.

Stando-Kawecka, B. (1998). "Odpowiedzialnosc nieletnich na tle nowej kodyfikacji karnej (Responsibility of Juveniles Under the New Penal Codification)," *Prokuratura i Prawo* (Prosecution and Law), 7–8: 29–41.

Stando-Kawecka, B. (2003a). "New Local Strategies in Individual Countries: Poland," in F. Dünkel and K. Drenkhahn (ed.), *Youth Violence: New Patterns and Local Responses – Experiences in East and West*. Mönchengladbach: Forum Verlag Godesberg, pp. 197–208.

Stando-Kawecka, B. (2003b). "Jugendstrafrecht in Polen," in *Jugend, Gesellschaft und Recht im neuen Jahrtausend. Blick zurück nach vorn. Dokumentation des 25. Deutschen Jugendgerichtstages vom 28. September bis 2. Oktober 2001 in Marburg*. Mönchengladbach: Forum Verlag Godesberg, pp. 419–511.

Stando-Kawecka, B. and Dünkel, F. (1999). "Strafverantwortlichkeit Jugendlicher in Polen," DVJJ-Journal, 10: 409–418.

Statistical Yearbook of the Republic of Poland (2003). Warsaw: Central Statistical Office.

Urban, B. (2000). *Zaburzenia w zachowaniu i przestepczosc mlodziezy* (Youth Crime and Conduct Disorder). Cracow: Jagiellonian University.

Wojcik, D. (1995). "Juvenile Delinquency and Victims of Crime," in J. Jasinski and A. Siemaszko (ed.), *Crime Control in Poland*. Warsaw: Oficyna Naukowa, pp. 73–76.

15

Restorative Approaches and Alternative Methods: Juvenile Justice Reform in the Czech Republic

Helena Válková

INTRODUCTION

With respect to per capita income and the standard of living, the Czech Republic (about 10.2 million inhabitants) belongs to the most developed central European countries that have joined the European Union on 1 May 2004.

There are at present five court levels in a three-instance system: district courts, regional courts, higher courts, the Supreme Court, and the Supreme Administrative Court. Alongside the system of ordinary courts, there is the Constitutional Court.

The sanction system makes a distinction between penalties, measures, and conditions. All these penalties can only be imposed after trial by the court. A number of alternatives to pretrial custody are available. Other alternatives are attached to a conditional waiver. Since the beginning of the 1990s, new forms of community sanctions have been introduced into Czech criminal law, without any remarkable pilots. That is why they were often introduced very quickly and the current law includes a varied set of alternatives (van Kalmthout et al., 2003).

The overall crime level of in the Czech Republic in the last 3 years, as expressed by statistical data, can be viewed as the continuation of a period of stagnation. In 2003 the police recorded a total of 357,740 crimes of which only 135,581 were solved.

Thirty-six crimes per 1,000 of the population were recorded by the police in the Czech Republic; the highest rate was recorded in the capital: 82 crimes per 1,000 of the Prague population (Marešová, 2003).

Considering the juvenile population there is a large gap in crime rates between 1993, which was the first year of the newly created Czech Republic, and 2003.

In 1993 there were about 540,000 juveniles in the Czech Republic, of which 10,110 were prosecuted (1,874 per 100,000 juveniles) and 659 were sentenced to imprisonment (122 per 100,000 juveniles). In 2003 there were only about 394,000 juveniles in the Czech Republic, of which 7,374 were prosecuted (1,870 per 100,000 juveniles), but only 213 were sentenced to imprisonment (54 per 100,000 juveniles). In fact, Czech criminal policy towards juveniles has been – at least according to statistical data – significantly milder in the beginning of the 21st century than in the last two decades of the 20th century.

J. Junger-Tas and S. H. Decker (eds.), International Handbook of Juvenile Justice, 377–396.
© 2006 Springer.

The following text will attempt to comprehend the important changes in penal policy that took place in the Czech Republic in the last 15 years, including a brief overview of the dynamics and structure of juvenile delinquency. Based on the development in the legislation area, a new law on the Judiciary in Juvenile Matters was adopted in 2003. The Czech lawmakers opted for an interesting solution covering, within one law, the issues of criminal liability, criminal proceedings and types of measures, including criminal sanctions that can be imposed on a juvenile age group, i.e., 15-, 16-, and 17-year-old persons. In the Czech Republic this age group consisted of 395,721 persons as of 31 December 2002. This law, within a specially modified civil process, also sets up a way of handling the case and determines the types of educational measures that can be imposed on children younger than 15 years for committed offences without the existence of the lower age limit for establishing this special type of liability.

A common feature and a leading principle appearing in the entire law common to both age groups, regardless of criminally liable juveniles or children not yet criminally liable, is the emphasis put specially on restorative approaches and alternative methods. In this respect, it is a brave legislative experiment since it is not clear how a more or less rigid criminal justice system in the Czech Republic is going to apply this in practice and whether this progressive concept will be successfully transferred from the letter of law into real life.

1. MAIN TRENDS IN JUVENILE DELINQUENCY

The Czech Republic – founded as of 1 January 2003 as one of the succession states formed due to secession of Czechoslovakia into two sovereign states, the Czech Republic and Slovak Republic, with its approximately 10 million inhabitants of which slightly more then one-tenth lives in Prague – belongs to the countries that in the last 15 years underwent rapid social, economic, and cultural development. Considerable changes can be also noticed in the demographic development where we can see a drastic drop in the birth rate accompanied by a growing average age of an individual that can lead to adverse socio-economic consequences since 1990. The trend can also be seen in the area described in this material, by decreasing absolute number of delinquent children and juveniles that can lead on one hand to positive changes whereby the referred demographic group gets more qualified attention than before; on the other hand, it is possible that a higher number of unnecessary interventions of formal social control would take place. However, this statement is only pure speculation since no serious research has been conducted on this topic within the Czech Republic (Hulmáková, 2005).

In the last decade it was often possible to encounter information on the negative development of youth crimes both in the mass media and specialized literature (Marešová, 1999). Based on police statistics it has become possible since 1989 to record a relatively considerable increase in the number of criminal acts committed by youth. These figures were growing rapidly for the juvenile offenders group particularly in the years 1990–1993. Then the growth slowed down culminating in 1996 by nearly doubling in comparison with 1990. However, since 1997 the number of criminal acts committed by juvenile delinquents has been dropping. In 2003 it was even lower than in 1989. The increase of delinquent acts (pre-criminality) for the group of children under 15 years was even more considerable. In 1993, in comparison with 1990, this number had nearly doubled, and in 1999 nearly tripled after reaching its maximum in 1990–2003. From 1996 to 1999 the situation was stabilized to a certain extent and since 2000 the number of these delinquent acts committed by children younger than 15 years has been constantly decreasing. A considerable decrease took place mainly in 2002 and 2003 with the year 2003 resembling the situation in 1990.

Graphs show a significant increase of the ratio of juvenile criminal acts on the total number of solved criminal acts. In comparison with the second half of the 1980s where the percentage was on average around 10.7%, or 1991–1994 around 17%, the highest percentage was in 1992 – 17.4%. However, since 1995 this ratio gradually reduced to below 8% in 1999. The next more significant decrease took place in 2002 and 2003 with juvenile offenders' share representing 7.2%. Also since 1990 the group of children younger than 15 years has seen an increasing ratio of solved delinquent acts even though not so significant as with the juvenile offenders. This trend lasted until 1996 where their share reached a maximum (7.4%), after which a constant, gradual decrease could be observed. The next more significant decrease can be seen in the years 2002 and 2003 when the percentage of acts committed by children under 15 years dropped under 4%.

Closer attention the bodies active in criminal proceedings, such as police, specially directed at juvenile offenders' such as could influence the increase of registered juvenile criminality and the increase of the percentage of juvenile offenders in the first half of the 1990s in addition to other factors contributing to a general criminality increase after 1989 in our state. Therefore, while assessing the extent of juvenile criminality, it is always necessary to bear in mind in addition to share in the total number of solved criminal acts, how many criminal acts taken from the total number of registered acts were solved at all. In view of the system of recording results and assessment of the CR Police work efficiency, as for the solved crime rate, it is possible that there are pressures within the police force to concentrate on the juvenile age group, while they are investigating the criminal act of offenders, since that is easier to "favourably" influence the percentage increase of the total solved crime rate.

These facts can be seen even more conclusively with the group of children criminally not liable yet due to their age. In these matters, the case has usually been suspended before the criminal proceedings have started.[1] If we consider

---

[1] Since the effectiveness of the law on the judiciary in juvenile matters from 2003, i.e., from 1 January 2004 the given case is being heard by the Juvenile Court investigating whether a child really committed the act.

insufficient guarantees of the rights of these persons, until the law no. 218/2003 Coll. on the judiciary in juvenile matters had become effective, the question is how many "solved acts" otherwise criminal would, if they went to court or at least into the preparatory proceeding, have their offenders proven guilty – meaning the children younger than 15 years really committed the delinquent act (Thomová, 2000).

It can be assumed that demographic influence played its role, decreasing juvenile criminality in the second half of the 1990s. Since 1993, we can observe, in the case of the juvenile age group, a consistent, gradual percentage decrease of this age group, taking into consideration the total number of inhabitants in the CR. Since 1989, this decrease is already noticeable for the age group of children up to 15 years.

The decrease of registered juvenile criminality in 2002 and 2003 could be partially caused by decriminalization related to damage limit changes covered by amendment of the criminal law no. 265/2001 Coll., and that is mainly for acts otherwise criminal committed by children younger than 15 years, whereby it showed a prominent decrease.

Also, it is possible to observe a similar trend for the group of children younger than 15 years who committed acts otherwise criminal. Since 1990, except 1994, the number of these persons had been growing despite a gradual decrease of this age group in the total population. Especially, the years 1995 and 1996 had seen a significant growth peaking in 1996 with more than three times more delinquent youth in comparison with 1990. After that, except 1999, their numbers gradually decreased. In 2002 this decline was very prominent.

To interpret data on registered criminality of children not criminally liable due to their age is also difficult for other reasons in addition to the above-mentioned problems. The statistics of various authorities monitoring this age group show discrepancies as for the number of delinquents due to their different focus and methodology. For example, the statistics of the CR Ministry of Interior and the CR Ministry of Justice contain data on offences of children younger than 15 years but their age is not closely specified. Therefore, it is very problematic to determine exactly at what age the offenders more frequently commit the offences or whether this age is decreasing in the last decades.

Very often the police and courts point at the increasing offence gravity, brutality, and aggression of children and juvenile delinquents while committing offences (Marešová, 1996a, b). Based on the CR Ministry of Interior statistical data, it is clear that criminal acts of violence[2] in the group of children younger

---

[2]It is necessary to add that the following acts are classified as violent criminal acts according to the statistical results recording of the CR Police Presidium: for example, forcible entry into dwelling pursuant s. 238 Penal Code or unauthorized intervention into rights related to a house, apartment or non-residential premises pursuant s. 249a of Penal Code, i.e., criminal acts unnecessarily connected to violence against a person.

than 15 years were on the increase from 1990 to 1997. Since 1998, with exceptions in 1999 when their number was the highest ever in a monitored period (1,468 acts) and in 2001, we can observe a decrease in violent acts. In 2002 and 2003 a more significant decrease of violent crime took place in comparison with the previous years. An increase of registered violent criminal activity of juvenile groups was recorded starting in 1990 and lasting until 1996. However, the number significantly dropped between 1997 and 2001. In 2000 the number of these acts was close to the situation of the early 1990s. Since 2001 this number had slightly increased. In addition, it is possible to state that the number of very grave criminal offences, murders or rapes, committed by youth does not considerably change in the course of time and represents only an insignificant part of their criminal offences. In the group of children younger than 15 years, three murders were committed in 2001. In other years of the monitored period no murder was registered and in the juvenile groups five murders were recorded per year, except 2001 with eight cases. The number of rapes was, in the group of children younger than 15 years, between 5 and 18 cases and in the juvenile group between 17 and 20 per year.

2. FIRST REFORM STEPS

Until 1990 Czechoslovak justice was only providing very limited possibilities while searching for procedures and solutions suitable not only for the offender but also for the aggrieved party and their closest social community. The situation has radically changed after 1989 with the first publications of materials looking for new paths and informing about foreign experience. Thus a new space has been opened for initial projects, pilot experiments, and legislative changes.

The Czech Republic now belongs to the countries that reflected some elements of restorative justice into its penal legislation during the last decade and enforced and applied those also in practice. The proof of that can be found in the nature of the adopted amendments and new laws attempting to modify in a better way the position of the aggrieved party, to introduce new, informal solutions of penal matters, to extend the catalogue of traditional punishments by alternative sanctions and also by Ministry of Justice statistics demonstrating these changes of penal policy on the specific figures about the numbers and nature of the imposed sanctions and applied procedures (Válková, 2003).

Already in 1993, i.e., in the first year after the break up of the Czechoslovak federation, the law no. 292/1993 of Coll. was adopted in the Czech Republic amending the Criminal Procedure Act by laying down the possibility of conditional discontinuance of criminal prosecution with the agreement of the offender for criminal acts with an imprisonment sentence not exceeding 5 years. This procedure, after initial dilemmas and hesitations, has become one of the most frequent ways of alternative solutions to criminal acts in the Czech Republic – for its simplicity, speed, and effectiveness.

Two years later the law no. 152/1995 of Coll. was embodied in the Criminal Procedure Act introducing a new institute of mediation that already counted on the active participation of the aggrieved party that also opened the possibility to agree on the way of compensating other harm than only damages quantifiable in money. This alternative sanction can only be applied to less serious and medium serious criminal acts not exceeding 5 years of imprisonment and naturally requiring the agreement of the offender and also the aggrieved party. However, the mediation in this case has not become a popular way to solve criminal acts in practice as opposed to the conditional discontinuance of criminal prosecution.[3]

Not only criminal procedure regulations but also the penal law have experienced changes in favour of alternative sanctions. In 1995 the sentence of community service order has been newly introduced (no. 152/1995 of Coll.), which meant the first breakthrough into traditional systems of repressively focused sanctions headed by the imprisonment sentence. Following this law, with the effectiveness from 1 January 1998 the possibility to apply supervision executed by the probation office was introduced for conditional discharge and for a suspended sentence (no. 253/1997 of Coll.). Position of the probation officer was additionally covered by a new law on the Probation and Mediation Service in 2000 (no. 257/2000 of Coll.). Thus organizational and personal prerequisites were formed for imposing and executing alternative procedures and sanctions and at the same time the conditions were created for application of restorative procedures upon solving criminal acts both inside and outside criminal justice.

3. JUDICIARY REFORM IN JUVENILE MATTERS

The last significant change, considerably strengthening restorative procedures in Czech criminal justice, is represented by the reform of the juvenile criminal law that was embodied until then with only into 25 criminal law provisions (14 in the Penal Law and 11 in the Criminal Procedure Act). That arrangement did not

---

[3]New criminal procedure institutes – conditional discontinuance of criminal prosecution and mediation – that were embodied in the Criminal Procedure Act by amendments in 1993 and 1995 and statistically reported by courts since 1994 and the state prosecution offices since 1995 – signal a significant growth and frequent application of conditional discontinuance of criminal prosecution that was applied in 1995 to 5,606 criminally prosecuted persons (i.e., 5.2% out of all criminally pro-secuted persons) and in 2002 already to 10507 criminally prosecuted persons (i.e., 11.3% out of all criminally prosecuted persons) while mediation is concerned its use in practice is sporadic: for example, in 1996 was applied only to 105 cases (i.e., 0.1% of all criminally prosecuted persons) and in 2002 to 387 cases (i.e., only 0.4% of all criminally prosecuted people were involved).

consider sufficiently the specifics of this offenders' age group. It took into account a partially different course of the criminal prosecution but with more or less the same degree of their criminal liability and, with few exceptions, with an identical catalogue of criminal sanctions, though with shorter period duration. Therefore, juvenile criminal liability and its consequences were affected to the full extent by the traditional principle of retributive concept of criminal law whereby the protection of society through punishments plays a key role (s. 2 of PC). The essential break-through took place in June 2003 and the law no. 218/2003 of Coll. was adopted. This law on juvenile liability for illegal acts and on the judiciary in juvenile matters (further only as the law on judiciary in the juvenile matters) consists of 99 articles not including stipulations amending the Criminal Law, Criminal Procedure Act, and other related standards with restorative justice receiving for the first time an unambiguous support and preference to retributive justice.

It is necessary to take into account that the Penal Code and Criminal Procedure Act were adopted in 1961, i.e., more than 40 years ago. In spite of their numerous important amendments from the 1990s in relation to the age group of youth, they have not seen more significant changes. At the same time, professional discussions conducted on the topic of a possible change of penal policy in relation to youth sig-nalled two entirely opposite approaches on how to address the existing situation from the criminal policy point of view (Zbornik et al., 1996; Lortie et al., 2000). One group of experts expressed their opinion that the criminality of youth (in three-quarters of cases it applies to property criminal activity, most frequently thefts of belongings from cars and burglaries into flats and cabins) had to be addressed by reducing the age limit of criminal liability related to the total tightening of the penal policy, includ-ing consistent application of penal sanctions against juvenile delinquents (Marešová, 1996a, b, 1999).

The second opinion group pushed through such penal policies that would put in place the effort to create, in the social environment of the juvenile delinquent, optimal conditions for himself or herself to abstain from criminal activity in the future while keeping the existing arrangement for criminal liability for a commit-ted criminal act (Válková, 2001). The age of the juvenile does not play a key role in this concept. Not only criminal law consequences but other non-legal aspects that the law reaching a certain age limit are considered to be more essential. The emphasis lies with the importance of the responsibility in general, that applies also for a child who is not criminally responsible, but in a specific case was able to judge his acts and control them. It is necessary to draw conclusions from his behaviour and within a specialized judiciary system to apply suitable reformatory measures.

This second group of experts dominated the area for the prepared reform of the juvenile criminal law. The result of their work was a draft of the new law with a modified title at the beginning of 2001: *Law on the Responsibility of Youth for Criminal Acts and on Judiciary in the Matters of Youth* (*Law on the Judiciary in Juvenile Matters*). This draft was submitted to the Government, approved and passed in Parliament for discussion. The Assembly of Deputies approved the draft in the first reading and Parliamentary committees were supposed to further discuss it. A turn of development took place in spring 2002 before the upcoming June elections when Parliament excluded the discussion of a new law from the agenda of the 49th sitting of Parliament with the justification that such crucial changes that come along with the reform have to be assessed by the next Parliament. Based on this it is clear that at that time a political will was missing in order to adopt a new criminal juvenile law.

The situation had become more favourable after the June elections in 2002 when the newly established government had decided to discuss the draft of the law again – in the fall of 2002. After the comments raised mainly by the Ministries of Education and Defence, two major changes took place: a newly suggested institute of protective family rehabilitation was omitted and the age group of young adults, i.e., persons from 18 to 21 years was excluded from the law. The last mentioned change significantly affected the original concept of the law that was supposed to represent a complex standard for youth who had not finished the process of their social maturing. Thus there is hope that through suitable and age corresponding measures it is possible to prevent recurrence of criminal activity more effectively than through the traditional criminal law for adult offenders. Incorporation of the age group of young adults faced, from the beginning, the strongest criticism addressing "too soft" handling of young offenders of criminal acts. Therefore, the government finally decided to exclude this entire area from the law and leave in the framework of the concurrently amended criminal law a possibility for the courts to impose in certain cases – with the exception of specially serious criminal acts – a sentence reduced by one quarter to that of a person close to juvenile age and further to apply some of the educational measures mentioned in the law on the judiciary in juvenile matters with the conditions stated for juvenile offenders.

This amended governmental draft of the law was discussed and approved by the Czech Republic Parliament on 25 June 2003. The President of the Czech Republic signed the new law under no. 218 published in part 79 of the Collection of laws, becoming effective on 1 January 2004. Thus a long-term process of preparation and legislative negotiations of the standard shortly named by the legislators as "law on the judiciary in juvenile matters" has been finalized.

The new law on the judiciary in juvenile matters (further only as new law) is outlined to specify the difference of proposed special legislation for acts committed by youth as opposed to general legislation contained in penal codes and related legal regulations. The meaning of a new legislative form is to lay out comprehensively in *an independent code* substantive law and procedural aspects of youth sentencing, newly constitute a system of specialized juvenile courts, and clearly define integral variety of possible reactions to juvenile criminal activity.

The new law modifies conditions, procedures, and decision-making in juvenile criminal issues and execution of the judiciary function over juvenile persons and procedures and measures adopted against children younger than 15 years. It means that the new law covers *two age groups of youth*: children *younger than 15 years and juvenile offenders* (juvenile offenders are those who at the moment of committing a criminal act have reached 15 years of age but have not exceeded 18 years of age).

The new law defines the principles of legal form that are based on the principle that all measures, procedures, and instruments covered by a new law have to be used for restoration of broken social relations, integration of the young person into the wider social environments and for delinquency prevention.

The new law is based mainly on the fact that youth with regard to their age specifics require a special method of handling within criminal proceedings. Therefore, it is necessary to address each criminal case of a juvenile delinquent and young adult individually with regard to all circumstances of the criminal act, personality of a young person and also considering the needs of an aggrieved party and interests of their close social circle with the objective to restore broken social and legal relations and in suitable cases to achieve that with the use of alternative ways addressing criminal cases. This new law is based on the assumption that youth do not have to be responsible for their illegal acts in the same way as persons older than 18 years but they should always bear the consequences of their acts appropriate to their age and when reached the level of their development. While discussing these specific issues it is necessary to find out whether the juvenile individual who is committing the criminal activity does not need the supervision, necessary restrictions, advisory assistance, and help due to his or her personal situation.

The principles mentioned represent *binding interpretation rules for* application of all provisions of the law. That is why the judges, state prosecutors, probation, and mediation service officers active in criminal issues of juvenile offenders will be selected from persons who have sufficient life experience, and will undergo further special preparation.

Differentiation of criminal liability is outlined according to individual age groups. A child who has not reached 15 years of age at the time of committing a delinquent act (crime) is not criminally liable. For a child who committed a delinquent act, measures necessary for the reform and protection can be used since these acts require a suitable intervention. These measures are imposed by juvenile courts not in criminal but in civil court proceedings either pursuant to this law or to the family law in relation to the law on social and legal protection of children.

A juvenile offender is already – similarly as it has been until now – criminally liable. The new law, however, reflects the reality that the degree of intellectual and moral maturity, especially around 15 years of age, is for juvenile offenders very different and stipulates that a juvenile offender who has not reached (at the time of committing the crime) a degree of intellectual and moral maturity in order to recognize its danger to society or to control his or her actions, is not criminally responsible for this act. Thus the new law introduced into Czech juvenile criminal law a new institute of relative criminal liability that means that not every youth is criminally liable after reaching 15 years of age as it has been until now.

A criminal act subject to court proceedings committed by a juvenile offender is called *a petty offence*. The actions of juvenile offenders have to achieve more than a small degree of social danger in order to qualify as a petty offence against the law (so-called material feature of a criminal act). The petty offences against the law are a form of juvenile delinquency that corresponds to the criminal acts committed by adults. Therefore, the Penal Code will be applied as a the petty offences against the law, with exceptions stipulated in the law on the juvenile judiciary.

The new law creates a certain hierarchy of mutually complementary procedures and penal sanctions in the area of reaction to juvenile criminality. These could be recapitulated as follows:

(a) Solution of criminal matter by *diversion of criminal proceedings* – this procedure with the use of specific meditation methods should be directed at mediation of broken legal and social relations by the criminal act while the final decision in the matter should contain, besides the solution of the life situation of the youth motivating him or her in a certain way into the future.

(b) *Educational and protective measures* – while imposing these less intensive sanctions it is necessary to respect the principle of proportionality in relation to the seriousness of the crime and to the offender and to consider mainly his or her benefit from the view of further personality growth.

(c) Imposing of *alternative sanctions to imprisonment* with probation elements and without them – the sanctions executed in the community with active intervention of the social environment of the juvenile and sanctions connected with the specific care of probation officers should be preferred; while considering the choice of the adequate criminal law sanction or suitability of discharge, the influence of the criminal hearing itself upon the youth should also be thoroughly considered.

(d) *Sanction of imprisonment* imposed according to the seriousness of the act as the *ultima ratio* criminal law recourse – the law allows to impose these criminal measures on the youth for a considerably shorter periods than on adults and with the fact that the order of their execution will be accompanied by a wide offer of integration measures and educational programmes that will assist them with their integration into society; concurrently the law relies on the educational support and assistance to the youth not ending by their release but continuing also after the execution of a criminal measure.

Sanctions of a similar nature can be used in different stages of the proceedings, proving the interconnection of the entire system. Finally, the whole range of applicable *alternative ways to criminal proceedings* allowing to decide a series of criminal matters outside the standard main hearing, creates also conditions for consistent differentiation and individualization of procedural forms of solutions to juvenile criminal activity while taking account of the nature of this activity and the offender. These are procedural alternatives for sentences.

The law on the judiciary in juvenile matters rates the following sanctions among these alternative ways of proceedings:

(a) Conditional suspension of criminal prosecution
(b) Mediation
(c) Abandonment of the criminal prosecution

The new law enlarges the already existing *types of diversions* for the juvenile category – conditional suspension of criminal prosecution and mediation – by another type of diversion – *abandonment of the criminal prosecution* of the juvenile offender. This instrument allows, providing that the conditions set by the law are met, the state prosecutor in the pretrial proceedings, and in the court proceedings the juvenile court can abandon the criminal prosecution and concurrently not proceed with the criminal prosecution on the ground of non-existence of public interest in further prosecution of a juvenile offender.

The purpose of the use of all measures and types of diversions against juvenile offenders is especially their protection of harmful influences, the creation of conditions for their sound social and mental development and their abstention from committing criminal activity. The execution of measures will be secured by the justice system with an important role assigned to the probation and mediation service.

Proceedings in juvenile cases are also addressed differently than in recent practice. Each case of a juvenile offender and a young adult has to be dealt with individually with regard to all circumstances of a petty offence against the law, respective a criminal act, the personality of the offender, needs of the aggrieved party, and interests of their close social environment, with the objective to restore disturbed social and legal relations. Procedures, measures, and solutions restoring these relations and contributing to the prevention of criminal activity should have preference before the procedures and measures of a repressive and retaliatory nature.

The juvenile court and a specialized state prosecutor should choose between hearing the case in standard proceedings, use of the possibility of a simplified proceedings, or *application of some form of diversions*. At the same time he should always request the opinion of a juvenile offender and thoroughly consider the interest of the aggrieved party. He or she should organize their activities in such a way to be able to use, in all suitable cases, appropriate alternative measures.

The use of the instrument of *custody* in juvenile criminal cases is an absolutely exceptional measure. It is necessary to use alternative securing measures for juvenile offenders instead of custody – specifically replacement of custody by a guarantee of a responsible person, supervision of the probation officer, promise of a juvenile offender, financial guarantee, placing the offender in the care of a trustworthy person, and also in the institutional care. Juvenile detention *cannot last more than 2 months*. After the expiration of this period the detention can be, under exceptional circumstances, extended for another 2 months based on court's decision. Such an extension of time can take place only once in the preparatory proceedings and once in the court's proceedings. If the juvenile offender is prosecuted for an especially serious offences against the law, the custody duration cannot be longer than 6 months. After the juvenile offender is released from detention, a probationary supervision can be ordered that can last until the end of the criminal proceedings.

The new law also establishes special *juvenile courts* whose function will be implemented by specialized panels of judges of general courts. For those courts where there will be more panels and they will form a special section of the court. The juvenile courts will pronounce sentences in criminal cases of juveniles and in the cases of delinquent acts committed by children younger than 15 years of age. As opposed to the general outline of local criminal jurisdictions the proceedings will be conducted by the court in the district where a child younger than 15 years or a juvenile person lives, and if he does not have a permanent residency there, where his whereabouts are.

The Probation and Mediation Service forms another main instrument of the new law. Its activity will be focused on wider possibilities to select alternative solutions to criminal cases of juvenile offenders and in the cases of acts committed by children younger than 15 years, on elimination of the consequences caused by his act and on the prevention of his further criminal activity. In this respect the new law strengthens the role of the probation officers and it charges them with more significant competences than the current legislation does.

4. CONCLUSIONS

Finally, let us go back to the recent past that offers the explanation why at the end the reform with such significant elements of restorative justice in the area of juvenile criminal law was successfully enforced in the Czech Republic at least at the legislative level.

Immediately after the change of a political regime in 1989 the attempts to reform current, repressively oriented criminal justice took place in Czechoslovakia. One of the first experiments of this kind was a project called "Non-judicial Alternatives for Delinquent Youth" (further only as the project) that was developed at the Institute of the State and Law of the Czechoslovak Academy of Sciences (Válková, 1991). The project was inspired by the German (TOA, Koeln) (Kawamura, 1989; Herz, 1991) and Austrian experience (ATA, Wien) (Jesionek, 1989) with so-called diversion of criminal proceedings applied first of all to juvenile and young adult delin-quents. The Czech authors chose the same approach when they initially addressed juvenile offenders since they presumed, similarly to their foreign colleagues, major acceptance of this age group by the public and the media.

Although the effort of the project authors was initially limited to its experi-mental testing within the capital city of Prague, a different mechanism of reaction to a committed criminal act by the delinquents (youth) was applied, probably for the first time in Czechoslovakia. Instead of a mere object of the State-imposed sentence, a juvenile appears in an active role of someone who still can, through his actions, redress, though only partially, consequences of his act with which he is directly confronted during an encounter with his victim. Also, for the first time a mere witness-aggrieved party becomes a participant whose purely subjective experiences, feelings and needs can be completely or at least partially met. To maximize the benefit and minimize the risks of such an encounter of the offender with the victim a third, in the conflict disinterested expert, enters the negotiation process, later called a mediator.

It is possible to state that it was particularly the effort to change criminal policy towards the youth that was behind the birth of the reforms in the area of new ways of handling the delinquent population and that played the role of "the Trojan horse" in the rigid system of the Czechoslovak criminal justice at the beginning of the 1990s.

New elements of restorative justice that had been experimentally tested at the beginning of the 1990s in the Czech Republic and incorporated into the general criminal law system could be at the beginning of the 21st century developed and fully applied within the framework of a successfully finalized legislative reform of the juvenile criminal law.

REFERENCES

Herz, R. (1991). "Dekonstruktivismus im Jugendstrafrecht. Taeter-Opfer-Ausgleich," *MschrKrim*, 74:80–89.

Hulmáková, J. (2005). "Vyvoj registrované criminality mládeže v ČR (Development of Registered Juvenile Criminality in the CR)," in J. Kuchta and H. Válková (eds.), *Základy kriminologie a trestní politiky (Basis of Criminology and Criminal Policy)*. Praha: C.H. Beck, pp. 280–286.

Jesionek, U. (1989). "Die Konfliktregelung im neuen oesterreichischen Jugendrecht," in *Festschrift fuer Pallin*. Wien: Manz Verlag, s. 161–181.

Kawamura, G. (1989). "Arbeitschritte bei der praktischen Durchfuehrung des Taeter-Opfer-Aus-gleichs," in *Arbeitsgruppe TOA-Standards*, s. 23–32.

Lortie, S., Polanski, M., Sotolar, A., and Válková, H. (2000). *Soudnictvi pro mladistve v Kanade a v České republice (Judiciary for Youth in Canada and in the Czech Republic)*, Prague: Ministery of Justice of the Czech Republic-Manuals, Vol. 59.

Marešová, A. (1996a). Sociálně patologické jevy a kriminalita mladistvych v kontextu vyvoje společnosti. (Social and Pathological Elements and Juvenile Criminality in the Context of the Development of the Society)," *České Vězeňství*, 3: 27.

Marešová, A. (1996b). *Kriminalita mládeže* (Youth Criminality). Praha: IKSP

Marešová, A. (1999). "Trendy kriminality mládeže (Youth Criminality Trends)," *Trestní Právo*, 9:16–21.

Marešová, A. (2003). "Summary: Criminality," in A. Maresova, V. Baloun, M. Cejp, D. Kaderabkova, and M. Martinková (eds.), *Kriminalita v roce* (*Criminality in the Year 2003*), Praha: IKSP, 2005, pp. 111–113.

Thomová, J. (2000). "K možnostem reakce na kriminalitu dětí mladších 15 let z hlediska současné a budoucí právní úpravy (As For Possibilities of Reaction to Criminality of Children Younger than 15 years from the Current and Future Legislation Point of View)," *Právní rozhledy*, 7: 317.

van Kalmthout, A.M., Roberts, J., Nijmegen, S.V. (2003). "The Czech Republic," in *Probation and Probation Services in the EU accession countries*, WLP, pp. 81–102.

Válková, H. (1991). *Mimosoudní alternativa pro delikventní mládež (MS-alternativa).*

Non-Judical Alternative for Delinquent Youth Project. Prague: Institute of the State and Law of the Czechoslovak Academy of Sciences.

Válková, H. (2001). "Jugendstrafrechtsreform in Tschechien in Sicht?" *MschrKrim*, 396–409.

Válková, H. (2003). "Od vězení k alternativním sankcím (From Prison to Alternative Sanctions)," in *Ve skužbách práva, Sborník příspěvku*. Praha: C.H. Beck, pp. 305–322.

Válková, H. and Kopoldová, B. (1996). *Prevé zkušenosti z pražského experimentu mimosoudního narovnání (First Experience from Non-judical Mediation).* Česká Lípa: Foundation Klíc.

Zbornik, F., Kotulan, P., and Rozum, J. (1996). *Trestni soudnictvi nad mladistvimi v CR a v zahranici. (Criminal Judiciary over Youth in CR and Abroad).* Praha: IKSP.

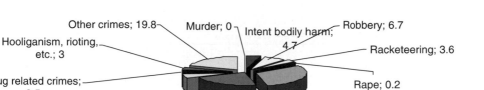

GRAPH 15.1. Structure of pre-criminality committed by children younger than 15 years in 2003 in %.

GRAPH 15.2. Structure of criminality committed by juveniles in 2003 in %.
Source: Statistical criminality overview 2003, CR Police Presidium.
http://www.mvcr.cz/statistiky/krim_stat/2003/index.html.

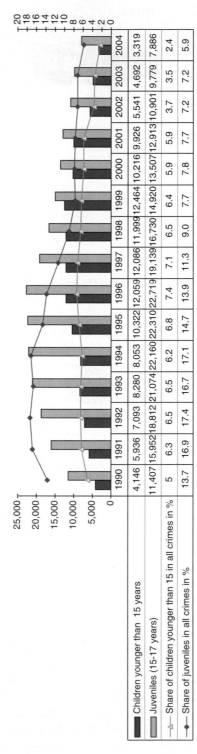

	1990	1991	1992	1993	1994	1995	1996	1997	1998	1999	2000	2001	2002	2003	2004
Children younger than 15 years	4,146	5,936	7,093	8,280	8,053	10,322	12,059	12,086	11,999	12,464	10,216	9,926	5,541	4,692	3,319
Juveniles (15-17 years)	11,407	15,952	18,812	21,074	22,160	22,310	22,719	19,139	16,730	14,920	13,507	12,913	10,901	9,779	7,886
Share of children younger than 15 in all crimes in %	5	6.3	6.5	6.5	6.2	6.8	7.4	7.1	6.5	6.4	5.9	5.9	3.7	3.5	2.4
Share of juveniles in all crimes in %	13.7	16.9	17.4	16.7	17.1	14.7	13.9	11.3	9.0	7.7	7.8	7.7	7.2	7.2	5.9

GRAPH 15.3.   Pre-criminality and criminality committed by youth in the Czech Republic in 1990–2004.
Source: Statistical criminality overview1990–2004, CR Police Presidium.

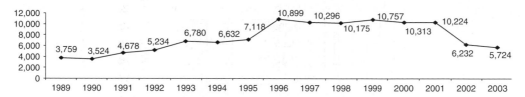

GRAPH 15.4. Pre-criminality of children younger than 15 years according to number of people in 1989–2003 in absolute numbers.
Source: Statistical criminality yearbook 2004, CR Ministry of Justice.

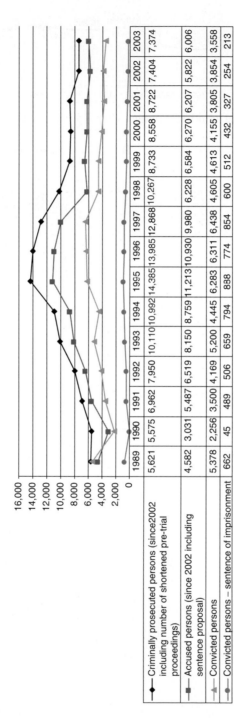

	1989	1990	1991	1992	1993	1994	1955	1996	1997	1998	1999	2000	2001	2002	2003
Criminally prosecuted persons (since2002 including number of shortened pre-trial proceedings)	5,621	5,575	6,962	7,950	10,110	10,992	14,385	13,985	12,868	10,267	8,733	8,558	8,722	7,404	7,374
Accused persons (since 2002 including sentence proposal)	4,582	3,031	5,487	6,519	8,150	8,759	11,213	10,930	9,980	6,228	6,584	6,270	6,207	5,822	6,006
Convicted persons	5,378	2,256	3,500	4,169	5,200	4,445	6,283	6,311	6,438	4,605	4,613	4,155	3,805	3,854	3,558
Convicted persons – sentence of imprisonment	662	45	489	506	659	794	888	774	854	600	512	432	327	254	213

GRAPH 15.5. Development of criminal policy applied to juveniles (15–17 years) in 1989–2003 in absolute numbers.
Source: Statistical criminality yearbook of the Czechoslovak Federation Republic State Prosecution Office (1991, 1992), CR SPO (1993) and CR Ministry of Justice (1994–2004).

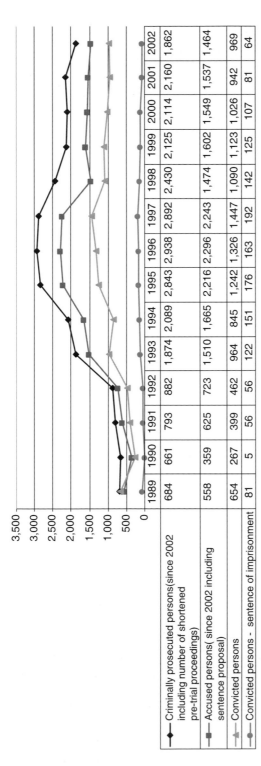

	1989	1990	1991	1992	1993	1994	1995	1996	1997	1998	1999	2000	2001	2002
Criminally prosecuted persons (since 2002 including number of shortened pre-trial proceedings)	684	661	793	882	1,874	2,089	2,843	2,938	2,892	2,430	2,125	2,114	2,160	1,862
Accused persons (since 2002 including sentence proposal)	558	359	625	723	1,510	1,665	2,216	2,296	2,243	1,474	1,602	1,549	1,537	1,464
Convicted persons	654	267	399	462	964	845	1,242	1,326	1,447	1,090	1,123	1,026	942	969
Convicted persons - sentence of imprisonment	81	5	56	56	122	151	176	163	192	142	125	107	81	64

GRAPH 15.6. Development of criminal policy applied to juveniles in recount of 100, 000 inhabitants of the respective age category (15–17 years) in 1989–2003.

Source: Statistical criminality yearbooks State Prosecution Office (SPO) of the Czechoslovak Federation Republic (1991, 1992), CR SPO (1993) and CR Ministry of Justice (1994–2003).

Statistical data on the age composition of the population as of 1.7. of a respective year (in 1989 as of 31.12.1989), Statistical yearbook of the Czech Republic, Czech Statistical Office, 1990–2003.

Note: Data on population for the group of 15–17 years of age was used between 1989–1992.

16

Welfare Versus Neo-Liberalism:
Juvenile Justice in Slovenia

Katja Filipčič

INTRODUCTION

Slovenia was part of the Austrian–Hungarian Monarchy until the end of 1918 when it became part of Yugoslavia. In 1991, Yugoslavia disintegrated and the independent Republic of Slovenia was established. Today it is one of the smallest European countries, with only 2 million inhabitants. Although the total population of Slovenia has been stagnating in the 1990s, its age structure has been changing constantly. The process of population ageing continues. According to the 2002 census the proportion of the young population (0–17 years) was 19.3%. Ten years ago, at the beginning of the 1990s, the proportion was 25%.

This paper discusses the evolution of Slovenia's juvenile justice system. It describes recent patterns and trends in juvenile crime, and the operation of the current juvenile justice system in Slovenia.

1. EVOLUTION OF THE JUVENILE JUSTICE SYSTEM

The Slovenian juvenile justice system developed under the influence of Austria. The Austrian Ministry of Justice decided in 1908 that all cases of juvenile delinquents must be dealt with by specialized judges at the general court. The first juvenile judge of the Austrian–Hungarian Monarchy (Fran Milčinski) was appointed in Ljubljana in 1909. A specific justice system for juveniles was officially created in the late 1920s. Yugoslavia enacted the first Criminal Code and Criminal Procedure Code in 1929, which also contained provisions pertaining to juvenile delinquents. Juveniles were divided in two groups:

1. Younger juveniles (between 14 and 17 years) were considered relatively irresponsible, the most important criterion being their level of maturity. The court could impose a sentence or educational measures only if their maturity was proven.
2. Older juveniles (between 17 and 21) were dealt with in the same way as adult offenders, although the penalties imposed on juveniles were less severe.

This system changed after the Second World War. The Criminal Code of 1951 divided juveniles into two age categories: younger (between 14 and 16 years) and

J. Junger-Tas and S. H. Decker (eds.), International Handbook of Juvenile Justice, 397–414.

older juveniles (between 16 and 18 years). Even more important was the conclusion about the eventual liability of the juvenile. Depending on that liability, the judge could impose an educational measure or a sanction. But the most important element was the orientation towards the personality of the juvenile and the emphasis on knowing the personal and family circumstances of the individual.

The Yugoslav Criminal Code was amended in 1959. An amendment to the law in that year brought a relaxation of sanctions, the removal of the penalty of life imprisonment, and the introduction of judicial admonition for cases "when grounds exist for the belief that the aim of punishment would be attained without the imposition of punishment". Several other security measures were also introduced. The provisions relating to juvenile offenders were also amended. Juveniles were no longer divided into the categories of "criminally responsible" or "irresponsible". The court could impose only educational measures in the case of younger juveniles (between 14 and 16 years); while imprisonment could only be imposed on older juveniles if the State had proved that the imposition of an educational measure would be inappropriate. A special category of young adults was introduced in the Criminal Code. Thus, it could be said that our system of dealing with juvenile offenders was established in 1959.

In 1974, the new federal Constitution of Yugoslavia strengthened the federal system and introduced a division of legislative competence in the area of substantive criminal law between the Federation and the Republics (Slovenia was one of them). The Code of Criminal Procedure remained a federal prerogative and was enacted in 1977. Under the Constitution of 1974, almost the entire general part remained the prerogative of the Federation, except the system of sanctions for juvenile offenders. The Slovenian Criminal Code of 1977 adopted the educational measures and sentences in the Yugoslav Criminal Code of 1959. The system of sanctions remained unchanged until 1995. Slovenia did not follow other European countries by introducing alternative ways of dealing with juveniles – diversion, restorative justice elements (Petrovec, 1996).

The present Criminal Code and the Code of Criminal Procedure were enacted in September 1994, and became law on 1 January 1995. No special Code for dealing with juvenile delinquents was created, but following the tradition from the Yugoslav juvenile justice system, it is part of the general criminal law (it is a special chapter in the Criminal Code and in the Code of Criminal Procedure).

2. TRENDS IN JUVENILE DELINQUENCY IN SLOVENIA

Over the last 20 years, Slovenia has not experienced a dramatic increase in the volume of juvenile crime. Approximately 4% of juveniles aged 14–18 (who fall under court jurisdiction) are dealt with by the police each year and less than 1% receives an educational measure or is sentenced by the court. As Fig. 16.1

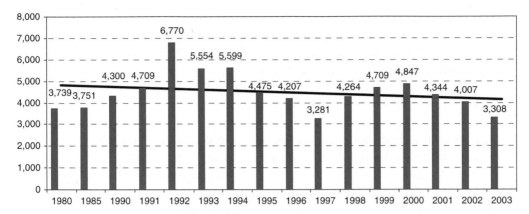

FIGURE 16.1. Number of reported offences committed by juveniles. *Source*: Adapted from Statistical Office of the Republic of Slovenia (2004).

indicates, reports of juvenile crime increased at the beginning and the end of the 1990s. This increase reflects several factors: societal change regarding reporting crime; a different way of collecting data, and better cooperation between police, school, and social agencies. The most important characteristic of juvenile delinquency in Slovenia is its decreasing share of crime in general. In 1977 juveniles accounted for 18% of all crimes; by 2003 this had fallen to 14%. However, while the volume of juvenile offending has been relatively stable, the rate of violent crime has increased slightly (Šelih and Filipčič, 2002).

3. THE QUESTION OF DIFFERENT AGE CATEGORIES

3.1. General Considerations

In 1995, new criminal legislation introduced some changes in dealing with juveniles who committed criminal offences. The age limit for "criminal" liability was not changed, and remained 14 years of age. Under the criminal law, young persons – the offenders – are divided into several groups:

1. *Children* (under the age of 14), who are not treated by courts, but by social welfare agencies (called Social Work Centres);
2. *Younger minors* (aged 14–16), against whom only educational measures may be applied;
3. *Older minors* (aged 16–18); as a rule, educational measures are imposed on them and only in exceptional cases may a special sentence be imposed (a fine or juvenile prison).
4. *Young adults*: those who have not yet reached the age of 21 by the end of a trial, although they were adults when committing a criminal offence (over age 18).

In the case of juvenile offenders, the court cannot apply the procedure for adult offenders and cannot impose the sanctions for adults, notwithstanding the seriousness of the crime. Juveniles cannot be transferred to the adult criminal justice system, however serious the offence.

3.2. Children Under Age 14

Slovenian courts deal in a special criminal proceeding only with those juveniles who have committed a criminal offence, and who, regarding their mental maturity (formally determined by the age of 14), understand the meaning of their conduct.[1] A perpetrator of a criminal offence, who was not yet aged 14 at the time the offence was committed, may be dealt with only by the social welfare agencies (called Social Work Centres), notwithstanding the seriousness of the offence and notwithstanding his actual level of maturity. Thus, the limitation is determined by the chronological age, and the courts may not change that in individual cases.

The analyses of some cases in recent years when children (allegedly) committed serious criminal offences have raised questions about the adequacy of such rules. It was found that the procedural protection of children treated by Social Work Centres which may impose committal to a juvenile institution (which is essentially similar to the institutional educational measures imposed by the court), was inadequate. These findings did not influence the proposals for the reduction of the age limits of children under the competence of the courts, but they further encouraged those who considered that specialized "family courts" should deal with all deviant behaviour of children and juveniles. Establishing these courts would mean the reduction of the social welfare agencies' competencies and a reconsideration of their role. Moreover, the issue still remains open and this is a matter for concern with respect to the protection of children's interests, as it is not clear what cases the courts would deal with (e.g., criminal offences in which children are victims, divorce procedures, adoptions etc.), and what kinds of proceedings would be used.

3.3. Young Adults

In 1959 Slovenian criminal legislation introduced the category of "young adults". Young adults are persons who committed criminal offences as adults (age 18 or more) but who were under 21 at the time of trial. As a rule, these offenders are criminally liable and they are sentenced as adults. In case a court ascertains, regarding the personality of a young adult and the circumstances in which the

---

[1] Article 71 of the Penal Code of the Republic of Slovenia "Criminal sanctions shall not be applied against minors who were under the age of 14 at the time a criminal offence was committed (children)."

criminal offence was committed, that the imposition of an educational measure is more appropriate than the imposition of a sentence of imprisonment, the court may impose certain educational measures on such person. In practice this option is rarely employed.

4. INTERVENTIONS OF THE PROSECUTOR

4.1. General Considerations

The police have to report all cases to the state prosecutor; diversion on the police level is therefore not possible. Our rules of criminal procedure follow the principle of legality of criminal prosecution. The state prosecutor is obliged to institute criminal proceedings provided there is evidence that a criminal offence was committed. Until 1995, there were only a few exceptions to this rule. "The expediency principle" was one of them, and was (and still is) operational in proceedings against juveniles in cases of less severe offences – for which imprisonment of up to 3 years or a fine is prescribed. The case could be dropped under any condition. The state prosecutor has the discretionary power to decide not to bring the case to court because the juvenile does not need any judicial intervention despite the fact he or she committed an offence. This is known as an unconditional dismissal.

The role of the state prosecutor dramatically changed in the late 1990s with the new competencies to dismiss a case (Šelih, 2000; Šugman, 2004). The state prosecutor may, with the consent of the accused and the injured party, decide to refer the case to one of two forms of alternative diversionary procedures: mediation or deferment of prosecution. The main criterion (but not the only one) for referring the case is the gravity of the offence. Until the last amendment of the Criminal Procedure Code in 2004, there were no criteria for the distinction of juvenile from adult cases when the court was dealing with criminal offences punishable by a fine or a prison term of up to 3 years. The amended Criminal Procedure Code introduced the possibility of dealing with juveniles in alternative ways in all criminal offences punishable by prison up to 5 years.[2] This change was introduced on the recommendation of prosecutors.

4.2. Mediation

The state prosecutor may refer the case to mediation and if the mediation process is successful, the charges will be dropped. Already in 2001 the prosecutor could refer the case to mediation even after filing the charges. Before deciding on the level of the sentence the state prosecutor has to consider the type of offence, its

---

[2] If the offender is an adult this is also possible for all offences punishable up to 3 years, but only for some offences punishable up to 5 years of imprisonment.

nature, the circumstances in which it was committed, and the personality of the offender and his or her past conduct. A juvenile is not required to formally admit guilt. However, mediation may be applied only with the consent of the juvenile and the injured party. Mediation can only be conducted by mediators (selected by a special procedure) who are placed on a list of enrolled citizens in the state prosecutor's office. Mediation cannot be performed by any third party. There are currently 194 specially trained mediators, a quarter of which are mediators in cases involving juvenile offenders.

The mediation process is carried out according to the following steps:

1. Selection of the case by the state prosecutor who refers the file to the mediator.
2. Contacting the juvenile offender and the victim separately: both have to give a written agreement to mediation.
3. Arranging a meeting between the juvenile offender and the victim. The juvenile has a right to parental assistance. The principle of confidentiality is respected.
4. Reaching an agreement that must be done within 1 month in written form: the agreement specifies material and/or immaterial reparation. The principle of proportionality is respected since the mediator has to ensure that the settlement is made in accordance with the severity of the criminal offence. If no agreement is reached, the mediation process is terminated; the mediator reports this to the state prosecutor who then initiates criminal procedures against the juvenile.
5. Writing an Interim report to the prosecutor.
6. Execution of the settlement by the juvenile: if the juvenile fails to execute the settlement within the agreed time period, the mediation process is deemed to have failed.
7. Writing a final report to the prosecutor: The whole file of the mediation process is sent to the state prosecutor, not just the report of the mediator. This means that the judge is informed of the content of the agreement and the behaviour of the parties during the mediation process. The principle of confidentiality is respected, since the judge may not use any information from the file as proof in later criminal procedures in the case of an unsuccessful outcome of mediation.
8. Dismissing the case; Successful mediation results in the dismissal of the case, the decision is final – no appeal is possible. However, in the case of successful mediation there may still be a trial if the prosecutor does not consider the reparation proportional to the seriousness of the crime. The question still remains whether he can use his or her influence to change the content of the agreement or whether he or she can only reject the agreement when it is deemed inappropriate – and proceed with prosecution.

A Supervision Committee supervises the mediation process. One member is the state prosecutor, the second is a representative of the mediators and the third a representative of the Ministry of justice. The amended Criminal Procedure Code introduced mediation in 1999 so we can analyse our experiences from the period 2000–2004. Despite this short period of practicing mediation, I believe that the concept of mediation between a juvenile and his or her victim satisfies the objectives of the Slovenian system of juvenile responsibility. The rate of success of the negotiated arrangements is almost 70% of all cases referred for mediation (in the case of adult offenders the rate of successful mediation is lower – about 50%). In 2002 the mediation process was successful in 256 cases. The number and the rate of successful mediation may be higher in other countries, but taking into account that these are the results of the first years of a completely new strategy in dealing with offenders, we are satisfied.

4.3. Deferment of the Prosecution (Conditional Dismissal)

The state prosecutor may drop the case if the suspected juvenile performs certain actions to remove the harmful consequences of the criminal offence. These actions may be: (1) elimination or compensation of damages, (2) payment of a contribution to a public institution or a charity, (3) execution of some community work. In approximately 80% of these cases juveniles fulfil the obligations and the case is subsequently dismissed. In 2002 the state prosecutor dismissed almost one-third of all cases; the reason of dismissal was the expediency principle in 29% (366 cases), mediation in 21% (256 cases) and deferment of prosecution in 9% (115 cases).

5. SENTENCING AND SENTENCES

5.1. The Composition of the Courts

In our legal system we do not have special courts for juveniles. Juvenile perpetrators of criminal offences are treated in the first instance by juvenile judges, followed by a panel for juvenile offenders at the level of district courts. Panels for juvenile offenders at higher courts and at the Supreme Court are competent for deciding legal remedies. Juvenile judges conduct a preliminary analysis of the case, which is the first phase of court proceedings against juveniles in which data and evidence are gathered, and preside over panels, which decide on the commission of a criminal offence and impose a sanction. Besides a professional judge there are two lay judges in a panel. The Criminal Procedure Code determines that lay judges are elected, as well as professors, teachers, educators and other persons experienced in the education of juveniles. Thus, a juvenile judge never decides on the perpetration of a criminal act and on the sanction by himself or herself but always together with two jurors. A panel decides the above-stated issues at "in camera" deliberation or at the main hearing (a fine, imprisonment and institutional measures may be imposed only at the hearing). A decision is reached by a vote of the panel members. Lay judges cooperate with a professional judge on equal terms in deciding on the liability of a juvenile and in selecting a sanction.

The courts in second instance and the Supreme Court panels for juvenile offenders are composed of three (professional) judges.

5.2. The Course of Proceedings

Procedures against juveniles are a special, yet fundamental type of criminal procedure. The juvenile has not only all the rights guaranteed to the adult offender, but also some additional ones, designed to diminish the possible detrimental effects of the procedure on the juvenile's development (Šugman et al., 2004). The proceeding starts with a preliminary phase, which may be initiated only at the request of the state prosecutor. The request is filed with the juvenile judge. The purpose of this phase of proceedings is to establish facts connected to a criminal offence and particularly to establish the circumstances necessary for the evaluation of the juvenile's maturity, the insight in his or her personality and the circumstances in which he or she lives. The preliminary phase is thus similar to the investigation in ordinary proceedings against adults with the difference that the goal of the investigation in adult cases is to investigate a criminal offence, while in juvenile cases the preliminary phase focuses on understanding the juvenile's personality. A further important distinction is that the preliminary phase may not be omitted, although this is possible under certain conditions in adult cases.

The Criminal Procedure Code prescribes certain steps that the juvenile judges must follow in order to establish the circumstances regarding the personality of a juvenile and the conditions in which he or she lives. In addition to the examination of a juvenile, the court must do the following:

1. Meet with the parents of a juvenile, his or her guardian, and other persons who could provide information regarding the circumstances. These persons have the obligation to testify with respect to the personality of a juvenile and the conditions in which he or she lives.
2. Request a report of a social welfare agency on these circumstances.

In order to determine the juvenile's state of health, his or her mental maturity and his or her psychological characteristics, a juvenile judge may order the juvenile to be examined by experts such as a physician, psychologist or teacher.

In proceedings against juveniles, a juvenile judge may order that during the preliminary phase the juvenile is sent to a diagnostic centre, is placed under the supervision of a social welfare agency, or is placed with another family if this is necessary to take the juvenile out of the environment in which he or she lived, or to be provided with assistance, protection, or accommodation. The measure ordered by the juvenile judge may last the entire duration of the proceedings, or the judge may end it any time. Appeal is possible against any of the above-stated measures to the panel for juvenile offenders at the higher court.

When the juvenile judge has examined all the circumstances referring to the criminal offence and the juvenile's personality, he or she sends the files to the state prosecutor, who may decide to file charges. When this happens, the juvenile judge may dismiss the case using the expediency principle, refer the case to a mediation process, or to a panel for juvenile offenders that subsequently decides upon the imposition of a sanction. The panel for juvenile offenders may impose sentences and institutional measures only at the hearing that is organized similarly to the proceedings against adults, the important difference being that the public is always excluded. The panel may also impose educational measures although not based on the available evidence, but rather on the basis of the material gathered in a preliminary phase. A state prosecutor, a counsel and a representative of a social agency may be present at the session.

5.3. Pre-trial Detention

A juvenile judge may order pre-trial detention against a juvenile on account of the possibility of escape or the danger of collusion. The Criminal Procedure Code stresses that pre-trial detention is to be ordered only in exceptional cases. A juvenile may be detained on the basis of an order of a juvenile judge for no longer than 1 month, while the panel for juvenile offenders (three judges) may, on the proposal of a state prosecutor, extend the pre-trial detention for a further 2 months. Thus, pre-trial detention at the time of the preliminary phase (before filing a charge) may not last more than 3 months, even in cases where the preliminary phase has not been completed during that time.[3] After filing a charge, only the panel for juvenile offenders may order pre-trial detention, and it must determine, every 2 months, whether the reasons for ordering detention still exist. In this phase of the procedure, pre-trial detention may last no longer than 2 years, which is the same as in proceedings against adult defendants.

The Committee on the Rights of Child of the United Nations, in examining the report of the Republic of Slovenia on the implementation of the Convention on the Rights of the Child in 1996, exposed the duration of pre-trial detention in proceedings against juveniles as a field where children's rights are not sufficiently protected. The UN committee did recommend shortening the duration of pre-trial detention. However, the statutorily determined duration of pre-trial detention after the filing of the prosecutor's motion for a sentence or an educational measure has remained unchanged. One of the reasons for this is the fact that pre-trial detention is rarely ordered, and even in these cases it lasts only a few months, for all proceedings against juveniles are, as a rule, completed in less than a year.

---

[3]Pre-trial detention during the investigation in proceedings against adults may last no longer than 3 months, and in cases of severe criminal offences (prescribed sentence over 5 years of imprisonment) no longer than 6 months.

Time spent in pre-trial detention is reflected in the imposed sentence of juvenile prison. However, that time is never included in the duration of an educational measure. Both older (between 16 and 18 years) and younger juveniles (between 14 and 16 years) may be detained, although juvenile prison may not be imposed on the latter, only educational measures. A juvenile must be detained separately from adult prisoners. During the time of detention, he or she must be provided with care, protection and all necessary assistance. Statistical data confirm the rarity of pre-trial detention; in most cases it does not exceed 2 months. For example, in 2000, the police dealt with 2,937 juveniles, of whom only eight were detained. An amendment to the Criminal Procedure Code in 1999 introduced alternatives to pre-trial detention. These may be imposed in proceedings against juvenile perpetrators of criminal offences. The alternatives include: home detention; a prohibition order with respect to certain locations or individuals; and reporting requirements (to the police station).

6. SANCTIONS AND MEASURES APPLICABLE

Less than one-third of all juveniles reported to the police are sentenced in the court (see Fig. 16.2). The reason is that the prosecutor and juvenile judge have the power to dismiss the case because of the expediency principle or to refer the case to mediation or to other forms of diversion (restorative justice elements).

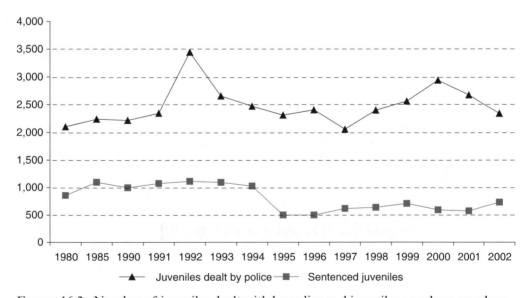

FIGURE 16.2. Number of juveniles dealt with by police and juveniles on whom an educational measure or a sentence was imposed. *Source*: Adapted from Statistical Office of the Republic of Slovenia (2004).

As Fig. 16.3 indicates, over the past 20 years the majority of sentenced young offenders had been convicted of property crimes. However, the proportion of property crime declined while the proportion of violent crimes increased. Two explanations account for this trend: (1) from 1995 on the state prosecutor and the juvenile judge have the possibility to use alternative measures in dealing with juveniles who committed minor offences: a lot of cases of property offences are diverted; the court is dealing just with juveniles who committed more serious offences; (2) juvenile violence is said to have increased over the last 10 years. However, despite the slight increase in violence, youth violence has not become a serious problem in Slovenia. Violent crimes committed by juveniles are not very serious – the majority being simple assaults and threats with a dangerous instrument in a fight or a quarrel. During the period under scrutiny, the number of the most serious crimes is stable; one or two homicides or attempted homicides and about 10–20 serious assaults per year.

6.1. The Purpose of Educational Measures and Sentences

The Slovenian criminal legislation reflects the perspective that a criminal offence committed by a juvenile is in most cases a manifestation of a personality disorder (Muršič, 2001). Thus, the purpose of a sanction is to ensure that the juvenile receives the necessary education to ensure appropriate personal development. Consequently, educational measures and sentences must not only provide for assistance and protection, but also for the supervision that the juvenile needs to rehabilitate or re-integrate in society.

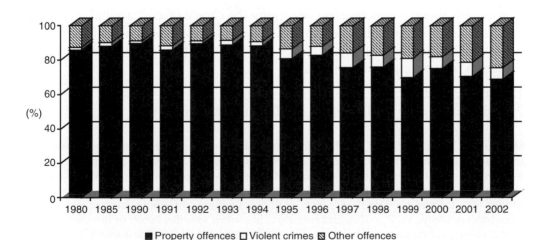

FIGURE 16.3. Juveniles on whom the courts imposed sanctions (educational measures or sentences) 1980–2002. *Source*: Adapted from Statistical Office of the Republic of Slovenia, (2004).

The chronological age of an offender is the fundamental criterion in the decision of a court whether to impose an educational measure or a sentence. A sentence (a fine or juvenile imprisonment) may be imposed only on older juveniles (aged 16–18), and only in exceptional cases. Upon the imposition of a sentence the court must state why it did not impose an educational measure in an individual case. In addition, the court's appreciation of how intensive care and assistance is expected to educate or re-educate a juvenile, is crucial.

Data show that the courts decided to impose an educational measure in approximately 98% of all cases. With respect to the choice among the six educational measures (one of them has eleven different forms), it is necessary to emphasize that for the purpose of educational measures, the seriousness of a criminal offence, which is of substantial importance for the determination of a sentence in adult cases, usually does not influence the selection of an educational measure. The deciding factors are the needs of the juvenile, as established by the court, for further education and re-education. The seriousness and nature of a criminal offence is only one of the criteria for the selection of an educational measure, and their effect is apparent only when there is the issue of whether a juvenile is to be committed to a juvenile detention centre. Social services and educational institutions have to send a report about progress made in the treatment of the juvenile to the juvenile judge every 6 months. Juvenile judges may stop the execution of educational measures on the grounds of positive treatment outcomes, or they may modify the imposed measure.

6.2. Educational Measures

A court has broad competencies concerning the choice of educational measures. It is primarily the juvenile's personality and not the seriousness of the criminal offence that will guide a judge in his or her decision. The following educational measures may be imposed on juveniles:

1. A reprimand;
2. Restrictions and prohibitions (11 different possibilities exist);[4]

[4]Article 77.2 of the Criminal Code "The following instruction and prohibition may be issued by the court to a juvenile offender: (1) to make a personal apology to the injured person; (2) to reach a settlement with the injured person by means of payment, work or otherwise in order to recover the damages caused in the course of committing the offence; (3) regular attendance at school; (4) to take up a form of vocational education or to take up a form of employment suitable to the offender's knowledge, skills, and inclinations; (5) to live with a specified family or in a certain institution; (6) to perform community service or work for humanitarian organizations; (7) to submit himself to treatment in an appropriate health institution; (8) to attend a session of educational, vocational, psychological, or other consultation; (9) to attend a course of social training; (10) to pass an examination for obtaining a driving license; (11) under conditions applying to adult offenders, prohibition from operating a motor vehicle may be enforced.

3. Supervision by a social welfare agency;
4. Committal to an educational institution;
5. Committal to a juvenile detention centre;
6. Committal to an institution for physically or mentally handicapped youth.

Data show that the educational measures in an open environment (reprimand, instructions and prohibitions, supervision by a social welfare agency) account for more then 90% of all cases. Over the last 20 years, the number of juveniles sent to an educational institution has decreased (in 1980, 14% sentenced juveniles were sent to an educational institution, in 2002 this fell to only 4%). Slovenia has eight institutions for juveniles who are in need of care and help. They can be put in an institution by a decision of a social agency if, for example, parents cannot take care properly of a child, if a child often runs away from home, if he or she fails to attend school, or by judgment of the court because he or she committed a crime. Regardless of the reason for being sent to an institution, they are all treated in the same way.

The capacity of these institutions is about 500 juveniles and just 10% (or fewer) of them are juveniles who are there by decision of the court. All institutions are organized as small communities (approximately 6 juveniles live in an apartment together with educators). In addition, there is one special institution for juvenile offenders – a juvenile detention centre with a capacity of 70 juveniles – for individuals who have committed more serious offences and who need special help and supervision. The juvenile can stay no longer than 3 years in an institution, whether it is an educational institution or a detention centre. After 1 year the juvenile may be conditionally released, and in that case the court may decide the supervision of the young person by the social service during the period of parole.

6.3. Youth Prison

As the most severe sanction, juvenile custody may be imposed only if two formal conditions are fulfilled:

1. when an offender is an older juvenile (aged 16–18);
2. when a juvenile has committed a serious criminal offence for which imprisonment of 5 years or more may be imposed.

In addition, the court must establish a high degree of criminal liability. The court determines the criminal liability of a juvenile in such a manner that it evaluates whether the juvenile was capable of understanding the meaning of his act, and whether he or she controlled his or her behaviour. Furthermore, it has to establish whether the juvenile was acting with intent or negligence. The court must consider these capacities as constituent parts of the juvenile's personality. Notwithstanding the prescribed sentences, the court imposes juvenile prison for not less than 6 months and no more than 5 years. In the case of criminal offences punishable by 30 years imprisonment (e.g., aggravated murder), the sentence of juvenile prison cannot exceed 10 years.

6.4. Fines

Since 1995, the court has been able to impose a fine on juveniles who (a) have been convicted of an offence punishable by up to 5 years imprisonment and (b) if the juvenile can pay the fine himself (because he or she has a job or a scholarship). A fine may be imposed in two forms: in daily amounts or in absolute amounts. In the case of default of payment, a fine cannot be converted into imprisonment (this is also the rule in the sanctioning system for adults) but must be converted into an educational measure (a reprimand, instructions and prohibitions, or supervision by a social welfare agency)

6.5. Frequency of Educational Measures and Sentences

Table 16.1 and Fig. 16.4 reveal that fines and juvenile prison are rarely used. After the adoption of the new Criminal Code in 1995 the following pattern of sanctions emerged:

1. To decrease the number of imposed reprimands which, according to judges, were imposed as an emergency exit due to the lack of other adequate educational measures,
2. The distinctive enforcement of a new educational measure (instructions and prohibitions) which represents one-fifth of all the imposed sanctions,
3. With the introduction of "instructions and prohibitions" the measure of supervision by a social welfare agency, which is often combined with some concrete instructions or prohibitions, has also increased.

TABLE 16.1. Juveniles on Whom an Educational Measure or a Sentence was Imposed, 1980–2000

Year	Total	Reprimand	Instructions and prohibitions[a]	Supervision by a social agency	Commitment to a juvenile institution	Juvenile prison	Fine[a]
1990	997	581	—	216	61	3	—
1995	499	290	14	146	41	7	1
1998	636	224	98	251	50	1	12
1999	706	237	130	285	36	4	13
2000	591	174	134	241	27	9	5
2001	571	167	104	270	20	5	5
2002	728	217	106	363	29	6	7

[a]Introduced by the Criminal Code in 1995.

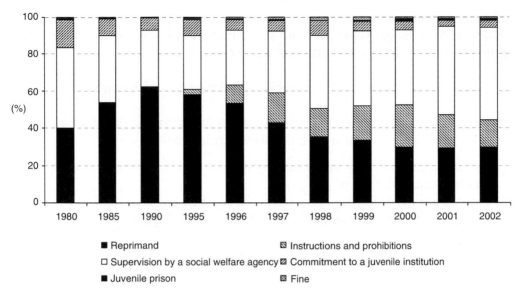

FIGURE 16.4. Frequency of educational measures and sentences. *Source*: Adapted from Statistical Office of the Republic of Slovenia (2004).

7. THE LIABILITY OF PARENTS FOR DELINQUENT CONDUCT OF CHILDREN

7.1. Criminal Liability

According to the criminal legislation, parents are not liable for criminal offences committed by their children, notwithstanding the age of a child. In Slovenia criminal liability may be only subjective; criminal liability for the conduct of others is not recognized.

The committed criminal offences of juveniles (under 18 years of age) may be, however, the consequence of neglect by their parents. In such cases parents may be liable for the criminal offence of "parental neglect and cruel treatment".[5] Thereby, it is important to emphasize that parents are not liable for criminal offences of their children, but are reproached of a separate criminal offence committed by the omission of their conduct as good parents. Thus, the consequences

---

[5]Article 201 of the Criminal Code: "(1) A parent, adoptive parent, guardian, or other person who seriously breaches his/her obligation of support and education by neglecting a minor whom he is obliged to take care of shall be sentenced to imprisonment for not more than 2 years. (2) A parent, adoptive parent, guardian or other person who forces a minor to work excessively or to perform work unsuitable to his/her age, or who out of greed inures a minor to begging or other conduct prejudicial to his/her proper development or who tortures him/her shall be sentenced to imprisonment for not more than 3 years."

of such omission are criminal offences of children. The causation between the omission of care and education and the commission of criminal offences by a child must be certainly (in addition to guilt) proven.

7.2. Civil Liability (Liability for Damages) of Parents

According to the Code of Obligations parents are liable for damage caused by their children, as determined by the following principles:

1. Parents are liable, notwithstanding their guilt, for the damage caused by their children under the age of 7.
2. Parents are liable for the damage caused by their children aged 7–18, unless they prove that the damage was caused without their guilt.

Thus, regarding the liability for damages of parents, the age of a child is of a substantial importance; for children under the age of 7, parents are objectively liable, for children over the age of 7 they are culpably liable (shifted burden of proof – their guilt is presumed, they themselves must refute this presumption).

8. CONCLUSION

In 1959, Slovenia created a welfare-oriented system for dealing with juvenile offenders. Since then, the juvenile criminal law has been amended several times, but the welfare orientation remains the main characteristic of the system, despite the more punitive orientation in dealing with adult offenders. Legislative reforms in the late 1990s introduced different forms of diversion and elements of restorative justice at the level of the prosecutor and the juvenile judge. Alternative sanctions have also been introduced, but juvenile judges have yet to use some of them (such as Community Service), mainly because of organizational problems rather than because of ideological obstacles.

REFERENCES

Muršič, M. (2001). "Socialnopedagoška diagnoza, študija primera na podlagi samopredstavitve (Sociopedagogical Diagnosis, Case Study Based on Self Presentation)," *Socialna pedagogika*, 4:469–491.
Petrovec, D. (1996). *Slovenia: Some Questions Concerning the New Criminal Legislation in Comparative Perspective* (Studies in Legal System: Mixed and Mixing). The Hague, London, Boston: Kluwer, 265–280.
Šelih, A. (2000). "The Prosecution Process and the (Changing) Role of the Prosecutor," *Crime and Criminal Justice in Europe* (Publications of the Council of Europe, 127). Strasbourg: Council of Europe, 93–108.

Šelih, A. and Filipčič, K. (2002). "Slowenien," in H.-J. Albrecht, M. Kilchling, (Ed.). *Jugendstrafrecht in Europa* (Kriminologische Forschungsberichte, Bd. 100). Freiburg i.Br.: Edition iuscrim, Max-Planck-Institut für Ausländisches und Internationales Strafrecht, 395–413.

Šugman, K.G. (2004). "European Public Prosecutor in the Context of Slovenian Criminal Law," *Slov. law rev.*, 1(2):123–136.

Šugman, K.G., Jager, M., Peršak, N., and Filipčič, K. (2004). *Slovenia: Criminal Justice Systems in Europe and North America* (Criminal Justice System in Europe, 20). Helsinki: European Institute for Crime Prevention and Control, affiliated with the United Nations.

17

Legal and Actual Treatment of Juveniles Within the Criminal Justice System of Bosnia and Herzegovina

Almir Maljevic

INTRODUCTION

Before getting into discussions on juvenile delinquency and juvenile criminal justice provisions in Bosnia and Herzegovina (BH), let us give a few introductory remarks related to the recent history of the country. Events that were taking place in the region of ex-Yugoslavia during the early 1990s are widely known and they are usually defined by the following words – crisis, disintegration, and wars. It would not be a mistake to say that the culmination of all these events, especially bearing in mind its duration and severe consequences, took place in BH. When it comes to war in BH, it should be recalled that it ended by the signing of Dayton Peace Agreement (DPA).[1] Although the DPA brought war to an end, it also defined a very complex, inefficient and complicated administrative and territorial state structure. From 1995 on BH consisted of two entities, namely the Federation of Bosnia and Herzegovina (FBH) and the Republika Srpska (RS) that are afforded a very high level of autonomy in exercising their constitutionally defined powers. FBH, as a bigger entity, is even more decentralized by being divided into ten cantons as separate units having their own assemblies and therefore constitutions too. Another separate administrative and territorial unit is represented by Brcko District of BH (BDBH) with a separate legal system including a separate criminal justice system.

According to Article III of the Constitution of BH (Annex 4 to DPA), BH is in charge of the international and inter-entity criminal law enforcement including relations with Interpol. All other issues related to criminal law are within the jurisdiction of the entities. Due to these facts, until July 2003 there were certain differences between the criminal justice systems of the entities, especially when it comes to provisions related to juvenile offenders. Another problem related to the issue of our concern, caused by this kind of state structure, is the nonexistence of all unified statistics, including statistics on crime related issues.

---

[1]DPA is concluded in Dayton USA and signed in Paris, France in December 1995. It is also known as General Framework Agreement for Peace (GFAP).

J. Junger-Tas and S. H. Decker (eds.), International Handbook of Juvenile Justice, 415–436.
© 2006 Springer.

1. CRIMINAL LAW REFORM IN BOSNIA AND HERZEGOVINA

The main characteristic of criminal law reform on the territory of BH during the period 1992–2003 was its great speed. It means that processes of criminal law reform were going on separately in both entities and in BDBH. Although rooted in the criminal law of former Yugoslavia, the three assemblies took different paths of progress toward harmonization of the criminal law with international standards. Fortunately, uncoordinated reforms stopped in January 2003 when BH, as a state, finally got its Criminal Code of Bosnia and Herzegovina (CCBH)[2] and the Code of Criminal Procedure of Bosnia and Herzegovina,[3] that have to be applied on the whole territory of BH. As new laws introduced a lot of new and modified legal solutions there was a need for immediate harmonization of existing respective criminal codes of FBH, RS, and BDBH. Luckily, it took only a few months until the new laws were in place.[4] Since there are no significant differences between the laws, in our further discussions we will primarily talk about laws regulating juvenile justice system on the state level.

2. GLOBAL OVERVIEW OF JUVENILE DELINQUENCY TRENDS IN BOSNIA AND HERZEGOVINA

As we have already said there is no state office of statistics in BH. Therefore, in order to get data on juvenile delinquency we had to look for it on the entity level. Surprising or not, we were able to get the data only in the Federal Statistics Office (FSO)[5] that provided us with partial information on juvenile delinquency in FBH. Although it was suggested to use only police statistics and self-report data when analyzing juvenile delinquency trends, due to the fact that self-report delinquency studies have not been conducted yet in BH,[6] and bearing in mind that police forces are organized on a cantonal level, it was quite impossible to collect the data as requested in the guidelines provided for the working group on juvenile justice. Therefore, we present the data as we got

[2]Criminal Code of Bosnia and Herzegovina, Official Gazette of BH, No. 37/03.
[3]Code of Criminal Procedure of Bosnia and Herzegovina, Official Gazette of BH, No. 3/03.
[4]Criminal Code of Federation of Bosnia and Herzegovina, Official Gazette of FBH, No. 36/03, Code of Criminal Procedure of Federation of Bosnia and Herzegovina, Official Gazette of FBH, No. 35/03, Criminal Code of Republika Srpska, Official Gazette of RS, No. 49/03, Code of Criminal Procedure of Republika Srpska, Official Gazette of RS, No. 50/03, Criminal Code of Brcko District of Bosnia and Herzegovina, Official Gazette of BDBH, No. 10/03, Code of Criminal Procedure of Brcko District of Bosnia and Herzegovina, Official Gazette of BDBH, No. 10/03.
[5]All data related to juvenile delinquency in this report are gathered from Federal Statistics Office's Bulletins for 1998, 1999, 2000, 2001, 2002, and 2003. These bulletins contain the data gathered in Federation of Bosnia and Herzegovina only.
[6]The very first self-report delinquency study in BH is currently being prepared by a group of international universities and institutions, including the Faculty of Criminal Justice Sciences, University of Sarajevo.

it from the FSO, assuming that those data are properly collected from the cantonal police forces. In our further discussions we will present certain trends in juvenile delinquency especially when it comes to juvenile crime rates, the structure of crime committed by juveniles, and age and gender differences.

The first thing we were interested in was to see how many juveniles participate in crimes committed in FBH if compared to adults. We were surprised to see that the relationship is very stable and that the participation rate of juveniles is remarkably low. As Fig. 17.1 shows it varies from 4.9% in 2001 to 6.7% in 2000.

Although it is common practice that, for comparative purposes, crime rates are presented per certain number of citizens (1,000, 10,000, or 100,000) we were not able to do so. It is because we were not able to get the data on the population of FBH, nor on the population of BH. In FSO we were told that the last known numbers are dating back to 1991, and war and after-war conditions changed these figures considerably. At this moment, there are only estimations but these vary significantly and cannot be used for our purpose. Therefore we decided to present the data on juvenile delinquency in absolute numbers.

Figure 17.2 shows that the number of crimes committed by juveniles in FBH is decreasing with an exception of 2002. It is very hard to say what the reasons for this positive trend are, since there is no single research conducted on this issue in FBH.

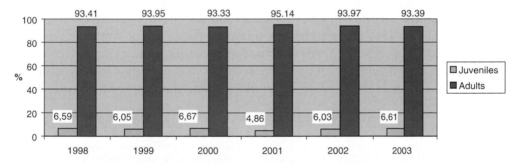

FIGURE 17.1. Participation of juveniles in total number of offences.

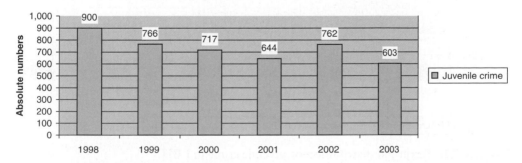

FIGURE 17.2. Reported juvenile offenders.

The problem we noticed in FSO's data is the fact that the number of reported juvenile offenders equates the number of offences committed by juvenile offenders. It is hard to believe that there was not a single juvenile offender who committed more than one offence nor that there were no offences committed by more than one juvenile. On the contrary, in informal discussion with one juvenile judge in Sarajevo, we were told that some juveniles were remarkably persistent in committing crimes, especially property crimes, sometimes committing more than 20 thefts or grand thefts within a short period of time. Also, the same judge says that juveniles commit crimes not only on their own but in coordination with their peers, or even jointly with adults. Therefore we think that the presented data do not represent the situation on the field and that we should be very cautious with our conclusions.

When it comes to the territorial distribution of juvenile delinquency in FBH (see Fig.17.3) it is a really remarkable finding that most of crimes committed by juvenile offenders are committed in four out of ten cantons in FBH. These four cantons represent urban areas in the country with Sarajevo as the capital of Bosnia and Herzegovina, Zenica and Tuzla as industrial centres and Una-Sana as a small canton in north/west part of the country on the border with Croatia.

Another interesting trend may be seen in the structure of crimes committed by juvenile offenders. Of course, there is no need to stress that juveniles mostly commit property crimes. Here we have to point out another shortcoming of the current crime-related data collection system. Surprising as it may sound, it is based on chapters of the criminal code and not on criminal offences. It means that it is not possible to say whether the number of, e.g., thefts, robberies, or burglaries increased or decreased. All we can say is whether some groups of offences are increasing or decreasing. As Fig. 17.4 shows it is obvious that the number of property crimes committed by juveniles decreased from 86.89% in 2000 to

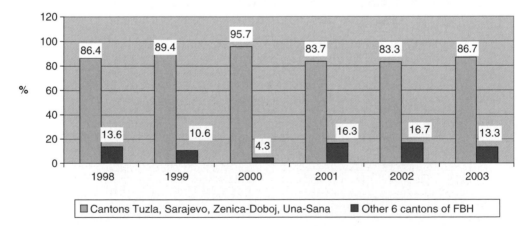

FIGURE 17.3. Territorial distribution of juvenile crime in FBH.

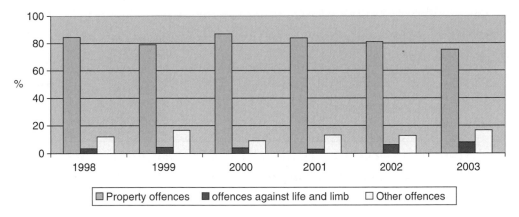

FIGURE 17.4. Offences committed by juvenile offenders.

75.37% in 2003. On the other hand, with the exception of 2001, it is remarkable that the number of crimes against life and limb (violent crimes) increased from 3.56% in 1998 to 7.99% in 2003, which means that juvenile offenders in FBH are getting more and more violent.

Even though we wanted to take a look at trends related to age differences in juvenile offending, unfortunately we were faced with the fact that FSO collects this kind of data only since 2002 (see Fig.17.5). Therefore we cannot talk about trends, but there are some very interesting findings. One should not be surprised to see that close to half of juvenile offenders in 2002 and 2003 were older than 17 but still younger than 18. On the other hand, we were surprised to see that more juveniles aged 14 participate in juvenile crime than those aged 15–16. Moreover, in conversations with the juvenile judge from the Canton Sarajevo we were informed that the number of children younger than 14, which are considered as not criminally responsible by the law in BH, and who are involved in crime increases.

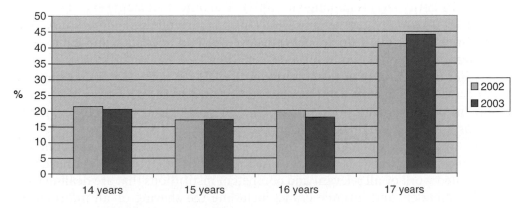

FIGURE 17.5. Juvenile offenders in FBH by age.

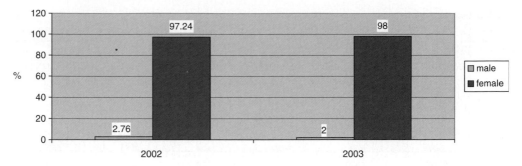

FIGURE 17.6. Juvenile offenders in FBH by sex.

Just as with age differences, FSO started to pay attention to gender differences in juvenile offending since 2002 (see Fig.17.6). Although we cannot talk about trends in female juvenile offending it is worth mentioning that females in FBH do commit crimes.

Other interesting data shows that within these 2.76% and 2.00% we have found females aged 14–17, just as for male juvenile offenders. Also, it is worth mentioning that females primarily commit property crimes (61.9% in 2002 and 50% in 2003).

3. THE PREVENTION OF DELINQUENT BEHAVIOUR IN BOSNIA AND HERZEGOVINA

In theory and practice, there is usually one question when it comes to the prevention of juvenile offending: are there more effective ways to prevent and reduce juvenile crime than those that are currently being applied? Unfortunately, in BH one should ask "is there any activity or program that is being implemented for the purpose of the prevention of such behaviour?" And again unfortunately, one has to admit that there is no strategy for the prevention of juvenile offending at the state or entity level (Damjanović, 2003). The only documents existing in BH that, at least partially, are dealing with issues of juvenile offending are Action plans for children. These documents are developed on both state and entity level and cover a range of activities related to children.

Within the Action plan for children in the BH we have only found that the task of analyzing juvenile delinquency is designated to the ministries of internal affairs, in other words to police forces. The purpose of this task is to create the basis for follow-up activities, including prevention.

The Action plan for children in the FBH is a bit "more detailed" and contains several instructions related to juvenile offending. The Plan requests continued and coordinated work of all relevant and competent institutions that are dealing with juvenile offenders and juvenile crime, including the sharing of all information gathered in the course of their work. It also requests that separate police forces in charge of dealing with juvenile crime should be established and that juvenile offences and juvenile offenders should be detected, reported and investigated in due time, primarily in order to curb juvenile delinquency more effectively.

The Action plan for children in the RS envisages that the core institution in dealing with juvenile offending is not the police but social welfare centres. According to the Plan in the RS it is a social welfare centre that requests the detailed information on juvenile offending from the police and then with the assistance of the police designs and implements follow-up activities including prevention.

As we may see from what has been mentioned before, it is obvious that the prevention of juvenile delinquency as some very complex antisocial behaviour, is viewed with enormous simplicity. Not only is there no attention paid to primary, secondary, and tertiary prevention, but the only institutions in charge of prevention of juvenile delinquency are police forces and centres for social welfare. Besides the noninvolvement of other institutions in preventing juvenile offending, there is also a need to stress that no action whatsoever is envisaged to be taken on a local, municipality or cantonal level.

When it comes to specific juvenile delinquency prevention programs, there are some isolated initiatives found in the Canton Sarajevo, both on the side of the Centre for Social Work and the cantonal police force. Still they could not provide us with more detailed information as activities were in their initial phase.

Due to this situation in BH, we do not have any evaluated, evidence-based programs in our country. During 2000–2003 there were two research projects[7] conducted on issues of juvenile delinquency in BH and both projects provided the recommendation that special attention should be given to a coordinated preventive approach to juvenile offending, not only by the police and social welfare centres, but also by schools, health services, the NGO sector and the local community.

4. POLICE INTERVENTION

In accordance with Article III of the Constitution of BH, that defines authorities and relationships between institutions of BH and the entities, internal affairs are under the exclusive authority of the entities. Therefore there is no state ministry of internal affairs, but two ministries on the entity level. The internal organization and powers of the police are defined by the law on internal affairs[8] and by the already mentioned criminal code and code of criminal procedure.

[7]Young people in conflict with the law in the light of topical problems related to juvenile criminal justice in BH, Open society Fund Bosnia and Herzegovina/UNICEF, 2002 and Young people in conflict with the law: A review of practice and legislation in Bosnia and Herzegovina in relation to international standards, Save the children UK/UNICEF, 2003.
[8]Law on internal affairs of FBH, Official Gazette of FBH, No. 42/02, Law on internal affairs of RS, Official Gazette of RS, No. 21/98, 18/99, 25/02, 43/02.

When it comes to the internal organization it has to be said that internal affairs in FBH are divided between the entity and the cantons, where the Federal ministry of internal affairs is in charge of terrorism, intercantonal crime, illicit trafficking of drugs and organized crime. All other offences are to be handled by cantonal ministries. Furthermore, it means that, due to the fact that juvenile offenders are rarely involved in aforementioned criminal offences, issues of juvenile delinquency are usually to be handled by the cantonal ministries for internal affairs. Cantonal ministries exercise their powers through cantonal units and through the municipalities' police stations. Police stations can be in charge of offences committed in one or more municipalities depending on the size of the municipality and the crime problems in the area.

Whereas the Federal ministry of interior is decentralized and coordinated, the respective ministry in RS is centralized and subordinated. The organization of police forces is unified and there is no division between different organizational levels, but the ministry of internal affairs of RS is in charge of internal affairs on the whole territory of RS and it exercises its powers directly on the field.

When it comes to juvenile delinquency it must be said that the division of labour in police forces is not based on the age of the offender but on the type of offences (e.g., units for offences against life and sex offences, units for property crimes, etc.). Therefore we do not have police officers, nor police units, specifically in charge of handling juvenile offending.

Speaking about the discretionary power of police forces in FBH and RS, when they deal with juvenile offenders, it should be noted that they do not have any special power. If a juvenile commits a crime, the police have to react in accordance with the principle of legality and have to take all necessary steps in detecting crimes and offenders, investigate the crime and bring the case to the prosecutor and than to a court.

There are some initiatives[9] suggesting the police to use diversionary measures for juveniles that come into contact with the police for the very first time. However, it is not known if the police exercise these powers, but since these powers are not defined by legislation in BH, if exercised, they would be illegal.

Police powers that could be used in dealing with juvenile delinquents are defined by the codes of criminal procedure. According to all criminal procedure codes in BH, as a result of the latest reform, it is the prosecutor who is in charge of initiating and conducting a criminal investigation.[10] Although officially in charge of the investigation it is not an exception that a prosecutor delegates his investigative powers to the police force. If a crime is reported to the police, depending on the penalty prescribed for such an offence by the criminal code, the police will have to inform the prosecutor (for offences punishable by 5 years of imprisonment or

[9]The handbook of principles and procedures, developed through cooperation of ministries of both entities and ICITAP, 2000.
[10]Article 216.1, CPC BH.

more) and then conduct the investigation under his or her supervision, or they will start conducting the investigation and inform the prosecutor within seven days about all steps and measures that they have taken so far (for offences punishable by up to 5 years of imprisonment). In order to perform these tasks, police forces or other authorized persons may obtain the necessary information from persons; they may make a necessary examination of vehicles, passengers and luggage; they may restrict the movement of citizens in a specified area during the time required to complete a certain action; they may take the necessary steps to establish the identity of persons and objects; they may organize a search to locate an individual or items being sought; and they may, in the presence of a responsible person, search specified structures and premises of state authorities, public enterprises and institutions, examine specified documents belonging to state authorities or public enterprises or institutions, and take all other necessary steps and actions.[11]

Other investigative measures that are usually performed in the course of investigation, but sometimes also during the main trial, include:

1. Search of dwellings, other premises and persons[12]
2. Seizure of objects and property[13]
3. A procedure of dealing with suspicious objects[14]
4. Questioning of the suspect[15]
5. Examination of witnesses[16]
6. Crime scene investigation and reconstruction of events[17]
7. Expert evaluation[18]

For certain criminal offences[19] some special investigative measures can be ordered by the preliminary proceedings judge upon the prosecutor's request. These measures include:

1. Surveillance and technical recording of telecommunications
2. Access to computer systems and computerized data processing
3. Surveillance and technical recording of premises
4. Covert following and technical recording of individuals and objects
5. Use of undercover investigators and informants

---

[11] Art. 219.1, CPC BH.
[12] Art. 51–64, CPC BH.
[13] Art. 65–74, CPC BH.
[14] Art. 75–76, CPC BH.
[15] Art. 77–80, CPC BH.
[16] Art. 81–91, CPC BH.
[17] Art. 92–94, CPC BH.
[18] Art. 95–115, CPC BH.
[19] For (a) Criminal offences against the integrity of Bosnia and Herzegovina; (b) Criminal offences against humanity and values protected under international law; (c) Criminal offences of terrorism; (d) Criminal offences for which, pursuant to the law, a prison sentence of minimum of 3 years or more may be pronounced. Art. 117, CPC BH.

6. Simulated purchase of certain objects and simulated bribery
7. Supervised transport and delivery of objects of criminal offences

If any of these measures are to be implemented, both by a police officer or a prosecutor, and in a case where a juvenile was the offender there are certain rights that a juvenile has and that have to be properly addressed. Besides some individual rights that a juvenile offender possesses just as all adult offenders,[20] there are some additional rights entitled to him or her as a juvenile. First of all, juvenile offenders can never be tried *in absentia*; he or she has the right to mandatory defence; neither the course of criminal proceeding against a minor, nor the decision rendered in that proceeding may be made public, nor may the course of the proceedings be visually or audio recorded, from the beginning to the completion of criminal proceedings.[21]

5. INTERVENTION OF THE PROSECUTOR

According to CPC BH criminal proceedings in Bosnia and Herzegovina can be initiated only upon the request of a prosecutor.[22] The prosecutor has the obligation to initiate criminal proceedings if there is evidence that a criminal offence has been committed,[23] unless a juvenile committed a criminal offence punishable by imprisonment up to 3 years or a fine. In that case, the prosecutor may decide not to adjudicate the case even though there is evidence that the minor committed the criminal offence, if he or she feels that it would not serve any purpose to initiate criminal proceedings against the minor in view of the nature of the criminal offence and the circumstances under which it was committed, the minor's past and his personal characteristics. In order to determine these circumstances, the prosecutor may seek information from parents or guardians of the minor and from other persons and institutions and when necessary, he may summon those persons and the minor to the prosecutor's office to obtain information in person. He may seek the opinion of the juvenile welfare authority concerning the usefulness of conducting criminal proceedings against the minor. If there is a need to study the personal characteristics of the minor in order to take a decision, the prosecutor may, in agreement with the juvenile

---

[20]Presumption of innocence, *in dubio pro reo*, *ne bis in idem*, right to participate in proceedings using its native language, to be informed about charges against him or her, right to a decision based on legally obtained evidence, right to compensation and rehabilitation, right to be informed about all his or her rights, right to a trial without delay.

[21]A juvenile judge in charged of criminal proceeding against a juvenile, has to inform a President of the court every 15 days about which juvenile cases are not closed and what are the reasons for such a situation.

[22]Art. 16, CPC BH.

[23]Art. 17, CPC BH.

welfare authority, send the minor to a juvenile home or institution for further examination, or an educational institution, but not longer than 30 days. Another situation when a prosecutor does not have to initiate criminal proceedings against a juvenile offender is when punishment or an educational measure is being executed. The prosecutor may decide not to charge the juvenile for another criminal offence if in view of the severity of that offence and the punishment or educational measure being executed, there would be no point in conducting criminal proceedings.

If in any of the two mentioned cases the prosecutor finds that it does not serve any purpose to conduct criminal proceedings against a minor, he shall inform the juvenile welfare authority and the injured party (victim), stating the grounds of his decision.

If a prosecutor decides to initiate criminal proceedings he or she is in charge of conducting all those investigative measures already mentioned in the previous part of this report. Even more so, a prosecutor is also in charge of ordering autopsy and exhumation.[24]

When it comes to the prosecutor's role in criminal proceedings it must be said that a prosecutor not only initiates criminal proceedings but also, after preliminary proceedings, submits a proposal to a juvenile judge to impose youth imprisonment or an educational measure on a juvenile offender.[25] He or she is also obliged to participate in the main court hearing[26] and has the right to use all regular (ordinary)[27] and extraordinary[28] legal remedies.

6. SANCTIONS AND SENTENCING[29]

The Criminal Code in BH, as most of the criminal codes in the world, makes a distinction between two categories of offenders – juvenile offenders and adult offenders, and provides different penalties or sanctions for these offenders. Sanctions that can be applied on juvenile offenders and conditions for their imposition are defined in Chapter X of the CCBH. Special provisions for juveniles can also be applied on adult offenders if they are tried for an offence they have committed as a juvenile and, exceptionally, to persons who have committed a criminal offence as young adults.[30] A person is considered to be a young adult if he or she is older than 18 but younger than 23.

[24]Art. 222, CPC BH.
[25]Art. 360, CPC BH.
[26]Art. 364.3, CPC BH.
[27]Art. 293.3, CPC BH.
[28]Art. 324–333, CPC BH.
[29]This part is based on Maljević (2004).
[30]Art. 75.2, CCBH.

According to art. 341 CPC BH a procedure cannot be initiated if it is discovered that a juvenile was younger than 14 at the time of committing an offence. It means that no one provision of the CCBH can be applied on the offender aged under 14 as he is considered a child and not criminally responsible. If the fact that the juvenile was a child at the time of committing an offence was not known to the police or to the prosecutor at the time when the investigation was initiated, and was discovered later on, the procedure has to be stopped and a competent centre for social work should be informed about the juvenile and the offence. Consequently, provisions of the CCBH can be applied only if an offender is aged 14 or older.

Regarding the sanctions that can be imposed on juveniles CCBH makes a distinction between *younger minors* (14–16), *older minors* (16–18), and *young adult* offenders.

Having in mind the nature of juvenile delinquency and the personality of juvenile offenders, it is understandable that CCBH provides different types of responses according to the committed crimes. There are four different types of sanctions prescribed for juvenile offenders. These are:

1. Educational recommendations
2. Educational measures
3. Juvenile imprisonment
4. Security measures.

Educational recommendations and educational measures can be imposed on all juvenile offenders, but juvenile imprisonment can be imposed only, and exceptionally, on older minors. Security measures can be imposed only in addition to juvenile imprisonment and to some educational measures.

6.1. Educational Recommendations[31]

Educational recommendations are a recent novelty in the criminal justice system of BH. They were first introduced in FBH back in November 1998, as a result of the need to harmonize criminal provisions in BH both with the European Convention for Human Rights and the Convention on the Rights of the Child.

The purpose of educational recommendations is to avoid the initiation of criminal procedures against juvenile offenders and to influence the juvenile offender so that he does not commit a criminal offence again. These recommendations can only be imposed on a juvenile offender by a competent prosecutor or a juvenile judge. Educational recommendations can be imposed on a juvenile only if:

(a) The offence he or she committed is punishable by imprisonment not exceeding 3 years or by a fine.
(b) The offender admits he or she has committed the crime and expresses willingness to make amends with the injured party.

[31]Legal definitions of educational recommendations, their purpose and conditions for imposition are defined in Articles 76–79. CCBH.

If these conditions are fulfilled, and a competent prosecutor feels, bearing in mind the nature of the crime, the circumstances under which it was committed, the previous life of the offender and his or her personal characteristics, that it would not be in the public interest to conduct criminal proceedings, he has to consider the possibility and justification of imposing an educational recommendation on that particular juvenile offender.

Educational recommendations can be divided into two groups according to who (competent prosecutor or juvenile judge) may order them. Recommendations that can be ordered by a competent prosecutor are:

(a) Personal apology to the injured party
(b) Compensation of the damages to the injured party
(c) Regular school attendance
(d) Attending instructive, educational, psychological or other forms of counselling.

Educational recommendations that can be ordered by a juvenile judge are:

(a) Working for a humanitarian organization or the local community
(b) Accepting an appropriate job
(c) Being placed in another family, home or institution
(d) Treatment in an adequate health institution.

When deciding whether to order an educational recommendation, the competent prosecutor or juvenile judge has to take into consideration all interests of a juvenile offender and the injured party.

Educational recommendations may be ordered for a period not exceeding 1 year, and during that concrete period the educational measure may be replaced by another measure or cancelled.

If a prosecutor or a judge thinks that imposition of an educational recommendation will serve the purpose of punishment, a specific one will be chosen in cooperation with the juvenile offender's parents or guardians and social welfare agencies. When deciding on which educational recommendation to impose, special attention must be given to the juvenile's regular school attendance or his or her work.

6.2. Educational Measures[32]

Educational measures may be imposed on all juvenile offenders. There are three different groups of these sanctions:

1. Disciplinary measures
2. Measures of intensified supervision
3. Institutional measures

[32]Educational measures are defined in Articles 80–94 of CCBH.

In the process of deciding which one to impose on a juvenile, the judge has to take into consideration two very important circumstances: to what extent the juvenile is neglected and the nature of his or her social environment. Circumstances that should also be considered are the juvenile's motives, his previous record and other circumstances relevant to the selection of one of the sanctions.

Disciplinary measures – a court reprimand,[33] committal to a disciplinary centre for juveniles – should be imposed on those juvenile offenders that do not need intense supervision and who live in an environment which does not encourage them to commit crimes, especially if their crime was a result of thoughtlessness or carelessness.

Measures of intensive supervision – by parents, adoptive parents or guardians, in a foster home or by the competent social welfare agency – should be imposed on those juvenile offenders who need re-education or treatment with intensive supervision, but, still, do not need separation from their living environment. These juvenile offenders had not had adequate supervision at the time it was needed and their crime was a result of neglect.

Institutional measures – committal to an educational/correctional institution, or educational corrective/reformatory institution, or other training institution – should be imposed on those juvenile offenders who need re-education or treatment with intensive supervision and should be separated from their current living environment. The assumption is that these juveniles have not had adequate care and supervision when it was needed, and their social environment is assumed to influence their misbehaviour.

6.3. Juvenile Imprisonment[34]

Since the purpose of educational recommendations and educational measures is primarily special prevention (to influence the offender not to commit a crime again), the purpose of juvenile prison is both special and general prevention (to influence the offender not to commit a crime again and to deter other juveniles).

Older minors who commit a crime punishable by more than 5 years of imprisonment as prescribed by CCBH may receive juvenile prison as the only penalty that can be imposed on juveniles. This penalty may be imposed only if the consequences of the crime are serious, and if the juvenile offender showed a high degree of criminal responsibility, so that these facts do not justify imposing an educational recommendation or an educational measure.

A term in Juvenile prison cannot be less than 1 year nor can it be longer than 10 years. Still, when deciding on the length of juvenile imprisonment in a concrete

---

[33]A court reprimand had been the educational measure and therefore sanction for juvenile offenders until last criminal law reform. Since August 2003 it is left out of criminal legislation in BH except in the CCRS. You can see the extent of its application during 1998–2003 period in our further discussions on Sanctions in practice under 7.5.

[34]Juvenile imprisonment is defined in Arts. 95–99, CCBH.

case, a juvenile judge cannot impose a sentence for longer than prescribed by law. On the other hand he or she is not limited by the minimum punishment prescribed for that particular offence.[35]

6.4. Security Measures[36]

Under the conditions determined by CCBH, and in addition to an educational measure[37] or juvenile imprisonment, three security measures can be imposed on a juvenile offender. These would be mandatory psychiatric treatment, mandatory medical treatment for substance addicted juveniles and forfeiture. Depending on the case, a judge may impose one or more security measures on a particular juvenile. These measures can be imposed on a juvenile offender only if there is a need to remove certain situations or conditions that might prompt a juvenile to commit again a crime.

Mandatory psychiatric treatment can be imposed on a juvenile if he or she committed a crime in a state of considerably diminished mental capacity or diminished mental capacity and if there is a danger that, because of his mental capacity, he might again commit a crime. It can be imposed in addition to juvenile imprisonment or to an educational measure. Its continuation is limited by the removal of the cause of his diminished mental capacity, but it can never last longer than the juvenile imprisonment or educational measure that has been imposed.

Mandatory treatment for substance addiction can be imposed on a juvenile offender who committed an offence under the influence of alcohol or drugs and if there is a danger that due to the addiction he or she might commit a crime again.

Subject to forfeiture can be objects used or intended to be used for the perpetration of an offence, just as those that resulted from the perpetration of an offence, if there is a danger that those objects will be used for the perpetration of other offences or if forfeiture is absolutely necessary on account of the protection of public safety or for moral reasons.

Article 80.5 of the CCBH is a very interesting provision, stating that the suspended sentence is a sanction that cannot be imposed on a juvenile offender.

6.5. Sanctions for Juveniles in Practice in FBH

The summary of sanctions for juveniles prescribed by CCBH offered an overview of more than 20 alternatives that a judge or a prosecutor can impose on a juvenile offender. As we have seen there are some sanctions with pure educational objectives, some with restorative ones, some are educational and rehabilitative and

[35]Art. 96.2, CCBH.
[36]Security measures for juvenile offenders are defined in Arts. 68–72, 74 and 102 of CCBH.
[37]The exception are disciplinary measures.

some, such as juvenile imprisonment, are retributive in nature. For the purpose of this report, aiming to find out what kind of approach (educational, restorative, rehabilitative or retributive) our judges and prosecutors have to sentencing of juvenile offenders, we tried to conduct a preliminary analysis of sanctions that had been imposed on juvenile offenders in BH. Due to the fact that there is no national research done on sentencing juvenile offenders we had to rely again on data gathered by FSO. Therefore we will present only the data that are related to sentencing juveniles in FBH.

Analysis of the data gathered by FSO in FBH provided us with some very interesting and worrying results. A brief look at Fig. 17.7 speaks for itself. As we can see the domination of only three sanctions[38] in the observed period is obvious. Judges in FBH are most likely to impose a judicial reprimand, intensive supervision by parents or guardians or intensive supervision by a guardianship institution (centre for social work).

Surprised with this kind of results related to the sentencing of juvenile offenders in FBH, we wanted to check if there would be some significant differences if the same data would be separately analyzed for two categories of juvenile offenders. As Figs. 17.8 and 17.9 are showing, there are no significant differences. On the contrary, we have found almost the same trends.

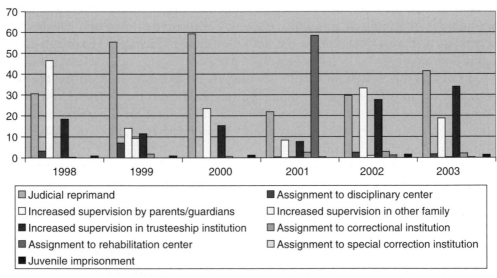

FIGURE 17.7. Sanctions imposed on juvenile offenders (1998–2003).

[38]As we could see the only exception is 2001 when judges imposed an assignment to a rehabilitation centre in close to 60% cases. Due to the fact that this sanction has never been imposed earlier, and only in less than 1% later in 2002 and 2003, and also having in mind other mistakes or shortcomings of the analyzed data, we dare to think that this 60% was wrongfully entered data in the database.

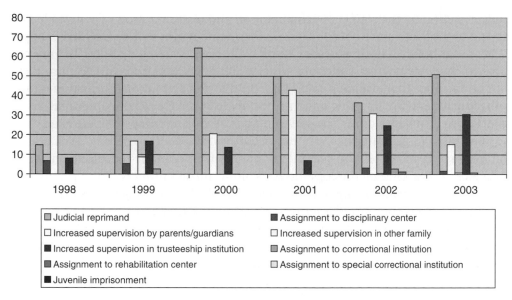

FIGURE 17.8. Sanctions imposed on younger minors.

Bearing in mind that, when deciding on which sentence to impose on a juvenile offender, a judge has to take into account all circumstances related to the committed offence, the juvenile's behaviour as well as his personality and previous behaviour and his current needs, it is our opinion that these results could be caused by several reasons. First, may be juvenile offenders and the offences they have committed in the observed period were of a such a nature that juveniles deserved nothing more than these, let us say soft and easy-to-implement sanctions. Second, maybe these juveniles deserved a bit harsher sentencing policy but

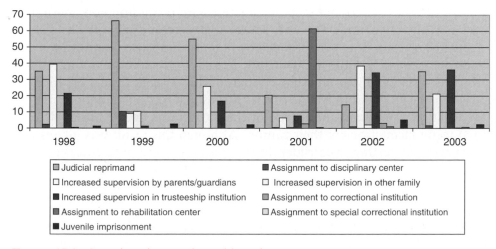

FIGURE 17.9. Sanctions imposed on older minors.

judges, acting on the course of rehabilitation and resocialization of a juvenile and trying to motivate him to become a valuable member of a society, decided to apply a bit softer policy. Third, which we think is the real reason, judges in FBH are not able to implement other sanctions on juvenile offenders primarily because there are no facilities that juveniles could be sent to for rehabilitation, correction or any other treatment. We find this one the most realistic reason, as previous analysis of the nature of juvenile crime showed that rates of violent crime are increasing.

The most important question that occupies our attention here is – What kind of message is being sent to juvenile offenders who commit repeatedly criminal offences? What kind of message do we send to those juveniles that are only one step away from committing a crime? Or what kind of message do we send to a juvenile who has committed a serious crime and is sentenced to intensive supervision by a centre for social work, especially if the supervision is not as intense as it should be? The author of the report does not want to be understood as advocating for a more repressive and more retributive approach to juvenile delinquency. On the contrary it is our intention to advocate for more individualized sentencing and to argue against improvisations that judges are forced to make.[39] Otherwise we would be advocating against the principle of legality. In the very end, if a juvenile needs treatment, then he is entitled to it and he has to have a possibility to exercise this right. The juvenile judge has to be able to make rehabilitation easier, since this is in the juvenile's interest, the interest of his family and in the interest of the whole society.

Unfortunately, when it comes to the implementation of educational recommendations as an alternative to sanctions and as an alternative way to solve a problem of juvenile crime, we cannot say very much. Since these recommendations are being imposed in order to avoid the initiation of criminal procedures against juvenile offenders, we could not obtain the data on its implementation from FSO. In other words, FSO nor the Ministry of Justice do consider the information on when and how educational recommendations are being imposed and implemented as really important. The only source that we could rely on was a study conducted by a group of experts, funded by the "Open Society Fund Bosnia and Herzegovina" and UNICEF in 2000/2001. Researchers surveyed 30 judges and 34 prosecutors in FBH. Results showed that, during 3 years from 1998 to 2001, only 10% of the judges applied one of the educational recommendations in their canton.[40] At the same time only 29.4% of the prosecutors decided to apply educational recommendations in their canton. Although this result was interesting, it is even more interesting to consider the reasons judges and prosecutors gave for

---

[39]By imposing only three, out of more than ten sanctions, judges are clearly sending a message that something does not function well in our criminal justice system. They are forced to look for more *in favorem* circumstances and to "close their eyes" on *in peius* circumstances, so they could justify their final decision.

[40]Similar results were found by Maljevic (2005) in his research.

not imposing these recommendations more often. Their strongest argument was the fact that there is no procedure prescribing the imposition of educational recommendations. In other words, the lawmakers introduced new ways of reacting to juvenile crime in substantive criminal legislation, aiming to achieve the harmonization of national legislation with current international legal standards in dealing with juvenile offenders, without prescribing procedural provisions for the implementation of the alternative measures. Next, another very strong argument was offered by 63.33% of the judges and 41.2% of the prosecutors, who reported they never had a case to which they could apply these recommendations. It tells something about the gap that exists between the conditions prescribed for the possible imposition of recommendations and the offences committed by juvenile offenders. In other words, the conditions prescribed by the law and required for the imposition of educational recommendations are defined in such a way that these recommendations can be imposed on very few criminal offenders only. One of the main obstacles in this regard might be the condition that restricts the imposition of educational recommendations to those offenders who commit an offence punishable by a fine or a term of imprisonment not exceeding 3 years. Our previous analysis on juvenile delinquency showed that juveniles are committing violent crimes and even when committing property crimes they do so in groups, or they are using force, which does mean a more serious qualification of the offence and as a consequence more severe punishment, sometimes even up to 10 years of imprisonment.

Although judges and prosecutors did not say anything about this, it is our opinion that there is at least one more reason for such a low rate of imposition of educational recommendations. Since for the very first time these alternatives to traditional penalties involve victims, families, communities and the government in solving problems of crime, these are clear examples of restorative justice notions in the criminal justice system of BH. Unfortunately, the term "restorative justice" in BH is known to a very small number of people. One can even name those police officers, lawyers, judges, prosecutors as experts in the field of law, who are familiar with the term. In order to implement these new measures it is absolutely necessary for a judge or for a prosecutor that he or she is familiar with the concept of restorative justice, that he or she believes in its philosophy and effectiveness, not only in the sense of reducing recidivism but also in the sense of increasing satisfaction on the side of victims and communities with the way in which the government deals with issues of crime and the way in which specific needs of offenders are evaluated and properly addressed. Therefore, it is our opinion that there is an urgent need for an intensive education campaign addressed to all stakeholders involved in the criminal justice system, but primarily judges and prosecutors as they are those in charge of implementing these modern measures.

The practical implementation of security measures for juvenile offenders is another interesting component of the current criminal justice system of BH. We have already said that these sanctions cannot simply be imposed on a juvenile offender but only in addition to imposed educational measures or to youth imprisonment. Analysis of the number of imposed security measures during the period 1998–2003 showed again one serious shortcoming of the current statistical package of information related to juvenile crime. We defined the data we found as "adjustment of data." Why adjustment? Let us take an example of the year 2003. As FSO data show, in 2003 there were 640 juvenile offenders charged and convicted for criminal offences. Out of these 640 juveniles, 292 received a sanction (educational measure or youth imprisonment), in 299 cases criminal proceedings were halted by the juvenile court and 49 juveniles received a security measure. If we sum up these numbers (292 + 299 + 49) we will see that the result is 640. What it means is that 49 juvenile offenders were punished by exclusively a security measure. Knowing that security measures can only be imposed in addition to an educational measure or to youth imprisonment, one may conclude that something is wrong with the data presented in FSO bulletins. In other words, these 49 security measures could be imposed only on 49 of 292 juvenile offenders who received a sanction. Therefore we argue that the data presented in the FSO bulletins are not reliable for serious scientific analysis and they should be taken as an indication rather than as a tool for exact scientific debate. Anyway, we will present the data on security measures in real numbers without drawing some reliable conclusions.

As we can see from Fig. 17.10, if we consider all charged and convicted juvenile offenders, security measures are usually imposed on less than 10% of all cases,

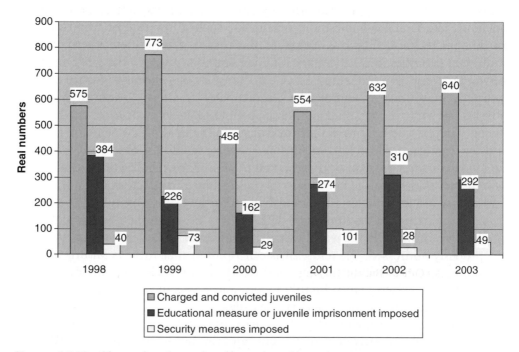

FIGURE 17.10. Charged and convicted/sanctioned/security measure.

with the exception of 2001 (18.23%). If, on the other hand, we compare this to those who were sanctioned by an educational measure or juvenile imprisonment, we will get completely different results. As Fig. 17.10 shows, the percentage suddenly increases and varies from 9.03% in 2002 to 36.86% in 2001. However, we did not present this result for any other purpose, but to illustrate how useless the data on security measures are.

7. CONCLUSION

The events from the very end of the 20th century in the Balkan region triggered not only reform of the criminal justice system in BH but also some apparent changes in trends of reported juvenile delinquency. Changes in the criminal justice system, based on international legal standards, are moving towards more substantial recognition of rights of a juvenile offender. Speaking about juvenile delinquency it has been found that their participation in crimes is rather constant (6–7%) and they commit more crimes in some parts of the country. It is also clear that juveniles are getting more persistent in committing violent offences not only on their own but also in cooperation with their peers and adults as well. Although the problem of juvenile delinquency in BH is perceived as very serious, almost nothing has been done in order to prevent it. The eyes of the society, wrongfully, are turned to the police (an institution without diversionary powers), prosecutors and courts. Despite the fact that a reformed criminal justice system provides the possibility for diversion of a certain number of cases involving juvenile offenders, prosecutors and judges do not use these possibilities primarily due to the lack of procedural norms defining the imposition and supervision of implementation of newly introduced alternative measures.

REFERENCES

Criminal Code of Bosnia and Herzegovina, Official Gazette of Bosnia and Herzegovina No. 37/03.

Criminal Procedure Code of Bosnia and Herzegovina, Official Gazette of Bosnia and Herzegovina No. 3/03.

Damjanović, O. (2003). Young people in conflict with the law: A review of practice and legislation in Bosnia and Herzegovina in relation to international standards, Save the children UK/UNICEF.

Federal Statistics Office's Bulletin (1998).

Federal Statistics Office's Bulletin (1999).

Federal Statistics Office's Bulletin (2000).

Federal Statistics Office's Bulletin (2001).

Federal Statistics Office's Bulletin (2002).

Federal Statistics Office's Bulletin (2003).

Law on internal affairs of FBH, Official Gazette of FBH, No. 42/02.

Law on internal affairs of RS, Official Gazette of RS, No. 21/98, 18/99, 25/02, 43/02.

Maljević, A. (2004). "Punishment of Juvenile Offenders in Criminal Justice System of Bosnia and Herzegovina," in G. Meško, M. Pagon, B. Dobovšek (eds.), *Policing in Central and Eastern Europe*, Dillemas of Contemporary Criminal Justice, University of Maribor.

Maljević, A. (2005). *Report on Judicial Approaches to Juvenile Crime: Explaining the Application of Educational Recommendations in Sarajevo*, The project was funded by Open Society Fund Bosnia and Herzegovina through the National Policy Fellowship Program.

Open Society Fund Bosnia and Herzegovina/UNICEF (2002). Young people in conflict with the law in the light of topical problems related to juvenile criminal justice in BH.

PART IV

Two Special Systems

18

The End of an Era? – Youth Justice in Scotland

Michele Burman, Paul Bradshaw, Neil Hutton, Fergus McNeill,
and Mary Munro

INTRODUCTION

Scotland is a small jurisdiction, yet it has a distinctive criminal justice system with unique institutional arrangements and certain political and legislative structures, which render it academically and politically interesting. Unlike other jurisdictions which have adopted neo-liberal policies, Scotland remains committed to a welfare state ethos that is expressed in the continuing commitment to social work with offenders and the welfarism of its youth justice system. The Scottish youth justice system is based on a core set of welfarist principles which stem from the work of the Kilbrandon Committee which reported in 1964. A key strength of the Scottish system is that it has thus far managed to avoid the more punitive and incarcerative aspects of other jurisdictions (most notably England and Wales), yet some recent policy and legislative developments that have impacted on the management of young offenders and the delivery of justice can be seen to pose serious challenges to the core Kilbrandon ethos.

Following decades of debate, a devolved form of government was introduced in Scotland in the late 1990s.[1] Devolution has been accompanied by a raft of legislative and policy changes, alongside a new emphasis on bottom-up policy development, partnerships and networks within Scotland. There has been the establishment of a Justice Department, and two Justice Committees. Following the new Parliament, there has been the assimilation of human rights into Scots law, the introduction of efficiency measures in the delivery of criminal justice and other changes, which include the restructuring of youth justice interventions, the introduction of antisocial behaviour orders, restriction of liberty orders (RLO), and electronic monitoring of young offenders, and the introduction of specialist youth courts. Increasing emphasis is placed upon inter-agency working practices to try to ensure effective delivery of criminal justice.

There are just over 5 million people living in Scotland with almost one in five (19%) being a child under the age of 15 years. The 2001 Census showed that 15- to 19-year-olds make up 6% of the population, as do 20- to 24-year-olds. Scotland

---

[1] Devolution was legislated for in 1998, elections for MPs were held in May 1999, and the Scottish Parliament assumed its full powers in July 1999.

J. Junger-Tas and S. H. Decker (eds.), International Handbook of Juvenile Justice, 439–472.
© 2006 Springer.

currently has one of the youngest ages of criminal responsibility in Europe (8 years) although the Scottish Law Commission has recommended that this be raised to 12 years.

In this chapter, we present a contextual overview of the Scottish youth justice and welfare system, tracing its genesis in the work of the Kilbrandon Committee, and discuss the implications of recent policy initiatives on the management and delivery of youth justice.

1. THE LEGACY OF KILBRANDON

The late 1960s and early 1970s in Scotland saw the inception of major changes transforming the ways in which the courts and services deliver youth justice. The most notable of these, the Children's Hearing System, was set up on the basis of recommendations made in 1964 by the Kilbrandon Committee.[2] Charged with finding solutions to the rise in the rate of juvenile delinquency in post-war Scotland, the Committee found that most cases coming before the juvenile courts were on offence rather than care grounds, and the majority of offences were trivial in nature. Over 90% of juveniles charged with offending did not dispute the charges made against them; and over a third of cases resulted in an absolute discharge or admonition (Kilbrandon Report, 1964). The Committee deemed the arrangements for dealing with children unsatisfactory, and recommended the removal of those under 16 years from adult criminal procedures (except for the most severe offences). Given the trivial nature of the majority of the cases, formal judicial proceedings were considered unnecessary and time-consuming. Furthermore, in Kilbrandon's view, the referral of children to the criminal courts for "juvenile delinquency" was best understood as a failure in the social education of children who were not amenable to voluntary measures of support and correction (Kilbrandon Report, 1964). The Kilbrandon Report put forward a set of rather radical and far reaching recommendations for a new national coordinated system to deal with children in need of compulsory measures of care. It proposed the separation of adjudication from disposition, and community participation in the system in the form of lay involvement in decision-making. It also promoted the importance of early intervention in a child's life. This new system was intended as the means by which the deficiencies of the pre-1971 systems were to be remedied, but it can also be seen as an important departure from the models of youth justice operating in other jurisdictions at the time.

Kilbrandon's recommendations are premised on certain key principles. Somewhat radically, the Committee maintained that the legal distinction and institutional separation between juvenile offending and children who were in need of care and protection was not meaningful, in that the underlying needs and circumstances

[2]Lord Kilbrandon was a senior Scottish judge.

of children in trouble – whether they were offending or were in need of care – were fundamentally similar. Children referred on different grounds have many needs, issues and problems in common; responses can and should be governed by the same principles, through the same processes. In a major departure from the adjudication and punishment model of youth justice, Kilbrandon proposed an integrative welfare-oriented approach, recommending a single system of civil jurisdiction for children brought before the courts for offending, for those beyond parental control and for those in need of care and protection. The recommendations were founded on the key principle that welfare should be the *paramount* concern in decision-making about children whether they are involved in offending or in need of care and protection. The welfare of the child "throughout their childhood" is the main objective of the system and the application of the welfare principle the key test guiding decisions concerning the necessity and extent of compulsory intervention in the child's life (Asquith, 1983).

The distinctive and innovative Children's Hearing System[3] was a direct result of Kilbrandon's deliberations. The Scottish juvenile courts as arenas of punishment were replaced by a more informal and multidisciplinary system with powers to make decisions about the social education and welfare supervision of the children brought to its attention, taking account of the child's needs.

Scotland has retained this system for almost 30 years, although it was given a new statutory framework by the Children (Scotland) Act 1995. Although responsibility for the Hearings was removed from Scottish local authorities in 1995, and a single Scottish Children's Reporter Administration (SCRA) was created to manage the service, the conduct of the system and its associated structures remain largely the same. The 1995 Act did, however, introduce some important qualifications to the *paramountcy* principle, which relate to circumstances where children are at significant risk of causing serious harm to themselves or others Kilbrandon (see Bottoms, 2004 for more detailed discussion). Specifically, the Act stated that the system could place the principle of public protection above that of the child's interests where the child represented a significant risk to the public.[4] The incursion of the risk principle is seen to pose a challenge to the ethos of Kilbrandon which privileges the interests of the child.

Today, the Children's Hearing System continues to lie at the heart of the Scottish youth justice system. It deals with children referred on care and protection grounds from birth up to the age of 16 years and with children referred on offence grounds from age 8 (the age of criminal responsibility in Scotland) usually up to age 16 (child offenders aged between 16 and 17 can be dealt with in the

---

[3]Established by the Social Work (Scotland) Act 1968 and implemented in full in April 1971.
[4]The risk principle was first introduced in 1983 by the Health and Health Services and Social Security Adjudication Act, which enabled the system to require a child to reside in secure accommodation where the child was likely to injure others.

hearings system, but they are more generally processed through the courts).[5] The central tenets of the System remain essentially welfarist: the continued emphasis on "needs" not "deeds"; that decisions should be made in the best interests of the child; the claim that offending is symptomatic of deeper psychological or social malaise; the focus on early and minimal intervention; an emphasis on informal, lay involvement, and; informal procedures which maximise the participation of children and their families in decision-making.

The grounds on which a child can be brought to a Hearing are diverse, and include because they are beyond the control of parents, are being exposed to moral danger, are likely to suffer unnecessarily or suffer serious impairment to health or development through lack of parental care, are the victim of a sexual, neglect or cruelty offence, are failing to attend school regularly, are misusing drugs, alcohol or solvents, or have committed an offence. The fact that this system combines both "criminal" and "care" cases is regarded by many as a key strength and has attracted praise and support within Scotland and internationally.

1.1. Children's Panels and the Hearing Process

The Children's Hearing Systems are essentially welfare tribunals headed up by lay "panels" of trained volunteers drawn from the local community.[6] There is a Panel for each local area, and currently across Scotland there are over 2,000 panel members. Professional staff with a social work or legal background are employed by SCRA as "Reporters" to the system. The role of the Reporter is to receive referrals of children and young people and initiate inquiries into their circumstances, in order to decide whether a Hearing should be called to consider compulsory measures of care and supervision. The main source of referrals is the police but other agencies such as social work or education and indeed any member of the public may make a referral to the Reporter. The role of the Reporter is discussed in more detail in section 5).

A Children's Hearing involves three lay panel members, the parents or guardians of the child, the child (in most cases), representatives from the social work department and the Reporter. There is also provision for parent(s) and/or the child to bring a representative (who may be a friend, another family member or a legal adviser). As Kilbrandon intended, the Hearings System separates the functions of looking at the needs of children from establishing guilt. The panels have

---

[5]Although the Hearings System can, in principle, deal with young people up to the age of 18, in practice, it tends to deal with those up to the age of 16, and the police tend to refer most offenders aged over 16 to the Procurator Fiscal (the public prosecutor in Scotland). In effect, then, the transition to court takes place at 16 years, although there is an option for Sheriffs to remit those up to 17 and a half years back to the Panel for advice and/or disposal.
[6]Panel members (aged 18–60 years) are recruited from the public, undergo selection and training processes, and are appointed by the Secretary of State for Scotland.

the power to order supervision in the community, as well as compulsory removal of children from their homes to schools, care homes or secure establishments.

1.2. Evaluation of the Children's Hearings System

Although widely regarded, the Children's Hearings System is not without its critics. Overall, however, there has been relatively little systematic evaluation undertaken. A three-part study of the System was commissioned in the late 1990s by the Scottish Executive (then the Scottish Office). The research found a lack of clarity about decision-making in the system, a fairly substantial drift in time intervals, and a failure to prevent escalation in offending among a small group of older male offenders at high risk of progression to the adult courts (and subsequently prison) (see Hallett et al., 1998; Waterhouse et al., 2000).

A later report by Audit Scotland (2002) which examined how the Children's Hearing System and the criminal justice system in Scotland deal with offenders under 21 years raised several further criticisms. The Report found a Hearings System that is under considerable strain as a result of internal and external resource problems; subject to delay and with a lack of available services. There has been continuing – and increasing – difficulty in recruiting lay panel members, and growing problems in finding social work staff to provide services for children. Clearly, the System has strengths but, as Whyte (2003) points out, some of its practices have weaknesses. In part, this has led to serious consideration in recent years by practitioners, academics, children's organisations and Government of the future and the way ahead for the Hearings System.

2. DEVELOPMENTS IN THE MANAGEMENT OF YOUNG OFFENDERS

2.1. Pendulum Swings?

Asquith and Docherty (1999) note that since the Kilbrandon Report, there have been at least three recurrent themes in the search for appropriate strategies for dealing with children and young people who offend in Scotland. The first is what they characterise as the "pendulum-like" swing between a punitive approach, and a more welfare-based philosophy. The second is the failure, despite the commitment given in Kilbrandon, to fully and systematically implement an early preventive approach in reducing numbers of children at risk of offending in later life. The third is the introduction of policies and practices which owe more to political ideology than systematic and rigorous research-based evidence (1999: 243–244). Such policies and practices, which are increasingly more punitive are in conflict with the more welfare-oriented philosophy laid out by Kilbrandon.

Since before devolution, there has been considerable public debate on crime and punishment in Scotland, with a particular focus on offending by young people. Many of the concerns mirror those expressed in England and Wales. In 1999, the Government announced its commitment to review youth justice. The Scottish Cabinet set up an Advisory Group on Youth Crime to assess the extent and effectiveness of options available to the Children's Hearings System and the criminal courts involving persistent young offenders, and to look at "the scope for improving the range and availability of options aimed at addressing the actions" of such offenders (Scottish Executive, 2000). Their report, published in 2000, identified responses to 14- to 18-year-old offenders as requiring attention. Although the Hearing System, as noted above, can deal with young people up to 18 years, in practice most of those over 16 years are referred by the police to the Procurator Fiscal (PF), and from there into the adult system. The Report noted the apparently sharp transition between the "needs" based approach of the Hearings system and the "deeds" based approach of the courts which occurs after the offender's 16th birthday, and stated that this approach is inherently contradictory (Scottish Executive, 2000). As McNeill and Batchelor (2002, 2004) point out, young people in this transitory position face a dramatic shift moving from the holistic approach of the Hearings system, which views their offending behaviour in the context of their needs and circumstances, to an institutionally and conceptually different system whose main goal is punishment. Furthermore, along with the changes in the focus and nature of intervention, is a concomitant change in the approach to children's rights as a citizen. There is a stark contrast in the shift from the notion of shared responsibility for the problems of children as espoused by the Hearings System (and the participation of the community in the System), to the notion of individual adult responsibility in the criminal justice system (McNeill and Batchelor, 2004: 13).

Whilst the Report acknowledged that the need to effectively address offending was becoming a dominant issue, in both Scottish political rhetoric and within the penal realm more generally, it put forward recommendations for a unified and balanced approach "combining care and protection with the public's concern" to address offending (Scottish Executive, 2000: para. 14). In this vein, the Report produced recommendations for a strategic multi-agency approach which would seek to balance the needs of the 16- and 17-year-old offender with public concern over the need to address offending behaviour, particularly for what the Report took to be a relatively small number of persistent offenders (c. 2,300) responsible for a significant amount of offending (i.e., 25% of all crime). It also envisaged a raft of services, a "range of accredited programmes and interventions available to children and young people who persistently offend" which would be accessible to the Hearings System, Reporters and PFs alike (Scottish Executive, 2000: para. 19).

Whilst the Report's recommendations were broadly accepted, they were never fully realised. The appointment of a new First Minister for Scotland,

Jack McConnell, in November 2001 signaled a toughening-up of policy towards young offenders. McNeill and Batchelor's (2002, 2004) analyses show that, in several key respects, developments in Scotland following this political appointment can be characterised as following a distinctively (and populist) correctional agenda, which "combines an fairly narrow emphasis on individual responsibility and personal (and parental) accountability for the behaviour of young people, with a practice focus on correcting personal (and parental) deficits" (McNeill and Batchelor, 2004: 13–14). That said, they maintain that this correctional drift in Scotland is not as pronounced as in England and Wales, and has had a more muted effect on practice, thus far. Nevertheless, McNeill and Batchelor (2004) also remark that hopes that the particular Scottish context with its welfare-oriented tradition of youth justice, might act as a buffer against the wholesale adoption of the correctional approaches and punitive penal politics that characterise other jurisdictions, may well prove "optimistic" and "forlorn" unless Scotland manages to retain some of the traditional strengths of the Scottish system.

2.2. Raising the Age of Criminal Responsibility

The Advisory Group on Youth Crime also raised the matter of criminal responsibility with the Group's report recommending a review of the case for raising the age of criminal responsibility from 8 years to 12 years, a recommendation accepted by the Executive. In October 2000, in the context of increasing concern about the way society should deal with young people who commit crime, the Scottish Law Commission was asked by Scottish Ministers to look at the rules on the age of criminal responsibility. Scots law uses two concepts of the age of criminal responsibility; one concerns a rule on criminal capacity, the other a rule on immunity from criminal prosecution. In Scotland, a child under the age of 8 years cannot be guilty of any offence, as they are considered to lack the mental capacity to commit a crime.[7] The age at which an offender becomes subject to the adult system of prosecution and punishment is 16 years; children below this age can be prosecuted only on the instructions of the Lord Advocate.[8] The Scottish Law Commission's recommendations, published in July 2001, called into question the need to retain the rule on criminal capacity, arguing that "the age of criminal responsibility is better conceptualised as relating to immunity from prosecution" and to do so would bring Scots law more into line with international conventions and legal systems operating elsewhere. The Scottish Executive undertook to consider the recommendations to raise the age to 12 years as part of its wider review of the Scottish youth justice system.

---

[7] Section 41 of the Criminal Procedure (Scotland) Act 1995.
[8] Section 42(1) of the Criminal Procedure (Scotland) Act 1995.

2.3. "Getting Tougher" on Young Offenders

In recent years, policy has shifted from a concern with the social and personal needs of young offenders to a focus on the nature and frequency of their offences. There is now an increased emphasis on investigation, risk assessment and surveillance. There has also been a number of policy initiatives aimed at enhancing the effectiveness of the system, including the implementation of national objectives and standards (2002); the creation of multi-agency youth justice strategy groups (2002) which have a key role to play in the planning and development of services. In addition to Scottish Executive policy development, the Justice 2 Committee of the Scottish Parliament is conducting its own independent *Youth Justice Inquiry* into the effectiveness of multi-agency working and to identify and assess the impact of gaps in service provision in the youth justice field.

Since coming to office in 2001, the First Minister has spearheaded a number of "get tough" initiatives, signaling youth crime and disorder as prominent political issues. In 2002, a "10 Point Action Plan on Youth Crime" was published (Scottish Executive, 2002b) which set out new measures to tackle persistent offending. These included Fast Track Hearings for offenders under 16 years; a pilot Youth Court for persistent offenders aged 16–17 years and a review of the scope for imposing antisocial behaviour orders, Community Service Orders (CSO) and RLO on persistent young offenders, all of which have been followed through in recent years. With its emphasis on persistent offending, the development and expansion of programmes based on "what works" principles (which are focused on criminogenic needs rather than a more generic welfare-based needs) poses yet more of a challenge to Kilbrandon's work. This 10 Point Plan also announced proposals for national standards on youth justice. A national target was set of a 10% reduction of young people who are persistently offending between 2000 and 2006. Other points in the Plan promote parental responsibility, and consider increasing the number of places in secure accommodation for young people.

Of particular resonance to the national standards objective, a Fast Track Hearings pilot, which specifically targets persistent offenders under 16 years was set up in a number of sites across Scotland in February 2003, in partnership with six local authorities.[9] It is important to note that the Fast Track Hearings remain essentially Children's Hearings and, as such, are governed by the welfare principle, and Panels employ the same range of disposals in Fast Tracks as any other type of Hearing. What is different about them is the speed with which referrals are processed, and the ways in which disposal options are better developed and resourced. The Fast Track pilot has four broad aims, which are to: reduce the time taken at each stage of decision-making; promote more

[9]Persistent offenders in the Fast Track pilot are defined as those individuals who have been referred for five or more offences in any 6-month period.

comprehensive assessments including appraisals of offending risk; ensure that all persistent young offenders who require an appropriate programme receive one, and; reduce re-offending rates. The pilot has been running since February 2003 and a full evaluation is underway. Early indications are that the shorter time-scales for dealing with persistent offenders are being met, and that both the level of offending and the re-referral rates of the young people participating in the pilot are decreasing (Hill et al., 2004).

Scotland has also seen the introduction of controversial pilot schemes for the electronic tagging of young offenders under the age of 16 years and, in June 2004, the introduction of the deeply contentious Antisocial Behaviour (Scotland) Act which, although not solely targeted at young people will, it is feared, impact exponentially on them. Indeed, when the Act came into effect, the Scottish press focused on the new civil powers to penalise children under 16 with headlines such as "New helplines for public to report unruly teenagers" (Adams, 2004) and "Warning over teen gang law" (Evening News, 28 October 2004).[10]

The Act includes a number of strategies to tackle antisocial behaviour, such as police powers to disperse groups of more than two people in designated trouble spots, the introduction of parenting orders, fixed penalty notices for lit-tering, vandalism, drunken behaviour and consuming alcohol in public places. There is a concern that the new legislation represents a new system of social control over children that parallels and, at least, cuts across the work of the Children's Hearings system. It is now possible for 12–16 year olds to be made the subject of Antisocial Behaviour Orders in the Sheriff Court's civil juris-diction, although a Children's Hearing must be held before such an order is made. If the order is broken, the young person will be reported to the PF. The outcome of subsequent court action might be a community reparation order;[11] a RLO (which may be combined with a supervision order) if the court is satis-fied that the local authority will provide services for the child's support and rehabilitation;[12] or another antisocial behaviour order. Young people of 16 and older may also be sentenced to imprisonment on conviction for a breach of an "ASBO." It is as yet too soon to report on how the new powers are being used but, in Scotland, as in England and Wales, such developments must be seen within the context in which a gradual elision has taken place between the com-munity safety and youth justice agendas, marking a shift from a more child-centred focus to a wider focus on the concerns of neighbourhoods and victims of crime and incivilities.

---

[10]Antisocial behaviour is widely defined as anything that 'causes or is likely to cause alarm or dis-tress' s. 143 Antisocial Behaviour (Scotland) Act 2004.

[11]An new order requiring anyone aged 12 and over to work 10 and 100 hours for the community that has been damaged. This innovation is to be tested in three Scottish cities from January 2005.

[12]The 'RLO' involves the electronic tagging of children to enforce an order restricting them to a specific place for up to 12 hours a day. This has been introduced in phases from April 2005.

The Antisocial Behaviour (Scotland) Act 2004 also has the potential for criminalising parents, where the proposed parenting orders are breached. A Sheriff may make a parenting order on the application of a Reporter or local authority if, for welfare or criminal conduct or antisocial behaviour reasons, the order is desirable to prevent the child from engaging in such conduct or behaviour, or to improve the welfare of the child. However, not all local authorities have services in place to provide the necessary support to parents on such orders.

Electronic tagging and monitoring of offenders over 16 years was first introduced in 1995 under the Criminal Procedure (Scotland) Act which allowed for courts to impose a RLO. From 2004, and introduced as part of the raft of policies to assist with meeting the target of reducing the number of persistent young offenders by 10% by 2006, young people aged under 16 years can become subject to Intensive Support and Monitoring Services (ISMS).[13] This is a new alternative disposal by the Children's Hearing System for young people who meet the criteria for secure care, that is: that the young person is likely to abscond and, if so, is likely to be at risk and; is likely to injure herself or others.[14] The conditions are to be applied where the Hearing believes it will help stop persistent offending or if the welfare needs of the child might be addressed through such a measure. Monitoring will essentially restrict young people to, or away from, certain locations at particular times.[15]

Although the Scottish Executive claim that ISMS are designed with welfare needs of the child in mind, it is hard not to see this and other similar developments as signaling a shift from the welfarist concerns and ethos of minimal intervention espoused by Kilbrandon. Of crucial significance here, is that these measures are being implemented in a context of falling crime rates, and in which convictions for young offenders under 21 years are decreasing (Table 18.1 shows that, overall, the rates of convictions of 16–21 year olds have decreased over the past 10 years), and offence referrals to the Children's Hearings System are relatively stable. Furthermore, as Stevenson and Brotchie (2004) maintain, there is perhaps an irony in these major changes in the penalisation of children's behaviour coming at the same time as a clear public rejection of proposals to abandon the Kilbrandon approach of responding to all children within a unified Hearings system that does not distinguish between "offenders" and other vulnerable youngsters.

[13]After public consultation, s. 70 of the Children (Scotland) Act 1995 was amended to allow for the alternative disposal of ISMS by Children's Hearings.

[14]The Scottish Executive anticipate that only a small proportion of 'persistent offenders' will be viewed as suitable for an ISMS. There are around 800 persistent offenders reported to the Reporter each year (Scottish Executive, 2004a) and about three quarters of young people who receive a secure authorisation are actually placed in secure accommodation.

[15]The maximum length of time a young person can be tagged for is 6 months with a review period after 3 months.

TABLE 18.1. Number of Persons with a Charge Proved per 1,000 Population, 1993–2002

	1993	1994	1995	1996	1997	1998	1999	2000	2001	2002
All persons										
Total	40	39	38	37	37	34	31	29	29	31
Under 16	0.3	0.3	0.4	0.3	0.3	0.3	0.2	0.1	0.2	0.3
16 years	42	43	46	44	42	42	36	26	27	31
17 years	109	103	110	116	112	103	94	82	79	77
18 years	142	136	142	153	148	130	116	114	114	109
19 years	137	127	126	135	138	126	115	104	111	113
20 years	124	125	116	125	124	115	107	99	107	108
Males										
Total	66	66	64	63	62	58	53	49	50	51
Under 16	0.6	0.7	0.7	0.6	0.5	0.5	0.3	0.2	0.3	0.5
16 years	79	81	85	82	79	76	66	48	50	58
17 years	201	193	202	214	204	189	170	148	146	141
18 years	258	251	263	278	271	235	210	205	209	200
19 years	249	231	229	246	246	228	204	185	198	204
20 years	222	227	206	224	221	203	191	174	192	189
Females										
Total	13	11	11	11	10	9	8	8	8	9
Under 16	0.02	0.03	0.06	0.05	0.04	0.02	0.02	0.03	0.02	0.01
16 years	7	5.9	9	7	7	8	5.8	5.4	4.3	5.8
17 years	20	16	18	21	21	20	19	17	15	16
18 years	27	23	25	28	28	27	25	24	23	22
19 years	27	22	24	25	27	25	25	23	25	24
20 years	28	25	24	26	26	26	25	24	23	26

Source: Adapted from Scottish Executive, *Criminal Proceedings in Scottish Courts*, 2002, Table 5.

3. TRENDS IN OFFENDING BEHAVIOUR

Accurate figures on the "true" extent of offending by young people are not available. Recorded crime figures do not include information about offenders. Data about the number, age and gender etc. of offenders only becomes available within the criminal proceedings data and the conviction data. Gathering comparable and reliable information about the numbers of young people going through the Children's Hearing System and the criminal justice system is rather problematic as some agencies count cases, not individuals (e.g., number of reports to the PF) and some young people commit more than one offence (and so can go though the system(s) more than once in any given year). An individual may be proceeded against on more than one occasion over the course of the year, with several charges involved on each occasion. Those under 21 are more likely than older offenders to be convicted on a number of occasions and hence to be counted more than once.

3.1. Young People in the Criminal Justice System

A review of the offender files carried out by the Scottish Criminal Records Office in 2001 revealed over 76,000 recorded offenders under the age of 21 years (including those whose cases were still pending). According to Audit Scotland (2001: 10) this represents one in twelve young people in Scotland.

In 2002, 24,881 (or 24%) of the 106,096 male offenders in Scotland with a charge proven against them were aged under 21 years. In the same year, 3,033 (or 16%) of the 18,499 female offenders in Scotland were aged under 21 years. The peak age of conviction was 19 years. For males and females aged under 21 years, 19% and 30%, respectively, of convictions were for crimes of dishonesty.

3.2. Referrals to Children's Hearing System

The original report of the Kilbrandon Committee made it clear that the majority of cases coming before the Scottish juvenile courts were on offence rather than care grounds, although the majority were of a trivial nature. Less than 600 of just over 22,000 children and young people were cases of persistent truancy, children "beyond parental control" or victims of neglect or abuse. In a study completed shortly after the inception of the Hearings System, it was revealed that offence referrals predominated. Of 678 cases, 73% were offence referrals, with only 5% for parental neglect or an offence committed against a child (Martin et al., 1981).

Today's figures are dramatically different from those of the 1970s when the Hearings System was first incepted. The pattern of referrals has changed and, currently, the majority of cases referred to the Hearings System are on non-offence or welfare grounds, as Table 18.2 and 18.3 clearly show. It is important to note that these tables record numbers of grounds referred to the Reporter, not numbers of children; a child can be referred on several grounds at any one time.

As Table 18.2 shows, since 1991, the numbers of referrals on offence grounds have increased steadily, from 25,155 in 1991 to 30,129 in 2002, an increase of 19%; yet as Table 18.3 shows, the increase in referrals on non-offence grounds has been much more marked, from 18,366 in 1991 to 45,436 in 2002, an increase of 147%. Clearly, the demand on the System has increased substantially, although, to put it into perspective, the Hearings System deals only with a small minority of children in Scotland. Recent SCRA figures (2002–2003) suggest this is less than 4% of children in Scotland, although it is up from 2.4% in 1992.

For the last 20 years, the referral rates on offence grounds have remained relatively stable for boys (around 40–45 referrals per 1,000 population in the 8–15 year age group), whilst the rates for girls have risen (from 8 referrals per 1,000

TABLE 18.2. Number of *Offence* Grounds Referred to the Reporter by Year

Year	Boys	Girls	Total
2002/2003	–	–	30,129
2001/2002	–	–	29,179
2000/2001	21,901	4,865	26,766
1999/2000	24,844	5,789	30,633
1998/1999	23,027	5,186	28,213
1997/1998	23,060	4,502	27,562
1996/1997	23,656	4,449	28,105
1995	22,826	4,780	27,606
1994	21,440	4,295	25,735
1993	19,610	3,510	23,120
1992	21,015	3,574	24,589
1991	21,851	3,304	25,155

Source: Adapted from SCRA Annual Report, 2002–2003.

population in 1985 to 12 referrals per 1,000 population in 2000–2001). The peak age for offence referrals to the Reporter is 15 years for boys and 14 years for girls (SCRA, 2002–2003).

In 2002–2003, a total of 37,727 children were referred, the highest since the Children's Hearings System began. This increase is almost entirely due to an increase in children being referred on non-offence grounds; for example, there was a 102% increase in children referred on non-offence grounds and a 7% increase in children referred on offence grounds between 1992–1993 and 2002–2003 (SCRA

TABLE 18.3. Number of *Non-offence* Grounds Referred to the Reporter by Year

Year	Boys	Girls	Total
2002/2003	–	–	45,436
2001/2002	–	–	39,148
2000/2001	17,334	16,062	33,396
1999/2000	19,681	18,859	38,540
1998/1999	13,875	13,264	27,139
1997/1998	11,878	10,880	22,758
1996/1997	10,544	10,075	20,619
1995	10,418	10,166	20,584
1994	9,805	9,724	19,529
1993	9,835	9,885	19,720
1992	9,446	9,112	18,558
1991	9,508	8,858	18,366

Source: Adapted from SCRA Annual Report, 2002–2003.

Annual Report, 2002–2003). The majority of children referred to the Reporter in 2002–2003 were on non-offence grounds with similar numbers of boys (14,092) and girls (13,004) referred.

As Table 18.4 shows, 38% of children referred to the Reporter were referred on alleged offence grounds in 2002–2003 (i.e., 14,404 children aged 8 and over). This was for a total of 45,413 alleged offences, of which girls were referred for 8,495 of these alleged offence (an average of 2.6 offences per girl) and boys were referred for 36,891 alleged offences (3.3 offences per boy).

Over three times as many boys were referred on offence grounds compared with girls. Although, for the third year running, the number of boys referred on non-offence grounds (14,092) exceeded the number referred on offence grounds (11,177). In 2002–2003, 3,773 children were referred to the Reporter on *both* offence and non-offence grounds (SCRA, 2004: 15).

The SCRA data on numbers of offences and numbers of referrals per child is interesting vis-à-vis the debate concerning persistent offending and whether or not it is increasing. Research commissioned by the Scottish Executive in order

TABLE 18.4. Children Referred to the Reporter, All Grounds, as a Proportion of the Population, 2002–2003

Grounds	Children[a]	Percentage of population (%)[b]
All grounds (0–15 years)		
Boys	22,591	4.6
Girls	15,136	3.2
Total	37,727	3.9
Non-offence grounds (0–15 years)		
Boys	14,092	2.9
Girls	13,004	2.8
Total	27,096	2.8
Offence grounds (8–15 years)		
Boys	11,177	4.3
Girls	3,227	1.3
Total	14,404	2.8
Referred on both non-offence and offence grounds (8–15 years)		
Boys	2,678	1.0
Girls	1,095	0.4
Total	3,773	0.7

Source: Adapted from SCRA Annual Report, 2002–2003.
[a]"Offence" and "non-offence" grounds include children referred on both types of grounds, so individual children may be counted more than once. However children are only counted once in the "all grounds" category.
[b]Percentage of population figures were calculated from the "Estimated population by age and sex, Scotland, 30 June 2002," General Register Office for Scotland.

to establish baselines for youth justice system performance, suggest that 7% of children referred on offence grounds are defined as persistent offenders[16] and that they are responsible for 33% of all offences referrals. Persistent offenders are concentrated in nine local authority areas covering, mostly, but not all, the major cities: 20% of all offence referrals originate in the city of Glasgow (PA Consulting, 2004).

Earlier work on offending children in Glasgow and referrals to Children's Hearings showed that the most persistent offenders tend to be referred at a relatively early age and that a substantial proportion had already been formally identified as children in need of care and protection. Overall, most offending amounted to "minor thefts, assaults and disorderly behaviour" and 86% of alleged offences were committed by boys (SCRA, 2003).

In a recent pilot study for research into the social backgrounds of children referred to the Children's Reporter, perhaps unsurprisingly, high levels of social adversity were found including parental drug and/or alcohol misuse, domestic abuse, mental health problems (Wallace and Henderson, 2004).

4. PREVENTION OF DELINQUENT BEHAVIOUR IN SCOTLAND

4.1. Early Age Prevention of Antisocial Behaviour

The importance of social welfare and educational intervention to prevent later antisocial or delinquent behaviour was implicit in the Kilbrandon Committee's influential and radical review of Scottish juvenile justice. However, although the importance of "early years" investment was stressed it was not coherently reflected in policy or resourcing. A major research review on children and offending in Scotland conducted in the mid-1990s maintained that "Early intervention should be acknowledged as a key guiding principle on which to devise a strategy for preventing crime by children and young people" (Asquith et al., 1998). Yet the reality of early age provision was found to be "minimal," not planned on a comprehensive basis, and "dependant on the goodwill of local authorities" (Asquith et al., 1998).

Is the situation any better today following the devolution of legislative responsibility for criminal justice, social welfare and health issues from London to the new Scottish Parliament? Several separate programmes targeting vulnerable young children were launched to support the new social justice agenda. For example, Sure Start Scotland aims to support families with very young children so that they have the "best possible start in life." However, it was not until the publication of the Scottish Executive consultation Early Years Strategy (March 2003) that programmes were brought together in an approach based on

---

[16]That is, a young person with five offending episodes within a six-month period.

the integration of services to meet universal needs, at the same time as target-ing families and children needing extra support. The strategy built on existing initiatives to promote an integrated approach to local needs assessment, ser-vice planning, and service development across key agencies (local government, health, voluntary organisations, and parents). Recent research suggests that in comparison to Sweden, the "impact of these policies has been constrained by UK wide childcare policies which have targeted public investment in early years on disadvantaged areas, while stimulating a private childcare market for work-ing parents" (Cohen et al., 2004).

4.2. Specific Prevention of Delinquency

> On purely practical grounds it would seem essential to provide for pre-ventive and remedial measures at the earliest possible stage if more serious delinquencies are not to develop (Kilbrandon, 1964).

Early intervention was always meant to be an essential element of the Chil-dren's Hearings System, and, in many ways, it remains an early intervention sys-tem for those children who would benefit from compulsory measures of care and protection. However, critics of the system say that it has never been resourced sufficiently to fulfil Kilbrandon's original vision of prevention through welfare or to deal with the special control problems of offending children.

As highlighted earlier, Scotland has witnessed successive "pendulum" swings between a punitive approach, and a more welfare-based philosophy. At present there seem to be two contrasting political narratives about young people and crime in Scotland. On the one hand, young people are scapegoated as the main perpetrators of general disorder and antisocial behaviour. Authoritarian and punitive responses are invoked such as electronic monitoring, eviction of "nui-sance" families from public housing, and increased police powers of dispersal of groups (Antisocial Behaviour Act 2004 (Scotland)). On the other hand, strate-gic approaches to the prevention of offending, especially the role of parenting, have been explicitly included in youth crime strategies. The Report of the Advi-sory Group on Youth Crime (2000) urged the new Scottish Parliament to place "greater emphasis on prevention, diversion and the concept of restorative jus-tice, including the victim perspective" in its youth justice programme. The Report also maintained that "Early intervention programmes delivered jointly through social work, health, housing and education can help here as can the wide range of social inclusion and community initiatives." General preventative programmes recognised the need for "increasingly effective universal provision for all children and their families to reduce or compensate for conditions which expose children to harmful behaviours of all kinds" (Scottish Executive, 2000).

Subsequently the 10 Point Action Plan (referred to earlier) identified two key strands of prevention: (1) the provision of educational, cultural, sport and voluntary activities for all young people to give opportunities to fulfil their potential, and; (2) early intervention measures aimed at tackling the root causes of offending behaviour, through a coordinated partnership of local authority departments, the police, parents, schools, health and the voluntary sector. Local youth justice strategy groups are charged with the development of effective preventative approaches by police, social work departments, schools, health professionals and so on, to avoid the need for children and young people to attend a Children's Panel: and to more closely integrate the youth justice system and an authority's service planning for vulnerable children. The programme also declared an intention to "identify how best to evaluate the impact that individual social justice programmes can have on reducing youth offending."

The Youth Crime Prevention Fund (£11 million over 3 years) was launched in October 2003 as part of this programme. The fund is to support new and existing projects that "reduce and prevent offending by young people through effective early intervention and by providing a range of support to children at risk of offending, their parents and families and by offering more effective support to victims."

4.3. Availability and Use of Evaluated, Effective and Evidenced-Based Programmes

The Freagarrach Project for persistent juvenile offenders is a pioneering project based in, Central Scotland. It was established in 1995 and is operated by the children's charity Barnado's, and funded by the Scottish Executive and local authorities. An evaluation of the first 5 years work indicated that offending by young people attending the project decreased overall by between 20% and 50% in their first year. The study also found evidence that the project had succeeded in reducing the risk of longer term offending (Lobley et al., 2002).

5. POLICE INTERVENTION

There is no national police service in Scotland and therefore no standard model for juvenile justice services across the eight regional police forces, even though all forces are now working towards national standards. The chief constable of each force carries ultimate responsibility for the work of the police in their area subject to the legal framework provided by statute and case law. At a national level the Deputy Chief Constable for Central Scotland Police briefs on, and coordinates, work on youth issues within the Association of Chief Police Officers Scotland (ACPOS) Sub-Committee on juvenile justice.

The police are key gatekeepers to the youth justice system. All "beat" police officers in Scotland are likely to encounter young people who are in trouble or at risk, and most Scottish police forces are believed to have appointed specialist officers with responsibility for youth issues across the whole force area. The role of the specialist officer is to take a strategic view of work with young people by police and to liaise with external agencies such as the criminal justice social work departments (local government) or voluntary agencies. For example, in the Strathclyde police force, which covers the Glasgow urban area and much of the west of Scotland, there are specialist juvenile liaison officers with administrative functions within each division.[17] These functions are (i) to process police reports to the Children's Reporter on both offence and non-offence grounds and; (ii) to coordinate the "contact card" system. Contact cards are filed by beat officers when they have reason to speak to a child, for example, out alone at an unreasonable hour, or causing some nuisance that falls short of criminal activity. The juvenile liaison officer refers the child to the Children's Reporter once three contacts are recorded.

5.1. Police Discretionary Powers in Juvenile Cases

There are three formal options for dealing with young people: a formal warning (for children who admit involvement in minor offending and where parents cooperate); a referral to the Reporter and: a referral to the PF (for serious offences). In practice, the police have a high level of discretion in decision-making, and this leads to concerns about variation in decision-making.

In practice, police officers do have discretion to administer informal warnings (an immediate "telling off") to children who are found to be committing a minor offence if they judge that to be an adequate response. Research has shown considerable inconsistencies in the practice of administering and recording warnings across the separate police forces (Audit Commission, 2002). In response to such criticism the Scottish Executive is currently implementing a national police restorative warning or caution system to take effect throughout Scotland by April 2006. Restorative cautioning has been piloted successfully in the Glasgow area since August 2003, but as yet there is no available evaluation of this system.

There has only been patchy availability of schemes offering a restorative option as an alternative to referral by the Reporter to a Children's Hearing, or local authority social work intervention. Pioneer diversion programmes such as the Fife Young Offender Mediation Project (begun in 1996 and evaluated by the Scottish Executive in 2000), have tended to be set up and managed as one-off local projects, usually by voluntary rather than official agencies. It is the Reporter who will use his or her judgement as to the suitability of a child for referral to such a scheme. However, the roll-out of the police restorative warning and conferencing programme

---

[17]A division is a territorial sub-division of a Police Force typically covering around 100,000 people and managed by a Superintendent or Chief Superintendent

referred to above, represents a significant step in developing a consistent service across Scotland.

5.2. Police Dealings with Children Under the Age of Criminal Responsibility

Children who have committed an offence under the age of criminal responsibility for whom an informal warning is inappropriate may be referred to the Reporter on non-offence grounds, for example, being beyond the control of their parents, and the local social work agency alerted. Where a police officer is called to a case of domestic abuse, for example, a report outlining the circumstances is forwarded to the Children's Reporter.

5.3. Protection of Procedural and Individual Rights of Juveniles Protected (Police)

Police procedures in relation to custody are defined by statute. Under the Criminal Procedure (Scotland) Act 1995 the police may detain a child up to 6 hours if they suspect a serious offence (imprisonable) has been committed. After 6 hours the child must be released or charged.

If a police officer arrests a child under 16 he or she must inform his parents, or other responsible adult, immediately. There is no obligation on the police to inform a lawyer on behalf of the child although in practice this should be done. Where a child is detained and charged with a serious offence or there is "reason to believe that his liberation would defeat the ends of justice" the child must be kept in a place of safety other than a police station until he can be brought before a court (usually the next working day). In practice this usually means a call to the duty social worker who will take the child to local authority residential care.

Where an "unruly certificate" is issued the child is taken to secure accommodation managed by local authority social work departments. The principle is that public protection from a child that presents significant risk to others outweighs the best interests of that child (see below for more detail).

Demand for such secure places outstrips supply. The result is that some 14–16 year olds (30 in 2002) are held in prison establishments, usually in hospital blocks. Most of these children were charged with crimes of violence. In response to concerns the Scottish Executive has recently commissioned research (due for completion in October 2005) into the quality and level of provision of social work secure accommodation.

Police practice in relation to juveniles is controlled by legislation and therefore subject to scrutiny by the courts. There is no independent police complaints body in Scotland although the Minister of Justice has recently confirmed that a proposal to establish one will be introduced during the current parliamentary session. At present complaints are handled internally within each police force (e.g., by the "Professional Standards Unit" within Strathclyde Police).

Her Majesty's Inspectorate of Constabulary for Scotland acts independently to promote efficiency and effectiveness across all police forces through force and thematic inspections. There have been no thematic inspections of work with juveniles nor is one planned in the current programme.

The ECHR was incorporated into Scottish law as recently as October 2000 and the degree to which police procedures comply in relation to children has not yet been tested.

6. INTERVENTIONS OF THE REPORTER AND THE PROCURATOR FISCAL

The current system allows that a child who has committed an offence may be dealt with in one of two ways – by the Children's Hearings System via a referral to the Children's Reporter or by the criminal justice process via a report submitted to the PF. However, as outlined above, the underlying philosophy of the system and the resultant procedure are such that the vast majority of cases follow the first route. It is estimated that, currently, just 0.5% of young people under 16 years who have committed an offence are prosecuted.

If a child is reported for one of the offences detailed by the Lord Advocate, the police must also provide a copy of the report to the Reporter. The PF and the Reporter between them decide who will take responsibility for the case. Generally speaking, even when the offence does fall into one of the categories defined by the Lord Advocate, PFs take note of the fundamental principle of child welfare legislation on which the Scottish juvenile justice system is founded and only retain the case to be prosecuted before the courts in exceptional circumstances. One fundamentally distinct difference between the two processes was determined by the Court of Session in considering the case of *S v. Miller* (2001a). In this case, the court concluded the Hearing is not determining a criminal charge in terms of art. 6 of ECHR. As previously stated, the overarching concern with the welfare of the child is paramount and a Children's Hearing does not determine a criminal charge. As such, no distinction is made between a child referred on offence grounds and a child referred on non-offence grounds[18].

This particular arrangement means that there are two key players who may intervene in any juvenile offence case either before it proceeds to the lay tribunal of a Children's Hearing or the formal prosecution before a criminal court. There is a significant and fundamental difference between these two systems worth reiterating. Whilst formal prosecution deals purely with offending, the integrated nature of the Children's Hearings System is such that it does not deal exclusively with children who offend but also considers cases where a child is in need of care and protection. As such, and as noted earlier, the Reporter can deal with a juvenile

[18]For a fuller discussion see *S v. Miller* (2001a).

offender for a range of reasons as well as the alleged committal of an offence. In 2002–2003, for example, 3,773 children were referred to the Reporter on *both* offence and non-offence grounds (SCRA, 2004: 15). Furthermore, research undertaken by Waterhouse et al. (2000) found that a large proportion of children referred on offence grounds had already experienced a range of social adversity and had a history of non-offence referrals in the system.

6.1. Interventions of the Reporter

The principles of diversion are very much a central part of the Hearing System. These principles are realised both in the diversion of cases from the courts to the Children's Hearing and also in the initial action taken by the Reporters in response to referrals. The Reporter has a key role in promoting the diversion and early intervention aspects of the system.

The Reporter has three principal initial functions in relation to cases where a child has allegedly committed an offence. The first is administrative in receiving and recording the referral. The second is investigative; the Reporter may require additional information when considering the case, such as information from social work services, the child's school, and the police. The third function is deliberative in that the Reporter must decide how the case proceeds: the Reporter decides whether there is sufficient evidence to support the grounds of referral, and where insufficient evidence is available no further action is taken in the case. This outcome occurs in only a very small number of offence referrals (7% in 2002–2003).

In cases where the child is already subject to compulsory measures of supervision, the Reporter may decide that the current measures can deal appropriately with the new infraction and that therefore the case need not proceed further. The case will only proceed to a Children's Hearing if the Reporter is satisfied that compulsory measures are necessary. This is an important power placing the Reporter in a crucial role which allows him or her to filter out cases where an offence has been committed but where the child is not in need of *compulsory* measures of supervision. In Kilbrandon's original conceptualisation, although the commission of an offence is one of the possible grounds for compulsory measures of care, in itself an offense is *not* a sufficient basis for ordering compulsory measures for care (Asquith et al. 1998: 425–426). Underpinning this important decision are the key principles of *paramountcy* which instruct that the Reporter's key concern is with the welfare of the child, and *minimum intervention* which stipulates that a requirement or order should only be made where "it would be better for the child that the requirement or order be made than that none should be made at all" (s. 16(3) of the CS Act 1995). Kearney (2000) calls the "no non-beneficial order principle."

A range of informal action is available to the Reporter when he or she has decided that compulsory measures are unnecessary. This may take the form of an informal discussion or warning involving the child and his or her parents or indeed, the Reporter may ask the police to warn the child. Alternatively, the Reporter may decide to refer the case to the local authority for "advice, guidance and assistance"[19] and suggest a period of *voluntary* support. The voluntary nature of this approach mean that it is only when the Reporter believes that such a measure is likely to be accepted by the child and/or family and furthermore, that it will prove beneficial to them that this mode of action will be employed. The voluntary measures available are varied in their content and range from vocational projects to restorative justice schemes.

The Reporter's discretionary powers are considerable, although there are moves afoot to structure, if not constrain, that discretion, partly as a result of apparent disparities in practice highlighted by a report by Audit Scotland (2002).

Statistics from SCRA show that these diversionary powers have increasingly been employed by Reporters in the last 10 years (see Fig. 18.1). In 1991, 31% of offence grounds proceeded to a Children's Hearing and informal action, including referral to the police or local authority, was initiated for 46% of offence grounds. By 2000/2001 however the proportion of offence grounds where the Reporter arranged a hearing had decreased by 7% and the proportion where the Reporter had decided to follow an informal route had increased by 7%. It is notable that the decrease in referrals to hearings and the concurrent increase in diversionary practice are most significant following the inception of the Children (Scotland) Act 1995 which installed the "minimum intervention" principle discussed above.

6.2. Interventions of the Procurator Fiscal

Whilst in the vast majority of instances of juvenile offending in Scotland the case is referred to and processed by the Children's Hearings System, each year a small number of cases are retained by the PF. There are parallels between how

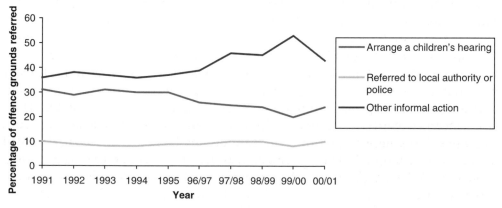

FIGURE 18.1. Trends in initial action taken by Reporters on offence grounds referred.

[19]Section 56(4)(b) of the Children (Scotland) Act 1995.

the Reporter responds to an offence referral as detailed above and how a PF responds to an offence report.

In similarity between the two roles, the PF receives all police reports, makes the important decision about whether to prosecute and then determines the venue and type of procedure under which the prosecution will take place. Furthermore, on deciding not to prosecute, the PF can choose to employ a range of diversionary actions. One key difference between the PF and the Reporter lies in the nature of these diversionary measures. In Scotland, the public prosecutor has powers under common law and statute to deal with cases reported to them by taking other forms of action apart from prosecution. The PF can issue a warning much like the Reporter although the Fiscal warning is of a more formal nature. Alternatively, the PF has a statutory power that allows him or her to make a conditional offer to the accused of a fixed monetary penalty.[20] Conditional offers such as fixed penalties or driving licence endorsements (e.g., penalty points) are often used for cases involving minor road traffic offences. For both the Fiscal fine and the fixed penalties for driving offences, the accused persons may reject the offer and the case will proceed to court, although it is notable that around 80% of these offers are accepted. The PF may also refer the accused to a diversionary programme involving the supervision of a social worker, psychiatrist or psychologist and reparation and mediation options are also available.

Whilst, strictly speaking, all of these diversionary actions are accessible to PFs when processing a juvenile offence case, as noted above only a small number of juvenile cases are retained by the PF. Generally speaking, when a PF does retain such a case it is with the intention to formally prosecute in court. Where a PF may feel it appropriate to divert the child from formal prosecution, this diversion will almost always be a referral to the Reporter. The spirit of the law underpinning the Scottish system of juvenile justice allows little scope for PFs to employ alternative diversionary measures for juvenile offenders.

As stated earlier, in 2002, the report by the Improving the Effectiveness of the Youth Justice System Working Group introduced a set of national standards specifically for youth justice services (Scottish Executive, 2002a, b). These standards recognise the importance of swift interventions for offence cases in the Children's Hearings System and a distinct set of time interval standards were drafted by the group which further reduce the acceptable time for each stage of the process: police reports must be received within 10 days of caution and charge date rather than 14; The Reporter must make a decision on the case within 28 working days of receiving the report rather than 50; and the first hearing should be scheduled to take place within 15 working days rather than 20. These standards are being applied in the Fast Track pilot project for persistent offenders, mentioned earlier, which is currently being operated in six local authority areas in Scotland.

---

[20]The levels of the 'Fiscal Fine' are set by an order of the Secretary of State, and are currently £25, £50, £75 and £100.

6.3. Pre-trial Detention

One particular and significant aim of the Scottish youth justice system is that no child shall be detained for any prolonged period of time except on the authority of a sheriff or a Children's Hearing. As such, the detention of young people who have committed offences *before* their case is considered by a Children's Hearing or by a judge in court, although possible, is rare.

Generally, a child who is arrested for an offence will be released on the basis of a legal requirement to attend at court or at a Children's Hearing on a future date when the case will be considered. In certain exceptions where the alleged offence is of a more serious nature, they may be detained in a "place of safety" (such as a residence provided by the local authority, a police station, a hospital, or other suitable place) until he or she can be brought before a sheriff or a Children's Hearing. In such cases the offence will be jointly reported to the PF and the Reporter. At the earliest opportunity, they will reach a decision on how the case is to progress – whether through the Hearings system or through the courts.

In those cases where the PF retains the case, the child will be brought before a sheriff in court on the next lawful day, and if it is decided to proceed to trial, and bail is opposed, the sheriff may order the detention of the child. Special considerations apply to the place where the child may be detained in this instance.[21] For children under 16, the child should be in the supervision of the local authority social work department rather than commit him or her to prison. If the child is over 16 and subject to a supervision requirement, the court may place the child with the local authority rather than in prison. Those children who are over 16 and not on supervision, and those between the ages of 14 and 16 who are "certified by the court to be unruly or depraved"[22] shall be committed to a remand centre where a place is available.

It is notable at this point that in the case of *S v. Miller* (2001a), judges in the Court of Session ruled that whilst the placing of a child in secure accommodation under the supervision of a local authority does amount to deprivation of the child's liberty in terms of art. 5 of the UN Convention on the Rights of the Child, this is justified for the purposes of "educational supervision" of a minor in terms of art. 5(1)(d). This arose from recognition by the Court of two significant points. First, the requirement for Children's Hearings to hold the child's welfare as their paramount consideration in making any decision and second, the obligation on managers of secure establishments in Regulation 4 of the Secure Accommodation (Scotland) Regulations 1996 to "ensure that the welfare of a child placed and kept in such accommodation is safeguarded and promoted and that the child receives such provision for his education, development and control as is conducive to his best interests."

[21]Section 51(1) Criminal Procedure (Scotland) Act 1995.
[22]Section 51(1)(b) Criminal Procedure (Scotland) Act 1995.

6.4. Guaranteeing the Rights of the Child in Situations of Pre-Trial Detention

The Children's Hearing (Scotland) Rules 1996 in Rule 11 gives the child and parent a right, separately, to invite a representative to attend a hearing. The representative may assist the person represented in the discussion of the child's case and can be anyone, for example a sibling, a friend, a teacher or a lawyer. In this context however, a lawyer does not attend in the role of a legal adviser and indeed until recently, there was no provision for paid legal representation at any Hearing. This particular position was not an objection to the presence of lawyers or to lawyers acting as representatives at hearings but instead to ensure that the children and other parties present could speak for themselves rather than have lawyers to speak "on behalf" or instead of them. In the case of *S v. Miller* (2001b), the Court of Session considered whether the non-availability of legal aid at a Children's Hearing contravened the child rights under art. 6(1) of the ECHR. The Court found that in certain cases, the absence of any possibility of paid legal representation may represent an infringement of the child's rights in this sense. Accordingly the Scottish Executive, in The Children's Hearings (Legal Representation) Scotland Rules 2001, provided for the appointment of legal representatives in situations where legal representation is required to allow the child to effectively participate at the Hearing; or where it may be necessary to make a supervision requirement which includes a secure accommodation authorisation.[23]

Where the child is brought before a sheriff in court, the case follows the normal processes of any case being brought from custody on a criminal charge, free legal representation is available automatically to the child. A duty solicitor is available at all Sheriff courts to advise and represent people held in custody at their first appearance.

7. SENTENCING AND SANCTIONS

7.1. Children Under 16

In 2002, 128 under 16 year olds had a charge proved against them in the adult court system (11 in the High Court[24]). Nearly all of these more serious offenders

---

[23]The rules do not extend to a pre-emptive appointment of a legal representative for custody or emergency hearings where a secure warrant may be considered. In *Martin v. N* (2003), the Court of Session ruled that this was not a breach of the child's ECHR rights even if a secure warrant was the decision. However, the ruling did recommend that in cases where the emergency hearing did issue a secure warrant, it should at the same time appoint a legal representative and arrange a further hearing as quickly as possible at which the legal representative can attend.
[24]Scottish Parliament, 4. October 2004, Answer to Question by Mr. Kenny MacAskill (Lothians) (SNP) (S2W – 10867).

were boys (125 boys, 3 girls). Of the boys, 23 were sentenced to custody (to be held in local authority secure accommodation).

In 2003–2004, 5 children under 16, sentenced by the adult court system, were held in adult prisons for a few days waiting transfer to secure accommodation. However, as has been explained above, it is also possible for children to be held in prisons under the "unruly certificate" procedure before sentence. Figures for 2003–2004 indicate that, of the 18 children affected, most (13) were held for under 14 days, usually in Young Offender Institutions.[25]

Children's Hearings have powers to make orders in the best interests of the children and local authority social work departments must implement these. The imposition of "compulsory measures of supervision" is the most common outcome and may include a variety of conditions such as where the child should live. The period of supervision is not defined but must be reviewed at least once a year. On 30 June 2003 about 1% (10,137) of children in the population were subject to a supervision order. This figure has remained stable over the last decade (Scottish Children's Reporter Administration Annual Report 2003–2004).

In 2003–2004 there were 242 admissions to secure accommodation. Of these, 71% come through Children's Hearings and the remainder through courts. The average number of children held in the system was 92 (15% up from 2000) and the average age on admission was 14 years and 5 months (*Children's Social Work Statistics 2003–4*).

As stated earlier, the new powers in the Antisocial Behaviour (Scotland) Act 2004 introduce electronic monitoring for under 16 year olds, intended as an alternative to placement in secure accommodation.

7.2. Young People of 16 and 17: Youth Court

There have been the introduction of a number of specialist courts in Scotland in recent years, including the drug court, the domestic abuse court, and the youth court. Some of these are still at the pilot stage. The Ministerial Group on Youth Crime (Scottish Executive, 2002a, b) recommended the establishment of a study of the feasibility of introducing a Youth Court for 16- and 17-year-old persistent offenders into Scotland. A Feasibility Group reported in December 2002 to the Justice Minister that a Youth Court was feasible under existing legislation, and shortly after, in June 2003, a designated Youth Court was established in one Sheriff Court as a 2-year pilot.

The first stage of the evaluation of this project has been published (McIvor et al., 2004). This evaluation covers the first 6 months of the pilot and is mostly concerned with procedures rather than outcomes. A second pilot Youth Court has now begun in a second Sheriff Court. The Scottish Executive intend, over the

---

[25]Scottish Parliament 19. 07. 04. Answer to Question by Christine Grahame (South of Scotland) (SNP) (S2W – 9381).

next few years, to extend the Youth Courts to all jurisdictions in Scotland subject to the results of the pilot evaluations.

The Youth Court is formally part of the Sheriff Court. There is no new legislation governing the court. Practitioners are guided by documentation produced by the Scottish Executive Justice Department. The target group for the Court are "persistent" 16- and 17-year-old offenders. The evaluation by McIvor et al. shows that, in practice, the police report all offences committed by 16 and 17 year olds to the PF who then decides whether these cases are suitable for the Youth Court or for the Hearings system.

"Persistent offending" is a criteria for allocation to the Youth Court. The definition of persistent offending used here is "at least three separate incidents of alleged offending in the previous six months" (including the current charge). The other criteria for allocation to the Youth Court are "contextual criteria" which lead the police and/or the PF to believe that the offender is vulnerable to progress to more serious offending which would diminish community safety.

The evaluation by McIvor et al. (2004) shows that almost twice as many offenders were referred to the Youth Court by the Fiscal on "contextual" grounds than on the grounds that they were persistent offenders. The "contextual grounds" used by the Fiscal were often the threat to public safety through carrying offensive weapons (possession of an offensive weapon is an offence). There is some concern expressed in the evaluation that this was a rather different interpretation of "contextual grounds" from that envisaged in the Executive's documentation where context referred to the domestic or personal conditions of the offender.

The feasibility study estimated that around 600 cases involving persistent young offenders would be referred to the Fiscal for the Youth Court in a year. There were 147 referrals involving 120 young people in the first 6 months of the pilot, far less than anticipated.

An important aspect of the Youth Court is the "fast tracking" of cases. Targets are set for each agency to try to ensure that cases are processed more quickly than would happen in the normal working of the Sheriff Court. The evaluation shows that these targets are largely being achieved. There have also been relatively small numbers of not guilty pleas and adjournments which have also resulted in speedier processing of these cases.

It is perhaps reassuring to note that, despite being presented as a "get tough" policy intended to tackle persistent and serious offending and promote community safety, another key stated objective of the Youth Court is to "promote the social inclusion, citizenship and personal responsibility of the young offenders whilst maximising their potential" (Scottish Executive, 2003).

7.3. Sanctions

The following sanctions are available to all of the courts in Scotland (including the Youth Courts).

(a) Prison
(b) Community Service Orders
(c) Probation
(d) Drug Treatment and Testing Orders
(e) Restriction of Liberty Orders
(f) Supervised Attendance Orders
(g) Fines
(h) Structured (and other) deferred sentences
(i) Absolute discharge, caution and admonition

7.4. Sentencing in the Youth Court

In the first 6 months of the Youth Court, deferred sentences were passed in 35 cases, a further 65 cases were sentenced (see Table 18.5) and 7 young people were found not guilty or had a plea of not guilty accepted.

As anticipated, the Youth Court appears to be making extensive use of the community sanctions which have been made available. As with Fast Track Hearings, these community disposals are better resourced than usual. Only 7 out of 100 cases have resulted in custodial sentences. The community sanctions were combined in diverse ways. No doubt these sanctions were intended to fit the circumstances of the case, but this raises possible concerns about consistency and proportionality in sentencing.

The Youth Court has also made extensive use of "structured deferred sentences." This requires some further discussion. Deferred sentences are commonly

TABLE 18.5. Disposals in the Youth Court, June–December 2003

Disposal	No of individuals
Probation	20
Fine	12
Probation and Restriction of Liberty Order (RLO)	8
Custody	6
Probation, RLO and Community Service Order (CSO)	4
Probation and CSO	3
RLO	2
Fine and CSO	2
CSO	2
Custody and fine	1
RLO and deferred sentence	1
Probation, RLO and fine	1
Probation, CSO and fine	1
Probation and deferred sentence	1
Admonition	1
Total	65

used in the adult court. A Sheriff will defer sentence for a period of time to allow the offender to demonstrate that he or she has changed their behaviour. If this is achieved, typically, the offender will be admonished on return to court. The Scottish Executive has provided the Youth Court with additional resources to fund programmes which can be attached to a deferred sentence. (These resources are not typically available in the adult court.) A "structured" deferred sentence means that the young offender agrees to participate in particular programmes. After the successful completion of these programmes, the offender returns to court and the expectation is that he or she will be admonished. The value of this sentence to the court is that it allows some work to be done to address offending behaviour without attaching a criminal conviction to the offender. The danger is that the offender is receiving a punishment which is disproportionate to the seriousness of the offence and that failure to complete the programmes to the satisfaction of the court may lead to an additional sentence. The range of services available to the court for a deferred sentence is similar to the services available for sentenced offenders.

Sheriffs can ask to review the progress of an offender on an order of the court. Although sheriffs in Scotland have always had the power to review court orders, this has not been a common practice. The evaluation shows that sheriffs have made use of their power to review cases. There is some concern expressed about the way in which review is exercised, some confusion about the purposes of review, concern about the sensitivity of information being discussed publicly in a review hearing etc. The Implementation Group are examining these issues.

7.5. Services Available to the Youth Court

There are a wide range of services for offenders available in the Youth Court. These are provided by a range of providers through the local authority social work departments. These include:

(a) Offending Reduction Programmes (offending is not the only choice,[26] PATH-WAY[27])
(b) Addictions services
(c) Remand fostering
(d) Family group conferencing
(e) Video interactive guidance
(f) Restorative justice services,
(g) Intensive intervention, mediation and reparation
(h) Intensive support, and a number of other social, cultural and educational programmes.

---

[26]Scottish Executive Youth Court Feasibility Project Group Report (2002), p. 10, *Offending is not the Only Choice*.
[27]Scottish Executive Youth Court Feasibility Project Group Report (2002), p. 11. *PATHWAY*.

A dedicated Youth Court social worker will write a social enquiry report (SER) for the court. The report will assess the offender using a risk/needs assessment instrument. An action plan will be drawn up by the social worker addressing the offending behaviour of the offender. The plan will identify particular services as relevant for the offender and may propose particular forms of intervention, but the role of the SER is solely to provide the court with information and the sentencing decision is made by the sheriff.

7.6. Sentencing of Young People aged 16–21 years

Nearly 10% (699) of all probation orders made in 2002–2003 were imposed on 16–17 year olds and about 20% (1,525) on 18–20 year olds. For community service, including probation orders with a condition of unpaid work the figures are about 7% (503) and 21% (1,542) (Criminal Justice Social Work Statistics, 2002–3).

Scotland has a high imprisonment rate overall compared with most other European jurisdictions. However there has been a reduction in the proportion of the total numbers of receptions into custody who are young offenders from 20.6% in 1994 to 15.1% in 2003. The absolute number dropped from 4,359 to 2,864 over that period. There has also been a 12% drop in the average daily population of young offenders from 720 (1994) to 577 (2003). Running contrary to this overall trend is the rise in numbers of young women going to prison but even this seems to be in reverse since peaking in 2002.

Table 18.6 shows the spread of court sentences for young people by gender in 2002. Custody as a percentage of all other sentences for 16–20 year olds has declined for young men. For young women, custody as a percentage of all other

TABLE 18.6. Spread of Sentences Imposed on Young People by Gender 2002

	Males					Females				
	Under 16 (%)	N	16–20 (%)	n	All (%)	Under 16 (%)	N	16–20 (%)	n	All (%)
Total	100	125	100	24,756	100	100	3	100	3,030	100
Custody	18	23	14	3,412	11	–	–	8	251	4
Community sentences	12	15	17	4,255	9	–	–	19	590	9
Financial penalty	22	27	56	13,880	71	67	2	47	1,424	71
Other sentences	48	60	13	3,209	9	33	1	25	765	17

Source: Adapted from Scottish Executive (2002) Criminal Proceedings in Scottish Courts, Table 11.

sentences rose markedly from 1997 (22%) and peaked in 2001 at 40%, dropping in 2002 to 30%.

Of all young people (1,979) received into prison in 2003, as many as 45% were there, not because they had been sentenced directly by a court, but because they had defaulted on the payment of an earlier financial penalty. However, this proportion has declined over recent years (1994: 53%) possibly as a result of the impact of alternative methods of fine enforcement such as supervised attendance orders. Even so, young people (and adults) continue to be imprisoned for this reason usually for very short periods. The time held in custody on default was 7 days or under for 71% of the young women and 52% of the young men (average 11 days) (*Prison Statistics Scotland 2003*).

There are no available statistics on the numbers of young people in prison. It is estimated that there is an average daily population of between 70 and 90, and that has been stable for the last 5 years or so. Although there were no statistics kept at the time, anecdotal evidence from prison governors[28] suggests that, during the time of the Borstals (i.e., up until the early 1980s) around 50% of the Borstal population were aged under 18 years. Currently, around 15–20% of the under 21-year-old prison population are aged under 18.

8. CONCLUSION

The rush to reform youth justice unleashed by the new Scottish government is but part of a radical programme of change across the criminal justice system as a whole against a background of seemingly unstoppable growth in the incarcerated population. There is a sense of needing to tackle long neglected issues. Nonetheless, the problem of crime in Scotland is seen by many to be essentially a problem of juvenile and youth crime. Dealing with this is a major political and social priority: government spending on youth justice is increasing significantly as policy changes and reforms and innovations across the complex system are negotiated and implemented.

In all this there remains the tension between the "correctional drift" seen elsewhere in the United Kingdom and the welfarism of the distinctive Children's Hearings approach to juvenile offending of which Scotland is proud. It might be that whereas the public rhetoric is punitive, the reality of work with troubled children and young people is more focused and constructive than before; that the idealism of Kilbrandon was a poor substitute for well resourced effective interventions in the lives of troubled children and that we are paying the penalty for this failure in record numbers in our adult prisons.

---

[28]By means of private correspondence.

REFERENCES

Adams, L. (2004). "New Helplines for Public to Report Unruly Teenagers," *The Herald*; 28 October 2004.

Asquith, S. (1983). *Children and Justice: Decision-Making in Children's Hearings and Juvenile Courts*. Edinburgh: Edinburgh University Press.

Asquith, S., et al. (1998). *Children, Young People and Offending in Scotland*. The Scottish Office, Central Research Unit.

Asquith, S. and Docherty, M. (1999) "Preventing Offending by Children and Young People in Scotland" in P. Duff and N. Hutton (eds.) *Criminal Justice in Scotland* Aldershot: Dartmouth.

Audit Scotland. (2001). *Youth Justice in Scotland: A Baseline Report*. Edinburgh: Audit Scotland.

Audit Scotland. (2002). *Dealing with Offending by Young People*. Edinburgh: Audit Scotland.

Audit Scotland. (2003). *Dealing with Offending by Young People: A Follow-Up Report*. Edinburgh: Audit Scotland.

Cohen, B., Moss, P., Petrie, P., and Wallace, J. (2004). *A New Deal for Children?: Re-forming Education and Care in England, Scotland and Sweden*. The Policy Press. University of Bristol.

Criminal Justice Statistical Bulletin: CrJ/2003/10 Criminal Justice Social Work Statistics 2002–03 Edinburgh: Scottish Executive.

Hallett, C. and Murray, C. with Jamieson, J. and Veitch, B. (1998) *Deciding in Children's Interests* Research Findings No 25. Edinburgh: Scottish Executive Central Research Unit.

Hill, M., Walker, W., Khan, F., and Moodie, K. (2004). *Fast Track Hearings Research: Interim Report Nov 2003*. Edinburgh: Scottish Executive.

Kearney, B. (2000). *Children's Hearing Systems and the Sheriff Court*. Edinburgh: Butterworths.

Lobley, D., Smith, D., and Stern, C. (2002). *Freagarrach: An Evaluation of a Project for Persistent Juvenile Offenders (Crime and Criminal Justice Research Findings No 53)*. Edinburgh: Scottish Executive Criminal Research Unit. Available at http://www.scotland.gov.uk/cru/resfinds/crf53-00.asp.

McIvor, G. et al (2004) *The Hamilton Sheriff Youth Court Pilot: The first six months* Edinburgh: Scottish Executive Social Research.

McNeill, F. and Batchelor, S. (2002). "Chaos, Containment and Change: Responding to Persistent offending by Young People," *Youth Justice*, 2:27–42.

McNeill, F. and Batchelor, S. (2004) *Persistent Offending by Young People: Developing Practice*. Issues in Community and Criminal Justice Monograph Number 3. London: National Association of Probation Officers.

Martin, F., Fox, S., and Murray, K. (1981). *Children Out Of Court*. Scottish Academic Press.

PA Consulting. (2004). *Scottish Youth Justice Baseline*. Glasgow.

Sawyer, B. (2000). *An Evaluation of the SACRO (Fife) Young Offenders Mediation Project*. Edinburgh: Scottish Executive.

Scottish Executive. (2000). *It's a Criminal Waste: Stop Youth Crime Now; The Report of the Advisory Group on Youth Crime*. Edinburgh: Scottish Executive.

Scottish Executive. (2001). *Blueprint for the Processing of Children's Hearings Cases: Inter-Agency Code of Practice and National Standards*, 2nd edn. Edinburgh: Scottish Executive.

Scottish Executive. (2002a). *National Standards for Scotland's Youth Justice Services: A Report by the Improving the Effectiveness of the Youth Justice System Working Group Edinburgh: Scottish Executive*. Edinburgh: Scottish Executive.

Scottish Executive. (2000b). *10 Point Action Plan for Tackling Youth Crime*. Edinburgh: Scottish Executive.

Scottish Executive. (2003). *The Report of the Feasibility Group on Youth Crime Pilots*. Edinburgh: Scottish Executive.

Scottish Executive. (2004a). *Children's Social Work Statistics 2002–3*. Edinburgh: Scottish Executive.

Scottish Executive. (2004b). *Children's Social Work Statistics 2003–4*. Edinburgh: Scottish Executive.

Scottish Executive. (2004c). *Criminal Proceedings in Scottish Courts 2002*. Edinburgh: Scottish Executive.

Scottish Executive. (2004d). *Police Restorative Warnings in Scotland: Guidelines for the Police*. Edinburgh: Scottish Executive.

Scottish Executive. (2004e). *Prison Statistics Scotland 2003*, Edinburgh: Scottish Executive.

SCRA. (2004). *Scottish Children's Reporter Administration: Annual Report 2002–03*.

SCRA. (2002). *Scottish Children's Reporter Administration: Annual Report 2001–02*.

SCRA. (2001). *Scottish Children's Reporter Administration: Annual Report 2000–01*.

Smith, D. (2004). *Parenting and Delinquency at Ages 12 and 15*. The Edinburgh Study of Youth Transitions and Crime. Research Report No. 3. University of Edinburgh.

Smith, D., and McAra, L. (2004). Gender and Youth Offending, The Edinburgh Study of Youth Transitions and Crime. Research Report No 2. University of Edinburgh.

Stevenson, R., and Brotchie, R. (2004). *Getting it Right for Every Child: Summary Report on the Responses to the Phase One Consultation on the Review of the Children's Hearings System*. Edinburgh: Scottish Executive.

Stow, L. (2004). "Warning Over Teen Gang Law," *The Evening News*, 28 Oct 2004.

The Children's Hearing Representative Group. (2004). *Report on Children's Hearings Time Intervals 2002–03*. Edinburgh: Scottish Executive.

The Kilbrandon Report: Report of the Committee on Children and Young Persons, Scotland (1964), Cmnd 3065, HMSO.

Wallace, K. and Henderson, G. (2004). *Social Backgrounds of Children Referred to the Reporter: A Pilot Study*. SCRA. Stirling.

Waterhouse, L., McGhee, J., Whyte, B., Loucks, N., Kay, H., and Stewart, R. (2000). *The Evaluation of Children's Hearings in Scotland*, Vol. 3: *Children in Focus*. Edinburgh: Scottish Executive.

Whyte, B. (2003) "Young and Persistent: Recent Developments in Youth Justice Policy and Practice in Scotland" *Youth Justice* (3) 2:74–85.

Court of Session Opinions

Martin v. N, 2004 S.L.T. 249

S v. Miller, 2001(a) S.L.T. 531

S v. Miller, 2001(b) S.L.T. 1304

19

Keeping the Balance Between Humanism and Penal Punitivism: Recent Trends in Juvenile Delinquency and Juvenile Justice in Sweden

Jerzy Sarnecki and Felipe Estrada

INTRODUCTION

Geographically Sweden is one of the margin members of the European Union. Sweden is also rather sparsely populated with a total population of 9 millions. During the last decades every cohort of children/juveniles consist of approximately 100,000. Since the age of legal responsibility in Sweden is 15 years and special legislation still applies for juveniles until they reach 21 years, the juvenile population could be said to consist of around 600,000. It is a well-established fact that the number of young people who have been reported for committing a crime has increased dramatically since World War II. This is not unique to Sweden and is often the same elsewhere in Europe (Estrada, 1999a). It is not unusual to see this change as continuous, that young people are becoming "worse and worse". An attitude like this obviously affects the measures that are involved in the development of juvenile crime. This report will present the measures against juvenile crime from a criminal (justice) policy perspective and highlight how this policy has changed over the past three decades. The report begins with a general background describing the history of the Swedish juvenile justice system. Thereafter the trends in juvenile delinquency[1] are analysed and the responses to crimes that are taken by the Swedish juvenile system are described in more detail. Finally we discuss how the current trends can be understood.

---

[1]The English concept "juvenile delinquency" has no direct equivalent in the Swedish language or in the Swedish legal system. Instead, in Sweden we usually speak of juvenile criminality, a concept which differs from juvenile delinquency in that it does not include so-called status offences, i.e., acts committed by juveniles which constitute a crime but are legal if they are committed by adults. The authorities' reactions in such cases have the character of social measures and are regulated by social legislation, not penal legislation. In this chapter the term juvenile delinquency is used synonymously with the Swedish concept of juvenile criminality and thus covers all acts which are subject to penal sanctions according to Swedish law.

J. Junger-Tas and S. H. Decker (eds.), International Handbook of Juvenile Justice, 473–504.
© 2006 Springer.

1. BACKGROUND – THE SWEDISH JUVENILE JUSTICE SYSTEM FROM A CRIMINAL POLICY PERSPECTIVE

Swedish criminal (justice) policy is characterised by its emphasis on a comprehensive perspective. In the national programme for crime prevention, it is thus stressed that criminal (justice) policy covers more than the measures against crime that the legal system carries out. Our report concentrates on the social and punitive side of criminal (justice) policy. Society's overall goal for criminal (justice) policy against juvenile crime in the post-war period can be said to be one *of diversion*. Criminal youths should be kept away from correctional treatment in general and prison in particular. In the post-war period, however, social reactions have changed. There is an emerging shift from treatment to punishment in programmes involving juvenile delinquents (For an overview of the situation in the rest of Scandinavia see Storgaard 2004).

Over the entire 20th century, it was clear in Sweden that measures against juvenile delinquents should be separated from measures against adult offenders.[2] As early as 1902, several laws were passed which followed this line of thinking. Instead of prison, "forced care" was introduced for criminal youths between the age of 15 and 17. In 1935, the Child Care Act was expanded to include young people between the age of 18 and 21. At the same time, youth prisons were established for young people who could not be treated within the social youth welfare system. Treatment in youth prisons was for an unspecified period of time, so that the time in prison was not set beforehand and was based on the needs of the young person and not on the act he or she committed.

After World War II, forced care was abolished and replaced by protective foster care in community homes. Prison sentences were limited even further for young people under 18. They were instead to be taken care of in the child care system, not in the prison system. This change was connected to a growing realisation of the negative repercussions on young people living in institutions. Youth welfare was increasingly aimed at preventive and supportive measures. Placing young people in institutions was reserved as a final measure. In the 1950s, a rather optimistic view prevailed of the chances of treating juvenile delinquents. There was a shift to thinking in terms of treatment rather than punishment.

In 1965, a new penal code was introduced which gave great support to the way of thinking that favoured treatment. Intervention against young people would be based on their personal circumstances. This meant that a more highly differentiated system of responses was developed. Youth prisons remained for young people who committed a crime for which the penalty prescribed was prison. Perpetrators also had to be between the ages of 18 and 20; only in exceptional cases were they under 18 or between 21 and 23. The time spent in youth prison continued to be unspecified. For young people between the age of

[2]This section is taken from Estrada (1999b) where additional Swedish sources also are listed.

15 and 17, the goal was to keep them away from the criminal care system and instead take care of them through the child care system. Responses that tended to involve treatment were now grouped under a penalty named "commitment to special care".

The treatment ideology underlying the penal code was criticised strongly from the very beginning. The debate focused on the lack of proportionality between the crime and its consequences. Given that the consequences were focused on the individual and not the crime, this opened the door for inhumane and unjust decisions according to some critics. It was further pointed out with growing frequency that treatment was ineffective. For an individual, it is humiliating to be locked in an institution no matter what name is given to this involuntary deprivation of freedom.

Thus by the end of the 1960s, the need for force and locking people up came under question. Positive effects could only be expected if the person receiving care was motivated by the treatment. Motivation was considered to improve if young people could be treated outside an institution. In the 1970s, there was thus a desire to avoid placing people in institutions and in forced care as much as possible. After a long debate, youth prisons were abolished in 1980. According to the new *Social Services Act* that entered into force in 1982, youth welfare would be based on voluntary commitment and mutual understanding. Forced care measures were allowed by the Act with Special Provisions on the Care of Young People (LVU). These forced care measures, however, should follow the intent of the *Social Services Act* and also be based on what is best for the young person. *Intervention should not be based on any interest to protect society or any similar aim.*

Responsibility for community homes was now transferred from the state to the county council, and their name was changed from community homes to Special Approved Youth Homes. The reasoning behind the rearrangement was that care should be provided nearer to home so that contact with family and friends could be maintained and so that continuity in treatment would be easier.

In the second half of the 1980s several revisions were made in the LVU with the aim of making the response from society faster and clearer. Demands for greater consequences, that is, increased consideration for the *seriousness of the act,* began to be made. A clear sign of the change in attitudes towards the role of the system of responses was given by the *Commission on Prison Sentencing* in 1989. The intervention of society is no longer justified based on the youth's need for care; rather, it is the seriousness of the criminal act that is the starting point in determining the consequences. *Equality before the law and proportionality replaced voluntary commitment and mutual understanding as guiding principles* (Tham 1995, 2001).

In 1993, *the Commission on Juvenile Crime* (SOU, 1993) presented its proposals for society's response to juvenile crime, which were essentially that there should be fixed, clear responses and that they should guarantee the citizen's protection under the law. The rules concerning the commitment of juvenile delinquents to social care were given a new form "so that punitively – motivated requirements for predictability, consequence and proportionality are given more space". Criticism aimed at youth homes administered by the county councils resulted in the establishment of National Board for Institutional Care (SiS) in 1993. The following year, the state assumed responsibility for youth welfare in the special approved youth homes.

Today, SiS has the responsibility for young people under 18 who have been sentenced to the new institutional care. The length of time for institutional care of young people is determined by the seriousness of the crime and is for no less than 14 days and no more than 4 years. Punishment is intended to be for a limited time. The proposal means that institutional youth care will in principle replace prison sentences for juvenile delinquents under 18. To give young people between the age of 18 and 20 a prison sentence as the consequence of their action still requires special circumstances.

Figure 19.1 gives a summary of the development in the number of young people in institutions in the post-war period. We can see that the number of people in institutions increased up until the end of the 1960s. In the 1970s, the number fell dramatically. The decrease ended in the 1980s and thereafter there is a slight increase in the 1990s (described in more detail below).

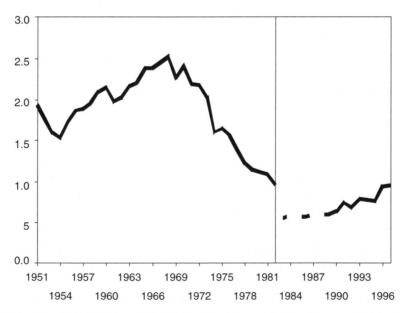

FIGURE 19.1. Young people aged 15–20 who have been admitted to community homes (or the equivalent) or prison on any given day, 1951–1982 and 1983–1997, per 1,000 inhabitants.

2. THE DEVELOPMENT OF JUVENILE CRIME IN THE POST-WAR PERIOD

Measuring the extent and development of juvenile crime is far from simple. Official crime statistics are the most accessible source, but they have their well-known shortcomings. Our knowledge, for instance, of an individual's propensity to report a crime, the work routines of the police or court routines and how they have all developed and changed over time is, unfortunately, far too unsystematic and insufficient. It is thus justifiable to remain somewhat sceptical about statistical pictures of crime as descriptions of the "real" development. In short, any attempt to produce an ideal description of crime trends should be based not only on official crime statistics, but should also utilise other statistics, such as victims studies and cause of death statistics, that are less affected by changes in the criminal justice system or in the methods used to produce the official statistics.

It is also well-known that the number of criminal offences registered in official crime statistics was much larger in the year 2000 than it was in 1950 and that this increase was to a large extent the result of an increase in theft offences (Smith, 1995; Pfeiffer, 1998; Estrada, 1999a; Westfelt, 2001; Falck et al., 2003). This is probably an expression of an actual increase in juvenile crime. But it is more uncertain what this increase looks like. Is it, as has often been claimed in both academic literature and public debate, a question of a continual, linear increase? Post-war criminological research into crime trends has been dominated by descriptions of an ever-increasing population of offenders (e.g., Wilson and Herrnstein, 1985; Smith, 1995; Pfeiffer, 1998). In more recent times, however, an alternative description has gained currency, highlighting a levelling off in this trend during the 1980s (Kyvsgaard, 1991; Estrada, 1999a, 2001; von Hofer, 2000, 2003; Westfelt, 2001). Figures 19.2 and 19.3 present these two alternatives. At the beginning of the 1990s, this question was debated in Swedish criminology. Which of the two descriptions holds true is of significance when the policy on juvenile crime is to be evaluated.

2.1. The Overall Crime Trend

Theft is the dominant – type of crime among young people. This has meant that the discussion about the development of juvenile crime has been about how theft has developed. In recent years, however, violent crimes among young people have become a more prominent issue (von Hofer 2000; Estrada 2001). Because violent crimes are far more unusual than theft, variations in violent crimes will disappear in general reports. In view of this, an analysis of general developments will first be given below and then followed by analysis of violent crimes.

Juvenile crime increased slowly in the first part of the 20th century (Fig. 19.4). It increased with greater speed starting in the 1950s, with the 1950s showing a doubling in the number of young people reported for committing a crime. This

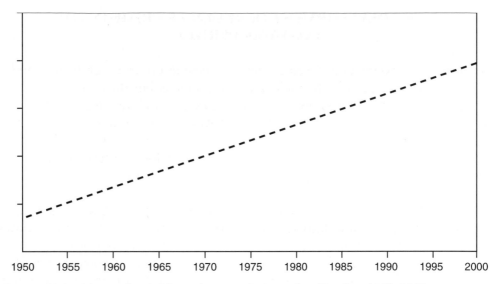

FIGURE 19.2. Alternative 1. Linear increase in juvenile offending 1950–2000.

strong rate of increase continued throughout the 1960s. At the beginning of the 1970s, the trend was broken, and since then there has been a *clear stabilisation in the statistics or even a decrease in the number of juvenile offenders*. The total level of police reported crime in Sweden increased up until the beginning of the 1990s, at which point it stabilised at a level slightly lower than that recorded in 1990.

The marked drop in theft convictions at the very end of the period should partly be seen in the light of major reorganisations of the police and the prosecutorial

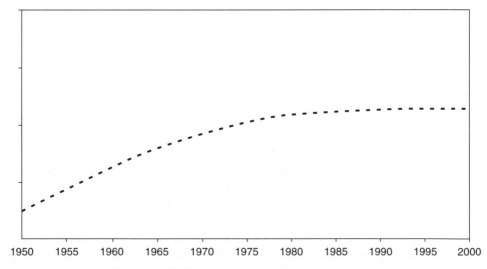

FIGURE 19.3. Alternative 2. Juvenile offending leveling off 1950–2000.

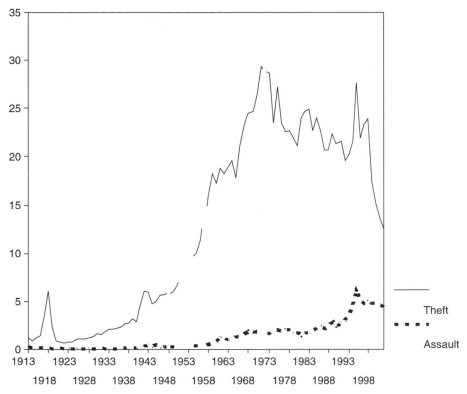

FIGURE 19.4. Youths aged 15–17 convicted of theft, respectively, assault 1913–2002 (per 1,000). Sweden.

systems in Sweden, which led to a loss of efficiency and to reduced output (von Hofer, 2003). This observation gives rise to the following classic question in relation to the use of crime statistics in general: to what extent are the described trends real, and to what extent are they simply the result of amongst other things procedural changes within the criminal justice system or variations in reporting behaviour? The most obvious answer is of course that both alternatives are true to a varying extent. In most of the countries in Western Europe, for example, statistics concerning *convicted* juveniles indicate a clear *reduction* over the last 20 years or so (as shown in Fig. 19.4; Estrada, 1999a). Those indicators which lie "closer" to the crime event however, and which are thus less sensitive to changes within the criminal justice system (such as statistics relating to suspects), suggest that the reductions are not real but are rather the result of "system effects" (a more detailed discussion is found in Estrada, 1999a). Thus the development in the number of young people suspected of committing crimes as outlined in the penal code has been stable for the last three decades in Sweden. Well worth noting is that the number of adults suspected has increased more or less in line with the development in reported crimes.

One problem with the crime statistics is connected to the decrease in the percentage of crimes that have been solved in the last few decades. A reduction in the number of crimes solved has been seen as suggesting a situation in which fewer and fewer criminal individuals are identified and reported for their crimes. It is therefore considered productive to check for such a relation by calculating the number of registered juvenile delinquents.[3] In that way, a "worst case scenario" on development is produced. These calculations, however, do not confirm that juvenile crime continued to increase at an unchanged rate over the entire post-war period. A reasonable conclusion is that, instead the number of juvenile criminals has been more or less stable in the last few decades. A reasonable hypothesis is thus that the increase in crime can be attributed above all to the increased number and activity of adult perpetrators. This interpretation is supported by the development in the types of crimes that are committed principally by young people. The number of crimes that are most closely identified as juvenile crimes has been unchanged while reports for other types of thefts, where young people constitute a smaller share of perpetrators, have increased.

2.1.1. Self-Report Studies

Alternative sources of information on trends in juvenile crime also indicate that the offending of young people has been relatively stable and may possibly even have decreased over recent years. The first large self-report study of juvenile crime in Sweden was conducted in the town of Örebro in 1971. Twenty-five years later, in 1996, this study was repeated using the same survey instrument (Ward, 1998). This study also indicated that variations in levels of self-reported crime were relatively small. Ward shows however a certain polarisation among the groups studied, with the group presenting the highest levels of criminal participation becoming both larger and more heavily involved in crime between the two surveys, whilst at the same time the size of the group reporting no involvement in crime whatsoever also became larger. National self-report studies were first started in Sweden in the mid-1990s (Ring, 1999, 2005). Since this point, four self-report surveys have been conducted on representative samples of pupils in school – year 9 (aged approximately 15 years). The findings from these surveys show that levels of self-reported drug offences and violent crime have been relatively stable between 1995 and 2003 whilst levels of theft offences and vandalism appear to have fallen off somewhat. The proportion of young people who report not having committed offences of any kind over the course of the previous year has increased somewhat from 19%

---

[3]The connection between the rate of crimes solved (the percentage of reported crimes that the police have solved) and the risk of discovery (the risk of a criminal being discovered and reported for a crime that was committed by him or her) is problematic. In essence, it can be said that the risk of discovery for the individual criminal has probably not decreased to the same degree as the percentage of crimes solved. This means that the calculations that have been made most likely overestimate the development.

in 1995 to 23% in 2003 respectively from 39% to 50% of the more serious offences. At the same time, it is worth noting that a large majority of the 15-year-olds surveyed (approximately 75%)[4] still report that they have committed one or a few offences during the past year. Relatively few youths report having committed large numbers of offences and the results suggest that the size of the group which is highly involved in crime has somewhat diminished.

Since property crimes dominate among the reported offences, the total level of self-reported crime has decreased. This decrease is greatest among the most socially well-adjusted respondents and those reporting the lowest levels of participation in crime, but it is also discernable among youths presenting much higher levels of delinquent participation and among those from socially disadvantaged backgrounds. It should also be pointed out, however, that the study includes a number of questions relating to the young people's experience of criminal victimisation. In contrast to the levels of self-reported crime, levels of reported victimisation as regards certain types of theft, threatening behaviour and violence remain fairly constant over the period examined. Taken together the existing data seems to suggest that *the post-war period does not appear to have been characterised by an ever expanding population of young offenders in Sweden.*

2.2. Juvenile Violence

Swedish criminologists are generally in agreement about the development of violent criminal activity among young people up to the 1980s (von Hofer, 2000; Estrada, 2001). Criminal statistics show that the number of young people prosecuted for assault remained at a low level until the end of the 1930s (Fig. 19.4). At the end of the 1950s, there was a clear increase. At the end of the 1960s, the increase stopped and up to the middle of the 1980s, the number of young people who were prosecuted for assault remained at a more or less stable level. Since the middle of the 1980s, assault statistics show a very large increase and in the 1990s we saw an increase in juveniles convicted for robbery (Fig. 19.5).

Some people, both academics and politicians, have interpreted these dramatic increases as reflecting a corresponding increase of juvenile violence. One problem with this interpretation is, however, that the increase is preceded by a clear change in public awareness of juvenile crime. "Youth violence" became the focus of the media in the summer of 1986, and politicians started campaigns, appointed commissions and amended legislation (Estrada, 2001, 2004). All of this may be considered to have affected citizens and institutions like the school's view on youth violence, and has therefore had an effect on people's propensity to report crimes. Our research shows, for example, that the number of cases of school violence

---

[4]If certain minor offences such as thefts from school or the respondent's home, and fare dodging on public transport, are ignored, the proportion of youths reporting having committed one or more (non-minor) offences during last year stood at 61% in 1995 and 52% in 2001 (Ring, 2005).

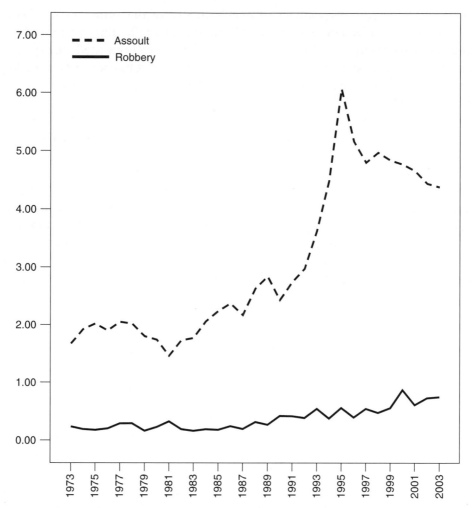

FIGURE 19.5. Youths aged 15–17 year olds convicted of assault and robbery, per 100,000 of population, 1973–2003.

reported to the police has increased substantially since the 1980s. An analysis of the police reports indicates that the explanation for the increase lies primarily in an increased reporting propensity. Significant changes have taken place in reporting routines (Table 19.1).

It is thus reasonable to question whether the official statistics on juvenile violence are the best source for describing the development of violent crime among young people in the period. In view of this, other indicators are of greater value.

2.3. Alternative Measures of Trends in Violence

Unlike the general levelling off described above the upward trend in violent crime is not corroborated by the available alternative indicators.

TABLE 19.1. Violence in Schools. Assaults on 7- to14-Years-Olds Reported to the Police. A Sample of Variables. Stockholm, 1981–1997 (%)

	1981–1992	1993–1997	Proportion of increase
Notifier			
Reported by victim or family	67	39	17
Reported by school	29	60	83
Method of notification			
Reported via visit to police station	67	39	21
Police called at school	19	9	2
Reported by phone, fax, other	14	51	77
Seriousness of assault			
Non-serious violence; violence leading to bruising, not requiring medical attention	33	49	61
Assault; violence leading to bleeding or requiring medical attention	46	41	37
Serious violence; violence leading to serious injury or emergency medical attention	21	10	2
Number of incidents	80–98	194–230	

$p < .01$ (for each variable). Variations in the number of incidents are due to missing data for the respective variables.

2.3.1. Victim and Self-Report Surveys

Since 1978, Statistics Sweden (www.scb.se) has carried out a nationwide survey asking a representative sample of 16- to 24-year-olds about their exposure to violence (see Nilsson & Estrada, 2003 for a presentation of this dataset). These victim surveys show an increase in the subjective experience of threats and violence. The level of more concrete episodes of victimisation on the other hand, and in particular of more serious violence, has remained more or less stable. A more detailed examination of these victim surveys suggests that juvenile violence increased somewhat from the mid-1980s to then level off again during the 1990s at the level of the late 1970s and early 1980s (Fig. 19.6). The statistics from victim surveys thus do not suggest a linear trend.

Since 1972, self-report surveys on drug use have been carried out in Stockholm among all students in year 9 (i.e., 15-year-olds). Between 1987 and 1998, these surveys also included questions on the students' experiences of violence. These surveys indicate that school children in Stockholm report neither that more of them have been assaulted, nor that more are carrying out assaults, nor even that they have witnessed more acts of violence during the years 1987–1998 (Estrada, 2001). Data for the years 1995–2001 from the nationally representative self-report study of crime among school children show stable response rates

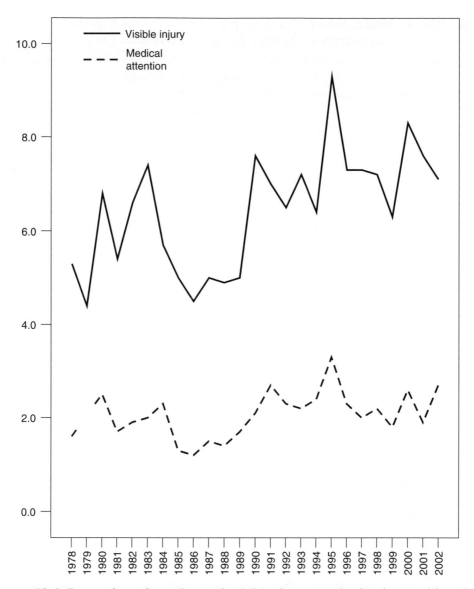

FIGURE 19.6. Proportion of youths aged 16–24 who report having been subjected to violence resulting in visible injury, or requiring medical attention, during the past year, 1978–2002.

in relation to levels of self-reported violent crime (Ring, 2005). A reasonable summary of the results of victim and self-report surveys is thus that they do not show a continual increase but rather that violent acts by youths have remained at a more or less stable level since the 1970s.

2.3.2. Hospital and Cause of Death Statistics

Since the end of the 1960s, Sweden has maintained a register of patients admitted to public hospitals. This patient register contains amongst other things details of the number of persons admitted as a result of assaults (Estrada, 2005).[5] There has been no general increase in the numbers admitted for hospital care as a result of violence (Fig. 19.7). The clear rise in numbers seen during the period 1968–1973 is probably most correctly interpreted as indicating the length of the start-up phase for the reporting system. It is interesting to note that the trend is reminiscent of the trend curve

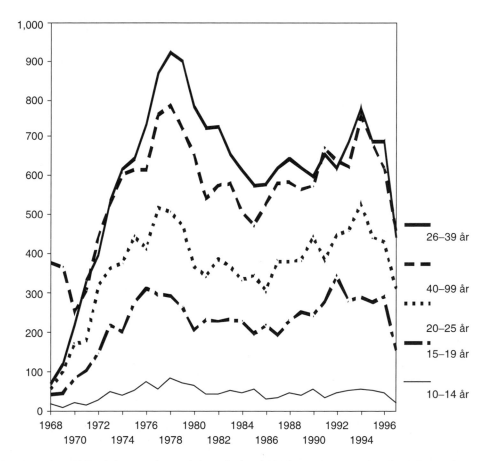

FIGURE 19.7. Absolute number of hospital admissions as a result of violence by age. Sweden, 1968–1997.

[5]Hospital admission statistics are presented in such a way that the same person being admitted several times during the same year will be counted once for each admission. The figures for 1997 should be regarded with caution since there has been both a change in the classification system and a drop in the quality of reporting.

indicated by the nationwide victim surveys presented above. The higher levels in the 1990s correspond well with those presented during the second half of the 1970s. Here too, the mid-1980s stand out as a low point. If the trends are studied in more detail, we find that the number of admissions among the youngest juveniles has fallen by 25% during the period 1990–1996 as compared with 1975–1979. For 15- to 19-year-olds, admissions during the 1990s lie at exactly the same level as they did during the second half of the 1970s, and for the older youths there has been a 5% reduction (Estrada, 2005). A reasonable summary is thus that the number of hospital admissions resulting from violence has remained at a more or less stable level since 1973 for youths aged 10–25 years. Whilst this does not constitute a direct indication that juveniles are not in fact committing crimes of this type, it does indirectly belie the perception that serious violence is on the increase among this group, since the perpetrators and victims of violence are most often drawn from approximately the same age group (Sarnecki, 2001).

The material from the patient register also allows us to follow the trend in the number of cases where the injury resulted from the use of a weapon. These cases obviously constitute a small proportion of the admittances but can be seen as an indicator of trends in more serious violence. Taken together the number of violent injuries resulting from stabbings or shootings has not increased during the period studied (Estrada, 2005).

Statistics relating to fatal violence are often seen as the most reliable indicator of the trends in violent offending since few cases will be unreported. Trends in fatal violence can therefore be used as verification for trends in types of violent offences characterised by a somewhat larger dark figure. Since the 1970s, violence resulting in death has not increased in terms of either the number of youths who are perpetrators or the number who are victims. The number of youths who die as a result of acts of violence has remained constant at approximately 16 individuals per year (Estrada, 2001, 2005). This suggests at the very least that any increases in juvenile violence that may have occurred have not affected the levels of the most serious forms of violence.

A reasonable summary of the results of victim and self-report surveys, hospital data and fatal violence is thus that they do not show a continual increase but rather that the number of violent acts committed by and against young people has remained at a more or less stable level since the 1980s. An integration of the interpretations of data drawn from alternative sources and crime statistics respectively leads therefore to the following hypothesis regarding violent crime in Sweden (and probably accurate for other parts of Europe too):

A change in criminal behaviour is not the principal reason for the rapid rise in the number of (particularly young) people being registered by the criminal justice system since the 1980s. This increase is rather the result of a marked shift in the way society responds to young people's actions. This change has occurred in parallel with an ideological shift, from the treatment ideology to a neo-classicist focus on just deserts, which has affected the politics of social control. Together, these tendencies have lead to an increasing propensity to report acts of violence, which has in turn led to a situation exhibiting all the classic characteristics of a deviancy amplification spiral (Hall et al., 1978; von Hofer, 2000; Estrada, 2001, 2004).

3. RESPONSES TO CRIMES COMMITTED BY YOUNG PEOPLE – A DETAILED DESCRIPTION

In Sweden the responsibility for responding to crimes committed by young people is shared by the social services and the judicial system (Sarnecki, 1991; SOU, 1993). The extent to which the judicial authorities and the social services share responsibility for the response to crimes committed by young people is mainly dependent on the age of the offender.

- For those below the age of 15, the main responsibility for the response to crime lies with the social services.
- For those aged between 15 and 17, (and in certain cases up to the age of twenty), the responsibility is divided between the social services and the judicial authorities.
- From the age of 18–20, the responsibility lies mainly with the judicial authorities.

3.1. The Judicial System: The Police

The Swedish justice system functions on the basis of the legality principle, which means that the police and other agencies within the justice system are obliged to intervene where the legal criteria that serve to define a criminal act are fulfilled. At the same time, however, the system allows for a large number of exceptions to this rule. In practice, therefore, as is the case in many other countries, the Swedish police have a large amount of discretionary power. When the police discover that a minor offence is being committed, their efforts are often limited to an order to cease and desist. If this is sufficient to stop the improper behaviour, the police do not report the matter. According to the legislation, the police have the right in certain cases to direct young offenders to repair the damage caused by their criminal acts. If the offender complies, the offence is not reported. In 1990, however, certain restrictions were introduced in relation to the police's right to exercise discretion in relation to the reporting of offences (RPS FS, 1990: 3).

According to Swedish law the police shall prevent, discover and investigate crimes. If a crime has been reported, the official task of the police is to investigate who committed the crime. As in most western countries, the police in Sweden have a low success rate (approximately 20%) when it comes to clearing up traditional crimes. This is true both for crimes committed by juveniles and those committed by adults. Nevertheless the police, and in particular those police who work with juvenile crimes, are familiar with most of the highly criminally active juveniles within a police district. The criminal activities of these young people are so extensive that even given the low risk of discovery, they will become the subject of a police investigation at some time or other. Furthermore, the police obtain substantial knowledge about the more active juvenile offenders through contacts with and interrogations of other juveniles, neighbourhood police work and other police activities.

In normal cases, the police are expected to investigate crimes committed by young people over the age of twelve, but such investigations are supposed to be carried out in collaboration with the social services. The principal objective with an investigation of this kind is to investigate the need for social measures. By law the police have the right to investigate crimes committed by younger children only in special cases. In addition, the last decade has witnessed a certain shift in praxis, such that schools, for example, have become more inclined to report offences committed by relatively young pupils to the police (see Table 19.1). The social services, however, still have the right to request that specific criminal investigations be suspended when they relate to persons under the age of 15.

Most investigations of juvenile crimes are relatively simple since the crimes committed by young people are usually not of a particularly serious nature. By law, the police are required to show great regard and care in their interrogations of juveniles. Parents and/or representatives of the social authorities should be in most cases present during an interrogation.

In different parts of Sweden the juvenile crime investigation issue has been resolved organisationally in variety of ways. In some areas, special units have been established which specialise in crimes committed by juveniles, or in some instances even certain types of juvenile crime, such as mugging, for example. In other areas, the less serious offences committed by juveniles are investigated by local community police officers whilst investigations into more serious offences are transferred to the central criminal investigation departments at the police district level. Irrespective of the way in which the police organise investigations of juvenile crime internally, this work always takes place in collaboration with the local social services.

If a suspect is under the age of 15, the police turn over the results of their investigation to the local social services. If the suspect is older then 15 the results of the investigation are turned over to the prosecutor. However, if the suspect is under 18, the social services are usually informed.

3.2. The Judicial System: The Prosecutor

According to current legislation, the police are to have a prosecutor assigned to an investigation if the offence is not of a "straightforward nature" and where there is a suspected offender aged 15 or older involved. In certain cases the prosecutor is the head of the formal investigation. The prosecutor is also responsible for deciding whether the suspect should be arrested and whether an application should be made to a court for a detention order. However neither arrests nor detention orders are utilised very often in relation to offences committed by juveniles. For an individual aged 15–17 to be detained during an ongoing investigation, the law requires "exceptional cause". One of the prosecutor's important tasks is that of deciding which measures should be taken regarding the suspect once the police investigation is finished:

- Should the preliminary investigation be discontinued?
- Should the prosecutor issue a prosecution waiver[6]?
- Should he or she issue a summary sanction order?
- Should he or she prosecute the suspect in court?

A preliminary investigation may be discontinued, for example, if it turns out that the act committed by the individual did not constitute a crime. The prosecutor may also find that the evidence is insufficient to warrant prosecution.[7]

A waiver of prosecution still constitutes a relatively common form of decision taken by prosecutors in Sweden (see Table 19.2) although its use has decreased substantially since the mid-1980s (Fig. 19.8).

TABLE 19.2. Convictions for 15- to17-Year-Olds, 18- to 20-Year-Olds and All Persons Sentenced by the Courts, or Awarded Prosecution Waivers or Summary Sanctions by the Prosecutor, 2001

	15–17 Years		18–20 Years		All ages	
Convictions	N	%	N	%	N	%
Imprisonment	3	0	733	7	11,113	10
Closed youth care	85	1	17	0	102	0
Psychiatric care	3	0	15	0	362	0
Probation	132	1	1,087	11	6,419	6
Suspended sentence	117	1	1,310	13	9,425	9
Care under Social Service Act	2,178	18	239	2	3,379	3
Fine by sentence	2,171	18	1,833	18	21,632	20
Fine by prosecutors decision	4,426	37	3,733	36	35,911	32
Waived prosecution	2,871	24	1,086	10	12,027	11
Other	43	0	280	3	10,341	9
Total	12,029	100	10,333	100	110,711	100

[6]A waiver of prosecution may be perceive as warning or conditional discharge and means that the guilty party will not be subjected to any further measures by the legal apparatus (on the condition that they do not commit any further offences) as a result of the act. However, the act will be considered a crime and will be recorded as such in the register of convicted persons. The prosecutor may issue a prosecution waiver in regard to less serious crimes but only if the suspect has admitted to the offence. In the absence of an admission of guilt, the matter must be tried by a court.

[7]The prosecutor may also discontinue a criminal investigation if the crime in question may be deemed to be insignificant in relation to another offence and if the costs of the investigation would assume unreasonable proportions, providing the sanction would not exceed a fine or a waiver of prosecution. In such cases however, the interests of other parties (e.g., those of the victim) may not be disregarded.

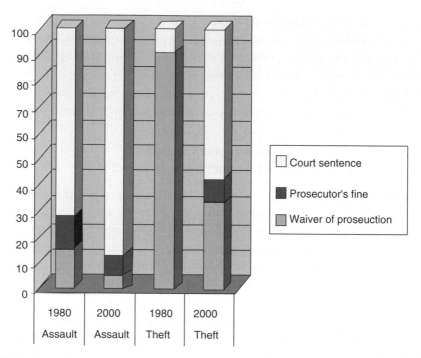

FIGURE 19.8. Youths aged 15–17 years who have been convicted by means of a court sentence, a prosecution waiver or a prosecutor's fine in 1980 and 2000, for assault and theft offences, respectively.

The Swedish Young Offenders Act (LUL 1964:167) gives prosecutors broad powers regarding the issuance of prosecution waivers when a suspect is below the age of 18, and in certain cases up to the age of 20. The rules are much more generous in relation to young people than older people. But the prosecutor may revoke a prosecution waiver if the young person returns to crime. In the legislation from 1988 on young offenders, the prosecutor's power to revoke such decisions was extended. The provisions regarding prosecution waivers were also made more formal and were to some extent given the form of a formal caution issued by the prosecutor to the juvenile and his parents. A further legislative change in 1994 (SFS, 1994: 1760) produced a situation whereby waivers of prosecution may in principal no longer be used for youths who have previously been registered in connection with offences.

Before a prosecutor issues a waiver of prosecution to a person under the age of 18, he or she often obtains an opinion from the social services if the offence is of a serious nature. When such a decision is issued it is often combined with the condition that suitable measures are to be undertaken by the social services. Prosecution waivers are issued only in extremely rare cases in relation to violent crimes or vandalism.

Another option available to a prosecutor is to determine the sanction for a crime himself or herself). The conditions for the prosecutor to be able to issue a summary sanction order are similar to those for a prosecution waiver: the crime must be relatively minor and the suspect must have confessed. In addition, the suspect must have accepted the size of the sanction. Summary sanction orders may be issued only in the form of day-fines, where the number of days is determined by the seriousness of the crime while the size of each day-fine is determined by the guilty party's economic circumstances. Approximately 33% of all the entries into the police register involve summary sanction orders. Among the youngest youths (i.e., those aged 15–17), the proportion is somewhat higher at 37%.

Finally, as was mentioned above, the prosecutor may decide to prosecute. Of the 15- to 17-year-olds who were convicted of offences in 2001, 61% received these convictions in the form of a prosecutor's decision whilst 39% were convicted by a public court, having been indicted by the prosecutor. The corresponding proportions for 18- to 20-year-olds were 51% and 49%, respectively. Thus the majority of the younger youths and approximately half of the older ones are convicted by means of a prosecutor's decision. By contrast, 15 years ago a significantly larger proportion (83%) of 15- to 17-year-olds were convicted by means of a prosecutor's decision as were 61% of the older group. Thus a considerably larger proportion and number of youths are today indicted for their crimes in a public court, whilst at the same time, the proportion and number of young people being convicted by means of a prosecutor's decision has fallen substantially.

3.3. The Judicial System: The Courts

When a prosecutor decides to prosecute an individual, his guilt and any possible sanction will be determined by the court. Of the approximately 4,600 juveniles aged 15–17 convicted annually by the courts in Sweden, 47% are sentenced to day-fines (the same type as can be decided upon by a prosecutor). A similarly common court-imposed sanction regarding juveniles involves being delivered into care in accordance with the Social Services Act. The proportion of sentences of this kind has doubled since the mid-1980s (Fig. 19.9) (see also Granath, 2002); the number of juveniles given a sentence of this kind has increased almost four-fold. This sentence means that the court transfers the responsibility of finding a suitable measure for the guilty party to the local social services board.

Approximately 11% of all registered offenders in Sweden are sentenced to prison. Prison sentences are employed very rarely in Sweden for persons who have not yet reached the age of 18.[8] Up until 1999, approximately 60 individuals per year

---

[8]According to Swedish law, exceptional cause is required before an individual aged between 15 and 17 may be sentenced to prison. The opportunities to sentence 18- to 20-year-olds to prison are also limited, although the legislation is somewhat less restrictive in this case and only reasonable cause is required.

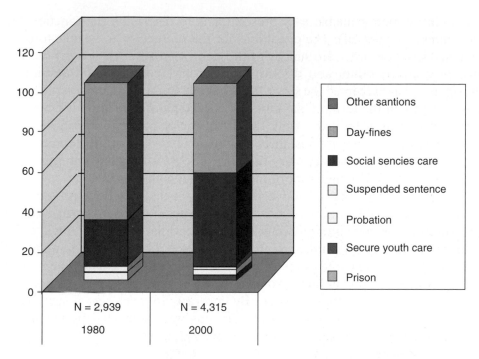

FIGURE 19.9. Comparison of distribution of court sentences for youths aged 15–17, 1980 and 2000.

aged under 18 at the time of their offences were sentenced to a prison term, whilst a further 25 or so were sentenced to a special form of probation that begins with a short stay in prison. Since the introduction of the new youth sanction *Secure youth care* in 1999, only very few persons under the age of 18 (to date no more than four per year) have been sentenced to prison (Fig. 19.10). Individuals in this age group are today in principal only sentenced to a prison term if they are of an age such that the length of a sentence to secure youth care would extend beyond the date on which they turned 21 years of age.

The fact that so few young persons are sentenced to prison shows that the intention of the new Act, i.e., to minimise the number of youths sitting in prison, has been achieved. The new sanction does in fact involve young people being sentenced to a fixed term sanction (which according to the intentions of the Act should be of approximately the same length as the prison term for which one would be sentenced as a young offender, usually approximately half the length of the sanction that an adult would have received for the same offence) but is served in an institution established for the care of young people (here referred to as a youth care facility). These are the same institutions where youths are placed in compulsory care by the social services (see below). These institutions are focused

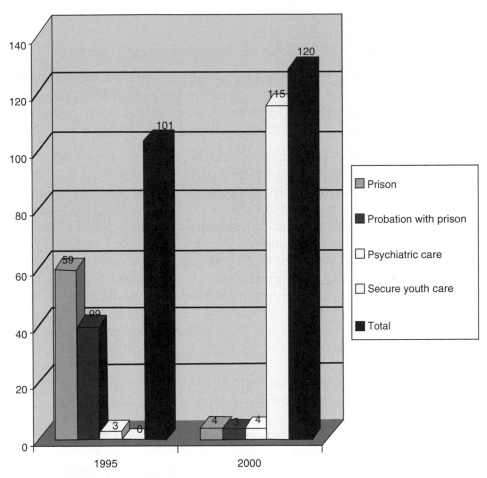

FIGURE 19.10. Number of youths sentenced to custodial sanctions 1995 and 2000.

on the treatment of young people and have a staff to "inmate" ratio (of) approximately three times that of prisons (approximately three staff members per youth in care). Over the course of 2000 and 2001, approximately 100 annually youths have been sentenced to the new sanction (of which approximately 85% were aged between 15 and 17 at the time of the offence, whilst the remainder were over the age of 18). This constitutes a slightly higher number than those who were sentenced to prison (including probation with a prison term) prior to the new Act coming into force. In addition, the introduction of the secure youth care sanction has led to longer custodial sentences. Youths sentenced to prison prior to 1999 served an average sentence of approximately 5.4 months. Youths sentenced to the new sanction, on the other hand, spend an average of 9.5 months in custodial care (Brå et al., 2002; Kuhlhorn, 2002).

The other sanctions which a court can use in sentencing minors are:

(a) Suspended sentences (approximately 1% of convicted persons aged 15–17 and 13% of those aged 18–20, were given this sanction in 2001) and,
(b) Probation (without prison) (approximately 1% of convicted persons aged 15–17 and 11% of those aged 18–20, were sanctioned in this way in 2001).

Some of the sanctions presented above may be combined with each other or with other forms of sanction. Thus probation may, for example, be combined with contractual care or community service. Combinations of this type are rare, however, for young persons under the age of 18. On the other hand, surrender into the care of the social services may be combined with the youth service sanction, which comprises community service specifically adapted to younger people. For approximately 20% of the 15- to 17-year-olds sentenced to care within the social services, the sanction is combined with youth service in this way. In rare instances, youth service is also applied in combination with probation for young people over the age of 18. Fines too may also be awarded in combination with other sanctions. Finally, young people are in rare cases sentenced to psychiatric care. This sanction is however extremely rarely used in relation to the youngest age group.

The distribution of sanctions in 2001 for all those convicted, and for young people aged 15–17 and 18–20, respectively, is presented in Table 19.2.

3.4. The Social Services

The social services do not have the task of punishing young people for their crimes. Therefore, when the social services make a decision regarding a measure suitable as a response to a criminal act, the decision should be based solely on the young person's social situation. (If an individual has a serious history of criminality, that is naturally included in the overall picture of his or her social situation.) Swedish law places the entire responsibility for responding to crimes committed by individuals under the age of 15 on the social services. Thus the criminality of this group is regarded as a social welfare problem.

Accordingly the social services have the aim of helping the young offender out of the social situation that is causing him or her to commit crimes. The measures vary substantially, depending on which factors are deemed to be causing the individual's delinquency. Several years ago there was a heated debate in Sweden about whether or not the social services should have the right to undertake coercive measures with regard to their clients. The opponents of coercion thought that if the purpose of the social services was to help an individual, then it could hardly be done against the individual's will. It was also feared that the social services' right to use coercion would make the development of confidential contacts between social workers and clients impossible. The supporters of coercive measures felt that in certain cases, for example, extensive drug abuse or substantial antisocial behaviour by young people, coercive measures were necessary, at least at the beginning of the treatment process.

The compromise finally reached was that the use of coercive measures would be limited greatly in the social legislation. In the Social Services Act (SoL) there are no coercive measures at all. This Act, which in most cases is also applicable to young offenders, states that those measures which have the aim of removing the causes of an individual's criminality are to be undertaken in terms of cooperation between the individual, his or her parents and the social services. Regarding individuals with minor criminal histories, these measures are usually limited to one or a series of talks with the young offender and his or her parents. If it becomes apparent through these talks that there are serious problems in the home (economic problems, internal conflicts, etc.), an attempt will be made to resolve these problems. The family is then given certain opportunities to receive economic support, therapy, a contact person and other forms of support. In certain cases the family may get a social worker who can meet with them at home over a longer period in order to help the family members resolve various problems (e.g., the family's economic planning, their leisure time problems, and conflicts in relationships).

In cases of extensive antisocial behaviour that constitutes a threat to a young person's ongoing development, a law containing coercive measures known as the *Act with Special Provisions on the Care of Young People* (LVU) may be utilised. Another law containing coercive measures which can be used by the social services is the *Act on the Care of Drug Abusers in Certain Cases* (LVM). The rules governing when an individual may be forcibly taken into custody for the purposes of social services care are very restrictive. According to the Social Services Act (1982) the local social welfare boards have the right to decide about taking a child or young person into custody for social care. These boards, which are made up of local politicians and reflect the political party breakdown at the local government level, have been established by law in every Swedish municipality. In the larger municipalities, additional local boards have been set up. All decisions on custody for social services care made by these boards must be approved by a county administrative court. These courts have an organisation which is completely separate from that of the criminal courts. Decisions arrived at in the county administrative courts may be appealed to higher courts.

In approximately 2,000 cases per year, the social services arrive at a decision to place a young person outside of the family home. In the majority of these cases (approximately 80%, see Table 19.3), the decision relates to voluntary care in accordance with SoL. The young person is usually placed in a family home or a so-called home for residence and care (HVB). HVB placements are also used relatively often in relation to compulsory (LVU) placements. (In 33% of compulsory care orders, the young person is placed in a HVB home).

TABLE 19.3. Youths Aged 15–17 Placed Outside of Their own Home by the Social Services in Accordance with SoL and LVU in 2001

Decision	N	%
Family home (SoL)	908	47
HVB-home (SoL)	643	32
Institutional care (SoL)	47	2
Other (SoL)	46	2
Family home (LVU)	26	1
HVB-home (LVU)	117	6
Institutional care (LVU)	201	10
Other (LVU)	7	0
Total	1,995	100

Source: Brå et al., 2002.

The most common form of placement used in connection with compulsory care orders is placement in a youth care facility. Unlike the other institutions, these facilities have the right to use compulsion to keep the youth in place, and they often have secure units. In addition to placements in accordance with LVU, and in rare cases SoL, youths sentenced to secure youth care are also placed in these institutions (see above). Thus both youths placed in care in accordance with LVU and those sentenced to secure youth care are given compulsory care at these institutions. The difference is that youths in the LVU group are placed in these institutions by the social services (once the care order has been confirmed by the county administrative court) and are discharged in accordance with a decision reached by the social services which must however be reexamined every 6 months, and which may in this context be appealed in the county administrative court, whilst those sentenced to secure youth care are placed in these institutions by means of a court sentence and stay throughout the term of this sentence.

It is common that young people who have been placed in youth care facilities by the social services or by the courts are there for the same reason – i.e., involvement in crime. The social services may however also take a decision to issue care orders and place youths in institutions (although not usually youth care facilities of this kind) as a result of other problems experienced by the young person, such as the parents inability to look after the young person, for example, and different forms of behaviour which are self-destructive but not criminalised.

3.5. Other Institutions

In Sweden, just as in other countries, there is a strong correlation between behaviour in school and criminality as well as other forms of deviant behaviour, both in the teenage years and in adulthood (Sarnecki, 1986, 1987; Ring, 1999). Swedish teachers recognise very well the symptoms related to a heightened risk for persistent criminality, alcohol and drug abuse, etc., even if not all teachers are conscious of how important these observations may be.

Schools usually have their own organisation for dealing with student problems. Many schools have a school psychologist, a social worker (school curator) and medical personnel (doctor, nurse) attached to them. These personnel, along with those heading the administration of the school and certain teachers, constitute a student care team which, among other things, has the task of deciding how to react when students show symptoms of deviant behaviour. Most schools also have teachers who are specially trained to take care of students with school problems, behavioural difficulties, etc. Initially schools try to resolve problems that arise by means of talking with the student and his parents. Another possibility open to schools is that of taking students out of normal classes and placing them in special education groups, where they may receive more support and be subject to more control. In certain difficult cases the students can be placed in special separate schools run by local school boards. The goal, however, is to separate students with adjustment problems as little as possible from other students and to make sure that they are kept in their ordinary classes to as great an extent as possible. In addition, according to current law, schools within the compulsory school system cannot completely exclude students from the educational system. Instead, students with serious problems among the older age groups are given the option of taking a part-time class schedule and working the rest of the time (without pay) at some workplace nearby. In such cases, the school is responsible for providing the student with suitable guidance.

In general, the school staff will initially try to resolve a student's behavioural problems themselves. The social services are usually not contacted until the measures put in place by school staff have been seen not to produce the desired results. Even though school personnel see their students' behavioural problems at an early stage, schools make relatively few reports to the social services. In Sweden, the level of cooperation between the social services and schools varies from municipality to municipality.

The social services and the schools are also supposed to cooperate with the mental health care authorities responsible for children and juveniles, which have an independent status in Sweden. Parents, especially parents of younger students with behaviour problems, are often given a recommendation to make contact with this institution which offers various forms of individual, family and group therapy. However, contacts with the mental health care authorities are in principle voluntary and in most places they do not accept clients who are not clearly motivated regarding treatment. Sometimes the social services also utilise psychiatric experts to analyse young people with more serious behavioural disturbances. Certain young people with substantial criminality in their backgrounds can also be taken in for observation and in rare cases even for treatment in the county's psychiatric clinics for children and juveniles.

In the context of the debate on juvenile delinquency, the issue of leisure time is usually ascribed major importance. Sometimes juvenile criminality is simply defined as a leisure time phenomenon. A significant portion of the leisure time activities available to young people in Sweden are either financed or directly organised by public sector agencies. The financing of leisure activities for young people is provided through payments to an extensive number of organisations. It is estimated that at least half of the young people in Sweden are members of one or more organisations, most often sporting associations. In many places, especially in some of the country's smaller cities, the degree of association membership is significantly higher. However, associational activity seems to a large extent to be characteristic for young people from socially well-functioning families and, accordingly, for young people among whom the risk of developing serious antisocial behaviour is relatively low. The number of organisations that successfully recruit young people in the risk zone for criminality, and that may serve as an effective alternative to their antisocial network is relatively small (Sarnecki, 1983, 1986).

As was mentioned earlier, the economic problems affecting Sweden at the beginning of the 1990s resulted in certain cutbacks within the public sector. The local authorities, which are responsible for schools, the social services and the leisure sector, have been forced to make savings and have done so primarily in areas of activity that are less well regulated in law than the social services. Amongst other things, substantial savings have been made in the area of leisure provision for young people and student care within schools. During the second half of the 1990s, as the economy has improved, more resources have once again been devoted to these sectors, but one has to work on the assumption that preventive efforts, not least within schools, are less comprehensive than they were previously. At the same time as the resources available to schools for social measures have been reduced, schools have turned to an increasing extent to the police for support in connection with criminality among pupils (Estrada, 2001). Several local authorities have made policy decisions that all crime in schools is to be reported to the police.

4. CONCLUSIONS

Sweden is a pluralistic welfare society with a highly developed public sector. Until the middle of the 1970s Sweden experienced a substantial increase in levels of criminality and other social problems among juveniles. From that point onwards the trends seem to have stabilised, and there are even signs that levels of juvenile crime may have diminished.

The ideas of welfare and pluralism also contribute to the relatively large amount of tolerance and humanity shown in Sweden towards persons who deviate from the norm. These ideas are considered to be important in the formulation of the measures to be used in relation to young offenders. Relatively substantial and long-term criminality is required before the authorities are allowed to undertake more far-reaching measures. The emphasis on treatment instead of punishment is also considered to be more humane, even though the ideas behind it have been questioned (Brå, 1977; SOU, 1993: 35). The criticisms directed at the strong treatment focus within the Swedish justice system, and primarily within that part of the justice system focused on young people, have comprised two elements. The one related to the lack of scientific evidence that treatment was an effective method, the other to the perception that the system was unfair. In the light of more recent research, the first of these arguments against employing treatment as a means of responding to crime has shown itself to overstate the case (e.g., Lipsey, 1992, 1995; Loeber and Farrington, 1998; Brå, 2001b). The treatment of young offenders has shown itself capable of producing positive effects, even if these effects are rarely all that strong (Brå et al., 2002; Andreasson, 2003). The criticism of the system's unfairness, on the other hand, is still relevant. In this context, a hypothetical case is usually referred to whereby two youths who have committed the same offence are responded to in quite different ways – one comes from a well-functioning social background and is merely given a caution, whilst the other comes from much more difficult conditions and is therefore taken into care and placed in an institution.

In general, one can argue that in Sweden, the 1980s and 1990s have been characterised by increasing levels of concern for juvenile violence which has been perceived both within the media and among the public as undergoing a substantial increase. Discussions of the trends in violent crime of the kind presented above seldom reach the public and tend to be contrasted in the press with descriptions of tragic and particularly bloody cases of violence. The general perception among the public at large may be assumed to be that the country has suffered a dramatic increase in the levels of violent crime committed by young people and other forms of serious youth crime. In the context of this climate of opinion, there is a general questioning of methods used to treat young offenders that are perceived to be too lenient. Certain treatment measures, such as taking youths with a long criminal record on sailing trips have been presented in the media as both ineffective and at odds with the public's general sense of justice. This atmosphere has led politicians to perceive a need to show that they take juvenile crime seriously, and in particular violent crime (Tham, 1995, 2001; von Hofer, 2000; Estrada, 2001, 2004). Many of the reforms of legislation and praxis relating to young offenders appear to have the objective of accentuating the idea that this is a problem that cannot be taken lightly.

The substantial reduction in the number of young persons convicted of crime has therefore been followed by a substantial tightening of both the law and its application in relation to young offenders. This has led, for example, to a dramatic reduction in the number of young people being awarded waivers of prosecution and to a larger number of youths being sentenced by the courts. This and a long list of other measures suggest that there are efforts afoot to limit the measures of the social services, which are perceived as rather diffuse by many, and instead to emphasise the more transparent means of dealing with young offenders that are manifested by the justice system. These efforts, however, have not been allowed to go so far as to sentence young people to prison. On the contrary, Swedish legislators have made it clear that they do not regard prison as a suitable sanction for youths. Placing juveniles in prison is regarded as inhumane and as running contrary to the UN's convention on the rights of the child. Parallel with the general increase in the severity of the response to juvenile crime, then, the prison sanction has in effect been abolished for the youngest individuals who have reached the age of criminal responsibility. Instead of a prison term, the sanction of secure youth care has been introduced, which takes the form of a treatment measure but which is imposed by a public court and in accordance with the proportionality principle. In this way, the "lenient" influence of the social services is removed from this sanction. Given the current social climate, however, the introduction of secure youth care has in fact had a "net-widening" effect, if not with regard to the number of youths being given custodial sentences then at least with regard to the length of the custodial sentences being imposed. Despite the fact that it was not the intention of the legislators, the courts appear to feel that they may sentence youths to a longer stay in a youth care institution than they could when the youths in question were instead being sent to prisons.

It is nonetheless highly doubtful that the influence of the social services over measures relating to young offenders has declined in any general way as a result of the neo-classicist trend witnessed within the Swedish justice system. It is true that the social services do not exert an influence over the length of stay in youth care institutions, but the treatment provided is nonetheless of a social nature and is provided in a collaboration between the National Board of Institutional Care, which falls under the Ministry of Health and Social Affairs and the local social welfare authorities. Further, the fact that a larger number of young people are being indicted and sentenced in public courts has resulted in more youths being delivered into the care of the social services. In connection with this sanction, the measures are formulated by the local social services even if the court has a certain influence over the way they are formulated.

The general conclusion of the above presentation is thus somewhat surprisingly that the combination of a general critique of the treatment ideology, a neo-classicist focus within the judicial system and a stiffening of sanctions against young offenders, has led to a situation where the influence of the treatment ideology and the social services has in fact become more powerful in relation to the way society responds to the crimes of young offenders. The fundamentally humanist view of youth crime and of measures for young offenders that has been dominant in Sweden over recent decades appears at least for the moment to remain intact, although the authorities have become more inclined to intervene against young offenders. The pressure from various quarters to change this system and to make it "more effective," or even simply "tougher," remains however. The Swedish Government recently appointed a new inquiry with the task of reviewing the way Swedish society responds to crimes committed by young persons. The Government's directive to the inquiry states amongst other things that "The measures taken are to be dedicated to preventing the youth from reoffending. The commission's objective, whilst maintaining the penal law principles of proportionality, predictability and consistency, is to make progress with the work to develop a sanctioning system for young persons whose content is both clear and instructional, and to create improved conditions, on the basis of the young person's needs, for a return to a life characterised by good social function, thus producing positive change" (Ju, 2002: 14). By means of these formulations, the Government appears to be opening the way for both a more powerful element of neo-classicist thinking but also a continued treatment focus within the new legislation. The future will tell which of these directions the inquiry and the future legislation will take and what the consequences of coming reforms will be for the system's humanist focus.

REFERENCES

Andreasson, T. (2003). *Institutionsbehandling av ungdomar. Vad säger forskningen?* (Institutional Treatment of Young People. What Does the Research have to Say?). Stockholm: Förlagshuset Gothia.

Brå (1977). *Nytt straffsystem* (The New Penal System). Stockholm: National Council for Crime Prevention.

Brå (1982). *De unga lagöverträdarna. Åtgärder vid brott av ungdomar under 15 år* (Young Offenders. Measures in Response to Crimes Committed by Youths Under Fifteen Years of Age). Stockholm: National Council for Crime Prevention.

Brå (2001a). *Kriminalstatistik 2000* (Crime Statistics). Stockholm: National Council for Crime Prevention Sweden BRÅ.

Brå (2001b). *Kriminell utveckling: tidiga riskfaktorer och förebyggande insatser* (Criminal Development: Early Risk Factors and Preventive Measures). Stockholm: National Council for Crime Prevention Sweden.

Brå et al. (2002). *Sluten ungdomsvård – en uppföljning* (Institutional Care of Youths – Follow-up). Stockholm: National Council for Crime Prevention, National Board of Health and, National Board for Institutional Care.

Estrada, F. (1999a). "Juvenile Crime Trends in Post-War Europe", *European Journal on Criminal Policy and Research*, 7(1):23–42.

Estrada, F. (1999b). "Crime," *Review of National Youth Policy. Sweden National Report*. Stockholm: The National Board for Youth Affairs, pp. 223–237.

Estrada, F. (2001). "Juvenile violence as a social problem. Trends, media attention and societal response", *British Journal of Criminology*, 41:639–55.

Estrada, F. (2004) "The Transformation of the Politics of Crime in High Crime Societies" *European Journal of Criminology*, 1(4):419–444.

Estrada, F. (2005). Trends in violence in Scandinavia. An exemplification of the value of alternative indicators of crime. Working paper 2005:4, Stockholm: Institute for Future Studies.

Falck, S., von Hofer, H., and Storgaard, A. (2003). *Nordic Criminal Statistics 1950–2000*. Report 2003, 3. Department of Criminology, Stockholm University.

Granath, S. (2002). *Påföljdssystemet för unga lagöverträdare 1980 – 2000. Förändrade reaktioner, förändrat samhälle eller förändrade brottslingar* (The Juvenile Justice System 1980–2000. Changed Reaction, Changed Society or Different Criminals). Stockholm: Stockholm University, Department of Criminology.

Hall, S., Critcher, C., Jefferson, T., Clarke, J., and Roberts, B. (1978). *Policing the Crisis. Mugging, the State, and Law and Order.* London: Macmillan.

Ju 2002:14. *Utredningen om översyn av det allmännas ingripanden vid ungdomsbrott* (Commission of Inquiry on Revision of Intervention in Case of Youth Crime). Online available at http://www. riksdagen.se/debatt/dir/index.asp.

Kühlhorn, E. (2002). *Sluten ungdomsvård. Rättliga reaktioner på de ungas brott förre och efter införandet 1999* (Institutional Care of Youths. Juridical Reaction on Youth Crime Before and After Introduction 1999). Stockholm: Statens institutionsstyrelse.

Kyvsgaard, B. (1991). "The Decline in Child and Youth Criminality: Possible Explanations of an International Trend", in A. Snare (ed.), *Youth, Crime and Justice.* Oslo: Universitetsforlaget.

Lipsey, M.W. (1992). "Juvenile Delinquency Treatment: A Meta-analytic Inquiry into the Variability of Effects", in T.D. Cook, D.S. Cooper, D.S. Cordray, H. Hartmann, L.V. Hedges, R.J. Light, T.A. Louis, and F. Mosteller (eds.), *Meta-Analysis for Explanation: A Casebook.* New York: Russell Sage Foundation.

Lipsey, M.W. (1995). "What do we Learn from 400 Research Studies on the Effectiveness of Treatment with Juvenile Delinquents?" in J. McGuire (ed.), *What Works? Reducing Reoffending: Guidelines from Research and Practice.* Chichester: Wiley.

Loeber, R. and Farrington, D.P. (1998). *Serious and Violent Juvenile Offenders: Risk Factors and Successful Interventions.* London: Sage.

Nilsson, A. & Estrada, F. (2003). "Victimisation, Inequality and Welfare during an Economic Recession. A Study of Self Reported Victimisation in Sweden 1988–1999," *British Journal of Criminology.* 43:655–672.

Pfeiffer, C. (1998). "Juvenile Crime and Violence in Europe." *Crime and Justice, A Review of Research*, Vol. 23, pp. 255–328.

Ring, J. (1999). *Hem och skola, kamrater och brott* (Home and School, Peers and Crime). Stockholm: Stockholm University, Department of Criminology.

Ring, J. (2005). *Stöld, droger och våld bland Sveriges elever* (Theft, Drugs and Violence among Swedish Pupils). Stockholm: National Council for Crime Prevention.

RPS FS 1990:3. *Polislagen med kommentarer* (The Police Act with Comments). Online available at http://www.polisen.se/inter/mediacache/4347/4734/2671/polislagen_pdf.pdf (2004–09–12).

Sarnecki, J. (1983). *Fritid och brottslighet* (Leisure and Criminality). Stockholm: National Council for Crime Prevention.

Sarnecki, J. (1986). *Delinquent Networks.* Stockholm: National Council for Crime Prevention Report.

Sarnecki, J. (1987). *Skolan och brottsligheten* (School and Crime). Stockholm: Carlssons.

Sarnecki, J. (1991). "Reaction to Crimes Committed by Young People", in A. Snare (ed.), *Youth, Crime and Justice.* Oslo: Universitetsforlaget.

Sarnecki, J. (2001). *Delinquent Networks: Youth Co-offending in Stockholm.* Cambridge: Cambridge University Press.

SFS 1994:1760. *Lag (1994:1760) om ändring i lagen (1964:167) med särskilda bestämmelser om unga lagöverträdare.*

Smith, D.J. (1995). "Youth Crime and Conduct Disorders: Trends, Patterns, and Causal Explanations", in M. Rutter and D.J. Smith (eds.), *Psychosocial Disorders in Young People. Time Trends and Their Causes*, pp. 389–489. New York: John Wiley & Sons.

SOU 1993:35. *Reaktion mot ungdomsbrott* (Reaction to Juvenile Delinquency). Stockholm: Ungdomsbrottskommitten. B Statens offentliga utredningar.

Storgaard, A. (2004). "Juvenile Justice in Scandinavia," *Journal of Scandinavian Studies in Criminology and Crime Prevention*, 5:188–204.

Takala, H. (2004). "Nordic Cooperation in Criminal Policy and Crime Prevention," *Journal of Scandinavian Studies in Criminology and Crime Prevention*, 5:131–147.

Tham, H. (1995). "From Treatment to Just Deserts in a Changing Welfare State", in A. Snare, (ed), *Beware of Punishment*. Oslo: Pax.

Tham, H. (2001). "Law and Order as a Leftist Project? The Case of Sweden", *Punishment and Society*, 3:409–426.

von Hofer, H. (2000). "Criminal Violence and Youth in Sweden: A Long-Term Perspective", *Journal of Scandinavian Studies in Criminology and Crime Prevention*, 1(1):56–72.

von Hofer, H. (2003). "Crime and Punishment in Sweden. Historical Criminal Justice Statistics 1750–2000", *Journal of Scandinavian Studies in Criminology and Crime Prevention*, 4(2):162–179.

Ward, M. (1998). *Barn & brott av vår tid?: självdeklarerad ungdomsbrottslighet 1971 och 1996: en jämförelse utifrån Örebroprojektets data* (Children and Crimes of our Time?: Self-Reported Juvenile Crime in 1971 and 1996: A Comparison Employing Data from the Örebro Project). Stockholm: Stockholm University, Department of Criminology.

Westfelt, L. (2001). *Brott och straff i Sverige och Europa. En studie i komparativ kriminologi.* (Crime and Punishment in Sweden and Europe – A Study in Comparative Criminology) Doctoral dissertation. Stockholm: Stockholm University, Department of Criminology.

Wilson, J.Q. and Herrnstein, R. (1985). *Crime and Human Nature.* New York: Simon & Schuster.

20

Trends in International Juvenile Justice: What Conclusions Can be Drawn?

Josine Junger-Tas

INTRODUCTION

Treatment of children, who are victims of the conditions in which they are living and children who have violated the law, is a reflection of a society's culture and value system. This treatment is a society's vision of children and youth and its views on how to socialize and educate children. In the last decades of the 20th century this vision has undergone drastic change, which led to considerable modifications of juvenile justice legislation both in North America and in Europe.

The main trend in juvenile justice in a number of countries has been more repressive, but not necessarily more effective. It is essentially this aspect that worries most of those who are working in the field. The question is what national and local authorities might do to reverse this trend, and in particular whether there exists in the western world other more effective and more humane ways to prevent juvenile delinquency and to deal with young offenders. In order to answer this question two reports are prepared. The first question, which is the subject of the present publication, presents an overview of the juvenile justice systems and legislation in 17 European countries and two North American ones: Canada and the United States. The reader will note that there are large differences among these countries in the way they have organized their juvenile justice systems. This is not only true with respect to formal organization but also in terms of the conception of what such a system should be, what policies are used to reach this goal and how to approach young people. Moreover, the differences are not random, but they are clustered among countries which are geographically close to each other.

Writing about juveniles,[1] delinquency and the juvenile justice system I use the definitions of the Council of Europe, defining a *juvenile* as someone who is criminally responsible but has not reached criminal majority. In this respect it should be observed that age limits clearly vary across countries. *Delinquency* refers to acts which are dealt with under criminal law, although some countries do include antisocial or deviant behaviour in their juvenile penal law. The *juvenile justice system* is a formal system that is part of a wide approach to delinquency, including the police, the pros-

---

[1] The words juveniles, young people and children are all included in this definition

J. Junger-Tas and S. H. Decker (eds.), International Handbook of Juvenile Justice, 505–532.
© 2006 Springer.

ecutor system, the probation system, and youth institutions, but also agencies such as health, education, and social welfare (Council of Europe (Rec. 2000, 20).

This chapter first looks briefly at why and how a separate juvenile justice system came into being and what the general trend of that system actually is. In that respect I also examine whether we need a juvenile justice system at all: maybe one criminal justice system dealing with juveniles and adults alike is to be preferred. This section is followed by the most recent law reforms which have been adopted in the countries represented in this book. A puzzling question in this respect is what might have caused the reforms and some hypotheses on that subject are presented. Finally, we try to draw some preliminary conclusions on the basis of the 19 different juvenile justice systems presented in this book. The conclusions point to important issues at stake, which will be extensively treated in a second publication.

The aim of the latter report is to examine these issues and to come up with a number of answers which might assist authorities to improve their juvenile justice system, and to assemble a number of realistic, preferably tested innovations in juvenile justice procedures and interventions.

1. A SEPARATE JUVENILE JUSTICE SYSTEM

The community's responsibility for deprived and delinquent children emerged in the 16th and 17th centuries. People slowly recognized that a situation in which children were the victims of economic and social misfortunes was not acceptable and that therefore more attention had to be given to the conditions in which children were raised. Though by present standards juveniles were punished in a barbaric way, including physical punishments such as flogging and branding, documents from that period indicate that some courts took account of the offender's age and meted out more lenient punishment to young people than to adults (Penders, 1980).

In the 18th and 19th centuries corporal punishment was increasingly seen as morally wrong and as an ineffective educational measure. Much higher expectations were placed on psychological interventions and on the education of children in Christian norms and values and on training in discipline and useful labour in an institution. It was the time when reformatories were created all over the western world (Rothman, 1971; Leonard, 1995). As a consequence of the size of the institutions, the emphasis on discipline, the many punishments – using violence and isolation – the central rehabilitative aim disappeared in favour of the dominant goal to preserve law and order within the institution. Despite the intentions of reformers, the institutions degenerated into youth prisons, characterized by constant overcrowding, large dormitories, strict work schedules, rigid discipline and punishment, and very little real education.

Different reform movements were active in the second half of the 19th century. In the United States, the Chicago progressive reformers, believed that in order to do something about deprivation and delinquency one had to consider the urban environment and the community setting. They campaigned for compulsory schooling and the abolition of child labour. This reform movement, which spread from the United States to Canada and Europe, was essentially the outcome of two important developments. The first was the urge to rescue children from the living conditions in an increasingly urbanized and industrialized environment. And second, the emergence of a different conception of childhood, related to social and economic change, such as the decline of the power of the father over his children, the creation of a public school system and the increasingly separate world of children and adolescents (Stearns, 1975; Shorter, 1975).

In the light of the new views on children and adolescents, it was felt that the state should intervene and take over the parental role (*parens patriae*) if parents abused their power or neglected their children. Together with a firm belief in education and rehabilitation, the stage was set for legislation on a separate jurisdiction for children, both in cases of children in need of protection and with respect to juvenile delinquents.

One of the first countries to create a modern child protection system was Norway with a law on the treatment of neglected children, enacted in 1896. The first juvenile court was established in Chicago by the Juvenile Court Act in 1899. The first juvenile justice legislation in Canada is the Juvenile Delinquents Act of 1908, while Belgium, France, and Switzerland enacted new legislation in 1912. Not all countries adopted the American juvenile court model. For example, although the first Dutch Children's laws, which specified the conditions that would justify state intervention to limit parental authority, dating from 1901, the institution of the juvenile judge and the supervision order as a civil protection measure were established only in 1922. In France specialized juvenile court magistrates were established only after World War II (Trépanier, 1999). In addition, as we know, the Scandinavian countries developed their own civil system of welfare boards.

However, as the juvenile justice system spread throughout the western world, whether in the framework of a separate juvenile court, a specialized juvenile judge or a welfare board, a number of similarities emerged. These include:

- Large discretionary power of the juvenile judge, based on the notion of *parens patriae*, who had to act "in the best interest of the child." The discretion was not limited to the juvenile judge but referred to all levels of the system: the (juvenile) police, the public prosecutor and the court. The focus of juvenile justice was the individual child and not the offence that was committed.
- Much emphasis on treatment in stead of punishment. Later on this led to a broadly supported extra-judicial diversionary practice, on the level of the police as well as on the level of the public prosecutor, often in collaboration with social agencies.
- Considerable efforts were made to reduce the formal character of court procedures.

- Hearings are not public and procedures are confidential to protect the juvenile's privacy.
- Because of the emphasis on treatment, rehabilitation and protection, the need for legal procedural rights, such as they existed for adults, was not felt.

The ideal was that of a juvenile judge who – as a medical doctor or a psychologist – would make a diagnosis of the problems and needs of the child, and then take the measures or impose the treatment adapted to those needs.

The separate juvenile justice system was undoubtedly based on humanitarian concerns. It does symbolize increased consideration for the well-being of children as well as more respect for their individual personality. It had its heyday in the 20th century and its philosophy remained practically unchanged until the 1970s. This is true for most of the western countries, but I would argue that in practice some differences emerged already between the United States and continental Europe. First, within 10 years of the Juvenile Court Act, new legislation was enacted in the United States, defining incorrigibility, growing up in idleness, gambling, loitering, begging and running away as "status-offences,"[2] thus justifying the intervention of the juvenile court. As a consequence many children were placed in large institutions for indeterminate periods during the first half of the 20th century. Of course similar behaviours occurred also in Europe, but they were usually not defined as offences but as problem behaviour, although they could lead to referring the child to the protection system. Second, most justice systems in continental countries did not include indeterminate sentences.[3] However, in Europe as in the United States, the child remained a powerless object in the hands of a paternalistic and patronizing judge.

2. CHANGES IN JUVENILE JUSTICE PHILOSOPHY

This system – also called the welfare system – persisted until about the 1970s. However, as a consequence of important social changes in western society since the end of World War II, including the increase in prosperity, higher levels of education, technological change, and emancipation movements, involving also the youth population, the system had become obsolete. People no longer accepted the absolute authority of a paternalistic judge over the lives of children, nor did the adolescents themselves. The first country to change was the United States, through the landmark US Supreme Court's ruling *in Re Gault* (1967) granting juveniles due process rights, such as notice of the charges, right to counsel, right to confrontation and cross-examination, and the privilege against self-incrimination. At the same time the ruling meant the disintegration of the protective system, based on the principle of the delinquent being mainly

[2]Status offences are acts that are defined as punishable behaviour because of the child's status as a minor.
[3]In some other countries there existed indeterminate (civil) sentences for mentally disturbed offenders. Such sentences had to be regularly reviewed by the director of the medical penitentiary.

a victim of circumstances and his environment. Since more rights usually entail more obligations and accountability, the juvenile justice system also reaffirmed young people's responsibility for their own actions and rediscovered free will. Disappointment with treatment results in general and with institutional treatment in particular (Martinson, 1974) affected the confidence in therapeutic interventions and prepared the minds for a renewed emphasis on retribution and punishment. Although the Supreme Court in the Gault case did not challenge the existence of the juvenile court, I would suggest that this ruling was the starting point for a gradual blurring of the distinctions between the criminal court and the juvenile court.

These neoclassical retributive principles are best expressed by von Hirsch (1976) in "Doing Justice: The Choice of Punishments," the report of a Commission set up to reform the American system of indeterminate sentences. The commission designed a system based on three related principles. First, the principle of *just desert,* meaning that the convicted person should receive the punishment he deserves for the crime he has committed. Second the principle of *proportionality*, which says that the punishment should be directly proportional to the seriousness of the crime. Third, the principle of *equality,* which states that like cases should be treated alike. Although the aim of Von Hirsch and his colleagues was to achieve a fairer and more just sentencing policy, the principle of equality in particular did mean that judges could no longer take into consideration the personal (mitigating or aggravating) circumstances for the offender, and this did affect their discretionary power.

Summarizing the main characteristics of the juvenile justice system as it is now established in North America and many European countries, the following elements seem to be of central importance.

- The offender is again viewed as a rational being with a free will. Consequently he is considered as fully and individually responsible for his actions.
- The focus is placed on the committed offence rather than on the offender.
- This implies increasingly notions of culpability and guilt as well as more severe penal intervention, at the expense of protection and treatment.
- The victim has gradually become the central figure in legal procedures, one of the consequences being a renewed emphasis on restitution and reparation of harm done.
- By awarding due process rights to juveniles, judicial procedures have again become considerably more formal than they used to be.
- Differences between the criminal justice system and the juvenile justice system have been reduced. Since both systems are increasingly alike, this trend did increase the number of transfers to adult court in a number of countries.

2.1. Do we need a separate Juvenile justice system?

In view of these fundamental changes in juvenile justice orientations some criminologists have stated that there is no need for a separate juvenile justice system.

They argue for a unified criminal justice system which processes all delinquents, be they young people or adults (Feld, 1998a, 1998b; Bol 1991). Feld argues that young people are often treated worse in the juvenile justice system than in the adult system, while Bol wants to abolish age limits because she claims that from a development point of view it is impossible to determine at what age children might be considered accountable for their acts. This opposition to the juvenile court raises the question whether there are valid arguments for pleading for a juvenile justice system that is separate from the adult criminal justice system.

Important statements on this issue are presented by a number of National and International bodies, which strongly emphasize the need for differential treatment of children as compared to adults. For example, the Council of Europe's recommendation of 1987 says in its Preamble:

> Young people are developing beings and in consequence all measures taken in their respect should have an educational character.

The National Council of Juvenile and Family Court Judges in the United States (1998) made a similar argument, stating that

> Children are developmentally different from adults; they are developing emotionally and cognitively; they are impressionable; and they have different levels of understanding than adults.

These statements have important implications for the treatment of juvenile offenders, indicating the need for a special system taking into account the differences between children and adults, in particular their age and immaturity (Howell, 2003, 148). On a more abstract level they suggest three principles that are central to juvenile justice: diminished responsibility, proportionality and room to reform (Zimring, 1998, 75–83)

Diminished responsibility refers to the question whether children are less culpable then adults for having offended. Children may lack sufficient cognitive abilities to realize what they are exactly doing and in particular what might be the consequences of their acts. Of course the older the juvenile the more he will be responsible for his acts, but even at age 14 and 16 he might be incapable of grasping the full meaning of his actions (Scott, 2000).

Proportionality refers to the mitigation of punishment because of children's lack of development of social and cognitive capacities. Zimring argues that punishments meted out to juveniles should be graduated in the sense that the older the child the more severe the punishment.

Room to reform indicates the importance of the kind of punishments that is meted out, considering what we want to achieve with punishment and what we would want to avoid. It means that we should strive for penal interventions that promote rehabilitation and the growth of young people into responsible citizens. The crucial importance of the latter principle is illustrated by a comparison of young people treated within the juvenile justice system and those that are transferred to the adult system (Bishop et al., 1996), showing that in terms of recidivism juveniles retained in the juvenile justice system did considerably better than juveniles who were transferred to adult court. Nearly one third of the transferred group was rearrested compared with 19% of the matched non-transferred group.

Finally, in terms of the purpose of the juvenile justice system the Council of Europe (Rec. 2000, 20) summarizes its principal aims as follows:

• To prevent offending and re-offending;
• To (re)socialize and (re)integrate offenders;
• To address the needs and interests of victims;

It should be observed that the latter aims do not mention deterrence and retribution. On the contrary, because the juvenile justice system recognizes the immaturity and special needs of young people it should be concerned in the first place with prevention, resocialization and making juveniles aware of the feelings of victims. In this perspective the juvenile court is truly guided by the "best interest of the child." It is precisely this orientation that makes the juvenile justice system fundamentally different from the adult criminal justice system, which thinking is dominated by the principles of deterrence and retribution. Since our purpose should be to foster the growth of children and young people into responsible citizens, we must cherish this different system and not abandon it.

3. RECENT TRENDS IN JUVENILE JUSTICE

However, the reality is that in the 1980s and 1990s one sees in a number of western countries the development of a system with a growing emphasis on punishment and a secondary role for rehabilitation. This happened first in the United States, but others soon followed.

3.1. The Anglo-Saxon Orientation

Far-reaching revisions of juvenile penal law took place in more than 90% of all American states between 1992 and 1995 (Snyder and Sickmund, 1999). These changes made it easier to transfer juveniles to the adult criminal justice system and to impose adult sentencing, including imprisonment. Accountability is increasingly translated by long-term imprisonment. Between 1992 and 1997 all but three states have changed their juvenile law, expanding the application of adult criminal law; offering judges more (adult) sanctioning options and allowing investigation, prosecution and trial in juvenile cases to be a public affair. Automatic transfer was required by law for some specific offences and in 20 states such transfer was possible for any offence. In 19 of 47 states the minimum age for transfer is age 14, in six it is 13. The confidentiality of legal procedures as well as the juvenile's privacy is no longer guaranteed because of the objective to make the public aware of the criminal behaviour of minors. Some states have introduced mandatory sentences for juveniles, which include long terms of imprisonment. In most of the states the main objectives of the juvenile justice system are expressed in the following way:

- To make juveniles accountable for their acts;
- To introduce effective deterrence;
- To protect the public against criminal behaviour;
- To balance attention paid to the offender, the victim and the community;
- To impose punishment that is proportional to the seriousness of the offence.

Although (some of) these objectives may be shared by many countries, the absence of any suggestion that young people should be rehabilitated and reintegrated in the community is striking.

There are a number of interesting differences between the United States and Canada, both in the underlying philosophy and in practice. Canada has been confronted with two big problems: the juvenile court was overburdened with non-serious cases, and youth detention was too frequently imposed, which was mainly related to the absence of sufficient alternatives (Doob and Sprott, 1999). It should be recognized that there is considerable variation in the practical application of the law among Canadian Provinces, which have great autonomy in the practical application of the federal law. For example, the Province of Québec has a more pronounced "welfare" practice than Ontario, as expressed in the number of juveniles in pre-trial detention and in custody.

In 1998 the federal government decided to replace the Young Offenders Act of 1982 by the new Youth Criminal Justice Act which came into action in 1999. The law specifies that a youth is accountable for his actions and places more emphasis on the offence than on the offender (Trépanier, 1999). However, despite pressures to lower the age of criminal responsibility, which was age 12, this was not followed by the legislators, so that children younger than age 12 continue to be dealt with by social agencies and youth protection services. Moreover, Canada has never introduced *sentencing guidelines,* neither in criminal law nor in juvenile penal law (Roberts, 1999). Also transfer to adult criminal justice requires elaborate procedures and is restricted to a small group of serious violent and sex-offenders, since practically all juvenile offenders can be sentenced within the framework of the new law. Therefore it is expected that not many more young people than was the case before (annually about 100) would be sentenced in the criminal court (Doob and Sprott, 1999). Furthermore, the new law has created considerably more possibilities to deal with cases informally and divert them from court, keeping young people in the community. In this respect the Federal government has made available funds to provincial authorities to develop initiatives in the field of juvenile justice, encouraging the development of alternatives for custody. The law states the following objectives for juvenile justice in Canada:

- To prevent crime by attacking the circumstances that lie at the basis of delinquent behaviour;
- To insure that young offenders experience significant consequences of their delinquent act;
- To rehabilitate young offenders and to reintegrate them in the community.

The difference with the United States is that the Youth Criminal Justice Act not only states that a young person should be punished, but explicitly states as one of its objectives that it strives for rehabilitation (Bala and Roberts, 2004).

Revision of juvenile justice legislation has also taken place in Europe. England changed its law in 1998 (Graham and Moore, 2004). The Crime and Disorder Act abolished the so-called *Doli Incapax* principle, according to which a child under age 14 "is not capable of doing evil things" and states that children are accountable for their acts at the age of ten. The law has created new preventive interventions for young children, such as the *Child Safety Order, Child Curfews,* and the *Parenting Order*. The latter orders parents to attend a Parent Training course and if parents do not attend they may be fined. The Police cautioning practice in the case of non-serious offences was considered too "soft" and was replaced by *Final Warnings*. By this measure the discretionary power of the police was seriously curtailed, and it considerably increased the number of prosecutions. The discretionary power of the juvenile court was also reduced, since in a number of cases the court could no longer use the option of the conditional dismissal. In addition, children aged 10–16 could be placed in pre-trial detention and a new *Detention and Training Order* may be imposed on all delinquents aged 15–17, as well as on "persistent delinquents" aged 10 and 11. All this makes the sentencing framework for young people more similar to that for adults. An innovation was the creation of multidisciplinary *Youth Offending Teams* which produce pre-sentence reports and intervene at every stage of the process. And indeed their effect was to speed up procedures and to supervise more closely young people when penal interventions were imposed by the court. Another innovation was that young first offenders are referred to *Youth Panels,* which make a contract with the youth and his parents specifying a number of behavioural requirements.

The English approach is more repressive than that of most other European countries, but it seems to be more pragmatic than that of the United States. This is shown by their efforts to translate the available research evidence on risk factors in child development that might lead to delinquent behaviour, into broad policies. In addition, the English government has invested considerable funds in generalized preventive policies and it made great efforts to develop a consistent and gradual approach to youth crime emphasizing more rational juvenile justice interventions. The latter is illustrated by a report of the Audit Commission of 2004, noting the following positive points:

- Young offenders are dealt with more quickly and juveniles more often receive an intervention;
- One third of offenders have to pay damages or to work for the victim (a *Reparation Order*);
- Reconviction rates after a *Reprimand* or *Final Warning* are 7–10% lower than predicted;
- *Intensive Supervision and Surveillance Programmes* (ISSPs) have proven to be a considerably more constructive and cheaper option for persistent delinquents than a stay in an institution: 6 months ISSP costs £8,500, while 6 months detention costs £25,400;
- Magistrates[4] are very satisfied with the services they receive from the *Youth Offending Teams,* which make pre-sentence reports, appear at the trial where they give information to the judge, execute ISSPs and impose Alternative sanctions.

The Audit Commission also noted a number of negative findings, the most important of which are the following:

- Although youth crime has stabilized, the public knows very little about the recent reforms and public confidence in the juvenile justice system is low;
- There are still too many petty offences brought to Court;
- Contact time of social workers in the system continues to be only one hour per week;
- Minority juvenile delinquents (especially blacks) are more often placed in pre-trial detention and get more often a custodial sentence than white young people.

The Netherlands frequently looks at England and Wales as a model for change in its juvenile justice system. Policies have become more repressive and although alternative sanctions are a preferred option for most juvenile judges, the capacity of judicial youth institutions has grown exponentially and more establishments are built. Just as in England more young people are sent to a closed institution, while increasing attention is placed on 'delinquent' acts of children under the age of criminal responsibility (12 years). Since these children are not criminally responsible they cannot be punished, but in this case the public prosecutor proposes to the parents to deliver an (educative) intervention. Although parents may refuse, most accept an intervention which has a definite "juvenile justice flavour" (van der Laan, 2004). The latest intervention introduced by law in England and as an experiment in The Netherlands is the ASBO (Anti Social Behaviour Order). Behaviours that are no criminal acts, such as nuisance behaviour, harassing or intimidation, excessive noise, rowdy behaviour, graffiti, drunken behaviour and fouling the streets with litter may be punished by prohibiting the young people entering defined areas, associating with certain people or going near a house where they cause trouble. ASBOs are civil orders made in court and they are in

---

[4]England has lay judges (Magistrates) which have only a basic knowledge of the law, but who are assisted by trained jurists.

effect for a period of 2 years. However, breach of the order is a criminal offence and may lead to placement in an institution. What this means is that acts that are no crimes may be punished as crimes if the young person breaches the civil order during the period of 2 years. Moreover, civil proceedings do not carry with them the same due process rights as penal proceedings.

Northern Ireland and the Republic of Ireland, also belong to this cluster of Anglo-Saxon countries. However, they have introduced important innovations in their system. For example, Ireland has changed its Children's Act (1908) into the new Children Act (2001). It is true that the new law is slow to be implemented and that young people are still incarcerated in an institution run by the Irish Prison Service. Moreover, the British example of Parent Orders is followed. On the other hand the new law has introduced preventive and diversionary practices as well as family conferences.

Northern Ireland has introduced a Youth Diversion Scheme in the form of restorative cautioning. Participation of victims is found to have advantages over traditional cautioning. The most interesting part of the new law is the introduction of restorative justice, implicating statutory youth conferences for all juvenile offenders up to age 18. The law distinguishes diversionary youth conferences and mandatory Court ordered youth conferences. The logical consequence of the latter procedure is that conferences may recommend a custodial sentence, although it is up to the court to decide on custody as well as on the length of the term. A somewhat problematic issue in this respect is the solicitor's role in the conference. The solicitor is not allowed to defend his client. He has only advisory capacity, since he or she is supposed to fully participate in the conference process.

So far the impact of legal change and practice in what may be termed the Anglo-Saxon countries has been real but it has limitations. Moreover, there are clear differences between these countries and other European states, in particular Southern Europe and East and Central Europe.

3.2. The Continental Tradition

In countries of continental Europe the tradition of the protection of youth is much stronger. For example, although France and Belgium struggle with growing repressive tendencies, they still have a law that reflects the "welfare" of juveniles. However, it is true that several specific retributive initiatives have been taken to deal with delinquent young people in both countries.

The French system is essentially dominated by the *Ordonnance of February 2, 1945,* including the principles of a special jurisdiction for juveniles, diminished responsibility of minors and priority of educational measures (Wyvekens, 2004). These principles are still upheld although they are under increasing attack for being too lenient. For a very long time the juvenile judge, who is competent in penal and civil cases, was the most powerful player in the game, as the prosecutor had little influence. This is now changing and a number of courts have prosecutors who are specialized in juvenile matters. An interesting French initiative is the neighbour-hood prosecuting offices, who deal with petty offences committed by adults and minors rapidly, mostly through a conditional discharge. This practice, legalized in 1993, is similar to several diversion procedures in other countries, since it includes reparation to the victim and/or community service. Taking into account the prin-ciple of protection in French legislation, the term "educative sanction" appeared in 2002, when a new decree made it possible to sanction children aged 10–13, who are not yet criminally responsible. Juveniles aged 13–18 can be fined, receive a Com-munity service order or may be placed in a closed educative centre. They may also be placed under supervision, eventually including a term in care for 6 or 12 months. Those aged 16–18 may be subjected to electronic monitoring, or be imprisoned.

Belgium had adopted a protection law in 1965, establishing criminal responsi-bility at age 18 (Van Dijk, 2004). As a consequence the youth court cannot impose any sanctions, but only educational measures. There have been several initiatives at the level of the prosecutor to develop community based sanctions, which tend to express some dissatisfaction with the law of 1965 and promote more punitive goals. Belgium is one of the few European countries to have developed the prac-tice of Restorative Justice, although unfortunately this is somewhat fragmented because of a lack of relevant legislation. Like other countries they apply Victim-Offender mediation and Community service. Transfer of 16- 18-year-olds to the adult court is possible. However, it should be observed that, contrary to its north-ern neighbour, The Netherlands, Belgium has very few institutions and there is only one federal correctional facility for boys aged 14–18. In Flanders the total capacity is 246 places, while the French speaking part of the country has 5 rather small youth institutions.

A clear example of the Welfare tradition is apparent in the German – and also the Austrian- legislation (Dünkel, 2004; Bruckmüller, 2004). Already in 1923 Germany created the option of educational measures instead of punishment and increased the age of criminal responsibility from age 12 to age 14. The legislative reform of the Juvenile Justice Act (JJA) in 1990 emphasized the importance of diversion both at the level of the prosecutor and the juvenile judge, distinguishing four levels, such as simple diversion and diversion combined with interventions of increasing seriousness, including educational measures or alternative sanc-tions. All formal sanctions are structured according to the principle of minimum intervention, with juvenile imprisonment as a last resort. Imprisonment includes a "short sharp shock" detention of a maximum of 4 weeks (*Jugendarrest*) and youth imprisonment for 14- 17-year-olds of 6 months to 5 years. Interestingly, young adults aged 18–20 may be sentenced according to the JJA, a practice that occurs frequently. Since 1953 all young adults (aged 18–21) are placed under the jurisdiction of the juvenile court, a procedure that has been followed by Spain in 2000,[5] as well as by Austria and Lithuania in 2001. This is all the more remarkable

---

[5]However, this has later been suspended till 2007.

since it goes counter to the tendency in many other countries to facilitate transfer to the adult criminal court of young people aged 16–18. In fact 62% of young adults in West Germany were sentenced under the JJA in 2001, while sentencing under the adult Criminal law occurred mainly for traffic offences. Although in essence welfare systems, Germany and Austria – similar to other countries – have introduced due process rights for juveniles. Also similar to other European countries is the fact that juvenile delinquency has remained stable since 1990, while violence rates in East and West Germany have grown closer because of a rise in West and a decrease in East Germany.

Diversion procedures in Germany account for 69% of all disposals. Short-term detention has been reduced from 11% to 5% in West Germany, unconditional youth imprisonment to 2%. Moreover, about 70% of youth prison sentences are suspended, making prison a real "last resort." Since 1990, however, youth prison rates have increased, not because of more severe sentences but because of the increase of juveniles sentenced for assault and street robbery (89% of the youth prison population is aged 18–25, while 11% is aged 14–18). Sentencing practices are not more severe in East than in West Germany, except for violent offences where sanctions in East Germany include more often short term detention. In terms of community sanctions Germany applies community service, social training courses, mediation and different combinations with reparation, restitution and the like. In conclusion, Germany's legislation represents a clearly different view of young people and of childhood than that of the more Anglo-Saxon countries such as England and Wales and Canada, but also of the Netherlands.

Austria maintains also some clear welfare principles. For example, age limits for criminal responsibility are 14–18, children below age 16 cannot be sentenced to prison, while young people aged 16 or more may be sentenced for a period of two weeks maximum. Austria has also established that "a trusted adult" by the child must be present in all police interrogations and pre-trial hearings by the juvenile judge. In addition, Austria adopted the day-fine system, where the fine is based on the daily income of a juvenile whether he is employed, receives pocket money or has a small job after school hours. An important element to add is that Austria as well as Sweden has an *Ombudsman* for children.

As noted by the authors the Greek law of 2003 was influenced by the German legislation, as well as by procedures in Switzerland and Italy (Spinellis and Tsitsoura, 2004). These substituted the earlier law of 1950, introducing diversion and mediation and increasing non-custodial measures. Greece has only two penal youth institutions where about 300 minors were housed in 2004. Moreover, a special Bill introducing special "Care Units" for young people with particular problems, such as drug addicts and delinquents with psychological or mental problems (as well as for children in need of protection) has included young adults up to age 21. Moreover, a most interesting innovation is the creation of an "Ombudsman for Children" who – among other duties – has to defend and promote children's rights.

The Spanish law of 2000 illustrates how in Continental Europe legislators are also grappling with the problem of how to deal with increasing pressures for harsher measures in juvenile justice. Spain is still suffering from the ETA and other terrorist activities which might explain some of the modification of the 2000 law, a welfare law with a great emphasis on the "best interest of the child." Similar to Canada the implementation of the law is delegated to the provinces which have great autonomy in a "quasi federal state" (Rechea Alberola and Molina, 2004) The law itself gives large discretion to the prosecutor for dealing with delinquents, while every province has a special juvenile section, including at least one specialized youth prosecutor. However, despite the introduction of restorative justice principles, implementation is variable over provinces which may be related to a lack of resources. Some provinces are collaborating with the Social services department and services provided by NGOs are requested for implementing restorative justice principles. Later modifications of the law were dominated by general deterrence principles rather than the "best interest" of the child, such as longer custody terms in the case of serious offences. However, statistics on interventions in 2000–2003 show that the effect of these modifications is not so great: although custody did increase, community measures also increased.

One other example of a typical "welfare approach" is the Swiss Juvenile Justice Bill of 2003, which acquired force of law in 2006 (Zermatten, 2004). Until that date juvenile law was part of the Criminal law, but the new law changes this. The current law is explicitly based on protection principles.

The minimum age of criminal responsibility was raised from 7 to 10 (despite pressures to raise it to age 12) and criminal majority is fixed at age 18. The juvenile judge is competent to hear both civil and penal matters. On the other hand due process rights for juveniles are recognized and have been adopted in procedural law, as is the case in most European countries. Custody, which had a maximum term of 1 year, has been enlarged to 1–4 years for young people aged 16 or over. However, the maximum of 4 years is reserved for serious violent offenders who committed acts such as serious assault and robbery. It is a remarkable fact that until recently Switzerland only had open institutions and that it has only recently made a start with constructing several closed institutions. Although Switzerland supports alternative sanctions, so far they have only introduced community service and mediation programs. A professional probation system is still lacking because of a shortage of qualified social workers. The case of Switzerland is interesting in that the country has tried to merge the protection system with the due process model. Elements that may have played a role in this moderate approach are the relatively small population size (7.5 million inhabitants), the strong informal social control still exercised in the many small cities and villages, and the fact that immigration from troubled regions such as ex-Yugoslavia and Albania is from a relatively recent date. Important social changes that happened all over Europe came to Switzerland somewhat later than to other countries.

In considering the Eastern European countries one may speculate that Germany's and Austria's welfare legislation has had some impact on recent juvenile justice legislative change.

For example, in reviewing juvenile justice legislation in the Czech Republic and in Bosnia, one may note this impact along with that of international Conventions, rules and regulations. Indeed, in 1993 the Czech law made conditional dismissals possible at the level of the prosecution, and this became one of the most frequent alternative disposals (Valkova, 2004). More importantly, the new law which was adopted in 2003, established the age of criminal responsibility at 15 and criminal majority at 18. The law explicitly emphasizes diversion of criminal proceedings, educational and protective measures, and alternatives to imprisonment. Custody is considered as a real last resort. In Bosnia the criminal law reform of 1992–2003 introduced due process rights, specified the role of the prosecutor as it is known in other European countries, established criminal responsibility at age 14 and introduced educational measures (Maljevic, 2004).

Looking at Poland, the biggest country among the new EU member states, the author states that there has been opposition to the welfare type juvenile justice legislation, which dates from 1982 (Stando-Kawecka, 2004). However, the author concludes that the welfare oriented principles of the Act have to a large extent remained unchanged. Poland has family courts with the juvenile judge the most powerful figure in the system. There is a strict separation between juvenile offenders and children in need of care and they cannot be placed in the same institution. Transfer to a criminal court as well as adult sentencing is only possible in the case of very serious offences. Both police and prosecutors have limited roles, since the family judge is competent at all stages of the proceedings and even conducts the preliminary inquiry when a juvenile is referred to the court. The 1982 Act provides for a great number of interventions ranging from a reprimand, supervision, placement in a foster family to a youth educational centre and including some restorative measures (although these are still rarely applied). The 1982 law was amended in 1995 as an answer to all those who found the prevailing juvenile law "too soft." However, both the amendment and the Penal code of 1997 introduced only limited changes, the most important of which are lowering the maximum age limit of criminal responsibility in very serious cases from age 16 to 15 and enlarging the possibility of transferring juveniles to the criminal court (although reducing the penalties for juveniles). Despite these legal changes, practice did not change very much: placement in an institution continues to be rare, educative measures being the main dispositions of the family court, with the reprimand and supervision by a probation officer and by parents being the most frequent ones. Restorative justice practices, such as mediation, repairing damages done, apologizing to the victim and the like are seldom imposed.

3.3. Welfare Boards and Hearing System

And then there are the Nordic countries, including the Scandinavian states as well as Scotland. They deserve a prominent place in this chapter because of their perseverance in maintaining a particular welfare system even when more punitive measures are imposed.

Scotland is a case in point, since it is upholding a welfare model that was created in the 1960s on the basis of the well-known Kilbrandon report.[6] The Scottish Hearing system was established in law in 1968 and is still going strong although important changes have modified juvenile justice in the last decade. It is based on a focus on the offender instead of the offence and does not separate children in need of protection and delinquent children. Children's panels, composed by lay people recruited from the local community were introduced. A hearing includes the child, his or her parents, a social worker and the Reporter, but there is no legal defence since that was considered unnecessary. When a case is reported to the Reporter, the latter may ask the social work department for a social background report. On the basis of that report he will decide on how to proceed. If a panel meeting is convened the welfare of the child must be the essential consideration, implying a reduction of the risk of reoffending and an increase social inclusion. Measures may include a warning, voluntary supervision from the local authorities, compulsory supervision and placement in an educative establishment. However, in the 1990s a more punitive approach was gaining ground and the juvenile justice system was reviewed, focusing heavily on both individual and parental responsibility. The hearing system was more or less reduced to treating the ages 8–16, while a pilot was set up for a Youth court, judging 16- to 17-year-old persistent offenders. In addition, Scotland has also introduced (the British) Anti-Social Behaviour Orders in order to ban "unruly" behaviour. In practice, however, the hearing system is still very much alive. All offenders aged 16 and 17 are referred by the police to the Procurator fiscal (the prosecutor) who decides whether the case should go to the Hearings system or to the Youth Court. Most of the sanctions imposed by the court are community based and only 7% result in custody. In addition, there has been a greater emphasis on evidence based interventions. Scotland will not abolish the Hearing system which made the country famous, and the authors conclude that "the work with troubled children and young people is more focused and constructive than before" (Burman et al., 2004).

With respect to the Scandinavian countries there is an interesting mix of the philosophy of "just desert" and the humane tradition for which they have always been known. Because of their intensive collaboration, Denmark, Sweden, Norway, and Finland have rather comparable legal systems (Kyvsgaard,

---

[6]Recommendations made by a Committee chaired by Lord Kilbrandon.

2004). For example, there is no separate juvenile justice system and in all of them the age of criminal responsibility is 15. Children under age 15 are dealt with by so-called welfare boards (social agencies), while young people over age 15 are dealt with by a criminal court just as adults. However, various sanctions and measures specially addressed to offenders aged 15–17, result in a more lenient outcome for this age group. When children under age 15 are suspected of an offence, the police may detain them but they have to immediately inform the Welfare board. It is up to the latter to decide what has to be done after an assessment of what kind of assistance is needed. It is the child's needs that dictate that decision and not the seriousness of the offence, which is a pure Welfare principle. Social interventions include practical assistance for the family, family therapy and also – with the consent of parents – out-of-home placement in a foster family or a home. Children and juveniles may be placed in secure accommodation, although this is mainly for observation. However, under age 15 this is very rare and such placement cannot exceed a period of 2 months (Sarnecki and Estrada, 2004). Young people aged 15–18 usually do not go to court, the dispositions being a fine or dropping the charges, sometimes with specific conditions, such as a fine or substance abuse therapy. Various sanctions are available if they end up in court, such as a "youth contract" (since 1998), specifying a number of obligations of the youth and his parents, probation and the most frequently used punishment, the day-fine. Alternative sanctions, such as Community service or mediation are rare. Imprisonment is seldom used for young offenders and judges must consider alternative ways of serving the sentence: the youth may be sent to a hospital, in family care or to a specialized care institution or clinic. In 2001 Denmark introduced a new youth sanction, covering three phases in 2 years: first the youth is placed in secure accommodation, followed by placement in an open institution. This may take 1½ years. The last phase is spent in liberty which is restricted by supervision and after care. During these 2 years the offender has to follow intensive social, educational and employment training programmes. Sweden has strongly been influenced by the "just desert" philosophy (Von Hirsch, 1976). However, although there were pressures to remove the responsibility for supervision from the social Welfare board and to give it to the court this was not followed by the government (Janson, 2004). In 1997 the government introduced a new sanction, "youth custody" for offenders aged 15–17, which made secure placement in the case of serious offences possible for a term between 2 weeks and 4 years. However, the young offender is to be transferred to an open institution as soon as possible. All in all the Swedish system is not very different from the other Scandinavian ones: it separates children under age 15, who are dealt with by social agencies, from those aged 15–18; young suspects (up to age 18) may only be arrested under very special circumstances and imprisonment is rarely used.

4. WHY DID THE JUVENILE JUSTICE SYSTEM CHANGE: SOME HYPOTHESES

Why has the juvenile justice system, in particular in western countries, undergone such drastic changes away from the welfare model? One of the reasons might be the belief of many people that the increasingly harsher system is a consequence of the rise in crime. As far as juvenile crime is concerned, there was a substantial rise between 1950 and 1980 in most Western countries, but the bulk of it was non-serious property and petty crime. Furthermore, there is no evidence for a similar rise in the 1980s and 1990s. For most European countries juvenile crime appears to be pretty stable over the last decade. Although in many states there has been a rise in violent crime, the question whether the increase in violent crime is as high as portrayed in police statistics or whether it is partly an artefact produced by defining more acts than before as crimes, an increase in reporting violent acts by the public, more alert police reaction to these complaints and better police registration due to the use of computers, is an unresolved question. An additional hypothesis is that the general stability in juvenile crime is the consequence of more severe sanctioning policies. Deterrence and incapacitation are supposed to reduce crime. However, American research has long since shown that the manipulation of penalties has only a marginal effect on crime rates (President's Commission on Law Enforcement and Administration of Justice 1967; Tonry 1995; Howell 1997). It does appear that changes in crime, particularly juvenile crime, are essentially unrelated to changes in criminal and juvenile justice policies.

An alternative explanation is that the new faith in harsh punishments is a consequence of increased mass media attention to serious, rare, and heavily dramatized crimes. This phenomenon is as frequent in Europe as it is in North America. As Tonry notes:

> We know that ordinary citizens base their opinions on what they know about crime from the mass media and as a result that they regard heinous crimes and bizarre sentences as the norm. They believe sentences are much softer than they are, and they believe crime rates are rising when they are falling. As a result majorities nearly always report that judges' sentences are too lenient. (Tonry, 2001, p. 57)

This distorts people's views on crime in general and it supports the assumption that the media contribute to create a climate of fear in which people believe that crime is fast increasing and that deterrence and retribution are needed to maintain sufficient social control. An additional problem is that politicians follow the media. They base their political actions on what they see as the public's feelings about the issues figuring in the media. As a consequence they exercise pressure on the government, prosecutors and judges to be firm and pronounce more severe sentences. The latter are not insensitive to the pressures of public opinion and tend also to support more repressive sentencing policies.

These explanations add to our understanding of the actual situation in criminal and juvenile justice. However, as far as western countries are concerned, some additional factors might be taken into consideration.

My view is that the present trend of meting out more severe punishments to adults and juveniles may be related to fundamental changes in the technological, economic, and social make up of Western society. Three phenomena seem to have special importance in this respect. These are changes in the labour market due to technological innovations, the impact of globalization on the Welfare state, and mass immigration.

First, technological change is causing the gradual disappearance of unskilled labour from the economy and the emergence of a strong service sector. The new jobs require considerable training, flexibility, and adaptability to changing circumstances, and high verbal, social, and communication skills. Increasing interdependence among people and institutions requires a controlled environment, reliable and predictable interactions, and a rejection of the use of violence. This is why modern society stresses strong control of emotions, a more deliberate and rational approach to problems, and a strong emphasis on internalized (moral) norms of behaviour. One result is high unemployment rates among those who cannot meet these requirements, among which many young people living in deprived neighbourhoods (Garland 2001, p.81). At the EU level 22% of today's youths do not complete any form of secondary education: this is 30% in Ireland, Italy, Spain and the UK, but is only 15% in the Nordic countries. In addition, 20% of the males are still unemployed 5 years after having left school (OECD, 1999). Furthermore, to the extent that there is a discrepancy between the behavioural requirements of post-industrial society and individual skills to meet them, unemployed and marginalized young people may resort to deviant and delinquent behaviour.

Second, western society has since long been based on a market economy. However, after World War II and until the end of the 1970s, negative effects on people's lives were cushioned by an elaborate welfare system that gave the state an important interventionist role. When, as a consequence of several recessions, this balanced system was considerably overextended, it was gradually dismantled in many countries. Although economic growth increased at first, this had also negative consequences. One consequence is growing social and economic inequality and an increase in poverty, in particular among families with children and lone mother families. Moreover, even when unemployment rates declined the number of families without an income through work increased (European Commission, 1999). Family unemployment has serious negative effects for children. A Danish study found that family unemployment doubles the risks of family break up and of later unemployment of the children. It is highly related to parental alcoholism, violence and incarceration (Christoffersen, 1996, cited by Esping-Andersen, 2002, p. 54). American research has shown that childhood poverty is strongly related to less schooling, more drop-outs, more criminal behaviour, more psycho-social disturbances and becoming poor parents themselves (Danziger and Waldvogel, 2000; Duncan, Brooks-Gunn et al., 1998). While these conditions contribute to the marginalization and social exclusion of deprived families with poor parenting skills, at the same time they create the need for tighter control on marginalized, unruly, undisciplined and delinquent young people. One of the answers to such social destabilization may be an increasing reliance on the criminal and juvenile justice system to restore some peace and order. This has led among others to justice initiatives, such as replacing the practice of dismissing juvenile cases by diversion programs, ASBOs, local justice offices where prosecutors and police do justice at the local neighbourhood level, intensive supervision programmes and, in particular, an increase in institutionalization. Social correlates of crime are no longer seen as significant, because of the emphasis placed on the individual, who has no self-control or lacks social controls and who deserves to be punished for his sinful acts (Garland, 2001, p. 102). One of the consequences is that countries that have an Anglo-Saxon tradition, such as the United Kingdom and the Netherlands, have seen their detention rates skyrocketing. On the other hand the Scandinavian countries, which have maintained a strong welfare tradition, still have very low custody rates. Other countries have not as yet developed a full-fledged punitive justice and control model, such as Germany and some of the East European states.

Finally, mass immigration is a third important factor, both in North America and in Western Europe. The United States and Canada have long been immigrant countries. In the 19th century, most immigrants came from Europe, but since 1950 about 18 million immigrants, most of them of non-European origin, came to the United States. At the same time, Europe received 15 million immigrants, many of whom were recruited as unskilled factory workers (Yinger, 1994). In fact immigration has never stopped, and there is a continuous flow of Third World labourers and asylum seekers to the Western world. The consequences are many. First, it is clear that new immigrants will affect the composition of the population. In Holland's big cities, the majority of children younger than 15 years belong to ethnic minorities. Similar trends are apparent in other big European cities, such as Paris and London. The same is true of Canadian cities such as Toronto and Vancouver. Second, changes in the labour market hit these groups particularly hard, with huge unemployment rates as a result. Third, a growing number of segregated and deteriorated city areas are emerging, housing an "underclass" population of mainly, though not exclusively, immigrants (Eisner, 1997).

These changes undermine society's stability and social cohesion and create mechanisms of social exclusion, producing widespread feelings of insecurity and fear: fear of the future, of unemployment, of poverty, of war and terrorism. They are projected on essentially two groups: a loosely defined group of ethnic minorities, including refugees and foreign labourers, and marginalized, deviant and delinquent young people. The latter are considered as threatening social peace and social cohesion to an even higher degree.

Gurr (1981) argued that in the 19th century the social institutions that did educate and socialize non-integrated persons into behavioural conformity, adequate social functioning, and respect for the prevailing value system – schools, factories, and military conscription – are in decline or have disappeared. The only norm-enforcing system that remains in full force and has the pretension to preserve social peace is the criminal and juvenile justice system. That system is increasingly intervening in people's lives, not just by detaining people, but also by extending its operations and control in the community. To the extent that social unrest, feelings of insecurity, and fear of the future remain prevalent, people will continue to expect the criminal justice system to pacify society and re-establish social cohesion. They will also continue to put pressures on the judiciary to punish and to put away those who are seen as disturbing social peace.

5. THE INFLUENCE OF INTERNATIONAL STANDARDS

Contrary to the United States which does not recognize and ratify international conventions,[7] there are important limitations to what European states can do in terms of general penal legislation or the unrestrained introduction of repressive innovations in Juvenile Penal law. Their actions are limited by International recommendations, rules and conventions.

For example, the most important legislation to which European laws are tested for conformity is the European Convention on Human Rights and Fundamental Freedoms (ECHR), which has been adopted in 1950 by the Council of Europe and which all members of the Council must have signed. The Convention is enforced by the European Court in Strasbourg and it has considerable influence on the national legislation of member states who adopted the Convention, since international jurisdiction supersedes national jurisdiction. Indeed national legislation is continually tested against ECHR provisions and the court's jurisprudence.

Expert committees of the Council of Europe also prepare Recommendations for the member states. One of the first on juvenile justice was Recommendation no. R (87) 20 on "Social Reactions to Juvenile Delinquency," while in September 2003 a Recommendation (Rec. 2003, 20) was adopted by the Council of Europe, recommending among others:

- A reduction of institutionalization
- Greater use of evidence based interventions
- Greater involvement of parents and
- Recognition of victims' interests.

---

[7]It should be observed that Canada does not share the views of the US in this respect: for example Canada did sign the Convention on the Rights of the Child;

A full-fledged Convention, which has increasing importance for Youth protection as well as for Youth justice is the UN Convention on the Rights of the Child (CRC) which was adopted in 1989 by the General Assembly and since then has been ratified by 191 countries. However, the Convention cannot be enforced by an International Tribunal. Every 5 years the UN Supervising Committee tests the measures taken by individual states to implement the Convention.

Articles 37, 39, and 40 of the convention are relevant for juvenile justice (Mijnarends 2001). For example Article 37 guarantees the rights of the child in the case of deprivation of liberty, while Article 39 emphasizes the duty of authorities to rehabilitate and reintegrate young people after detention. Furthermore, Article 40 guarantees the establishment of a juvenile justice process that is respectful of a juvenile's rights.

Of course the question is whether the convention will be observed by the UN member states that have ratified it. It is to be expected that efforts to observe the provisions will be strongest in Western democracies where the legal profession and the media play an important role. I think that the convention's main importance lies in the values it represents and its moral appeal to realize these values in practice.

Moreover, UN congresses have adopted Standard Minimum Rules for the Administration of Juvenile Justice (The Beijing rules) in 1985, and Rules for the Protection of Juveniles Deprived of their Liberty (the Havana rules) in 1990. The Beijing rules include important notions such as the well-being of juveniles, the minimum age for criminal responsibility, proportionality of the penalty to the act, and taking into account mitigating circumstances. The Havana rules are concerned with juveniles in detention, stating as the main objective the reintegration of the juvenile, and his right to adequate treatment and contacts with his family (Mijnarends 1999, 2001).

In addition, nongovernmental organizations, such as UNICEF, Defence for Children, and Amnesty International do also critically review juvenile justice proceedings. For example, the Netherlands has been criticized for not providing sufficient information to children about their rights and for their policy in child abuse cases (Defence for Children International 2000).

One may expect that the impact of the UN Convention on the Rights of the Child will increase over the coming years. Nonetheless I feel that the unifying influence of the Court in Strasbourg on the legislative process of member states, through its jurisdictional powers in the field of human rights and jurisprudence, will probably be greater.

6. CONCLUDING REMARKS

An overview of the 19 national reports displays many differences. Indeed there seem to be essentially three clusters of juvenile justice systems. The first cluster includes the English speaking countries, with the exception of Scotland but including the Netherlands. It is essentially "justice" oriented, characterized by a retributive, sometimes repressive, approach, placing a strong emphasis on the juvenile's accountability, "just desert" principles and parental responsibility for their child's behaviour. This does not mean that in these states juvenile justice systems are completely similar. On the contrary there are differences in emphasis on some aspects of the system between for example the United States and the Republic of Ireland or Northern Ireland. It is clear that the United States represents these characteristics in its extreme form. However, it is surprising to note to what degree England and also the Netherlands have adopted both the rhetoric and the practice from the United States, particularly the growing institutionalization of young people. On the other hand most of these countries – while subscribing to the general just desert philosophy – have also introduced on a large scale alternative sanctions (Canada, the UK, and the Netherlands), restorative justice (Northern Ireland) and preventive and diversionary measures (Ireland, the Netherlands, and the UK).

Furthermore there is a second characteristic distinguishing these western countries from the others and that is their pragmatism and strong emphasis on "what works" including evidence based interventions, as well as prevention. There is a great interest in better ways to prevent crime and a conviction that we can and should make considerably more effort to reduce juvenile crime by preventive measures. For example, reading the research literature, there is overwhelming empirical evidence showing that interventions at an early age are considerably more effective than interventions in adolescence or adulthood (Tremblay and Craig, 1995; Rutter, Giller, and Hagell, 1998). Or as others have put it "...remedial policies for adults are a poor (and costly) substitute for interventions in childhood" (Heckman and Lochner, 2000; Esping-Andersen, 2002, p. 49). Moreover, the Anglo-Saxon tradition implies a strong empirical research tradition which is unfortunately absent in many continental European countries. This means, among other things, that the prevention of crime has become a specialist discipline in criminology, based on developing, implementing and evaluating interventions, both preventive as well as treatment programmes. As a consequence of these research efforts most of new and innovative interventions that are applied in juvenile justice and preventive programmes in Europe were originally developed in the United States and Canada. Since considerable resources are invested in developing, testing and demonstrating their effectiveness by sometimes long term effect evaluations, such programmes then find their way to other countries.

The second cluster of countries mainly covering continental Europe is still very much "welfare" oriented. This is perhaps best represented by the German approach of juveniles and young adults, but one sees a similar approach in many continental European states. Western European states, such as France and Belgium also have a strong welfare legal tradition, although there are pressures to change this and create a more retributive system. It is clear that some adaptations are made (France), but the essential protective system laid down in the

Ordonnance of 1945 is still adhered to and has a strong foothold in the country. In an important study Whitman (2003) has shown that throughout history both France and Germany have developed an essentially humane approach of criminal offenders based on respect and rejecting practices of their degradation. It is interesting to note that we are finding the same essentially humane approach in these two countries with respect to juveniles.

However, this approach is also characteristic for other continental countries, such as Switzerland, Spain, and Greece, as well as the Eastern European states. What is striking about the latter is that despite a huge rise in delinquency after 1998, when communism was dismantled, their juvenile justice systems have not taken over the harsh juvenile justice orientation of the United States. In reviewing their juvenile justice legislation adopting diversionary measures and alternative sanctions, some of these countries may have undergone western European influences and those coming from the Council of Europe, but the fact remains that their welfare approach is clear.

A third cluster is formed by the Scandinavian countries and Scotland. The four Scandinavian countries have very similar juvenile justice systems. Because of their relationships with Anglo-Saxon states the "just desert" philosophy gained in importance particularly in Sweden, although we also see some "just desert" innovations in Denmark for example. In practice this means placing more emphasis on the offence, as well as on the responsibility of the juvenile for his actions and on the proportionality principle. However, despite these new accents in juvenile justice the countries have remained faithful to their welfare boards, their restraint in punishment and institutionalization and their emphasis on treatment interventions. They are also receptive to "what works" principles and evidence based interventions and they are strongly relying on empirical research in guiding policy. A similar story may be told about the Scottish Hearing system although the British influence is strong as is clear from the introduction of parenting orders and ASBOs. However, they are proud of their own Hearing system and the changes that that have been introduced will be limited and won't destroy their essential welfare approach.

The question is, however, what we may expect in the future?

In 1984 Malcolm Klein published the book *Western Systems of Juvenile Delinquency*, including eight North American and Western European countries. This was the time when the "cold war" determined our lives and when there were only limited contacts with Eastern Europe. Since 1989 the world has experienced a social and economic metamorphosis leading among others to the recent admission of ten of the "new" European countries in the European Union. Many of these new countries, whether they belong or not belong to the EU, are now changing their juvenile justice legislation.[8] In this respect it is not surprising that

---

[8]At the moment of finalising this publication, this author has been approached by the Republic of Kazakhstan which intention is to create a juvenile justice system.

in transforming or creating their system they are looking to the West and tend to adopt the conventions and recommendations of the Council of Europe and the United Nations. Some of them have also looked at other countries as an example to follow. To the degree that the EU, despite its regular crises, will continue its march towards a growing economic and political unity, homogenizing tendencies in the penal field will also grow. However, one may expect that EU countries, despite pressures to conform, will preserve a large degree of autonomy in their practical implementation of juvenile justice legislation, as is clear, for example, in federalist countries, such as Canada and the United States.

Consequently, I think that scientists, as academics and as socially responsible individuals, have the specific responsibility to reflect on – and propose to our respective government's new ways to improve juvenile justice procedures and make them more effective as well as more humane. In this respect and as a preliminary conclusion based on the review of these 19 juvenile justice systems, I want to suggest that it would be important to try to merge the empirical "evidence based" approach of the Anglo-Saxon states with the essentially humanistic juvenile justice tradition of continental Europe. Both systems have negative *and* positive characteristics and our task – as I see it – would be to work towards a system that serves best the needs of children as well as the requirements of postmodern society.

REFERENCES

Audit Commission (2004). *Youth Justice 2004: A Review of the Reformed Youth Justice System*. London: Belmont Press.

Bala, N. and J. V. Roberts (2004). "Canada's Juvenile Justice System: Increasing Community-based Responses to Crime," Paper presented at the Conference of the European Society of Criminology, Amsterdam, 25–28 August.

Bishop, D. M., C. E. Frazier, L. Lanza-Kaduce, and H. G. White (1999). *A Study of Juvenile Transfers to Criminal Court in Florida*. Washington DC: Office of Juvenile Justice and Delinquency Prevention.

Bol, M. (1991). *Leeftijdsgrenzen in het Strafrecht*. WODC, Arnhem, Gouda Quint.

Bruckmüller, K. (2004). "A Protection Model," Paper presented at the Conference of the European Society of Criminology, Amsterdam, 25–28 August.

Burman, M., P. Bradshaw, N. Hutton, F. McNeill, and M. Munro (2004). "Trends and Developments in Youth justice in Scotland," Paper presented at the Conference of the European Society of Criminology, Amsterdam, 25–28 August.

Christofferson, M. (1996). *Opvaekst med Arbejdloeshed*. Copenhagen: SFI.

Council of Europe (1989). *Social Reactions to Juvenile Delinquency*, Recommendation No.R (87) 20, Strasbourg.

Council of Europe (2005). *New Ways of Dealing with Juvenile Delinquency and the Role of Juvenile Justice*, Recommendation No. Rec. (2003), 20.

Danziger, S. and J. Waldvogel (2000). *Securing the Future: Investing in Children from Birth to College*. New York: Russel Sage.

Doob, A. N. and J. B. Sprott (1999). "Canada Considers New Sentencing Laws for Youth: a Sheep in Wolf's Clothing," *Overcrowded Crimes*, 10 (2): 5–11.

Doob, A. N. and J. B. Sprott (2004). "Youth Justice in Canada," in *Youth Crime and Youth Justice: Comparative and Cross-National Perspectives,* M.Tonry and A. N. Doob (eds.), *Crime and Justice,* vol. 31. Chicago: University of Chicago Press, pp. 185–243.

Duncan, G., J. Yeung, J. Brooks-Gunn, and J. Smith (1998). "How much does Childhood Poverty Affect the Life Chances of Children," *American Sociological Review,* 63: .406–423.

Dünkel, F. (2004). "Juvenile Justice in Germany: Between Welfare and Justice," Paper presented at the Conference of the European Society of Criminology, Amsterdam, 25–28 August.

Eisner, Manuel (1997). *Das Ende der Zivilisierten Stadt? Die Auswirkungen von Modernisierung und Urbaner Krise auf Gewaltdelinquenz.* Frankfurt/New York: Campus.

European Commission. *Social Protection Report.* Brussels: DGV.

Esping-Andersen, G. (2002). "A Child-Centred Social Investment Strategy," in Esping-Andersen (ed.), *Why We Need a New Welfare State.* New York: Oxford University Press.

Feld, B. C. (1998a). "Abolish the Juvenile Court: Youthfulness, Criminal Responsibility, and Sentencing Policy," *Journal of Criminal Law and Criminology,* 88: 68–136.

Feld, B. C. (1998b). "Juvenile and Criminal Justice Systems," in M. Tonry and M. H. Moore (eds.), *Youth Violence.* Chicago: Chicago University Press, pp.189–262.

Garland, D. (2001). *The Culture of Control – Crime and social Order in Contemporary Society.* Oxford: Oxford University Press.

Graham, J. and C.Moore (2004). "Trend Report on Juvenile Justice in England and Wales," Paper presented at the Conference of the European Society of Criminology, Amsterdam, 25–28 August.

Gurr, T. R. (1981). "Historical Trends in Violent Crimes: A Critical Review of the Evidence," in *Crime and Justice: An Annual Review of Research,* vol. 3, Michael Tonry and Norval Morris (eds.). Chicago: University of Chicago Press.

Heckman, J. and Lochner, L. (2000). "Rethinking Education and Training Policy," in S. Danziger and J. Walfvogel (eds.), *Securing the Future: Investing in Children from Birth to College.* New York: Russel Sage, pp. 47–86.

Howell, J. C (1997). *Juvenile Justice and Youth Violence,* Thousand Oaks, California, Sage

Howell, J. C (2003). *Preventing and Reducing Juvenile Delinquency: A Comprehensive Framework.*

Janson, C.-G. (2004). "Youth Justice in Sweden," in *Youth Crime and Youth Justice: Comparative and Cross-National Perspectives,* M. Tonry and A. N. Doob (eds.), *Crime and Justice,* vol. 31. Chicago: University of Chicago Press, pp. 391–443.

Junger-Tas, J. (1996). "Youth and Violence in Europe," *Studies on Crime and Crime Prevention,* 5 (1): 31–59.

Kyvsgaard, B. (2004). "Youth Justice in Denmark," in *Youth Crime and Youth Justice- Comparative and Cross-National Perspectives,* M. Tonry and A. N. Doob (eds.), *Crime and Justice,* vol. 31, University of Chicago Press, pp.349–391.

Leonards, Chr. (1995). *De ontdekking van het onschuldige criminele kind: Bestraffing en opvoeding van criminele kinderen in jeugdgevangenis en opvoedingsgesticht 1833–1886.* Hilversum: Verloren.

Maljevic, A. (2004). "National report on Juvenile Delinquency and Juvenile Criminal Justice-System of Bosnia-Herzegovina," Paper presented at the Conference of the European Society of Criminology, Amsterdam, 25–28 August.

Martinson, R. (1974). What Works? Questions and Answers about Prison Reform," *Public Interest* 35: 22–54.

Mijnarends, E. M. (1999). *Richtlijnen voor een Verdragsconforme Jeugdstrafrechtspleging, 'Gelijkwaardig maar minderjarig.'* Dordrecht, The Netherlands: Kluwer Rechtswetenschappelijke publicaties.

——. (2001). "De betekenis van het Internationaal Verdrag inzake de Rechten van het Kind voor het Nederlandse jeugdstrafrecht," *Tijdschrift voor Familie- en Jeugdrecht* 23(11): 302–307.

National Council of Juvenile and Family Court Judges (1998). *The Janiculum Project: Structural, Procedural and Programmatic Recommendations for the Future Juvenile Court.* Reno, Nevada.

OECD (1999). *Employment Outlook*. Paris: OECD.

Penders, J. (1980). *Om sijne Jonckheyt*. Utrecht: Rijksuniversiteit Utrecht.

President's Commission on Law Enforcement and Administration of Justice (1967). *The Challenge of Crime in a Free Society: A Report*. Washington, DC: US Government Printing Office.

Rechea Alberola, C. and E. Fernandez Molina (2004). "Report of the Spanish Juvenile Justice System," Paper presented at the Conference of the European Society of Criminology, Amsterdam, 25–28 August.

Roberts, J. V. and A. von Hirsch (1995). Statutory Sentencing Reform: the Purpose and principles of Sentencing, *Crim. L. Q.* 37: 220.

Rothman, David J. (1990). *The Discovery of the Asylum: Social Order and Disorder in the New Republic*, rev. edn. Boston: Little, Brown.

Rutter, M., H. Giller, and A. Hagell (1998). *Antisocial Behaviour by Young People* New York: Cambridge University Press.

Sarnecki, J. and F. Estrada (2004). "Juvenile Crime in Sweden – A Trend report on Criminal Policy, the Development of Juvenile Delinquency and the Juvenile Justice System," Paper presented at the Conference of the European Society of Criminology, Amsterdam, 25–28 August.

Scott, E. S. (2000). Criminal Responsibility in Adolescence: Lessons from Developmental Psychology, in T. Grisso and R. G. Schwartz (eds.), *Youth on Trial: A Developmental Perspective on Juvenile Justice*. Chicago: University of Chicago Press, pp. 291–324.

Shorter, E. (1975). *The Making of the Modern Family*. New York: Basic Books.

Snyder, H. N. and M. Sickmund (1999). *Juvenile Offenders and Victims: 1999 National Report*. Washington, DC: US Department of Justice, Office of Justice Programs, Office of Juvenile Justice and Delinquency Prevention.

Spinellis, C. D. and A. Tsitsoura (2004). "Juvenile Justice in Greece," Paper presented at the Conference of the European Society of Criminology, Amsterdam, 25–28 August.

Stando-Kawecka, B. (2004). "The Juvenile Justice System in Poland," Paper presented at the Conference of the European Society of Criminology, Amsterdam, 25–28 August.

Stearns, P. N. (1975). *European Society in Upheaval: Social History since 1750*, 2d ed. New York: Macmillan.

Tonry, M. (1995). *Malign Neglect: Race, Crime, and Punishment in America*. New York: Oxford University Press.

Tonry, M. (2001). "Why Are U.S. Incarceration Rates So High?" in Michael Tonry (ed.), *Penal Reform in Overcrowded Times*. New York:, Oxford University Press.

Tremblay, R. E and W. M. Craig (1995). "Developmental Crime Prevention," in M. Tonry and D. P. Farrington (eds.), *Building a Safer Society: Strategic Approaches to Crime Prevention*, pp.151–237.

Trépanier, J. (1999). "Juvenile Courts after 100 Years: Past and Present Orientations," *European Journal on Criminal Policy and Research,* 7 (3): 303–327.

Valkova, H. (2004). "The New Juvenile Justice Law in the Czech Republic," Paper presented at the Conference of the European Society of Criminology, Amsterdam, 25–28 August.

Van der Laan, P. H. (2004). "Juvenile Delinquency and Juvenile Justice in the Netherlands," Paper presented at the Conference of the European Society of Criminology, Amsterdam, 25–28 August.

Van Dijk, C. (2004). "Juvenile Delinquency and Juvenile Justice in Belgium," Paper presented at the Conference of the European Society of Criminology, Amsterdam, 25–28 August.

Von Hirsch, A. (1976). *Doing Justice: The Choice of Punishments – Report of the Committee for the Study of Incarceration*. New York: Hill & Wang.

Whitman, J. Q. (2003). *Harsh Justice – Criminal Punishment and the Widening Divide between America and Europe*. New York: Oxford University Press.

Wittebrood, K. and M. Junger. (1999). "Trends in Geweldscriminaliteit," *Tijdschrift voor Criminologie,* 41 (3): 250–268.

Wyvekens, A. (2004). "The French System of Juvenile Justice," Paper presented at the Conference of the European Society of Criminology, Amsterdam, 25–28 August.

Yinger, J. Milton (1994). *Ethnicity: Source of Strength? Source of Conflict?* Albany: State University of New York Press.

Zermatten, J. (2004). "The Swiss Federal Statute on Juvenile Criminal Law," Paper presented at the Conference of the European Society of Criminology, Amsterdam, 25–28 August.

Zimring, F. E (1998). *American Youth Violence*. New York: Oxford University Press.

Subject Index

The index was made following the order of chapters as they appear in the book.

Author Index

The index was made following the order of chapters as they appear in the book.